The Pathology of Mind

The Pathology of Mind

A study of its distempers, deformities and disorders

Henry Maudsley
Introduced by Sir Aubrey Lewis

Julian Friedmann Publishers London

This edition first published 1979. The text is based on the 1895 edition.

In the United Kingdom by Julian Friedmann Publishers Ltd,
  4 Perrins Lane, London, NW3 1QY

In the United States of America by St Martin's Press Inc.,
  175 Fifth Avenue, New York, NY 10010

Introduction © Sir Aubrey Lewis

All rights reserved

United Kingdom ISBN 0 904014 42 8
United States ISBN 0-312-59806-8

Library of Congress Catalog Card Number 78-61468

Introduction typeset by T & R Filmsetters
Printed and Bound by A Wheaton & Co, Ltd, Exeter, England

THE TWENTY-FIFTH MAUDSLEY LECTURE
HENRY MAUDSLEY: HIS WORK AND INFLUENCE

By Aubrey Lewis, M.D., F.R.C.P.
Professor of Psychiatry, The University of London

Reprinted from the 'Journal of Mental Science,' April, 1951, by kind permission of the Editor.

The keen pleasure I felt when I was invited to deliver this lecture arose not only from the honour which it conferred, but also because it offered an opportunity to link again the lecture founded in Henry Maudsley's memory with the hospital which is the living witness to his wisdom and generosity. The first Maudsley Lecture was given by Sir James Crichton Browne, a contemporary and friend of Maudsley; the second was given at the Maudsley Hospital by Sir Frederick Mott, who had seen much of him during the last decade of his life. Since then very few of those called to give this lecture had had any personal contact with him, and it seems appropriate that now, a hundred years after Maudsley entered University College Hospital as an apprentice, when he has become for most of us a shadowy figure of the Victorian past, I should attempt to revive the memory of what he did during his life and consider how his work lives on after him—most of all in the hospital and school where I, and so many more, have the privilege of working. Before I do this I would like to recall that on the list of Maudsley lectures there is the name of Edward Mapother, a man singularly close to Maudsley in temperament and outlook, who carried forward the Maudsley Hospital in the spirit of its Founder's intention, and who would have been ideally fitted, in the 1939 lecture entrusted to him, to deal with the theme I am entering upon; unfortunately the war and his failing health came between, and Prof. Mapother never delivered the lecture. Sir James Crichton Browne compared Maudsley with Mercier; I compare Maudsley with Mapother, and recognize that in each generation there are men of rare gifts, severe in self-discipline, with strong and consistent purpose, who, in psychiatry as in other fields, accomplish much good and leave behind a lasting memorial.

Henry Maudsley was born in 1835. He grew up in a notable time; "of all decades in our history, a wise man would choose the 1850's to be young in," says Mr. G. M. Young. The giants were on the scene: Faraday, Clerk Maxwell, Darwin, Lyell, Owen; Carlyle, Tennyson, Ruskin, Dickens, Matthew Arnold; Herbert Spencer, J. S. Mill, Lecky; and as many more. There was intense intellectual activity and material success, self-questioning also, and social and spiritual discontent. Maudsley, however, was not at first much exposed to this revolution of ideas. He was born on a farm in the West Riding of Yorkshire, not far from Settle in Ribblesdale, of a family of yeomen who had been settled there for two centuries and more. "My father was a stolid Tory all his life, and quietly fixed to old ways of thinking and doing. He once told me, when I rebelled against traditional custom, that what was good enough for my forefathers was good enough for me," he says in a fragment of autobiography, which the kindness of Dr. Henry Maudsley of Melbourne has put at my disposal. Maudsley paints a drab picture of his childhood, after his mother had died; he attended the Giggleswick school, where " we had to construe the Latin and then repeat the appropriate rule from the Eton Latin Grammar without in the least understanding what the words meant. Similarly, in the upper school, besides arithmetic I went through a part of the first book of Euclid without any comprehension of the problems, learning the letters of the lines and angles by heart and repeating them offhand and instantly forgetting them. The little instruction which I obtained was probably not mainly due to the system there, but in part also to the fact that I was a day boy who had to walk over two miles to the school and back daily in summer and winter, in rain and snow. It was a hard time, but use and no experience of anything better made it tolerable, as it does everything else. Still it was a succession of sombre and dreary years, for my father was so profoundly afflicted by my mother's death, to whom he was ardently attached, that his natural silence was increased and hardly a word ever passed between us boys and him except when absolutely necessary." There were, however, some enlivening people—his paternal uncle John, a wayward, philosophically minded, well-read man; and his maternal aunt, Elizabeth Bateson, a philanthropist of the true Victorian breed, who conducted schools, and after a quarrel with the vicar of Bolton set up her own dissenting chapel at Kellett. "I owed more than I can reckon to her," says Maudsley, " for the poetry which she used to repeat to me, and I, having got it by heart, used to rush into the kitchen and declaim it to the servant. To that early and useful instruction I owe, I believe, any quality of style in my writings." It was this aunt, Elizabeth Bateson, who had him sent, when he was 14, to be a private pupil in the house of the Rev. Alfred Newth at Oundle. There his world opened out. His teacher was a good classical and mathematical scholar, widely read in general literature, who took him through Homer and the great Greek tragedians and historians, and of course, the Latin writers: Thucydides and Tacitus made a lasting impression on the boy, and so did the " Prometheus Bound " of Aeschylus; no doubt the theme of man's futile struggle against necessity, which recurs so often in Maudsley's writings, got something of its imprint from that tragedy of rebellious pride.

To University College Hospital Maudsley went in 1850, after he had matriculated; he was apprenticed for five years to Clover, who was then the Resident Medical Officer. He tells us that he was self-assertive and stubbornly rebellious against all control, " as I have always been," and that he did not avail himself of the opportunities the practice of the hospital afforded, so that Sharpey, the Professor of Physiology, remarked, " Maudsley has great abilities, but he has chosen to throw them into the gutter." Maudsley's terse comment is, "Happily I managed to pick some of them up again before they entirely rotted." His capacity for memorizing from books and for expressing himself well enabled him, he says, in spite of his wild curses, to gain a scholarship and a rouleau of gold medals. When he had his degree he designed to be a surgeon, but his lack of means and some trifling miscarriage of letters hindered him in this; so he decided to enter the East India Company's service. As they required their doctors to have spent six months in an asylum, he took a post as assistant medical officer at Wakefield, where he stayed nine months, and got on famously with his "congenial Yorkshire countrymen." From then there was no more talk of surgery or the East India Company; psychiatry had marked him for its own. A brief spell at Brentwood (where, I regret to say, he took a strong dislike to the people of Essex) was followed by a decisive event—his appointment as Medical Superintendent of Cheadle Royal.

He was only twenty-three, he had had no lengthy or formal training in psychiatry and no experience of administration, he had scamped his clinical studies, and he had vacillated in his career; his teachers did not think he was steady or tractable. What chance would he have had before a selection committee nowadays? What chance even of being "short-listed"? Those hard-headed Victorian committeemen in Manchester gave over the conduct of their new Royal Hospital for the Insane to this clever, headstrong, handsome young Yorkshireman. His success in the post was outstanding, and their courage and judgment bore richer fruit than they could foresee, and in a wider field. I think it is worth pausing to consider whether we are not in danger nowadays of becoming hidebound in our demands upon every aspirant, whatever his talents and promise; no doubt our requirements are the safe and right ones for the majority of candidates, but we have no great cause to preen ourselves on our skill in selection or our readiness to back a winner when we make comparison with our staid forefathers of a hundred years ago. To go no further than neurology and psychiatry. Hughlings Jackson, born in the same year as Maudsley, was on the senior staff of the National Hospital by the time he was 27, and of the London Hospital at 28; Griesinger, Maudsley's nearest counterpart in Germany, had, like him, neglected his regular classes as a medical student, had been self-willed and impatient of control, and had no more than two years' mental hospital experience when he published, at 28, his great textbook which radically influenced German psychiatry and made him its accepted leader. The range and content of psychiatry have been much extended in the last hundred years; but it is still, I think, true that a man of exceptional powers can acquaint himself in a few years of concentrated observation, reading and reflection with all the current knowledge he needs and can use, while the rest of us work our way steadily through the appointed stages of a lengthy training. If we force the Maudsleys and Griesingers of our day to delay their productive time until they have satisfied our normal and regular demands upon the would-be psychiatrist—and worse, until they have completed their "analysis"—I think psychiatry may suffer. Our difficulty, obviously, lies in knowing how to distinguish between the slick, hasty smatterer claiming privilege, and the impatient man with an original mind, fertile, selective and independent.

I have called Maudsley's appointment to Cheadle Royal a decisive event. He stayed there only three years, but in that formative time he learnt to know his subject and himself in a way that had not been possible before. He set about the practical business of his charge with sense and energy, effecting many improvements and some enlargement; he thought deeply, read much and wrote profusely and experimentally, stretching his literary limbs. In these writings there is explicit statement of most of the ideas that were to occupy him for the rest of his life.

His three Annual Reports at Cheadle Royal (for access to which I am much indebted to Dr. Roy) exhibit a mature and conscientious outlook. In the first he emphasizes the importance of treatment early in the illness, and points out that the supposed causes of insanity in each case are by no means definite efficient causes, that there are commonly many partial causes or conditions of the disease, some predisposing, some exciting, and that "the bodily derangement which so commonly exists in cases of insanity cannot be always regarded in the light of a cause; it often partakes as much of the character of effect. The physical acts on the mental, and the mental back again on the physical, and vice versa—cause and effect acting and reacting, and mutually aggravating one another. The old rule that 'the cause having ceased, the effect ceases' is false almost as often as it is true; the effect often continues after the cause has ceased, and, thus abiding, becomes in its turn a cause." Disturbance of the emotions and morbid introspection are the most conspicuous features of insanity—" the insane walks along, in many cases, the embodiment of an exaggerated emotion. . . . There is no boundary line between sanity and insanity; and the slightly exaggerated feeling which renders a man 'peculiar' in the world differs only in degree from that which places hundreds in an asylum. He who is eternally contemplating his own feelings can scarcely be pronounced to be perfectly sane "; exaggerated and distorted emotion leads to exaggerated and distorted ideas; if the ideas are lively and active, it is mania; if gloomy in character, it is melancholia. Hereditary predisposition is a most important cause, though often hidden by relatives who deny the facts: " Where hereditary predisposition exists, a cause so slight as to be inappreciable to observers is often efficient to produce the disease." As for treatment, he describes at length the many occupations and amusements which are arranged for the patients, and he denounces a " system which permitted to the insane only the monotony of a lifelong incarceration, and the inestimable privilege of wishing, like Hafiz, ' to break up the tiresome old vault of heaven into new forms '." In his report of the following year Maudsley refuses to classify as " recovered " those who were well when they left the hospital, but might not remain so, and he adds, as we might to-day, " a candid experience in the treatment of insanity must teach the wisdom of a discreet scepticism with regard to very high percentages of so-called recoveries." He remarks on the mild form of lifelong susceptibility to breakdown which makes the mental hospital a haven for some people: it might seem a painful thing to deprive of liberty persons who appear so little ailing, were it not that a repeated experience has shown it to be really a vain folly, if not a positive cruelty, to send them forth into the trials of life, when they are utterly unable to encounter them." He deplores the "strange, foolish and unjust prejudice" about insanity: "the slightest consideration would teach that an unavoidable affliction cannot be counted as a shame or disgrace." Heredity, again, receives much notice: he deplores the dysgenic consequences of women leaving hospital to conceive more children who may inherit the disease; and *à propos* of the frequency of insanity in unmarried people, he refers to the harmful postponement of the age of marriage, because civilization multiplies tastes and causes luxuries to be regarded as essentials of life. A discussion of will and the power of emotion foreshadows his later writings on free will and responsibility. Degeneration, as Morel understood it, and the "neuropathic taint" also begin to appear: "inherited weakness of any kind, unless there has been the compensation of a good education and a happy collocation of circumstances, must be exhibited in some form of weakness or other, whether it be as drunkenness, crime, immorality or insanity. . . . Families, like trees, often grow till they have attained their greatest development, then begin to decay, and ultimately die out." He reverts, in the tones of a preacher, to the theme "that it is a grievous mistake to neglect the formation of character as an aim of existence"; when he dilates on this the future sceptic is out of sight, and the yeast of authentic Victorian earnestness is at work. In this report, as in the previous one, he shows a close acquaintance with the classical text-book of Esquirol. His last report, much briefer, in 1861, makes two cardinal points: First, that on no account should lies and stratagems be used to get the patient to hospital; secondly, that mental disorder is to be considered an illness, not a visitation—" truth has as much force with the insane as with the sane, and it would seem to be the simple right of those who are afflicted and need control, that they should have the truth spoken to them"; moreover, "in place of the sufferer being sent to the hospital with the utmost secrecy as if some great disgrace were to be concealed, he is sent distinctly for the medical treatment of a disease, just as he would be placed under medical care for any other bodily disease." You will notice that word "other"—much of Maudsley's thought and writing was devoted to maintaining that insanity is a bodily disease.

I have dwelt upon these reports because they show us, so early in his life, Maudsley the psychiatrist, humane, practical, honest and outspoken, voicing in 1860 opinions which still in our day have to be asserted, which indeed many people suppose to have been unthought of until our generation asserted them.

Alongside Maudsley the psychiatrist there was then, and for the rest of his life, Maudsley the philosophic inquirer; Maudsley the positivist, to whom metaphysics was anathema. It is in the nature of our subject that every thoughtful psychiatrist can choose only between having his philosophic standpoint explicit or leaving it implicit; a philosophic standpoint of some sort he must have. Consequently the problems that troubled Maudsley are the perennial basic problems of us all. His views on them are inextricably woven into the fabric of his psychiatry, but his approach is that of his time and—need it be said—of his personality.

The first article of his that was published was on the "Correlation of Mental and Physical Force, or, Man, a Part of Nature," which appeared in October, 1859, in the *Journal of Mental Science*. It said substantially about metaphysics what he was still saying in "Organic to Human" nearly sixty years later—that man's consciousness and moral nature and all his other psychological attributes are closely dependent on the physical structure of his brain. Much influenced by Grove's recent book on the correlation of physical forces, Maudsley argued, with skill and fervour, that the same continuity exists between mental and physical as between the various sorts of physical force; he inveighed against man's vanity in measuring himself against and apart from the rest of nature, his abuse of the power to see things in words, and his propensity " to ignore himself as a material being and to speculate loosely and dilate rapturously on his mental being." Metaphysics, says Maudsley, is the vanity of vanities, its study a vexation of spirit, because it concerns itself not with phenomena but with the hypothesis of essence. He regrets, moreover, that "so eminent a philosopher as Auguste Comte should be one of those who have endeavoured to place science and religion in antagonism to one another." Repudiating "pure materialism," he glances at the universe in its gradual evolution, in which mind appears as one of the sequent effects in its due time and season, and he concludes that all forces are " but modes of manifestation of one force—the Will of God—manifest in highest form and with least obscuration in the temple of man's body."

This young philosopher and medical superintendent, who freely quotes Mill and Faraday, Spinoza and Leibnitz, St. Paul and Shakespeare, was the child of his time. In the late eighteen-fifties man's place in nature was a topic uppermost in the minds of thinking men. The conflict between the evolutionists and theologians like Bishop Wilberforce was already joined, though, of course, the *Origin of Species* had not yet been published and only a précis of Darwin's manuscript had been read before the Linnaean Society. Herbert Spencer had expressed in his *Principles of Psychology* a genetic and materialist view, rather loosely formulated, of the mind and its significance in evolutionary progress through differentiation, and he had objected to the hypothesis of special creation of species, just as Maudsley after him objected to the hypothesis of special creation of consciousness and moral feeling. Other influences producing the intellectual and spiritual turmoil of that generation were to be found among the philosophers —Sir William Hamilton, James and John Stuart Mill, Bain, W. A. Carpenter, Mansel. The Germans Schelling and Herbart, and the French physiologist-philosophers like Cabanis and Bichat, also exerted indirect influence and were closely read by Maudsley.

There is little, I think, in that first essay of Maudsley's that is not to be found in other writings of the time; what is significant is that here was a young psychiatrist well versed in the great argument, bold and confident enough to take a stand which compelled the attention of philosophers, and evidently determined to carry these vigorous principles into his study of morbid as well as normal mental states and activities. He had not defined his position rigorously or consistently, as Croom Robertson and Stout sharply pointed out when examining his views some years later; his version of positivism (shorn of ritual and ethic) seems to have been, not philosophy acting in the service of natural science, to use R. G. Collingwood's phrase, but rather natural science acting in the service of psychology; and he attacks metaphysics with some of the metaphysicians' own weapons—a dangerous venture, but the Maudsley of the *Physiology and Pathology of Mind*, of *Natural Causes and Supernatural Seemings*, of *Responsibility in Mental Disease*, was clearly presaged in the article by this audacious newcomer of 1859.

In 1860 he published two articles, both dealing with literary genius; one of these, much influenced in content and style by Carlyle, is about Edgar Allen Poe; the other examines discursively the insanity of many a famous man, and in one passage foreshadows Maudsley's treatise on psychiatry—" this must be the aim of a philosophical history of madness, should it ever come to pass that such an one is undertaken, a history which should aspire to establish some principle or principles but which, at any rate, should not be content to occupy itself with a catalogue of appearances. . . . In an account of insanity in any form there are thus two elements to be taken into consideration, one almost as important as the other; these are the subject and the environment, the man and his circumstances, subjective force and objective forces, both passive and active; and the problem for solution is, what there was in the one or in the other whereby harmonious co-operation between them became impossible and a discord was, of necessity, produced . . . materials (for a general history of insanity written in a philosophical spirit) lie in profusion around every one who has devoted himself to the care and treatment of the insane." In this essay, testifying in its gusto and exuberance to its author's comparative youth, he expresses a young man's conclusion—that " the act of dying is generally very agreeable." It is noteworthy that shortly before his end, as a tired old man of 81, solitary and disillusioned, he repeated this belief in much the same language, in the characteristic essay on " Death " that appeared in *Religion and Realities*. His account of various eccentrics in the 1860 essay is delightful in its tolerant enjoyment of absurdities; for example, his story of Thomas Wirgman, the philosophical goldsmith, who persuaded the Guardians of St. Pancras to allow him to try out on the pauper children his system of metaphysics, which was to bring universal peace and virtue on earth by teaching a " grammar of the five senses."

In the next year Maudsley, no doubt stimulated by the fierce controversy between Owen and Huxley, wrote a learned and elaborate article on the "Genesis of Mind," in which the problems of cerebral development are surveyed. It is notable for the plain indications of Herbert Spencer's influence and for its more than Tennysonian confidence in man's upward progress; as for the former, one can understand Herbert Spencer's petulance in his letter to Tyndal in 1868, wherein he complained at Maudsley's barely acknowledged but heavy indebtedness to him. Maudsley's confidence in man's future, expressed with a simple and—to our embittered view—naïve faith, is startling, coming from a man who is now remembered as a pessimist. In 1860 all is for the best in the evolutionary survival of the fittest; the degenerate and the primitive are being eliminated as "humanity, in its progress upwards, fashions the supporting stem only by sacrificing the early branches. All observation proves that mankind is advancing. The beings of the present civilization are evidently superior to those of any past civilization, and the beings who now make barbarism appear to be disappearing from the earth." "When we reflect that moral principles are not merely intellectual speculations but actual laws of nature, as certain and uniform in their operations as are the physical laws there is every reason to anticipate that, as the recognition of the physical laws, has added so greatly to the power and comfort of mankind, so the practical realization of the moral laws in the conduct of life will increase the happiness, advance the mental development and, perhaps, insure the stability of nations." " In place of degeneration and destruction from ignorance of, and disobedience to, the physical laws, there are development and salvation from knowledge of, and obedience to, them. . . . As soon as ever men have attained to a sincere, intellectual recognition of the causes and laws of events, there inevitably springs up the correlative moral cognition. . . . We have a certain guarantee of moral progress." " Love and virtue must replace cruelty and vice: that . . . simple scientific observation of the natural course of the development of mind compels us gladly and confidently to anticipate; it is the realization in general practice of those sublime principles which revelation has inculcated. And such, happily, will be the functional expression of the superior type of brain amongst modern civilized nations." "Advancing knowledge is becoming conscious of the love that there is in every apparent evil. In fact, the wider and deeper our insight becomes, the more clearly do we perceive love working in every event of nature, all-embracing, all-supporting, all-powerful." These millenarian rhapsodies are strange; Maudsley was no Pangloss, nor was he writing a Bridgewater treatise, but he echoed the hopes of his time; and he was not the first to base his assurance of Utopia upon a pessimistic view of man's past state, from which a rational progress should henceforth redeem him. The development of this notion of progress in the nineteenth century, the confusion between the biological conception of progress through natural selection and the humanistic conception of it through the working of man's moral nature; the contrast, superficial but striking, between the optimists and the pessimists; the struggle to relate, if not to reconcile, religious with biological views of man's past and future—these are familiar to us in the pages of Ruskin and Carlyle, Herbert Spencer, Mill, and many more of the noted men of that time. Darwin himself wrote, at the conclusion of the *Origin of Species*: "As natural selection works solely for the good of each being, all corporal and mental environment will tend to progress towards perfection." I need not stress further the obvious similarity between Maudsley's views and those which agitated or comforted his generation, but his profession gave a special bias to his statement of these views and later led him away from them. He wrote, when he was 60, " a physician who had spent his life in ministering to diseased minds might be excused if, asking himself at the end of it whether he had spent his life well, accused the fortune of an evil hour which threw him on that track of work. He could not well help feeling something of bitterness in the certitude that one half of the disease he had dealt with never could get well, and something of misgiving in the reflection whether he had done real service to his kind by restoring the other half to do reproductive work. Nor would the scientific interest of his studies compensate entirely for the practical uncertainties, since their revelation of the structure of human nature might inspire a doubt whether, notwithstanding impassioned aims, paeans of progress, endless pageants of self-illusions, its capacity of degeneration did not equal, and might some day exceed, its capacity of development." That is a profoundly disillusioned, unhappy conclusion. It would be easy to read into it an unrelieved pessimism, but in later writings of his we find again qualified optimism, weighed against qualified pessimism; scepticism rather than despair. There were, as Maudsley himself maintained, two warring strains in him: " I have always thought and said," he wrote in his autobiography, " that the paternal and maternal were never vitally *welded* in me, but only *riveted*." He was, he tells us, in his youth self-assertive, but at the same time a tormenting critic of himself. His friends described his " difficult personality, his tart replies and scathing judgments," while they recall also his " genial look and friendly interest." He was, indeed, by no means a sociable, affable doctor, full of the team-spirit, who would demonstrate to the world that the psychiatrist is a good fellow; but he was not a Timon or Thersites either. He recognized the vigorous intrinsic animality in human beings, while he abhorred its manifestation in cruelty and deceit. As he grew older he took it more and more for granted, though he never quite reconciled the moral aspiration that had been so strong in his youth and was still quick in him as an old man, with the resigned, half-doubting meliorism that represented his final standpoint as philosopher-psychiatrist.

The warring strains in him, which he attributed to the intellectual tough-minded inheritance from his father and the emotional, religious warmth from his mother, asserted themselves in other views that appear often in the writings that stretch over sixty years. He denounced introspection and metaphysics, yet he constantly returned to the metaphysical problem of the mind-body relationship, which fascinated him (as it has always fascinated psychiatrists): he inveighed against the tyranny and deceit of words, especially of newly invented words, but he laboured to be eloquent and he proposed new coinages (such as "paramorphic" and "boulepsy"); he was a Positivist who rejected the ritual and religion which was the mainspring of Comte's teaching; he detested the brutishness, and worse than brutishness, men can display, yet he extolled war in language that shocks us: "War in one shape or another, open or disguised, has plainly been the divinely appointed instrument of human progress, carnage the immoral-seeming means by which the slow incarnation of morality in mankind has been effected"—we have to remind ourselves that this also is the language of Tennyson's Maud, that it was commoner, and certainly easier, then than now for war to be misconceived as a heroic and beneficient instrument of natural selection. There are other contradictions evident in his writings, but these, so far from indicating weakness, bespeak, I believe, Maudsley's criticism of doctrines prevailing in his time—doctrines which he espoused, it is true, and which he enriched from his experience as a psychiatrist; but this very experience and the tenacity and candour of his mind compelled him to doubt their general application. In some matter on which he wrote he was no wiser than his generation, but his chief inconsistencies bring him closer to modern views than a consistent adhesion or opposition to the opinions of his time—I mean the period between 1860 and 1890—would have permitted. This is illustrated by his views about the pathology of mental disease, which I shall mention presently.

It is well, moreover, to remember that Maudsley was fond of contrasting the two types of creative mind; thus in 1866 he wrote that the men who influence mankind fall into two classes—"men of wide intellectual grasp, vast wisdom and serene energy; and the men of limited vision, intense feeling, and impetuous energy"; thirty years later he is more biting about the second class—"persons who are clever but flighty, talented but unstable, intense but narrow, earnest but fanatical; all sorts of persons who, plunging into new movements, good or bad, and pursuing them with intemperate, perhaps distempered, zeal, lack the just balance of the faculties, the calm equilibrium of a stable mental organization, the true proportion or mean of nature which is the highest sanity. In the end the result is some such misproportioned incongruity as the philanthropic zealot, reeking of self, whose testimony or character no prudent man of the world could trust, or the intensely neurotic investigator, aspiring to be scientific, who, seeing nothing else, is utterly untrustworthy as an observer." In his latest book, written shortly before his death, he returned to the theme: "The plain truth is that the pessimist observes sincerely, thinks fully and feels deeply.... Pessimism is alike the stern conclusion of thinking reason and the pious confession of reverent religion.... Optimism, on the other hand, is the practical expression of unthinking feeling." There can be no doubt that he knew himself to belong to the more mournful company, though sometimes feeling the energy and often enjoying the faith and exultant vitality of the optimists.

The writers whom he most often quotes are significant: Goethe perhaps more than any other; Shakespeare, the Bible (especially Ecclesiastes and Isaiah), Milton, Bacon, Pascal, Montaigne, Robert Burton, Sir Thomas Browne, Gibbon, Amiel; and of philosophers, Locke, Hobbes, Hume, Hamilton. These are lofty minds, often of a sombre and sceptical cast, like his own. Then there are the medical and scientific authors with whom he was evidently familiar: Darwin, Huxley, Carpenter, Laycock, Prichard, Brown-Séquard (but he never quotes Galton, and seldom Hughlings Jackson, though he and Jackson were both close to the thought of Herbert Spencer and had other things in common, including their Yorkshire origin; perhaps Hughlings Jackson's fear and contempt towards the mentally ill, which Savage noted, rather alienated Maudsley, who felt a close and sympathetic kinship with the insane). With the German and French writers of his middle life he was as familiar as with his English contemporaries; but he seems not to have kept up his psychiatric reading after the eighties and nineties as much as his general reading (which included Karl Marx's writings).

I come now to Maudsley as physician and psychiatrist. He had a high conception of what a doctor's life should be, and it would be hard to find a more outspoken panegyric of the value and opportunities of our profession than that contained in his introductory lecture delivered to the medical students at University College, London, in 1876, while he was Professor of Medical Jurisprudence there. Throughout his life he tried to keep abreast of clinical and scientific developments, as his 1905 British Medical Association Lecture in Medicine showed; indeed his familiarity with then recent developments in physics is startling to a reader to-day; he stresses, for example, the importance of the demonstration that matter can be resolved into moving electric charges, and he says, " a living cell seems but a gross thing. Concentrated within its little body are subtle and intense forces continuously and quietly working which, if let loose in large explosive display, might suffice to blow up the chemist and his whole laboratory." It is his psychological rather than his general medical and scientific standpoint that is chiefly of interest to us.

Maudsley entered psychiatry at a time when the prestige of English and Scottish philosophers stood high throughout the learned world for their psychological speculations, and when British psychiatrists enjoyed very little regard outside these islands Pinel's strictures upon them had not been lived down, and only J. C. Prichard's writings and Conolly's had attracted some attention or excited controversy abroad. When the young Maudsley in 1867 published his *Physiology and Pathology of Mind* it was promptly acclaimed by Westphal, in Griesinger's new journal, as the most important psychiatric work to appear in that year, one which he hoped might long exercise an influence on our science. Similarly, Ribot gave the book warm but discriminating praise a few years later, by which time it had been translated into German, Italian, French and Japanese. Henceforward, until well within this century, few of the most prominent psychiatrists of other countries failed to show some acquaintance with Maudsley's writings and views, either on psychiatry in general or on those special questions of psychosomatic relations, criminal responsibility in mental disease, and the psychology of " supernatural seemings " to which he had devoted particular books. Although Bucknill, Daniel Hack Tuke, Clouston and some others later became known abroad, it was Maudsley that taught German and French psychiatrists that they could not safely disregard everything in our psychiatry except "no restraint." I think the same may be said of the Italian psychiatrists but I know too little of them, apart from Lugaro and Tanzi, to be sure. At all events, the publication of *Physiology and Pathology of Mind* was a turning point in English psychiatry; it presaged the end of the period in which psychiatry rested on a magma of empirical observations and windy philosophizing, and it embodied a critical synthesis of biological and other scientific advances so far as they had an evident bearing on mental activity, in health and disease. Moreover, it took account of what the French and the Germans were then so vigorously contributing to psychiatric theory and observation. I would not like to give an impression that Maudsley appeared a giant among the English pygmies; I have been convinced in reading those early volumes of the *Journal of Mental Science* that in the Association of Medical Officers of Asylums and Hospitals for the Insane there was as much capacity and erudition as might be found now in a much larger circle of our members, and perhaps more vitality than is commonly exhibited in a professional association when it has become large and prudent. Only an arrogant and ill-informed psychiatrist in our day would look down on the men who contributed to the advance of our subject in the mid-Victorian period. But though these contemporaries of Maudsley were men of considerable stature, they had not the grasp, the acumen and the facility of expression which made his work outstanding and potent. He had something important to say on many topics that are fundamental for psychologists and psychiatrists, and he said it insistently, pointing to recent discoveries and, still more, to some recent and old absurdities which were, in his eyes, strangling progress.

On these matters he felt so strongly that he wrote intemperately. His attacks on introspection were violent, beyond what he could justify in his later writings; but he was battling less against introspection and metaphysics in psychology than against that irrational dualism which denied that mental activity could be studied by the scientific method on the ground that it was exempt from any laws of predictable succession. Hence his diatribes, and his vehement assertion that psychology was cerebral physiology. Hence also his lifelong concern with the problems of will in disease and crime. As early as 1863 he had shown his bitter indignation at the way popular clamour and legal pedantry could cause a manifestly insane murderer to be hanged, and he could never stomach the argument that man has a dual composition—body (including brain) acting in a way determined by its structure and history, and mind, which having free will, is to be judged and held accountable quite otherwise than as the body is.

This is the place to consider Maudsley's view about consciousness—obviously a crucial issue in his campaign against dualism. Briefly, he held that consciousness is the adjunct of mental function, merely lighting up a small part of the mental process;

never preceding or dictating a mental occurrence, but only accompanying it or following it. The motives of behaviour "are very mixed, and their main work is unconscious." He was, of course, familiar with the views of von Hartmann, Schopenhauer, Beneke and other philosophers on this matter, and in his insistence from the beginning on a wholly physiological psychology he took account of the difficulties which the fact of consciousness had presented to these writers. He never succeeded in resolving the problem—who has?—but his standpoint about consciousness was, in essence, not different from that of, say, Lashley, allowing for the vast disparity in the relevant knowledge available to the two men. His constant stress upon the immense importance of the processes that occur unconsciously has led a psychoanalytic writer, Christoffel (to whose essay Dr. Stengel directed my attention), to claim him as in some sort a forerunner of psychoanalysis. I do not think the claim can be sustained. "Unconscious" was for Maudsley a negative psychological term of description; he applied it to cerebral happenings which in his view provided the whole dynamic of mental life, in contrast to the small segment of those cerebral happenings illuminated by consciousness, which the much-abhorred metaphysicians liked to study by introspection. As soon as some of his contemporaries attributed to "subliminal consciousness" a mental force and quality of its own, he was up in arms; he called it a signal example of clever beguilement by words, and jeered at this "subliminal consciousness which can do marvellous things—as well indeed it may, being a positive consciousness, created out of negation, . . . a something which is and is not at the same instant." There can be no doubt that the Freudian conception of the Unconscious was alien to Maudsley's thought, though it should be said that in many respects he was in sympathy with the psychoanalytic attitude; he constantly stressed the animality of human beings, their control by forces which they denied or ignored, their inner conflicts, the power of unsuspected or curbed sexuality (especially in women) and the passionate urges of the child. On the last matter his words may be quoted: " Whoever observes sincerely what a child's actual mind is, without being biased by preconceived notions of its primal purity, innocence and natural inclination to good, must see and own that its proclivities are not to good but to evil, and that the impulses which move it are the selfish impulses of passion. Give an infant in arms power in its limbs equal to its passions, and it would be more dangerous than any wild beast."

It would be impossible in this lecture to set out the chief features of Maudsley's clinical and theoretical psychiatry. I can only say that I have compared his book with Kraepelin's, published at about the same time (Maudsley's third edition and Kraepelin's second), and Maudsley's does not suffer by the comparison, though there are very wide differences in style and method; Kraepelin's is a text-book, Maudsley's a treatise. It would be a most valuable formative experience even now for young psychiatrists of ability to read Maudsley's major works; there they would meet a powerful critical intellect, versed in clinical practice, impatient of shams, and capable also of fertile synthesis. Maudsley's originality appears in his assertion of opinions, then heterodox, and even now fancied by many to be banners first inscribed and flown in our own enlightened day. I will mention a few of these. He maintained that the psychosomatic relation is a reciprocal one occurring within a complex but unified organism, "each part of which calls the furthest brother, which acts upon the rest of it and is reacted on by it." He emphasized that emotion affecting every part of the body is "rooted in the unity of organic life," and he asserted that "it is in the natural order of events that continuance of perverted function should lead to organic disease." He required that treatment should be adapted to the particular patient—"always the rule of rules should be to treat an individual who is sick, not an abstract disease." Narcotic drugs should be used with the greatest restraint. He rejected the claim of men like Schroeder van der Kolk to have discovered in the morbid anatomy of the brain the pathology of mental disease. "The morbid anatomy of insanity," he wrote, "would take little room were speculation rigidly excluded and it limited to what is actually seen and known. Nor does that which is seen, it must be confessed, throw much light on the symptoms.... The intimate chemical and molecular changes which are presumably the conditions of mental disorder go on in a domain of nature the subtleties of which far exceed the subtleties of observation." In another remarkable passage he suggests that it might be easier to conceive what nervous disorder means if, "instead of thinking of the body as a material structure built up of so many organs, one were to abolish in imagination the gross matter, to think it clean away, and to conceive its organs as so many and divers complexes of very fine and active vibrations bound within the forms and shapes of the different organs and united by the most complete harmony of inter-nuncial vibrations, the whole organism being the formal unison of these multitudinous and various complexes of energies." In all his writings on this theme, even where he falls (like every medical writer of his time who dealt with it) into "brain mythology," he displays a prescient imagination; thus, in melancholia (for which no one had then suggested leucotomy) he speculated about the "exorbitant and predominant almost exclusive, activity of certain brain tracts charged with sad feeling"; and in mania he guessed that "the functions of the most fine and special traceries of the cortical reflexes are suspended or effaced, being too delicate to lend themselves to the currents of turbulent energy which now pass along courser channels." Crude as these surmises are, they are perhaps no cruder than those will seem in fifty years which now, to us, represent the striking discoveries recently made in cerebral physiology, applied to the problems of mental disease. Still, these opinions of Maudsley's are at best speculations, unsupported by any evidence. Where he dealt with more substantial matters, Maudsley again strikes us as an anticipator of our practice. He even suggested, in his Goulstonian Lectures in 1870, that if we had the power to induce general convulsions in some cases of acute insanity, "we might, for the time being at any rate, cure the insanity." Not only in his precepts for treatment but in his general approach there is much that psychiatrists of our generation consider it important to reiterate. He emphasized the need for a full, searching life-history of the patient; causes are multiple, the notion of cause itself needing reconsideration and restatement; inherited predisposition is the most potent influence, but the actual outbreak of illness depends on whether circumstances of upbringing and subsequent life have been propitious or unpropitious; patients have often had the ill-fortune to be twice penalized, first in a bad inheritance, and secondly in a bad training given them by those who gave them that inheritance; there must therefore be " close and diligent study of the particular qualities of individual character, mental and bodily, and an exact exposition of its relations to its circumstances ... a patient unfolding of (the person's) action on circumstances and of their action on him." The effect of circumstances, acting on a suitable inheritance, may be not insanity, but a lesser mental deformity or nervous obliquity, or it may be crime; crime " is clearly sometimes the result of an actual neurosis which has close relations of nature and descent to other neuroses."

There is a further topic to be mentioned among the many which might be taken to illustrate Maudsley's expression of views now sometimes trumpeted as up-to-date corrections of the unwisdom of our predecessors—it is classification. I single it out because Dr. Gregory Zilboorg, in his erudite *History of Medical Psychology*, has been severe upon Maudsley in this particular. He says that " the classificatory effort of Maudsley appears unenlightened; were it not for his insistence on careful historical studies of each individual patient, one could not easily discern the human being behind the classificatory frame," and he says that Maudsley was " purely materialistic and purely descriptive "—a remark often made nowadays about Kraepelin too. As early as 1859 you will recall Maudsley had written that " a philosophical history of insanity ... should not be content to occupy itself with a catalogue of appearances." In his *Pathology of Mind* he followed at first, with patent misgivings, the classification of Esquirol; he was critical of Skae's ambitious scheme, though recognizing the practical if limited usefulness of singling out mental diseases regularly associated with a bodily disease; and he similarly appraised Morel's scheme of classification. The note on classification in the second edition, 1868, states his very reasonable position. In 1879, in the third edition, he gives a brief, clear explanation of his grounds for adhering, for the present, to a simple symptomatological classification; " this necessity of calling up by a general term the conception of a certain co-existence and sequence of symptoms is a reason why the old classification holds its ground against classifications that are alleged to be more scientific; it is good as far as it goes, but it by no means goes to the root of the matter; whereas the classifications which pretend to go to the root of the matter go beyond what knowledge warrants and are radically faulty." Finally in 1895 he says quite explicitly in the Preface, " A leading aim through (the work) having been to clear the ground by endeavouring to think the subject into simplicity and to set forth the results in as plain language as possible, I have purposely avoided mention of the numerous and elaborate classifications which, in almost distracting succession, have been formally proposed as exhaustive and tacitly condemned as useless. For the same reason I have shunned the use of the many learned names—of Greek, Latin and Graeco-Latin derivation—which have been invented in appalling numbers often to denote simple things and sometimes, it may be feared, with the effect of confounding apprehension of them. Insanities are not really so different from sanities that they need a new and a special language to describe them; nor are they so separated from other nervous disorders by lines of demarcation as to render it wise to distinguish every feature of them by a special technical nomenclature."

I have dealt a little more fully with this matter than its intrinsic importance warrants, but as Dr. Zilboorg has been so damning in his main comment on Maudsley, largely on the score of his classificatory procedure, I thought it proper to clear the issue, in the hope that Dr. Zilboorg in subsequent editions of his justly esteemed book will give due recognition to Maudsley's outstanding merits among nineteenth century psychiatrists.

So far Maudsley appears as the brilliant iconoclast, the erudite reasoner who could expound lucidly the principles of physiological psychology, the sage, the far-sighted writer on clinical psychiatry. His influence, in spite of his unsociable ways, was immense, and was not limited to the narrow circle of psychiatrists and psychologists; Darwin, for example, quoted Maudsley frequently in the *Descent of Man* and in the *Expression of the Emotions*. Professor Boring, of Harvard, the discriminating historian of experimental psychology, wrote in 1929 that the first edition of Maudsley's *Physiology and Pathology of Mind* was a " very influential book which forms the background for the tradition for medical psychology in Great Britain." I need not amplify such a judgment or look closely into the indirect means whereby Maudsley's influence extended beyond the range of those who knew him or read his books. It is clearly also difficult or impossible to separate his influence from that of precursors and contemporaries with whom he had much in common; still more difficult to separate or trace it in successors who have incorporated his views along with much knowledge which was not available to him and many opinions which would have astounded him. It might therefore be assumed that his influence, though great in his active period, became steadily less manifest and less potent as the decades passed. If his works had consisted solely of his writings and clinical activity, that would be so, and he would now be a fading, Victorian figure, no better known to the psychiatrists of a later day than, say, Hack Tuke, Magnan or Kahlbaum. But Maudsley, the sceptic, the childless pessimist, decided upon a constructive act which would project his intention further than books or talking could; he created a living organism, to be his heir. The steps he took have been described by Sir Frederick Mott, who acted as go-between in the drawn-out negotiations between Maudsley and the London County Council that started in 1907, but the genesis of the project lay further back. While he was at Cheadle Royal, Maudsley had urged the need for early treatment. Then, in his early days as a rising consultant in London, he had evolved plans for such early treatment in concert with that earnest champion of family care, " my friend Baron Mundy, M.D., of Moravia," and others of Maudsley's circle, who used to meet (as Crichton Browne tells us) at a Soho restaurant to discourse about the future of psychiatry and the betterment of mankind. I had supposed these plans of Maudsley's to be pioneer efforts until I chanced upon the paper in which Samuel Gaskell, in 1860, when he had become Commissioner in Lunacy, advocated voluntary treatment, free from legal forms, so that remedial measures might be instituted early and for a class of patient, with mild forms of disorder, who would not " resort to asylums as at present constituted." Maudsley must have read this paper with conviction, and still more he must have been impressed by the reiterated views of his father-in-law, Conolly, regarding the need for schools for clinical instruction in the nature and treatment of mental maladies. Thus Conolly, in 1862, four years before his death, told our predecessors in this Association that schools for psychiatric instruction were the " great want of our profession, and a great impediment to any progress in it. . . . Until you have these schools, you will never be able to command men to take positions of great importance—not such as you would sometimes wish could be found." It was not, however, until 1907 that Maudsley could begin to give practical effect to these ideas implanted so long before. Mott, who had been one of his pupils at University College and who was now Pathologist to the L.C.C. Mental Hospitals, wrote a proposal after visiting Kraepelin's Clinic at Munich, in which he urged the creation of a similar University psychiatric hospital in England which should be devoted to early treatment, research and postgraduate training. This accorded well with Maudsley's views; he got in touch with Mott and made his offer of £30,000 to the London County Council if they would build the hospital, subject to its association with the University of London; this offer, supported by A. J. Balfour and Arthur Rucker, the Principal of the University, was accepted by the London County Council in 1908, but there were delays; the site was not chosen until 1912, nor the building completed till the end of 1915. Before Maudsley died, he had seen the hospital, under Mott's energetic guidance, doing some of the teaching and pioneering work which he wanted, though, of course, it was not until 1923 that it was opened to fulfil all the purposes which Maudsley had outlined in the article he wrote for the *Archives of Neurology and Psychiatry* in 1909.

It is not for me to examine what effect the existence and activities of the Maudsley Hospital have had upon the advancement of psychiatry, but it is clear that the hospital has been the instrument whereby Maudsley, after his death, continues to be a potent force. If, however, its work were not carried out in his spirit and to further his aims, it would not be Maudsley's inheritor and agent, but his unfaithful steward, writing an ironical footnote on the vanity of human wishes. I have tried, therefore, with such knowledge of Maudsley's views and character as could be got by steeping myself in his writings, to picture him returning to the scene and judging us in the light of his purpose. Two things are certain: that what he saw and disliked he would condemn in good set phrase or scathing epigram; and that everything new or supported by new knowledge would be brought to the bar, not so much of his former opinions on the matter, as of his standards of truth and scientific method, and of his requirement that it should be relevant to the understanding of human nature in health and disease.

I think, when we were planning how to welcome this most worshipful and august of visitors, and thinking how we might fitly conduct our founder to show him to what uses his gift had been turned, we would decide to bring him first to Professor Meyer. Not that neuropathology had been his concern—he was always a clinician who had no laboratory experience or any evident taste for experiment; but because the work done in that department, the outlook and method, the nexus with clinical problems and opportunity, are in the fullest accord with the beliefs he expressed in the *Physiology and Pathology of Mind*, in *Body and Mind*, in *Organic to Human*, and in many essays and addresses. He would even find kindred interests in what may be called the by-ways of Professor Meyer's department; I recall, for example, that he wrote, as long ago as 1867, " It is deserving of remark that the different nervous centres of the body manifest elective affinities for particular poisons. . . . That medicinal substances do display these elective affinities is a proof, at any rate, that there are important though delicate differences in the constitution or composition of the different nervous centres, notwithstanding that we are unable to detect the nature of them. It may be also that there is shadowed out in these different effects of poisons on the nervous system a means which may ultimately be of use in the investigation of the constitution of the latter "—a prescient statement, ensuring his delight on finding how fully Dr. Meyer had turned his prediction into fact.

Where we would wish to take him next I am not so sure; electroencephalography would surely fascinate and delight him, as a fresh disclosure of those delicate traceries and enural activities about which he constantly surmised; or biochemical studies, esoteric to him as to most of us, but in keeping with his faith in the importance for mental disorder of general metabolic and cell chemistry; these might be the most obvious activities to show him next. But if we delayed his entry into the clinical territories, it would probably be at the risk of a sardonic inquiry as to whether we treated any patients nowadays. We would therefore be brief in detaining him while we explained the subtleties of the relation between the Institute and the Hospital, and the closeness of our connection with other medical schools of the University—a matter always near to his heart—and told him also of the auspicious union effected so lately between his Hospital and that ancient and notable hospital of which his friend Savage was the head, and which had had, long ago in the days of Henry the Seventh, a Thomas Maudsley as its Master and Warden. When in his visit he came to the wards he would find, I think, much being practised which he had advocated and prized—the careful inquiry into history; the regard for physical examination; the concern with individual needs and constitution; the avoidance of liberal sedation; the dislike of rigidity and dogmatism, whether in diagnosis or treatment, theory or practice; the emphasis on the continuity or communality of healthy with morbid; the care for hereditary and eugenic considerations; the social approach to the study and treatment of childhood deviations, of occupational inadequacy, of neurotic deformity and suicidal despair. What he would say about our psychopathology and psychotherapy is a matter for wide conjecture; I think the Jungian doctrines would excite his warmest invective, and the Freudian perhaps his coldest approval—in parts; but seeing that at the hospital we are not all convinced of the rightness of the same theory of psychopathology or the same method of psychotherapy, he would, I imagine, concede that in matters such as these, admitting of legitimate differences of opinion and practice, it is fitting that a University School should allow teachers of proved capacity and experience to put their several standpoints *sine ira et studio*—or at any rate *sine ira*. Then, in the psychological department, he would certainly be pleased to find an animal laboratory and a child development unit, for he had said that the study of the plan of development of mind, as exhibited in animals and in infants, would furnish results of the greatest value and be essential to a true mental science. What he would make of the statistical methods and the study of personality through tests is a hard question, for he liked objective methods and rigorous logic, but had no taste for mathematics. It is significant that in his paper on " The New Psychology " in 1900 he repudiated those psychological studies of animals and of children which used terms without definition and made observations without objectivity, and he extolled the experimental method, declaring that " to express the results in arithmetical numbers or algebraic formulas is a method of demonstration which cannot fail . . . to bring psychology into touch with realities and to put positive meaning into its language." At the same time he castigated psychophysics for its aridity and neglect of individual differences, and said that though measurements might be " multiplied and accumulated world without end, yet if they remain scattered, incoherent, fragmentary heaps, they will only be monuments of sterile industry—monumental mockeries of knowledge." So it may be guessed that his judgment of our statistical labours in psychology would be favourable, but reluctantly so, since the bent of his mind was away from ready acceptance of such concepts as the statistical aggregate and uncertain inference, but this may be a hasty conclusion. It is well to remember what Maudsley said at the end of the soundly but rather destructively critical paper which I have just referred to: " I conclude that man as a whole is a larger affair . . . than any single method of minute inquiry—be it chemical, physical, pathological, microscopical, or psycho-physical —will ever unfold. . . . There is work enough for as many methods of study of mind as are rationally based: have the definite aim of a concrete mental organisation to be studied, and work definitely and progressively for it by observation of facts, exclude not one another, but know that in the end they must bring, and, knowing, strive to bring their results into harmony."

I have said very little about Maudsley's personal life, partly, of course, because the data are meagre, but chiefly because he has plainly shown how he detested to see the trivial and private details of a man's life exposed after his death. Neither have I dwelt upon the themes, few but rather striking, on which the knowledge or the sentiments and experience of our later time would judge him to have been wholly mistaken. Each generation, as Maudsley himself often said, has a common heritage of ideas; each individual mind reflects the thought of its time; and the men of each generation are apt to look kindly but loftily upon the errors and defects of those who preceded them. Few, however, who had become familiar with his thought would feel disposed to condescend to Henry Maudsley, or to dwell, in extenuating advocacy, upon any mistakes into which he fell. He was, I have said it already, a man of incisive and tenacious intellect, a man gifted with unusual foresight, capable of planning and enforcing a great constructive design, such as I believe the inception of the Maudsley Hospital to have been. To his contemporaries at different phases of his long life he seemed other than this; there seem to have been times when they thought him a bitter recluse, given over to mordant nihilism. But they mistook the appearances. It is true, as he once scribbled on a blank page of the *Physiology of Mind*, that he never hated people, but often felt contempt; his contempt, however, was as free from bitterness as his social brusquerie was without malice or any unkindness. I may conclude with recalling the occasion when Maudsley delivered his Presidential Address to this Association; it was in 1871. When he had finished, Clouston took part in the discussion and said: " Dr. Maudsley's address has been one of utter and entire scepticism. He treated three subjects: the prevention of insanity; the sending of patients to asylums; and the treatment by sedatives. And he answered them (thus): Insanity cannot be prevented until we arrive at some future state of human existence in which we shall all live in the light of right reason; patients get much better out of asylums than in them; and do not give sedatives as you will probably poison your patients." When Maudsley came to reply, he said: " I think Dr. Clouston accurately described my paper as one of scepticism, but in accepting this description of it I would use the word not in an ill sense, as Dr. Clouston might do. I would remind him that scepticism was a very good word before it got an ill meaning: that fundamentally scepticism, and episcopacy, and bishop have the same root; that they all come from the Greek word Skopeō which means to examine, to look to." To examine, to look to—that is what Maudsley always did; he examined the knowledge of his time that had a bearing on psychology and mental disorder, and he looked well to it that out of his consideration of these things should come as much gain of truth, of benefit to the mentally ill, of continuing advancement of psychiatry, as his powers could compass. Such a sceptic we do well to honour.

PREFACE

THE first edition of *The Physiology and Pathology of Mind* appeared in 1867, and a second edition in the following year. In 1876 the first part of it was published as a separate volume entitled *The Physiology of Mind*, and in 1879 the second part followed in separate form as *The Pathology of Mind*. This book, although retaining the old name, is virtually new; for while old matter has been left out and much fresh matter added, the whole has been recast, the form of its presentation changed, and the text entirely rewritten. As it would not have been proper to give it a new title, since it deals with the same subject as the former treatise, and necessarily incorporates the revised substance of what was contained in it, I have retained the old title, only adding a supplementary notification of the present scope of the contents. As it is now, the work may be said to present the last ripe fruits of observations and reflections the first green fruits of which appeared so long ago:

A leading aim throughout it having been, if I may so say, to clear the ground by endeavours to think the subject into simplicity and to set forth the results in as plain language as possible, I have purposely avoided mention of the numerous and elaborate classifications which, in almost distracting succession, have been formally proposed as exhaustive and tacitly condemned as useless. For the same reason I have shunned the use of the many learned names — of Greek, Latin, and Græco-Latin derivation — which have been invented in appalling numbers often to denote simple things, and sometimes, it may be feared, with the effect of confounding apprehension of them. Insanities are not really so different from sanities that they need a new and special language to describe them; nor are they so separated from other nervous disorders by lines of demarcation as to render it wise to distinguish every feature of them by a special technical nomenclature. The effect of such a procedure can hardly fail to be to make artificial distinctions where divisions exist not in nature, and thus to set up barriers to true observation and inference. Without doubt the ground now is encumbered with a deal of rubbish which must be cleared away before the foundations of good building can be laid.

The foregoing dates may serve to prevent the reader who meets with opinions, perhaps terms and phrases of expression, which he may have met with in contemporary writers (abroad or at home) on mind and its disorders, from jumping off-hand to the conclusion that I have taken from them what I may have taken only from myself. Among less curious experiences of the same kind, it has twice happened to me to stumble accidentally in journals on articles which I should have said to be nearly exact copies of articles by me, had it not been that the writers of them published them as original. A chapter in the last edition of this book having appeared in such original guise, I may now guard myself against any worse charge than that of having been a little beforehand in saying what somebody had in mind to say in due course later.

CONTENTS

PART I

THE NATURE AND CAUSATION OF INSANITY

CHAPTER I

	PAGE
INSANITY: WHAT IS IT?	1

CHAPTER II

CAUSATION OF INSANITY—*SOCIOLOGICAL* . . . 21

CHAPTER III

CAUSATION OF INSANITY—*MALFORMITIES OF MIND* . . 63

CHAPTER IV

CAUSATION OF INSANITY—*PATHOLOGICAL* . . . 93

PART II

THE SYMPTOMATOLOGY OF INSANITIES

CHAPTER I

INSANITY WITH DEPRESSION—MELANCHOLIA . . . 163

CHAPTER II

	PAGE
MELANCHOLY WITH DELUSION	188

CHAPTER III

INSANITY WITH EXCITEMENT—MANIA	234

CHAPTER IV

MANIA	262

CHAPTER V

INSANE DEFORMITIES OF MIND	297

CHAPTER VI

CONDITIONS OF MENTAL WEAKNESS—
1. IDIOCY AND IMBECILITY 334
2. DEMENTIA 345

PART III

THE CLINICAL VARIETIES OF INSANITIES

CHAPTER I

INSANITY OF CHILDREN	364

CHAPTER II

ADOLESCENT INSANITIES	387

CHAPTER III

INSANITY AND CHILD-BEARING	415
INSANITIES OF THE DECLINE OF LIFE	420
SENILE INSANITIES	426

CHAPTER IV

	PAGE
GENERAL PARALYSIS	435

CHAPTER V

EPILEPTIC INSANITY 477

CHAPTER VI

ALCOHOLIC INSANITIES	492
INSANITY AND PHTHISIS	503
INSANITY AND GROSS BRAIN-DISEASE . . .	507

PART IV

THE MORBID ANATOMY AND TREATMENT OF INSANITY

CHAPTER I

THE MORBID ANATOMY OF INSANITY 515

CHAPTER II

TREATMENT OF INSANITY 530

PART I

THE NATURE AND CAUSATION OF INSANITY

> Fortes creantur fortibus, et bonis
> Est in juvencis, est in equis patrum
> Virtus, nec imbellem feroces
> Progenerant aquilæ columbam.
>
> HORACE.

> Wohl dem, der seiner Väter gern gedenkt,
> Der froh von ihren Thaten, ihrer Grösse,
> Den Hörer unterhält und still sich freuend
> An's Ende dieser schönen Reihe sich
> Geschlossen sieht! Denn es erzeugt nicht gleich
> Ein Haus den Halbgott noch das Ungeheuer;
> Erst eine Reihe Böser oder Guter
> Bringt endlich das Entsetzen, bringt die Freude
> Der Welt hervor.
>
> GOETHE'S *Iphigenie auf Tauris.*

CHAPTER I

INSANITY: WHAT IS IT?

BY insanity of mind is meant such derangement of the leading functions of thought, feeling, and will, together or separately, as disable the person from thinking the thoughts, feeling the feelings, and doing the duties of the social body in, for, and by which he lives. Alienated from his normal self and from his kind, he is in the social organisation that which a morbid growth is in the physiological organism: something which, being a law unto itself, in the body but not of it, is an alien there, a morbid kind, and ought in the interests of the whole either to be got rid out of it or sequestrated and rendered harmless in it. However it has come about, whether by fate or fault, he is now so self-regarding a self as to be incapable of right regard to the notself; altruism has been swallowed up in a morbid egoism.

Forasmuch, however, as societies differ much in different ages, places, and peoples, and in different social sections and strata of the same people, it does not fail to happen that thoughts, feelings, and acts which are natural and avowedly sane at one time and in one medium are unnatural and pass for insane at another time and in another medium. He who has in him the current social nature of one epoch and is suited to live in it may be quite out of harmony with the social thought and feeling of another epoch and unsuited to live in it. Were anybody nowadays to build a column sixty feet high and to live on the top of it, occupying himself from morn to eve with repeated bendings of his body from forehead to feet, until curious spectators tired of counting the number of his prostrations, he would without doubt be thought mad; but when Simeon Stylites, performing a Christian plagiarism of pagan examples, built his lofty column and acted in that way he was esteemed a signal example of religious devotion and extolled as a saint. As all living things are in a continual flux, never constant in one stay, but are by change brought to perfection and then by continuance of change to decay, it comes to pass that religions, like empires, decay and die, and that in the whirligig of time it is the lot of the distinguished saints of one religion to be accounted madmen or impostors by the partisans of a succeeding religion. There have been savages who have deemed it piety to kill and eat their aged parents when these had become burdensome to themselves and to them, and others who, counting it no shame to perform their sexual functions in public, have thought it gross indecency to eat in public. What would be thought now in any civilized country of a person who practised the piety of those or the open intercourse of these savages? When the belief in witchcraft was as strong and general in all countries as it is still among barbarous peoples, the complaint of any one who proclaimed himself bewitched was received as awful truth, and the malignant witch forthwith sought out, tortured, and put to a cruel death; but if any decently educated person were to believe himself bewitched at the present day he would be thought to labour under an insane delusion and to need medical treatment. Every day in the lowest strata of society a person says and does habitually that which, were it said or done by a person of the more refined classes, would infallibly denote mental disorder in him. So much do the particular conditions of the society in which the individual lives fix the meaning of his thoughts, feelings, and acts, and so incumbent is it to weigh them critically when judging what is or is not madness in a particular instance. Nay more: to take exact account also of the particular circumstances of the incident in question; for that which would be a natural and fitting act in its proper circumstances might be so extraordinary an offence against propriety in other circumstances that it could then proceed only from aberration of mind.

Insanity means essentially then such a want of harmony between the individual and his social medium, by reason of some defect or fault of mind in him, as prevents him from living and working among his kind in the social organisation. Completely out of tune there, he is a social discord of which nothing can be made. What is the nature of the fault in him? It may be simply a natural defect or congenital deprivation of mind, one or more of its faculties being absent or stunted owing to defective cerebral organisation; in which case the person is *idiot* or *imbecile* according as the degree of mental deprivation is greater or less. Or the fault may be a derangement of mental functions not originally defective, owing to disorder of their extremely fine, complex, and intricate nervous substrata; in which case he is deranged, out of his mind, *insane* or *lunatic*.

Obviously the derangement may be brought about in two ways—either mainly from within, when there is much natural infirmity and instability of the mental organisation, or mainly from without, when a powerful extrinsic cause of disorder acts on a mental constitution in which there is little or no intrinsic fault. The strongest mind in the world could not help being overthrown by such external cause as severe injury to the brain, or gross disease of it, or by the flow of a much vitiated blood through it; and in that case the derangement might properly be described as accidental or occasional. But when the alienation of mind is the result of a great native instability thereof, whereby it easily topples over, or is the culmination of an irregular and perverted development of faculties, whereby it has grown awry into such disproportion or actual deformity of its parts as to be incapable of social functions, or easily to become so on the occasion of a slight external shock or strain, the disorder is essentially natural or intrinsic. Most instances lie between these extremes of strong and weak mental organisation; they represent a conspiracy, in varying contributory proportions, of external and internal factors. Few are the cases in which, when an outside event overthrows the mind, it is not right to suspect and, suspecting, to search for the secret coefficient of an infirmity of mental constitution, whereby a sorrow, need, trouble, or other adversity which glides easily off persons of a more robust nature causes a kind or degree of commotion of mind fatal to its balance.

It is the custom to speak of insanity as disease of mind, but in a large class of cases it is not disease in the ordinary sense of the term so much as distortion or deformity—that is, growth gone awry. Unpropitious conditions of nurture and training have conspired with an innate bias of nature to produce such a wry and disproportionate growth of one quality or set of qualities of mind, such a want of proportion or *ratio* of them, that the person is *irrational;* the exaggerated growth then becoming the predominant note of a particular variety of insanity. Since the mental distortion may be of every degree and kind, so slight as to be no more than eccentricity that is consistent with sanity or so great as to go beyond the bounds of reason, it is not possible to draw a distinct line of division between sanity and insanity. There exists no such separating boundary on the one side of which lies positive disease and on the other side not; there will always be persons whom some will think mad and others think not mad, or who might be thought mad in one place and time and not in another place and time.

In speaking of insanity as *disease of mind* the difficulty lies not only in defining exactly what is disease, but also in obtaining a clear and exact idea what mind means. The notion of a spiritual entity which exists and can be diseased apart from the body is pretty well obsolete, albeit many of those who make this acknowledgment in the general, having made it, go on forthwith to speak of its functions in the particular, especially of imagination, moral feeling, and will, as if they had abstract being, and it were a derogation from their dignity to think of them as dependent on a physical basis. Failures of morality and will therefore they view not as faults which are avenged on mortals by process of natural law in this world, but as sins which will be avenged on immortals in a world to come. Were they to substitute the term mental organisation for the term mind on every occasion of its use, forming for themselves a conception of an area somewhere instead of a metaphysical point nowhere, the exercise might be profitable and its results fruitful in giving substance to thought and meaning to words. Anyhow, that is what the practical psychologist must needs do who can find no footing for himself in metaphysical abstractions, but has to deal with the defects and disorders of the fine and complex nervous plexuses which subserve all mental functions, the highest equally with the lowest—with defaults, that is, of the mental organisation.

What is the mental organisation? The key of its structure and function is a simple reflex or excitomotor act. The type of its structure is, on the one side, a sensory or afferent nerve along which, in response to an impression made on its endings, an ingoing current passes to a central nerve-cell, and on the other side a motor or efferent nerve connected also with the nerve-cell, along which the resulting outgoing current passes to the muscles that react on the outer world. Such simple nervous structure by which a message is received from without and fit reaction made to it is practically the entire nervous system of the lowest creature which owns one, and it is the basis of the more complex structures that subserve the adjustments of the highest creatures to their external conditions; for it is by the multiplication of cells and fibres, and by complication of tracts and connections, that their nervous structures, however complex, are built up. In the complex plexuses formed by the multiplication and complication of cells, fibres, and connections, there are the obvious means of associating several ingoing currents proceeding from different sensory endings and of making fit distributions of energy and different combinations of distributions along several tracks or lines of conduction. Moreover, in the ascending scale of animal organisation from the more simple and general to the more complex and special structure there is a further complication of different levels of nerve-plexuses; and it is obvious that in the superposition of areas of higher level of reflex action with which areas of lower level are connected, and in the more abstract superordinate functions of which their lower functions are represented, there are the means by which pregnant impulses may descend from the higher areas of the nervous hierarchy to the several subordinate centres and be there suitably analysed, as it were, and distributed.

Considering that there are some hundreds of millions of nerve-cells and fibres in the cerebral cortex of man, that every cell which is not unattached has its own connection or connections, and that every one of the multitude of fibres goes separate to its destination, whatever that be, imagination may go some way to realise how exceedingly fine, numerous, intricate, and complex are the nervous networks which constitute the mental organisation. There are abundant means of physical reflection to serve all the purposes of mental reflection, more perhaps than have ever yet been made full use of by minds of the largest capacity; indeed it is a specious surmise that there are multitudes of available cells in the cortex waiting to make their connections as fast as new observations and reflections shall require and use them to register newly discovered relations of things.

As the mechanism of a simple reflex act is the elemental type of the complex mental structure, so the simple reflex act is the elemental type of the complex mental function. To receive an impression and to make a fit reaction to it, either in order to embrace the stimulus when it is agreeable and useful or to repel and evade it when it is painful and hurtful, that is the fundamental factor in all mental function; the most complex of which represents essentially, though in abstract representations, by cortical registrations— as it were by a system of algebraic symbols—the greatest number of the fittest movements in answer to the greatest number of fitting impressions. Many small creatures are admirable in the adaptations of their acts to their ends, being more perfect than man in that respect, but the range of their impressions is very limited and special compared with the wider and ever-widening range of experience which his senses open to him; they are perfect machines for their comparatively narrow ends, their more simple nervous system being wholly appropriated and, as it were, stereotyped to certain set uses; whereas his complex nervous system is a progressive and perfecting machine plastic to the new uses which his pains and gains through the ages gradually incorporate into it. What could be more clever than a bee along the tracks of its instincts, what more stupid than a bee outside them? Growing reason is the progressive gaining by experience of what, in elementary form, is innate or instinct in many of the lower animals.[1] Purposive reflex action without conscious design we call instinct, and the more complex the act the more wonderful the instinct, but purposive action consciously adapted is called reason, because it is desire guided to its end by experience. At bottom the latter is just as reflex as the former, and the former as essentially reason as the latter, instinct being formed reason and reason instinct in process of formation; or they are both alike acts of reason, if that description of them be preferred, the one of implicit the other of explicit reason,—the actual processes of the same nature, however we choose to name them.

That the fit adjustment of movement to impression is the

[1] Having found the powers to do a variety of acts instinct in different animal organisations, men have thereupon made *instinct* a substantive faculty and treated it as an explanation. It would be just as good an explanation to make of *innate* or of *implant* a substantive faculty and thereupon to ascribe them to it. That so much time and work have been given to tedious doubts and discussions whether such animals as dogs and horses possess reason is a proof how little psychology has been a science of observation, and how much its concern has been with words not things; since there was not an intelligent shepherd or groom who could not at any time, had the problem been intelligently put to him, have settled it off-hand and was not daily solving by his daily management of these animals. The question, Are animals machines? might profitably be supplemented by the question, Is reason mechanical? That is to say, organic machinery in mechanical making.

quality of perfect reflex action is plain enough, but it is not so plain that it is the fundamental quality of the more complex process of reason or intelligence. Nevertheless that is so; to perceive or be sensible of a coexistence or sequence of impressions and to determine consciously fit actions in relation to them is to distribute the æsthesodic or afferent impulses through central junctions along nerve-tracks whose union in function shall effect the desired end; and that is to act with purpose after reflection—in other words, to understand and will. The true nature of the process is masked by its complexity, and especially by the symbolic representation of bodily functions through the highest cortical reflexes of the brain; but still more masked perhaps by the presence of consciousness and by the traditional misconception of what it is and does in mental function. It has been very difficult to persuade the speculative psychologists who elaborate webs of philosophy out of their own consciousnesses that consciousness has nothing to do with the actual work of mental function; that it is the adjunct not the energy at work; not the agent in the process, but the light which lightens a small part of it. In no case does the consciousness of a particular mental state go before and dictate it; it comes into being only with the actual state, attending or following it; no one is ever, nor for the life of him could ever be, conscious of the state until the state *is*. We may put consciousness aside then when we are considering the nature of the mechanism and the manner of its work, for it is a pretty safe assumption that when the same act is performed consciously on one occasion and on another occasion in exactly the same way unconsciously the same mechanism has been at work. Dreams and the dreamlike products of imagination might occasion less surprise to psychologists could they but see and acknowledge that the brain has and performs mental functions and get rid of the notion that it does not and cannot perform the functions we call memory, reason, and imagination without extraneous metaphysical help.

Nothing is more certain than that when we have done

an act a thousand times, whether it be an act of bodily skill or an act of judgment, we can do it better without consciousness than with it. Every immediate perception or apprehension is a proof of this; for although it appears to be instant and instinctive, it is actually, in origin and nature, just as much an inference as any act of judgment or long discourse of reason which we perform deliberately; neither more nor less than gradually learnt motor adaptation to special sensory impression — literally, the right *apprehension* or grasp of the object. The forms of objects and their various qualities are essentially such fit motor apprehensions. But because the process of learning begins with life and goes on continually and insensibly through it, its steps lapse in consciousness and the apprehension which had to be tediously acquired comes to seem immediate and intuitive. In like manner a judgment which, being well based on sound experience, is instantaneous and instinctive, is so because the steps of its process have lapsed in consciousness. In both perception and judgment, the premises being given, the conclusion which follows inevitably in every soundly constituted mind is just as necessary a reflex act or effect as is the infant's sucking when the mother's nipple is put between its lips.

I may set it down then that in the development of the functions or so-called faculties of mind we have to do with a process of gradual mental organisation after the type of reflex action—in fact, with the formation of a number of special and complex interlinked cerebral reflexes. Consciousness attends the process of adaptation, tentative endeavours, the practice of means to ends, the steps of organisation; it lapses when skill is perfect, whether it be skill of thought or skill of action. An angry wasp stings instantly with perfect art and skill, because a perfecting practice through the ages has been embodied in a most fit mechanism, owing to a process of extinction of the wasps which did not, and of the survival of those which did, succeed in so defending themselves : it does not now need to remember how to sting because its memory is so complete as to be unconscious, working so well that it does not know that it is at work. In like manner, when any one is an instinctive thief or liar, as the best thief or liar always is, or a born poet, as the true poet must be, he is so because the foundation of the fit nervous structure has been infixed in his constitution by prevenient bane or prevenient grace; that is to say, by the ancestral exercise of a predisposing function before ever he was begotten. All the pains and practice in the world could never make a great criminal of a person who entirely lacks criminal proclivities, any more than they can make a great poet of one who toils and moils painfully to manufacture consciously the inspiration which is not in him. Great artist of his kind will neither of them ever be. Virtue itself is not safely lodged until it is so grounded inward in the nature that it is a habit and its exercise a pleasure; so long as it is self-conscious it is not fixed and stable, being at best in process of formation rather than formed, its reflexes not firmly and definitely organised. Of vice too it may be affirmed that it never reaches its skill of perfection until it is sublimely unconscious of itself and, masking its wiles and guiles, its shifts and deceits, its essential egotistic foulness, in the guise of virtue or the garb of religion, gratifies itself from superfine moral motives and is vain of its superlative virtue.

Not only does special function imply special structure, but special structure means the incorporation of that kind of function which has been the condition of its formation. Organic growth has taken place along the lines of habitual activity, and that form of nervous system survived in development which was the most fit to survive in the actual conditions and because it was most fit. The difference in structure and form between the simple nervous system of a creature low in the scale of organisation and the complex nervous system of another high in that scale represents the form, measure, and means of the difference between the few, simple, and general reflex acts of which the one is capable and the many complex and special relations with the external world which the other has. With the progressive increase and specialisation of these relations the progressive development of the nervous system has gone along; its formal structure in each species incorporates the accumulated experience of the species in its progressive adjustments to its surroundings, and accordingly it displays explicitly when it functions what it contains implicitly. The stimulus which acts on it excites not merely a simple, direct, or plainly proportionate reaction, which ceases when it ceases to act, but effects that are indirect, circuitous, complicated, continuing when the stimulus ceases, and reaching back in secret and silent operation through the embodied history of the species. Moreover the specific nature of an organism necessarily determines and limits the number and kind of its relations to the external world and renders it incapable of the special responses thereto of a differently constituted organism. Thus it comes to pass that every species of organism has its own world: the worlds of a tiger and of a tiger-moth are two quite different worlds, one as good as non-existent to the other; and the eternal truths of the wisest monkey's mind are not the eternal truths of a human mind. The very different and at the best very limited relations of organisms to the external world we might compare to the graduations of a thermometrical scale; one scale is divided into more and another into fewer degrees, and there is no limit to the number of possible divisions; but in every case, whatever the length of the scale and the number of its divisions, there is an ungraduated infinity below the lowest and an ungraduated infinity above the highest degree. Knowledge is but a little gleam of light between two infinities of ignorance—the infinitely little and the infinitely great; it is just as impotent to reveal the microcosm of self as the macrocosm of the universe.

That human minds differ much in their natural capacities, some being capable of developments which others could never attain to, whatever training they might undergo, is an obvious truth; and it is not less certain, albeit less obvious, that such differences go along with differences in the complexity of the structure of the cerebral cortex. We cannot demonstrate arithmetically that the nervous plexuses are fewer and more simple in the cortex of one brain than in that of another on the same level of general civilization, seeing that it is impossible to make the innumerable nice countings and measurings necessary to prove it, but they are notably fewer and more simple in the brains of the lowest savages than in the brains of the highest races of mankind. The superior structure is the embodiment of superior function which has been developed through the ages; and therefore no amount of education, even were it begun from the first and continued to the last hour of life, could raise the low savage, who lacks the nervous substrata of the highest mental functions, to the level of the civilized person who possesses them. The former lacks by nature that which the latter has lost by disease when he is the outcome of a morbid degeneration of kind and, sunk to a congenital idiocy by reason of defective nervous plexuses, is less capable of ordinary intellectual and moral culture than the low savage. It is at the beginning of the development of mind in the lowest specimens of the human kind, who have not yet a full human heritage, and at the end of the degeneration of mind in its highest specimens, who have lost it, that we discover plain evidence of structural defects which, though inferred with certainty, are not manifest in the intermediate stages.

Not that the defects in such case must needs be actually missing cells and fibres; for these might be there in full number and yet be unfit to subserve the proper faculties, either because of some defect of their quality or because of the absence or fault of the requisite fine connecting processes. It is not enough to have a line of nervous conduction laid if it be so badly laid that it will not conduct, nor to have the full number of lines laid if the junctions of tracks are wanting; in neither case then would there be the capability of a proper mental organisation. The cortical plexuses neither act all together nor act at random when they discharge the several functions of mind, any more than the muscles do when they perform bodily acts. Definite combinations or patterns of nerve-tracks are formed to serve the different requirements of sensory impressions and motor reactions; and these central patterns or forms of associated tracks are more or less temporary or permanent according as they minister to temporary needs or to fixed habits of function. In some brains it would seem that certain associations of tracks, ready-formed or easily formed, constitute natural endowments of structure and are the foundations of special bents and aptitudes of mind; an ancestral mental habit having presumably endowed the offspring with such a trend and aptitude to the exercise of a particular function and to the acquirement of an instinctive excellence of it in consequence. What other explanation can be given of singular tricks of gesture and even peculiar modes of thought or expression exhibited sometimes by a child which never had the opportunity of learning them by imitation of a father or a grandfather whose characteristics they were? or of the signal talents of a special kind which are met with occasionally in persons who in all other respects are no better than imbeciles?

In the varying firmness of an organised tract of thought lies the explanation of the effects or the non-effects of education to undo it. For it may be so firmly set that a systematic training to a new order of functions will not permanently dissolve it, the propensity to fall back into the old form and to resume the old activity being irresistible; or the association of its parts may be so loose that another kind of training than that to which it owed its formation breaks it up easily and uses them for the organisation of other forms of activity. In the latter case education and training may do much to mould mental formation; in the former, they can do little to change the innate set lines of function into the maturities of which the mind is destined to grow. If there takes place inwardly and invisibly in the combinations of nerve-tracks something like that which takes place outwardly and visibly in the combinations of muscles to perform complex movements—which are notably first associated fitly by tedious exercise, afterwards act together easily, and at last can only with difficulty be dissociated—it is easy to perceive that to undo a mode of thought might become as hard a business as to undo an accent of speech. Man's constitution responds best to cultivation and training, right or wrong, for the highest organism is always the most modifiable, and most modifiable in its highest developments; his complex nervous system affords the conditions of many and various incidences of impressions and of many and various reactions thereto, as well as an available store of plastic substance to undergo new organisation. The character of the ant or the bee, its nervous plexuses being comparatively few and simple and set to certain definite functions, it would be vain to expect to modify materially, whatever changed circumstances it were placed in and however soon in life the experiment were begun.

In man also there are certain fundamental lines of thought, feeling, and action which have been infixed in the organisation through the ages of its fabrication and which no education could subvert. To require him to move off them would be as ridiculous as to require the bee to move off its instincts. Such are (*a*) the forms or categories of the understanding in his intellectual life; (*b*) the forms of pleasure and pain in his life of feeling; (*c*) the forms of bodily activity in his motor life: all alike the necessary consequences of the present physical structure, sensory and motor, of the human body. They are implanted powers of, and at the same time the limitations to, the variety of thoughts which he can think, of feelings which he can feel, and of deeds which he can do; to transcend them he would have to transcend his present structure. The infinite variety of human nature, when we look critically into it, is reduced to basic lines of somewhat mechanical repetition, with variations that are themselves repetitions. For the life of him man could not now invent a new virtue or a new vice or a new movement, any more than he could invent a new form of thought—would be as stupid in that respect as a bee outside its instincts.

If a mind be free from dominating proclivities, still more if training be applied specially to foster suitable proclivities in it, then it may almost be moulded to any pattern, though not to any height, of thought and feeling that is wished, provided that exclusive training be begun early enough and uniformly enforced long enough. Get exclusive hold of it from its first dawn, subject it systematically to a special class of impressions and to an answering set of reactions, sequestrate it from all conflicting and distracting impressions, and exercise it constantly in the way in which it is desired it should think, feel, and do,—the certain physical effect is the formation of a mental organisation which shall discharge that function and take pleasure in discharging it; which shall function in one sort of belief and practice in one age or country and in another sort of belief and practice in another age or country, and which always shall resent and recoil from any alien function. How can a being so manipulated, trained, and manufactured to a set form of mental growth by tradition, special education, custom, and habitual practice in relation to special conditions of environment, observe, reflect, and judge in relation to matters outside his range of set functions? It would be as reasonable to ask one species of insect to have the sensibilities and to perform the acts of a different species. How can a Mussulman who has been taught to spell the Koran, to read the Koran, to write the Koran, to recite the Koran, as his sole school-lesson, and to believe that there is nothing true outside the Koran, and whose ancestors have done the same thing for more than ten centuries, have any real sympathy of feeling and thought, a real community of nature, with a Christian, or do otherwise than loathe, hate, and despise him? The two beings are of the same animal species, but they are now virtually of different mental kinds. But why multiply instances? There is not an inconsistency or contradiction of thought and conduct, however flagrant, which may not exist in the same individual; not a folly of belief nor absurdity of practice, however monstrous, which has not been cherished piously somewhere or other at some period or other of human history.

Having a firm grasp of the principle of the reflex structure and function of the brain, and of the mode of building up of a mental organisation, it is easy to understand how the most distorted mental mouldings are inevitably accomplished when they are resolutely put in hand and steadily carried through. That is done for the individual by artificial selection which he does for himself by natural selection, when, owing to the strong base and bias of some such passion as pride, suspicion, jealousy in him, which takes all impressions and turns them to its nature and nurture, his mental development is warped into deformity or actual insane delusion. Then he is utterly incapacitated from getting into true relations with men and things, his deformity precluding a just mental contact: he lacks a rational basis of nature, that just proportion of parts whereby they act in harmony among themselves and in fit adjustment to the outer world. Now, as everybody fulfils the capacities of being more and more fully in proportion as he multiplies and makes more intimate his relations with nature, social and physical, and becomes a more and more complete part of it in a circuit of intaking and outgiving, receiving and reacting, feeling and doing, it is obvious that so far as he stands out of it by any intemperate development of self, any growth of it which is not justly motived by external conditions, he is a social malformity and an encumbrance or injury to the social organism. Wrong thoughts and feelings there will always be from inadequate attention, bad reasoning, passion, prejudice, tradition, custom, and other common causes of error, to be corrected by better information, sounder reasoning, and more wholesome social sympathy; but they are widely different, at any rate in degree, from those firm sets of the mental organisation underlying fixed morbid habits of thought and feeling, not to be corrected anyhow, which mark certain types of character and, if not actual mental derangement, are well on the road to it.

That which disease or distorted development does for the individual when it produces a dominating delusion or a prevailing cast of deluded thought with its corresponding hallucinations and conduct is very much what the so-called mesmeric or hypnotic operator does for his subject when he puts him into the hypnotic state. What may we suppose to take place when a person is thrown into such a trance in which, machine-like, he is governed by the suggestions which the operator makes, touching, tasting, seeing, hearing, thinking, and doing just as he is bid? That by the special suggestions made the fit tracts of his brain are stimulated to a separate and pretty nigh exclusive activity, while the function of the remaining tracts are suspended. Thereupon he cannot choose but perceive as he has been made to think; must translate every impression on sense into the language of the solely active idea and shape it to its features, or else have no consciousness of it at all. He cannot possibly perceive in the terms of ideas that are entirely inactive. The one active cerebral tract is virtually the whole and sole mind which he then has, and to obey it in sense and act is a compulsive necessity. For the time being he is as effectually severed from full mental contact with things as if he had been educated through life to exercise that tract and none other, or as if he were a madman dominated by its morbid growth and function. There is good reason then why persons of weak and unstable nervous temperament can, while persons of strong and compact mental organisation cannot, be thus put out of possession of themselves, and why those who have frequently allowed their mental being to be thus dislocated become so unstable at last as to fall out of mental joint at the least suggestion. Nay more, there are persons who under enthusiasm or other mental excitement can perform a self-hypnotism and afterwards so cultivate the acquired function by strain and practice as to repeat the operation at will with the greatest ease. That is the explanation of the success of those hypnotics who, when told that they will fall into a trance at a certain hour on a certain day, fail not to do it; the explanation also of the hysterical trances of the religious ecstatics which, like epilepsy and other abnormal nervous functions, have been ascribed to supernatural causes; the explanation again of the set forms of thoughts and feelings into which all fanatics and very many who are not fanatics fall instantly when, confronted with unwelcome facts absolutely opposed to what they believe, they blindly ignore them in blind ignorance of their own blindness.

Enough has been said to make plain where the physical disorder lies in mental derangement and how exceedingly fine, complex, and intricate is the anatomical structure concerned. The problem of the physician is to find out by what causes and in what ways this fine and complex substratum of the mental organisation is deranged: whether by such gross disease as apoplexy, tumour, softening of the brain, and the like, in which case the mental impairment, being regarded as a by-event, is not technical insanity; whether by such intimate and insensible molecular disorders as give rise to the commonly recognized forms of insanity; whether by such positive fault of structure as is the frequent cause of idiocy. At the bottom of all mental impairment there is impaired structure of some kind, at the bottom of each particular mental disorder the fitly disordered structure.

The two guiding reflections to be kept in mind are: first, that the mental organisation has been perfected by a gradual development through untold generations and embodies in its formal structure the acquisitions of the race through the ages, from the first gains of culture to the latest gifts of heredity; secondly, that the plan of its complex structure and function is the simple structure and function of a reflex act. It follows then that the study of its pathology must in every case be of two kinds—first, historical and social, and secondly, strictly pathological.

The study of the individual as an element of social pathology will plainly be a long, laborious, and difficult business of the future. For it will be a study of the progressive formation of the social being and of the causes, nature, and features of its disruption when his social nature is going through the regressive processes of being unmade. Nevertheless, if psychology is ever to be a solid and fruitful science, it must cease to take the individual and his qualities for granted as something final, behind which it is vain to go, and must search out the differences of individual minds and how they have come to be. What the astrologer aspired to do when, noting these differences of character and the need of an explanation of them, he thought to find it in the aspects of the planets under which persons were born; what the phrenologist thought to do later when he claimed to discover the seats of the faculties of mind by inspection of the protuberances of the head;—that the psychologist must some day do by patient scientific study of individual character as the natural product of organic processes of mental growth and decay. Hitherto he has been so high in the clouds of speculative abstractions that he has not been in the least touch with the real being of flesh and blood who plods painfully on the ground; therein not unlike the shoemaker who, able to discourse largely and learnedly about shoes, was not able to make or to mend one. Having obtained his exact knowledge of individual characters and found out what the different qualities mean, he will have no difficulty in tracing the growth of false fashions of temper and thought into the excesses which become insanities, whether in the course of individual life or in the course of pathological development from generation to generation.

The strictly pathological study of insanity will perhaps show that disorders of the mental organisation run parallel to disorders of the lower nervous centres. A disordered reflex act may be taken as the type of the disorder of the most complex mental functions, provided that due allowance be made for the fact that we have to do not with simple and direct reflex action, but with special and complex reflex action taking place indirectly and circuitously, in many windings long drawn out, through the intricate and complex network of the cerebral cortex in which is intreasured the capital of human experience. The inquirer who translates the terms of the morbid functions of the lower nervous centres into terms of morbid cerebral functions finds himself in presence of the varieties of mental derangement. What is mania but the counterpart of convulsions, at a higher remove or level? What is torpid melancholia but the counterpart of sluggish and pretty well palsied movements, at a higher remove? What is a morbid distortion or deformity of mind but the counterpart of a fixed spasm or deformity of movement? What is absolute dementia but a lasting paralysis of mind? Lessened and increased irritability, lessened and increased sensibility, neuralgias, and their kindred nerve-storms on the afferent or sensory side; violent and irregular movements, spasms and convulsions, partial or complete paralyses on the efferent or motor side;—these are the varieties of morbid function which are represented in the mental disorders of the cerebral cortex. Like them, they may properly be described under the headings of—I. Depression; II. Excitement; III. Perversion or distortion; IV. Weakness or privation of function.

Note.—More detailed arguments in support of the propositions set forth in this chapter will be found in two articles in *Mind*, viz :—
1. "The Physical Conditions of Consciousness," vol. xiii. No. 48 ;
2. "The Cerebral Cortex and its Work," vol. xv. No. 58.

CHAPTER II

CAUSATION OF INSANITY

In pursuance of the study of the causation of insanity from the social and from the physiological sides, I go on now to inquire:—

I. How is it that a man gets on so ill among his fellows in society as to break down into madness and be no longer of one kind with them?

II. What is the nature of the pathological processes at the bottom of the disorder which, thus driving him mentally astray, makes him a degenerate or morbid kind?

Living in a social medium and in a physical medium, he is liable to disorder in both relations.

I. SOCIOLOGICAL.

The Social Nature.

To live in social relations implies a social nature within as well as a social medium without, for were there no community of kind such inter-relation could not be. Envy, emulation, malice, hatred, vanity, ambition, and the like human passions exist only in relation to beings of the same kind: even a fool does not envy a good-looking horse nor hate an ill-doing machine. Because all men are of one kind they are so infected by a panic of terror among themselves that they behave as foolishly and frantically as a flock of silly sheep, but they are not similarly affected by a panic among sheep. Neither actor nor orator would derive inspiration from a gazing herd of bullocks, bovinely attentive as they might be to his eloquent words and antics, but he inflames and is in turn inflamed by the sympathetic fire of his human audience; and it is proof how much of his kind there is in every performer that he keenly relishes the bellowing applause of a mob to-day which will bellow in as loud applause of his rival to-morrow. Flattered and fooled by a like applause the exultant demagogue foretells the progress of mankind to perfection along paths determined for it by the voice of the majority, although he knows well that the wise nowhere constitute the majority and that the rule of fools does not end well. Lacking a social medium for its nurture and display, hysteria would not attack the solitary inhabitant of a desert island; it would hardly be inspired to perform to the unheeding stars. In the absence of their proper stimuli how can the fit reflexes take effect?

To comprehend what an individual is socially it is necessary to qualify the customary and in some respects misleading notion of individuality. The conception of the individual as separate from nature, set over against it in a sort of antagonism, living in and for himself, and in a continual conflict with his environment to maintain his being, springs from a partial and one-sided view of things. A truer and more fruitful conception would be that of every creature as an organ and function of nature, and of man as, in addition, an organ and function of humanity—as essentially part of while apart from nature. As a mere organic being, indeed, his conflict with his environment would soon end disastrously for him, since the breath of man is fatal to man, did not physical nature come in friendly aid to disburden him of the noxious products of his own activity and to render them innocuous; and in like manner, in a social organism, the noxious anti-social products of its own activity would be fatal to it did not the social environment take order to render them innocuous. No individual of to-day could ever be what he is had there not been social nature before him in a human past from which he is descended and were there not around him a social medium in and for and by which he lives and has his being : always is he part and parcel of his age and place, never the separate and self-determining being which he, considering himself as beginning and end in himself, appears to himself.

His faculties of mind and body and all the means and appliances which they now make easy and skilful use of for his purposes represent the slow accumulated gains of multitudinous generations of men in sequent toil of progressive adaptations to the external world. So and not otherwise has the complex reflex structure of his organisation been tediously built up. Not a word that is spoken, not a gesture that is made, not a garment that is worn, not a tool that is used, not any article of daily use or ornament, but has been formed and perfected to its present uses by the intelligent industry of men through the long procession of the ages and is the incorporation of their intelligence. Thus the spirits of the dead are everywhere around and within us, in everything we use and in everything we think, feel, and do, and it is in literal truth in the lives of the living that the dead live and by the lives of the dead that the living live. Separated from the social organism, of which he is element or unit, the whole working in him and he in it, the individual could no more live and function than an organ or a structural element of the body which, dreaming itself self-sufficing, should forget its dependence on the whole and start life on its own account. The essence of mad and of bad wrong-doing, that which makes the one disease and the other crime, is that it is anti-social ; the individual being very much in the social what a diseased organ is in the physiological organism, something separate, out of harmony and unity with it, alienated from it, in fact too individual. The limit of the sanest activity of self is the fullest development thereof consistent with the good of the whole : a man should love and esteem self just so far as the love and esteem of the social body for him for his uses to it can go along with his self-love and his uses of it.

To describe a being as anti-social is not to say that he is anti-natural. Just as disease is as natural as health and to die as natural as to be born, so a madman, a criminal, an anarchist is just as true a social product as a philosopher or a saint. The seeming anomaly or mischance has not come by chance but by natural laws of growth and development, an event in an organic process of human becoming: not in independence of an antecedent past, unfathered and self-sufficing, nor in nakedness of faculty, but bearing a special heritage of good or ill; a heritage of sufficient ill to wreck life sometimes, whatever its circumstances, at other times of sufficient evil force to do that only when it meets with fit coefficients in circumstances. Whatever the mortal be, he fulfils the final purposes of fate, whatever they be, albeit to us, viewing him from the standpoint of mankind as centre and end of creation, he seems to miss his purpose in the universe. But no one does that really: for the faults and the failures, the vices and the crimes, the deaths and decays of man on earth, not less than his glories and his grandeurs, his virtues and his triumphs, his births and growths, fulfil with unfailing certainty the dark decrees of destiny.

What does the social nature of man mean physiologically? Manifestly something of quite different physical constitution from anything else in the world; something which exists not in inanimate nature and exists in rudiment only in animate nature other than human. Not that a part of his nervous system is necessarily therefore of higher chemical composition, or even of more complex molecular structure, than any part of the nervous system of the lower animals; the signal perfection of social life worked out by the mere nervous system of such creatures as bees and ants, without the postulate of either a supernatural or a psychical intervention, would indicate that it was not; but certainly a superadded structure of more complex combinations of nerve-tracks comes into function. In the long process of human evolution higher and finer cerebral reflexes have been formed, special social and moral reflexes, by virtue of which he is capable of feeling and fitly responding to a class of impressions to which lower organisms, wanting them, are insensible. To make a mental abstraction of these functions and to call the abstraction a moral sense may help us to appreciate the special nature of moral feeling and to realise that it must have its special organic mechanism, but the ill effect of so naming it has been to dissociate it from matter and to transform it into a metaphysical entity. As wrongly as mischievously; for it is essentially an apprehension, connoting a motor as well as a sensory element, and, like other apprehensions, denotes special nervous adjustments to special impressions, the functions of special reflexes. Let disease raze out these fine patterns of cortical reflexes which subserve social sensibilities, and the whole social nature of the individual is a "razed oblivion."

Granting that the social nature is a product which has come to be by a slow process of becoming during the long time the world has lasted; not a process of ten thousand, nor of ten thousand times ten thousand years, but a process of accumulating minute changes which, infinite time being given, must have ended so, as inevitably as minutes make the hour and hours the years, we may grant also that the general law of development which has governed the process during the unrecorded ages was the same law which is proved to have worked within the short compass of recorded time—namely, the law of the more complex and special development at the cost of the more simple and general. Thus has profitable social function been built up into special mental faculty, special purposive adjustment into special form of structure in the mental organisation, which thenceforth must needs, when suitably stimulated, display explicitly in function what is implicit in structure.

The highest nature of man might seem to contradict the law of natural selection by which the strong crushes out the weak, inasmuch as it inspires him to succour the afflicted, to help the needy, to heal the sick, and generally to do to others as he would have others do to him. But here one may reflect that the struggle for existence has been transferred from the individual to the social organism, of which he is an element, and which exists only by virtue of some suppression of the purely self-regarding impulses of individuals, their altruisms going to constitute its egoism. His direct interest is to subdue these impulses, because it is his interest to belong to a social union which may maintain itself against similar organisations in the fierce competition and can exist only by virtue of sacrifices of self. If he fail to organise in his social and national spheres, he will be helplessly at the mercy of others who, being strong in union, will not fail, the moral law notwithstanding, to use their united strength to crush him. Contemplating the moral sense with all the ecstasy of rapture which the contemplation of it and the starry heaven excited in Kant, still a man cannot choose but confess that altruism has not counted for much in conflicts between rival nations nor has had much visible operation in the competitions of trade and commerce. Have not nations owed their formation as much to brotherly hate as to brotherly love—more perhaps to the welding consolidation enforced by the pressure of hostile peoples than to the attractive forces of their components? And what is the spur of commerce but competition? War in one shape or another, open or disguised, has plainly been the divinely appointed instrument of human progress, carnage the immoral-seeming means by which the slow incarnation of morality in mankind has been effected.

When we look at facts sincerely as they are, not satisfied to rest in a void of speculative idealism and insincerity, we perceive that in every department of life the superior person uses his superior powers to the inevitable detriment of the inferior person, even though he may afterwards dispense benevolently out of his superfluity to some of those who fall by the wayside. The moral law only works successfully as a mean between two extremes, excess of either being alike fatal. He who aspires to love his neighbour as himself must at the same time take care to love himself as his neighbour, making himself his neighbour while he makes his neighbour himself; his right duty being to cultivate not a suicidal self-sacrifice which would be a crime against self, but just that self-sacrifice which is the wisest self-interest and just that self-interest which is the wisest self-sacrifice. So he obtains the utmost development of self within the limits of the good of the whole. He will not go very far in morality if he compound for lack of self-renunciation on his part by a special indulgence of his own self-love in dictating sacrifices to other people. Were men to carry the moral law of self-sacrifice into rigorous and extreme effect they would perish by the practice of their virtues. When they had succeeded in eradicating competition, in making an equal distribution of wealth, in prolonging the feeblest life to its utmost tether, in banishing strife and war from the earth, in bringing all people on it to so sheep-like a placidity of nature that they would no more hurt and destroy, and to such an ant-like uniformity of industrious well-doing that no one would work for himself but every one for all, they would have robbed human nature of its springs of enterprise and reduced it to a stagnant state of decadence. A millennium of blessed bees or industrious ants! For it is the progress of desire and the struggle to attain which keeps the current of human life moving and wholesome alike in individuals, in societies, and in nations. Not to go forward is to go back, and not to move at all is death.

The social constitution of his age and place being incorporate in the individual, he is necessarily susceptible to special mental impressions, and therefore to possible causes of mental disorder arising out of its conditions. Is he now, then, by reason of his complexity of social nature, more liable to insanity than his more simple-minded forefathers were? Does insanity increase with civilization?

That is a simple question which, though it might seem to admit of an exact answer, has not yet been answered exactly. Savages neither take care to keep statistics nor to keep their insane alive, and the statistics of civilized peoples with regard to insanity are still recent and imperfect. Without doubt there has been a great increase in the number of registered insane persons during the last fifty years, but the very greatness of that increase might have suggested to everybody, as it always did to cool and competent observers, that it was not due simply to an increased liability of the people to madness. Obvious objections present themselves to so hasty an inference : first, there is certainly not the great difference between the civilization of to-day and that of fifty years ago to warrant the attribution of the great increase of insanity which has been registered in that time to an acquired liability; secondly, the registered increase is almost entirely in pauper patients, not in those who, being able to pay for their maintenance in asylums, might be supposed equally, if not more, liable to suffer from the overstraining conditions of a more complex civilization; thirdly, there are weighty and sufficient reasons, arising out of successive legislative enactments for the better care and more stringent registration of the insane in an increasing population, to account for the greater part, if not the whole, of the increased numbers. A little critical observation shows abrupt bounds of increase after each new act of legislation concerning them. Putting aside conjectural speculations, all the positive evidence, including that of the latest English census, goes to show that there has not been any material increase of insanity out of proportion to the increase of the population.

We may dismiss then all speculative opinions about the evil effects of excitement and overstrain as unnecessary to account for an increase which is not real or is really small. Similar lamentations concerning the hurry of life have been common in past times, especially by those whom, age having dulled their desires and weakened their energies, it has hurried past. Certainly it might be supposed that a complex mental organisation, being constructed of more special and delicate parts which must work together in relations of the nicest precision, would be liable to more faults of construction and to more occasions and varieties of derangement, by virtue of multiplied susceptibilities, increased impressionability, and more complex workings, than a simpler mental organisation whose various parts have less fine and complicated relations. The Australian savage, whose language wants words to express moral ideas, of which his mind is destitute, his simpler brain not embodying in its reflex structure the accumulated social heredity which a civilized brain imports, clearly cannot go mad because of a breach of the moral law, nor ever present an example of true moral insanity; before he can undergo moral degeneration he must first be humanized and then civilized; and that is a process which he is not more likely to survive than the many savage or barbarous people who, having been subjected to it, have died of it. Being the fit product of his time and place, and his immoral doings the right things for him to do then and there, he is necessarily unfitted to feel, think, and act in the vastly more complex conditions of civilized existence, where his natural ways and doings necessarily cause him to be treated as noxious vermin. A precocious savage who had the ill fortune to develop a moral sense among savages would probably have no greater chance of survival than a tiger which developed a sudden horror of bloodshed; and a low savage in civilized society must needs fare almost as badly as a carnivorous animal would fare in a land of herbivorous animals which it was forbidden to eat.

On the other hand, it is not difficult to bring forward reasons in support of the opinion that a higher mental development must tend to prevent insanity. There will be more chances in breeding of neutralising and in the end eliminating a morbid taint, not only by reason of a greater variety of choice open to individuals who marry, but also in the greater number of possible neutralisations from the union of more complex germ-plasms. Moreover, the full and varied exercise of mind elicited by a variety of interests is no less conducive to health and strength of mind than a full and varied exercise of the body is to its health and strength. The intellect suffers more from rusting in disuse than it ever does from its utmost use. One fact which the statistics of insanity in England has clearly shown is that the purely agricultural counties furnish the largest percentage of insanity in proportion to the population; that is to say, there is most madness where there are the fewest ideas, the simplest feelings, and the coarsest desires and ways. That the agricultural labourers should thus yield the largest percentage of insanity is plainly but poor support to the opinion of its causation by over-stimulation and overstrain of mind.

The opinion that special mischief is done, not so much by mental overwork in itself as by worries and anxieties attending it, the wear and tear of emotion, has a better show of foundation in fact. Here again, however, there are countervailing reflections which invalidate too absolute a conclusion. In the number, variety, and succession of emotions there is a large element of compensating good, enough perhaps to counterbalance the possible ills; for it is certain that one grief drives out another and so prevents it from taking on the irrational proportions which it might do were it left to fill the mind. Railways and steamboats may have done more to prevent insanity by the variety, than they have done to produce it by the hurry, of life which they have occasioned.[1] The more numerous and various the impressions to which a mind is subject in the complex relations of life the less likely is its balance to be upset by the exaggerated preponderance of any one of them. That is the disastrous discovery which the man of many

[1] I may call attention here to an instructive observation by the author of *Old New Zealand* (1863): an admirable little book instinct with the practical insight of a sagacious observer who was familiar with the native customs and character of the New Zealander in old times and describes the alterations which had taken place. The most marked alteration was the decrease of suicides. Formerly suicide was of almost daily occurrence: when a man died it was almost a matter of course that his wife or wives hung themselves. He has known young men, often on the most trifling affront or vexation, shoot themselves. Not one suicide occurs now, he believes, for twenty when he first went to the country. The reason is that the minds of the natives are now filled and agitated by new ideas, new wants, and new ambitions, which prevent them after a single loss or disappointment from feeling as if there was nothing left to live for.

affairs and responsibilities sometimes makes for himself when, retiring from active business because of the worries which it occasions him, he finds himself a victim to many petty agitations and apprehensions which he cannot shake off and to disperse which the simple monotony of his life affords no help. He cannot get away from himself because he has nothing to lay hold of outside himself and no resources in himself: founders in a weltering sea of self for want of way on his life-craft.[1] Simplicity and dulness of emotion are not any more than stupidity of intellect a preservative against insanity; it is more easy for a dull and idle mind to worry itself into madness over the little things of domestic life than for an alert and active mind to break down under the vast responsibilities of an empire. On certain unstable temperaments the circumstances of active occupation exercise a beneficial steadying effect, however they may seem to strain and distress them; for the conditions of social action impose restraints which operate to maintain a balance of faculties prone otherwise to fly astray into acute or to go awry into chronic disorder. When a person of that temperament goes mad from overwork it is probable he would have gone mad sooner but for his work.

It is not easy for the individual to realise how much he owes to the restraints and supports of the social fabric in which he is an element, and which, like the atmosphere, always and insensibly surrounds him. There could not probably be a greater danger to the balance of any mind than to be exempt from the bonds and pressure of the surrounding social system. Let a man have uncontrolled dominion over the whole known world, without being constrained into a certain sobriety and solidity of character by the responsibilities and labour of maintaining his empire, he would most likely be a monster like Nero or Caligula,

---

[1] I call to mind a zealous man of business who, having by a life of diligent labour and almost miserly economy attained his ambition to leave a fortune of half a million at his death, retired in order to enjoy the fruits of his labour. But he then worried so much over little things, a weed in his garden-walk, for example, and was so miserable, that in a little while he shot himself.

notwithstanding that he might, like Nero, have been a great artist had he been a private person subject to and subdued by the usual social restraints.¹ Destroy the social structure of a nation, as in the French Revolution, and then behold what monsters of apish deformity and tigrish ferocity the individuals are capable of becoming. We see the same principle at work on a small and meaner scale when a wife, the conduct of whose life has been fair and regular in the domestic system established during her husband's life, goes her way quite astray when his supporting and restraining hand has been removed by death.

One thing we may feel pretty sure of, that if insanity be on the increase among civilized peoples the increase is due more to their pleasures than their pains—to idleness, luxury, and self-indulgence more than to work, thrift, and self-denial. It has been noticed again and again that the largest number of admissions into county asylums take place not in bad times when workmen are on strike and forced into self-denial, but in times of prosperity when trade is flourishing and wages are high; the principal reason for which is that there is more intemperance and dissipation when wages are high and work plentiful.² At the present day it is the fashion for men to pity themselves and to be pitied because they have to work hard for a livelihood. Craving leisure to cultivate their higher or indulge their lower natures, they despise the real discipline and self-denial involved in hard work well done, the self-discipline by which their uncultivated forefathers made a strong nation. To shirk work or to do it badly in order to have time to practise self-culture is a new method of going to work to make virtue by a process of unmaking it. When such strain of self-indulgence pervades all the classes of a nation in all the relations of

---

[1] Qualis artifex, pereo! Artist even in his "spintrian recreations."
[2] In the Report of the Lancashire County Asylum at Prestwich for 1878, it is noted that the admissions were less during the hard times. A similar observation is made in the Report of the West Riding Asylum for 1879; and again in the Report of the Glasgow Asylum for 1870 it is pointed out, "That all the sufferings and sorrows of the past two years in this district have done little to increase the number of insane."

life, it marks a decay of those hardy virtues by which a sound and strong social fabric was built up; the corruptions which then ensue and spread will not fail to show themselves in manifold degeneracies of individual vice, crime, and madness, and, inasmuch as individuals make the nation, in its corruption and decadence. Neither for nations nor for individuals is it well when, waxing fat and doing what they lust, they are deaf to the eternal lesson of renunciation which is the hoarse-sounding refrain of the human hours.[1]

Family Nature.

The same law which has governed the evolution of species has presumably been at work in the formation of the special qualities that distinguish families. How else have its distinctive features, good or bad, been fashioned and fixed in the particular stock but by the fostering and preservation of a variation of feature, physical or mental, because it was an advantage in the circumstances, or because it was a distinctive mark, or because it was made a habit of the family nature for some reason, or perhaps because it was a stable organic type? Is there a family at the present day which has not a certain sneaking pride in its special characteristics, even when they are in no sense marks of superiority, and a certain instinctive dislike or distrust of characters in a member of it that are unlike those of the stock? Why should a child be pleased to be told, and its parents be pleased to tell it, that it is like its father or its uncle or its grandfather, when it would be better for it perhaps to be like a better person? If that be so now when railways, steamboats, telegraphs, and other means of quick and easy communication have liberated thought and feeling by breaking down the barriers of separation and so tended to make men tolerate differences and be more

[1] Entsagen sollst du sollst entsagen,
Das ist der ewige Gesang
Der unseres ganzes Leben lang
Uns heiser jede Stunde singt.

alike, it is easy to understand how much more power the sense of distinctive separation had to enforce a particular mental and bodily type in the more simple and constant conditions of primitive human life, when the weight of tradition and custom of thought, feeling, and conduct was practically irresistible.

The savage tribes of Africa which, after their several fashions, gash their faces and rub powder into the gashes so as to produce lasting hideous deformities, do it as a mark of tribal distinction, wanting no better reason or sanction than the custom of the tribe, and each is ready to attack at sight the tribe whose differently deformed features is a sufficient war-signal. Therein they are moved by the same principle as that which actuates a community of ants instantly to set on and tear to pieces an intruder from a strange community; which actuated the Homoousians and the Homoiousians when they slaughtered one another in tens of thousands because of a quarrel about a diphthong; which has instigated untold persecution, hatred, and bloodshed because of a difference of opinion respecting the removal or the retention of a foreskin; which inspires the fashionable fool of the day who looks on the person as an inferior being who does not mutilate words exactly as he does in pronunciation, or grimace in face or gesture exactly as he does. " You pierce your nose or pronounce a word in this fashion; embrace me, you are my brother: you pierce your ear or pronounce the word in that fashion; you are vermin and I will kill you:"—such has been the uniform way of mankind in its slow travail towards a universal brotherhood.

The bent of the family to accentuate and perpetuate its distinctive traits has been qualified by the mixtures of families in breeding, since such intermixtures must tend to merge the family traits, prone otherwise to become marked and set, into the species. By sending propagation back to the original plastic substance of the germ which retains the power to make variations, the living and forming as distinguished from the fixed and practically dead structure, it has done the sort of service which a young, fresh, and vigorous nation of barbarians does when it sweeps over an effete civilization and helps perchance to regenerate it; the service which war has so often done by breaking down barriers of separation and mixing peoples in spite of themselves. If it ever saddens the heart of the philanthropist to reflect on the little way which Christianity has made by its moral inspiration to abolish war and to unite mankind in one brotherhood of love, he may still philosophically admire the mighty work which it has done to further human progress towards universal brotherhood by the wars which it has instigated, sanctioned, and promoted. For assuredly it has been the frequent fate of the righteous to wash his footsteps in the blood of his enemy; and it is a sober historical truth that if the earth were now to disclose its blood and no longer to cover its slain, the race of man on it would be drowned in the blood and buried deep under the carcasses of his kind.

The evil operation of family sympathy to cherish and foster a particular quality of the stock is often exemplified in a striking manner when a morbid strain of mind runs in the blood, as the old saying was, or is graved in the nerve-structure, as we should say now. Instead of being checked or modified by suitable training, the morbid bent is treated as if it were something of finer texture than the qualities of the kind and deserving a more tender management; thus it is fomented and developed by clannish sympathy, wittingly or unwittingly, until it grows into a positive alienation from the kind. Whence it came? what it means? and how it will end?—these are questions not so much as propounded for inquiry; it is taken for granted as either an accidental thing that requires no explanation or a mysterious thing that admits of none; whereas it is truly a natural product of organic development, no more an accident than a distorted tree or a deformed animal is an accident. The kind of function displayed by it is the result of the incorporation in the individual brain, the structuralisation in its mental organisation, of the kind of function which has been performed by its ancestors; either of exactly the same kind of function, or of allied bad function which in process of interbreeding has issued so. Just as everybody is and does what he has learnt to be and do, so he is and does what his forefathers have learnt to be and do, in so far as he has not been made by training to unlearn it. Such working of family selection to foster a strain of morbid quality may incidentally remind us that the law of natural selection works as efficiently to do ill as to do well—indifferently to make the knave or the saint according as the environment best suits the development and survival of the one or the other.

Nothing has done more to put man out of understanding of his true position in nature, as well as out of conceit with it, than the metaphysical doctrine of freewill. It has been an insurmountable hindrance to the recognition of the truth that there is no motion of any kind in him, whether of mood or thought, of will or deed, which is not just as necessarily determined physically, although by subtile, hidden, intricate, and circuitous paths, as the motion of a magnetic needle. To say in general terms that the individual is a product of the human past, and then, instead of diligently searching out the steps of the entire process of his becoming in the particular, to assume a cataclysm and a thereupon supervening order of quite spiritual events, such as self-creating will and absolute moral feeling which transcend all physical determinants, is to say and unsay in the same breath, beguiling the understanding in a traffic of words. What does the simplest thought, feeling, or inclination mean in its inmost origin and being? Nothing less than the whole body and mind of him, whose it is, and all that has gone before him through an unlimited past to make him what he is: all his own past life and all the past that has gone before it in the line of its causation. Undetermined motion of will with such a weight of antecedence is therefore either a nonsense of thought within the human domain or a thought-transcending identification of opposites outside the human domain. The very nerve-structures of the brain which minister to mood, thought, and impulse, the intimate molecular groupings of their elements as well as the forms of their structure, are they not essentially the concentrated incorporation of multitudinous experiences, the quintessential abstract of past perfected relations, and their least affections or motions the stirrings of secret vibrations that echo backwards through a virtual eternity? No plummet, either of introspection or observation, can sound the bottom of the individual nature; out of its unlit depths of being from time to time come faint airs and floating echoes of an infinite past—melodious or discordant ghost-tones, as it were—which determine present moods and, more often than we think, present acts; and of them consciousness can no more give an account than it can of the first thrill of a young man's or maiden's love. So far from will being undetermined except by itself, the supreme function of mental organisation which will represents is the most determined event in all the wide world, the last consummate issue of its long organic travail. It is nature, come to self-consciousness in man, striving with deliberate purpose to better itself; and with all the awkward misadventures that mark self-conscious doings.

Individual Nature.

Besides the social nature which man has acquired in the course of his development through the ages from an animal basis, and the different family stocks into which it has branched, together predetermining the fundamental lines of his mental structure and function, every individual has also his own special nature: he is one with his kind, comes of his family, and is himself. He is himself because the transmission of qualities from parent to child is not a case of reproduction or imitation wholly, it is a case of production or variation also. Unknown compositions of parental qualities take place in breeding whereby the offspring's qualities are not all either simple repetitions of those of either parent nor yet mere varying intermixtures of them, but some are varieties or new products; new at least in respect of their immediate components, albeit perhaps nothing new, nothing strange, in respect of what has been some time in the infinite past, may be now somewhere in the infinite present, and will be again in the infinite time to come. To the possible number of these variations it is impossible to fix a limit, they are for us practically infinite. For when we reflect on the number and variety of the elements which go to form the human organism, on the complexity of the intimate molecular constitution of each element, on the intricate interplay of molecular energies, on the diversity of the many parts and organs of the body, and on the manifold and special relations involved in the complex unison of the whole, we can neither gauge nor guess what happens in the way of new features of body and mind when two persons enter into organic union to generate a third. Instead of the crude conception of the material body as comparatively inert structure, we have to think of it as quivering throughout with multitudinous motions inconceivably fine, complex, intricate, and active, whose harmonic whole it represents.

Individual variations have plainly not as a rule continuity of being from generation to generation, are not fixed and inherited but fluent and fugitive; not steadfast and lasting but ever forming and unforming in the changes and chances of human reproduction : belonging to the individual they for the most part die with him. Happily so perhaps, since otherwise families might go off into wide differences of development, becoming at last almost different kinds, just as men and women might have done had not the sexual qualities of father and mother been distributed in common, though in different measure, to boy and girl. Moreover, there might have been the risk of a term to development, no scope in fact for variations, because of the using up of the plastic, unformed germinal substance available for the compositions and decompositions necessary to produce new variations. Mankind might at last be stereotyped in certain set impressions and in a sterile immobility, as the lower animals for the most part are now, and as old worn-out nations and families, having exhausted their germinal plastic energy and retained set forms of structure, commonly the vicious forms of regression, tend to become. Formed structure and plastic unformed substance might be compared respectively to matter in its fixed and inactive crystalloid state and to matter in its mobile and active colloid state; the formed structure being the stable framework of vital activity, the differentiated and specialized mechanism or vehicle of life, whereas the plastic forming substance is the living and working life-stuff which lends itself to inventive variations and new organisation. It might be expected therefore that the formed structures which constitute the general framework of character would pass from parent to child and that individual variations would not pass with anything like equal certainty, if at all.

Those who uphold the doctrine that acquired characters are not inherited have much to say in support of their opinion, and they cannot easily be dislodged from it so long as they are free to postulate whatever secret modifications in germ-plasms and whatever secret causes of them the immediate exigencies of theory require. But is it right to limit the modifiable plastic substance of the organism to the germ-plasm? The developing part of man is his brain; it is through it that nature is carrying forward its line of organic evolution; its plastic elements therefore might conceivably be respondent to and retentive of impressions made on the individual by the special experiences of his life. Man's all-pervading presence and dominant ascendency as lord paramount of the earth has practically put a stop to the development of variations in other animals, except such variations as he chooses to cultivate in domestic animals for his pleasure or his profit; in sole possession of the leading line of organic evolution, having usurped and engrossed in himself the plastic forces which make for progress, he has condemned other branches of animal life to a sterile immobility, and one after another they are becoming extinct. A little while, indeed, and it will be as if they had never been, as it is now with many species; a little while longer doubtless, and it will be as if he had never been, as it is now with many varieties, races, and nations of his kind. To allow organic evolution to proceed along other than human lines it would be necessary to sweep the whole human race off the face of the earth. It is not then in the comparatively fixed structures of the body that we ought rightly to look for evidence of the heredity of recently acquired individual characters; to conclude positively against such heredity because the child of a person who has lost a finger is born with the full number of fingers, or because a cat which has had its tail cut off has not tailless kittens, is very much like what it would be to conclude that a baby cannot grow because a full-grown man cannot grow, or that a man cannot change his mind because he cannot change his bones. In the plastic substance subserving the development of the mental nature, if anywhere, the evidence of transmission of acquired characters or at least of acquired inclinations or biasses might be found. Such evidence as there is needs to be more severely tested than it has been; but there is enough of it at least to suspend the denial, if not to warrant the opinion, that the germ-plasm of an individual is affected by the special mental and bodily conditions which prevail in him during its formation, can acquire a special bias in consequence, and may carry it into the next generation, either as a direct reproduction of quality, or indirectly through the unknown neutralisations and modifications which take place in the union of different germ-plasms.

Here, however, we are confronted with the obvious fact that genius is not transmitted to the offspring. The sons of really great men, notwithstanding the social advantages which they enjoy, so far from being great, are usually small men; a fact so notorious as to have been proverbial.[1] It looks as if the stock, having accomplished the supreme effort of a brilliant flowerage, must revert to the mean or go backwards below it. That may be so when and because the potential energy of the stock has been expended in an elaborate blooming of genius; still the open display would

[1] Heroum filii noxæ et amentes Hippocratis filii.

have been impossible but for the fund of great quality latent in the stock, notable perhaps in the quiet father or grandfather, the mother or grandmother, who made no show in the world and was perhaps bigger potentially than the eminent offspring was actually. That the high or highest quality of genius which we call imagination should not be transmitted by heredity is not the conclusive argument against the transmission of acquired faculty which it looks at first sight. Imagination is not really an acquired faculty in the proper sense of the word; it is not something that is acquired or can be acquired by any labour of thinking; it *is* or *is* not, a vital gift of nature, independent of individual will, blossoming as it lists, working spontaneously and vanishing in its work. Not therefore in it, but in acquired modes of thinking and feeling, in those set habits of mind which are formed by the ways and circumstances of life, ought we to look for evidence of the possible hereditary transmission of a bias from parent to child; neither in the most set framed structure nor in the most mobile and plastic developing substance which ministers to, and, as it were, foretells structure, but in the intermediate region of aptitudes and talents.

Imagination is essentially productive. Its almost exclusive possession by man is proof of a plastic substance and energy in his brain which is lacking in the brains of the lower animals. Memory, understanding, and reason some of them share with him in greater or less measure; and although the share be meagre at best, yet in sufficient quantity and quality to prove that those mental functions proceed not from anything special to him, but are the proper functions of a certain nervous organisation which is only more special, more complex, and more plastic in him. But productive imagination they have not; the best resemblance of it that the best of them has is a limited reproductive imaging of experience, which is quite a different thing. Inspired by the evolutional *nisus* of nature, imagination's plastic stress creates the ideals which are aspired to and informs the arts by which they are realised; it is the function of a developing mental organisation, in it is immanent

> the prophetic soul
> Of the wide world dreaming of things to come.

The wide world cannot now dream of things to come and strive to become them along any other than human forms of thought. Nor in them when old age has rendered the mental tissue of the individual stiff and rigid, and he lingers on the stage, dead matter practically, waiting to be superseded by younger persons in whom the immortal plastic substance is fresh and capable of new organisation. Nor at any time in a great many persons whose mental tissues become fixed and rigid in set forms of thought and feeling long before they suffer the hardening changes of age. Being thus the most plastic and least set function, not fixed but fluent, that which makes variations, it results naturally that imagination is the most individual and least transmissible faculty, and that great poets and other persons of genius who bequeath their most fixed qualities of character do not bequeath it to their children.

Whether acquired characters of the individual are or are not transmitted by heredity, they are the least likely thus to pass. The qualities of the kind, being deepest, most fixed and durable, descend with most certainty; the qualities of the stock, being more fixed and durable than the individual qualities, with more certainty than they; and the qualities of the individual, being least stable, with least certainty. So when the mental qualities are stripped off in retrograde succession by disease the individual loses first his best social or moral qualities, after that his family qualities, and last of all his general human qualities. Going through the regressive degenerations of madness, he ceases first to be himself, then loses his social and family nature, and last of all has nothing human left but the form and name of his kind.

Everybody's mental constitution being determined primarily and mainly by his inheritance from his forefathers, and secondarily and in less degree only by the circumstances of his life and training, the fundamental lines of his character which have been laid down in the past fix for him, and would, had we full and exact knowledge, fix for us the education of which he is capable and, if so be, the degeneration to which he is doomed. To know what any one is really it is necessary to know the stock from which he proceeds; to know what he has "become," to know the process of his "becoming." That which education can do is to *educe* or bring into development the inborn capacities or faculties; it cannot instil them when they are not there nor eradicate, though it may modify and repress, them when they are there. How very slow and gradual a process the business of modification by education and social training is appears by the little effect which the moral medicaments of ages have yet had to correct a portion only of the large dose of original sin in human nature. Individual development must needs take place in the main along the lines of structural organisation and the person grow into the maturities of the tendencies, good or ill, which constitute his original mental nature. When he has been forced and fitted into a special mould of character by an adapted special training, begun soon in life and applied steadily throughout it, he is liable easily to lose his acquired, and to revert to his real, nature, like a domesticated species of animal turned wild, if the special conditions of his manufacture are entirely removed. A man struggling against his nature is like the ancient Grecian fighting fruitlessly against the fate foredoomed to him by the oracle; he goes painfully about to fulfil his destiny unwittingly by the very means which he employs to evade it; the long, subtle, and winding tracks which he devises and pursues to combat or circumvent it become the fit chain of events, circuitous but certain, devious but definite, by which its dark decree is ultimately accomplished. Eddying in never so blind uncertainties, he is driven along by its deep and noiseless current and forced to obey his being's law.[1]

[1] Es glaubt der Mensch sein Leben zu leiten, sich selbst zu führen, und sein Innerstes wird unwiderstehlich nach seinem Schicksal gezogen.—*Goethe.*

A thorough inquiry into the causes of insanity can never properly begin and end with the particular event. In the great majority of instances the inclination to go mad is not, any more than the inclination to be bad, an acquired faculty but a possession of the original nature; the acting external cause being the occasion rather than the cause of the mental overthrow, the *occasional* not the *efficient* cause. Seeing that it is the natural function of women to bear children and that not one out of a hundred mothers becomes insane after childbirth, most of them suffering little more from the everyday transaction than they would do if another and nicer way had been ordained for the generation of mankind, it is manifestly not good science to call childbirth a cause of insanity. In like manner when one person, undergoing a moral shock or the wear and tear of anxiety, becomes profoundly melancholic, while another person, going through a similar experience, is not seriously hurt in mind, it is not the whole truth, but a misleading half-truth, to describe the moral trouble as the cause. The latter, exempt from some flaw or infirmity of mental constitution which the former had, has not suffered the same kind or degree of mental commotion; possessing a more stable mental structure, he has not afforded to the external cause the internal coefficients essential to its ill effects. Is there one of the usually enumerated causes of insanity which does not act on hundreds of persons without causing it for every case in which it does cause it? And if injuries and other overwhelming damage to the mind-tracts are barred, is there a single external cause of madness or perhaps any concurrence of such causes which can positively be depended on to produce it? If the answer be that the external stress might be so great as to break down any mind, however well organised, it is not conclusive; one may still suspect that there are persons who, though they might die, could not go mad, from the overstrain.

The inward and outward conditions and the modes and degrees of their co-operation to produce insanity it is impossible to describe in general terms; error lurks inevitably in such generalities. Persons differ widely in characters; they are enterprising and timid, prudent and rash, liberal and parsimonious, frank and false, proud and humble, ambitious and retiring, gentle and aggressive, pitiful and cold-hearted; and each variety of character or particular humour, having its own adjunct pleasures and pains, presents its special susceptibilities where a moral cause will strike it with most effect. The calamity which would hurt one seriously might not do the least hurt to another: the liberal man might lose a fortune with equanimity, when a similar loss might drive the miser mad; the proud man be overthrown by a blow to his self-love which would leave the lowly-minded unhurt; the loving husband be sunk in despair by the death of his wife, while the man of little love but self-love was not seriously put out by the event. A general enumeration of the moral causes of insanity, without searching inquiry into the particular coefficients in each case, how barren of real instruction it must necessarily be!

Not only are the susceptibilities of individual character to be taken account of, but there are the particular susceptibilities incident to the particular ages or seasons of life, when particular organs or systems of organs are developing or declining. The years of man's life may be divided into periods of 15 years: the period of childhood up to 15 years; the spring of adolescence from 15 to 30 years; the summer of full manhood from 30 to 45 years; the autumn of declining from 45 to 60 years; the winter of old age from 60 to 75 years. In childhood, the lymphatic system and lower nervous centres being active, scrofula and epilepsy are the hereditary diseases most prone to show themselves; at puberty, the vascular and muscular systems being in vigorous motion and the sexual system coming into function, inflammatory diseases, especially pulmonary, hysterical disorders and adolescent insanity are in evidence; in manhood, rheumatism and gout attest, the former a muscular system which having reached its active prime now discloses a native strain of weakness, the latter a decline of the forces of nutrition and assimilation predisposed to such failure, while brains at all inclined to disorder encounter abundant occasions of it in the wears and tears, the strains and stresses, the joys and woes of the most busy period of work and pleasure; in the autumn or fall of life, the visceral organs, the vital sources of the energy of feeling and will, decline in vigour, whence follows a tendency to local congestions, hypochondria, and melancholia; in old age, degenerate tissues declare themselves in apoplexy, senile dementia, softening of the brain. It is not only, however, that hereditary disease-tendencies are prone to develop at special seasons of life, but that mental character differs greatly at these different seasons; its moods of feeling and manner of thinking witness to the different bodily conditions. The world being thus seen in very different lights in the changing seasons of life, the moral as well as the physical causes of mental disorder act then with very different effects; practically they strike different individuals.

Furthermore, the particular circumstances of a moral catastrophe make all the difference in the world in its effects on the mind. The respected citizen who falls into fornication when on a visit to London or Paris is probably not much troubled in mind by his misdoing; but if he go similarly astray in the little country town in which he dwells he might fall into a positive melancholy of despair from the fear that what he has done will be known and talked about. In that case when he came to tell the penitent tale of his sin and sorrow, it is pretty certain that his mental disorder would, in a classification of causes, be set down to remorse, the so-called remorse being really the dreaded shame of being found out. The present need of psychology is not any addition to the superfluity of vague disquisitions which yield no practical fruit in the end, but close and diligent study of the particular qualities of individual character, mental and bodily, and an exact exposition of its relations to its circumstances: a scientific demonstration of the strict order and necessity of the chain of events of the person's life-history by a patient unfolding of his action on circumstances and of their action on him. Sane or insane, a man's history is his character, and the full and exact explanation of his position in life, whether eminence or madness, would be the full and exact disclosure of his character.

Hereditary Predisposition.

What is it that he inherits who inherits a predisposition to insanity? How far is he the thralled victim of an evil fate? In the first place, it is certain that he does not inherit actual madness, since no one is born mad; he inherits only a predisposition to it, which may be either strong or weak: so strong in a few instances as to burst forth and wreck the mind in childhood; so weak in some instances as to lie dormant and not issue in actual derangement; of such force in other instances as to be kindled into flame by the evil troubles and vicissitudes of life. There is the essential madman, as he might be called, who, the victim of fortune's might, goes mad however propitious the circumstances of life—who would go mad in heaven were he there, being what he is; the *occasional* madman who, the victim rather of fortune's spite, goes mad because he has the ill chance to be thrown into specially adverse circumstances or to meet with a specially bad conjuncture of them; and between the two extremes there are madmen who represent all degrees and varieties in the relative co-operations of the internal factors of character and the external factors of circumstances.

In the second place, he who inherits a predisposition to insanity does not necessarily get it from a parent who happens to be insane; no, not even though his father was insane when he was begotten or though in madness his mother conceived him. He gets it from where his parent got it — from the insane strain of the family stock: the strain which, as the old saying was, runs in the blood, but which we prefer now to describe as a fault or flaw in the germ-plasm passing by continuity of substance from generation to generation. Thus it comes to pass, on the one hand, that the child of an insane parent is perhaps never insane at all, and on the other hand that the child of a sane parent, who has an insane uncle or aunt, becomes insane. Nothing is more striking in the histories of families that have histories than the close likenesses of bodily features or of mental qualities or of tricks of gesture or gait which crop up in members who are generations apart; with small variations the present individual is a signal reproduction, almost a copy sometimes, of a more or less remote ancestor whom he lives over again; for all the world as if there was nothing new but that which is had been before: a memory of what, but for an accident, might, in our brief records, have been lost in oblivion. Nor is the likeness only to an ancestor in the direct line of heredity, it may be to a member of a collateral branch; then a child not specially like its parents shall reproduce the mental or bodily features, or both, of an uncle or aunt, or of a cousin at different removes. Despite the frequent interminglings of different strains of qualities by the union of the germ-plasms of the two parents in successive generations, the predominant strain of the stock might chance to determine from time to time the same combinations and developments in much the same mould. A rare throwback necessarily, if it ever be, since in the multitude of possible combinations there is scope for almost infinite variations. As might be expected, this kind of reproduction is much more often evident in particular traits of feature or character, and is then sometimes seen only or particularly in individuals at particular periods of life; is perhaps only caught momentarily as a transient gleam, unfamiliar and unexpected, on particular emotional occasions that stir the being to its depths. Now and then a person may detect in his own face in the looking-glass a momentary flash of expression of the sort which he will find formal in the portrait of an ancestor or perhaps of some living relative, near or remote. In the same way silent memories of strange feeling shall startle and move him. Beneath every face are the latent faces of ancestors, beneath every character their characters.

In all hereditary transmission there is then a deep silent stream of tendency which is of more importance than what we see here and there on the surface. A son, who cannot in the nature of the case exhibit them himself, still conveys his mother's special feminine qualities to his daughter, having them latent in him, as he has in him the rudimentary representatives of the special female organs; in like manner, a daughter conveys her father's special masculine qualities to her son, having them latent in her, as she has latent in her the rudimentary special male organs. Everybody, male or female, is essentially male and female. Two brothers may differ more in superficial features of body and mind than two strangers, while two strangers may be very like in superficial features; still, notwithstanding the difference on the surface, we are sensible of a fundamental identity beneath diversity in the brothers and, notwithstanding the surface-resemblance, of a fundamental diversity beneath apparent identity in the strangers. In spite of their facial unlikeness two brothers or sisters are sometimes like two separate cords stretched side by side and tuned in unison, when, the one being struck, the other vibrates also and sounds the same note; wherefore here and there madness or suicide seems to be positively infective, the discordant note in one member of a family striking an answering note in another when the two live together in daily converse and do the same things in the same ways day by day.[1]

Manifest then is the good reason of the maxim which I have many times insisted on—that a good use to make of relations is to teach self-knowledge. In one or other of them

---

[1] I remember three elderly maiden sisters, living together, two of whom, when the third fell into a mania of persecution, were infected with the same delusions eventually. And there are on record instances of twins who, like in features and dispositions, have become insane about the same time and had the same kind of insanity—even sometimes when living apart. Amongst other instances: "Suicidal Insanity in Twins," *Annales Médico-Psychologiques*, 1863; "Exalted Delusion in Twins," in the same journal for 1873; "Melancholia in Twins," *Journal of Mental Science*, vol. xxviii. p. 539; "Mania in Twins," in same journal, p. 540.

a man shall see in overt display qualities which, being latent in him or, if not quite latent, silent and subtile in their secret workings, he was perhaps unconscious of: implicit qualities which from time to time in the changes and chances of life shall unawares sustain or betray him. If the devout prayers to have grace enough to fulfil the elementary principles of morality by keeping the ten commandments be a tacit confession on the Christian's part that the moral nature of the human kind is yet so unstable, its tenure so precarious, that there lurks in everybody the potentiality to break them, much more is the open development of any special vice or virtue in one member of a family proof of the potentiality of that essential vice or virtue in other members of it, notwithstanding that it may not show in them or may show in another form.

Having clearly apprehended the conclusions, first, that a person does not inherit insanity but a tendency or predisposition to it, and, secondly, that the tendency is inherited from the stock, not from any particular development of it in the parentage, it is easy to understand that it is not in special individual outcomes, but in the foundations of the family nature, that we must search for the principal factor in the causation of insanity. Nowise extraordinary therefore is the apparent caprice with which mental disorder shows itself in a family, skipping one generation to come out in another, appearing in different forms in the different individuals attacked. Nowise extraordinary again this occasional event: that a son or daughter becomes insane, neither of whose parents have been insane, but afterwards one or other parent becomes insane; then the morbid strain in the stock has developed more quickly through the weaker offspring, perhaps in connection with the effects of pubescence operating on a frailer nervous constitution, than in the parent, where it may have come on only with the degenerative changes of age.[1]

---

[1] I have elsewhere referred to the cases, recorded by Dr. Skae, of a blacksmith in the Edinburgh Asylum who imagined himself King of Scotland, and of his daughter, an inmate of the same asylum, who believed herself to be

A predisposition to insanity not being the heritage of something definite and known passing from one generation to another in a definite and constant way, but rather of an uncertain bundle of obscure tendencies which break up into various distributions, therefore it is impossible even to guess with any confidence what the issue shall be in a particular case. Can anybody venture to foretell the features or the disposition or even so much as the sex of a child whose parents are well known? Or to predict that the son or daughter of an insane parent will have the same form of insanity or be insane at all? Except in melancholy and in dipsomania, it is unusual for the disease to pass by descent in the same form. Nor need the unsound strain in the stock show itself in any form of actual insanity; it may appear in some allied nervous disorder — in hypochondriasis, in suicide, in epilepsy, in dipsomania, in weakness of mind, in neuralgias, in stammering, in chorea, in spasmodic asthma, in some periodical nerve-storm of abnormal character; as, conversely, these disorders of one generation may in their turn forebode some form of insanity in the next generation. Such sequences are often described as transformations of neuroses, as though the epilepsy of the father were transformed into the insanity, or the insanity of the father into the epilepsy, of the son; which is much as if one were to say that the roses of one year are transformed into the roses of the following year. The more exact truth is that the insane variation is not inherited, but that it is the native fault or flaw in the germ-plasm of the stock which, revealing itself in the neurotic weakness, issues in this or that particular nervous disorder—first and foremost, according to the fortune which it meets with in the union of germ-plasms, and, secondly, according to the external influences which chance to work on it from the first conception of the germ unto its full development in the

a Royal Princess. Not that the daughter inherited or even shared her father's delusion, for she perceived clearly that he was insane, as he on his part perceived that she was lunatic; but the morbid outgrowth of a morbid quality of the stock in process of degeneration appeared at an earlier age in her than in him.

mature individual. He, unhappy mortal, has often then the ill fortune to be twice penalised : first, in his evil inheritance, and, secondly, in the evil training given him by those who gave him that inheritance.

How different are the fortunes of the children of a family in whose stock runs a strong strain of madness ! Seldom do they all go mad, although that happens now and then.[1] Taking account of the children of a number of unsound families, what might we expect to find among them ? One a born idiot or imbecile, although perhaps showing special aptitudes or talents quite out of keeping with his general lack of intelligence, such as a wonderful memory for dates, words, tunes; another going hopelessly insane early in life, most likely at or soon after puberty; a third, eccentric in his mode of thought, feeling and conduct, while still manifesting a strain of genius of a narrow and special kind; a fourth falling into mania or melancholia in connection with child-birth, or change of life, or circumstances of moral trouble; a fifth showing no positive mental derangement at any period of life; a sixth, epileptic or the victim of some other life-long nervous trouble. That no careful collection of instances showing the exact results of a distinct insane taint on the children in a large number of marriages has ever been made, must be noted as a lamentable want in morbid psychology.[2] There is the same lack of exact information

---

[1] I can call to mind three such instances in my experience—two families of four children each, and one family of three children, where all became insane eventually. In the *Journal of Mental Science* (April 1881) an instance is given of a family of eleven children seven of whom were imbecile, and another instance of a woman who had four imbecile children, all illegitimate and each by a different father. Probably the woman herself was a vagrant imbecile who yielded herself to the brutal embraces of every man whose lust she provoked. From the Report of the Northern Hospital for the Insane of the State of Winconsin, U.S., I take this extract :—" In one of our patients we have the following history : the father eccentric ; the mother died insane ; the eldest child, a son, became insane and shot himself ; the second child, the eldest daughter, is now in the hospital ; a second daughter is insane, and an inmate of another hospital ; another daughter became insane, and committed suicide by taking poison ; another daughter, insane, hung herself."

[2] The difficulties of getting accurate information are insuperable. There is hardly a sin in the calendar of which some persons had not rather be suspected

with regard to the effects of parental epilepsy on breeding: all we can say is that some children might die at early ages from convulsions, that some might be epileptic, that others might be insane, and that some might be neither insane nor epileptic. In all these cases the neuropathic diathesis is the fundamental fact; its proteiform outcomes, sensory, motor, mental, and trophic, are uncertain and incalculable.

The uncertainties of heredity might have been predicted as necessary consequences of the neutralisations, occultations and variations of qualities which take place in the union of germ-plasms. What are the possible effects of such union on a particular quality of character, healthy or morbid? (*a*) A direct increase or intensification of it; (*b*) a decrease or mitigation of it; (*c*) a neutralisation of it whereby it is kept in suspense and is dormant for a part or the whole of the individual life; (*d*) a modification of it whereby a variation is produced.

As germ-plasms are constitutionally well or ill suited to combine, some uniting well to produce good compounds while others are so ill-sorted that they combine only to generate weak and unstable products, so they are sometimes incapable of combining organically to propagate at all. Those of different species do not combine; for some unknown reason the germs from two individuals of the same species who are both in good health of body and mind are sometimes infertile; those of the most widely

than of having an insane relative. I remember one gentleman who was desperately anxious to prove and have it certified that his married son's insanity, of hereditary origin, was caused by syphilis, which there was no evidence he had ever had. The sister of an outrageously insane lady strenuously maintained that the latter was not insane at all, only shamming insanity in order to be relieved of the presence of her husband. An indignant old lady, the aunt of a gentleman who was hopelessly insane, wrote to me thus:—"I think it right to let you know that there is *no* insanity in my family, not the slightest trace of it, and that the state of my nephew's mind has been *entirely* brought on by drinking." After giving humiliating details of his drunken degradation, she went on to say—"It is a cruel and wicked thing and a shame to try and make out my nephew to be insane. . . . It is a stigma on the family, when there is no reason for it."

separate varieties of the human kind are either incompatible, or only combine to produce hybrids which for the most part unite in themselves the vices and lack the virtues of either stock; and in idiotic specimens in which degeneration has reached its worst, impotence, sterility and consequent extinction of the line ensue. For it may be taken for granted that no experimental attempts to propagate a race of undoubted idiots, however diligently and with whatsoever artificial aids pursued, would succeed.

On the other hand, when the germ-plasms are best suited to combine and conjugation is at its best, they issue in so excellent an incorporation of the outward relations of the kind, such inbred essential aptitudes, as transcend and anticipate the slow gains of individual experience, requiring the mere touch of experience to quicken them into their superior and almost intuitive function. The product is that excellent variation or sport which we call genius. Sometimes, again, much to the prejudice of the consistency and unity of the individual's life, the leading paternal and maternal qualities seem to lie side by side, mixed rather than combined, so that he is not a welded unity of being, but at the unforeseen sway of the one or the other main factors in his composition, according as either is in the ascendant; now driven perhaps to impulsive action and outburst of feeling by the maternal strain in him, and now subdued by the deliberate and critical spirit of the paternal strain which does not fail to torment him by sitting in cool judgment on his expansive outbursts. Thus he suffers through life the pains and penalties of a distracted unity of nature, getting perhaps the imputation of inconsistency and insincerity when he is really consistent with his ill-compounded nature. Obviously the manifold circumstances of life might do much in such cases to influence the development of character according as they favoured, by natural selection, the growth of the paternal or the maternal side of his nature.

That definite laws of composition govern the unions of germ-plasms is certain notwithstanding that the processes are much too subtle, intricate and complex to be found out by any present means of research. In time to come men may succeed in learning the laws of human composition so well as to be able to use their knowledge to breed virtue or vice methodically into or out of a family. But that interesting day, if it ever come, is yet far off, and it will be a curious thing for the philosophic observer of the time, when it comes, to see whether they will set themselves to breed more of the self-indulgence of vice or of the self-sacrifice of virtue into themselves. Meanwhile, however, we are almost entirely ignorant of the qualities which do and do not mix well in breeding; cannot even say positively how far consanguineous marriages are hurtful.

Is it a well-founded opinion that such marriages breed degenerate offspring? A series of careful inquiries by Mr. G. Darwin inclined him to doubt whether they had any ill effect, but the difficulties of obtaining reliable information were so great as to warrant no positive conclusion.[1] The researches of Charles Darwin into the effects of cross-fertilisation and self-fertilisation in plants proved that cross-fertilisation was followed by larger and better growth, by enlarged capacity to resist adverse external influences, and by increased fertility; that in fact the introduction of a fresh stock to remedy the evils of interbreeding is as marked in plants as it is known by breeders to be in animals. But when he prosecuted his inquiries farther he found that cross-fertilisation by plants which have been reared in the same external conditions is not beneficial, and that its benefits were due to the different conditions to which the individuals had been subject in previous generations and to the differentiations thereby produced in them. His conclusion was that self-fertilisation was injurious because of the absence of such differentiations; a conclusion which agrees with the experience of breeders of animals who, when they intend to breed from males and females of the same stock, separate them and place them in widely different conditions, and so get good results.

[1] *Journal of Statistical Society*, June 1875.

Applying this principle to the human kind, it may be supposed that where there are essential differences between cousins because of their representing different lines of heredity their wholesome differentiations of nature might prevent any ill effects from interbreeding and they might intermarry with as little hazard almost as two strangers in blood; all the more safely if they had been bred and reared in very different external conditions. But if there is a distinct line of fault running in either stock, such as madness or deafness or consumption, then intermarriage would be wrong even if the cousins were unlike; for the morbid taint, though not manifest, might still be latent in the one taking after the sound line of heritage and, being transmissible, serve to intensify the bad strain in the next generation. Should there be such unsoundness in both families, whether blood-kin or not, but especially if so related, intermarriage would be a wrong which neither the rash ardour of love nor the selfish interests of family ought to excuse. It is an old theory that parental madness is most likely to be transmitted to the child which most resembles in features the insane parent; but it is subject to these qualifying considerations—first, that a resemblance in disposition does not always go along with a resemblance in features, since a child may be more like one parent in features and the other parent in disposition, and, secondly, that a marriage with the offspring that was unlike the insane parent in both features and disposition would still involve the risk of an occultation of qualities in it which might be transmitted to and developed in a succeeding generation.[1]

Putting aside conjectures concerning complex organic processes that are yet inscrutable, it is broadly evident that

---

[1] Bémin, a French author quoted by Ball (*Leçons sur les Maladies Mentales*, p. 375) found that of thirty-one children born of incestuous intercourse between father and daughter, mother and son, brother and sister, nineteen were idiots and one epileptic. But to quote that as convincing evidence of the degeneracy caused by consanguineous breeding is absurd. What was the mental condition of the parents who abandoned themselves to such incestuous vice? It is not improbable that they were weak-minded or idiotic.

in every stock there is going on, regularly or irregularly, a process either of regeneration or of degeneration. On the one hand, no family can continue long in one stay of perfect soundness, but when at its height, like everything which grows, it begins to decrease, keeping in perfection but a little moment: its culmination in genius the probable knell of its decay. On the other hand, there appears to be at work a silent tendency in nature to restore an insane stock to a sound type, if regeneration be possible, or to end it if its degeneration be such that it is too bad to mend; the social organism, when not itself rotten, possessing a certain *vis medicatrix naturæ* which is charged with the mission of healing or ousting what is amiss in it. For just as the function of a diseased organ or part of the body, being a disadvantage to it, will not be welcomed and fostered in the physiological commonwealth, and thus survive and be perpetuated, so insane thought and feeling, being antisocial, gets no sympathy nor sustenance from the general social atmosphere of healthy thought and feeling—albeit sometimes specially nursed and fomented by like wry-minded cliques or sects—but meets instead with a surrounding hostile resistance, the still, steady and continued pressure of which through generations makes quietly for sanity. That which has a fairly sound basis tends to grow sounder, that which has a very unsound basis to grow worse, and the worse the derangement the more sure it is to be eliminated by extinction.

The two principal modes by which an insane strain in a family is worked out of it are, first, propitious unions in marriage with sound stocks whereby it is attenuated, neutralised, perhaps ultimately extinguished, and, secondly, propitious dispositions of the circumstances of life whereby salutary differentiations of individual character are effected: the first without doubt the most effective, but least within control, since men are obliged, because of ignorance, to trust mainly to the chapter of accidents; the second, albeit more within control, not designedly adopted and methodically pursued, since they are content to trust to chance and to indulge a tacit belief or hope that nature will have a special care of the fortunes of so superior a creature. Without doubt many a one has broken down in insanity who might have gone through life successfully had he been transplanted early into new and different social conditions from those in which the insane strain was bred——conditions adapted to the disuse of old and the use of new tracts of mental structure. Not that the circumstances of life can be depended on to change a character; but a character has several facets, so to speak, and circumstances are several also, wherefore they may influence its formation and destiny by their special appeal to and development of a particular aspect of it.

Time and chance play a mighty part in the circumstances which make or mar a career. When we see, as we sometimes see, one son of an insanely predisposed stock arrive at a position of eminence, poetical, artistic, scientific, or political, while another son ends his days in a lunatic asylum—and I have known several such instances—the different results are not always nor entirely due to differences of innate faculty; they may be due in part, perhaps wholly, to the different circumstances, propitious or unpropitious, in which the respective lots of the two lives were cast. Many an obscure person whom the world never heard of, had time and place suited, would have done as great things as the greatest have done. With mortals it befalls as with seeds of equal quality: some falling by the wayside among thorns are choked by the fierce struggles of competition; some on the stony ground of poverty and adversity are starved; some light on good ground where they take root, spring up, and bear fruit a hundredfold. It is not to be doubted that many men of as good natural genius as Shakspeare's have lived and died in obscurity for him whom, owing perhaps to the accident of a youthful indiscretion having thrown him into the exact circumstances fitted to feed and develop his dramatic genius, the world brought to a glorious maturity; that many soldiers have died in nameless obscurity who might have rivalled Napoleon in achievement had they opportunely chanced, like him, on the fit events and circumstances to elicit the display of their powers. Of the greatest scientific discovery ever made it is true to say that, had its author lived a hundred years sooner, he would not have made it, and that, had he lived a hundred years later, he would not have needed to make it. The way of nature is a way of infinite experiments and infinite failures; it is a rare chance when the fit variation is put in the exact circumstances fit to make the best of it, a common chance for the variation and the circumstances to be misfits.

As a tendency to variation is often a distinct feature of a stock in which nervous disorder of one kind or another runs, it is obvious that, when the mental variation and the circumstances do not fit, the result will sometimes be a breakdown of mind. The variation which is not balanced by solid qualities of character is apt to be eccentricity, which unpropitious circumstances may force or crush into madness. For the eccentric person is one who, though not insane, does not run on the common tracks of thought and feeling; whose thoughts fly off from them at all sorts of tangents in quips and cranks and zigzag flashes; who has strange and startling feelings of things, takes topsy-turvy views of them, conceives and prosecutes out-of-the-way curiosities of inquiry; who is prone to singularities or oddities of behaviour; who in fact is a shock, piquant or painful, to the customs and conventions of thought, feeling and action. The world and its ways, as they strike his senses, do not stir those set forms of nervous adaptation, those fixed moulds of thought, which, translating impressions into their forms, represent the customary thought and feeling; the unstable junctions of his thought-tracts or thought-forms are more easily dissolved and new and transitory junctions more readily formed; therefore it is that he is prone to look at things in novel aspects which may be witty, humorous, comical, fantastic, or grotesque, and is sometimes addicted to punning on words.[1]

[1] Who but a person of that temperament could have conceived the fantastic notion of the discovery of roast sucking-pig by the accident of the

Eccentricity of this sort may obviously be of all kinds and degrees from mild and odd to grotesque and silly, running through a scale reaching from actual insanity to the borderland of genius. On the one hand, it may ripen into insanity when it is not counterbalanced by a strong judgment which fits the individual to weigh things, himself included, in their just proportions, to look at himself in self-critical manner from the outside, and, if need be, to satirise himself as a fool among fools. A sense of humour is a saving health in time of need. On the other hand, the zigzag lightnings of thought may perchance be flashes of inspiration or true imagination, the novel feelings fresh sensibilities to custom-staled impressions, the alien impulses happy rendings of the enslaving bonds of tradition and convention. The light may be irregular, partial and fitful, but still light from heaven; the path-breaking energy fitful and fanatical but still not lead entirely astray.[1]

Here then is manifest the reason of the common saying that genius and madness are near akin. But the genius which is thus closely allied to insanity is of an inferior order—intense, narrow, hysterical, explosive, not calm, large, whole and constructive. Between veritable madmen who exhibit fitful flashes of irregular genius—madness streaked with genius—and persons of real genius who display eccentricities of thought, feeling, and conduct that smack of madness—genius streaked with madness—there is a number and variety of persons who are clever but flighty, talented but unstable, intense but narrow, earnest but fanatical; all sorts of persons who, plunging into new movements, good or bad, and pursuing them with intemperate, perhaps

burning down of a house and alleged a consequent Chinese practice of burning down houses in order to have roast sucking-pig? Perhaps, like most original thoughts, something of a plagiarism, after all! Bacon speaks of persons of a certain character as persons who would burn a house to roast their eggs.

[1] Therefore it is that the best mind might sometimes obtain inspirations or hints from the judicious observation of erratic impulses. "He hath a devil: why hear ye him?" is the first impatient exclamation. But further reflection may discover inspiration in the seeming madness. The simplest facts might often teach great discoveries were they seen as they are and not seen partially through traditional and conventional spectacles.

distempered zeal, lack the just balance of the faculties, the calm equilibrium of a stable mental organisation, the true proportion or mean of nature which is the highest sanity. In the end the result is some such misproportioned incongruity as the philanthropic zealot, reeking of self, whose testimony or character no prudent man of the world could trust, or the intensely neurotic investigator, aspiring to be scientific, who, seeing vividly what he thinks and seeing nothing else, is utterly untrustworthy as an observer.

Every genius being more or less special and limited, there are manifold varieties. A genius in one may be a fool in another domain of thought. What comparison is possible between Chateaubriand and Shakspeare, between Jean Jacques Rousseau and Goethe? In some persons the manifestation of genius is no better than an expiring flash of degeneracy : they are the degenerates or decadents of a stock which sparkles in its ashes. So far from the highest genius being akin to madness, the very principle of its being is the negation of the essential character of madness. A mad Shakspeare or a mad Goethe is not so much as conceivable, a mad Chateaubriand or a mad Rousseau very easily conceivable. Music of mind, as of a vast orchestra in which many and divers instruments, being many seeming one, unite in concord of well-tuned sounds —that is the outcome of the highest genius. He is at one with himself and at one with nature; they are of one mind and he its perfect organ, the nature-made mean by which nature is made better.

That which genius and madness have in common at bottom is a tendency to variation, something mobile and plastic, not formed and fixed, predisposing to new modes of thought and feeling, and to new fashions of expression in word and deed. But with this mighty difference: in the one, a solid foundation of well-ordered experience laid in the mental structure, over which the instructed imagination broods silently, shaping it according to true-informed laws of form and harmony, and thus fashioning something which, essentially natural, yet surpasses every concrete example in nature—forms in sculpture, scenes in painting, characters in drama and novels, inventions in science, realised ideals in every art; in the other, no such basis of informed order and instructed experience in the mental structure, but an empty and flighty imagination which, wanting the substance, forms, and balance of experience, works to fashion the barren and fantastic fabrics of fancy, uninformed and abortive, and only a little less foolish than the anarchic creations of madness or the convulsive doings of hysterical social reformers. The former represent the informed and restrained work of disciplined capacity—of reason ; the latter for the most part the incontinent and deformed work of undisciplined incapacity—of unreason. So far from reason and imagination being antagonistic or incompatible in the same person, as some ignorantly suppose, the highest reason is pre-essential to high, sane and whole imagination. But inasmuch as the wise in the world are few and the foolish many, it does not fail to happen that the feeble and futile products of strained imagination, no matter how devoid of reason and reality, are usually the most extolled and most in demand.

On the whole it must be confessed to be a rare fortune when the variation-tendency in an insane stock gets itself developed into genius. Most often the development is into twists and obliquities and deformities of mind which, albeit they fall short of actual insanity, are peculiarities that bespeak ill-laid mental foundations—the tokens of an insane temperament. Of such mental deformities there are several varieties which might repay exact study and description. They mostly lack, as the basis of their being, a good sound animality to hold in salutary check the vagaries of an over-sensitive and unstable nervous system, a wholesome solidarity of body and mind, and they are prone to develop pathologically into positive insanity in the individual or in the next generation.[1] Certain leading varieties I go on to sketch.

[1] *A good sound animality:* a very different thing from the prurient lubricities and overstrained sensualities into which such persons are prone to run, who are sometimes as hysterical and unwholesome in their sensualities as in their general modes of thinking, feeling, and doing.

CHAPTER III

CAUSATION OF INSANITY

Mental Malformities—Varieties of Insane Temperaments

MOST striking perhaps is an acute and extreme suspiciousness of nature which incapacitates those who have it from putting trust in anybody or anything. They cannot help looking always for the hidden evil motive, and, believing it to be there when they cannot gauge or guess it, are only the more suspicious of subtler guile in face of frank simplicity; on a tiny basis of proof they are ever ready to build a monstrous superstructure of surmise. And forasmuch as men, whatever they think or profess, are moved at bottom mainly by motives of self-interest, an extraordinarily keen faculty for prying into secret and selfish motives, though it often overreach itself, fails not now and then to make wonderful hits, such as look like flashes of inspired insight. Still it is a vicious habit of mind, hurtful to him who possesses or is possessed by it, for it cuts him off from wholesome social sympathy and converse, is a hindrance to the free development of mind in other and healthier channels, and is prone to grow out of all sense of proportion until it becomes positively irrational. Every one has essential need of his kind for his proper development, so long as he cares to be one of his kind: if he is good and wise, for the good which he does to himself in doing good to it; if frail and foolish, for the good which it does to him in doing its own good. In spite of, nay in virtue of, their distrustful natures, these persons are the frequent and fit prey of knaves who make their profit out of them by flattering and feeding their suspicious foibles; and they, when they realise how they have been duped, naturally have their suspicions strengthened by their latest experience. So they travel farther and farther away from the just mean of a prudent caution, the virtuous mean between the defect which is folly and the excess which is vice or disease. For what is every virtue but a mean or equilibrium between two extremes which are vices? Take one of its opposing supports away, it falls into the vice of the other.

Those who have to deal practically with insane persons cannot fail to observe sometimes how marked this morbidly suspicious temperament is in their near relatives. It is a curious thing to see how these, imbued with a radical sympathy of nature with the patient, will then shrink from acknowledging, although obliged practically to accept, the insanity; how they will explain, excuse, minimise one insane thought, feeling, and act after another until they have proved it not to be madness, and it only remains to wonder at the necessity of treating as a mad whole that which is not madness in any single particular. Moreover, they will suspect, question, censure, carp at every particular restraint put on his sensitive nature, exacting a mode of treatment which shall ignore his insanity, and ending perhaps, if one who lacks the foundations of sanity does not get well, by believing that the disease was rendered incurable, if not actually caused, by the treatment. A much-enduring husband, whose wife, being of that temper, has finally become insane, is pretty sure to have all the blame of her illness put on him by her like-tempered family, notwithstanding that he may have been a pattern of weak conjugal devotion. They have not the least capacity to go in feeling beyond the range of family, being completely engrossed in a narrow and intense family selfishness, although capable of practising towards one another, and of exacting from one another, much self-sacrifice within the family circle.

An allied development of an insane strain is into a narrow, keen and intense egotism which entirely disables the individual from viewing anything in the world from another standpoint than that of his own sensitive self-love. To apply his mind simply and closely to facts so as to get just impressions of them, to envisage circumstances calmly and adequately, is impossible to him, for his sensibilities are concentrated into one keenly tender point of self which precludes full and sincere contact with them. Incapable therefore of true observation, right reasoning and a rightly instructed judgment, he concludes from his own passionate feeling and regards its intensity as a supreme test of certitude. That a proposition is distasteful is a sufficient reason that it is untrue. The more vividly he is affected by a conclusion, pleasantly or painfully, the more sure he is of its truth or falsity and the more insensible to all opposing or qualifying considerations. All that, or only that, is right which he thinks and feels. This is the man who exults in the spiritual intuitions of feeling and despises the low material gains of the plodding understanding.

On the whole, despite his keen self-love and lofty self-conceit, he is an unhappy mortal himself as well as the cause of no little unhappiness to others, who have in the end to bear his burdens, to suffer for his selfishness, to expiate his errors, to make atonement for his wrong. Is it not an almost atrocious irony of nature that a wise man is given understanding in order that, by foreseeing calamities which he cannot prevent, he may be crucified daily by folly? a good man moral sensibility that it may be outraged every hour of his life? a prudent man foresight and self-control that he may feel acutely the sin of recklessness and self-indulgence which the self-indulgent never feel? a sincere man veracity of nature that he may suffer the pains of hiding and the penalties of speaking the truth? But the law of atonement is the principle of the social system, by sole virtue of which it continues in being. The few wise and good in the world expiate the follies and frauds of the many foolish and wicked; on them is laid the burden of its grief and guilt, by them is the social system leavened and made whole, and they are the sacrifices for its sins.

The one thing which this keenly self-sensitive being cannot feel, cannot so much as suspect to himself, is that he exists for the species, not the species for him. Real social feeling he has not in him. If all the world agree on a certain course of action for its welfare and he likes it not, he holds at heart that his repugnance, which is the more intensely conscientious the more it quivers with hurt self-love, should override the common judgment and interest of all the world in his own case. Deep in his inmost nature is the implicit conviction that laws are made for other people not for him to obey; benefits created for other people to confer as a matter of right, for him to receive as his due without sense of obligation and without gratitude; self-denial a proper discipline and self-suppression a proper aim for others, but the one an offence to his superior nature and the other a sin against it; the passionate ebullitions of his inflamed self-love proofs of a noble zeal and enthusiasm for humanity. Meanwhile, he is pretty sure to put the comfort of his favourite dog or cat before that of any form of humanity in the concrete except himself. A narrow fanaticism of belief, religious, social, artistic, or philanthropic, suits the intense strain of his spasmodic nature and is self-flattering proof of a superiority which is thought by him spiritual but is hysterical. Into its current he flings himself with passionate ardour, measuring its righteousness by the intensity of his personal feeling, recking not that a belief may be convulsively strong and yet as worthless as a convulsion, seeing only what agrees with his exclusive tract of thought and feeling, and seeing no wrong in wrong-doing to do its service. Exploding in shrill horror and shrieking conceit at a single sensation-hurting spectacle of present pain, he is incapable of looking before and after at the larger issues involved; attaches more weight to a fanatical scruple of his own than to the welfare of a community or a nation; talks humility with the pride-cant which apes it; dilates loftily on purity in the unclean spirit of prurity.

Such a being usually obtains more indulgent appreciation and less critical scrutiny than he deserves, provided that his fanaticism take not the form of philanthropic Anarchism, because of the presumed goodness of his motives and aims. But the sober truth is that few persons are more essentially selfish and less trustworthy in the ordinary relations of life. Moreover this also may be truly said of his class: that of all wry-minded beings they are the least capable of a wholesome development and afford worse stuff to breed from than some persons who are downright insane. A child sprung from a clean-minded madman might have a better chance of a sound nature than a child bred from one of them; for while an attack of madness need not always be of the essence of the character, but may be in great measure accidental, this unsound nature, being essentially degenerative, is pretty sure to show itself in the offspring as crime or madness.

To take due note of this type of mortal and to define his nature scientifically is not to deny his uses in the social economy as a quickening and propulsive force. Nature needs and uses all sorts of instruments and does a vast amount of work by means of weak and ill-made ones, for the most part getting out of each the exact work which it is best fitted to do. For him personally too it is no doubt better to develop as he does than to become actually insane or criminal, which might be the other issues of his degenerate temperament. What it behoves men to perceive and ponder is that, however good his moral uses, he is still personally selfish and unsound, of essentially immoral structure. Moreover, it ought not to be granted offhand that his fanaticisms and strained fancies and follies, whether in music, painting, poetry, social or political work, are in the end more useful than hurtful to society; they may be none the less pernicious because a great or small number of likeminded persons, fired with an equal ardour of self-love and self-esteem, confederate to foster and further them. When a whole people, seized by a frenzy of hysterical emotion, plunges headlong into some fanatical folly, taking leave of sense and reason for the time, like a crowd in a panic of fright, save only a small minority who are overwhelmed by the rush or compelled to stand helplessly aside, the best hope for society may be that they will spend the fury of their rash enthusiasm in noise and tumult and not carry it into equivalent action. For it is not by the multiplication of fools that wisdom is manufactured, still less higher wisdom in ever higher terms of the multiplication; folly is none the less foolish nor a mad thing any the less mad because a multitude, inflamed by contagious sympathy, combine to do it. Meanwhile this reflection is always available by way of cool consolation : that in the manifold and intricate relations of a complex society the irrational zeal of one person or sect of persons is perchance checked, qualified or counteracted by an irrational zeal of another sort, and thus out of the collision and conflict of fanatical forces a fairly rational resultant ensues.

As the wide world affords no worse stock to breed from than the extremes of these degenerates, the pity is that they are not satisfied to propagate their missions without propagating their kind. Considering the weak and ill-constructed germ-plasm which the narrow intensity of their natures implies, and the further special distortion of its frail and faulty nature which the essential hypocrisy of their lives probably imparts to it, the world might well dispense with its continuation, much more with its deterioration, from generation to generation. A good fund of sound animality is not only an excellent, nay a necessary, basis of a strong, sound and manly mental organisation, but it is an indispensable condition of sound and vigorous procreation. Let a man strain to the utmost his aspirations and efforts to rise from the sensual to the spiritual by putting off the animal in him with its affections and lusts, the reproductive process, loving or lustful, is still an essentially animal function, entails the animal use of his body, and requires the right animal vigour. He who, aiming to soar to a soul's utmost spiritual heights, emasculates manliness and calls the result saintliness, has no right to propagate sexually at all. It may be that man is destined to become less prolific as he becomes more neurotic or, as some might prefer to say, more spiritual, and one day perhaps to reach the spiritual ideal of a saintly emasculation, when, no young, fresh and vigorous barbarian stock being any more available to renovate his animal nature, he will end on earth; either because of actual physical impotence to propagate successfully, or because, disgusted by the process and its results, he agrees with one consent to forego such propagation for some threescore years and ten. But he is more likely perhaps, if we judge the future by the past, to perish by the various vicious abuses and excesses of the function which he has used the powers of his superior reason to devise and indulge.

Proceeding with the consideration of varieties of unsound neurotic temperament, I may advert to a class of persons who, without the intense egotism and explosive hysteria just described, indeed being of fair moral structure, are still debarred intellectually from a sincere and wholesome contact with facts, and therefore from a thorough veracity to them, by reason of a too quickly sensitive and irritably impatient temperament. So sensitive is such a one to the pain of impressions which do not agree with his feelings and notions that he shrinks from them; they are hurts and offences, not, as they should be, instructions; to be confronted with them is to be affronted by them; he cannot for the life of him so attend quietly and patiently to unwelcome facts as to mark, learn, and inwardly digest them. His sorely tender self prevents him from apprehending truly, as an inflamed finger prevents him from grasping firmly. The result is that he fails throughout life to take what is repugnant to him into his mind, to embrace and hold fast that which it ought to teach him, and so to make it part of a well-knit and consolidate mental structure as ever afterwards to be disciplined to front, feel, and think it truly.

Nor is that the whole mischief. Ignoring or shirking,

consciously or unconsciously, repugnant impressions, by taking refuge in feelings and notions that suit the bent of his temperament, he strengthens it by exclusive nurture and exercise, thus growing more and more unable to get into true relations with men and things and to apprehend them as they are. Those who are in daily intercourse with him, knowing and fearing the outbreaks of his sensitive irritability, are tempted to conspire with his nature to withhold disagreeable impressions from him, even expressions only of simple disagreement, in order to avoid occasions of painful collision. Thus he is let go his way: his life becomes an unwitting development of the tendencies of nature which his endurance-shirking forefathers have determined in him and he by culture upholds and strengthens. In the end he is ill furnished to encounter the strong trials and unforeseen calamities of life which cannot be evaded.

An outlet of escape from rude realities which such a one is inclined instinctively to seek and find, is into the comfort of some idealism—religious, poetical, or artistic, perhaps alcoholic—where unlicensed imagination and sentiment can have things their own way. But his art fails not then to suffer as much by running away from realities as his intellect and character do by his evasions of what is repugnant to them. Its elaborations, feeble, fanciful, and artificial, are likely to be nothing better than strained and futile endeavours to express sentiments that have no substance and thoughts that have no form; not, as he fondly imagines, sentiments that are ineffable and thoughts too deep for words, but imbecilities of both, expressing themselves, as imbeciles do, in laboured contortions of meaningless expression—in hysteric art for art's sake.

Another manifestation of the undue sensitiveness of the neurotic temperament is an excessive nervousness of one kind or another. Persons of robust nature have no idea what such nervousness means—to them it seems ridiculous and contemptible—nor can they realise in the least what tortures they suffer who are afflicted by it or what agonies of resolving they go through in nerving themselves to do things which cause no uneasiness and no effort to ordinary mortals. Nevertheless it would cost these victims of quaking nerves less to face a battery of artillery in action than it costs them to face a simple interview on a trivial business which they shrink from, knowing well the while that there is no need to fear and how ridiculous their fear seems. The nervous anguish which seizes them is not indeed fear; it is more incapacitating than actual fear, which they would combat better, nay, welcome as a relief in comparison with what they feel. Nor is it cowardice, for they exert a courage to act in spite of it which a coarser nature, were it half as much afraid, might be incapable of. It is an overwhelming moral qualm, an undefined reeling anguish of apprehension, which completely shatters self-confidence; a sort of tremulous perturbation in the moral sphere which may be compared to the visible agitation of movements shown by a very nervous person in the performance of, or the failure to perform, a nice act of manual skill under the influence of great emotion.[1]

Akin to this condition of mind, but special in some respects, is an extreme shyness, which is the unfortunate disqualification of some nervous temperaments. Only those who have it can know how sore an affliction it is and how great a let and hindrance to them through life. Nay, it sometimes wrecks a life. For as the unamiable proclivity of mankind, as of other animals, is to set upon and persecute any individual of the species which differs from the conventional type, it happens that when a nervously sensitive and shy boy is sent to school he is teased and bullied there because he is not like other boys. If he

---

[1] I have known a strong and healthy man physically, very successful as a practical engineer, who all his life could not for the life of him sign his name in the presence of any one who was watching him. Another gentleman wrote to me with regard to an interview, nowise formidable, which, after intense suffering and paroxysms of almost suicidal despair, he had nerved himself to go through with :—"Of course it seems very ridiculous now, but if the rewards of bravery were properly distributed, I should now be wearing a V.C. for not running away on Sunday night."

meets with no one to understand him, to show him sympathy and kindness, he gets more and more estranged from his fellows, more and more feels himself a peculiar and separate being, suffers, mopes and pines in solitude, and in the end is so shattered mentally perhaps as never in after-life to get over the injury which has been done to him. Even if he does seem to get over it, still it leaves an undertone of self-distrust in his character which is an abiding prejudice and painfully weakens him on occasions when he has most need to be strong. Moreover, as there is no absolute forgetfulness, but that which has been once in the mind can return in memory, it may revive in bad dreams or sad wakings of the night and thus in old age add to the bitternesses of physical and mental decadence.

Whatever shape it has—and many are the forms and ways it takes—an excessive self-consciousness is the sorest of human afflictions. It may be questioned whether any malady in the world causes so much suffering as the malady of it; for malady it is, being the sure sign of nerve-weakness, natural or acquired. Is it not veritably in the long run more painful than cancer, more paralysing than paralysis, more demoralising than despair? When the natural tendency of the individual to be always thinking and fearing what somebody is thinking or saying of him, even though the somebody is a mere nobody, is intensified by an unwise education which inculcates self-inspection, and tends absurdly to magnify the importance of self instead of being blunted by an education which insensibly merges self in the not-self, the fostered and isolating infirmity is prone to grow into a morbid sensitiveness and excess which is positive alienation of mind. Endless then are its torments: in one it is fixed on some imagined disfigurement of nose, mouth, face or head which he or she is convinced that all the world notices, which is a perpetual subject of tormenting reflection and an insurmountable hindrance to natural social intercourse; in another, on an ever-urgent impulse to do, or an ever-quivering fear of having done, some ridiculously foolish or wrong act, when neither in the hazard of doing nor in the fear of having done it is there real belief; in a third, on some scruple of conscience which, revived as soon as resolved, is magnified out of all sane proportion, until it so fills the mind as to make it a waste; in a fourth, on some penitential retrospect which could not receive more attention and be deemed of more moment if it concerned the salvation, not of one mortal, but of the whole race of mortals. Oftentimes, in consequence of the want of proportion and unity in the mental structure, an irresistible propensity to give a testy attention, absurdly inordinate and inopportune, to unessential details, and an utter inability to see things in their just proportion and as a whole, evince a lack of ratio in mind which verges on irrationality. As the healthiest and happiest organism is unconscious of its organic functions and only becomes conscious of them when they go wrong, so the healthiest and happiest self is least conscious that it is a self; it is going wrong when it is acutely self-conscious. The fall of man from bliss to woe having been a fall from an unconscious unity with nature when, though naked, he was not ashamed, to a self-consciousness and separation from it, when shame sewed fig-leaves to cover his nakedness, it may be a tacit stress of his nature to get painfully back, through all the slow and tedious acquisitions of consciousness, to the blessed unconscious unity from which he was in an evil hour seduced.[1] The tree of knowledge is not the tree of life.

Another manifestation of an unsound strain of temperament is an outrageous vanity. Social in essence and in a measure excusable, if not laudable, seeing that it springs from a love of the approbation or admiration of the kind, vanity may yet grow in a weak character to such a height of folly that it is positively insane. How deep in human nature its social roots lie is shown by the pains and labours men will undergo in its service; for

---

[1] The peremptory demand in the garden of Eden, "Who told thee that thou wast naked?" was followed instantly by the question, "Hast thou eaten of the tree whereof I commanded thee that thou shouldst not eat?" The taste of knowledge was the bane of happiness.

there is not an absurdity of dress, not a grotesque affectation of behaviour, not a folly nor heroism of action, of which they are not capable, even though it be the sacrifice of life itself, in order to gratify this poor passion which, preached against ever since preaching began, has not been in the least weakened by the persistent onslaught. Could anything be more ridiculous, from an outside standpoint, than the heroic things men will do to gain the applause of their fellows in one part of the world, or in one section of society, or in one kind of pursuit, while perceiving and despising the folly of those who are doing equally heroic performances of another kind for the same motive in another part of the world, or in another society, or in another pursuit ? Although vanity is a meaner passion than pride, mean enough for petty revenges, and betrays a weaker character, since pride may be the attribute of a strong character, strong enough to be magnanimous, (being founded on a contempt of vulgar opinion and, in proper degree, conducive to the maintenance of personal self-respect and dignity), yet both passions, when they are related to unworthy objects and developed extravagantly, become unsound distortions of mind and may then grow into such disproportion as to be irrational. What a pretty folly it is for any one to be vain or proud of his defects, because they belong to him, or to his family, or to his caste, or to the silly shibboleth of his special faith!

Here, however, a real difficulty presents itself—the difficulty of keeping a just mean between a disdainful defiance of social opinion and a slavish subservience to it, of combining the maintenance of individuality with a due assimilation of the social medium. To be overmuch governed by circumstances is to have no character at all, while not to be influenced justly by them is to miss the salutary restraints and discipline under which a character grows in. strength and proportion, and in the result to develop an individuality not well balanced and consolidate, if not actually distorted and eccentric. No man can divorce himself and live aloof from his social medium; wherefore, if he chance to fall on evil times and to live in the foolish medium of a foolish age, he cannot help it, he must be content to be more or less a fool of his time and medium.

Still another outcome of an insane temperament is an extreme avarice. Its worst display is seen in the sordid miser who, sacrificing his life to his greed, starves himself to death in order to add to wealth which he has no need of and of which he makes no use when he has got it; who, losing sight of the end in the means, since riches, like manure, are useless unless spread, toils meanly for the means as an end; who grows in greed as riches increase, since it is not want but possession which breeds avarice, and is essentially poorer as he grows richer, since the greatest avarice is the greatest poverty. He is the incorporation of a natural passion, itself in moderation a virtue, gone astray out of bounds into the exclusive growth of a virtual madness; the evil habit of his life so rooted in his nature and with such a vital hold of him that to eradicate it would be to pull up his being by the roots. An example well suited to prove that a person may systematically mould and manufacture himself to be the rigid machine of any special folly of belief or vice of conduct if only on a fit foundation he exercise the fit training continually and exclusively for the desired end. Less extreme manifestations of the same passion crop up as little meannesses, petty avarices, miserly wiles and guiles, tricks and shifts of cupidity, in the characters of persons of good social position who in other respects maintain a high standard of honourable behaviour. So misplaced and incongruous in them do these mean things seem that it is a surprise to see them exhibited at all, a greater surprise to see that they occasion no sense of shame when exhibited, a still greater surprise to see, should some shame be shown, that they are still exhibited in spite of it. But the fault is ingrained in the individual nature, and it will appear, if full inquiry be made, that a strain of mental unsoundness commonly, of moral unsoundness certainly, runs in the stock.

These inborn faults of an unsound nature do not go on to end in actual insanity usually; on the contrary, they continue for the individual life without much change, getting perhaps their pathological development in the offspring. Still they are all essentially antisocial, tending to injure the social organisation and to cut off the individual from fit function in it, and some of them of such antisocial kind and degree as to be immoral. Not that there is essential difference of kind between faults and sins. Sins are faults writ in finer type, faults, that is to say, of the finest reflexes of thought and feeling which have been the developments of Judaism and Christianity. To the ancient Greek and Roman, who had not the least conception of what moderns mean by sin, they were faults or vices, though none the less social offences. Christendom counts them wicked and calls them *sins* because it holds them to be the offences of an immaterial spirit, bodily imprisoned for a while in time and space, against a divine Being who may be relied upon to mete out due punishment to it for them when it is disembodied by death. But this preternatural view of them need not for ever preclude scientific study of the natural laws by which they have come to be natural events and by which, being breaches of physiological and social law, they inexorably work their punishment on earth in the injury which they do to the individual and to the social organism.

Not only has sin been taken out of the domain of natural causation and scientific study, but the supernatural haze of sin-notions has, by its theological implications, prevented simple and searching inquiry into the constituent factors of individual character as social causes and effects. Blinded by the conception of sin as an offence against a supernatural power, it has been impossible for the individual to see that sin is foolishness in the natural world and to realise his responsibility for being sin's fool.[1] If it were desired to breed a degenerate human being, sinful, vicious, criminal, or insane, what would be the safest recipe? To engage his progenitors in an antiphysiological or antisocial life: to impregnate

[1] To apprehend the scientific truth and its moral: "Through thy precepts I get understanding ; therefore I hate all evil ways."—Psalm cxix. 104.

them thoroughly with alcohol or with hypocrisy, with syphilis or with selfishness, with gluttony or with guile, with an extreme lust of the flesh or an extreme pride of life. When mankind has learnt the ways by which degenerate beings have come to be, it will be able to lay down rules to prevent their production in time to come; but in order to do that, it must substitute for the notion of *sin* and its consequences in a life to come after death the notion of *fault* of organic manufacture and its consequences from generation to generation in the life that now is—must not rest satisfied to look outside nature for supernatural inspirations, divine or diabolic, but seek for natural inspirations within itself which it can observe, study and manage.

A scientific view of natural things might be easier to those whom theology has blinded to the facts and laws of the natural world if they would reflect on another and striking instance of the effects of an insane heredity—namely, the example of a complete absence of moral sense in a child of civilized parentage. Such a noxious product of degeneracy now and then presents itself: a creature of such antisocial bias, so destitute of moral sensibilities and their fit reactions, so imbued with vicious inclinations, that it is truly a moral imbecile whom no culture, gentle or severe, be it never so patient, will raise to the level of moral feeling and conduct; and yet so young in years that there can be no question of real responsibility in its case. It is just a precocious prodigy of evil proclivities—proclivities to lie, steal, cheat, deceive, hurt and destroy, and exhibits a cunning, a pertinacity, and a skill in its evil doings, which, outgoing experience, bespeaks an inspiration or instinct of nature that gives and surpasses understanding. Its depravation means a congenital moral deprivation. Devoid of the finest and most tender cerebral reflexes or of the inspiring feeling to quicken them into function, it has never had the finishing social touches given to its mental organisation; is therefore out of place among beings whose natures have put on the conquests of culture, though it might be in place among the amoral savages of Terra del

Fuego. Meanwhile it is neither causeless nor lawless, it is product and proof of degeneracy of the kind, and in most cases may be traced, when close inquiry is made, to extreme moral obliquities, or criminal tendencies, or actual crime or insanity in the family stock from which it has sprung. Doves breed not kites, nor do grapes grow on thorns in the moral any more than in the physical world.

Having now come to the confines of crime, a brief survey of the relations of the criminal nature to unsoundness of mind will be in place.

The Criminal Nature.

As crime and madness are both antisocial products of degeneracy, the aim of a fruitful inquiry must be in each particular instance, criminal or insane, to discover its origin in the family stock, to unfold its relations to the circumstances of life, and to trace its growth or decay from generation to generation. A little reflection on the varieties of insane temperament will serve to show that the innate fault tends to run naturally in one of two directions when it undergoes pathological development: either into such morbid maturity, by natural selection of what favours and fosters its growth, that mental obliquity becomes mental deformity which is avowedly irrational; or into one or other of the manifold varieties of criminal degeneracy. When crime makes a startling appearance in a respectable family, without any extraordinary temptation of circumstances to provoke it or without any special warping of the individual's nature by bad training, we may be sure that he lacked sound moral fibre and suspect an evil strain in the line of his heredity. Not that there must have been overt crime in a preceding generation, but there was probably some such weakness or vice of nature as showed itself in guile, duplicity, low cunning, trickery, treachery, mendacity, or like manifestations of moral rottenness. Shifty lines of structure had somehow been laid in the foundations of the individual nature by shifty lines of function in the past:

the fathers had eaten sour grapes and the children's teeth were set on edge; having sowed iniquity, the children reap crime.

In this relation it is necessary to take note of the subtle and specialized developments which crude antisocial impulses undergo in the complex and special conditions of modern civilized society. The coarse crimes of our ruder forefathers, like other social products, have taken fairer and finer shapes and wind through more subtle, devious and tortuous tracks, so that they do not brutally shock and hurt sensibilities, as their coarse originals would now do; so fair are their refinements that the evil loses its horror by losing its grossness, so transformed are they that they no longer seem deformed. But not therefore less pernicious, since, artistic suggestions of wickedness, like artistic suggestions of nakedness, are more insidiously tempting and more demoralising than naked grossness. Instead of the vile wrecker who by false lights lured the labouring ship on to the rocks in order to plunder it, we have now the far-scheming wrecker of large commercial enterprises who, though he might recoil from wrecking a ship, feels no qualm in making his vast profits out of the widespread ruin which he cunningly plans and ruthlessly accomplishes; instead of the vulgar gambler who loads the dice and marks the cards, the speculating gambler of the Stock Exchange who concocts and spreads false reports, bribes false witnesses, and heaps fraud on fraud to serve his base ends; instead of the highway robber demanding boldly the money or the life of his victim at the certain risk of his own life, since he was sure to be hanged if caught, the treacherous promoter of fraudulent companies who makes an immense fortune by despoiling thousands of persons and is not hanged, not so much as in effigy. Is it truly a well-based hope that the sum of morality on earth is growing steadily greater and the sum of immorality less?

Now if a man pursue these or like paths of fraud he is none the less criminal because, opinion being infected by an evil commercial spirit, it is not customary and would not be safe to call him so. Moreover, his criminal doings will not fail to have their consequences in the vitiation of the stock and in the evil legacy which he leaves to his children and his children's children; and if his son, lacking criminal subtlety and reverting to the gross basal strain, perpetrates an open robbery or forgery, his crime is only a cruder outcome. Here as elsewhere in the process of degeneration, the more specialized and complex refinements lapse, while the more simple and stable antisocial proclivities in the stock remain and manifest themselves in grosser forms. So it is that the moral guile of one generation goes before the gross crime of a succeeding generation.

So gross sometimes is the antisocial product in this process of degeneration that it is not anyhow capable of being repressed or even of being so manipulated as to find outlet in the subtler and more sinuous refinements of crime. This is the case with a vagrant class of more or less weak-minded criminals, well known to prison officials, who spend most of their lives in prison, being no sooner released from one punishment than they incur another; persons of irremediable moral and intellectual weakness, congenitally destitute of moral feeling and constitutionally incapable of moral conduct. Lacking the curbs of moral sense and reason by which the natural organic appetites are checked and guided in persons of full mental organisation, how can they, in face of the special and complex conditions of civilized society, satisfy those appetites but by acts that are necessarily antisocial? How exhibit them otherwise than in their brutal simplicity, naked but not ashamed, pretty much as they were exhibited in the premoral ages of human life on earth, stealing if they will not starve and appeasing lust by rape or by unnatural offences? Like savages in contact and competition with civilized peoples, such low social beings, in their struggle for existence with higher social units, can only maintain themselves, if they cannot or will not serve others, by low cunning, lying, stealing, treachery and crime.

We have not, however, to do with a faulty nature of that

simplicity and crudity in the majority of criminally-disposed persons, the proclivity being seldom of such compulsive force as to assert itself whatever the external conditions. It may be so weak as to be repressible by circumstances or to require favourable circumstances to develop its activity. Circumstances count for much in the destiny of the potential criminal. On the one hand, there are thousands who are not criminals because they are not at all, or not opportunely, or not strongly tempted by the circumstances of their lives to do amiss; on the other hand, there are thousands of criminals who are so only because time and chance have been unpropitious to them by exposing them unprepared to the sudden and urgent temptation, or gradually to the slow sap of insidious temptation, or untowardly to a conjunction of circumstances suited to put a great strain on the weak fibres of their natures. How many persons there are in a large city who are moral, nay how many who do not commit robbery or other crime, simply because of the strong ally which gaslight is to morality! How many who preserve the name, while lacking the principles, of morality! Considering how weakly organised in human nature morality still is, how precarious its stability, and how possible it always is that what one man has been and done other men may be and do, it is a pretty safe conclusion that any child reared in criminal surroundings and trained in criminal ways would become a criminal. Human nature needs the continual support of good social conditions to hinder it from running back to barbarism, not otherwise than as domesticated animals need the continuance of domestic conditions to prevent them from reverting to the characters of their wild ancestors. Many men therefore have good reason to bless, not only the prevenient grace of their genitures, but also the special providences which ordained the propitious circumstances of their lives. The reflective observer, mindful of the little things and the thousand accidents which make or mar human careers, will acknowledge that the Romans had better reason for the altars which they erected to

Fortune than for the altars they erected to other gods or goddesses.

It is easy to make too much of criminal instincts or dispositions and tempting to be content with them as a sufficient explanation of crime. But no criminal is really explicable except by an exact study of his circumstances as well as his nature; when there is a struggle in him between social habits and savage instincts it will depend much on the surroundings which shall gain and keep the upper hand. Take a person with loosely knit nervous centres, one or other group of which might easily be dissociated into criminal or insane development by circumstances; nay, take the more decided case of a person in whom the special bias or growth of one or other group predisposed to a particular line of criminal conduct;—it is still possible that a strong passion, such as avarice or ambition, by summoning and bending his collective energies to a definite end and thus giving aim and unity to them, might keep him straight in life. Given an equally loose and antisocial predisposition in two persons, the worse might be less likely to fall into madness than the better moral nature; for while the one, unable to adapt itself to the complex social conditions of the higher social life, might go out in immorality and the antisocial ways of crime and so spend its energies definitely, the other, equally unable to adapt itself to the higher social conditions but having no outlet in the lower conditions of immorality and crime, might break down and scatter in mental disorder. Thus an immoral or actual criminal life might positively save a person from madness, and a duke's daughter become insane where a dustman's daughter remained a sane prostitute or thief.

It is not possible to draw a distinct line of demarcation between insanity and crime, either when we have to deal with them socially as events or when we investigate their causation in a scientific spirit. There are criminals who are more mad than bad, insane persons who are more bad than mad. One thing one may safely do—rest on the broad truth that a man's nature is essentially a recompense or a retribution.

Bad strains of structure being the structuralisation of bad function in the past, and the pleasure of every organ being to perform its function, his pleasure, like his tendency, will be to perform the function pre-ordained in his structure—to go astray in madness or in iniquity when the forefathers have preformed him for that function.

Moral Causes of Insanity.

Considering then in the light of foregoing reflections the common causes of error of observation and reasoning—the various biasses of prejudice, passion, temper, interest and the like, which turn the mind from the straight paths of truth, it is manifest that they are just the causes which, when carried to excess, tend towards madness or other mental aberration. The structuralisations of wrong tendencies are so many incarnations of error. What is beauty but sublimed truth of character? In the character, as in the flower, fragrance is incarnate radiance. What is positive insanity of perception, thought, feeling and conduct but a kind of ugly hypertrophy of common error of seeing, thinking, feeling and doing? From such common errors, through set forms of faults in the varieties of insane temperament, to extreme insanities there is no break of continuity in the process of mental degeneration. What are false fashions of temper, feeling and thinking essentially but so many unsoundnesses of mind in themselves and so many predispositions to the developments of disease when they are allowed to grow to irrational heights in the individual or through generations? If a man observe not the laws of nature to obey them, his sin will be avenged on him and on his children unto the third and fourth generation. To be unwilling or unable, out of prejudice or prepossession of any sort, to look sincerely at facts and to get into true relations with them entails inevitable retribution in the growth of prejudice and in proportionate privation of good mental food and faculty; to vitiate judgment with passion or self-interest is to minister then and thereafter to demoralisation

of self; to suffer a foolish pride to hinder wholesome social
communion is to lose the social stimuli and restraints of
healthy growth and to become more and more deformed
and lame in mind in proportion to the degree of exclusive-
ness; to be blind, out of envy, hatred, or malice, to the
just merits of others is to suffer by the moral blindness
and to go the right way to make the blindness lasting;
to be wholly destitute of charity is to give the pride of
intellect free play to puff up and lead astray. Growing
wrong habitually from any such causes, he grows into
a deformed organ of such wrong-doing, a machine of
special perverted reflex action, reaping at last the character which is the fruit of the habits which his disposition
has sown.

In the mental organisation, as in other organisations,
being comes by doing. Its order of development in the
human kind is—first, to act together, which is social
co-operation, enforced rudely by primal human necessities,
for men work together before they feel or think together;
then, in quiet sequence which is almost concomitance,
to feel together, which is social feeling or *consentience*,
for those who work together soon get a consent of feeling;
lastly, to think and feel together, which is *conscience* or
moral sense, for they who reflect on what they are feeling
and doing together, with and for others and others with and
for them, perceive that they ought not to do to others what
they would not have others do to them. Could a man
live alone on a remote island, without need of intercourse
with his kind, his moral errors would be innocuous, seeing
that, lacking nurture, they would lose their nature; he
might have all the social vices and virtues under the sun,
and it would be all one as if he had them not so long as he
had no one in relation to whom to feel and exercise them;
but having to live and act in, by, and for a social organisation
of which he is a unit, his moral errors are antisocial evils or
sins which, hindering its full functions, lame and deform his
nature. Now it is only a question of degree and kind of
fault how far antisocial feeling, thought and conduct, passing

through their divers forms of degeneracy, must go before it becomes madness or crime.[1]

The usually enumerated causes of insanity are too vague and void to have any scientific value. Even when the disorder is known positively to be hereditary in any one, we are little wiser, if we stop there, than we should be if we were told that it was owing to a particular conjunction of the stars at the time of his birth. How far grief, remorse, disappointed love, domestic cares and anxieties, jealousy, pride and the like are really the causes which they are said and appear to be; whether more members of one religious sect than another go mad in proportion to the numbers of the flocks of each fold; what is the ratio of insane to sane persons in this nation and in that; whether one kind of occupation is more likely to cause insanity than another; whether men or women are the more liable to go insane; —these are questions too vague and general, too wanting in precision, to admit of instructive answers. The most diligent and painstaking statistical inquiries in respect of them serve at most only to indicate the line along which closer inquiries must be prosecuted and more exact knowledge sought. One thing we may conclude certainly of all moral commotions and mental overstrains which cause insanities: that they do it by straining or breaking the molecular ties of the nerve-structure and so injuring or destroying its vital elasticity.

The question what religious denomination is the most fruitful soil of insanity cannot be answered without going much deeper in inquiry than statistics take us. For as it is not the religion which makes the character, but the character which suits itself with the religion, it comes to pass that the Christianities of different nations and persons are as different as their characters. Suppose it were established that two Plymouth Brethren go mad for one Roman Catholic, out of an equal number of adherents of the two sects, as

[1] Self is, as it were, the centre of gravitation of the individual round which he revolves, but, as a sound member of a social organism, he is made to revolve also round its centre of gravitation.

is a not improbable ratio, the conclusion that the former religion is twice as liable to cause insanity as the latter would be unwarranted. What was the peculiar temperament or special education which made one a Plymouth Brother and the other a Roman Catholic? Most likely the Plymouth Brother had an insane temperament which sought out by an elective affinity the narrow religion most suited to its narrow spirit. Certainly there is no more weak, unstable, self-deceiving and shifty nature in the world than that which finds its joy, perhaps its refuge, in the special shibboleth and practice of an extremely keen, narrow, exclusive and egotistical religious profession.

When overwork is the assigned cause of insanity, in nine cases out of ten it is not the real factor; for either the overwork never existed at all, and was wrongly fixed on as cause because the man, broken down by other and more sensual causes of exhaustion, could not do his wonted work, or it was work which, for other reasons than its direct stress, entangled him in wearing worries and anxieties. It is the wear and tear of emotion, not of work, that is the real hurt, the heart-work not the head-work; not the work which a man can do, but the work which, thinking he must do, he cannot do. Now the work which he can do and is a pleasure to him when he is strong and well becomes work which he cannot do and is a strain and pain to him when his nervous energy has been weakened by causes of physical exhaustion. Moreover, work which he will some day do with ease may be an almost intolerable anxiety to him at the outset, before the habit of its accomplishment has made its burden easy. When work causes worry and the worry sleeplessness in any one, we may be sure that, either from its character or from conditions in him, it is too great a strain on his nervous energy.

Of the multitude of diligent and minute inquiries which have been made in order to settle statistically whether men or women are the more liable to insanity, it may be said at once that they have not repaid the tedious labours which they have cost. The two clear results of them are to prove that women have, in their special function of child-bearing, a special occasion of mental disorder, and that more men than women fall victims to general paralysis; both which must needs be, seeing that it is not the function of men to bear children, and that women are not exposed, like men, to the most efficient causes of general paralysis. But whether more males than females go mad, on the whole, either by reason of native structure of mind or of their different conditions of life, must be set down as uncertain; and the uncertainty, after so many laborious inquiries, is presumptive evidence that the liability is pretty equal in the two sexes.

As it is impossible to separate the moral and physical causes of mental disorder, seeing that every moral feeling has its physical basis and what is a moral trouble in one may not be so in another physiological state, it is obvious that the ultimate aim of inquiry must be into the nature of the weakness of mental organisation, native or acquired, which is the determining condition of the breakdown. Here, I think, two kinds of fault might be distinguished and specified. First, the fault may be in the complex molecular constitution of the nerve-element itself, whereby it is either unduly susceptible and unstable, too apt to discharge its energy and to let the explosive commotion spread from molecule to molecule by a quick sympathetic infection, or is insusceptible and inert, sluggish to react and slow to conduct impressions. These are undoubtedly primary and fundamental qualities of nervous composition which powerfully influence education and have far-reaching effects on individual mental development.

The second and perhaps secondary fault is in the confederation or association of the nervous plexuses or so-called centres which unite to form the structure of the mental organisation. Loosely linked and ill-balanced among themselves, they are an unstable confederation which easily falls to pieces under shock or strain; or they are not well federated because one or other of them obtains an undue development, and, not kept in proper check, grows to such a predominance as to lead to deformity and disorder of mind. Then the central government—that is to say, psychologically, the will—which should represent the collective energies of the co-ordinate parts, fitly linked and balanced, and working diversely to one end, is weak because the several states, loosely held together, are not bound in compact solidarity of function ; or it is weak because, one state having too much and another too little representation in it, the supreme government is not the compact and justly balanced expression of all the interests and forces of the federal union : being not well proportioned, not truly *rational*, the tendency inevitably is to a dissolution which is irrational. What is right for a part in a mental organisation, as for a state in a confederacy, for an individual in a community, for an organ in an organism, is the utmost fulness and freedom of individual function consistent with the good of the whole, every good to self which is not a hurt to the community—the blessed mean between extremes, perfection's law, which it is so good to aim at in everything, so hard to attain to in anything.

Conformable with the two kinds of faults of mental structure specified are the two principal modes in which the causes of insanity act to produce it. Either the derangement comes on suddenly and is widespread, a general mania betokening the direct implication of the whole area of the mental organisation ; or it comes on gradually and is partial, when it presumably implicates chiefly and directly a part only of the mental area, the rest of it, if it suffer at all, being affected indirectly. When delirious mania follows a great physical or moral shock, it is evident that the mind is as generally, though not quite as deeply, involved as when it is delirious in fever; whatever the intimate molecular condition of things, it is of such a character as implies the spread of the disorderly motion over a large area ; no effective resistance is offered to the propagation of disorder from molecule to molecule, or from one group of nerve-plexuses to another. Nevertheless there is still a certain measure preserved in the most frantic mania which is not similarly preserved in delirium; more or less system is manifest in the disorder, all is not absolute incoherence; the functional forms of the associated tracts are not entirely broken up, as they are in delirium; even at the worst there are fragments or remnants of method which float as wrecks on the tumultuous sea of disorder. In the second mode of invasion, when the mental derangement comes on gradually and is partial, there is manifestly not the same molecular instability, not at any rate the same tendency of the disorderly motions to spread quickly far and wide over the mental area; either they are not sufficiently active, or more resistance is offered to the conduction of disorder, which gets itself established locally in the limited area of a morbid habit, other forms of mental function being unaffected. These differences in the limitations and dispersions of disorder may be due in part to the nature of the extrinsic cause of disturbance, but in the main they are certainly due to the native quality of the mental structure or of the nervous federation or of both.

To have a well-built and stable mental organisation attests the virtues of forefathers who built wisely in welldoing of thought, feeling and conduct. If a bad passion or vicious impulse or false thought or evil desire invades a mind of that sound composition, it is an invader in a hostile territory, meets with no sympathetic welcome, encounters instead a silent strength of resistance which, being infixed in structure, is molecular, and for the most part unconscious. There is no need to raise a signal of alarm and busily to muster the forces necessary to combat it, for the silent repugnance of a good nature is enough. Whosoever must go about to summon consciously the forces of virtue in order to think wisely, feel rightly and do well on the occasion of a temptation to do wrong has not a mind thoroughly well-fashioned, stable and sound, but at best a moral character which is in process of formation, forming not formed, and therefore not whole and thoroughly stable.

He has to take pains to do for himself what his forefathers have not done for him—namely, to lay up a silent fund of moral capital in mental structure. Nor is he safe to succeed always in his encounters, since he is liable to be taken unawares at a disadvantage and, betrayed by his nature, to be foiled at last, after many heroic victories, on the occasion of a sudden or subtle temptation. Virtue is never surely fixed until it is infixed in structure, never more virtuous than when it knows not that it is virtue.

The deeper and the more real inquiry is, the more plain it is that the present need of psychology is the study of the individual and of the manner of his becoming. Empty generalities and barren speculations ought once for all to give place to particular observations and exact scientific investigation. The practical problem is the organic manufacture of a good mental organism—the best instrument of its kind for social purposes; and the test of the worth of psychology as a science will be the exact knowledge of the processes by which that result can be achieved. Individual instances are therefore the proper subjects of study: if well constructed, how was the excellent product formed? if ill constructed, what was the fault in the process of manufacture, and how can it be mended? The questions are simple enough, but the answers to them involve many very complex and difficult researches. What exactly are the differences between individuals and what do the differences mean? How have they been brought about by formation from generation to generation, so far as they are constitutional, and by the exercise of individual function, so far as they are the result of training and circumstances? What were the relations between the individual and his circumstances—how they acted on him and he on them in the vicissitudes of life to determine his life-history? What are the developments, modifications, neutralisations, occultations and variations which a particular family or individual quality, morbid or healthy, undergoes in the intermixture of individuals through generations? What in fact are the laws of human composition and decomposition? of human evolution and of human degeneration? If these are the questions which have to be faced and answered in order to lay the basis of a positive psychology, it is obvious that the beginnings of its foundations have not so much as been laid; but it is obvious also that, once founded, it cannot fail to grow and to displace the vague speculations and barren disquisitions which, plentiful as profitless hitherto, have not been of any practical use either for the breeding of children, or for the guidance of education, or for the conduct of life.

A sanguine belief in the evolution of the human race to ideal heights of intelligence and holiness in times of knowledge to come may properly be tempered with the reflection how easily and quickly it loses a truth or a virtue which it once possessed. Its dates are brief and therefore it continually admires as new what has been before of old. There is no novelty in the discovery that the present doings of one generation are processes whereby intelligence and virtue and continuation of being, on the one hand, and folly and vice and decay of being, on the other hand, are structuralised in the mental constitution of succeeding generations. That a good man leaves an inheritance to his children's children, that the seed of the righteous shall never beg his bread, that the seed of the evil-doer shall not be renowned, that the house of the righteous shall stand, that the posterity of the wicked shall perish, these and the like utterances of prophetic inspiration were based on implicit intuition, if not on explicit recognition, of the laws of human evolution into good and lasting social products and of human degeneration into bad and corrupt anti-social products. And are we to think it was a new truth when the Jewish prophets proclaimed that the incorporation of righteousness in its structure made for the endurance of a family and the incorporation of iniquity for its decay? I would as soon believe that the sun rose and set for the first time two thousand years ago as believe that so obvious a truth of human experience was not perceived by some one two thousand times two thousand years ago.

It is easy for the race as for the individual to lose what it has cost it great pains to gain; for the undoing of a good fabric of mental organisation is a much quicker and shorter process than the building up of it. Two or three generations of progressive degeneration suffice to produce a pretty complete moral and intellectual devastation, whereas the successive labours of multitudes of generations have been required to weave the delicate traceries of nervous networks which subserve the highest moral and intellectual functions. If the continuance of the processes which bring nations and families to perfection leads inevitably, after that, to their decadence, it is obviously deserving of consideration whether the line of the human career on earth is a line of destined progress, interrupted it may be but on the whole advancing, or whether it is not a series of cycles of progression and retrogression—of pulses and intermissions, like the processes of organic life, of systole and diastole, of rhythms of movement and rest. Is there any surer principle of immortality in a complex social body than in a complex organic molecule? Vice, crime, disease, decay and death are just as natural and necessary events as virtue, health, growth and life; ever-present processes that are kept in check while evolution is in full vigour, they will increase when it has reached and passed its height: their presence and function now are the augury of a larger presence and function some day. The long, long time the world has lasted and the infinite travail of it to bring life on earth to its present development! The short time and the little change that will be necessary to bring it all to an end as a tale that is told!

CHAPTER IV

CAUSATION OF INSANITY

II. *PATHOLOGICAL.*

I.—*The Organic Mechanism and its Reactions.*

GIVEN the individual constitution, such as it has come of the long travail of the past, an organic product to the creation of which all things from the beginning have ministered, I go on to consider it now as what it simply and essentially is—an organic mechanism placed in social and physical conditions to which it must adjust itself or which it must adjust to itself in order to live at all, and make the best mutual adjustment in order to have the best life and function. Moreover, because in its nature all things have silent intelligence one with another and each with the whole, therefore the greater in number, the wider in range, and the more special in character the relations between it and its surroundings, the fuller and keener will its life be. In this process of interrelation it is acted on and reacts, suffering passions and performing actions, combining impressions in perception and reflection, and responding to them through fit volitions; such action and reaction being the physical basis of its various sensations, feelings, thoughts and wills. Were the relations between an organism and its medium the most special full and fit of their kind possible, action and reaction would be everywhere opposite and equal. There would be no passion then in the sense of suffering, because there would be a perfect equilibrium between feeling and doing; an aggregate of perfect reflexes might function so exactly and completely on every occasion that consciousness would be swallowed up in the victorious achievement of ideal perfection. Let a man of the fullest possible mental capacity get into the completest relations with the external not-himself, the separation between him and it would be as if it were not; he would act perfectly from instinct without need of reason, his divinings being discoveries, his aspirations prophecies, his performances instincts: he might get a long way back towards the Paradise in which his first ancestor was before, eating the forbidden fruit of the tree of knowledge of good and evil, he obtained the fatal gift of consciousness.

The relations of the organism to its external stimuli are strictly matters of definite law, not in any way accidental, and capable of being expressed some day in mathematical ratios. The stimuli to which it is sensible are fixed, limited, special, subject to minimum and maximum limits of physiological operation, between which alone life has its being; so relative and finite their operation that there is nothing more imbecile than to speak as if man's susceptibilities were the measure of nature's forces, no more ludicrous spectacle in the world than that of the philosopher who aspires to set forth the *first principles* of things. When the external stimulus is in excess, whether because too powerful or too prolonged, passion or suffering ensues, which is felt either as pain or distress or anxiety or dread or tumultuous feeling of some sort, and, if not completely paralysing, issues in irregular, involuntary, distracted and quasi-convulsive movements. The greater the discord the more painful the consciousness when the discord proceeds from such disproportionate external action and consequent incapacity of any fit internal reaction. For according as the impression is more strange, vast, undefined and confounding, so is the feeling of dismay more vague, vast and appalling, no motor adjustment to it being possible:

the external agency is formless, inapprehensible, overwhelming, not capable of being expressed in words of definite meaning, capable only of being signified vaguely by terms that are negations of definite conceptions. Therefore it is that the stupendous catastrophes of nature have always had a singularly demoralising effect on mankind, the more awfully so the more mysterious their causes, and that darkness and solitude, especially in strange and unknown places, still terrify persons who are just as safe there as if they were at home in noonday and company. It is with them as with the child which is thrown into a convulsion of fright by the apparition of a new and strange object. If there be sufficient personal reaction to prevent utter demoralisation in face of these overawing aspects of nature, and the man, instead of falling on his knees, aghast, utter, and helpless, stands erect, resolute and defiant, the spice of bravery adds just the necessary element to make him seem sublime—to his kind. Here however, as always, it is proper to keep a certain mean, lest otherwise the sublime degenerate into the ridiculous; for while Prometheus defying Zeus is a spectacle of sublimity, Ajax defying the lightning is only a ludicrous spectacle of folly.

When the external stimuli are in defect, being insufficient in quantity or not of the right quality to satisfy the instinctive needs of the organism, then also there is a painful consciousness, which shows itself in discomfort, dissatisfaction, unrest, craving and the like feelings of unfilled want or desire. The potential energy locked in organic structure craves to be actual, but lacks the proper stimulus to elicit it. This is evident enough in the two fundamental appetites, the self-conservative and sexual, and it may be traced through all the elaborate superstructure of complex and special developments which they undergo in their final constitution of mind, animal and human. So it is that while the organism is in full life and energy it misses and craves the stimuli of a full activity, nay even creates them ideally when it cannot have them actually, expecting in eternity what it cannot taste in time; but when life and energy wane, then desire dies and ideals fade, and stimuli from the outer world, once its want and joy, are pain and weariness to it. To the heaviness of the night no morning of joy succeeds. Bereft of potential, how can it wish to display actual energy? Then at last it craves nothing but rest and peace. Why cannot you let me alone? is the natural cry of the dying person whom the superfluous attentions of affection are tormenting in order to keep him alive.

It is obvious that all persons have not the same scale of natural sensibilities and therefore do not live in exactly the same external world; diversities in degree and character of sensibilities make divers worlds to divers persons, and divers strange worlds to the same person when his senses are disordered. One half the inhabitants of the earth differ greatly in respect of a whole class of impressions from the other half by virtue of differences of sex, either half having special sensibilities which the other has not. Again, there are great differences in the same person at different ages; although there is continuity of being from infancy to old age, yet the child and the old man are not the same person in any real sense, differing more in tastes, thoughts, aims, feelings and inclinations than two persons of the same age and similar dispositions; so much so that it is an abiding puzzle to pious persons what form of character the immortal self will have. Which changing self in the flux of its mortal pilgrimage shall it be to enjoy the eternal bliss or suffer the eternal pains of immortality? As the lowest savage and the highest saint belong to the same human kind, the one is no less entitled than the other to indulge immortal longings; but seeing how vastly different their sensibilities and capacities are and how eternal a punishment to the one the fit eternal joys of the other might be, it is evident that in heaven, as on earth, there are many mansions. Always let it be understood that we have to do with definitely constructed organic machines adapted to work in special conditions, having their special differences of structure which condition strictly their functions, and that no training can ever make one be and do exactly like another.

Besides the differences of sensibility springing from sex, age, and state of civilization in beings of the same kind which affect so much their relations to external stimuli, there are special differences of individual constitution; for no two persons are ever exactly alike—could not perhaps for the lives of them, if they did nothing else but try, manage to cough or sneeze exactly alike, and might each be known as well by his sneeze as by his name were the proper attention given to it. Very singular sometimes are these differences of personal equation, connoted but nowise denoted by the large word *idiosyncrasy*: here and there in the world is a person who faints at the smell of a rose; another who turns pale, pants and feels sick when there is a cat in the room, whether he knows it is there or not; another who cannot eat a strawberry or a shell-fish without having a rash break out on his skin; another again in whom the smell of a hare brings on an attack of asthma; and another who has other extraordinary susceptibilities. These curious instances are well suited and might be used to arouse attention, by their uncommon character, to the common facts and subtle workings of individual sensibilities which, being less manifest, are apt to pass unregarded. Two general reflections they might further suggest: first, concerning the intimate sympathies and repulsions which secretly pervade all nature, organic and inorganic; secondly, concerning the sensibility of the nervous system as an exquisitely delicate reagent, surpassing in that respect anything which the most subtle chemical agent or the minutest microscopical observation can reveal.

Of the manifold ordinary personal diversities there are some which, being found frequently together, have therefore been grouped together as general qualities of certain temperaments. Hence the descriptions of such temperaments as the melancholic, the sanguine, the lymphatic and the nervous, which were made much of once but are little heard of now, not because there was not a basis of truth to them, but because they were not sufficiently definite and constant to be of real use. Moreover, the temperaments got themselves so mixed up in many cases, and the descriptions and designations had to be so blended and qualified in consequence, that in the end there was no sure ground to stand on. The psychologist who is not satisfied to treat of the operations of many minds of different qualities as if he were dealing with one general mind in the abstract may justly regret that little or nothing has been done, since their abandonment, to observe and describe accurately the diversities of individual minds. How is it that many theoretical books are written concerning pleasure as a motive of human action but no practical book is written to explain why one man's pleasure is another man's pain? or why the pursuit of desire is a pleasure and its fulfilment often a pain?

One thing which the constitutional differences of temperament perhaps at bottom mark are differences of excitomotor or reflex irritability, albeit differences not easy to apprehend and describe definitely. The nervous temperament signifies quick excitability, rapid conduction, and mobile reaction; whence ensue, in the domain of consciousness, keen, vivid and fleeting feelings, quick and changing desires, flashes of unstable and volatile thought, capricious wills, eager and hurried movements: a tendency of the individual to over-express himself and to create thin ideals. The melancholic exhibits slower but perhaps softer and deeper sensibility, tardy conduction, rather sluggish outward reaction; whence brooding moods, deep longings rather than quick desires, a proneness to over-meditation and consequent pessimistic insight and outsight which, according to the person's character, may have humorous or cynical expression, wills dilatory in formation but obstinate in action, slow, heavy and deliberate movements: a general disability of the individual to get himself adequately expressed and to create ideals, a disposition rather to create anti-ideals, if I may coin the word. The sanguine temperament is characterized by active but not very delicate sensibilities, easy conduction, full and free outward reaction ; whence brisk and buoyant feelings, eager desires, thoughts more rapid than deep, optimistic outlook, strong self-confidence, energetic will and conduct : the individual expresses himself adequately, having, by virtue of equivalence between stimuli and action, rapid easy-flowing currents not prone to run off into branch-lines or side-issues nor to be impeded by inhibitions from them.

There are undoubtedly such broad native differences of constitution denoting different modes of working of the reflex mechanism of the mental organisation ; but in practice we find them much mixed, and may suspect that the best balanced mixture constitutes the best temperament. The sanguine temperament is the happiest : it thinks and expresses easily what it feels, and does not feel more than it can think and express ; sees and desires conformably and has no difficulty in equivalent action ; not creating fantastic or impossible ideals, like the nervous temperament, nor failing to create ideals, like the melancholic temperament. The latter is the least happy : it does not easily think and express what it feels, and feels more than it can think and express ; but it is more solid and sincere in thought than the sanguine temperament, which is apt to be superficial, or than the nervous temperament, which is apt to be fanciful, flighty and inconstant. Optimistic, pessimistic and spiritualistic views are the respective outcomes of the sanguine, melancholic, and nervous temperaments, and for each temperament the view of life is truest which fits it best. Which the truest abstractly ? Probably the melancholic temperament sees most truly because it sees most deeply and steadily, being under no glamour, like the sanguine, which is fired by brisk blood, or the nervous, which is stirred by over-excitable nerves.

These temperamental differences may be exhibited, in some measure, by the same mind in different bodily conditions. The same person shall then be nervous, melancholic, or sanguine according to the present state of his nervous system, and will feel, think and act in each state just as three persons of different temperaments might do. When either a surprise of joy or an alcoholic or like chemical stimulant animates the melancholic or lymphatic temperament for the occasion with the glow and brisk energy natural to the sanguine temperament, it presumably does so by stimulating its molecular excitability and conductivity and thus producing temporarily a similar physical state of things in the intimate nerve-structure. As the internal condition of things varies so will the effects of the same external stimulus vary, that which is adequate at one time being inadequate at another and that which is normal in one condition being excessive in another; the difference going even to the virtue of one phase becoming the vice of another. A slight noise striking a painfully sensitive ear causes an abrupt start as great as, or greater than, that caused by the loudest noise striking a sound ear suddenly; and a word or a tone of voice which passes indifferently in good health will occasion an outburst of anger or of tears in a sick and sensitive mind: the jarring effect in both instances as essentially physical as the spasms or convulsions which a breath of air or the touch of a gentle hand is sufficient to start in hydrophobia. To know exactly what has caused madness in any one it is necessary to know both the native build of the constitution and its special condition at the time; not only the stress which it was framed to bear naturally but the capacity to bear which it chanced to have then and there. How often has the battle been lost because the general's nerves were at fault? Or the nation perished because the ruler was brain-sick? How many epoch-making changes have been worked in the world by the providential means of morbid states of thought and feeling? Battles and realms, triumphs and tears, storms and calms, the raging of the sea and the madness of peoples are alike natural events of the universal becoming and unbecoming of things and alike fulfil the universal plan.

An excessive expenditure of nerve-force by the drains and strains of life signifies the exhaustion of its potential energy; and that means the lowering of the threshold of sensibility, whereby the stimulus which would naturally be agreeable or indifferent and issue in the calmly continent action of strength is disagreeable or painful and issues in the incontinent, explosive, even purposeless action of weakness. Not only is the person more sensitive in the lower regions of sense, but his mind is more self-conscious throughout; he is brought temporarily to the condition which in a measure is natural to a weak and unstable nervous constitution, which is affected by weaker stimuli, is prompt to react in unquiet and confused fashion, and is easily exhausted. It is the reserve force of potential energy which imparts quiet confidence and the strength to be still. To the individual a just and stable level of sensibility is as blessed a mother-gift of nature as a low level of sensibility and self-consciousness is a life-long prejudice; for it is not only in respect of outer stimuli, physical and social, that it works well or ill, but also in respect of the internal organic stimuli: irritable sensibilities of mind, on the one hand, radiate easily and far into vasomotor and other sympathetic disturbances, functional and nutritive, of the organic viscera; on the other hand, deranged stimuli from the organic system affect quickly and actively the whole temper of mind and its consequent moods of thought and feeling. The philosophy which avails one person to teach patience and self-control avails not another whose lowered level of nervous inhibition supplies the many easy occasions of distempered mind: how should it when at its best philosophy can never preach directly to the organic system?

The three principal ways by which an external stimulus strains and perhaps overstrains the nervous equilibrium are—(*a*) Because, as just pointed out, it is too powerful in itself or is made so by occasional causes of weakness in the individual. (*b*) Because, albeit not excessive in itself, it is made so by a too prolonged action or a too frequent repetition, since the continuance of a strain which is ever so little in excess is fatal at last. Engineers know well that numerous repetitions of a strain on iron or steel, so moderate in itself as to be borne safely, will cause a fracture at last by rending the ties of the molecules and destroying its elasticity. A snowflake is a light enough thing in itself, but a steady succession of quietly-falling snowflakes builds the suspended avalanche which the vibration of a voice precipitates destructively into the valley below. (*c*) Because of the sudden stroke of the shock, the momentum of a moderate blow being thereby made equal in effect to that of a heavier burden which, imposed by degrees, has its increasing stress lessened by custom of endurance and power of accommodation. These are necessary considerations to be borne in mind when seeking to estimate the moral causes of insanity in a particular instance.

Apart from the force of the impression, its novel nature or strangeness is especially disconcerting and disturbing. So disquieting and repugnant has every new thing been to mankind from the cradle of its being that the wonder perhaps is that it has managed to widen and perfect its experiences as it has done. Always the first impulse of vexation, anger, or fear has been to resent and reject the new experience; and times without number have men made martyrs of those who opened new paths of knowledge, only afterwards, when they learned to reap the fruits of labours which they despised and rejected, making heroes, saints and myths of the pioneers.[1] It is effect and evidence of man's superiority over other animals and of his larger possession of

---

[1] *Myths.*—The illustrious being who lives through the ages, extolled and magnified, is never the real being who lived, seldom even much like him, but just an ideal being whom mankind has created to fulfil its imaginative desire: the real Hercules as like the fabled Hercules "as I to Hercules." He who has lived long enough to read the biographies of men whom he has known or the histories of events in which he has been concerned will justly suspect what a farrago of fancy and fable history mostly is. Most often the real pioneer of progress is forgotten, no mention of his name being heard of; he falls in a fight which, for all he can see, is a lost fight for a cause that perishes with him. In the fulness of time another takes up the cause, carries it to success, because the world has now grown to the level of its appreciation, and reaps in joy and glory what his forgotten forerunner sowed in solitude and tears. When he has made the new truth plain even to the capacity of fools, naturally the fools hail him as the discoverer.

the evolutional *nisus* that although, like them, he is quick to repel and evade a new impression and averse to encounter it again, prone and pleased always to go on in the old ways of thought, feeling and conduct, yet he learns by experience in the person of one of his kind, commonly a young member who, perhaps half-mad, is inspired by the adventurous impulse of development and successful perchance where many have failed, not to yield to his repugnance.[1] He applies himself in the end to the new experience, getting from it such sensations as it is capable of exciting in him and making fit motor adjustments, and thus goes on to gain new and special sensibilities in the sensory sphere, new and finer sentiments in the emotional sphere, new, subtler and wider thoughts in the intellectual sphere. By assimilating, instead of rejecting, new things, provided always in due relations to old experience, he develops new forms of nerve-tracts and increases the complexity of his mental organisation; thus he makes for himself by degrees a more special and complex reflex mechanism.

The novel impression is not unwelcome only because it is strange and there is nothing in the mind near enough akin to welcome and attach it, but it may be positively painful because the perception or apprehension of it involves the breaking-up of some existing forms or patterns

[1] The young of birds and beasts are really adventurous, and might perhaps, if unchecked, make new developments, but they are so shut in to old habits and ways by the balance of animal life on earth, and by the dominating preponderance of man, that their adventures end badly for them, well for their enemies that feed on them. Having no superior, man has free scope to develop when he is not crushed out by his kind in the struggle for existence. However, it is that very struggle which, forcing him to do or die, has been the making of him ; war with nature and his kind the great instrument of his progress ; for by the compulsion of necessity he has been forced to make the best of nature, conquering by obeying it, while the hostility of his kind has served his social development by compelling and welding individuals into tribes and tribes into nations. Had he not hit on the way of social union he might, like his pre-simian forefathers, been forced to take to life in the trees and to develop quasi-simian habits of body and mind. He has become social and is becoming more so almost in spite of himself, because he finds his profit in it.

of nerve-tracts, the blocking of certain wonted channels along which the nerve-currents run easily and the making of new channels—the dispossession, that is to say, of some preconceived tastes, feelings, notions or prejudices in the mind which are incompatible with its assimilation. To unmake a form of thought and feeling by which the mind is thus preoccupied or prepossessed excites a painful consciousness, the more painful the harder it is to unmake, and to make new adjustments is a strain that is often a pain; and this albeit the undoing and new-doing, though painful in the particular, are the demolition of prejudice which is for the good of the whole. Given an unstable and ill-fashioned organisation to begin with, the commotion of the necessary disorganisation and reorganisation of thought-tracts may overthrow the weak balance. There are persons whose minds give way because, placed in new circumstances of responsibility, they are unable to make the new mental accommodations and to perform the new duties required of them, or do so only at the cost of a ruinous wear and tear of anxiety; not otherwise than as some aged persons have died after being moved from old and familiar into new and strange conditions of life, who would have gone on living automatically had no change been made in their habits. Perhaps nothing is more trying to any mortal, especially to one of sensitive fibre, than the first year of his career of serious life-work, when he has to face responsibilities that are strange to him, to adapt himself to novel requirements, to blunt by use the too keen edge of self-consciousness, and gradually to make himself the automatic mechanism of fit functions. The revolution of self which takes place naturally at puberty has the same disturbing effect as the revolution produced by new external conditions, since it makes a new self with new sensibilities, desires, and thoughts, thereby so changing the aspect and meaning of old conditions as to make of them a new world requiring new adjustments; wherefore the revolution is not without risk to an unstable mental equilibrium and may chance to overthrow it.

A knowledge of the construction of the individual organic mechanism and of its special modes of reacting to impressions, as well as of the exact nature and particular circumstances of the acting cause, is indispensable to a true scientific exposition of its sufferings and doings, sane or insane. There is no profit, much deception, in mere generalities. Meanwhile it is better, staying in a confession of ignorance, to wait for the slow gains of exact and positive inquiry than to delude oneself with empty words which, offering a show of knowledge, are a proportionate hindrance to its progress.

2.—*Organic Causes of Mental Disorder.*

Passing from the external causes of mental disorder, what are the causes, other than hereditary infirmities of structure, which tend to produce it? They are causes which act from within the body to derange the reflex mechanism of the mental organisation, and they act upon it just as they do on the more simple reflex mechanism of the spinal cord. I shall include them summarily under two principal headings: (1) The flow, quantity and quality of blood in the brain; (2) The states of other organs of the body.

(1) Given the particular nerve-cell or nerve-element, it must be fitly nourished in order to live; and inasmuch as it is not, like a protoplasmic Amœba, independent, able to move about and to seek and obtain its nourishment directly from without, it must have proper nourishment brought to it in proper channels. This function the blood-vessels accomplish, and, like other functions, it may be done well or ill. Whether a too quick or a too slow circulation of blood through the brain does ever, by itself, cause mental derangement may justly be doubted. It is the commonest observation that congestion of the brain originating in causes outside it does not give rise to delirium or insanity, and that congestion of the brain is

found after death in cases in which there was no symptom of mental derangement during life. Something more, which is of the essence of the cause, is wanted for the special effect to follow. Moreover, it has been known since the time of Hippocrates, that the symptoms which go along with bad congestion of the brain—swimming in the head, dulness and confusion of thought, disturbances of sense and movement, and in extreme cases delirium and convulsions—are very much like, indeed indistinguishable by themselves from, those produced by too little blood in it.

The vascular changes in the brain and its membranes which are met with in connection with mental disorder are concomitances or effects rather than causes; no more the primary agents in initiating and keeping it up than the hyperæmia of alcoholic excitement is the cause of drunkenness, or the hyperæmia of the spinal cord in strychnia-poisoning the cause of the fatal convulsions. As drunkenness is due to the direct action of alcohol on the nervous element, so mental disorder is due directly to disordered nervous element. A man does not feel ashamed because he blushes, but he blushes when he feels ashamed. Indirectly, however, there can be no doubt that a continuance of disorders of circulation, congestive or anæmic, in the extremely fine and delicate structure of the brain, most richly supplied of organs with blood and most sensitive to changes in blood-pressure and blood-composition, may lead to disorders in the nutrition and function of the nervous elements, and thus secondarily become causes of insanity where there is any weakness predisposing to it. The sudden vasomotor contraction of the pallor of fear and the sudden vasomotor dilatation of the flush of anger have their consequences, if we may believe Cohnheim, in an increase of the porosity of the blood-vessels whereby, after the storms, both white and red blood-corpuscles as well as serum transude. In either event, whether the blood-flow be too little or too much, it is easy to conceive that the result to the nerve-element might be practically the same —namely, a hindrance to the processes by which fit material of nutrition and fuel of function are supplied and the refuse of nutrition and function is carried away. To the welfare of the inhabitants it is equally adverse whether they cannot get food brought to them or cannot get refuse carried away, so long as proper circulation of life-stuff is prevented. The nerve-element, like the inhabitant, will not only suffer because it is not properly fed, but will poison itself with the waste products of its own function, if they are not duly cleansed away through proper drainage-channels.

It is the *quality* not the quantity of blood which is of most moment. Here there is wide scope for many mischiefs. What are the exact nutrient products supplied by the blood to each structure and what the exact waste-products excreted by the structure, in the infinitely complex processes of metabolism, we know not and shall not know until minute chemical researches have been carried much further than they have reached yet; but it is certain that such substances are highly complex, very unstable, and prone easily to undergo changes of composition which, seemingly very small, transform them from beneficial or harmless into noxious or virulently poisonous compounds—from elements of composition into elements of decomposition of structure. Indeed, considering how many the changes and how great the possible differences of properties in consequence of the minutest changes of composition, the wonder is that the organism does not poison itself at any moment of its life. As the brain has the most complex chemical constitution in the world, its known components numbering, it is said, as many as three hundred bodies or compounds, it is obvious that there are in it room and occasion for multitudinous faults in the processes of nutrition and function — the processes of anabolism and katabolism. Without knowing the exact vitiations and their exact modes of action, a rude mental picture of the very complex nervous elements lying bathed in a vitiated or actually poisonous fluid is enough to show that, short of actual death, the effect will be either to oppress their intestine motions or to stimulate them into explosive disorder.

How quickly and seriously the brain is affected by vitiated blood is shown experimentally when alcohol or belladonna or a like comparatively gross chemical agent is introduced into it. A drunken man notably exhibits the abstract and brief chronicle of insanity, going through its successive phases in a short space of time: first, a brisk flow of ideas, inflamed emotions, excited talk and action, aggressive address, unusual self-confidence—a condition of stimulated energy with weakened self-control so like the sort of mental excitement which goes before an outbreak of mania that the one is sometimes mistaken for the other; next, as in insanity, sensory and motor troubles, incoherent ideas and conversation, and unreasoning passion which, according to the person's temperament, is expansive, quarrelsome, melancholic or maudlin, and which may sometimes, as in insanity owning one cause, go through these stages in succession in the same individual; lastly, a state of stupidity or stupor which might be called and is essentially a temporary dementia. As the disorder begins and ends within the compass of a few hours instead of being spread over months or years, the artificial drama is a copy in miniature of the ordinary symptoms and natural course of an attack of insanity. Happily the drunken man comes to his senses so soon as the alcohol has been burnt off in his body or excreted from it; not otherwise than as the mad spinal cord which has been poisoned by strychnia comes to itself if the body be not killed outright before there has been time for the poison to be discharged by the excretions. Where there is weakened nerve-element to begin with, alcohol acts with special disintegrating force; a small dose being apt to produce drunkenness, and a large dose a positive temporary madness, in persons who have suffered at some time a severe injury to the head, or had a serious attack of insanity, or who have inherited a strong predisposition to insanity, as also in women and children. The reason is obvious: where *co*-order is weak *dis*order is easy, and where a function is disposed to go wrong in a particular way any cause which disorders it will be likely to make it go wrong in that way.

A large dose of atropine will in like manner derange a mind completely during the time of its operation. Here, as with so many other drugs, individual temperament counts for much in the special complexion of the symptoms. Usually they are these—very restless and very incoherent delirium, vivid and changing hallucinations, busy, jerky and aimless movements of disintegrated volition; but now and then, probably in stronger minds more able to resist disintegration, the delirium keeps so much measure of intellectual coherence, and the acts show so much method, that the disorder looks like a brief insanity; indeed, any one who saw the patient for the first time, not knowing what he had taken and not noticing his dilated pupils and dry throat, might well think him simply mad. The active delirium which, instead of its usual narcotism, morphia causes from time to time in persons of a special idiosyncrasy I have known to be similarly mistaken for mania by an experienced medical man.

Mental disorder of the opposite and depressed kind is an occasional effect of lead-poisoning. The symptoms, which are those of deepening failure of physical and mental power, betoken direct damage to the molecular energies of the nerve-elements: in the sensory and motor domain, lowered sensibility and muscular tremors declining into paralysis; in the higher mental domain, loss of memory, weakened intellect, deadened feelings, and general prostration of faculties; meanwhile, as accompanying or sequent effects of the decline, hallucinations of sight and hearing, neuralgic pains, epileptiform attacks and paralysis. In the order of deterioration I might broadly signalize three degrees or stages, though the features of them get mixed, partly because of the different degrees in which different parts of the brain are affected, and partly because of the unknown ways in which a morbid condition of one part of the brain affects other parts, either to stimulate or inhibit their functions. First, there is prostration and dulness of sense, movement and thought, which, though weakened, are not abolished; then follow irregular and uncertain reactions of the nervous elements against the noxious agent, shown in the hallucinations, the delirium, the convulsions, for excito-motor loss in one part may be increase of it in another part; last event of all is paralysis or extinction of function. In the result we have an artificial dementia produced by a known poison of the nervous system; a dementia which, were other evidence of lead-poisoning overlooked, might be thought, and once used to be thought, the effect of natural disease.

It is interesting, though not as instructive as it may some day be, to take notice of the two very different moods exhibited in the mental weakness caused by lead-poisoning. In the one, the patient, all unconscious of his sad incapacity, manifests a good humour and complacent self-satisfaction which give him the look of a person suffering from general paralysis; in the other, he is miserable, irritable, suspicious, distrustful, and believes himself an object of persecution. On what physical differences do the differences of mood depend? That we know not; but it is plain that the molecular differences, whatever they be, lie very near one another, since one mood may follow the other abruptly in the same person; as near perhaps as the molecular differences of ice and ice-cold water. It looks as if ever so little a turn or contraction of the nervous molecule in the brain made the difference of heaven and hell in a mind, as a little further turn or contraction makes the difference of function and no function of it.

Ergotism, a disease so called because presumably caused by the use of rye-bread tainted with ergot, is characterised by symptoms of great nervous and mental deterioration. They are, in the first place, sallow complexion, creeping or burning sensations in the hands and feet, fulness of the head and giddiness, flickerings before the eyes, dulness of perception, loss of memory, and a profound feeling of mental incapacity and distress. Were a patient to present himself to a physician with a wailing story of such symptoms, without affording any clue to the cause of them, he might be thought to be suffering from simple nervous depression or debility, if he were not set down as merely hypochondriacal, and might fail to obtain all the sympathy and attention which he deserved.[1] In further course, by a sort of feverish reaction of menaced nerve-element, follow mental excitement, muscular jerkings, tonic or clonic spasms, dazzled vision, and perhaps epileptic fits. Sensibility is blunted, the pupils are dilated, menstruation is suppressed, and there is motor ataxia. Going along with these symptoms, or sequent to them, in irregular ways are wandering delirium, utter incoherence of talk, and epileptic fits when these have not, or more of them when they have, occurred already. Lastly, a stupor ensues from which the patient recovers or which deepens into coma ending in death. These are the symptoms when they are not, as they are said to be sometimes, those of joyous exaltation with ideas of grandeur; they are of much the same kind as, but deeper in degree than, those caused by belladonna, and, though more acute, not unlike the chronic symptoms of an ordinary case of paralytic dementia which goes on to a fatal termination. They witness to direct and deepening injury of the sensory, motor and ideational tracts by the toxic agent in the bad bread.

One instructive instance more may be adduced. *Pellagrous insanity*, which gets its name because of an exanthema of the skin (the so-called *Pellagra*), some authors ascribe specially to the use of diseased Indian corn as food, albeit others consider it to be rather a profound cachexia owing to general bad nutrition and wretched conditions of life. Diarrhœa, emaciation and feebleness are early symptoms nowise distinctive, but a special feature is a very gloomy dejection and apathy, a sort of fatuous melancholy in which a propensity to suicide is common. The propensity has been said to be specially, almost exclusively, to suicide by

[1] The obscure nervous symptoms of slow arsenical poisoning are liable to be similarly misconstrued when their real cause is not suspected.

drowning; for which reason one author has proposed to call the disease *Hydromania*.¹ The truth probably is that the sufferer, weary of an intolerable misery, only throws himself into the water because the inviting river is always near at hand and it is the suicidal fashion of the district to end life so, since men, like sheep, are infected by the contagion of example and follow one another fatuously; or it may be that, fearing he shall do it, he is seized with a mental vertigo at the sight of water and precipitated into doing it by the very dread of doing it.

These examples suffice to show the effects of direct injury to the nervous system by poisons introduced into the body from without. Of the morbid action of poisons bred in the body we cannot speak with the same certainty, because we know neither what they are, nor where they are bred, nor how they act. But there can be no doubt of their existence and of their action to produce mental disorder, especially where a predisposition to it has implanted a susceptibility, and gives a formal direction, to their morbid action. How different the world looks according as the liver is or is not acting well! So familiar is the experience that a person seldom goes melancholy but the disorder is set down to an indolent liver. Doubt, despair, even suicide, on the one hand; faith, hope and life-love on the other hand;—these are determined respectively by some minute and subtile organic compound which has been either insufficiently or sufficiently manipulated before its discharge into the blood-stream. In like manner the presence of some malformed nutrient product in the blood of gouty patients, or of some waste-product which has been incompletely broken up or

[1] To ascribe death by drowning to water-frenzy and then, turning the English into Greek, to make the name a disease and consider it an explanation, is an example of a favourite practice in medical treatises, not only in respect of varieties of insanity but in respect of many other diseases. Having regard to the baneful habit, one cannot help thinking that if a generation of medical workers were compelled to abandon all their Greek, Latin and bastard phraseology and to construe it into plain English, the result might be a purging of vision, a clarifying of ideas, and such a discovery of word-obscured relations of things as would be a great push to progress.

incompletely removed, is sometimes the cause of a genuine melancholia, during which they are perhaps free from their regular attacks of gout, getting them back again when they lose their mental disorder. It was so with the eminent politician Lord Chatham, whose frequent gouty seizures left him for two years while he was deeply melancholic and whose melancholy in turn left him when his gout came back.[1]

The excess of uric acid which is found in the blood and urine of these gouty persons is only the ultimate product and gross token of latent and subtile changes in the intimate metabolic processes. So likewise is it with the states of disordered urine which are known as *oxaluria, phosphuria,* and *glycosuria ;* states which are frequently accompanied with symptoms of much mental discomfort or distress and sometimes with severe depression, anxious apprehension, and extreme irritability. In *glycosuria* the melancholy is inclined to be of a whining and wailing character, tedious and chronic, largely hypochondriacal in its complexion; whereas in *oxaluria* certainly, perhaps in *phosphuria* also, it is usually, I think, of a more keenly apprehensive character, with sharper irritability and more acute nervous agitation. In the former the symptoms bespeak a more oppressive, in the latter a more irritant, action; differences of mental reaction which doubtless betoken subtile differences, not yet discoverable chemically, in the compositions of the noxious products formed. The nerve-element shows itself a finer analyst than the chemist.

It is only now, for the first time, that inquiry has entered on the track of the minute chemical changes which are the conditions and accompaniments of disease. The result is such a revelation of the intimate activities of the infinitely little that the doctrine of inert matter might now

---

[1] A not less striking and perhaps more genuine transformation than that exhibited by him in the House of Lords when, carried there, his limbs swathed in flannel, a sad, sick man, resolute to raise his dying voice on behalf of his country, he rose slowly to his feet with much apparent pain and difficulty in order to speak, but forgot his sufferings and flourished his arms vigorously as soon as he was inflamed by his own eloquence.

be relegated to class-rooms of moral philosophy or to the regions of nature 300° below zero. That proteids are taken in the food and undergo a series of definite changes in the body before they are converted into its proteids is a broad and well-known truth, but it is only beginning to be demonstrated how subtle are the changes of composition and how momentous the resulting differences of properties. Theoretically it would hardly have been expected that albumoses are formed during digestion which, if they get into the blood or tissues, are positively poisonous and must, in order to become innocent and useful, undergo further changes in the later stages of digestion. But so it is: the work of the first stage of digestion is to do exactly what certain micro-organisms or so-called bacteria do—namely, to produce albumoses that are poisonous. These compounds bacteria go on to split up into virulent non-proteid bodies, alkaloids and ptomaines, whereas in the due processes of nutrition they undergo a higher conversion into the beneficent proteids of the body. Such and so many are the dangers which everybody runs every moment of his life in the building-up of his tissues, escaping death only by subtilties of distance compared to which a hair's breadth might be called immense space. And it is probable that he runs no less dangers in the waste or decompositions of them; for although their proteids are changed eventually into such comparatively harmless crystalline bodies as urea, uric acid, kreatin, and the like, yet the intermediate decompositions before they arrive at these gross and stable products may be fraught with perils. Such diseases as hydrophobia, tetanus and diphtheria yield fearful proof how powerfully the poisonous products of bacteria can act on the nervous system.

Of especial interest in this connection is the gradual mental deterioration, sometimes a positive insanity, which almost invariably occurs in *Myxœdema*, and is presumably due to the lack of a factor in the process of healthy nutrition which is supplied normally by the thyroid gland. The first symptoms are great mental lethargy with depression, sensation is blunted, memory dull and defective, thought slow and heavy, feeling deadened, and power of attention enfeebled; later on, more acute symptoms, melancholic or maniacal, sometimes appear; and the final result, when recovery does not take place, is great torpor and weakness of mind. Now the special interest of the disorder is that a remarkable improvement of the bodily and mental symptoms, which may go on to entire recovery, soon and steadily follows the administration of the juice or of portions of the thyroid gland of a sheep to the patient. The mental disorder is caused by something lacking in the blood by reason of the atrophy of the thyroid, and it is cured by the artificial supply of the lacking element. Manifestly ductless glands have, like the thyroid, their internal secretions that are essential to bodily nutrition.

It is probable that some toxic product of metabolism is the cause of the acute gouty mania which, breaking out after the cessation of the inflammation of the joints, is characterised by fierce frenzy, heat of head, and fever. Ending favourably in milder cases, it passes into inflammation of the membranes of the brain, serous effusion and fatal coma in the worst cases. May it not be too, that the singularly sanguine hopes and expectations of the phthisical patient who projects on the very edge of the grave what he means to do in years to come, long after he has rotted in it, are the effect of some organic or lower chemical product of metabolic composition or decomposition? If so, the so-called *phthisical mania* described sometimes as a special variety, albeit perhaps only mania of one or another phase of the phthisical temperament, may own the same direct cause in whole or in part. What, again, of the acute mental disorder which now and then occurs in the course of acute rheumatism, the swelling of the joints subsiding meanwhile? It is marked by great excitement and rapt incoherence, sometimes by violent quasi-choreic movements of all the voluntary muscles, which are perhaps followed by temporary paralysis; and after the excitement is past, there may be mental torpor and confusion, or depression with taciturn and moody suspicion. The delirium of acute fevers is probably due to the direct poisoning of the brain by the products of bacterial activity and is most likely to occur where a weak brain is predisposed to disorder, since the weak part is the place of little resistance and in the physiological as in the social organism to be weak is to be miserable; and the mental disorder of intermittent fever has been observed, like the fever, to recur in tertian or quartan attacks.

After the subsidence of acute fevers and of acute disease like pneumonia and influenza, when the temperature has fallen to its normal level and the patient seems to have entered on the straight path of convalescence, a mental derangement sometimes comes on, whether there was or was not delirium during the fever, but which anyhow is quite different from the delirium of the acute disease. It is an ordinary insanity, due probably to the ill effects of the fever on the nutrition of the brain, and has no distinctive form: it may be maniacal and violent; or melancholic with delusions of persecution; or a sub-acute chattering incoherence with mobile delusions which are sometimes of an exalted sort; or lastly, especially after acute rheumatism or pneumonia in a debilitated nervous constitution, an almost acute delirious mania. The name by which it is commonly called is *post-febrile insanity*.

Enough has been said to illustrate the effects of organic or purely chemical substances on the cerebral reflexes of the mental organisation. These effects are—either (*a*) so to depress as to disorder their functions; or (*b*) so to stimulate as to disorder their functions; or (*c*) to cause such extreme molecular change as to extinguish their functions. The respective outcomes, in consciousness, of these different effects on the complex cortical reflexes are—(*a*) such states of depressed feeling, ideation and action as characterise melancholia; (*b*) such states of excited feeling, ideation and action as characterise delirium and mania, the degrees and extent of disorganisation producing corresponding differences in degree and extent of mental and motor disorder; (*c*) such impairment or destruction of feeling, ideation and action as constitutes dementia and perhaps paralysis.

When these states of mental disorder follow so-called moral causes they must own similar molecular derangements to those which toxic agents produce. A painful moral shock to a sensitive and unstable mental organisation is as positive a physical hurt, and hurtful in the same way, as a chemical or organic poison; and a stroke of grief which kills a person kills, like lightning, by physical shock, the mental perturbation in the one case and the death in the other being the effect and evidence of the physical commotion. The actual working agent is not the hurt to self-love but the hurt to the organic self, and the cry of hurt self-love is the language of the organic suffering. No wonder then that reflection does not cure hurt self-love, as it might be expected to do were it an affair of pure reason only, but acts instead oftentimes as a corrosive; for right reflection cannot reach the physical perturbation and still it, while wrong reflection is provoked by it and helps to keep it up. If there be a strong well-compacted mental organisation, the moral shock does little harm, because the molecular commotion does not increase and spread beyond due bounds, being checked and restrained by the wholesome resistance of surrounding cerebral structure; but if the mental organisation be essentially weak, then the disturbance is prompt to spread into wide disorganisation : in either case a brain, well or ill informed structurally in the past, is doing its unconscious work in the spirit of its construction. Philosophy will not make a man bear a mental pain, any more than it will make him bear a toothache, patiently, if the underlying physical conditions do not make the pain comparatively easy to bear and the philosophy comparatively easy to practise.

3.—*Sympathy or Reflex Action.*

Forasmuch as the nervous system is the great internuncial and central co-ordinating mechanism of the body whereby each part is made member one of another and all parts are members of one body, the part having fellow-feeling or acquaintance with the whole and the whole with each part, it is obvious that there are manifold occasions of its derangement incident to the discharge of the complex functions of life. Essentially an infinitely complex union of reflexes which have their afferent stations to receive and their efferent stations to discharge in every part of the body, it results that a scratch on the toe may be followed by convulsions, a tape-worm in the gullet by a violent and fatal delirium.

Two reflections may be made with respect to these internuncial functions. The first is that in no case can the routes of intercommunication between organs be entirely inactive, even when they seem so; always must some quiet current be passing along them in order to keep up the common understanding, since thus only can there be an organic whole and the different members be members one of another. Not only is every organ, by virtue of its formal structure and the resulting complex of energies which are its function, represented in the central nervous system, but it is in constant silent communication with it while life lasts; there is no complete rest, no absolute stillness, not even in sleep, until death. It must needs be therefore that latent currents traverse the brain continually in all directions below the level of consciousness and make their silent contributions to the larger waves of thoughts and feelings that are outcomes in consciousness. Potent though latent, since it is these sub-conscious workings of the elements of feeling and thought which, fermenting in unconscious depths, issue in the upspringing of an idea or an invention, in the outburst of unexpected and apparently unmotived passion, perchance in an unforeseen deed of grand inspiration.[1]

[1] Here I may notice a signal example of clever beguilement by words. It has long been the custom to speak of the *unconscious* workings of the brain as taking place *beneath the threshold* of consciousness. An ingenious author has lately hit on the idea of translating *below the threshold* into Latin, christening it *subliminal*, and of then applying it as an adjective to con-

A second reflection is that a law of life, alike in the whole and in its integral parts, is probably a law of alternating activity and repose, a rhythm of rest and motion, a sort of systole and diastole. Just as there is not complete inactivity of living nerve-structure, albeit it may seem to be inert, so its energy is not uniformly continuous, however it may seem so to gross sense. A sensation comes into being and rises to its height by summation of insensible pulses, sometimes perceptibly by sensible pulses or throbs when it mounts to acute pain. Muscular contraction is in like manner the summation of a succession of invisible pulses, of the essential character of which the visible tremors of muscular weakness afford evidence; while the stiff obstruction and jerky movements of lamed muscle in disease witness to the impeded flow of the regular contractile pulses and to their irregular and explosive discharges. Not otherwise does the calm mood of self-contained feeling and the unity of steady will signify a good nerve-tone in which the rhythm of molecular motion is quiet and uniform, not interrupted, irregular, explosive. When irregular and explosive motions of feeling are carried beyond a certain measure, the result is exhaustion and apathy of mind; for mental torpor is the pathological sequel of mental excitement, as paralysis is the pathological sequel of convulsion.

If every bodily organ is represented in the brain, directly or indirectly, through fit internuncial mechanism, being translated there into its proper cerebral movements, it is plain that disorder of it may produce cerebral effects otherwise than through the blood which it fails to nourish or purify as it should do—in fact, by sympathy through the nerves. Because an ill-functioning liver occasions gloom and despondency, the whole trouble in melancholia

sciousness. What was unconsciousness because it was below the threshold of consciousness thus becomes a special consciousness nominally below, actually above, its threshold; a *subliminal* consciousness, which can do marvellous things—as well indeed it may, being a positive consciousness created out of negation, an essential contradiction in terms, a something which is and is not at the same instant.

is often imputed to it, even when it is really only suffering in common with other organs in consequence of central nervous depression. Thus it gets the credit or discredit of a movement of which its disorder is a prominent event only; not otherwise than as a great man, getting his name fixed to an epoch of thought, obtains the credit of creating that which for the most part creates him. Does the liver deaden the mind, or is it the low nervous energy of the dull mind which oppresses the liver? It is obvious that either may be the order of events: a disordered liver will sadden the mood, and, conversely, a sad mood will disorder the liver, just as a brisk-acting liver will quicken the spirits, and animated spirits will stimulate the liver to work well. In like manner, fright produces heart-anguish, and, conversely, heart-anguish produces fright. The order of events is a mechanical to-and-fro process of telepathic conduction in which either end may be the beginning; the deranged organ producing its disturbing effect by the induction of corresponding troubled movements in that part of the brain in which it has central representation and from which they spread by a subtile radiation; and such central disturbance with its accompanying mood, when otherwise caused, tending to cause a corresponding disturbance of the organ.

But for the absolute and gratuitous separation made of mind from body, the sympathies of body and mind need not have been the mysteries they have been. In order to get clear and exact ideas, it is necessary to go below such things as the bad mood and the bad bile to the physical motions which underlie them and of which they are the exponents. When hope, inspiring the belief of recovery in sickness, animates the elements of the ailing structure with new energy, or when despair deepens their distress; when the forcible suggestion made with absolute assurance and received with absolute credence turns enkindled energy into a special channel of activity and so heals by faith; when the specific imagination excites the special organ;—in these and the like instances it is not the conscious state which acts on the conducting nerves and is acted on by them; the desire or notion, as such, no more acts on the body than the pointer on the works to make the watch go. The power which does the work is in the molecular machinery; it is the letting loose of the potential energies of special structure when liberated by suitable impressions; and it is only when the potential energy has become actual that it can be conscious. The spectacle of two young lovers who, billing and cooing, cannot get too near or be too long together, is suited to awaken a pleasing sympathy, perhaps to inspire a poetic rhapsody, but the power which does the real work of drawing them to one another is as unconscious as gravitation. The conscious feeling is the effect and evidence, not the cause, of the attraction. When all is said, to fall in love is, like a fall downstairs, essentially physical and might, like it, be called accidental, since it is neither foreseen nor intended. In like manner when the vascular and muscular tones, and through them the intimate processes of nutrition and secretion, are said to be affected by mental moods, it is not the mental mood which causes the underlying nervous commotion that acts on the muscular elements, it is the nervous motion which expresses itself alike in the mental mood and in the vasomotor changes. Always it is one part of a complex organism, each part of which calls the furthest brother, which acts upon the rest of it, and is reacted on by it, by physical ways and means.

The union of mind and brain in so much of the work done by the brain and in all the work done by mind has made it hard to realise how much mental work the brain does habitually by itself without help of mind, and how it is the brain that does the work when they work together. Having abstracted mind from brain, metaphysics then denied to the brain the power of doing intellectual work. Thence the necessity of assuming that, when any one follows a train of thought without being conscious of it, and is aroused to consciousness only by the result, he is all the while thinking consciously without being conscious that he is conscious,—anyhow, whether conscious or subconscious, is working purely mentally. Thence also the never-failing wonder at the wonders which the brain does in dreams, when it not only manufactures fantastic products of all sorts but reasons sometimes as logically as when awake, and performs feats of novel and vivid imaginative creation which it positively cannot do when it is awake and has the mind to help it. The wonder must remain a wonder so long as all the virtue of its work is ascribed to the mind; so long, that is, as the illuminator of a part of what it does is assumed to be the agent of all that it does intellectually.

The brain can so measure time during sleep that a man shall wake at the hour at which, before going to sleep, he resolved to wake. When it estimates time in the day, as it does when one who, while so occupied in some pursuit as to give no thought to the clock, still judges pretty accurately what o'clock it is, the supposition is that his mind gives momentary and intermittent attentions to the lapse of time, and that the nature of the pursuit affords some measure of it. But as that explanation will not apply to sleep there is nothing for it but impotent wonder. The real wonder, if we consider, would be if the brain by itself took no note of time, seeing that every organic process takes its special time, that every such process sends its special measured thrill to the brain, and that the brain, as central unifying organ of the complex organic mechanism, presides, marks, regulates and directs. How could it do that if it could not keep time? No one is surprised when a man consciously measures time by counting the minutes and hours, translating his own muscular action into terms of external motion, nor would it be much of a surprise if, instead of counting by minutes, he counted 25 respirations or 70 pulse-beats for a minute and multiplied them by 60 to measure an hour: why then wonder that the brain, in whose nature and function time and proportion are ingraft, does that unconsciously and even makes more delicate time-registers of the finer and more subtile organic processes? Had the brain not that unconscious faculty, the cleverest consciousness might labour in vain to count.

Viewing the close interdependence and unity of the various nicely fitted parts of a complex organism, it is inconceivable that a disorder of any part of it can ever be quite isolated. Moreover, the finer and more complex the harmony of an organic whole, the more easily is it deranged. A centre of disturbance strikes a jarring note which spreads widely, as if by electro-magnetic radiation, and mars its mute music; and so it comes to pass that the full organic harmony of the best mind's best tone seldom lasts long. All too soon is the soul's lyre put out of tune: now and then only for a brief moment is there a full sense of a joy of existence; by and by some discord here or there in the organic unison reveals itself in a disturbance of the tone of feeling, which may range from simple irritable unease to profound misery and unrest. While the multitudinous quiet currents which unceasingly pass from the various organic processes to the brain, albeit in silent unconscious flow, fail not thus to affect our moods and thoughts in the busy day, their operation is more distinct in the night when, the senses being shut in sleep, they have the field to themselves and become the exciting causes of dreams. Infusing the ground-tone of feeling, they indirectly thereby inform the dreams which ensue; so that from this standpoint the dreams of an oppressed heart, of labouring intestines, of a troubled stomach, of a disordered liver, of irritable genital organs, are severally worthy of discriminating study. In such dreams the ingoing currents are presumably discharged irregularly in intermittent jerks or shocks, instead of flowing quietly in their normal gentle and regular pulsings.

Furthermore, there is this to be said: that it is just possible that all modifications of feeling and being do not come from without through the known channels of sense and the internal impressions of the organic life. The particular circuit of interrelation with the cosmos which every human being forms is not one of conscious and occasional function only, it is one of unconscious and continuous function also; and it may be that there are ever-flowing currents along it of which we know nothing. Who can say whether the undulations of ether which are light to our eyes may not affect our bodies unconsciously in other ways? Or that these may not be affected in unknown ways by electro-magnetic forces, or by still more subtile forces of the operation of which we are entirely ignorant? When we think that it is in ourselves we are thus and thus, the real determinant may be outside us, near or far away, inscrutable, we know not what nor where—in the air, in the planets, in the space-filling ether, somewhere and somehow in the infinite not-ourselves. The senses, which are so many specialisations of one sense, and at the best most relative and finite, do but break up the unity of nature, fashioning it fragmentarily in the individual according to the forms and measures of his feeble apprehensions; and the utmost that he can know of himself is no more complete measure of the infinitely minute operations of his body than it is of the infinitely vast operations of the universe.

It might be easier to conceive what organic disorder generally and nervous disorder in particular mean if, instead of thinking of the body as a material structure built up of so many organs, one were to abolish in imagination the gross matter, to think it clean away, and to conceive its organs as so many and divers complexes of very fine and active vibrations bound within the forms or shapes of the different organs and united by the most complete harmony of internuncial vibrations; the whole organism being the formal unison of these multitudinous and various complexes of energies. Thinking in that way, we may easily comprehend how extremely delicate and intimate are the sympathies of these organic energies and how a note of discord must propagate itself in waves that spread widely in all directions, and especially in certain directions, until its force is spent: may comprehend the instant jarring or sympathetic effect of a look, a tone, a gesture, a gait, an attitude, or some more subtle influence which is felt instinctively throughout the whole being, but passes apprehension and explanation. There must be some good reason why one person is inclined instantly to hate another whom he has never seen in his life before, because of a look, or a tone, or a gesture, and to hate him more than he would hate a known murderer. What is fine form but visible harmony? what is harmony but invisible form? To the poet's soul the stars discourse music and all nature reveals forms of harmony.

Organisms, like instruments of music, differ greatly in quality of tone, and no two of them have exactly the same tone. Intellects differ in degree, not in quality; an intellectual machinery, so to speak, when properly constructed and worked, must give out certain products, just as the calculating machine does. But people differ greatly in quality of feeling and will, which spring from the depths and express the essential character of the organisation. Thought is, like action, secondary to feeling, which goes before it in the order of development and, underlying it, gives it its motive power; ideas are only clear or obscure, definite or vague, not able to supply any force, requiring to be infused with energy from the affective life; a means through which the forces of desire obtain their fulfilments in suitable actions. Without appetence or inappetence all the ideas in the world might pass coldly through the intellect and it not experience the least motive of affection or repugnance to one more than another. What would the most clear and distinct idea of embracing a beautiful woman avail without the fit feeling or desire? Speaking physiologically, it is the latent nervous motion which expresses itself in feeling that is translated into the larger visible motions of action.

The happiness of the individual and of others depends much more on his tone of feeling than on his intellect. A very little thing will move a man in his inmost, reaching the very structure of his being, when it is in tune or out of tune with its fundamental note. What a ridiculous unreason it is for any one to be more distressed by a little waste or the loss of a few shillings which he will never miss, than by the loss of a thousand pounds which might be a serious hurt to him, or to get wet and run the risk of catching his death of cold rather than be at the expense of a small cab-fare! But the truth is that the little loss or expense occasions the more painful jar to his nature because it goes counter to the principle of its manufacture; it is the hurt spirit of his prudent or penurious forefathers crying out in him. Reason may prove to him by conclusive demonstration that he is vexing himself foolishly, but reason speaks like a fool, or at any rate discourses in vain, when it argues against feeling; to convince, it must have feeling agree with it, when it may speak folly and be thought wise.

No true interchange of thought can take place between two persons of equal understanding who are on different planes of feeling, nor will discussion between them then do more probably than inflame feeling. The wise man of the world who would convince an opponent, how does he proceed? By admitting his opponent's view of the side or aspect of the question in which it is possible to agree with him,—and the foolishest opinion has commonly some partial facet of sense,—he captures self-love and thus intones feeling in his favour, going on afterwards to lure him by gentle insinuation into uttering as his own the opinions which he subtly suggests. When two persons get into a fanatical sympathy of feeling, there is no limit to a common credulity; they are capable of believing together that they have seen the sun shine at midnight in London or Paris—all the more positively if they feel themselves to be thereby placed on a pedestal of moral superiority over the rest of the world which denies it.

The fundamental tones of a person's feeling are determined by his birth and breeding—that is to say, primarily by the mode of manufacture of the organism through foregoing generations, and secondarily by the moulding effects of education and environment: the former necessary to the grounding of fine feeling in the nature, which fails not then to come out always on occasions of stress and strain in life; the latter serving to produce a more superficial culture, which is prone, when the former is lacking, to give way to the ingrained coarseness of feeling on such occasions. The changing tones of present feeling are mainly effects of concord or discord of the complex organic harmonies. When a disagreeable impression or a jarring thought or an organic derangement strikes a note of discord, the first and mildest effect is a disturbance of the mental tone, a *dysthumia*, on which follow, summoned to its sessions, the sympathetic sad thoughts, the *dysnoia*. The order of events, so started, might be broadly and briefly represented thus: good or bad digestion, *eupepsia* or *dyspepsia*, entails good or bad mood of mind, *euthumia* or *dysthumia*; good or bad mood of mind, in further sequence, entails brisk and easy or heavy and gloomy thought, *eunoia* or *dysnoia*. May it not be that not digestion only, but every organic process of the body, has its special *euthumia* and *dysthumia* and in further sequel its conformable cast of glad or sad thought? Forms of feeling are perhaps determined by the several fashions of the internal organs, as forms of thought are by the several fashions of the special senses.

Obviously feeling lies much nearer the organic life in its nature and workings than thought; inhabits the whole body, so to speak, whilst thought is limited to the brain. Proofs of this organic kinship are evident not only in the disturbance of the emotional tone by organic derangement, which may itself be such as not to be otherwise appreciable, but also in the usual bodily accompaniments of emotion; for emotion hardly ever occurs without some sensible physical change and is loudly signalised by veritable bodily commotions when it reaches the pitch of passion. To suffer emotion or passion is to feel "moved" and moved in one's inmost. Emotion is essentially, as old language termed it, commotion: witness the ·effects on muscles, as seen in laughing, shrieking, gesticulating, trembling; on secretion, as seen in weeping, sweating, dryness of mouth, disordered stomach and liver and the like; on nutrition, as manifest in various bodily wastings and disorders, especially in the overlooked beginnings of disease; on the vasomotor system, as shown by blushing and pallor and lividity. Rooted in the unity of the organic life, it is feeling, not thought, which constitutes the real basic unity of the "ego," all whose passions and emotions are determined in character according as their exciting causes, being pleasant, help or, being painful, hinder its self-expansion. To pursue what is pleasant and profitable and to eschew what is painful and hurtful is the fundamental note of the organic life, as of all life, and the nervous mechanisms of thought and action are the means and instruments subserving these fundamental functions; thoughts the fit means or channels, fashioned through the ages, by which the forces of desire obtain their fulfilments, coarse or refined, in fit bodily actions.

The cerebral hemispheres virtually represent an aggregate of the complex elaborations and refinements which the fundamental reflex acts of self-preservation and self-propagation have undergone in the process of development from the animal to the human basis; and the unity of their functions which, looking merely to their structural separateness, might apparently be dual, rests on the unity of feeling inspired by the basic unity of the organic life. Therefore it is that trifling derangements of the viscera disturb the mental mood, disquieting the "ego," that severe disorders or injuries of them, alarming it, cause instantly an extremity of apprehension and moral collapse which seem out of all proportion to the present hurt and danger, and that the decline of their energies, weakening it, is followed by a loss of the relish and love of life and sometimes by a deep melancholic dejection. It is not for the most part that brains wear out in old age, many times they would go on longer if they were properly fed with energy from below, but the organic functions decay and fail; it is their failure which causes desire to wane and the grasshopper to be a burden; they are the source of life's energy and relish, and in their integrity and vigour lies the secret of a fresh and active old age. To live for ever, having got rid of the flesh with its appetites and lusts, would be to have a vapid and joyless immortality, the one long bootless desire of which would be an impossible suicide.

Distemper of feeling being the earliest exponent of a derangement of nerve-element, it is in accordance therewith that positive insanity begins generally with disorder of feeling. Such disorder is in fact the foundation of it, its mainstay while it lasts, and its sequel sometimes after intellectual disorder has disappeared. Seldom does it break out without a preceding period of uneasy mental depression, and in a large class of cases depression is the predominant note throughout. But the disorder of feeling in the various insanities may range from nethermost depths of woe to heights of ecstatic joy: on the sad side, all the strange and disquieting sensations, the overwhelming feelings of bewildering distress, the nameless horrors, shapeless fears, raptures of anguish, distracting impulses which are felt in different cases of melancholia, and some of which in times past were ascribed to possession by evil spirits; on the joyful side, ecstasies and raptures of bliss which, being ineffable, once were, and still sometimes are, accounted supernatural transports, and have played their distinguished parts in the religious history of mankind. In the varieties of disordered feeling there is a large domain of yet unsurveyed experience deserving and likely some day to repay exact observation and classification.

The way is to take too little account of the part which feeling plays in determining thought. When any one has sad or glad thoughts it seems as if he were sad or glad because of his thoughts, whereas his thoughts are sad or glad chiefly because of his underlying feelings. What profits it a man to *know* that he is himself when he *feels* that he is not himself? What concern is to him to *know* that he will die, until, age having spent his energies, he *believes* that he will die? The misery of the melancholic who is tormented with revolting thoughts and is full of remorse in consequence is not really because of their independent nature and sway, as he imagines; he knows their odious character and loathes them—would give anything to be rid of them; he might, indeed, have them or the like of them come into his mind casually, unfelt and unapproved, and, being able soon to chase them away, be little troubled by them.[1] But he has strange and horrible feelings which inspire and keep up the detestable thoughts and imaginings; and those he cannot anyhow dismiss. Therefore it is that the ideas and images are the loathed compulsions and repulsions which they are. So likewise is it when, being stirred by morbid feeling, he makes, against his will, the veriest trifles matters of meditative anguish and of tormenting wills and nills, notwithstanding that all the while he knows well that he is worrying himself about something which it is utter folly to heed. The worst misery in the world, so insupportable as to compel suicide sometimes, is a feeling of wretchedness which cannot be formulated, vague, vast and overwhelming, shapeless and nameless. He who, being in good health, would gain a notion, faint perhaps at the best, of what such feelings are, let him call back to mind, and so far as he can to feeling, the strange, distracting and indefinable horror, with its quaking sense of an appalling disintegration of self, which he has ever had in his worst night's worst dream; for dreams sometimes fashion terrors of feeling which no ordinary working experience can parallel. He might think also of the vague, sad feeling which, after a feverish night of bad dreams, sometimes lingers in the mind through the following day, shaking the foundations of self and tinging with gloom every experience and prospect. Not that the dreams caused the abiding feeling; they were the outcome of its silent inspiration during sleep, and the subsequent dejection of the day doubtless betrayed the partial persistence of the physical conditions of the sad feeling.

[1] Evil into the mind of God or man
May come and go, so unapproved, and leave
No spot or blame behind.
Paradise Lost, Bk. V. l. 117.

Of the opposite state of elevation of feeling and accompanying exaltation of thought no better physiological example could be adduced than that furnished by the fresh and jubilant feeling, the keen joy and relish of being, the enthusiasm of thought and energy incident to the entrance of the reproductive function into the mental life. As the chief pleasures of human life, sensual, emotional, and ideal, spring from it, men have naturally been much occupied, and still are much occupied, in singing and saying and otherwise uttering and expressing the same old story of its joys in endless variations, many times without suspecting what it is that they are expressing or labouring to express. Away with dull melancholy, sour cynicism, selfish forethought, crabbed pessimism, while its currents are at their best thrill of energy in the brain; life is earnest, desire boundless, enthusiasm glorious, love divine, language inadequate to express the ineffable rapture of being. All the more is this so, seeing that the entrance of sex into mind is something more than the mere awakening of the special organs to active functions and their special workings on it; it is the entrance of the individual into the productive life of nature and of it into him, a partial transformation of him out of individuality into oneness with nature, and therein a sort of temporary blending of the finite with the infinite. Individuality is a prison out of which the ecstasies of love and religion transport temporarily, restoring for the moment the great unity of nature.[1]

How different does life look to him in whom the productive passion has expired prematurely! Stale, flat and unprofitable then seem the uses of the world. There is no more powerful cause of mental depression, no more direct

[1] Some creatures are notably so rapt in the ecstasy of the sexual orgasm that they may be mutilated without showing any sense of the injury done to them. Flowers and the songs of birds are the tokens of the reproductive transport of nature ; flowers being the dress of love and the songs of birds love-songs. Men find these very beautiful in themselves and think of them as specially designed to gratify their senses. But is it not that they are beautiful, by secret sympathy of being, because they are expressions of the generative energy of nature in which men share ? And most felt or beautiful in spring when the sympathy of a common thrill is active ?

cause of suicide sometimes, than the loss of productive vigour while other bodily organs feel no loss of vigour. By the abstraction of its energy from the forces of the organic life in the brain their level is so far lowered; so much vital inspiration has, by the extinction of its source, been subtracted from the stream of organic energy supplied to the brain, whose functions are duller and lack zest in consequence. Although a similar disillusionment is brought about by its natural decline with the decline of life, yet as the decline is then gradual and goes along with the general failure of bodily functions it is less acute and is more soberly felt.

Why do the old man and the young man view life so differently? Not because of differences of intellect, since their respective intellects may be instruments of equal power which ought therefore to produce equal products; nor altogether because of the experience which age has had, since age in full animal vigour preserves its interest and faith in life, and there is notoriously no fool more buoyant with illusion than the old man who, enamoured of a young woman, fondly imagines the spirit of youth renewed in him. The differences of feeling make the different worlds. The one, sharer in the evolutional joy and energy of nature and fired by its glow, is thrilled by its prophetic promise of things to come—has desire, hope, enthusiasm and imagination; the other, now without part in it, is used and useless, disillusioned, sad. The truth is that nature, being interested in the individual mainly or only as an instrument of its development by the propagation of his species, lures him to it by his lust and fools him in it by his fancy, but is not concerned afterwards, when he has served his end, to make life happy and glorious to him or even so much as always pleasantly endurable. Yet he is not then given over to absolute despair, since the evolutional instinct inspires him with the hope and comforts him with the belief of everlasting felicity in a life after death. In life and in death it is the great creator of ideals.

That different molecular states of nerve-element, easily propagated from molecule to molecule in structure of the same *kind*, are the basis of sad and glad feelings is beyond doubt, but what they are we know not in the least; for they belong to a domain into which our senses, with all their aids, cannot yet penetrate. One may surmise that melancholy represents a sort of contraction or chill, joy an expansion or glow, of molecular motion; in which case such terms as contraction and dilatation of spirits, used of old to denote sorrowful and joyful moods respectively, had an unsuspected basis of physical truth, as most terms founded in popular experience have. In this connection it may be useful to reflect on the effects which such definite physical causes as cold and heat have on mental and nervous function. Cold notably benumbs sensibility, lowers the rate of conduction by nerve, dulls feeling, slackens movement, deadens thought; it congeals the nerve-molecules, as it were, thereby so obstructing and retarding their motions as, when extreme, to reduce the individual to a state of mindless torpor. We may safely assume, without calling in the aid of experimental psychology to measure the exact degrees of retardation and diminution of reaction-power in a person who is gradually being frozen to death, that it would not be easy to thread a needle, or beget a child, or discover the differential calculus on the top of a polar iceberg. The effect of heat, on the other hand, when not carried beyond physiological limits, is to sharpen sensibility, to quicken conduction by nerve, to animate thought; it thaws the obstruction of the molecules, so to speak, releasing and quickening their motions. Therefore it is that, when carried to excess, it upsets their stability and gives rise to the irregular and explosive discharges of delirium. With nervous molecules, as with planetary masses, an equilibrium between attraction and repulsion is necessary to normal function—the just maintenance of a certain mean—beyond which, on the one hand, their motions are hindered and contracted, and beyond which, on the other hand, they become irregular and explosive.[1]

---

[1] The following experiment, accidentally made, is instructive :—Four boys, of ages varying from six to ten years, who, after being exposed for some time

Of the inflaming effect of heat we have an example in fever where a transient excitement is, soon followed by delirium, while the opposite effect of cold to brace up unstable molecules and nerve-centres is exemplified by the drunken man who pulls himself together by dashing cold water on his head. Instructive again in this relation are the marked temporary revivals and the rare recoveries of intelligence which take place in some cases of chronic mania or of torpid dementia under the influence of acute fever, when nothing seemed less likely. The effect of acute fever on a sane mind being delirium, its equivalent effect on the sluggish function of an insane mind may well be such a quickening of molecular energies as reanimates the torpid intellect, a kindling of activity which is an ignition of thought. Such recovery is usually temporary only, albeit now and then it chance to be lasting, for the inflamed energies abate with the abatement of the fever and the stagnant stupor of mind returns.

Joy and grief evidently lie very near one another in the region of molecular physics; a very little difference of motion makes the difference between the one and the other. No wonder then that melancholy and mania alternate with each other in the same case or are so mixed that it is hard to say which name ought to be used; or that, the innate tone of the mind-structure being a determining factor, the same sort of moral or physical cause so acts on two different persons as to produce mania in the one and melancholia in the other. Consider the action of morphia, a drug which in small quantities causes depression of the spinal cord in the frog, retarding conduction and lowering reflex action, but in larger quantities excites

on a sledge to a cold of from 16° to 20° below zero, were brought into a room heated by a stove to a high temperature, went completely deranged, exhibiting great excitement, delirium, and hallucinations; all which disappeared entirely after a long sleep, leaving behind no recollection of the mental disorder (*Centralblatt für Nervenheilkunde*, No. 6, 1881). In these cases there was probably vascular contraction followed by vascular dilatation; still the vascular change by itself would not have produced the mental effects, although it might contribute to the nervous commotion which did, while the molecular changes might have produced them without the vascular changes.

its activity, producing convulsive discharges of energy; events in the function of the spinal cord not unlike, if not strictly parallel to, those which show themselves in the cerebral cortex as melancholy and sequent mania. Nay, this happens exceptionally, that a dose of morphia which in the great majority of persons would certainly cause narcotism, fails entirely to have that effect, because of some constitutional peculiarity, but gives rise instead to a very active delirium which has been mistaken for mania, or to convulsions which have been mistaken for the convulsions of strychnia. To describe mania and melancholia as two distinct diseases is hardly more scientific than it would be to describe the same man as two distinct persons, according as he was running or walking, laughing or crying.

The multiform phenomena of hysteria are well suited to illustrate the various degrees, sorts and anomalous mixtures of disordered nervous functions—including thought, feeling and will—and to attest their dependence on passing molecular derangements. In them the unity of the ego, the spiritual freedom of the will, and the abstract glory of the moral sense are confronted and affronted by multitudinous examples of the disintegration of the ego, the servitude of will, and the degradation of moral sense: degenerative effects which, extreme while they last, still often go just as quickly as they come. So acute sometimes is the sensibility of the body or of a part or patch of it in hysteria that the least touch causes agony; so deficient at other times that a pin thrust into the flesh elicits no sign of pain. Of such insensibility it used to be thought, when it had been pronounced hysterical, that no more need be said; as if it then were only seeming and it was a pretty trick of simulation to be a pincushion and evince as little feeling when pricked. But the excess of feeling and the absence of feeling are both real and have their real causes in passing molecular conditions of the nerve-element which dislocate function. Equivalent derangements in the highest cerebral tracts of thought and feeling, irregular in place and character, suffice to produce the moral insensibilities and perversities, and all the numerous vagaries and caprices of thought, feeling and will which characterize hysteria; just as similar derangements are at the bottom of the more plainly physical disorders—stammering, spasms of the glottis, facial paralysis, trismus, aphemia, amaurosis, epileptiform convulsions, pyrexia, local atrophies, and other sensory, motor and trophic disorders—that are met with in different cases of hysteria, and are now and then cured offhand by something which, inspiring a fit animation and co-ordination of the cerebral centres, quells the riot and restores order.

In severe organic disease of the brain such as abscess or tumour of it, there is sometimes in the parts outside the area of directly destructive action a physical condition of things which expresses itself in symptoms so like those of hysteria that they cannot be distinguished from it; an acquired molecular instability and weakness presumably similar in nature to that which is constitutional in hysteria. The consequence is that the patient is hysterical *plus* his organic disease, and that if the local damage be so situate as not to betray its presence by its own direct symptoms the demoralisations of character which he exhibits may be thought hysterical only. What can be more hysterical in feature than the complaining misery, the anomalous sensations of distress, the vague apprehensions, the extreme enervation of will which sometimes precede actual softening of the brain? It cannot be too distinctly borne in mind, in relation to all cerebral disease, that the direct physical effect of debilitated nerve-energies and loosened mental organisation is demoralisation of will, showing itself in self-indulgence, indolence, loss of self-control, moaning self-pity, sorrowful sighings, abject weakness of will, exaggeration and even simulation of symptoms of suffering; that the failure of will and its deepening degrees means an increasing dissolution passing into disruption of the federal union of nerve-centres, whereby the present thought or feeling, losing its proper inhibitions, has unbridled sway and way; that, in fine, to the full and free exercise of sound and strong will the substratum of a normal process of molecular energy and of a compact federation of nerve-centres are indispensably necessary.

Having traced feeling into the organic life and thence into the molecular derangements which are at the bottom of its various disturbances, ranging from states that are almost subconscious to the most appalling anguish, I go on now to inquire how the internal states of disorder express themselves outwardly. However they be caused, whether by bad blood, or by organic derangements, or by impressions from without, the perturbations must discharge themselves somehow. Their principal lines of discharge, determined by the reflex mechanism of the nervous system, are (1) trophic, (2) motor, (3) ideational—that is, in nutrition and secretion, in movement, and in thought.

4.—*Modes of Disordered Nervous Discharge.*

(1.) *Trophic.*—When reflex action is spoken of, it is usually understood of the transference of activity from a sensory to a motor nerve; the occurrence of disordered sensation or disease in one part of the body in consequence of disordered sensation or disease in another part of the body being ascribed to sympathy. But as sympathy only means fellow-suffering, by itself explaining nothing, we must push inquiry down to its mechanism, which is reflex nervous structure, and suppose that every such mechanism may serve as the means or channel of a particular sympathy. Except by reflexion from one to another sensory nerve, how can we explain such phenomena as the pain in a knee which bespeaks disease of the hip-joint, the facial neuralgia which is caused by toothache, the toothache which is felt in a neighbouring or opposite tooth to the diseased one? What again is to hinder the reflexion from being, as it apparently sometimes is, from a motor to a sensory nerve, or from a sensory nerve to a nerve concerned in the processes of nutrition and secretion? Wherever the channel is, there presumably may the morbid current run. In the varied phenomena of disease, and especially of disease of the brain, there are doubtless numerous instances of intricate pathological sympathies or morbid reflexes which have not yet been accurately observed and duly distinguished.

When the outgoing current of nervous disorder effects nutrition, it may do so in two ways—either by acting directly on the ultimate elements of the tissue, or indirectly through vasomotor contractions and dilatations.[1] Of the latter action such phenomena as the pallor of fear, the blush of shame, the red suffusion of rage, the livid green of envy, are familiar evidence; evidence which might justify the expectation of similar vasomotor effects from disturbed nerve-currents, and of consequent disorders of nutrition and function, in the internal organs of the body. May not these blush or turn pale, weep or be tearless, so to speak, from emotion? It is impossible to separate the vascular effects from the direct action on the element of structure, and to say how much is due to the one and how much to the other when desire quickens a secretion, or passion poisons it, or grief slackens it, or fear suspends it; but we may feel pretty sure, whatever the exact operation be, that the processes of nutrition and function which have no visible secretory outcome, albeit some of them have their internal secretions, are affected in a similar way. The sorrow which has no vent in tears may make other organs weep.

Contrast the very different looks of him who, favoured in love, is in the presence of her whom he adores, and of him who is the victim of a disdained suit: in the former,

---

[1] The vasomotor nerves are, as it were, the mechanical means of regulating the supply of blood according to the demands of function: little function there is little blood, much function much blood, disordered function disordered blood-supply. If a function is stimulated to activity from the central nervous system, whether consciously or not, the special vasomotor apparatus responds in reflex fashion to the activity. But the sympathetic nerves act also directly on the elements of tissues, as Claud Bernard showed.

bright eyes, animated features, alert movements, quickened pulse, elated energies; in the latter, dull eyes, pale and heavy features, languid movements, low pulse, deep sighs, general apathy of mind and body. The symptoms caused morally in the one are just the symptoms which a strong heart and high vascular tension would cause physically; in the other they are those of a weak heart and low vascular tension. If we suppose these opposite states—of nutrition inspired by joy and hope, and of nutrition infected by grief and despair—to continue for a long time, it is easy to understand how there shall be in the one buoyant health and vigour, with strong resistance to the omnipresent and ever-active causes of disease, and in the other languor and decline of health, with little power to withstand their insidious attacks. People do not die of actually broken hearts in the real world as they do in novels, any more than they think and feel in the real world as they do in novels, and grief is but a slow murderer at the best; nevertheless long-standing grief, and especially the grief that does not weep, may lay the foundations of chronic disease and powerfully second its progress, while the depression of a great sorrow, paralysing the vital energies temporarily, might open a breach and give an easy victory to the noxious agents of acute disease. The deadliest message which the brain can send to a diseased organ, is it not a message of despair?

That bodily processes are affected by attention to them is a familiar experience. But to ascribe the effect to attention and to accept that as an explanation is to traffic with words, not to deal with things. Attention is no more than a general term; there is no abstract faculty of attention which exists apart from each particular act of attention and can apply itself or be applied here or there, as may be required. There are as many attentions as there are particular acts of attention, and there are as many particular losses of attention as there are attentions. Instead of thinking of the mental process only, it is necessary to think of the underlying physical process, of the concrete particular implied by the general term. That is the special tension or latent stimulation of a particular nerve-tract, its definite tending to a particular end, the attention being the necessary accompaniment and mental expression of it. All such concrete acts have something in common, being of the same kind, just as all acts of walking have, but they are many and various in degree and quality and no more due to an abstract power of attention than the manifold acts of walking are due to an abstract power of walking. To train a person to give attention to a thing is to train or fashion the particular attention by exercise, when he has the proper nervous substratum of it, not to teach him to apply an abstract something which exists abstract in the background.

The tension of a particular nerve tract established, the current of response along it which a proper idea or object is fitted to excite is more readily excited, flows more quickly, is not easily distracted. That is why attention to a pain increases it, as attention to something else, when a pain exists, lessens or suspends it; and it is why the hypochondriac becomes a bundle of pains when, having given up pursuits which occupied his attentions and his energies, his attentions are attracted to and fixed on his sensations and his energies spent in stirring and exasperating them. It is no pleasure to him to be absorbed in them, and he would be infinitely glad to ignore them, but the state of their nervous substrata enforces and makes attention; and when that molecular state is altered for the better, whether slowly by the good effect of some interesting pursuit, or quickly by a sudden moral commotion, or perchance by the unknown working of some acute disease, his enthralled attention is gradually, it may be instantly, emancipated. Again, consider how, when there is an exceedingly sensitive and irritable state of the nervous system, the least sound jars and the least jar is positive torture followed instantly by motor starts that are almost convulsive; so keenly sensitive is the sufferer and so quick to react that he seems to be straining and expecting to hear the sound, almost to anticipate it before it is actually made. Doubtless subconscious or nascent motions are the physical basis of the quasi-expectant attention; not otherwise than as in such normal physiological acts of attention as listening intently, straining to see, expecting to touch, and the like, by which the particular sensibility is increased, there is a degree of subactivity of the several nerve-tracts which, when it reaches a higher pitch, is actual seeing, hearing, feeling—the hallucination thereof if there be not the fit outward impression, the actual perception if there be. How could a person in the hypnotic state feel a sharp pain at the spot where he is told authoritatively that he has it, or cease to feel a pain when he is told that he no longer feels it, if the attention were not bound rigidly to the physical state? To be told that a woman is hysterical and that, being hysterical 'she is devoid of will, without power of attention, and wrong in her moral feeling, is not to learn much—if we stay there; what is required to carry inquiry from words to things is a knowledge of the intimate nature and exact seat of the nervous disorder of which the lost will, impaired attention and perverted moral feeling are the effects and exponents. The organic mechanism being the unity it is, might not the wonder be if such disorder producing such mental effects were not reflected in the processes of nutrition?

(2.) *Motor.* — That a disordered nervous state will discharge itself in disordered movements is a familiar fact on which it would be superfluous to expatiate. What is wanted now is a closer examination and more exact discrimination of those motor outcomes, which vary in character from spasms and convulsions at the bottom to the purest voluntary movements at the top of the scale. The classification of movements into voluntary and involuntary is crude and artificial; an arbitrary sorting of different things into two separate compartments and an assumption thenceforth that every deviation, however great, must always belong to one or the other. Meanwhile, between them occur manifold deviations which belong to neither but exemplify every sort and degree of mixture of voluntaryism and involuntaryism.

Like attention, will is not an abstract unity, constant and definite, which is only lamed in its manifestations by the imperfect means of its performance. There is no will apart from each particular act of will, and there are as many wills as there are such particular acts; therefore all degrees and kinds of disintegrate will are met with in practice. Every purposive act has its own will, and every such will requires the integrity of the special nervous substratum subserving its particular function; when that mechanism is impaired in any part of its sensori-motor tract the integrity of the volition in action is proportionately impaired. Moreover, the particular will-faculty of the particular purposive act must be built up gradually by culture and practice; it may be a late acquisition which is unstable and easily lost, or it may be so grounded in the nature that it is merged and disappears in automatism. Therefore it is that, as pathological observation demonstrates, the particular wills of particular acts may be impaired or abolished while the several wills of other acts are unimpaired, or that the single wills of single acts may survive amidst the general wreckage, like columns, broken or entire, of a ruined temple which still stand upright in its ruins; so giving rise to the manifold and divers disintegrations of will which, despite the postulate of its metaphysical unity, are met with in the concrete.

Because to do definitely implies an intuition of the aim or end of the act and power over the fit means to do it—both no less indispensable notwithstanding that, though consciously acquired, they are eventually implicit and unconscious—therefore every such act is liable to impairment in respect of these two functions. The aim may be there while the means of fulfilment fail, the person thinking the act but being unable to do it, or the means may be unimpaired while the aim fails, the person being unable to think the act. It is just as it is in the sensory domain when a person sees an object plainly but, being mentally blind, is unable to recognise its meaning, or sees it with his mind's eye, but, being blind of his eyes, is unable to see it visually. The plainest exemplification of the twofold motor failure is furnished by the aphasic disorders of speech, the analysis being made easier in that case because there is the conception of the word or name to mark the end and its pronunciation to mark the means; but the principle is true of other purposive acts which have not their several signs, like words, to mark their special aims or ends.

Consider the simple illustration of a person set to write whose fingers are benumbed by cold or commencing nervous disease. His hand-writing is altered and impaired; so much so that it resembles generally the shaky hand-writing of an old man, and in particular perhaps that of his own father or grandfather when he was an old man. The specialisations of sensibility and movements necessary to the special and easy flow of the individual letters and their junctions are enfeebled or lost and he is reduced to dependence on the more fixed and coarse structural lines of the family stock, those which die last in decay; in default of the finest sensori-motor reflexes uses a coarser type. Accordingly he does the act slowly, by efforts and jerks, instead of easily, smoothly, and almost unconsciously; he has to exert more wills to execute its details and does it ill as a whole. Precisely the same kind of laming effect is caused by an excess of self-consciousness, or, speaking more correctly, by the nervous commotion which excessive self-consciousness betokens. A person who writes his name easily and freely when he is not thinking about it may, if asked to do it in another's presence, or if he does it consciously in answer to a request for his autograph, write it in a constrained, less regular, and somewhat jerky fashion; for each stroke then is apt to be dwelt on and to require a degree of voluntary accentuation in order to get itself begun and done, while the transitions from stroke to stroke are stiff and laboured, not free and flowing. It may happen that the nervous agitation and impotence are so great that he cannot write his name at all. So it is with every complex act of bodily skill—mounting a restive horse, riding it easily, jumping a stiff fence on horseback, playing a difficult ball at cricket, making a clever stroke at billiards, performing a brilliant acrobatic feat. In all such cases the free and uniform flow of the currents along the special tracts which are the exact and efficient means of the special performances is impeded; they are interrupted and irregular, either being obstructed by the disturbing impact of currents from other tracts that are in needless action, or perhaps being distracted by diversion on to other tracts; for that is probably what the intervention of consciousness as self-consciousness means physically. In the "nervous" act of a person in a "nervous" state, consciousness is an intruder, superfluous and mischievous, unable to suppress itself wisely; there is a fussy concern about the doing instead of a quiet unconcern in doing. The individual takes a great deal more pains and seems to exert a great deal more will to do the act because the whole will of it has gone to pieces, and the fractions of decomposed will are represented in the conscious labour and pains. Too self-conscious, he is nervous; nervous, he is too self-conscious: the two states alike the effects of the same physical conditions. The one whole compound will of the perfect act being disintegrated, the result is a condition of things, in the regressive order, very like that which prevailed in the progressive order when, learning to perform the act, he had to compound his several wills into the unison of one complex will.

The uncertain, jerky and spasmodic movements of stammering belong to a class of movements that are intermediate between voluntary and purely spasmodic; they are involuntary in quality while maintaining the voluntary form in whole or in parts; although exaggerated in manifestation, still retain so much form as removes them from the category of quasi-convulsive *movements* to quasi-convulsive *acts*. It is easy to note, in the case of a bad stammerer, how the disorder spreads from the mouth, where the obstruction begins, to the facial muscles and thence perhaps widely along channels of least resistance until the whole body is convulsively agitated. Behold a person then who seems to be vainly using all his muscular resources in order to bring out a little word! But in truth he only makes matters worse and worse with every increment of self-consciousness; his violent agitations, self-conscious and motor, represent a broken-up will, the true being and function of which, if whole and sound, would be their suppression into itself.

As will undergoes an increasing complexity of composition with every rise in dignity and the superior will is compounded of many inferior wills, so its decompositions in different cases witness to all degrees and sorts of fragmentary will-functions. Of these broken-up wills the actions of insane persons afford abundant illustrations, as will be exemplified later. For the present, one example will suffice by way of exposition of the steps of a deepening decomposition of will. In ordinary adolescent insanity we observe these symptoms progressively—first, pert, self-willed, capricious and contrary behaviour, inconsistent with natural respect and consideration for parents and others, marking the loss and the lost check of the highest social reflexes; next, turbulent conduct of a maniacal sort, wanton and wilful-looking, such as jumpings, shoutings, singings, yellings, grimacings, and acts of mischievous violence, marking further loss of inhibitions and further displays of wills gone convulsive; then, as the disorder deepens, the aimless iteration of the same half-sentence or sentence or of the question which may chance to have been put, or the automatic repetition or stubborn meaningless continuation of some act such as pushing, grabbing, striking, or resisting, having voluntary form without voluntary quality; last, quasi-cataleptic states in which, the patient standing or lying still or stiff, the limbs obstinately resist attempts made to bend them or only yield slowly to such attempts. These degrees of degeneration have all a singularly wilful look; they are will disintegrated into so many wilfulnesses; nowise entirely involuntary and actually spasmodic. It might help to a better apprehension of the nature of them and their like to compare certain physiological acts—notably, the movements of sexual congress which, begun voluntarily and practised consciously at first, are stimulated sensorily by degrees into involuntary and quasi-convulsive action, the more convulsive the more intense the final orgasm. Some children may be tickled through every grade of movement from simple laughter into convulsions.

Many more intermediates between will and convulsion, varying in the degrees of their voluntary and involuntary components, are exemplified by the disordered acts and movements of hysteria, chorea and epilepsy. The epileptic convulsions caused in young and susceptible women by the infection of example, the dancing epidemics of the Middle Ages, the quasi-convulsive antics of the shakers, the jumpers, and other religious corybants, are further instances in point; as also are the self-induced trances of the hysterical ecstatic, and the artificial disintegrations of will produced in so-called mesmeric or hypnotic experiments. When we reflect how many such morbid nervous phenomena have been, and some such still are, attributed to supernatural spiritual influx, as epilepsy and madness once were, and how much of the world's inspiration has proceeded from morbid nervous function, the question might arise whether illusion and madness are not the real inspiring forces of human progress, and whether, if it ever come to pass in human nature that reason predominates over the more animal force which imparts feeling and creates illusion, life will have motive to go on living.

Some nervous individuals, especially women, among the inhabitants of the *Eastern Archipelago* and other parts of the world, are liable to strange seizures that are of a very instructive character in relation to disorders of will. On being startled or excited suddenly, the person becomes what is called *lata*, losing all control of will and calling out, so long as the fit lasts, the name or imitating the action of that which, seen or heard, produced the startling impression. According to the degree of alarm the symptoms may last for a few minutes only or for the greater part of a day. For example, a young woman, having one day unexpectedly encountered a large lizard, was seized with a paroxysm; dropping down on hands and knees to imitate the reptile, she followed it through mud and mire until stopped by a tree in which it took refuge. Another woman who had been startled by treading on a venomous snake became so *lata* or fascinated that she vibrated her finger in front of its head, in imitation of its vibrating tongue, until the irritated creature struck her: she died within an hour.[1] In these cases there is not an entire loss of consciousness nor yet a pure automatism, for how could the organism do automatically special purposive work which it had never

[1] A *Naturalist's Wanderings in the Eastern Archipelago*, by H. O. Forbes. One may observe exactly the same kind of thing sometimes in a bird frightened and fascinated by a cat.

Dr. J. D. Thornton, of the United States Marine Hospital Service, gives some details, in the *New York Medical Record*, of the class of French-Canadians among whom the peculiar hysterical affection called "miryachit," or "lata," is prevalent. They are known as "jumpers," and are found especially among the lumber-men—French-Canadians, who go over into Maine and the other lumbering districts. Dr. Thornton says: "One or two instances will be sufficient. Recently one of them, a French-Canadian of small stature, came out from an adjacent camp to the post-office. Just as he was about to ask the postmaster for his mail, he being a total stranger to the official, a man of sixty-five years of age, some one, knowing the fellow to be a 'jumper,' mischievously cried out, 'Grab him by the throat!' The fellow sprung like a cat, and grasped the old man by the throat, and held on until removed, the irate postmaster pouring forth torrents of invectives on the poor fellow, who really was perfectly guiltless. Another unfortunate wood-chopper had just come into camp from two days' work, and was standing near the large camp-heater, in which was a very hot fire, when some one cried, 'Grab the furnace!' No sooner were the words said, than the poor fellow obeyed the order, and, as a result, left a scorched pattern of each hand on the nearly red-hot pipe, thus rendering him unfit for his work in the woods for some weeks. I could, were it not for taking up valuable space, enumerate instance after instance fully as peculiar as the above. In brief, it may be stated that at any time and under any circumstances, with the slightest provocation, and almost instantaneously on being spoken to, one of these fellows will obey any command, imitate any action, without regard to its nature, trivial or serious. He will leap on to a table, or over a stove, or into a river or pond; throw any article or weapon he may have in hand in any direction indicated; will repeat any sentence or exclamation. So serious a matter is this, that many of the lumber-men absolutely refuse to admit a man known as a 'jumper' into their camps."

done in its life before ? Alarmed and drawn against their
will to the object, the fascinated beings cannot form the
will to escape; they are dominated by the particular will
to act in the ridiculous way described, for other mental
functions are suspended. Being easily made to imitate, such
persons are apt to be teased by their companions who play
tricks on them for sport, by throwing them into this
abnormal state, and thus, like the hypnotic performer,
further damnify a native weakness of nervous organisation
by forming and keeping up a habit of mental dislocation.

Psychological language does not lend itself to the
appreciation and description of such examples, since it
obliges us either to describe a person as acting by will
against his will, or to call involuntary what is plainly
more than half-willed—in any case to ignore the essential
continuity of nature's process. The whole difficulty of
course springs from the metaphysical conception of will as
an entity which either is or is not and, always keeping
its unity, is incapable of disintegrations and fragmentary
functions. The real truth all the while is that will
is the expression, in terms of mind, of the unity of
action for definite ends of the various confederate nervous
centres of the cerebral cortex—of particular groups of them
for particular wills and of the unity of the whole for the
highest will-expression—and that the different disintegrations of their functions are so many forms of disintegrate
will; fragments, so to speak, of a shattered will which, like
fragments of a shattered planet, now make and traverse
their several orbits. This is the conception which we
must form and hold in order to discriminate and classify
the disordered actions of insanity.[1] The subject is an

[1] These quasi-automatic or spasmodic actions of separate wills and fractions
of broken-up wills stand in need of a special name in order to be truly dis-
criminated and understood. It remains for some one to invent for them some
such name as *Boulelepsy* (meaning will-spasm), and to call them *Bouleleptic*,
or perhaps—more euphoniously—*Boulepsy* and *Bouleptic*. To call them
psycho-motor is not fitting, since every act, normal or abnormal, inspired by
any function of mind is *psycho-motor*. I have discussed them at length in
*Body and Will: An Essay concerning Will in its Metaphysical, Physiological
and Pathological Aspects*, 1883.

organic mechanism in wrong action, and the problem is to find out the various conditions and modes of its wrong action when it goes wrong.

(3.) *Ideational.*—The third channel through which disordered nervous action discharges itself is disordered idea. I go on now therefore to consider the mad thoughts which madness thinks. What is it which, imparting their special lineaments to the insane ideas or delusions in a particular case, gives the derangement its own complexion? Whence do the delusions derive their contents?

The predominant mood, according as it is bright or sad, no doubt determines the general hue of the delusive ideas; an insane person who is melancholy no more thinks bright thoughts than does a sane person who is sad. But it is not easy to say, it is often impossible to guess, what is the origin of the specific form and character of the particular delusion. Sometimes it is evident that special sensations, clear or obscure, are at the root of it. The natural and necessary tendency, when a strange sensation is felt, is to describe it in terms of a familiar sensation, since, having no language of its own, there is no other language available, and to ascribe it to similar causes, since of such only is there available experience. The inflamed conjunctiva feels as if a grain of sand were irritating it and can hardly be persuaded otherwise; when there is active congestion of the internal ear, it hears the buzzing, rushing, hissing or roaring sounds of objective experience; and the reviving sensation of a numbed nerve is felt and described as the prickings of pins and needles. Were there a conviction that the proper external cause was present in such case, there would be actual hallucination. That is no doubt very much what happens when the sharp cutting pains felt in their legs and arms by persons suffering from alcoholic insanity instigate the insane notions that their bodies are being cut by knives or broken glass. In like manner the rats, mice, beetles, serpents or other creeping things which in delirium tremens are seen to run or crawl over the floor or bed may spring from strange creeping sensations of the skin due to the paralytic injury which alcohol is known to do to the peripheral ends of its nerves. The pretty constant characters of such hallucinations in delirium tremens certainly point to the insane idealisation or allegorical interpretation of sensory stimuli that are themselves pretty constant in character. Considering then the variety of our sensations and that disorder of each sense may instigate its illusive objective dramatizations in terms of its special experience, it is easy to see that disordered sensations will have much to do with inspiring insane delusions and even informing their structure.

Here it may be proper to take note of two modes of mental interpretation which, though they pass into one another, may be broadly distinguished—namely (*a*) the conscious and, as it were, pathologically logical interpretation, and (*b*) the unconscious and allegorical interpretation. In the first case, just illustrated, an insane person, afflicted with abnormal sensations that are strange and bewildering, imagines some extraordinary cause of so extraordinary an experience and so tries to explain to himself what he suffers; if he labours under an insanity of persecution, he concludes that they are caused by his enemies who are using magnetism, mesmerism or some other mysterious agent to torment him. He explains the unknown, not in terms of the known, since he does not know what he is talking about, but of mysterious and impossible powers which his ignorance ascribes to known agents. It is a pathological ergoism, so to speak. In the second case, the interpretation comes from mental operations which go on below the level of consciousness and has no known logic in it; like dream-creations, it is an allegorical interpretation done by the brain unconsciously, in virtue of workings of which we know nothing and conscious reflection could not follow nor ever devise. The strange, various and unexpected delusions of insanity, no less than the fantastic products of dreaming, are ample evidence of inherent cerebral plastic processes which go on at random, when they are not bound down to some logical order by the ties of experience.

The main determining stimuli of these morbid dramatizations might, I think, be classified thus : (*a*) Impressions made on sense from without the body ; (*b*) Internal impressions from the viscera and other organs of the body ; (*c*) Stimuli arising from the state of the blood, both as regards supply and composition ; (*d*) The unexhausted effects of recent experiences, whereby lately vibrating parts are prone to be stirred easily into renewed vibration ; and (*e*) The proclivities of the mental organisation, as determined by hereditary causes and the special experiences of life. They are just the conditions to be taken account of in an exhaustive study of the causes and characters of dreams.[1] As they have been previously treated of generally as causes of mental disorder, it will suffice now to adduce a few examples of their special action in determining the special features of the particular mental disorder.

Obscure intimations from irritable sexual organs, special probably in character albeit not definite sensations, impart special features to the complexion of the insanity which occurs soon after puberty and in some unmarried women. Feeling the stirrings of a new and strange function, with the dimmest idea only of its nature and fulfilment, perhaps perplexed and troubled by confused dreams which it inspires, conscious also of a void without being conscious what the void is, the maid imagines that some one who has never given a thought to her is in love with her, goes on to believe that he is in secret intimacy with her by mysterious sympathy, ascribing to outward agency her peculiar sensations, and ends perhaps by thinking that she is going to have a baby, notwithstanding that her conception in that case must have been immaculate and miraculous. That the special organ, having its special representation in the supreme centres of the brain, gives its colour to the feeling and form to the thought, without conscious co-operation, just as it does in dreams before instinct has been enlightened by experience, is not really more strange than that a male

---

[1] In the last edition of this book I traced their action on the causation of dreams in special chapters on *Dreams, Hypnotism and Allied Mental States*.

and female should, without previous instruction, discover the pre-established harmonies of their bodies and make the odd and, but for inspiring instinct, unimaginable, procreative use of them which they do. The nervous mechanism subserving the instinct incorporates in its structure a long history of experiences through the ages, and the obscure stirrings of these silent memories at nature's appointed season inspire or, as it were, revive thoughts and feelings in the individual consciousness which the compound instinct holds latent in its composition.

There is a kind of organic intelligence between the different organs of the body, the effect and exponent of their essential sympathies as constituent parts of an organism which still is *one*, whereby the brain feels the special effects of disorder in any one of the organs, without a corresponding special consciousness. The consciousness, if any, is a general consciousness only of discomfort or uneasiness. Beneath that, however, there is the deeper *special* intelligence which the brain has of the disorder of the *particular* organ. So perhaps it has come to pass that dreams of bodily illness have sometimes had a prophetic strain, a person having dreamt that he had a particular disease which neither he nor any one else suspected he had, but which nevertheless soon afterwards developed itself openly. Galen relates the story of a man who, having dreamt that his leg was turned into stone, soon afterwards was struck with paralysis of the limb; and similar instances, too many and marked to be set down offhand as mere coincidences, have been recorded by other authors. Many sad examples have been recorded of women who, suffering from disease of the reproductive organs, have been afflicted with grievous delusions betokening a special morbid origin: that they were violated nightly in their sleep, that they were with child by some supernatural agency, that horrible and disgusting feelings, ideas, and visions were excited in them by diabolic agency. To the last category one may relegate the sorceresses who professed and sometimes believed that they had intercourse with the devil at their midnight orgies, or that demons lay with them in the night, and who, being believed by other persons, were burnt alive at the stake.

How far each thoracic or visceral organ can, like the sexual organs, determine its specific mood or tone of feeling directly, and indirectly its accordant manner of thought, and how far therefore each may determine the character of the dream of sleep and of the delusion of madness, it is impossible to say with any certainty. But it is conceivable that all the visceral organs may have their several relations with modes of feeling, as definite and constant in character as the relations which the special senses have with forms of thought. Certainly the moods of feeling and thought which accompany disease of the lungs are very different from those which accompany abdominal disease; and inflammation of the gastro-intestinal mucous membrane notably occasions a gloom and anxiety which are not felt in inflammation of the bronchial mucous membrane. Speaking generally, there is a tone of despair in disease of the abdominal viscera which there is not in disease of the thoracic viscera.[1] The surgeon who, having performed an operation on the abdomen, has in mind the possible occurrence of peritonitis, views with apprehensive alarm a look of anxiety in his patient's countenance, before he finds the signs of local inflammation. Hitherto the mental symptoms of different bodily diseases have not been studied systematically, and one may search through treatises filled with elaborate descriptions of the symptoms, courses and morbid anatomy of them and not discover that they have any mental symptoms at all. Nevertheless patient and accurate observation of them might be of great scientific value.

Passing now from organic stimuli, without going into further detail, the important part played by defects and derangements of the muscular sense in the determination of the character of mental disorder merits special notice.

---

[1] The different effect may of course be mainly, perhaps entirely, due to the intimate concern of the abdominal organs in the manufacture of proper nutritive matter for the blood and to the poisonous action of vitiated blood on the nervous system from a failure in some organ of the process.

Consider the effects of loss of muscular feeling in such an instrument as the hand: inability to grasp nicely and fitly if the feeling be defective only, and inability to grasp an object at all if the feeling be abolished, unless, by fixing the eyes on it, the sense of sight is made to take the place of the missing muscular sense and thus to instruct the proper muscles what they have to do and what they are doing. The necessary ingoing current being wanting, how can the special reflex of the fit perception or apprehension take place? The muscular sense has lost its memory, and the sight has to remember for it. When sight thus takes on the work of the missing sense, all goes well so long as the instructing current from it runs, but if the person turns his eyes away from the object held in the hand, he lets go his hold unconsciously and drops it instantly. Now if the entire loss of the muscular sense causes such complete impotence, is it not likely that defects and disorders of it may be occasions of hallucination and delusion?

The special discriminations of each sense require and imply the most nice motor adaptations. Refinements of touch, of colour, of tone, of taste and smell are possible only by virtue of corresponding fine and exact waves of motor tension; without the exact degree of muscular contraction sensibility could not be exact nor the special fine impression be perceived. Why does a black eye impair vision? Not because the eye itself is hurt, but because of the stiffness of the bruised muscles about the eye, the nicely adjusted contractions of which accompany and are the conditions of exact vision. Were there the same stiff incompetence without any bruise or swelling the sight would still be impaired, and if all the proper ocular movements were similarly lamed there would be no look of intelligence in eyes which would then exhibit the vacant lack-lustre gaze of a drunken or idiotic person. How keen and quick an intelligent dog is to perceive its master's mood in the expression of his face and to answer it by the fit look and attitude! It reads the subtile language of his features when he perhaps is unaware himself of any change of them; the fine muscular contractions of the differing moods are enough to excite its discriminating apprehensions. Consider again how two strangers meeting and passing in the street sometimes cast mutual glances of uncertain recognition, so that either thinks the other must know him; the fact being that the one involuntarily puts on a certain inquiring gaze which is perceived and answered instantly by a corresponding gaze of the other. Destroy the muscular sensibilities of the fit movements, and the two would meet and pass with as blank indifference as two masks. It is impossible therefore for the victim of a mania of persecution who believes that people look at him significantly wherever he goes not to provoke and notice their strange looks. What is so-called mind-reading but muscle-reading through movements so fine as to be discernible only by a practised sensibility? What is mind-utterance in all its forms but so many most special and delicate muscular actions? How could mind ever be at all but for the motor factor which, built into its structure, constitutes half its organisation?

Pondering these things, it is a proper inquiry whether much of the painful feeling of mental impotence in melancholia be not due to sluggish muscular feeling. Lamenting the dull feeling of deadness or emptiness which he has in his head, over which perhaps his hands are passed restlessly in vague movements of distress, the patient affirms that he cannot think or feel things as he used to, cannot mentally grasp them, that they have a look of shadowy unreality and excite no interest; all which must needs be if the barrier of a dulled muscular feeling, interposed now between him and the outer world, prevents the adequate apprehensions. If certain minute tensions of the muscles of the forehead, eyes, nose, mouth, together or separately, are necessary to exact perception and thought, as I believe they are, being indeed constituent parts of their reflexes, it follows that when they fail there will be a feeling of deadness or emptiness and an impotence to feel, perceive, and think normally. Thereupon the bewildering sense of incapacity acts in turn to aggravate the misery of the general nervous depression of which it is an effect, and in further result perhaps inspires delusions in the person that he has committed some great sin and has been smitten with a curse in consequence; having lost interest in his family and his natural feeling of affection for them, as he thinks, he reproaches himself for his deadness of feeling and construes it into proof of his wicked state. On the other hand, an opposite state of excited muscular feeling is seen in the extreme muscular irritability with its accompanying great and dangerous irritability of temper, of the epileptic maniac.

States of the muscular system are determining factors in the characters of some dreams—probably in dreams of flying through the air, of falling down a precipice, of desperate struggles, and the like.[1] In like manner the hallucinations of holy persons, men and women, such as St. Dunstan, St. Christina, and others, who believed that during their spiritual transports they rose bodily from the earth and floated through the air, might doubtless be prompted by extraordinary states of the muscular sensibility; having

---

[1] Not necessarily so, since the notion of flying, etc., in dreams may arise from the change of the apparent magnitude and position of the images excited in the brain, when the change is such as a change of distance and position in ourselves in relation to them actually would have produced. Such changes in position and magnitude being constantly associated with motion in ourselves when we are awake, it follows, as Hartley pointed out (*Observations on Man*) that in dreams we infer the motions from the changes of magnitude and position. Much of the wonder which dreams occasion arises from our habit of thinking of their events as we think of real events—that is, in their terms of thought; for which reason we transfer the wonder which we should properly feel if they were actual events to what ought not to cause any wonder, they being what they are. We wonder at the rapidity of events in dreams, where a life-drama is enacted in a short time: why? The dream is but the running over a register in the brain which, though it is the register of a lifetime, only requires a glance to read, and drowning persons sometimes think they read in such a flash of consciousness. Though London and New York are two thousand miles distant on the earth, they are side by side in the brain; so near that a microscope might be required to prove their separateness: is it any wonder that the dreamer should pass instantly from the one to the other? Between the death of Cæsar and the death of Napoleon there is a distance of centuries in time, but if the nerve-current of the one follows immediately the nerve-current of the other in my brain, what wonder that I mix them in the same dream?

motor hallucinations they believed that they made movements which they did not make, just as when they had hallucinations of vision they believed they saw scenes which they did not see. So it is with those insane persons who, lying in bed, imagine that they are moved up and down, or that objects around them sway up and down or swing to and fro, or that walls and ceilings rise and sink, open and shut; and with those who declare that their arms and legs fly through the air, or, conversely, are too heavy to be moved at all by them. Still more is it tragically so with the maniac who, having an extraordinary feeling of bodily lightness, believes that he can fly and throws himself out of a window in consequence; and ludicrously so with the general paralytic who, impotent to govern and use his palsied movements with effect, boasts exultantly of his wonderful agility and prodigious bodily strength.

In the decline of old age the muscles grow stiff, dull and weary; they cannot easily adapt themselves to new combinations of movement; they do what they have been used to do, but slowly and heavily, without the grace, ease and suppleness of their former state. If the exceeding fine movements that are the conditions of perception and thought are in a like case, the inevitable effects will be such dulness of perception, sluggish thought, and loss of fine discernments as mark the mental decay of old age, and, in its extreme degree of senile dementia, sink into impotence to perceive accurately and to think coherently. Note how tardily the features of the old man whose brain is beginning to soften stumble into the recognition of an acquaintance who meets and accosts him unexpectedly; at first, a blank look of vacancy, and then after a little staggering hesitation, as if an obstruction were being slowly overcome, the stealing of a gradual animation into the lines of the fit expression. The motor apprehensions of the recognition are slow and tottering like the gait, quavering like the speech. In further process of senile decay the stumble is into a recognition which is no recognition at all; for by reason of the persistence of the old habits or set forms of nervous action when there is no longer the power to combine movements into new forms or to make nice adaptations of the old forms, it comes to pass that one person is mistaken for another and a perfect stranger greeted as an old friend; perceptions take the old forms which survive best in the general ruin. Even then, however, under the impulse of a strong emotion, a transient revival of intelligence can take place, the discharge of nervous energy being powerful enough for the occasion to force its way along the sluggish molecules and to quicken them into a temporary restoration of their former activity.

Thus much with regard to the effects of defect and disorder of muscular sense. The relations of disordered blood-flow to mental disorder have been previously discussed, and it only remains to point out here that the blood is certainly a possible factor in determining the character of the delirium and hallucinations. The rate of its flow through the brain manifestly affects the rapidity and the character of thought and feeling. Sluggish laboured thought is never cheerful thought, and sluggish thought is the accompaniment of dilated vessels and sluggish circulation; on the other hand, brisk and easy thought is cheerful thought, activity pleased with itself, happy to be, and a free and active circulation is the necessary condition of it. However, neither circulation nor thought must exceed a certain mean of activity, else it will become superficial, pass the continent bounds of form and order, and topple over into incoherence, albeit, being rapid, it is still joyful: nothing equals the exhilaration and joyous self-confidence of commencing mania. In acute sthenic mania of the frantic sort, where there is evidently an active determination of blood to the brain, the accompanying explosive excitement of the nervous molecules expresses itself in hallucinations of flames of fire, blood-red atmosphere, roars of cannon, and the like; a furious anarchy of the senses going along with a corresponding delirium. Certainly the maniac who, like the furious epileptic maniac, sees things in blood is prone to be very dangerous.[1]

In the end the most important factor in determining the form of the delusion probably is the individual character as it has been fashioned by the joint action of the inborn nature and the circumstances of life : what a man's forefathers have felt and thought, as embodied in the foundations of his nature, and what he has felt and thought, as the result of his own life-experience. There are varieties of natural disposition in men, just as there are varieties of dogs and horses, which cannot be transformed into one another; and we may expect such various dispositions as the timid and the courageous, the retiring and the ambitious, the guileless and the suspicious, the sanguine and the despondent to testify of themselves in their habits of insane, as they do in their habits of sane, thought. While the spirit of an insane delusion may be inspired by the leading passion or inclination of the individual mind, its special form or structure might witness to the special life-experience. Neither in madness nor in sanity is it easy for any one to go against his nature. And his nature, were there an exact and full record of ancestral characters for generations back, he might find to be essentially the reproduction of one that had already been; its differences superficial and owing to the very different circumstances of the changed world in which it has to act.

[1] A red colour is associated with excitement, a bull being notably enraged by it, and the blind man imagined scarlet to be like the sound of a trumpet.

PART II

THE SYMPTOMATOLOGY OF INSANITIES

WHO can sufficiently speak of these symptoms, or prescribe rules to comprehend them? As Echo to the painter in Ausonius, *vane, quid affectas*, etc., foolish fellow; what will? If you must needs paint me, paint a voice, *et similem si vis pingere, pinge sonum:* if you will describe melancholy, describe a phantastical conceit, a corrupt imagination, vain thoughts and different; which who can do? The four-and-twenty letters make no more variety of words in divers languages, than melancholy conceits produce diversity of symptoms in several persons. They are irregular, obscure, various, so infinite, Proteus himself is not so divers; you may as well make the moon a new coat, as a true character of a melancholy man; as soon find the motion of a bird in the air, as the heart of man, a melancholy man.—Burton's *Anatomy of Melancholy.*

CHAPTER I

INSANITY WITH DEPRESSION——MELANCHOLIA

COULD we imagine the intensification and perpetuation of the dark moods of passing gloom to which most persons are liable, when for the time light seems to have gone out of life, or of that essential despondence of nature whereby some persons are addicted to see everything in black, we might go some way to realise the sad feeling which is the dominant note of this form of mental disorder. But only a short way, since to realise it justly would be nothing less than to have it actually. The sad feeling is the note of lowered energy in the inmost elements of the mental organisation: exhausted by excess of function, or depressed by causes which obstruct function, or lacking the food of function—for their fire of life may be burnt out or choked out or starved out—its structural elements suffer and reveal their suffering in consciousness by despondent sadness and apathy, by despair and life-weariness. Unapt or unable to react rightly to their fit impressions, the activity which should be pleasing is labour and pain to them. Relish of life is the glad expression of its full throb of being, and hope its highest relish, both therefore felt most in the exuberant vigour and enthusiasm of youth and young manhood; disrelish of life or life-weariness the sad expression of low vitality, and despair its saddest outcome, most apt to be felt when passion wanes with waning life, and most of all felt when its slow-labouring processes verge to their close. How can nerve-element feel impressions with interest and react to them with vivacity, respond by fit motions within to motion from without, when its own intestine motions are feeble and flagging? How take hearty hold of the things of the world when the essence of its nature as living organic element, that which is its very principle of individuation, is well-nigh extinct? The slow-sad gait and heavy look of the melancholic are the visible bodying-forth in mass of the sluggish molecular processes that are latent and invisible; life-weariness and death-longing their outcries in consciousness.

Given then enfeebled or oppressed nerve-element, its direct outcome in consciousness is a feeling of sad dejection out of which in further course gloom-engendered thoughts emerge and rule. Well or ill, one who is sad cannot think glad thoughts. If his sadness be due to misfortune, bereavement, soured hope, disdained affection, crosses or losses in business, or other sufficient blow to self-interest or self-love, his dejected mind rallies, when in good health, and presently recovers its tone; his grief was natural grief proceeding from a natural motive and proportionate to its cause. But if his sadness is due to internal failure of the springs of reaction, without external cause or in measure and duration out of all proportion to such cause as there may have been, then it is morbid. It is not unnatural to weep, but it is not natural to burst into tears because a fly settles on the forehead, as I have known a melancholic man do. The sad feeling goes before the sad thoughts, summoning them to its gloomy sessions and holding them in attendance there by an elective affinity; in it they have their roots and from it draw their nurture; not otherwise than as happens in bad dreams where the basic feeling of oppression, whether proceeding inwardly from organic derangement or outwardly from occasions of moral depression, formulates itself in afflicting ideas and visions of the night. As fear is the instant passion of nature when a danger from without threatens the continuance of self, being the cry of the alarmed instinct of self-conservation, so inversely the morbid enfeeblement of the supreme nerve-energies of the brain translates itself mentally into a vague fearfulness; an instinctive alarm of the *ego* which, feeling itself threatened, but not knowing how, is apprehensive in face of an unknown danger. Lacking nervous vitality, the individual lacks courage and energy; he is cowed by what, were he well and strong, would cause him no uneasiness. The springs of life strengthened, the fears vanish instantly and there is left only wonder that it could ever have had the overmastering hold which it had. " It is perfectly amazing that I could ever think so, yet I am sure that if I felt again as I did then, I should think so again." Such is the astonied comment of the melancholic whom restored health has exorcised of the horrible fear and congruent gloomy notions which possessed and entranced him.

Simple Melancholia.

Thus it is that a person is sometimes wrapped in the unspeakable gloom of profound mental depression without any or at least without proportionate disorder of thought. Unutterably sad without knowing why, he cannot conceive what has happened to him, so strange and changed does he feel; he is not himself nor the world itself, loss of sense of personal identity and of the sense of outward reality going along together; everything seems unreal, mechanical, image-like, the show not substance of itself; he cannot think or act to any purpose; feels no interest in his affairs with which he was hitherto pleased to employ himself, nor in his family towards whom it is now a bitter self-reproach and an exasperation of his misery that he has lost all natural affection. Not knowing what he fears, he is full of fear; knowing that he has nothing to fear, he still fears. Terrible and incredible are the petty vacillations and paltry irresolutions which besiege and torment him; decisions in trifling matters cost agonies of effort, or cannot be made; he can no more will to do a little thing than he could will to walk down the street on red-hot

ploughshares; is in a fever of trembling agitation at the
mere notion of having to do what, were he well, would not
cost him a tremor. All the while he is capable of perceiving and judging rightly objects, affairs and events, but
they have a strange, separate, remote look; just as if they
were the mere shows of themselves or as if a veil were let
down between him and them. And truly no thicker veil
could well be interposed between him and them than that
of paralysed interest. Nothing else can he think about
but himself and his woes; he would fain communicate what
he feels to be incommunicable; conscious the while how
weak it seems on his part to give way to womanish wailings
and in amaze at the abject wretch which he is. Although
a strong man physically, he tells his sad tale with quivering
lips, tears in his eyes, tremor in his voice, perhaps with
outbursts of convulsive sobbing.

His clear consciousness adds a keener pang to his
misery; not only because it makes him a spectator of the
inglorious spectacle in which he is an actor, but because it
lets him perceive how impossible it is to make other
persons realise what he feels, bewildering and inexplicable
as his state is to himself, and how overcharged his plaints
appear to them. Nevertheless he recounts his sufferings
with weary iteration day after day as if they had never
been told before; for it is a momentary relief to talk of
them and to solicit and elicit the repeated assurance of a
recovery which, though he hears it gladly at the time, he
fails to hold. One way of escape alone suggests itself, dim
and undefined in his mind and shrunk from with horror
at first, but viewed more nearly and clearly when he feels
his misery too great to be borne longer : it is suicide.

How is the pride of intellect brought low! That a man
should perceive and know and understand and reason perfectly and yet be unable to deliver himself from the bondage
of such an unreasonable oppression! Keenly conscious of
the unreason of his despair, he cannot reason it away: he
might as well hope to argue himself into feeling cold when
he is in a burning fever, or into feeling hot when he is

shivering in the cold fit of an ague. An apt illustration of how little avail a discourse of reason is to recommend life when the organic sources of feeling fail; how powerless is the instrument when the energy to work it is wanting! Little helpful, if not keenly irritating, even maddening, is the advice of friends who demonstrate to one thus oppressed the groundlessness of his sadness and urge him to throw off his depression, to banish his fears, to interest himself in his affairs, to rouse himself to work, to distract himself with amusements. As if he would not be unspeakably glad to do so and it were not the very essence of his misery that he cannot! The bad effect of such a jarring appeal, ill judged when well meant, is perhaps to make him feel how impossible it is for them to understand his suffering, how far away they are from the least appreciation of it, what an impassable gulf lies between him and them, and to drive him into a deeper and more silent despair. The promises of religion and the consolations of philosophy, so inspiring when not needed and so helpless to help when their help is most needed, are no better than meaningless words to him; things present and things to come of equal unconcern; hope an empty mockery, for he expects without hope and awaits without desire; life a living woe, not life but a long death in life. In his person he might well feel the awful pronouncement fulfilled—"Behold I take away from thee the desire of thine eyes with a stroke."

Such are the distinctive features of a class of cases of mental depression. Although they are characterised by a most afflicting impotence to think, feel and act, there is neither delusion nor actual disorder of thought. Accordingly it is the custom to describe them as examples of *Simple Melancholia* or *Melancholia without Delusion*. Melancholy they are, but *melancholia* they are not in strict sense, since there is no real derangement of mind; there is only a profound pain of mind paralysing its functions—an essential *psychalgia*. Nevertheless they are attended with worse suffering than actual madness is, because the mind being whole enough to feel and perceive its abject state, they are more likely to end in suicide. Sometimes this kind of mental affliction goes no further, recovery taking place in due time when it is sought in the right way, but in other cases it is the prologue of deeper disorder.

In another and somewhat deeper form of disorder there are, along with the like feeling of miserable depression, exaggerated woe-born apprehensions of a harassing and tormenting kind; not always fixed, but sometimes changing, although one sort of them may predominate. Perhaps it is an apprehension, vast and formless, of something dreadful without knowing what, an undefined feeling of awful wretchedness, a vague and nameless horror, but commonly it takes a more or less definite form: a dread of going mad, a dread of having brain-disease, heart-disease, or some other fatal disease; a dread of impotence; a dread of doing harm to self or others, and like dreads of a brain-sick fancy. The sufferer cannot go near a precipice, or a railway train in motion, lest he should be beset with the temptation to throw himself down the one or under the other; cannot bear to look at a newspaper, because his eyes fasten instantly on the report of any horror in it; cannot see a knife without falling into an agony of fright lest he should yield to an impulse to use it against his wife or children or against himself.

Or the apprehension is retrospective: he fixes on a sin of omission or commission in his past life, or on some trivial error not worth a flitting pang of regret, magnifies it mightily, charges it with the most exaggerated consequences, and is in a fever of remorseful agitation. A prevailing dread is of having done some wrong which cannot be undone; he would give the world to be able to unsay a particular say, unthink a particular thought, undo a particular deed. He threw the blame of his offence when at school on an innocent schoolfellow who was punished for it and cannot rest now, thirty or forty years after, until he has sought him out and made atonement; he bought or inherited shares in a brewery and has no peace of mind because of tormenting scruples of conscience regarding the sin of profits made in such a business; or, having sold his shares in order to appease his scruples, he is no less afflicted because he has injured his family by giving up a good investment which he could ill afford to do, or because, by selling his shares, he has been guilty of shifting their burden of iniquity on to some one else.

Ludicrous sometimes is the disproportion between the troubled apprehension and its assigned motive: he touched a ladder accidentally as he passed under it in the street and is haunted with the fear, which all the while he knows to be unfounded and foolish, that it may have fallen down and killed somebody; he has misgivings lest he dropped a spark from his candle and is in a fever of apprehension that the house may be burnt down; he said or did something in company and is tormented with the insistent imagination that it may have been construed in an ill sense, although he had not the least ill meaning. Every mischance is a misconduct, every misconduct a crime. There is no end to the possible occasions of self-torture, for the least remembrance may suffice to stir it; nor does the ridiculous inadequacy of the circumstance, glaring as it is to lookers-on, avail in the least to stop the recurring round of anguish. And forasmuch as there is neither reconciliation nor revenge in the grave, the self-torment is all the worse when the morbid apprehension fixes on an imagined defect of duty or affection towards one whose death has precluded the possibility of atonement. Continuing in weary round from day to day and week to week, the misery from time to time mounts to a panic of anguish. Such morbid magnification of the minute usually, perhaps invariably, betokens an hereditary factor in the causation.

An instructive demonstration of the evils of acute self-consciousness and minute introspection! Instead of acknowledging once for all that what has been has been and thereupon going on so to act in the present as to determine well that which is to come, a morbidly hypersensitive self, lost to all sense of proportion, paralyses action in the present and spends life in vain regrets and remorses about a past upon which not Heaven itself has power. Such is its monstrously disproportionate estimate of itself in relation to the notself that it cannot work in silent subordination to the whole, suppressing its wails when it suffers, but would have the universe to stand by in order to attend to its sorrow. "Behold and see all ye that pass by, if any sorrow is like unto my sorrow which is done unto me!" It is the same overestimate and indulgence of self which caused the fault that now finds relief in incontinent self-reproach. But in truth the exaggerated self-consciousness is but the effect and evidence of nerve-weakness. To increase it by unwise exercise is to become more and more unhealthy. Sickly musings of solitude, penitential reflections, sigh-laden retrospections of remorse are not wholesome to form and strengthen but hurtful to weaken and deform character, whether they are the bitter self-indulgences of a morbid disposition or the intemperate exercises of religious superstition.

In another group of cases of simple melancholy the cause of affliction is a morbid impulse to utter a bad word or to do an ill deed. The impulse is bad enough, but the essence of the misery is not always so much the fear of actually yielding to it as the haunting fear of the fear; it is that which is the perpetual torture, an acute agony when active, a quivering apprehension of recurrence when quiescent. Sometimes the impulse is of a dangerous character, as when it prompts a father to kill himself or urges a mother to kill her children; not unfrequently it is an impulse to utter aloud a profane or obscene word or to do an indecent act; now and then it is the impulse to do some meaningless and absurd act which has taken hold of the fancy and will not let it go, and to repeat the act over and over again, since thus only can peace of mind be obtained. In one person who had been used to travel by railway all his life, it was an inability to stay in a railway carriage so soon as the train was about to start or began to move, the feeling of distress being so intolerable as to impel him to yell aloud and to jump out at any cost. Such impelling feelings have been described as compulsive or coercive ideas, but it is not really the idea which compels, the driving force is not in it but in the insane feeling which presses to its discharge along the track of the idea; for the sufferer is all the while perfectly conscious of the character of the idea, loathing and abominating it. Bad as the impulses are, worse still perhaps is the persistent intrusion of evil thoughts, horrible and detestable, into the mind, despite the most earnest wish to turn and keep them out. They come and stay there against the will, a haunting horror, a maddening torture; agonies of praying are as futile to exorcise them as agonies of will to expel them; turning the mind into a perfect hell they render life an intolerable burden which a dim hope of relief, or perchance a certain procrastinating indolence of nature, or a shrinking dread of the unknown, alone prevents being violently put an end to.

It is not easy to persuade him who suffers in one or other of these ways that he is not doomed to madness, or that he has not the mortal disease of brain which he fears he has. Notwithstanding that he has had previous attacks of the same kind from which he recovered, he always declares the present attack to be different from and much worse than any former one and is sure he cannot possibly get well again. There is a feeling of eternity, no feeling of time, in relation to it. Of the worst grief at its worst there is always, when in health, a tacit or subconscious instinct of ending; but here an all-absorbing feeling of misery so usurps the being that there is no real succession of feelings and thoughts, no sense of time therefore, a sense only of an everlasting is and is to be. Could he so much as look forward to recovery as possible, the budding hope would itself be proof that his nervous plexuses were stirring intimately to regain their proper tone and form and that he was on the mend. To inspire a gleam of real hope in the gloom of melancholy is to initiate recovery, it is to plant a morrow in the midnight of its sorrow: to infix a distinct belief of recovery is almost to guarantee it.

The conviction of despair does not fail to be nourished and strengthened in many cases by strange and alarming sensations which occasion infinite distress and apprehension. Painful they are, but not definite pains; alien alike in place and character, they do not run in the category of ordinary pains, and the resources of pain-descriptive language are exhausted in the futile attempts to express them. It is necessary to drag into use all the terms which the known pains of physical injury and suffering suggest, such as cutting, shooting, piercing, burning, tearing, stabbing, throbbing and the like. In despair of success, the sufferer is driven to the last extremities of exaggerated expression: the pain is just as if a thousand knives were driven into his brain, or a saw were sawing it, as if his nerves were red-hot iron, as if vapours were boiling in his spinal cord, as if a multitude of fine wires were aflame in his loins and legs, as if galvanic shocks were rending his body. These exaggerated descriptions have two reasons of their being: first, like such words as absolute, infinite and eternal, they mark the negation of definite conception and are impotences of thought; secondly, they are vain endeavours, by their strong colouring, to excite in the minds of others a proportionate feeling of the really ineffable misery of the strange and bewildering sensations. They are endeavours not to convey ideas, but to express feelings that are inexpressible.

Where have these sensations their seats? Anywhere and everywhere, but principally in the head, along the spinal cord, in the precordial, epigastric and pelvic regions. Alarming shoots and rushes of distracting sensations from the epigastrium towards the head; throbbing, burning, creeping, crawling sensations in the spinal cord; sensations of fulness, soreness, deadness, of cracking, tilting, wobbling, of contraction or clamp-like constriction of the brain; shooting pains, as of red-hot iron, or sensations of numbness, pricking, soreness along arm or leg, coming on suddenly and accompanied by extraordinary and disproportionate mental distress;—these and like anomalous pains, indeterminate in place and character, betray profound derangement of the sensory system. Two things are conspicuous with regard to them: first, the impossibility under which the sufferer is of conveying to others a notion of their nature and of what he suffers; and, secondly, their extreme disabling effect on him. For these reasons they appear to onlookers to be exaggerated and hypochondriacal. But in truth it is their bewildering strangeness and anarchic disorder, inexpressible in the terms of any known language, that appal and confound him who, feeling as if his personality were deliquescing and he were sinking through the foundations of his own being, has his sense of self distracted and his self-confidence completely shattered. He could better bear the terrible pains of a cancer than bear them; and, as a matter of fact, while few persons commit suicide who suffer the definite pains of cancer many persons commit suicide who suffer these distracting pains. Of all the pains of consciousness the most painful is the sense of the mental self going to pieces, as the most painful of unbeliefs is the loss of belief in self.

Signal features of some of these cases of melancholy, occurring often in connection with storms of disordered sensations, are periodic paroxysms of indescribable anguish, veritable panics of nameless terror and distress. The patient is seized with a horrible fearfulness and trembling, without knowing what or why; a soul-shiver, which seems to contain the quintessence of horror, apprehension and anguish. He is not unconscious of surrounding objects, albeit they have a shadowy and phantasmal look; his consciousness of them dim and distant, much like that of a person who is transported out of himself during a panic of fright when the house is on fire, or is confronted with the appalling vision of sudden death in another form. Sometimes the paroxysm is preceded immediately by a rush of strange and riotous sensation towards the head from the region of the heart, or of the epigastrium, or of the pelvis, perhaps with a feeling of heat, a ringing in the ears, or a roaring in the head, the skin of which, however, is not necessarily hot or flushed; for the rush is not a rush of blood, though it feels like it and in some cases is accompanied or followed by it. While the panic is at its worst the sufferer feels urgently impelled to violent action of some kind, he cares not nor scarcely knows what, as a discharge or relief of it—to rush wildly out of the house, to shriek or yell aloud, to smash furniture, to do something desperate to himself or to others. After it is over, when he comes to himself, he is feeble, trembling, exhausted, panting, perhaps bathed in perspiration.

What is the nature of the seizure? Manifestly it is a violent nerve-storm of some kind, not unlike an attack of epilepsy in its mode of onset and character. Were it preceded or followed by loss of consciousness and convulsions, or even by a momentary loss of consciousness without convulsions, it would without doubt be called epilepsy; and in the present state of knowledge, no name serves better perhaps to convey a notion of its nature and relations than that of mental epilepsy. Whatever it be called, it is an explosive discharge of nerve-force in irregular fashion, attested on its sensory side by the wild panic and on its motor side by the desperate acts of frenzy: a neuralgic storm of anarchic sensations issuing in psycho-motor convulsive deeds. The impulse to self-destruction, or the deed, when it is done, is the fit outgoing response to the ingoing current of riotous sensation which occasions the apprehension of mental dissolution—the pathological unloading of it; not otherwise than as, in the domain of physiological function, the spasmodic action of the sexual orgasm is the outgoing muscular response to the ingoing increments of sensation which accumulate until they reach the self-absorbing crisis of discharge. Were it possible for any one to conceive and feel a tumult of painful sensation just the opposite of the voluptuous intensity of that orgasm, he might perhaps thus obtain a sort of conception of the all-absorbing anguish of a melancholic rapture.

In this relation we may reflect that quiet currents of nerve-force from all sensory endings of nerves, not from those of special senses only, probably proceed continually during waking life, and in less degree during sleep, keeping up at the lowest a certain tonicity of the muscles and a certain susceptibility of sense; that to be inactive and still is not strictly a cessation of energies at work, but a cessation of the so-called life of relation—that is, of the outward and visible relational activity of the animal life; and that a man not only feels and moves, but lives and has his unconscious being, as part of a circuit with external nature, ever receiving and giving, inspiring and exspiring, assimilating and excreting, feeling and doing, knowing and acting. There is a positive difference between a sleeping and a dead man in regard of sensibility and muscular tonicity which is evident in the attitude of his body; indeed, it is unlikely that a living man ever loses all sensibility and tonicity except perhaps when, falling from a housetop or knocked down by a railway-engine, he collapses entirely and drops, limp and formless, like a bundle of old clothes. So it comes about that the above-described nerve-storms occur, like storms in external nature, as violent disturbances of natural processes; just in fact as such spasmodic physiological acts as coughing, sneezing and sexual spasm are intensifications of natural movements. Instead of silent pulses there are throbs and pangs; instead of quiet oscillations there are explosive discharges.

The impulse to suicide is prone to spring up in these melancholics, even when they are not rapt out of themselves in panic-stricken frenzy. Sane enough to feel keenly what they suffer and to contrast their woeful deadness of feeling with the joyous energy around them, crushed to despair by the serene continuity of things in contrast with the sad discontinuity of their interest and work in them, in the world but not of it, sufferers not doers;—they cannot bear the burden of a lame and wretched existence longer. Having life enough to react passionately against the oppression they labour under, they have not life enough to inspire the energy of systematic outward doing: were they more mad they would be less sad, because they would then be so much out of relation with the course of things around them as to feel not much, or not at all, their estrangement from men and things. By open discourse or by covert hints they disclose the impulse, and being met with unsympathetic remonstrance, or with joking banter, or with a boisterous cheerfulness which, although designed to rally and cheer them, is perhaps most wounding to them because it is so essentially discordant, say no more of their temptation but prove its reality by succumbing to it.

Then the self-sufficient folk who, despising medical warning, were sure that those who talked of suicide never did it and proud of the rude vigour with which they had bid them pull themselves together and not talk such nonsense, move heaven and earth to have the death pronounced an accident. Having sent the patient to the Swiss mountains or to travel elsewhere by land or sea, where he had the best opportunities of suicide and when he was no more competent to take interest in new scenes than a paralysed man to embrace Venus; most likely too without proper attendance, because they were sure it would drive him mad to put such indignity on him, who in his heart would have been secretly glad perhaps of such protection against himself; they put forth the report of death by apoplexy, or by heart-disease, or of an accidental fall down a precipice in the attempt to pluck a rare alpine flower, or of a loss of way in the snow and death by exposure and exhaustion, or of an unlucky fall overboard. If he shot himself at home, the gun went off accidentally when he was carrying it carelessly or cleaning it at midnight; if he threw himself headlong out of a window, it was an accidental fall in consequence of an attack of giddiness to which he was constitutionally liable; if he drowned himself, leaving behind him a letter of woeful farewell, it was because he was seized with a sudden cramp while bathing with his clothes on; if he flung himself in front of a railway-engine, he was taking a walk along the track and made a rush after his hat which was blown off at the inopportune moment; if he died by poison, it was from an overdose of a drug which he took by misadventure. In nine cases out of ten nine persons out of ten suspect or know what the real event was, but in due decorous conformity with the rules of social convention that things shall be what it is agreed to call them, not what they are, every one professes to believe an account which everybody knows it is a pretence on the one side to put forth and on the other side to believe.[1]

Suicide of this sort, springing from suffering that is intolerable, is natural in motive and logical in fact, whatever may be thought of it from a moral standpoint. The outcome in consciousness of the sum of the despair of the life-lacking organic elements, it is a supreme, final, and—if I may use the word in this connection—fit act of adjustment to the outer world with which the individual can contend no longer. As always, man seeks his happiness and acts from self-interest—even when he hangs himself. He who is in good health and has a keen gust of life cannot in the least realise that any one can seriously wish to be rid of it, any more than he who is in the full vigour and enthusiasm of youth can realise the life-weariness of old age when the waning forces of life extinguish its desires and foretell its ending. So unnatural does a disgust of life appear to him that he cannot believe it sincere in another, or at least thinks it foolish weakness; and he feels the common arguments against suicide to be unanswerable, as they always are, so long as they do not require a real answer and until they are answered by the event. The truth is that the love of life is at bottom the capacity of organic element to feel agreeably and to respond fitly to the stimuli of its environment—to take interested hold of them—the translation of which into a

---

[1] From the same amiable hypocrisy it proceeds that the suicide, when it cannot be made out to be accidental death, is ascribed to temporary insanity. Mankind will not admit it to be in the order of human nature that anybody should be sanely sick of it and its aims.

higher plane of feeling is desire and effort. When that capacity is faint or extinct, arguments to prove the worth of life are vain and meaningless; they come like wind and like wind they go. For it is not the arguments in favour of living that inspire the love of life, it is the love of life which infuses force into the arguments; just as always it is the particular passion which summons and marshals reason in its favour, not the arguments which convince the passion. The good reasons for living are but modes or ways of exhibiting how desire, if it exist, may pass to varieties of gratification; if it exist not, they are so many tantalising incitements to despair.

Not that the entire loss of desire is most adapted to breed despair; matters are more peaceable then than when desire is not quite extinct. It is where the contest between the antagonistic forces is going on, where the love of life is struggling against its own ebb and there is not yet complete impotence of desire and acceptance of defeat, that the misery is greatest and the danger most urgent. Therefore it is, on the one hand, that perfectly sane persons who are horribly depressed kill themselves deliberately, and, on the other hand, that quiet melancholics go on for months or even years, with no wish to live but without taking active measures to die, and yet at last, with no change in circumstances or in their ordinary conduct to lead to the expectation of such a catastrophe, quietly hang or otherwise kill themselves; overtaken perhaps by a sudden surprise that they had put off the business so long, or hurried by the provocation of a fitly presenting opportunity out of the indolence of nature which had made them put it off from day to day.

Of the motives which consciously hold a person back from suicide, religion and love of family are thought to be the strongest; at least they are the restraints most often urged and professed. There is at bottom an instinctive shrinking back from the headlong leap out of warm and known being into the cold and dark unknown. Even the sceptic who scouts the notion of a future life in another world exhibits an aversion, notwithstanding his despair, to be suddenly the nothing that he was ere born to living woe. But the repugnance is vastly increased when the belief is entertained that after death there is a judgment to come. Nearer, however, and stronger on the whole to restrain, is the love of family; for as motives decrease in force as they increase in distance it comes to pass that an eternity of bliss or pain counts for less in effect on to-day's conduct than the prospect of to-morrow's joy or woe. To leave wife and children without support and protection, perhaps destitute, to the trials of a rude world, weighted too with the heavy consciousness of a parent's suicide, might certainly seem so abhorrent a thought that it is surprising it is not more deterrent than it proves to be. More surprising no doubt than it would be were the secrets of all hearts and hearths made known. Deterrent it is so long as the sufferer can feel and think for others, but it necessarily ceases to be so when his whole being is rapt in a transport of despair and for him others practically cease to be. One motive, not much confessed, which operates strongly to withhold the would-be self-slayer, and which perchance is the secret real motive when higher motives are professed, is a sensitive repugnance to hurt himself; the odd inconsistency of the thing, if any inconsistency in human conduct were odd, being that the timid fear of inflicting a short pain operates effectively in persons who describe the agony which they suffer every moment as frightful, inconceivable, unendurable. Now and then a melancholic will commit suicide from the very fear of death which is his continual torment thus ending by the certainty of the worst the intolerable apprehensions of suspense. The act is logical implicitly whether conscious reasons do or do not agree with it: the only remedy for the malady of life when it has become insupportable. Feeling has its reasons which reason cannot fathom; it is not from reason that life is loved, any more than it is from reason that young men and maidens fall in love.

The truth is often that neither the doer himself nor

any one else can say what is the real motive which either hinders or actuates self-destruction. When done, it is done perhaps on a sudden impulse, half-intended only, at random, after having been long mused upon; like Hamlet's vengeance which, lingeringly meditated, resolved upon, and put off through the scenes of a five-act tragedy, was accomplished at last by mere accident and might not have been accomplished at all but for that. A petty annoyance, a momentary chagrin, a paltry quarrel, a domestic jar, might seem a ridiculously small cause, but it is enough when it serves to precipitate the brooding event: it is the occasional not the efficient cause, just as the mean squabble is which perhaps lets loose at last the storm of long-impending war. A dozen times the person may have been on the verge of doing it and not have done it, and yet he does it next time because a child's cry, or the bang of a door, or a room in disorder, or an angry word has aptly added the weight of motive necessary. Certainly, if the man were strong and well, he would be no more affected by such trifles than he would be by the inundation of a Chinese province and the drowning and starvation of a hundred thousand of its inhabitants, but in his low, irritable, and very impressionable state of mind they suffice to produce a violent explosion.

Not less notable also is the trivial circumstance which sometimes prevents the carrying into effect of a predetermined suicide. A person on the way to drown himself, being spoken to casually by an acquaintance whom he chances to meet, has his resolve dissipated by the simple incident and returns quietly home: when he started off to do it, all the molecules of his being were magnetically attracted and set to a certain pole of purpose, so to speak, but the intervening circumstance was enough to dissolve the attraction and to let them return to their old positions. I knew one lady who, having gone a long distance to the banks of a canal with the determination to throw herself into it, was deterred at the last moment by the suddenly occurring idea of the disgusting spectacle which her dead body would present when it was dragged out of the water. She proved the sincerity of her self-destructive longings by taking poison three weeks afterwards. Probably she was self-deceived as to the real motive which held her back from drowning herself; it may have been the cold and dismal look of the water when she saw it. Motives are very mixed and their main work is unconscious in real life; it is only when fancy-made in psychological novels and poems that they are capable of precise and pretty analyses.

There are many persons who are able to commit suicide when the starting effort entails the full consequences, all the intermediate action between the first motion and the end being necessary sequence, as when they pull a trigger or throw themselves from a housetop, who would be incapable of it were they obliged to sustain and continue the effort in order to complete the business, as they must do if they cut their throats. Thus it is that some who try and fail never try again. Others again might be said to do it against their real wills; for they make a feigned attempt which, once initiated, precipitates them to an end which they did not sincerely intend or at most only half-intended. This is the case especially with hysterical and hypochondriacal melancholics who, playing to an audience whom they aim to alarm and convince, are prone to exaggerate mad behaviour in order to produce a stronger effect on its sympathies or fears: they are not really, as they might seem to be, sane persons who are feigning insanity, but insane persons, a feature of whose malady is a tendency to simulation. Certainly time and chance happen largely to those who embark on suicidal meditations and ventures, a power above their reach, in whose rigorous employ they move and of whose operations they are but little incidents, fulfilling or thwarting their intents.

It would be an easy and might not be an unfit reflection here—How great and momentous the issues that hang on the meanest event! That the least accident of time, circumstance or temper should decide whether a man shall live or die, when his life or death may determine the fate of a family or a nation! But mean and mighty things in a brief scene of time between two eternities are alike little things. There is hardly a career which men are agreed to think great but has been ·determined by the merest chance, while a thousand careers that might have been great have been marred by petty accidents. From the standpoint of the whole there is neither great nor small; the most trivial event, not less than the greatest, has needed to produce it all that has gone before it from everlasting, is linked inseparably to the whole, and will have its consequences to everlasting; in blind collusion with the dark decrees of fate the incident, be it only the fall of a leaf, at the appointed time meets with its secret co-efficients and produces the foreordained catastrophe. Considered objectively as a physical event, suicide is just a natural event of the human dispensation, a necessary incident from time to time of the course of its organic evolutions and dissolutions, and no more out of keeping than any other form of death. It seems unnatural because mankind, having a tacit prejudice that the universe has been made for it and not it for the universe, accepts not death sincerely as a fit event, but thinks it a principle of morality to avoid it as long as possible in the actual world and a principle of piety to abolish it in an ideal world to come. Even the flaming preacher or the ascetic priest who has all his life been proclaiming the miseries of this sinful world, and looking forward with joyful hope to a life everlasting in unspeakable bliss, is strangely tenacious to stay where he is when the time comes for him to go; he clings stubbornly to life day after day when he is surely dying of a mortal disease or when the last faint sparks of life are flickering in the ashes of senile decay.

If a man knows not exactly why he kills himself when he is unhappy, he knows still less why he is tempted, as he is sometimes, by an urgent, persistent, scarce resistible impulse to kill some one else when, so far from wishing to kill anybody, he loathes the horrid temptation, suffers agony because of it, and is maddened by the fear of yielding to it.

Nevertheless that is one of the tormenting forms of the melancholy which I am now considering. Odious and horrible as the impulse is to him, and frantically as he prays and struggles to get rid of it, he is in a perpetual agony of apprehension that it may some day overcome his resisting forces. So it does sometimes, but not nearly so often as one would expect who listened for the first time to the tale of his woe: how violently the impulse urged him; how desperately he fought against it; how fervently he prayed to God to be delivered from it; how he trembled all over in agitation and alarm; how the perspiration poured down his body; how utterly spent he was after the agony of the panic was over. For although the affliction is continuous, it rises to a nervous crisis of acute distress from time to time; the acute exacerbation being comparable, on a higher nervous plane, to the throbbing increments of pain which rise to a pitch of fierce anguish in a neuralgia or a colic.

For the most part in these cases it is a horror and agony of apprehension which the patient suffers, rather than a real risk which he combats; and against it he tries to safeguard himself by warning those whom he fears he may injure to get out of his way or by getting out of their way. Many years ago I knew a gentleman who, being afflicted with the impulse to kill his wife and children, used to lock himself at night in the bedroom which he occupied alone and put the key on the sill outside the window, in order that, if over-tempted and nearly overcome, he might have just time and sense enough, before he succumbed, to push the key into the street and so to render it impossible for him to get out of the room. He felt compelled to give up a house which he inhabited in the neighbourhood of a high tower because of the continual provocation which the tower was to his dread that he should yield to the unceasing prompting to ascend it and throw himself down from its top. Though he gave proof of the sincerity of his fears and of the severity of his sufferings by leaving the neighbourhood, I felt no serious apprehension of a catastrophe in his case, and I never heard that he did kill either himself or any one else.

These suicidal and homicidal impulses are of the same nature as other less dangerous but much afflicting impulses which befall in persons of morbid nervous temperament who have undergone a drain of nerve-force; the two principal conditions of their occurrence being innate nerve-weakness and outward strain or drain. The cause of the drain may be any one or more than one of the many causes of nervous exhaustion; chief among which are overwork, worry, anxieties, shock and—great though least regarded cause—sexual excess in legitimate or illegitimate way. The fundamental fault of nervous structure is probably a loose-knit federation of cerebral centres, the inhibitory ties being weak, and a consequent disposition on the part of separate thought-tracts to take on a separate and in the further event a quasi-spasmodic action. Once the irregular action is established, it is a torment to the individual no matter what the particular tract and its conscious idea or impulse be. Thus he is in despair because he has the urgent impulse to do some ridiculous thing which it has come into his mind to do and has no peace until he does it; or cannot help repeating an act foolishly over and over again, only because he feels he must, when he would be only too glad to have done with it; or is constrained to think of doing an indecent act and is in a fright lest he should some day do it; or feels impelled to utter aloud a blasphemous or obscene word, and is obliged either to bite his tongue to prevent himself from speaking or to compromise matters by whispering the word to himself; or is urged by a morbid spirit of metaphysical curiosity continually to ask himself the reason of this and the reason again of that reason and so backwards the reasons of reasons without end; or has his attention strangely attracted to a particular word or number and ever afterwards is compelled to notice with surprise with what extraordinary frequency that word or number recurs in a way that seems more than natural.

If we may believe those who suffer in these ways they go through almost as much mental anguish in their conflicts as those who are suicidally or homicidally possessed—that is to say, if they resist the impulse, since to yield to it is a transient relief; only transient, however, because, if pacified to-day by indulgence, it returns to-morrow or sooner with all-triumphant vigour or is succeeded by an equally ridiculous fellow of it. There is no salvation in giving way to foolish or vicious impulsions; for the nervous system is prone to repeat the act which, whether good or bad, it has done before and thus by habit steadily to build function into structure. To do ill habitually is to structuralise iniquity and to make its practice a natural and pleasant function. Why it should have been so ordained in human events we know not, since it might conceivably have been different, but the hard fact is that the painful way of self-discipline, not the easy way of self-indulgence, is the stern law of right development, the way of righteousness in little as in great things. It is better for the soul's sake to suffer the afflictions of Job than to enjoy the felicities of Solomon. So it comes to pass that the morbid-minded persons who yield to their impulses in order to pacify them run the risk of finding themselves in the end possessed with seven devils worse than the exorcised one and their lives a sevenfold servitude to their impish promptings. Although those who resist steadfastly (and they who are prompted to a criminal or otherwise compromising act commonly do) suffer mightily in the conflict and on each renewal of it feel afresh the keenest dread that their better self will be vanquished, yet they mostly come off victorious and in the end recover their mental balance.

How to do best in order to subdue the present temptation and to lay the good foundations of recovery? To inhibit and starve morbid function by discharging the energy of it into other channels of activity, either of thought or of movement: of thought, by a resolute and steady application of mind to wholesome intellectual work, so as to strengthen sound and weaken unsound function, seeing that it is of no avail to try to effect a violent diversion during the tumult of the panic; of movement, by the temporary expedient of active and even violent exertion of some sort, were it possible, at the time of the crisis, since no one who was racing for a wager or for his life would be sorely troubled with the impulse to utter obscene words or to do an indecent act. Secondly, by closing the channels of nervous exhaustion, whatever they be, and strengthening the bodily health in the best approved ways. There is no magic in medicine to dissipate incontinently the troubles of a mind so diseased; therein the patient must minister to himself; but there are physics of mind at the base of all its psychics whereby energy used in one way inhibits its use in another way—used in a good, inhibits its use in a bad, way.

Forasmuch, however, as a person's thoughts and feelings answer to and are kept up by his circumstances, his daily life becoming a routine of almost mechanical reactions to the recurring impressions, and the depression may be so deep as to swallow up all his energies, so that he cannot so much as think of a world outside his woe, or care in the least for its interests and doings, it is necessary often to give him the invaluable external help of a complete change of surroundings. The transplantation into new conditions will supply incentives to new thoughts and feelings and do for him gradually and unconsciously the first steps of that which he cannot do for himself. What change will be best in a particular case is a question to be decided by the wisdom of an experience that is mindful to take exact account of individual character, habits, and tastes, as well as of the disease. Here, indeed, it is that the would-be-skilled adviser sometimes makes signal mistakes; having certain set rules of treating the disease, he applies them indiscriminately, doing with minds as he would do with bodies, were he to take it for granted that they had all the same appetites and required the same diet. The right psychological insight into character and the true imaginative sympathy with individual mental moods are rare and more rarely available for systematic use; so that the specially suited individual treatment, which affords the best promise of success in all cases and some promise even in bad cases, does not get itself applied opportunely, wisely and steadily. The true imaginative sympathy needed is as far as possible from the blind sympathy which, fostering the disease by yielding to every exaction of morbid feeling, proves in the end more mischievous than a stern and unsympathetic treatment. At the bottom of all sympathy there should be salutary good sense keeping up a firm reasonableness of self-control and pressing quietly, with tender tact and steady insistence, to right doing.

So much for the character and symptoms of simple melancholy or melancholy without delusion. It may be itself the whole and sole disorder, continuing for a few weeks or in some cases for months or longer, when it passes away and the patient recovers his natural spirits and the full use of his gloom-eclipsed faculties. But in other cases it is the prelude to melancholy with delusion; either a short prelude only, or a long, dragging and tedious prologue.

CHAPTER II

MELANCHOLY WITH DELUSION

In this form of depression the sad feeling is accompanied by a fixed sad idea or by a set of fixed sad ideas which crystallise, so to speak, out of or about it. The nature of feeling, sound or unsound, is to find fit expression, either in ideas which it infuses or in acts which it instigates. Out of the melancholic gloom emerge dimly and shape themselves by degrees positive delusions of thought which, outcomes of it, seem thenceforth to be sufficient explanations of it. Not a conceivable misfortune or calamity that may not be the fixed form which the woe takes, and never from the beginning of the world was a miserable wretch in so woeful a plight. Absolutely sure that he has committed the unpardonable sin, although he has no notion what that sin is, and that there is no hope for him in this world or in the world to come, he groans an unspeakable grief; he has been a hypocrite all his life and it is too late now to repent; his business is ruined, he is brought to beggary, his wife and children will have to go to the workhouse; he is full of self-reproach, lamentation and mourning for some sin of omission or commission, in business-transactions or private relations—neglect, error, or fraud—which, though it is not the crime which he now magnifies it into, may not always be so entirely imaginary as his friends suppose; he maintains that he has been guilty of embezzlement or forgery in consequence of which his friends shun him, his acquaintance speak ill of him, strangers in the street jeer and mock at him, and the police are watching or pursuing him; he has contracted a loathsome disease which has made his body a source of foul infection and will cause him to be done away with in some unheard-of horrible manner; or he is afflicted with a disease the like of which was never seen before and which will doom him to endless suffering, since, notwithstanding it, he never can die a natural death. Such and of such character are the plaints which the sufferer makes, every sufferer deeming his estate the worst: of all the sad cases ever heard of in the world none ever equalled his. Always it is some irremediable calamity, often huge and vague, which a disordered imagination constructs as the adequate or inadequate form and expression of the misery.

In the ideal calamity we distinguish the form and colour of the thought and feeling of the age, nation and special surroundings; for an insane person cannot, any more than a sane person, get outside the social and intellectual atmosphere of his time and place; to do that would be nothing less than to get out of his own mental being. A savage might be sunk in an abysmal melancholy of remorse because his filial piety accused the neglect on his part to kill and eat his aged parent; a Moslem lady, because she had exposed her face unveiled in the street; an English lady, because she had shown her leg when lifting her dress, albeit quite unconcerned at the public exposure of her naked back, shoulders and breasts. If a Christian were pursued by the Furies to-day, as Orestes was of old, it would be as wonderful an anachronism as if Orestes in his day had been pursued by a devil who was not then invented. In the Middle Ages when witchcraft flourished in Europe and pious Christians showed their holy zeal by hunting out the witches and getting them burnt alive, the witches were the terrors to melancholics which the police are now; and at that time it was plainly impossible for the patient persecuted by voices to believe, as he often does now, that the persecuting voices were conveyed through a telephone. The awful conviction that an almighty and merciful God had singled him out for everlasting torment, as a fearful example and warning to mankind, because of a sin which he committed blindly, if he committed it at all, and which other persons placidly commit daily, never could have fascinated with its horror one whose mind was not imbued with the doctrine of Jewish and Christian scriptures. But its monstrous irrationality does not shock the reason of him who believes, on the authority of those scriptures, that God specially commissioned an evil spirit to lie to Ahab with the express purpose of luring him to his destruction. During the commotion occasioned by the murders of the notorious so-called "Jack the Ripper"[1] in Whitechapel, there were melancholics who, immensely overrating their genius, imagined that they were, or would be suspected of being, that unique criminal. With changing times and events the ideas of melancholy change; it is the inspiring feeling of misery which remains fundamentally the same. Sane or insane, as the ever-recurring rhapsodies and threnodies of poets prove, man goes on expressing or striving to express the same elemental feelings in different forms, only performing variations of the same old tunes.

The sad feeling in which the melancholic mind is engulfed takes away nearly all feeling else of the real world and its doings. The persons and events thereof seem far off, aloof, as if they were not real but were forms lacking substance, the figures and shows of a pageant; not because they are far off and unreal, but because the deadened feeling, precluding an interested touch and hold of them, thus interposes an impassable distance. To a paralysed man

---

[1] *Jack the Ripper:* So brief is the duration of great fame or great infamy that the exploits of this notable criminal are already well-nigh forgotten, though they excited a sensation throughout the world at the time, and a panic in Whitechapel where they took place. Within a short space of time and a narrow compass of space he cut the throats of several women of the unfortunate class and ripped up their bellies. Their bodies, mutilated in the same way, were found lying in different streets almost immediately after death, but not the least trace of the murderer was ever discovered. He has enjoyed a nameless fame.

who cannot walk a step a mile is infinity; to a man who, sick unto death, cannot live out the day, to-morrow is eternity: to the former it is all one whether he is asked to walk a mile or ten miles; to the other, all one whether he is asked to interest himself in the mightiest or the meanest event. What lover, infatuated by his passion, would not rather have a city destroyed or a navy sunk than have his mistress's little finger ache? What fond mother, wrapt up in her only child, would not in her heart of hearts care less that a thousand red Indians should be slowly starved to death than that it should suffer a day's fierce pain? Would all the arguments in the world convince her that its death, A.D. 1894, was not a bigger event than the death of a Chinese baby in the village of Chungpew, B.C. 1894? Of all relations space and time are the most relative; when the sense of relation is lost, they are practically meaningless.

According to the measure of his self-absorption is the manner of the deluded melancholic's look and conduct. Most often the absorption is not so complete and disabling as to prevent him from going about, with drooping head and slow-sad gait, desolate and in misery; and even perhaps doing as much as attend mechanically to his affairs, without heart in them or hope of them. For it is not his understanding of things but his relish of them which is at fault; not knowledge but desire and energy which fail him. It costs him infinite effort to make the least exertion; being in a waking nightmare he feels, like one in a real nightmare, as if he could not move to help himself. At the same time he is capable of giving an intelligent opinion about his affairs, though he protests that he cannot grasp them in the least and that it is absurd to ask him about them; nay, may even be tranquil and quietly interested when diverted from his morbid self on to lines of rational conversation and occupation. Immediately afterwards, however, he sinks back into brooding gloom and the monotonous unloading of it in groans and moans, in lamentation and wailing, in restless pacings and agitated movements, in ejaculations of distress and gestures of despair.

Two things are evident: first, that he is not so completely engulfed in misery as he looks, not always nor all unhappy; secondly, that his expressions of affliction outgo the reality. He is not actually so unhappy as one who, labouring under extreme depression, has his whole thought saturated with woe; for the delusion has concentrated the sadness and precipitated it, so to speak, into a definite and apprehensible form, to which some kind of mental adjustment may be made. Always is it the vague, the vast, the unknown, the incomprehensible and ineffable, to which no reflex adaptation can be made, that occasions the most bewildering fear, the most impotent credulity, the most abject prostration of mind; so soon as something having form, something definite, which may be in a measure grasped and talked about, has been set up as an explanation —so soon, that is, as he has ceased to drift on a sea of sorrow without a shore—there is comparative tranquillity of mind. If fear invented the gods, it relieved and assuaged itself by the invention. Nor does it matter much what the imagined cause is provided only that it obtain belief and the mind relief: it is all one whether it be Jove or Jahveh who thunders, so long as it is somebody who can be invoked and propitiated. The nature of man being to believe, he will necessarily, in default of the true, believe the false. The melancholic who is in a pitiable state of frenzied agitation because of the fear of death becomes comparatively calm when he has definitely resolved to kill himself and set himself deliberately to plan and provide the means. Uncertainty and vague apprehension cause agitation of mind; rest and tranquillity follow the decision, good or ill, that has been definitely made, the creed that is definitely believed, the despair that is definitely accepted. So it comes to pass that the melancholic manages to make some sort of adjustment to the woeful delusion which has got itself formed in his mind and goes on for the most part in monotonous iteration of it with a sort of mechanical composure. Damned to all eternity or certain that he will not live out the day, he performs the operations of his daily life as if death and damnation were ordinary incidents of it. His groaning ejaculations of distress or moaning supplications to God, aloud or under his breath, do not preclude observation of passing events and are perhaps interrupted by a natural comment on them from time to time: the wailing refrain to himself of "God have mercy on me," as he walks along the street, by the casual remark "What pretty eyes that lady had!" In the end it looks sometimes as if he were averse to part with his delusion.

The truth is that even in the depth of his woe he is prone to overcharge and exaggerate its utterance unconsciously, out of the desire and endeavour to produce in others an equivalent impression of the sufferings which he feels at the same time that they cannot be made to realise and suspects they think not so real as they are; and that, after the worst is over, he repeats mechanically the cries, when he no longer feels the grief, of despair. As many sane persons are prone to do, such melancholics say more than they mean in the endeavour to make others feel what they mean: they do not suffer as much as they think they do nor think they suffer as much as they say they do. They are like infatuated lovers who, straining ludicrously the capacities of language in their vain endeavours to reveal to one another what they feel, invoke eternities and infinities, trying thus to express in terms of extension the intensities of their present feelings; or like the religious ecstatic who, under the spell and stress of indefinite feelings which he deems divine, exhausts infinities, inconceivabilities, ineffabilities, and the like thought-void terms when he vainly strives to describe the rapture which transported him. The need of such much-labouring persons is a clever Socratic midwife to help them not only to bring forth, but thereafter to perceive the abortion which it is that they have brought forth. So too the zealous bigot who, ardent to exhibit his immense sense of the significance of sin, proclaims with flaming eloquence the sinner's doom of unspeakable torment through all eternity enjoys the self-discharging exercise and does not really mean the damnation which he thus fiercely denounces; his big and burning words are the pleasing outlets of big and hot feelings, not the expressions of definite thoughts or belief. He is eased by such utterances of inflamed nonsense. Some persons, when they call a man a scoundrel, mean no more than that they do not agree with him.

Another circumstance which tends to kindle suspicion that the melancholic's story outgoes the reality of his sufferings is the huge disproportion between the alleged offence and the tremendous consequences with which he charges it; the misery is declared to be so great while the fault is seen to be so small. And truly, were a man's external world outside him, there would be cogent reason in the suspicion that when anguish of mind because of some petty offence, real or imagined, makes as much show of sorrow as that which goes along with the delusion of eternal damnation, there must be some exaggeration in the expression of it. But inasmuch as everybody's outward and visible world is fashioned inwardly and invisibly within him, it ought not to surprise us that the melancholic mind moulds its world to its will and cannot then throw off notions which are absurd and inconsistent to the common sense of a child. What mind held in the thrall of a particular passion or prejudice ever can so detach itself as to see and judge things as they are? The monster in possession devours all impressions and wrests them to its nurture and nature.

Any one who lived with a melancholic for twenty-four hours and watched his ways and doings could not fail to think him one of the most self-indulgent, perhaps selfish, of mortals. Certainly his doings have all the look, if not the substance, of selfish indulgence; for it is of the essence of insanity to inhibit the higher, and to accentuate the lower qualities of a character. He makes not the least useful exertion himself and, when urged to it by others, soon leaves it off; bewails the ruinous condition of his affairs,

which he knows at the bottom of his heart a steady
examination of them would not confirm; neglects his dress
and becomes more and more careless of personal cleanliness
out of an indolent dislike of exertion; eats slovenly and
voraciously while complaining of distaste òf food and of
intense discomfort after it; or eats insufficiently and capriciously while complaining of never feeling satisfied; shuns
society because he feels obliged to exert self-control in company, and seeks only surroundings in which, being under
no sense of restraint, he nurses his malady; laments his
sexual impotence while he refrains not from provoking
the proofs of it; accuses his relations of unkindness and
torments them with his irritability and exactions at the
same time that he refuses to be separated from them and
cannot bear them out of his sight; cares only to wail his
sad case and to rehearse over and over again the monotonous tale of his misery in the same weary words. The
one positive pleasure which he might appear to have is
the pleasure of being miserable: he woos grief as if he
were in love with it, hugs despair as if it were his bride.

But is all this self-indulgence the selfishness which it
looks? It is the indulgence of a partial, maimed and
morbid self, not of a whole, sane and true self. He is
simply a reflex organic machine whose sensibility to feel
and power to apprehend and act in all relations are lessened
or suspended, because it is set to a certain special abnormal
action and, locked in disorder, cannot adjust itself otherwise. Not indulgence, therefore, but impotence is the real
note of its nature. The probable pathological condition of
things is an exorbitant and predominant, almost exclusive,
activity of certain brain-tracts charged with sad feeling—
not unlike the sort of activity which has motor issue
otherwise in spasm or convulsion of muscles—entailing a
molecular sluggishness and, according to its degree, a
lessened or suspended function of other tracts. The man
is mesmerised by his misery, so to speak, entranced or
possessed by it; and, like the mesmeric or hypnotic subject,
he cannot do what he is forbidden by his possessor to do and

cannot help doing what he is bidden to do. The result is that for the most part he does those things which he ought not to do and leaves undone those things which he ought to do. For him, too, if he would have health in him, the stern and salutary law of right doing is to do what he leaves undone and to leave undone what he does: to leave off his plaints and wailings and to apply himself to reasonable work of some kind, were it only the smallest fraction of work.

According to the degree of exclusive action of the morbid brain-tract and its more or less isolation, is the degree of incapacitation of the directly unaffected tracts and by consequence the special complexion of the disorder. The delusion may have weak hold, when it will come and go and mix among other thoughts, without blending into true communion with them—as happens at the beginning of the derangement when it has not yet got its full hold and towards the end thereof when it is losing its hold—and there will then be little or nothing noticeable in the patient's appearance and conduct; or it may have so strong a hold as to keep exclusive possession and practically to paralyse other thought-tracts, when the appearance and conduct, translating the inward state of things, will tell the tale. In the one case he shows the presence of mind, for the mind, being there and only maimed locally, can be solicited to a present use; in the other, an absence or eclipse of mind, because the function of the largest area of it is suspended.

When the delusion has got partial hold of the mind or full hold of a part of it only, there is nothing to preclude perfect lucidity in relation to matters that lie outside its sphere of influence. But the difficulty in a particular case is to make the delimitation of that influence, which for the most part is more deep, subtile and widespread than appears on the surface. That a person thus afflicted should perceive plainly the derangement of another person similarly afflicted, while unable to appreciate his own alienation, which meanwhile is gross and palpable to his fellow-sufferer, is a surprise to the sane person who, seeing the mote in his neighbour's, cannot see the beam in his own eye; but it is perhaps a more reasonable surprise how wanting in logic his conduct is from the standpoint of his own deluded thought. He does not reason rightly from his wrong premises, inasmuch as he does not do those things consistently which, were his delusion true thought, he ought to do, and does those things which, were it true, he ought not to do. Being compelled in the general to live, move and be with his kind in the real world, a unit of a community, in spite of his special morbid thought by which he is so much estranged from it as almost to belong to another sphere of being, he does for the most part as others do, his special creed notwithstanding, and while believing and maintaining that he cannot and does not. He is a dissevered being, virtually two selves not one self, drawn in two different directions, one self having to retire and be silent when the other self takes the lead and acts. Just indeed as his body disposes of the food which perchance he has the delusion never does pass or can pass into his stomach or beyond it, so likewise much of the ordinary tenour of his daily life is a practical refutation of the delusion that he will be carried off in the night to a death of torture and never see another morning.

In insanity no more than in sanity is belief usually the consistent outcome of a fully developed character. In the sane it is mostly the partial result of a nature moulded in a particular fashion by training and circumstances, in the insane the result of brain-tracts distracted into disorder by disease. What is human history but a long record, amazing or amusing, of the inconsistencies and contradictions of human beliefs and actions? Is it possible to pronounce any inconsistency too monstrous ever to have proceeded from one and the same person? However logic may boggle at the conclusion theoretically, it is necessary to avow practically that in the dispensation of human things it is not forbidden to a person to be two beings, now one and now another, when he is not an incoherent interplay between the one and the other.

Melancholia with Stupor.

One form of melancholy has received the special name of *melancholia cum stupore* or *melancholia attonita* because of the blank and torpid, sometimes quasi-astonied, look of the patient, who exhibits the spectacle of an almost complete mental and bodily inertness. His state is an inert stupor.[1] As there are necessarily different degrees of such stupor, to which different aspects of manner and behaviour answer, one might, I think, describe three varieties:

(*a*) In a cataleptic or quasi-cataleptic variety the mind is held in the grip of some vast and fearful delusion which dominates his whole being. His eyes have the fixed look of astonied horror or are sometimes tight closed in a spasmodic way; the features are contracted; he stands, sits, kneels, crouches or lies all day in one almost motionless posture, so little sensible to stimulation that snuff applied to the nostrils does not provoke a sneeze, and a sharp pin prick elicits no more sign of response perhaps than a quiver of the eyelid or a low grunt; he makes a stubborn passive resistance to everything done for him or which it is proposed he should do, even to taking food of any kind, and his arm or leg, if lifted up, sometimes keeps that attitude for an indefinite time, only falling back slowly into a position of rest. In this state he remains for days, weeks, even months, sleeping badly, and so rapt from natural thought and feeling in a morbid ecstasy that he is sometimes, but not always, insensible to the ordinary calls and instincts of nature. When he recovers he remembers and can give an account of the paralysing horrors which entranced him, as well as of the things that went on around him when he seemed unconscious of them. This is one form of so-called melancholy with stupor; a *melancholia attonita* proper, in which the person, rapt in an ecstasy of horror, is mind-locked, not mindless.

---

[1] *Inert stupor* has apparently been found too vulgar a term to describe the main feature; for one author has proposed to transform it into *anergic stupor* and to mark a variety of disease by the bastard name.

Inquiring how it comes on, we find that it is most often a development of ordinary melancholia, the patient passing from the state of active misery and the expression of it by word and deed into this quasi-cataleptic ecstacy or rapture of horror. But it may be caused quickly, almost instantaneously, by a great moral or physical shock. In one memorable example that fell under my notice it followed an astounded coachman's discovery of his faithless wife in the act of adultery with his master in the stable. Though the patient was more like an inert mechanism than an animated being for a whole year, requiring to be moved from place to place against his passive resistance, and standing all day long, like a statue, wherever he was placed, he woke up suddenly to lucidity and rational conversation one morning, relapsing into stupor the next day.

(*b*) A second condition of stupor is the lethargic form. Here, however, there is a complete or pretty nigh complete blank or waste of mind; there is no melancholy proper. The features are flabby and atonic, the eyes dull and vacant, no dream of horror in them, the pupil is commonly dilated, there is dull sensibility or it may be insensibility of skin, and the bodily movements are without form, flaccid and inert. The habits are dirty, but the sleep is fairly good. The patient does not resist stubbornly, having not mind enough for that; he is passive, without initiative, and must be moved about mechanically. When he recovers he cannot tell what he thought of during the seizure or says that he thought of nothing. This form of so-called *melancholia cum stupore* represents a state of things which is more properly an acute dementia, and is usually called so when it befalls suddenly from some great physical or moral shock. Essentially it is more a mindless or demented than a melancholic state; the vacant eyes, the toneless features, the insensibility and inert apathy of body tell the same story of a more or less complete paralysis of mental function. It is a sort of mental palsy which may be caused suddenly in feeble and neurotic subjects by a great mental or physical shock or by causes of nervous exhaustion; sometimes it supervenes on existing mental disorder rather abruptly in such persons. Between its state of mindless stupor and the previously described state of mind-rapt stupor, there are actually in nature all degrees of intermediate states of mixed desolation and horror of mind; they bridge the artificial gap between a demented waste and the melancholic cramp of mind in which nine-tenths of it are paralysed because one-tenth of it is in spasm.

(c) A third form might be described as the quasi-somnambulistic variety. Although there is no inert stupor, there is a stupor of perception, since the patient is so absorbed in his delirium that he cannot perceive. He is not in actual torpor, either rigid or inert, but, absorbed in his delirium, keeps on repeating automatically the same exclamations of reproach, fear or distress, unregarding what is said or done to him; not unconscious of surroundings, he is not conscious of them in their full and true character, for he is only sensible to impressions so far as he can translate them into the forms of his deluded notions and thus add fuel to his distress, taking no notice of such as he cannot so transform. His delirium is like the dream of the somnambulist; like him, he is awake only to impressions that are suited to or can assimilate with the current of it; and his conduct is dominated by its peculiar activity. The state is really an aggravated and more active state of ordinary delusional melancholia, the mind being more rapt in delirium, and it passes in one direction by intermediate instances into it, and in another direction by intermediate instances into *melancholia attonita*.

As it is not nature which makes divisions but man who imposes his divisions on it, the prudent inquirer will not make too much of them. What is called stupor is not really a definite and fixed state, of such constant quality and quantity as to denote a special nervous disorder; it is no more than a descriptive name comprehending very different degrees of mental obscuration and palsy which go along with several forms of mental disorder. In its slightest degrees stupor is a not unfrequent symptom after ordinary mania, in deeper degree after puerperal mania; in still deeper degree for a short time after epilepsy and acute alcoholic delirium, and for a longer time after mania in young, frail and neurotic subjects; it is conspicuous sometimes in the so-called mania of persecution when this reaches the climax of *melancholia attonita;* and it is occasionally observed in the course of general paralysis, alternating then perhaps pretty regularly with periods of exaltation. In fact, there is not a single form of insanity in which it may not be met with in greater or less degree. Last and best evidence of the absurdity of counting it the mark of a separate disease, the same patient who is in a state of speechless stupor one day shall be in a raving excitement the next day, passing abruptly from the one to the other state.

How far the stupor is from being so fixed and complete as it appears to be, when it looks fixed and complete, and how purely functional the disorder beneath it then is, we perceive both by the sudden way in which it may come and go and by the remarkable remissions and variations of symptoms. Occasional quite sudden restorations to lucidity last for a day or two or only for a few hours and go as suddenly as they come. Moreover, when the patient is restored to his right mind, he can give a pretty good account of what went on around him during the seeming suspension of it; he was nowise the senseless block he looked. Nor is his incapacity to make the least exertion always as genuine as it appears to be; for he may seize his opportunity and exert himself to make his observations when he thinks himself alone and unwatched.[1] I knew

[1] Morel relates the case of a woman, *æt.* 40, who was insane for many years, having at first strong delusions of poisoning, but falling afterwards into such a state of inertia and stupor as to be thought demented. She was indifferent to what went on, motionless, and answered all questions in low and mechanical monosyllables. All the while, however, she was writing down secretly day by day on concealed pieces of paper most complex delusions of persecution, not of poisoning only but of other persecutions, and also the incidents of the day, after her fashion, and the answers to the questions to which she was dumb.

one gentleman in this condition who had to be carried from
bed to couch and back day after day for nearly two years,
never doing the least thing to help himself during all that
time, not so much as moving hand or foot voluntarily, never
speaking a word or taking a morsel of food that was not
forced down his throat, who nevertheless, when he believed
himself alone, sometimes raised himself in bed on his
elbow and looked about him, and, after his recovery, had
a very fair knowledge of what had taken place in the world
during his torpor. The Franco-German war had been
fought during the long period of his transport, and he had
gathered from the reading and conversation of his attendants
and from furtive glances at newspapers a very fair knowledge
of its events. He was able also, after his recovery, to recall
and relate the horrors by which he had been fascinated and
paralysed. Evidently there are either temporary relaxations
of the spasm of morbid thought from time to time, especially
when, the patient being alone, it is not kept up by the misinterpreted impressions of persons and things which, thus
misinterpreted, act as stimuli to it by their presence; or,
not being so complete as to produce entire paralysis of other
mental functions, there is sufficient activity of them to
maintain some consciousness of surrounding things, notwithstanding that there is not the capacity to perceive
them as they are and act rightly in relation to them.

Moreover, far from being uniformly the torpid beings
which they seem generally, some of these patients make
occasional demonstrations of activity: one may struggle
blindly and stubbornly against being dressed, put to bed,
washed, and the like; another strike out suddenly when
irritated by a jeering or otherwise provoking remark; a
third may startle those about him by interposing quietly
a relevant and rational remark in reference to something
which is being talked of in his presence; a fourth, suddenly
and without warning, make a desperate and frantic attempt
at suicide; another utters or mutters mechanically the same
words or exclamations of bewildered despair continually;
and others show by a quick turn of the eye, by the con-

traction of a feature, by a decent movement to adjust a disordered dress, by some intelligent gesture or attitude, that they are not entirely cut off from relations with the course of things around them. If an attempt be made by words or acts to provoke or irritate the patient to step out of his torpidity he will sometimes, while remaining still or silent, show in his countenance, perhaps by a blush or by the filling of his eyes with tears or by a quiver of features, that he is touched sensibly by what is said or done to him. In like manner, when he is fed by the stomach-pump because of his stubborn refusal of food, he may betray his angry affliction or resentment by facial contortions or by energetic struggles of resistance. They make a great mistake who, having the charge of such patients, assume that it matters not what is said or done in their presence.

Terrible, though inadequate, is the story which, after recovery from the delusional form, the patient tells of the nightmare of horror in which his mind was fixed. He was in hell and the persons about him seemed devils whose attentions were modes of torment; or he was encompassed by flames of fire through which hideous faces mocked or menaced him; he was surrounded by brigands and murderers whose pistols were pointed at his head; he was on the edge of a bottomless abyss into which, if he made one step forward, he would plunge headlong; he was an unspeakably loathsome object at which birds, beasts, trees, assuming monstrous forms, grimaced and mocked; he heard indescribable noises and fearful sounds, such as mortal never heard before, or the piercing and heart-rending cries of tortured relations, or threats of the most horrible torments, or one imperative voice which commanded him not to utter a word or, with resistless force, fixed him in immobility by the awful warning—"Stir a step or move a limb, and you are a dead man." Not Dante with all his intensity of imagination could ever reach to the delineation of such a hell as a mind thus possessed makes for itself. Meanwhile he hears and sees what is said and done around him, but is utterly unable to respond by putting the motor system in proper use to apprehend it, or to act in relation to it, for that system is locked in impotence by the cramp-like action of the morbid thought-tract and the paralysis of the rest of its machinery. The condition is essentially like a nightmare, although it is actually a daymare. As in dreams, too, sense of definite time is lost: on the one hand, the patient sits, stands, or crouches motionless hour after hour and day after day in one position, as if frozen there, without apparent weariness and probably without consciousness of himself as an object distinct from objects around, looking as if, were he not disturbed, he would remain so for ever; on the other hand, to him hours seem days, days months, months years, for there is no succession of events in the stagnant contents of his consciousness to give measure and meaning to its experience.[1]

With the mental torpor go other symptoms of sluggish vitality. The temperature of the body is lowered, very much as it is in hybernating animals, and in like manner the respiration is slow and shallow. The pulse is small and slow; there is much vasomotor relaxation; and the extremities are inclined to be cold and blue, with a tendency to œdema and, in the worse cases, to purpuric patches. Saliva dribbles from the mouth and mucus hangs from the nose. A general atonic state of the tissues of the body betrays the absence of the proper animating nerve-force. Tactile sensibility is much blunted, sometimes nearly extinct; there is then no reaction even when the back of the throat is tickled, and the pupils respond not to light. But here also the semblance of loss is often much more than the actual loss; for it is plain that some patients feel in a measure when they are tickled or pricked, who either suppress or are powerless to express their feelings.

[1] In the Report of the Montrose Asylum for 1881, Dr. Howden relates the case of a melancholic patient with delusion who was admitted in 1860. Two years afterwards he became quite mute and was reported to be demented. But in 1875 he began to speak in a scarcely audible whisper, and, going on to improve, was discharged in 1881. On recovery, he said that the period of thirteen years of silence was a complete blank to him and appeared as if it was only six or seven years. His silence all that time was due to a feeling that he had not the power to speak.

So much for melancholy with stupor. The signal antithesis of it is what is called *acute melancholia*. Then there is acute and irritable distress, apprehensive disquietude, feverish agitation, active anguish; for the constitution is not sunk submissive under the stroke of oppression and, moaning its fate, tame to despair, but, possessing energy enough to resent its suffering, it rebels passionately against it in demonstrative exclamations and acts. The two opposite spectacles of melancholy might be compared to the opposite effects produced by a terrible fright on two differently constituted persons or on the same person in different circumstances: in the one case, he is so completely paralysed by it as not to make the least effort to help himself; in the other, he instinctively puts his self-conservative energies into agitated struggles of defence or escape. What then are the prominent symptoms of acute melancholy? Restless pacing up and down the room or unquiet wanderings from room to room, ceaseless lamentations and ejaculations of distress, cries and shrieks of apprehension or despair, perpetual moanings and groanings, rocking of body to and fro, wringing of hands, beating of head and face or rubbing of the skin into sores, pulling out of the hair, biting of nails to the quick,—these and like gestures and acts of unrest and grief betray the active misery which, agitation being its chief note, has sometimes received the name of *melancholia agitata*. Between it and the opposite state of melancholic stupor, however, there are intermediate cases marked by varying states of torpor and agitation; indeed the same patient may be in an apathetic stupor at one time and at another time in a state of frenzied agitation. Very near situate in such cases are the pathological conditions of stupor and storm. Painful to behold as the exhibitions of acute misery are, there is still so much look of mechanical monotony in them and they are reiterated in such a quasi-automatic fashion that the dispassionate observer might be tempted sometimes to ask himself whether the patient really feels as much misery as the show of feeling might indicate, and whether, if he did, he could continue in such good bodily condition as he maintains. He certainly can check them for a time when he thinks fit and even forget to display them when his attention is attracted elsewhere. Perhaps it is that they are continued in a measure as habit when their original motive has waned much in force. However that may be, just as there are transitional cases, marked by varying degrees of excitement, between torpid and acute melancholy, so from the acute form we may pass by intermediate steps of still increasing excitement to an *acute delirious melancholy*, in which the disorderly doings are disconnected, fractional, tumultuous and involuntary. It has its counterpart in an *acute delirious mania* from which it differs only, so far as it does differ, by its prevailing note of acute fear and by the more monotonous march of its symptoms.

Acute Delirious Melancholia.

What are the leading features of acute delirious melancholy? Most notable is a vague and very agitated apprehension, an acute panic of distress, which every sight, sound, word or circumstance seems only to stimulate. Instead of impressions being apprehended rightly, they are misapprehended and, however innocent, misconstrued into the language of its frenzy. The patient defends himself against help and everything done for him with shrieks and cries of alarm, with gabbling exclamations, with aimless movements of frantic resistance. No heed is given to food which, when offered, is pushed aimlessly aside or frantically rejected; words of comfort and reason are addressed in vain not to deaf ears but to ears deaf to their meaning, being repelled as if they were fierce menaces to life; familiar objects are in vain presented to eyes which, seeing, see them not as what they are; attempts to do service and explain its nature are met perhaps with senseless resistance and disconnected exclamations of distress. "I won't be made an animal. I won't be made an animal," was the frenzied refrain of a woman who pushed, clutched, struggled, writhed, twisted in a panic of senseless antagonism to everything done for her, until she died from exhaustion.

The acts, so far as they bear the stamp of form, are for the most part movements of vague and violent resistance or defence, instigated by formless terrors or wild fragmentary delusions: quasi-convulsive pushings, strugglings, kickings, strikings, contortions, rigid clutchings and headlong rushes, which are much automatic although with maintenance of voluntary form. Besides these there are sometimes grimacings and gnashings of teeth, sobbings, howlings in regularly sequent jerks, rigid tremors of arms and legs, or rhythmical movements of them repeated with mechanical uniformity and kept up with astonishing persistency. Now and again a frenzied self-abuse adds a more repulsive feature to the mad whirl of disorder. Without doubt these acts are essentially involuntary, albeit, having the voluntary form, they are *acts*, not mere disordered movements — formally purposive movements, whole or fragmentary, but violent and without present purpose. It might help to a better understanding of their nature to reflect on the shrieks, and howls, the muscular contractions and bodily contortions caused by the acute pain of physical torture; which are manifestly neither purely voluntary nor purely reflex, but rather reflex movements aggravated voluntarily or voluntary movements intensified into spasmodically reflex.

Day and night generally the frenzy goes on, with little or no true sleep, until the patient's forces are spent and death ensues. Not that the course of things is one of uniform fury; there are usually remissions and sometimes singularly lucid intermissions, followed soon by exacerbations of panic and outbreaks of violent struggling. It is throughout difficult to get food of any sort taken, even when it is forced into the mouth; at last even liquids are not swallowed, owing perhaps in some degree to loss of sensibility and of reflex muscular action. As the exhaustion increases, a typhoid state supervenes, with fœtor of breath, subsultus tendinum, and diarrhœa; and sometimes bronchitis, congestive pneumonia, and gangrene of the lung are incidents of the decline and hasten the fatal ending. Recovery, albeit exceptional, does now and then take place.

Remaining Symptoms of Melancholia.

Having described the special features of the opposite extremes of melancholia, namely, the torpid and the delirious varieties, it remains now to complete the description of its ordinary symptoms. The organic functions, like the thoughts and movements, are generally dull and sluggish, except where there is active irritation and agitation: the pulse usually feeble and toneless, perhaps irregular in force and frequency, sometimes intermittent, but in cases of excited melancholia tense, quick, full, with strong heart-beat, as if there were some irritating impediment to the circulation in the capillaries to be overcome; tongue apt to be foul and frequently coated with a thick whitish fur; digestion performed without sense of satisfaction, if not with actual discomfort, the process feeling to the patient no better than if it were the digestion of wooden food by a wooden stomach, and being perhaps accompanied or followed by large and frequent eructations of wind; the bowels constipated because partly of defective or disordered action of the liver, partly of atony of the muscular walls of the intestines, partly of dulness of sensation whereby desire of relief is not felt or, if felt, not attended to and by attention quickened; sexual desire and power nearly or entirely extinguished. All reflexes, mental as well as bodily, are blunted and slackened.

General dulness of tactile sensation is evident in some cases, and in the quasi-hysterical and ecstatic patients local patches or areas of complete insensibility occur in irregular fashion. Perhaps the gnawing of the fingers to the quick, the rubbing of deep sores on the face, head or neck, the plucking out of the hair, even of every hair on the body sometimes, which is done without any sign of pain nay, with apparent relief, may be due to disordered sensation or be unconscious efforts to provoke a missing sensibility. Not improbably too a bluntness of the tactile and organic sensibilities has its share in the causation of that strange feeling of changed self and of the incapacity to realise the feeling of a true self which is so keen a distress in simple melancholia and, in further degree, is at the bottom of the delusions of the melancholic who asserts that he has no throat, no stomach, no intestines, or the like. There is a low fund, therefore a low supply to the brain, of the visceral energy which, imparting the inspiration of feeling and being the real organic basis of the *ego*, is the deep source of vigour, self-confidence, and of the relish of life. In some cases there is easy and profuse sweating, and it is curious to notice occasional examples of partial sweatings, one part or perhaps one half of the body being in a sweat while the rest of it is dry. Presumably the double brain divides its work and sets its different parts or its two halves to different tasks.

Such bodily derangements, though often met with, together or separately, are neither characteristic nor constant; for it is certain that profound melancholy may come on and go on, especially when of hereditary origin, without appreciable bodily disorder. A patient who complains of suffering the utmost distress after taking food will nevertheless eat gluttonously; and it is impossible to believe of another that if his agony of mind and body were so great as he describes it, he would not become emaciated and exhausted, whereas he actually keeps up or even gains weight.

Sleep, the last refuge of the unhappy, is often denied to the unhappy melancholic. At worst, he cannot get to sleep at all, but tosses about all night on his bed in restless anguish of mind; or he sleeps for two or three hours when he goes to bed, after that waking suddenly to begin a revolving round of thought-torture and getting no more sleep for the rest of the night; or he has short snatches of unquiet slumber disturbed by horrid dreams; or has sleep so light, so shallow that it is no sleep (a "thin sleep," as one patient was wont to call it) which can hardly be distinguished from waking, and he protests that it was not real sleep or that he has not slept at all. It is an error to speak of sleep as if it were of constant quality when it really differs as much in quality as it does in quantity. One might conclude sometimes that the sensory and motor centres were asleep while the psychical centres were painfully awake, for the patient is persecuted with horrid dreams and visions; so vivid sometimes that they persist for a short time as hallucinations when he wakes, his overridden senses only gradually recovering their power of apprehending objects.

On the other hand, there may be neither comfort nor refreshment in sleep because it is too absolute, the self having been so completely cut off from its relations with the external world and extinguished temporarily that there is an uneasy sadness on waking, a sort of uncanny feeling of losing self too much, and the recurrence of such sleep is dreaded rather than desired. Perhaps some metabolic product has been formed in or entered the blood which has acted like a narcotic on the brain and put the organic life too much to sleep. The melancholic who labours under delusions of persecution, getting sleep of this heavy sort, may come to think that it is not natural sleep and to suspect that drugs have been administered secretly to him in order to throw him into a state of stupor in which his enemies can practise on him as they please. One observation may, I think, be made with regard to sleepless patients—that while it is difficult or impossible for them to sleep in the silence, solitude and darkness of night, because the torturing thoughts then have free play for undistracted activity, they can sleep in the daytime when persons are moving about and noises going on in the streets; indeed, they sometimes help by sleeping in the day to spoil their sleep at night. Noises that are unheeded, above all things not awaited with listening expectation, sometimes help rather than hinder sleep. Instead of seeking for perfect quiet and solitude at night

they might do better to place themselves in the midst of
noise and movement, no matter how great these were so
long as they were pretty regular and monotonous.

There are conditions of the nervous system in which
sleep will not come, however urgently longed for and whatever be done to entice or enforce it. Bad nights in which
little sleep can be got are usual before melancholia, but in
some cases there is a sleeplessness which is positively acute.
It is not then a matter of simple irritability of brain and
of unrest of mind, for there are palpitations of the heart,
flutterings of a disordered sympathetic system, and a keen
agitation of distress like in kind to, but less in degree than,
that which occurs in melancholic panics. In one case
which came under my notice a lady who had been
previously a little out of sorts only, went to bed feeling
then pretty well; but she could not sleep at all, had
distressing palpitations of the heart and was overwhelmed
with an indefinable anguish: the sort of apprehensive
anguish which those who have gone through it wonder
how they could have gone through, and declare they
would not go through again for worlds. Next day she
seemed to be fairly well. But in the night the bewildering
anguish recurred and this time passed directly into acute
melancholia. In all its degrees of disorder there is no
greater enemy to sound sleep and happy moods of mind
than a disquieted sympathetic system.

Thus much concerning the ordinary features of melancholy and their general pathological import. Certain marked
features, oftentimes but not invariably present, justly deserve
special notice. These are suicide, homicide, and hallucinations.

Suicide.

So much has been already said of suicide that little
more need now be said. By the deluded melancholic it
may be done not only from inability to bear the burden of
misery any longer and from other motives of a more or less
rational sort, but at the direct prompting of his hallucina-

tion or delusion. He obeys the dictates of an imaginary voice which urges him to kill himself or reproaches him as a wretched coward who has not the pluck to do it; he feels himself a useless castaway and so great a burden to his family, who, he thinks, are weary of him and his woes, or are being ruined by the expense and trouble to which he is putting them, that he resolves to rid them of him; he starves himself to death under the deluded conviction that being penniless he cannot pay for food, or that his gullet is closed, that he has no stomach and intestines, and that consequently no food can pass into or through him; he is such an odious and loathsome wretch that he ought not to live a minute longer among his kind; he believes that he is afflicted with a serious disease which must prove fatal and, tormented with the perpetual fear of death, dies to be rid of the fear.

The occasion of the suicide may be a paroxysm of panic under the stress of which he throws himself into the fire or out of the window or from the top of the stairs, not having deliberately premeditated the deed beforehand or not having had sufficient motive power to do it. Because of his liability to such sudden panic or rapture of anguish, it is always rash to let the tranquil melancholic who has suicidal feelings be alone; for although dull and sad ordinarily, he is liable to be swept away into a convulsive act of despair at which he is amazed himself perhaps when it is over, wondering how he could have done such a dreadful thing, able only to say, "I did not know what I was doing:" "I could not help it:" "Something came over me." Moreover, it is sometimes the opportune means of doing the ill deed which makes the ill deed done in such circumstances; a momentary relaxation of watchfulness provokes him to take eager and instant advantage of the occasion which may not soon recur. "I only left him for a moment," is then the stupid excuse offered by those who, having been solemnly warned never to lose sight and touch of him, cannot be made to comprehend, after the event, that a moment's negligence is just as sufficient as an hour's for an act that requires a moment only for its doing.[1] An intermitting vigilance is possibly fraught with more danger than the allowance of free opportunities would be, since that which may be done at any time is perhaps never done, the person putting it off to another opportunity and resting tranquil in the assurance that he can do it whenever he is minded. It is a matter of fair argument whether some suicidally inclined melancholics would be as likely to kill themselves were they supplied with the easy means of doing so, as they are when they are subjected, night and day, to a constant and irksome supervision, which being a perpetual reminder, becomes at last a provocation to evade and defy it. Lastly, the suicide is done without having been the end directly designed, when it is the sequel of serious injury self-inflicted in obedience to delusive impulse; as, for example, when a patient cuts off his arm to prevent himself from killing himself, gouges out his eye because it has been the offending organ, tears out his tongue for the same reason, cuts off his genitals or otherwise horribly mutilates himself, under the belief that it is better for him to enter heaven maimed than to burn whole in hellfire.

Of all causes of suicide, however, none is more powerful than the implicit note of constitutional life-weariness which an inherited tendency to suicide implants. Many memorable examples have been recorded of its frequent occurrence in the same generation and in successive generations of a family. When a nature is thus suicidally intoned, a slight cause serves to strike and stir the vibrating impulse in feeling and thought; then the deed is determined, dared and done as if it were an ordinary event of daily life rather than an extraordinary event ending life. The man puts off life with as little concern as he would put off his stockings; doing it quietly, when no one in the least expected it, and perhaps

---

[1] *Sight and Touch.*—The common note of warning is "Never to lose sight of him"; whereby it does not fail to happen sometimes that the anxious guardian, obeying the injunction to the letter, *sees* his patient throw himself in front of an incoming locomotive engine at a railway station.

after discussing plans for the future which might seem to show that he did not expect it himself. That is the fundamental motive of the startling suicides which are done by young persons and even children, who, however, do not realise fully what they are doing; *that* or a marked strain of melancholic inheritance. A nature mindful in its inmost how the past was sad forefeels and shuns the inanity of that which is to come. The loss of a favourite pet, a quarrel with a comrade, a mother's scolding or a father's rebuke, the threat of a trivial punishment, the refusal of a looked-for holiday, any petty cross or loss then becomes an adequate motive.

Certainly a mean enough motive for so big a deed were the conscious motive ever the full motive! But it is in truth the smallest part of it, the mere occasion of the explosion: where there is suitable explosive substance the least spark or tap suffices to cause the explosion, whereas a shower of sparks or a thousand taps fall inert when they meet with no answering welcome. To a thoroughly life-loving nature a suicidal thought is a jarring discord which makes no way into its intimate recesses; to a suicidal-toned or life-sick nature it is a concordant note which passes in long reverberating echoes through its inmost elements and stirs the whole being to its unison. The practical lesson therefore is that when the suicidal strain runs in a family the mildest melancholic who thinks and talks placidly of suicide as if it were something abstract in which he had only a speculative interest cannot be trusted not to do it. He will do it even in extreme old age, when at most he has but two or three years more to live, because he has got intolerably tired at last of the monotonous and wearisome round of buttoning and unbuttoning which he has been doing all his life.[1]

[1] As an old farmer in Scotland, eighty years of age or upwards, did some time ago, alleging that motive. Seneca observed long ago—*Cogita quam diu eadem feceris; mori velle, non tantum fortis aut miser, sed etiam fastidiosus potest.* A line somewhere in Virgil expresses the same thought —*tædet cæli convexa tueri.* Hafiz sought another, perhaps a better, way of breaking the monotony of seeing the same tiresome vault of heaven: "Crown me with roses, let us drink wine and break up the tiresome old vault of heaven into new forms!"

Homicide.

Another tragic outcome of melancholic feeling and delusion from time to time is homicide. A dejected, poverty-stricken mother, sure that she is going to die of a disease which she has not got, or going out of a mind which at its best was not much to go out of, or going to be sent to the workhouse or to the gaol, kills her children to spare them the misery and corruption in store for them on earth and to send them in their innocence to heaven, and perhaps kills herself afterwards; or a melancholic husband, harbouring a groundless suspicion that his wife is abandoning herself to other men, kills her and his children also in a fury of rage and despair. The poor man, having keen imagination, suffers its vivid tortures until he can bear them no longer; for to have imagination and to suspect a wife or mistress of secret infidelity is to be perpetually conceiving the occasions and realising in imaginative detail the minute circumstances of the offence. A hypochondriacal melancholic, believing that his manly vigour has been wasted, and irremediable injury done to his brain by medicines or other measures which he has taken to cure himself, only with the effect of having got worse, or by the mysterious means of persecution which his enemies secretly employ to ruin him in mind, body and estate, makes a fatal assault on the person whom he imagines to be maltreating him. Especially dangerous to the person whom he thus suspects is the melancholic who believes that he is being subjected to some wicked process of secret emasculation. Another melancholy victim of a mania of persecution, wearied out by his reiterated and futile appeals to the authorities for an impossible help or redress, resolves in despair to enforce public attention to his wrongs by shooting some highly placed person whose lofty eminence attracts the discharge of his insane vengeance. In the ears of another melancholic an imperative voice keeps on crying "kill," "kill," "kill," until he either kills himself or, driven desperate by its insistent torment, kills some one in order to bring matters to a crisis and anyhow force a change of things. Another, who believes himself to be the wickedest wretch on earth, fit only to be hanged, yielding to the logical impulse to fill up the measure of his iniquity and be visibly to all men what he feels he is privily, aims to fulfil his fate by doing murder and being hanged for it; or he conceives the notion of killing some one and being hanged for it in order to avoid the crime of killing himself, which he might otherwise be irresistibly tempted to do.

Such and of such are the homicidal melancholics. For the most part they know well what they do when they do murder, and are quite aware that it is wrong in the world's estimation. As the criterion of responsibility established by English judges is a knowledge by the madman of the nature of the act which he does, not the existence of power over himself to do or not to do it, the melancholic is strictly entitled to be hanged when he kills somebody. The principle on which the legal dictum and his right rest is a very simple one when clearly conceived and formulated—that a man in convulsions is a strong man, and that he is criminal if, being conscious of them, he does not stop them by his will. *Conscious sui* is decreed to be the equivalent of *compos sui*, even when the person is not himself but another self. The pity of it is that the essence of insanity is to disorganise, first functionally and last structurally, the supreme nerve-tracts in which the transformation of the forces of passion into the energy of will takes place and self-mastery resides.

Hallucinations.

Hallucinations of sense are not uncommon features of melancholia, especially in its acute forms; most common those of hearing, though not a sense escapes. Whether the hallucination begins first in disorder of sense, as it may do, or in disorder of thought, as it often does, there is no question that disordered sense and thought conspire to mutually aggravate one another. Sane or insane, the senses cheat the understanding and are in turn cheated by it. How else could every infatuated lover discover the incomparable charms of his particular mistress? In all the world none more fair to him than she! Not a piquant deformity would he have away, not a pretty caprice absent, her childlike prattle not a whit other than it is. After marriage, when his lapsed senses resume their functions, his flushed feeling sinks into sobriety, and his understanding is purged of its fond glamour, he easily discerns the uncomeliness in her features, the ill temper in her caprice, the silliness in her talk, which no one else ever failed to see. By the same law of mutual deception the persecuted melancholic, having a bad taste in his mouth, believes that he is being poisoned, the notion suiting aptly with his gloomy and suspicious tone of thought, or, believing that he is being poisoned, asserts that he tastes arsenic in his food, notwithstanding that arsenic, were it there, would be tasteless; the preoccupied sense and the preconceived idea conspire successfully to prevent accurate experience of sense and thought. It is a strange thing to see how completely delusion of thought can dominate sense; a frenzied melancholic mother will refuse good food and frantically resist the administration of it, because she believes and protests that she is being fed with the flesh of her own murdered children. Hallucinations of smell sometimes engender, and are in turn engendered by, notions of stinking odours, poisonous or putrid, or by other like insane imaginations; hallucinations of sight are sustained by or sustain notions of secret signs, offensive gestures, significant movements, which are believed to be made in pursuance of a hostile system of persecution, or to be deliberate exhibitions of scorn and contempt by friends, acquaintances, and even strangers. The man does not see with his eye but through it, and when an unsound mind looks through a sound eye it shapes what it sees to its own features.

Most instructive of all are the different sorts of hallucinations of hearing, because in their features we can trace something of the genesis of hallucination and the steps of its growth to maturity. Before a distinct voice is heard to tease or torment, there is perhaps a period when a blasphemous, obscene, or otherwise detestable thought or word intrudes into the mind against the patient's will and vibrates there persistently; it is loathed and lamented as a wicked thought, odious and horrible, deemed perhaps evidence of sin, if not of actual Satanic possession, fought against in agonies of fervid will and prayer; but it is known to be a thought only, is not believed to come actually in auditory guise. The next step, however, is to hear it as an internal voice, not from without through the ears, but nevertheless distinctly as a word which is supposed to be produced somehow in the head from a distance by mysterious agency, magnetic, telephonic, hypnotic, or telepathic. Whatever the unknown means by which the thing is done, there is absolute certitude that it is done somehow, however extraordinary and incredible the affair seems; the very impossibility of explaining the operation becoming, in face of the very vivid experience of the effect, a help to compel belief. Like Tertullian, the sufferer believes because it is impossible, and, like St. Theresa, believes the more the more impossible it is. Considering the matter pathologically, we may conceive that the proper excito-motor current of the word in the cerebral cortex is persistently active, without being so active on the one hand as to pass to the subordinate sensory centres, where it would be heard as a word in the ears, or to the subordinate motor centres, when it would be uttered or muttered in speech by the person himself. Indeed, in such case, his acute dread sometimes is that he will be forced to utter it aloud in spite of himself; obliged then to exert all his forces of self-control to hold it in, he is perhaps driven, in despair of complete victory, to compromise matters by whispering it inaudibly.

The last step in the evolution of the hallucination is the heard word, which is then as distinctly audible as if it were spoken by some one, as it is now believed to be. Here, however, we may sometimes note a precursory stage when the word is not yet distinctly articulated, but there is a sort of confused sound or whisper heard which has no particular meaning and which afterwards only becomes a distinct voice. Then the excito-motor current has presumably overflowed its cortical bounds and excited its proper terminals in the sensory centres; just the same parts as the words spoken to the ear would excite, and therefore with just the same result. Of its nature there is not any further question in his mind, it is the actual voice used by his persecutors for their evil purposes; one of which is perhaps to drive him mad by their devilish production of these hallucinations in him, or at any rate to cause him to be thought mad. Counterpart, on the motor side, of the audible voice on the sensory side is the utterance of the distressing thought or word aloud, the excito-motor current of the cortex then discharging itself on its proper motor terminals. There are patients who are continually afflicted by the horrible thoughts which the voices suggest to them, others who are afflicted by the fear of their impotence to refrain from uttering the horrible thoughts aloud.

Such is one way in which a hallucination may be conjectured to arise, grow gradually and maintain itself—by the inspiration of a false notion. But it is pretty certain that it can also be formed without the priority and without the privity of false thought—in fact, directly from morbid sensory irritation. Of this mode of causation we have ample proof and example in the spontaneity of the abrupt, diverse, and transient hallucinations of delirium tremens, when there are vivid visions of rats, mice, serpents, and other creeping creatures on the bed, the floor, or the walls of the room, though the patient was not expecting anything of the kind, and could not, had he wished, have created the strange medley; in the strange smells perceived, in the well-defined figures seen, and in the sounds or actual voices heard sometimes before an epileptic or apopleptic attack;

in the voices which now and then seem to shape themselves into articulate forms out of the noise of a common tinnitus aurium; in the hallucinations of sight, surprising to the patient by their unforeseen diversities, which may accompany the optic irritation of commencing blindness; and in the familiar phenomena of dreaming. To say that thought is concerned in the origin of such hallucinations would be ridiculous, but we are not therefore entitled to limit their origin to subordinate sensory centres and to exclude the cerebral cortex from any part in their manufacture. The working of the mental mechanism is one thing, the consciousness thereof another and incommensurate thing; the latter being like moonlight unto sunlight, a reflection only, luminous not warming. Of all hallucinations it might be said, in the language of psychology, that they are either of psychical origin or of sensory origin or of joint psychical and sensory origin.

A curious rarity is when hallucinations are different in the two ears. On the one side a threatening voice has harassed the patient and on the other side a reassuring voice has consoled him.[1] An exaggerated illustration of the common mental dialogues of daily life in which a person, going in imagination through a discussion with another, hears arguments, as it were, internally and confutes them, puts questions and answers them, makes reproaches and remonstrances, and even carries it so far sometimes as to gesticulate and talk aloud to himself in the street without being aware of it. In dreams it is the dreamer who makes his own points and puts and solves his own riddle. If the two hemispheres of the

[1] Morel relates the case of an old woman who, ordinarily calm, gentle and well-behaved, was subject to attacks of excitement during which sometimes she stopped her left ear and struck that side of her head violently; at other times, she burst out in explosions of laughter, running out then into the yard and gesticulating violently. The explanation of these seemingly incomprehensible acts was the hallucinations of a double voice: on the left side, a demon voice which sometimes made indecent proposals and urged her to dishonourable acts, and at other times said pleasant and laughable things; on the right side, the voice of a good angel which, undertaking the answers to the other, enabled her to remain quiet and tranquil ordinarily.

brain act separately and differently in such soliloquies, then it is easy to understand that their dissentient action might be the cause of a double personality in some cases of mental disorder—of two seeming personalities in one body, the one inspiring one kind of thought and impulse, the other a quite different kind of thought and impulse.[1] Less rare than double hallucinations, though infrequent, is hallucination on one side only.

An ever new surprise in spite of old experience is the absolute credence given to a preposterous hallucination by a person who in other respects exhibits just discrimination and sound intelligence. On the false testimony of one sense he believes in an impossible occurrence when he has at hand his other senses and other persons' senses, and their reason as well as his own reason, to correct the wrong evidence. Willing to allow that the common sense of all the world is likely to be wiser than the opinion of a single individual, at any rate in a matter that lies within common experience, he has not the common sense to make application of the rule in his case. For him the particular experience is so exact and positive, so vivid and persistent, that there is no gainsaying it, amazing and incredible as it seems; its very incredibility, fascinating and subduing his reason, helps to make it credible. Like a religious truth, he *feels* it to be true with a certitude which to *know* it to be true could never give him. Where would the province of faith be were its function only to establish truths which reason suffices to establish? Its just function begins where reason ends, for it is to make that credible which to reason is incredible.[2] Ignorant of the physiological mechanism and working of his brain, he cannot comprehend how it should play him a gross trick of deception, and can-

---

[1] Regarding the double action of the brain, I may refer to an article by me on "The Double Brain" in *Mind*, vol. xiv. p. 54.

[2] "Methinks there be not impossibilities enough for an active faith . . . yet do I believe all this is true, which, indeed, my reason would persuade me to be false: and this, I think, is no vulgar part of faith, to believe a thing not only above, but contrary to, reason, and against the arguments of our proper senses."—Sir Thomas Browne, *Religio Medici*.

not be brought to see that a natural interpretation, when such a one is offered to him, is not equivalent to an insulting denial of his positive experience. Were he clever introspectionist enough, he might perchance succeed in detecting and catching the idea or word in his mind at the instant before it became audible as a voice; all the more so as its sayings are usually of the stuff of his ordinary thoughts and doings and concerned with his daily occasions, being very much the thoughts that would pass through his mind in its habitual self-dialogues; and in those instances in which he could not thus catch it before its transformation, he might, were he able to reason quietly and fully about the matter, convince himself by a cool and critical examination of the conditions of its occurrence that the words were inspired within and not uttered without him. The woman mentioned by Baillarger, the voice of whose persecutor could in many repeated trials invariably tell correctly whether a number of coins taken at random in her hand was odd or even, discovered by experiment that the voice, which always answered rightly when she herself knew, was capable of giving a wrong answer when she did not know, the right answer; like other cunning prophets, ranging in rank from equivocating oracles to vulgar fortune-tellers, it was liable to blunder badly when it had not secret sources of information or inference to rely on.

In like manner, the person who, speaking more languages than one, is persecuted by voices, does not fail to notice that he is persecuted most in the language which he knows best, and least in the language which he knows worst. I remember one gentleman who, after full argument, was half inclined to acknowledge that the persecuting voices in his case, ascribed by him to the revengeful machinations of offended freemasons, might sometimes utter what had been in his mind the instant before, but who repudiated strenuously the suggestion that a Hindustanee word used by the scoundrels unexpectedly from time to time could possibly have come from himself, though he understood Hindustanee; it was positive proof to him of its external origin, since he was sure that he was not thinking in the least of Hindustanee at the moment. Perhaps his thought-centres were not, but evidently his auditory centres were. The abrupt sensorial excitation of a word and its distinct audition, without previous thought of it, might be found to be an occasional occurrence by every one who took the pains to observe himself attentively; when he is walking along the street or sitting quietly in his room he may hear an unbidden word as suddenly and distinctly as if it had been actually spoken, and be uncertain for the moment or for ever afterwards whether it was spoken or not. Were the level of inhibition of his nerve-centres lowered in consequence of irritable activity or actual disorder, it is obvious that such sensorial experience might very well happen more often and more vividly; in which case his mind would be likely to welcome and work it into its train of morbid thought, receiving it as confirmatory evidence and using it to strengthen the fabric of delusion.

The lesson of the whole matter is simple—to wit, that a man may be trained by education or distrained by disease to believe anything. Just as by fit training begun early enough and steadily continued long enough a mind may be moulded to certain tracks of thought and feeling, off which it cannot get to perceive, feel and judge otherwise, so by disorder of its mechanism it can be brought to function mainly in special morbid tracks of thought and belief, off which it cannot go to see and judge things as they are. Then its unity is no better than a flattering figment of philosophy; part of its functions have either grown to such a fixed fashion by exclusive exercise, or been so severed from the confederation of faculties by disorder, that they work aloof from the rest, which on their part cannot possibly now act in concert with them. The same bodily person is two different beings mentally according as the limited area of his mental organisation which lies on the one side, or the larger area of it which lies on the other side, of the line of separation—the unreasonable or the reasonable part of him—is in function.

Notwithstanding that all hallucinations, those of hearing more especially, have a bad prognostic import, they may disappear when they are associated with bodily derangement and active mental disorder; the hope then is that they will disappear with the acute perturbation of the system. It is when the excitement is past and the mind has settled quietly into morbid ruts of action, and the bodily functions proceed with sluggish regularity—the processes of mind and body, alike indifferent to their alien presence, going on with equanimity despite a trouble which could not fail to disturb them were there full unity of being—that they mean settled chronic disease and are signals of despair.

Another weighty factor of which due account ought to be taken in estimating the ill-boding import of hallucinations is the sound or unsound structure of the individual character. Is the foundation of nature sound and stable? or is it frail and faulty? There are certain ill-constructed minds which, not overstepping the bounds of conventional sanity, are loose, incompact, wanting in unity of being? unable to get into sincere and wholesome contact with facts and to take and keep a steady hold of them, they flicker and flash at seeming random from notion to notion in abrupt and mobile ways; it is impossible to get a truth into the bottom of minds which are so superficial that they have no bottom to reach; like shallow streams, which are incapable of whirlpools, they are incapable either of an absorbing passion or of consistent feeling. Of their possessors it might be said that much or most of their habitual observation and thinking is no better than hallucination and delusion. The correlative defect in the moral sphere is usually a surcharge of suspicions and distrusts, insincerities and deceits. Offcomes commonly of a degenerate nervous stock, they have inherited the disposition to instability and incoherence of thought and feeling; in such degree too perchance that the best training in the world avails not to overcome it effectively. No wonder then they and their like, when they have morbid hallucinations, do not get rid of them; these are far too much at home from the first in the mental constitution, find much too congenial fellowship there, to be dislodged and go, once they have got fair footing: to unfix their fast foundations would be to root up a nature and to unmake a character. To a sincere, well-tempered, and sound nature, on the other hand, a hallucination, if it comes, is so alien that it comes as an intruder, meets with no welcome, and does not easily obtain fixed footing.

The Course and Ending of Melancholia.

Having now dealt with the serious adjuncts of melancholy insanity—suicide, homicide and hallucinations, it remains to consider what is its usual course and what are its customary endings. Seldom does it run a uniform course, either upwards to the best or downwards to the worst issue. It would be strange if it did, seeing how inconstant are feelings even in sane persons, ever passing, as they do, from gleams of joy to clouds of gloom. Exacerbations and remissions occur irregularly, one knows not why; and it is not uncommon for complete intermissions to take place, the patient abruptly coming to his right mind for a day, or a few hours, or only a quarter of an hour, and then as quickly falling back to be as bad as ever again. Sudden and transient recoveries of this sort, which are like passing rifts or patches of blue in a cloud-covered sky, ought not to excite undue hope on the one hand, nor the quick relapses in their turn to unduly dishearten. Though the abrupt sanity may chance to last, it seldom does; and the relapse does not lessen the prospect of ultimate recovery, which comes permanently to pass usually by a process of gradual amendment. However, it is a gratifying surprise now and then to see an attack end abruptly which has been going on wearily for months and shown no sign of real abatement during all that time, and still up to the crisis, seemed perhaps to be in full fury and strong in fixed delusions; after a wretched night of fierce anguish and frantic unrest, in the morning it is gone. Why it goes then for good and did not go before is as great a mystery as why in another case it goes for an hour or a day only and then comes back. In one of my patients who was subject to recurrent attacks of deep melancholy the welcome augury of recovery was a happy dream which she invariably had a night or two before the cloud of woe suddenly dispersed : it was thus that the organic life, forefeeling it, foretold the impending change.

The course of simple melancholy which does not end prematurely in suicide is most often to recovery. Not without the risk of a relapse some day. Such risk is least where the inborn sanity is greatest, and greater or less according as the influences to which the individual is exposed in the changes and chances of life are untoward or propitious. In delusional melancholy recovery takes place in as many as half the cases; usually within from three to twelve months from the beginning of the illness, now and then after two years, in some few and rare cases even after several years. The chances of recovery decrease as the duration of the disease increases. An immediate stimulus and sustaining aid to recovery in long-lasting cases will be found sometimes in a complete change of environment, even if the change be only from one asylum to another which is nowise superior; for the change breaks the routine of morbid reaction to familiar impressions to which the mental machinery has become set, and, by soliciting new actions in answer to new impressions, opens to it the way and the chance of righting itself. To uproot and transplant, the wisest measure often at the beginning of the illness, succeeds unexpectedly sometimes after its long continuance, when other measures have failed. But seldom; one reason being that it is seldom tried. For the fervent interest of relations, who at first deem no pains too great to have the patient cured, cannot help waning gradually with waning hope as time goes on; then motive is wanting to actuate new measures, beset with troubles and offering a forlorn hope only, in order to bring back to social life one whose place in it has perhaps been filled up and whose return to it, after so long an absence, might be embarrassing.

Recovery not taking place, what are the issues then? (*a*) A chronic course of continuing woe and woeful delusions, with a gradual weakening of mind; less real feeling of distress, however obtrusive the show of distress, expressed in an automatic or quasi-mechanical way by words, gestures, physiognomy and gait; in the end perhaps a state of completely demented melancholy. (*b*) An apparent recovery which, however, is not real recovery, but only a passing state on the way to an attack of mania or of general paralysis; for both these forms of derangement are sometimes preceded by a longer or shorter period of more or less melancholy, which is then generally of the simple kind. (*c*) Death: a seldom event seldom due directly to the melancholy, except in the acute delirious form; most often caused by intercurrent thoracic or abdominal disease, especially where food has been taken sparingly or refused persistently and the vitality thus brought to a low ebb. Then a low congestive pneumonia is apt to supervene which, going from bad to worse, lapses sometimes into actual gangrene of the lungs. Or death takes place in consequence of gradual exhaustion, food not being taken in sufficient quantity, or, if taken, not availing to sustain the strength of life; for a time comes in the process of increasing nervous exhaustion when the tissues rebel against food which they cannot assimilate and when a heart, not itself diseased, ceases to beat more. After such a death, any one who goes diligently to work to search out the cause of it in the body may fail to discover a distinct morbid structural alteration of any kind in any part of it; the utmost that he shall find being perhaps a look of general wasting. Forasmuch then as death is an exceptional end of melancholia and there is nothing in the disease itself directly to cause it, the sufferer cannot comfort himself, nor his friends mitigate their grief, with the prospect of a premature deliverance from the sad burden of his life: despite his mental affliction, he may well live out the full measure of his days.

Varieties of Melancholia.

Thus much concerning melancholia in its simple and delusional forms. Several varieties of it have been described; and there is nothing to prevent as many more being discovered and described by any one who chooses to lay hold of the principal feature of the prevailing delusion or apprehension, to give it a special big-sounding name, and thereupon to use the name to denote a variety of disease. In that way it is easy to manufacture as many varieties as there are modes of distress or forms of grief-utterance: a *religious melancholia*, when the delusion is of being outcast from God and given over to eternal damnation; a *dæmono-melancholia*, when there is a delusion of possession by a demon or evil spirit which constrains and uses its victim to feel, think and do what he abhors as wicked and most foreign to his nature; a *melancholia metamorphosis*, when the patient protests that he is not alive now, since it is not he but his dead body which is walking about, or that parts of his body have been changed, other matter than human or other organs than his having been put into him or on to him, or that he is altogether no longer human but animal; a *panphobia*, when he is in a perpetual agitation of apprehension and alarm—in the uttermost fright of everything and everybody; a *syphilophobia*, when he is in a special fever of terror of infection by syphilitic disease and anxiously discovers evidence of it in every pimple on his body, in every discoloration of his gums, in every furrow of his tongue, in every strange sensation which he feels; an *agarophobia*, when he cannot attempt to cross an open square or place without being seized by an overwhelming and incapacitating distress, not a giddiness but a distracting mental fright and impotence to move; a *claustrophobia*, when he cannot for the life of him remain alone in a room, because, feeling as if the walls were closing in on him, he is overcome by an awful and indescribable agony of stifling apprehension and must rush out. These and the like shapes or forms of melancholic apprehension are simply different symptoms exhibited in different cases, and some of them together or successively in the same case.

Hypochondriacal Melancholia.

One variety of melancholy may justly claim a brief special description—namely, the so-called *hypochondriacal melancholia*, in which there are the strangest fears and fancies of impending or actual bodily diseases. It is not a special disease, but its symptoms give a special complexion to the depression of melancholia, into the ordinary form of which they pass by transitional instances; sometimes too they so mask the more serious symptoms of positive organic brain-disease as to lead to a wrong diagnosis. Of this form of melancholy three degrees or varieties might be distinguished.

(*a*) *Simple hypochondria:* where the person, filled with fearful fancies about his health, imagines that he has got heart-disease, stomach-disease, brain-disease, or disease of some other organ, and is for ever prying into his sensations, examining his eyes, scrutinising his tongue, feeling his pulse, inspecting his excretions, and going from doctor to doctor to tell over the tedious tale of his sufferings and apprehensions. By habitual attention to sensations and signs which have unluckily attracted his notice, some nerve-weakness in him having been probably the primal, and being still a continuing, cause of their importunity, he has so fostered them that they have obtained a tyrannic hold of him and he can think of little else; for although his daily work, so long as he goes on with it, diverts his attention temporarily from them, yet so soon as his mind is free they invade and possess it again. Being unable, by reason of their obsession of him, to give proper attention to passing events, he naturally forgets what he has not noticed, and thereupon concludes that he has lost his memory and is surely losing his mind. Rational otherwise, he is in respect of his fears quite out of reason; however many and strong the authoritative assurances which he seeks and obtains to the contrary, he cannot believe that his morbid sensations betoken no mortal disease. Of these hypochondriacs far the worst are those who fix on the sexual organs as the sources of their troubles and apprehensions, since nothing has a more demoralising effect on human kind than the imagination or certitude of something amiss with them. Depression deepening into suicidal despair or, if the calamity be imputed to a particular person, flaring into homicidal violence may be the upshot.

This sort of hypochondriacal melancholy is specially apt to occur during the periods of adolescence and decline: in adolescence, because of the new and strange sensations and vague subjective moods which are the mental effects of pubescence; in the decline of life, because of the natural waning of physiological sensations and powers and the equally natural occurrence of morbid aches and pains which are not known and owned to be what they are. There are persons who fall into despairing alarm because they cannot eat, sleep, and procreate as well at fifty as they could at twenty-five years of age; nothing will persuade them that their condition is not portentous and unnatural, much less reconcile them to it as the natural effect of decay.

Obviously this hypochondria is very near akin to hysteria. The symptoms which would be ascribed to hypochondria in a man would be described as hysteria in a woman; in fact, the male hypochondriac is sometimes as hysterical as a woman, the hysterical woman essentially hypochondriac. The difference, such as it is, is not in the sensory but in the motor symptoms—in the convulsive tendencies of hysteria—which, especially in their aggravated form of hystero-epilepsy, merge on their side into the convulsions of actual epilepsy. There is no real line of division between those different forms of nervous disease; they pass into one another by transitions.

(*b*) A worse form of hypochondriacal melancholy is *crazy* or *delusional hypochondria*, as it might be called, in which all sorts of foolish delusions shape themselves to meet the exactions of the disordered sensations. Seldom, if ever, a further pathological development of the simple form, it is essentially, I think, an hereditary insanity which takes the hypochondriacal type. In a state of agitated alarm because of absurd delusions concerning the cause and nature of abnormal sensations which trouble him, the patient's mind is in other respects singularly clear and intelligent. It is an ever-recurring wonder that one who can discuss and judge sensibly all things but himself and his imagined diseases should be so utterly irrational when he comes to judge and talk of them. Flickers or specks before his eyes portend a rapidly approaching blindness, red gums signify putrid disease of them, and a dry throat means syphilis or cancer of it; his stomach is contracted, or his intestines are displaced in some unheard-of way; his head is growing smaller or deformed, and his eyes have been strangely dislocated in their sockets; his brain has wasted so that he cannot think, or it is melting away and gradually running down his spine into his genitals. One patient is in incredible distress because he is sure that his genitals have shrunk or altered in form, or that they and other organs of the body have been strangely displaced, and in spite of exact measurements and the most positive assurances, remains unshaken in his belief. Another protests that his nose or other feature is distorted, and consults medical man after medical man about it, soliciting and, if so be, undergoing an operation to have put right that which is not wrong. A third imagines that his gullet is contracting or actually closed, so that no food will pass through it, or that he has no stomach, or that his bowels never act, while he is all the while taking food or having it regularly forced on him in spite of his protests. A fourth declares that his nasal mucus is purulent matter which flows from his brain and is gradually wasting it, or that the bronchial mucus which he spits up consists of rotten fragments of his lungs. There is no delusion too absurd to be believed and to be defended stoutly against every assault of argument and the weightiest dicta of authority. Ignorant and uneducated persons may go so far as to believe that serpents or other vile creatures have got inside them and are the cause of what they suffer; and here and there one will still be found to maintain that an evil spirit, such as entered into the herd of Gadarene swine and bedevilled them to their destruction, has taken possession of him and is tormenting him. Such beliefs are not matters of reason, they are quite contrary to it; being matters of feeling and faith, they are impregnable to reason, for it is nothing else than want of reason to endeavour to confute by reason a belief which is the express negation of it. It is the morbid feeling, not the morbid notion in which it takes form, that is the real malady.

The worst thing in respect of these deluded hypochondriacal melancholics, torments to themselves and to others, is when they fix on some innocent person who has had to do with them and accuse him as the cause of their sufferings—it may be a medical man who has prescribed for them or some one else who has tried to help them—and in the end make an exasperated, perhaps a fatal, assault on him. Others of them, weary of what they suffer and of their bootless quest of relief, turn desperate hands against themselves and commit suicide; those whose trouble lies in the abdominal viscera and the genital organs being most likely to do that. The extremity of the deed, whether homicidal or suicidal, is proof of the extremity of sufferings which an onlooker might be inclined to think somewhat unreal in character and much exaggerated in expression.

(c) A third variety I might designate *demented hypochondria*. In it the patient exhibits delusions of the most demented stamp with regard to his bodily condition, although his mind then, apart from them, is not always so weak as their enormities might indicate. They, however, are of a monstrous absurdity—for example, that his legs are not his legs but other legs which have been put on him; that his blood is at a standstill, or is not blood at all, but a putrid, red fluid which has been infused into his veins; that his nerves are not nerves but red-hot wires put in their place; that his brain has been taken out of his skull and replaced by some other substance; that his body is cut to pieces every night and put together again every morning. His preposterous dementia is not invariably harmless, since he sometimes makes an abrupt attack on an unlucky person against whom a sudden blaze of suspicion chances to spring up and direct his fury. Like the second variety, it is not a development of simple hypochondria; it is a native insanity which takes the special complexion. A pronounced example of it is sometimes met with in general paralysis of the melancholic type. On the other hand, the features of simple hypochondriacal melancholia are now and then so extreme as to raise a doubt whether it is not going to be general paralysis; a doubt which is only settled at last perhaps by the patient's recovery.

It is in the first form or degree of disorder alone that recovery can be reasonably expected. Then it is sometimes brought about by the slow salutary effects of time, or by the revolutionary action of intercurrent bodily disease, or by the lucky development of an interest in life which drags the patient out of himself. If he does not recover, he often goes on for years without much change, retaining his mental powers generally in spite of his fears and fancies about his health. In some instances the hypochondria develops into a mania of persecution; it may then end in exalted notions of personal greatness.

CHAPTER III

INSANITY WITH EXCITEMENT—MANIA

Simple Mania or Mania without Delusion.

THE intensification and perpetuation of the opposite moods of feeling and thought to the dejection and woe of *melancholia* is the basal note of the mental disorders that are included under *mania*. At its outset in most cases, throughout in a few cases, there is in mania an extraordinary excitement, without positive derangement, of feeling and thought: quickened thought flushed with elated and aggressive feeling, but not actually deluded or incoherent; the heat, fire and motion of inflamed thought and feeling, so to speak. The *ego* being in a state of ignition, the result is extraordinary mental activity of a sort, and a signal display of self-assertion and self-sufficiency. Apprehension is quick, conception prompt and easy, memory instant and acute, will swift in origin and execution, action bold, alert and energetic; a sanguine self-confidence thinks nothing difficult to plan, nothing hard to accomplish. Timidity and reserve of character are supplanted by their opposites; one who is naturally shy and self-contained becoming bold and familiar in his address, free and jocular in speech, lively in repartee, prone to make clever and caustic sallies, and quick to take up and turn to sarcastic or equivocal meaning any innocent expression that can be so twisted. However timid and vacillating by nature, he now exhibits extraordinary decision, nerve and daring: will make a speech to a large audience, and make it fluently, who would not dare to open his mouth in public if he were himself; or ride to hounds with a dash and daring which amaze his friends at the time and himself afterwards when he comes to himself. It is possible that he recites from memory passages of poetry which he could not for the life of him remember at his normal level, or that he makes rhymes which he calls poetry. As thoughts spring up easily and abundantly, so he finds an equal ease and freedom of expression in language. He is not unlikely to entertain projects of business, travel, pleasure, perhaps marriage, which are foreign to the principles of his sane and sober self.

There is no let or hindrance now, as in melancholy, to the expression of internal states in outward activity, no burden of the incommunicable, no crushing weight of the world's authority to cow him, but a confident standing, a soaring sense of deliverance from bondage of thought and feeling, a realisation of the joy of living never experienced before, a supreme satisfaction with self, a glorious conviction of mental freedom and power. Never was there a more absolute certitude of free-will, and, correlate thereof, never such a feeling of triumphant superiority over circumstances which formerly overawed him. So signal is the transformation of the character for the time being that the spectator, suspecting the nearest cause, asks himself "Has the man been drinking?" or, amazed at his fire and eloquence when the excitement has a religious strain—" Is he inspired?"[1]

These things betoken exalted reflex action of the cere-

---

[1] The most subtile and complete details of the mental experiences of one who has gone through an acute mental derangement which I know of, are given in the *Le Rêve et la Vie* of Gérard de Nerval; nowhere else have I seen anything to compare to it. "Je vais essayer," he says, "de transcrire les impressions d'une longue maladie qui s'est passée tout entière dans les mystères de mon esprit ; et je ne sais pourquoi je me sers de ce terme maladie, car jamais, quant à ce qui est de moi-même, je ne me suis senti mieux portant, Parfois, je croyais ma force et mon activité doublées ; il me semblait tout savoir, tout comprendre ; l'imagination m'apportait des délices infinies."

bral nerve-tracts. Their excitability being augmented and their speed of conduction quickened, ideas rise instantly, flow swiftly, and strike more easy and varied associations; not well-worn associations only, but occasional and disused associations, whence abrupt revivals of forgotten thoughts and feelings; while the transient chance-formings of new track-junctions give rise sometimes to novel turns of thought, puns of speech, sporadic flashes of seeming inspiration. The normal set of the nervous molecules along beaten tracks being dislocated by their extraordinary intestine motions, an aptness to the formation of new and fleeting junctions is the consequence. The glowing feelings of elated being are the direct mental outcome of the physical excitement; the thoughts and deeds the congruent modes or forms in which they obtain expression; and the individual, erect in body and mind, fronts the world with such a confident spirit as old experience backed by philosophy could never give him. As the outer world is to everybody just what he apprehends and as he apprehends it, the sense of personal power and freedom is necessarily increased when his motor centres and their higher representatives in the cerebral cortex are in a state of excited and quasi-inflamed activity; when they are strong the world is weak, and when they are weak the world is strong, not otherwise than as when they are giddy it turns round. The real world of his normal self in its due form and proportions is for him as if it were not, and in its stead he deals with the show of the world as it is presented in his inflamed mind; accordingly he deals with it with much the same triumphant freedom and confidence as he does in pleasant dreaming. The condition of things is like in kind to, though less in degree than, that which will hereafter be noticed at the beginning of general paralysis and

Je les étonnais (mes amis) par une éloquence particulière, il me semblait que je savais tout, et que les mystères du monde se révélaient à moi dans ces heures suprêmes." After two acute attacks from which he recovered, he committed suicide by hanging himself when he was in the restless, wandering, sleepless state which foreboded another attack.

goes on then to the exultant development of wildly extravagant delusions of grandeur.

The contrast with melancholia and the meaning of the contrast merit attention. In melancholia the malady seems to weigh on the sensory or ingoing nervous current, is attended with more sensory disturbances, and has the note of sorrow and self-distrust, because of the inability to communicate or utter adequately the internal states; in mania, it affects the motor or outgoing current, is accompanied by great motor activity, and has the note of joy and self-conceit, because of the free and easy expression of the internal states. The instinct of every self is to seek happiness in activity outside itself and to be happy in so uttering itself; sensation discharges itself in movement, passions seek or crave for their objects when these are not present to gratify them, intelligence devises ways and means to fulfil desires; therefore any obstacle in self to such free activity outwards is felt sadly as a repression and depression of self, any help or furtherance of it joyfully as an expansion and elevation of self. The idiot who is its mother's joy because she joys to spend her love on it, itself delights in its hideous howls and grotesque contortions; the rapture of the combatant in game or war is in the eager struggle not in the victory; the chief happiness of the philosopher is in the pursuit not in the attainment of truth; and all alike would be terribly distressed to have their self-utterances suppressed. As for the man of sentiment, the relief of his incontinent feelings is a necessity of nature which, like other necessities of it, he would deem it an outrage on humanity to be debarred from.

The exalted nervous energy of mania is not limited to thought, feeling and conduct; it is felt also in the functions of nutrition and secretion. So animated is the visage sometimes that the person looks ten years younger; the dull eye becoming bright, the complexion fresh and blooming, wrinkles disappearing from the care-worn face, and the hair growing less gray. The pulse is strong, the appetite voracious and nowise dainty, the digestion equal almost to any task put on it, and the general movements remarkably free, vigorous and alert. With these effects of rejuvenescence may go a revival of sexual desire and an increase of sexual power and a temporary restoration of the overpast sexual functions of women. All that is wanting to fill up the full measure of wellbeing, although the patient is not troubled by the want, is sleep; for he sleeps little. The animated physical effects, like in kind to the vivifying effects which a new joy in life works naturally in a person worn and prematurely aged by grief and anxiety, testify to the sprightly intestine motions of the nervous elements; they are their outward and visible translations in physiognomy, gestures, movements and acts. Could this signal joy of life, of which mental and bodily activity is the natural exponent, not the consciously sought anodyne, last without toppling over into disorder, even a philosopher might breathe a regret that his nervous system had not been permanently tuned to the high note of premaniacal exaltation.[1]

Thus far there is neither distinct delusion nor actual incoherence of thought, only a kind of brain-ignition. It is a condition which may be compared well to the first stages of inflammation of structure when there is a struggle between the antagonistic forces of order and disorder, before the equilibrium is overthrown and the latter gain the day and have their way. Its present nature is not always recognised as the serious thing it is, until it is made plain by the sequel. At the best, the exaltation and activity are not the pure gain they seem to be; with the excess of energy there is a default on the side of the most specialised refinements of thought and feeling; for along with the show of increased

---

[1] Those who have this exalted temperament, in less degree, as a natural endowment, exult in the joy of living and insult over the mean views of life entertained by those who have an opposite temperament. They have no doubt of the superiority of their own natures, and confidently prescribe their modes of feeling, thought and action as right and a remedy for the temperament which is incapable of them. Meanwhile, the one mind cannot enter into the feelings and thoughts of the other; there is an impassable gulf between them.

mental power there is a failure or loss of the most nice and delicate shades or tones of sensation, feeling, and thought which constitute the grace or fragrance of a character and are the perfume of social intercourse. That means that the functions of the most fine and special traceries of the cortical reflexes are suspended or effaced, being too delicate to lend themselves to the currents of turbulent energy which now pass along coarser channels.

For what do we behold? Forward address instead of quiet self-restraint, gross familiarity of behaviour instead of calm reserve and dignity, exultant self-satisfaction which is apt to become insulting rudeness, sharpened insight into the foibles and faults of others expressed in incontinent criticism or sarcasm, which may not be altogether unmerited, and would-be-forgotten incidents of their lives raked up in a mercilessly keen memory and commented on with unbridled license of speech. The modest maiden, Ophelia-like, makes immodest allusions, the grave matron wanton hints of lust by word or look, and the sober elder who has been a pattern of decorous gravity in his neighbourhood displays something of the sentiments and conduct of licentious youth. The inflamed and engrossing sense of self entails a proportionate insensibility to the refinements and rights of the social not-self, albeit not wilful nor even conscious; it erases the refined sensibilities, the decorous reticences, the gracious restraints and the gentle sympathies of social intercourse, —the culture-conquests of evolution. Nor them only at the worst; for then the finer sensibilities of the special senses are blunted or abolished, and the super-elated being, without repugnance, even with seeming zest, will eat coarse food, drink sour wine, listen to bad music, praise poor pictures, endure foul smells, embrace common sluts, all which would be abhorrent to his true self. From the first, then, there is a deterioration of the moral and social self which, as matters get worse, passes sometimes into the deeper dissolution evinced by brutal disregard of others, reckless contempt of proprieties, even coarse neglect of decent behaviour.

This condition of mental intoxication often precedes the

outbreak of acute mania, it may be for a few hours, it may be for a few days or longer. It is called *simple mania*, because it is mania without delusion, a mania of feeling and conduct rather than a derangement of intellect; but the name is not very suitable since it does not denote definitely the disorder and does connote indefinitely more disorder of reason than there actually is. Although commonly, it is not invariably, the prelude of mania; sometimes it is itself the whole drama, lasting for weeks or months, or even longer in a few instances, without going down into deeper degeneration. In that case it is pretty sure to recur some time or other, or from time to time, either as a simple so-called *periodic* or *recurrent mania*; or as an *alternating insanity*—that is, a recurrent insanity in which the excitement is regularly followed or preceded by a corresponding period of abject depression and apathy, the so-called *folie circulaire* of French authors. However it occur, it marks a less degree of disorganisation of mind than the delusional mania to which it is the frequent prologue and to which it leads naturally in the course of further pathological development.

Acute Mania.

Inquiry into the previous history of a person who has fallen into acute mania will generally discover a period of passing mental gloom and uneasiness, so brief sometimes as to be hardly noticed, before any show of excitement. Dejected and disquieted in mind, he knows not what ails him but feels anxiously that something ails him. His condition is a painful out-of-sortness—a *dysthymia* or *psychalgia*—showing itself in gloomy and irritable mood, nameless anxiety, haunting foreboding of ill, with which go vague and disquieting discomforts in head, chest or abdomen, great unrest, bad sleep and horrid dreams. In quest of relief, he feels impelled to wander restlessly from place to place, and is prone to drink much fluid, perhaps to take alcoholic stimulants. Disappearing suddenly perhaps after a duration varying from a few hours or days to as many weeks, the gloom is followed by the excited state of jubilant thought and feeling, which goes on then to run its shorter or longer course.

These opposite-featured precursors of acute mania I might compare to the chill and contraction of a part and the sequent warmth and dilatation which go before inflammation of it: first a chill then an ignition of thought, a contraction followed by a dilatation of spirits, as old writers would have phrased it. If the slow thought and sad feeling of melancholy denote sluggish molecular motions and dull reflex action, and the brisk thought and lively feeling of mania sprightly molecular motions and rapid reflex action, it is easy to conceive how close the intimate physical conditions of the two mental states lie to one another, much as the complexions of their symptoms differ; how quickly alternations of them may take place, as they do abruptly sometimes; and why it is that depression followed by excitement is the common and almost natural order of onset of acute mania.

Nor need it be a surprise that the great elevation of mind should increase until it topples over into the frenzy of acute mania. Then excitement goes on to rise, order and unity of mind to fall in proportion; ideas are rapid, incomplete and incoherent, the currents of them being interrupted before they are finished, and crossed at random by other ideas which in turn do not get themselves finished; actions eccentric and absurd, disjointed and aimless, turbulent and destructive. The symptoms presented in the general are these: an urgent desire to be moving and doing, wherefore the person, instigated by pure internal unrest, wanders from home without knowing why or whither, or is restlessly occupied in senseless acts; an incessant loquacity in harsh tones which have lost their finest modulations, with little or no coherence in what is said, even when it is not, as it sometimes is, the mere physical excitation of speech without thought; loud declamations, singing, and bursts of meaningless laughter; fitful and abruptly changing moods, an air of expansive cordiality being pulled up short and displaced instantly by a menacing glare of angry suspicion, and friendly salutations turning in a moment to coarse abuse or bitter imprecations, should a passing look, gesture, or word of the interlocutor chance to be misliked and misconstrued; unresting activity in walking backwards and forwards over the same piece of ground, in tearing up weeds, grass, flowers, in turning things upside down or in changing their places, in pulling off and putting on the clothes, and the like. A sane person cannot realise the acute internal disquietude which the patient feels in consequence of the agitation of his nervous elements; he is "frantic mad with evermore unrest!" Neither in moods, nor in thoughts, nor in deeds usually is there constancy or coherence; a sound, a sight, a word, a gesture which catches a momentary attention suffices to cause an instant and abrupt change. Sometimes, it is true, a more lasting mood of suspicion, pride, or other passion imparts a measure of system and continuity to the delirium by summoning accordant thoughts to its sessions and holding them to a degree of unity and form; but for the most part the moulds or forms of thought are temporarily dissolved, their neurotic patterns broken up, and all sorts of faulty junctions and unions, partial, irregular and fleeting, made in consequence. The outcome is a discordant turmoil, "like sweet bells jangled, out of tune and harsh." Withal there is commonly a sense of glorious satisfaction with himself, an exultant and sly joy in the consternation and confusion which he creates, an immensely jubilant feeling of freedom and power. Never is mortal more pleased with himself, never more sure of his free-will, than when, clean gone self-astray in passion or in madness, he is not himself.[1]

[1] Describing the gradual increase of his excitement, Gérard de Nerval says :—"Je chantais en marchant un hymne mystérieux dont je croyais me souvenir comme l'ayant entendu dans quelque autre existence, et qui me remplissait d'une joie ineffable. En même temps, je quittais mes habits terrestres et je les dispersais autour de moi. . . . Une ronde de nuit m'entourait ; j'avais alors l'idée que j'étais devenu très grand, et que, tout inondé de forces électriques, j'allais renverser tout ce qui m'approchait. Il y avait quelque chose de comique dans le soin que je prenais de ménager les forces et la vie des soldats qui m'avaient recueilli."

The higher inhibitions of thought and feeling gone, the lower passions surge to the front in turbulent welter and actuate the conduct. Sexual feeling, prone and prompt to be coarsely obtrusive, shows itself in equivocal words, in lascivious gestures and attitudes, sometimes in acts of repulsive lust. It is a strange thing to see, although it be instructive evidence of the inmost contents of human nature, what a foul and shameless fury of inflamed lust a chaste and decent woman can become when her mind is decomposed into mania. More startling perhaps is the spectacle of a modest maiden, whose virgin nature might be expected to be innocent of the least stain of impurity, displaying a knowledge of sexual relations and of their vulgar vocabulary which seems miraculous, since it is thought incredible she could ever have learned it. Understanding of reproductive means and ways comes by the inspiration of nature, but not their descriptive language. Rightly considered, we are in face of nothing very wonderful nor very dreadful. Who hid such import in the gesture-language of love? Who taught their skill to the unpractised instruments of procreation? Good people would have the maiden incurious about an instinct which transforms her whole nature, physical and moral, and is the secret inspiration of her hopes and faith, nothing less than her being's main end, because the modesty of convention, forbidding the acknowledgment of it and hardly allowing it a name, bids her blush at the open mention of its organs and office. But it is a tacit conspiracy to be wilfully blind to the actual. To suppress curiosity instigated by an instinct whose promptings cannot be suppressed is impossible; it will put forth its feelers with stealthy ingenuity, and an elective affinity will not fail, consciously or unconsciously, to guide it to the fit tracks of inquiry. Is it not true that the chastest maiden, innocent herself of the moving reason, is stirred more by the lustful look and bold address of a rake than by the ingenuous face and shy respect of a homebred bashful youth? What are the graceful tricks of modesty, the innocent coquetries, the shy, half-retreating advances, the half-beseeching repulses, but the subtle social wiles and guiles of expression by which women unconsciously dissemble desires and feelings which they are debarred the freedom of showing but which nature has not debarred them from having? However revolting the spectacle, it is natural therefore for lust to show itself in coarse form when all the decent drapery of sex has been torn away by disease—all those refined ideas and feelings, that is to say, which have been evolved socially through the ages to cover its animal nakedness and to raise its human dignity.

So much for the outward and visible complexion of acute mania: what passes within is a tangle of confusion passing discernment. No sane mind can possibly enter into and realise the tumultuous disorder of a mind involved in frenzy; to do that would be to be actually and equally deranged.[1] Many times no doubt mad acts which seem unmotived have their obscure and partial motives in disordered feelings and notions of which the patient may think to give some account to himself; but at other times they have no definite feelings or notions beneath them, being as direct outcome of violent nervous excitation and its consequent intolerable unrest as if they were the effects of electric stimulation of the cerebral cortex. So also is it sometimes with the inexhaustible overflow of incoherent speech, which then betrays the mere urgent utterances of excited speech-centres, not any antecedent thought even of a fragmentary sort, and is such a manifest relief to the patient that he will not check it when he can and cannot check it long. In the worst cases all the mind-centres are so deeply disordered that consciousness itself is disintegrate. The result is that the movements of the maniac exhibit, proportionately to the disorder, all degrees of the undoing or dissolution of will—steps of a regressive process of *devolition,* if I may coin the word—from acts that have all

---

[1] It is related of one man that he strenuously tried it, and with an unexpectedly successful result: the Rhetorician of old who, in order to represent the madman with perfect art, entered so deeply into the character that he became the madman which he strove to realise.

the air of being wilfully exaggerated and perverse, through psychomotor displays where the voluntary forms are preserved in fractions or fractional groups, down to the entirely loose and incoherent vagaries which evince and express a completely shattered will. No one can ever understand the real nature of these examples of decomposed will who, viewing them from the standpoint of mind in disorder, tries to discover a mental explanation of them and to set it forth in the language of psychology. The truth is that psychology has no terms for them, and that its principles exclude their existence. Let him view them from the standpoint of a physical disorganisation which causes a disintegration of mind, substituting the informing conception of a definite mental organisation for the barren notion of abstract mind, and he will then be in the right way to perceive what they really are and what decomposition of will means.

Feelings and ideas are no less broken up, confused and incoherent than movements. In a sane person who is in good health the feelings are more or less definite and constant in relation to circumstances, but in the maniac they are fragmentary, incoherent, tumultuous, and transient, the least stimulus, whether adapted or not, exciting them to the most irregular and uncertain explosions. So strangely out of character are they that they come not within the category of ordinary experience and cannot be described in its language: they are ineffable.[1] The outer world to him is quite other than it is to the sane mind, for it is shaped to the features of his fragmentary and incoherent ideas; its impressions cannot help taking the forms and colours which his thoughts and feelings impose on them, so far as they take form and colour at all; they are therefore as good as non-existent save as they are thus taken into the wild currents and translated into the language of the delirium.[2]

[1] One may compare them with the ineffable feelings of the ecstatic creature, religious or erotic, as I have done at length in my book on *Natural Causes and Supernatural Seemings*. As in the "speaking with tongues," a new language is sometimes necessary and invented to express them.

[2] "Tout se transfigurait à mes yeux ; chaque personne qui m'approchait semblait changée, les objets matériels avaient comme une pénombre qui en

Thence follow inevitably all sorts of false perceptions; familiar faces seem as strange faces, whence utmost distrust of them, and strange faces as familiar, whence attempts to embrace them; men seen as disguised women, and women as disguised men; the familiar surroundings of home repudiated as strange and foreign, and friends tendering aid as enemies threatening life; real voices misheard and unreal voices heard to insult, impute, accuse, threaten, or command, or the ears filled with confused sounds, shrieks of torture, ringing of bells, explosions of firearms, and the like; food rejected as poison, meat as human flesh, milk as lime, and the foulest matters devoured with apparent avidity;[1] stinking, stifling, or putrid smells vividly smelt without outward cause, and no disgust felt of real and repulsive odours; up-and-down, to-and-fro, or swinging movements of the walls and floor of the room and of things in it, owing to the exteriorisations of deranged muscular sensations; strange shocks, thrills, creepings, tinglings, shootings, numbness, contractions in the limbs and other parts of the body, ascribed to secret electric agency or to other hidden machinery of mischief. Thus in the worst event every impression from without upon every sense becomes a stimulus of disorderly feeling and disorderly acts.

In vain is the right impression made on sense when, mind being severed from sense, the power of interpreting it is lost—that is to say, when the cortical reflexes which condition the fit forms of mental apprehension are themselves broken up, or the paths between sense and them obliterated; with chaos within, the outer world is just the chaos which is madly felt or thought, for the material of experience is necessarily wrested into the shattered shapes of formless thought and feeling. Some persons strangely wonder that a madman, able to see things clearly, does not

modifiait la forme, et les jeux de la lumière, les combinaisons des couleurs se décomposaient, de manière à m'entretenir dans une série constante d'impressions qui se liaient contre elles."—*Gérard de Nerval*.

[1] One lady, who had been fed forcibly with milk during her acute illness, informed me, after recovery, that she had refused it because she was convinced that it was lime-wash which was being forced on her.

see the world as they see it—that, seeing, he does not perceive; the true wonder is not that he sees it so differently, but that any one wonders at him for seeing it as it actually is to him. Could we get inside his brain and realise for one minute the anarchy of it, there would be nothing surprising in the looks, gestures, words, cries and deeds which, like him, we should perform; so far as they had psychical motive, they would be in relation to the real world of insane experience, however much out of relation to the real world of sane experience.[1]

In the foregoing portraiture of acute mania, I have brought together symptoms which, although most of them are met with at one stage or another in the worst cases, together or separately, vary in degree of severity and in mode of distribution in different cases, and sometimes in the same case at different times; presenting, in sum, every kind and degree of mental disorder from simple mania where, beyond undue excitement of thought and feeling, it is not easy to discern where the disorder is, to furious frenzy where, the mind completely disrupted, it is impossible to discover where disorder is not. Individual cases will of

[1] Dr. Kandinsky, a physician of Moscow, who, after being insane two years, recovered, has given a detailed account of the race of delusions and involuntary thoughts in his mind and of the various wonderful and lively hallucinations which he had. Of his numerous hallucinations he says that not more than one-tenth of them had any relation to the delusions and involuntary thoughts.

It is in the contents and workings of dreams that we find the resemblances of the contents and workings of mania. The same tricks of mental dramatisation are played, and the same liberties taken with space and time. Having conceived the notion that matter perishes not, but is modified : that we live in the race and the race in us—Gérard de Nerval says—" Cette idée me devint aussitôt sensible, et comme si les murs de la salle se fussent ouverts sur des perspectives infinies, il me semblait voir une chaîne non interrompue d'hommes et de femmes en qui j'étais et qui étaient moi-même; les costumes de tous les peuples, les images de tous les pays apparaissaient distinctement à la fois, comme si mes facultés d'attention s'étaient multipliées sans se confondre, par un phénomène d'espace analogue à celui du temps qui concentre un siècle d'action dans une minute de rêve. Mon étonnement s'accrût en voyant que cette immense énumération se composait seulement des personnes qui se trouvaient dans la salle et dont j'avais vu les images se diviser et se combiner en mille aspects fugitifs."

course differ according to the particular symptoms which predominate. In some the derangement affects principally the feelings, these drawing in their morbid train conformable delusions or a system of subservient reasoning; and the patient is then sullen, suspicious, haughty, reserved, according as the dominant feeling of his systematised mania determines, breaking out quickly, when thwarted or opposed, into angry and incoherent declamation or denunciation and violent conduct. In other cases there is an endless stream of rapidly flowing ideas in incoherent tracks and a corresponding outflow of them in unceasing loquacity. The degrees of increasing incoherence of speech which may be noticed in different cases, sometimes in the same case at different stages, are these: first, distinct remains of logical associations of ideas, more or less complete, whereby fragments or remnants of correct reasoning are displayed; secondly, associations of ideas through like-sounding words, so that thoughts follow one another, albeit essentially unrelated and incoherent; thirdly, a mere rattle of words or of parts of words, or of invented words that are no words, associated by assonance and alliteration, and an utterly meaningless and incoherent gabble in consequence; lastly, a purely physical excitation of speech without thought. The special complexion of a third type of case is imparted by an unceasing bodily activity of some kind: one is restlessly busy all day in acts of meaningless purport; another is involved, body and soul, in violent explosions of frenzy; a third is addicted to stripping himself naked, to self-abuse, and perhaps to an accompanying mad religious rant, for it is curious to see how prone, by some tie of secret sympathy, a strain of religious raving is to go along with nakedness and self-abuse.

These different features do not mark varieties of disease, but differences in character, degrees and distribution of symptoms of disorder; they may be seen sometimes in the same case at different stages of its course. By fixing on a particular symptom and giving its name to the cases in which it is prominent, it is possible to manufacture in mania, as in melancholia, any number of varieties, such as religious mania, erotomania, dipsomania, pyromania, kleptomania, nymphomania, and the like. But the distinctions are superficial; and the big names, if taken to be more than descriptive conveniences, are more harmful than useful, since they are likely, as I have before argued, to be straightway converted into pathological entities and to become ever afterwards hindrances to true observation and thought. Perhaps a *chorea-like* mania might merit a special description because of the special and specially congruent character of the motor and mental symptoms: perpetual movement hither and thither without notion of whither, unceasing repetitions of monkey-like grabbings and grimaces, clapping of hands, odd antics of body and arms, confused pushings and pullings, howlings and laughings, iteration of meaningless sentences or half sentences in automatic gabble; all aimless, jerky, disjointed, quasi-mechanical. There is no purpose in the patient's actions, whether generally as regards conduct or specially as regards particular acts; the latter are incomplete and quasi-spasmodic, one not getting itself finished before another, meeting, crossing, or joining it, distracts and frustrates it; and the consequence is that, volition being more disintegrated, he is less amenable to rational appeal or control than more violent patients often are. The interest of the special features is the spectacle which they furnish of a thoroughly disintegrate mental organisation, and of the fractional functionings of its separate parts in ideation and action.

Although it passes human penetration to discern order in the complex and confused disorder of acute mania, still one may indicate degrees of deepening disorder and their significance. Note how purposive movements and the forms of will behind them—acts and their wills—are decomposed and dissolved, so to speak, in increasing degree: first, undue excitement of normal movements, with loss only of the delicate modulations or refinements which, representing the latest and finest organisation, make the grace of them, and with no more loss of consciousness than the unconsciousness of the loss; secondly, wild and turbulent, yet systematised movements presenting all the show of inflamed will and consciousness, albeit with the large and calm self-control of true will gone, and the patient, entirely unconscious of his loss, exulting in his wild doings;. thirdly, as will be illustrated in detail later, dissevered and fragmentary acts which, although voluntary in their particular forms, are really involuntary, if not convulsive, in their manifestations, all semblance of integral consciousness and will being lost; lastly, at the worst, convulsive movements with positive abolition of consciousness and will. Such are the successive stages of *devolition*.

Course and Duration of Acute Mania.

The course and duration of acute mania are alike most variable. Sometimes it is a passing storm, raging for a few hours only, a *mania transitoria*, though that is an exceptional event; most often it goes on from day to day, from week to week, from month to month, now abating and on the seeming wane for a while, now reviving and flaring again into fury. Seldom does it proceed on an even level of excitement; remissions commonly and occasionally actual intermissions of symptoms—so-called *lucid intervals*—alternating with frenzy. Were it not for these remittent and intermittent respites, it could not well go on as long as it often does, without either spending itself or spending the patient's forces. Why it ends at last in a particular case it is hard to say, as it is hard to say beforehand when it will end. Too often the first promise of cessation is the disappointing lull of a remission only.

The remissions in the course of acute mania are more or less periodic. They may be for a few hours in the day, or on alternate days, or monthly, or perhaps at particular seasons of the year, or quite irregular. Why they should be daily in one case and monthly in another we know not in the least, any more than why one of two persons, ague-struck, should shiver every third day and the other every fourth

CHAP. III   *INSANITY WITH EXCITEMENT—MANIA*   251

day. When they take place monthly it will be a fast faith, which no argument will shake, that the moon provokes the recurrence. It is pretty sure then to have been noticed that the symptoms were worse at the full moon, albeit they were just as bad or worse at other times of the month; and the unfailing coincidence will be solemnly vouched for by persons who are such good observers that, although seeing the heavens every day of their lives, they have not the least idea in what part of them the new moon is first visible. The event which fulfilled expectation has been noted, while the events which went contrary to it have been overlooked; not otherwise than as the answered special prayer fascinates the awed attention, while no notice is taken of the multitude of special prayers that obtain no answer. Better reason is there for faith in monthly exacerbations when they are noticed in women at their menstrual periods or what, were these functions not suspended or extinct, would be such periods.

Actual intermissions of symptoms amounting to intervals of perfect lucidity are not so common as remissions. Still they sometimes occur suddenly and unexpectedly, perhaps when matters look their worst, the frenzy disappearing for an hour or so, or for a few hours, or for a day, and then returning as abruptly as it went. If the abrupt change to quietude takes place when the symptoms before it were more than usually fierce and there was nothing in them, unless it were their fierceness, to foretoken it, we might suppose that the violent molecular agitations of the disordered thought-tracks had been exhausted by the excessive discharges and a comparative peace established, whereupon the normal junctions of the tracks were restored and the train of thoughts turned on to their proper lines. Fortunate, though infrequent, is it when the junctions then continue right and recovery is stable and lasting; too often the restoration of energy during the lucid lull is the occasion of the renewal of the molecular commotion and its disorderly discharges.

Sometimes the lucid intermissions between attacks of mania are so long that the sane intervals equal or exceed the insane periods of the person's life; who is then practically two persons, since he has two alternating lives the respective thoughts, feelings and doings of which go on apart. The disease is really a recurrent disease after varying intervals of sanity, and it is known as *recurrent* or *periodic mania*. Between the paroxysms the mind may be so clear and natural that no one perceives any fault in it; sometimes, however, a close scrutiny detects a bluntness of it, as if it had suffered a sort of contusion, manifest in some apathy of feeling, an appreciable intellectual sluggishness, an indolent-looking inability to settle to a steady pursuit, a slight deadening of the finest social feeling. The time and reason of the recurrences are alike unknown; a short change of mood, either a sad mood of sudden irritability or a glad mood of lively energy, ushers in the mania, which bursts out quickly and quickly reaches its height, and then, after running its regular course, subsides as quickly, leaving the person as he was before it. The attacks are almost exact repetitions of one another; in the same order the same feelings, the same delusions, the same peculiarities of dress and demeanour, the same doings come on, keep on, and go off on each occasion. There is an accuracy of memory in the morbid drama surpassing that of conscious performance, the perfection of a memory which remembers not that it is remembering; a mechanical performance of an elaborate series of mental functions which suggests at one and the same time a mechanism of mind and the complexity of the mechanism. Why the disease should thus recur, and recur in similar paroxysms, we cannot tell; as with epilepsy, the nervous constitution carries in itself from the past the unknown conditions of the recurring storms.

As the normal functions of the nervous system are periodic, not constant, it would perhaps be remarkable if its disordered functions had not their remissions and intermissions. May it not be that the ebb and flow of its functions is a note of man's remote sympathy with day and night, summer and winter, moon and tides, and other periodicities of nature? These periodicities having been constant during the evolution of nature on earth from its primal elements to its present organic level, it is reasonable to suppose that the nervous system will contain implicitly in its nature and display explicitly in its functions a law of periodicity.

Granting a general tendency to periodical return, the uncertain periods of particular recurrences of mania must be admitted, like the fits of epilepsy, to be determined by internal conditions or external influences which are yet unknown, though without doubt bodily states, habits of life, seasons of the year, atmospheric states, and the like, have their effects. An alternation of action and relaxation seems to be a natural law of all nervous action, sound and unsound, and to show itself in more or less regular variations of excitement at different times of the day. Certainly periodicities are more frequent in nervous than in other diseases; they are more frequent in women than in men; and among mental disorders the tendency to them is greatest in hereditary disorders, where the nervous equilibrium is naturally unstable.

The large periodicities of nervous function attract easy notice, but the regular successions of minute intermissions, the waves or pulses which are the necessary conditions of the apparently continuous vital functions, are not so much regarded. The pauses between the constituent pulses of a sensation are as distinct probably as between the pulses of the heart, were our senses only fine enough to perceive them. To us who live within, and in relation only to, a little span of space and time the immeasurably small and the immeasurably great are alike infinite and unknown worlds. The infinitely little is nowise appalling to us because we are so vast in relation to it, whereas we are awed by the infinitely vast because in relation to it we are but atoms of atoms: to an infinitely minute being, however, the distance between the constituent atoms of a molecule might seem infinite space, while an infinitely big being might feel the fixed stars press too closely on him. Nay, it is easy to conceive of oppositely acting drugs which might go some way to produce, by their effects on the nervous system, those opposite feelings. Be that as it may, and however it be with the intimate pulsings of life, there can be no doubt that exhaustion of nerve-energy owing to a continuance of violent action entails a remission of fury, until the gradual accumulation of excitable potential energy by process of nutrition reaches the unstable level of a fresh discharge under the impact of ordinary mental and bodily stimuli. Hence the rule of wise treatment in acute mania: to withdraw the patient from all but mild and monotonous external impressions. Hence too, let me add, the evil of unwise treatment, that is, to constrain the nerve molecules into a forced quiet by repeated doses of narcotic drugs, released from which they recoil in violent commotions proportionate in their rebound to the previous tense restraint. An artificial periodicity of higher pulse-waves of excitement is established and the conditions of a subsequent more pernicious exhaustion prepared and made ready—the way of dementia is made easy.

Remittent or intermittent, acute mania runs its uncertain course to recovery in about half its cases. A full restoration of the person to his old self takes place when those who, appalled by his fury and hideous transformation, could never have believed it possible. "This is not my husband!"—"This is not my wife!"—"It is impossible I should ever feel the same love and trust as before," is perhaps the despairing thought, felt, if not formulated, at the bottom of the sad heart. It may well seem so at the time; yet with the restoration of the true self fears and suspicions fade away, sympathies revive, former contacts are restored, and the return to old intercourse, which appeared incredible, is natural and costs no qualm.

How does the patient himself feel when he comes to himself? Can he ever forget the horrible experience which he had and the degraded being that he was? Yes; here also oblivion waves its tranquil wing over the terrible past, and the events of it, as they recede into dim distance, fade and dislimn like a cloud in the sky, or like the visions of a bad dream. For it was not his true self, not the "I" that he is now, but a transformed and other self, the "I" that he was then, who went through them in quite strange circumstances; so that, to him now restored to his true self and to his normal circumstances, they wear a far-off alien look, having the pale and shadowy forms, without the substance, of experience. They are remembered historically, without the feelings which made them real at the time, as one remembers a dream, or the events of childhood, or the experience of some other period of life when virtually another person in other place or circumstances: to realise them truly in remembrance it would be necessary to be the self of them again.[1] Therefore it is that he who is subject to attacks of recurrent mania remembers better, during an attack, the thoughts, feelings and events of a former attack than he does when he is his sane self; he has the most real memory of them then because he can and does think, feel and act them again. Moreover, in silent and subtle aid of forgetfulness, self-love, resenting the humiliation of its abject overthrow, fails not to contribute; eager to discover or ingenious to devise in the special causes and circumstances of the attack explanations and extenuations and excuses of its worst features, it persuades itself that these were aggravated, if not caused, by the treatment pursued, or at any rate would not have been what they were had wiser measures been adopted.

Recovery, when it takes place, usually looks complete. Friends perhaps notice nothing wrong in him, and strangers would not suspect that he had been out of his mind. The only prejudice which he has suffered is that he lives thence-

---

[1] "Ego sum," was the eager exclamation of the mistress, surprised by the cold indifference of her former lover whom she met after a long absence again. "At ego," inquit, "non sum ego." The patient may even sometimes look back with a sort of longing envy to the happiness which he felt in his madness. Charles Lamb, speaking of his insanity in a letter to Coleridge, says, "I look back on it at times with a gloomy kind of envy; for, while it lasted, I had many hours of pure happiness. Dream not, Coleridge, of having tasted all the grandeur and wildness of fancy till you have gone mad. All now seems to me vapid, comparatively so."

forth under the suspicion and risk of a recurrence of the malady some time or other; a risk greater after some forms of mania than others, greater or less according as the future conditions of life are adverse or propitious, always greatest where it is most hereditary. Some there are who, having had one attack, perhaps early in life, go on to the end of their lives without ever having another; others who, having had more than one attack, yet pass their last days in peace and sanity; more perhaps who, having recovered from a first or even second attack, eventually die insane. Absolute assurance either of safety or of peril it is permitted to no mortal to give in the present state of human knowledge, and to no mortal to have in the manifold vicissitudes of human life.

The paramount question in a particular case is naturally, What is to be the issue, immediate and remote, in this case? Putting aside propitious or unpropitious conditions of life, that depends most of all on individual character, and this in turn on hereditary antecedents. The outlook is bad when the foundations of the mental nature are bad. As it is not the heat pain and redness of an inflammation, but the inherent vitality of the structure, which determines whether the inflammation shall undergo resolution or the structure dissolution, so it is not the violence of the mania, but the inborn structure of the individual mind which determines whether disorder shall deepen into disorganisation or shall pass away. A brain of grossly defective structure shows its fault plainly enough by such positive mental privation as we designate imbecility or idiocy; in such case the recovery from an attack of acute insanity never could be mental recovery. But a brain of deficient structure or vitality in which the weakness, being latent, does not show in childhood while performing childish functions, may still show its native infirmity by its inability to subserve the new mental developments which should take place at puberty, and by its consequent break-down under the stress of adaptations to the new relations and functions of life. Then the mental disorder befalling in an inadequate organ, and because of its inadequacy, will be prone to run rapidly into dementia.

In this relation it is proper to remember and reflect that bad foundations of mental structure are laid, not by positive madness only in the parental stock, but by such wrong and unwholesome mental development in it as is essentially lack of sanity of mind, though not technically insanity. There is a class of beings, essential degenerates, as irksome to others as they are satisfied with themselves, who display naturally such one-sided exaggerations of some qualities of character, such stunted developments of other qualities, such moral and intellectual obliquities, that it cannot justly be said of them that they are in right minds when they are not out of their minds; for they are truly wry-minded beings in whom the right mind is a wrong or deformed mind. They provoke a special irritation, not because they have deformed minds, for a deformity of mind might excite compassion, as a deformity of body does, but because, being deformed, they will have it that it is not they but the well-formed in mind who are the deformed. An attack of mania befalling one of them comes not as a stranger into strange surroundings, an exoteric calamity, but rather as an acute consummation of a native psychopathy; an esoteric development, whose germ lay in the same egg and quickened with the character. After the storm they are likely either to lapse into chronic insanity and to remain in it for the remainder of their days, or, if they recover, to have a relapse or relapses some time from which they do not recover. Dark and dubious as the future is for them, it is perhaps worse for their children, who are born with such unsound mental tendencies, and reared in such unsound mental atmosphere, that their degenerate mental structure gives out early in life and runs quickly to irremediable disorganisation.

Not that every degree and sort of neuropathic inheritance is fraught with so serious a risk. It is a question of kind and degree of degeneracy. Not a few persons having inherited a morbid strain of mental structure still recover from acute mania; for their heritage may amount to no more than an unstable equilibrium, prone to be overthrown suddenly and perhaps as suddenly restored. This is especially the case where there was an external cause of mental disturbance in some physical or moral shock, some stress or strain, not apparently adequate in itself but adequate in the case, and where the disorder was acute. Then the mental equilibrium may be restored as suddenly as it was lost. It is in frail and faulty constitutions, where the hereditary infirmity shows itself by positive signs of degeneracy, physical and mental, and the insanity comes on without any signal external cause, that the disorder, which from its outset and even in the acutest phase may then exhibit notable demented features, is prone to become chronic and progressive. In such case the vital elasticity is small, there are no reserve-forces, and when the first feeble line of defence has been overthrown by the storm of the attack, the disaster degenerates quickly into irretrievable disorganisation of mind. Always the most constant danger of hereditary mania, its essential risk, is the danger of a recurrence; for the tendency to recurrence springs, like the tendency to occurrence, from the same unsound source—a faulty foundation of nature.

Does recovery from acute mania, hereditary or not, always leave the person more liable to a second attack? Does it add anything to the native predisposition, supposing him to have one? It certainly adds to the apprehension of a second attack, since, but for its occurrence, no one might have thought of expecting an attack at all; and always thereafter the same nature exposed to similar and equal causes of disturbance may be expected to react in the same disordered way. Without doubt too it adds something to the strength of the apprehension, by adding something, however little, to the native predisposition; for the nervous system has a certain inclination, strengthened by every repetition, to go the way of function it went before, never forgetting absolutely, but building up habits, good or bad, into structure. No one can escape from the past which he has made for himself in himself, any more than from the more deep-laid past made for him in him by his forefathers: together they go far to make his destiny.[1]

This observation may also be made: that recovery from acute mania is not invariably quite so perfect as it looks, at any rate in the first instance. It may be hard to say what the change in the person is when he comes to himself, and those who know little of him may not notice any change. But his friends and those who know him intimately feel that he is not quite his old self, that somehow there is a difference, subtile but sensible, though they cannot say exactly what it is; perhaps a blunting of the finer sensibilities of his nature shown by lessened delicacy of feeling, coarser self-regard, and ruder self-will—a certain bloom and refinement of character, the grace of the fashion of it, gone—perhaps a loss of elasticity of mind shown by some apathy and indolence of thought and conduct. Ever so little damage has been done to the delicate texture of the mental organisation—to wit, a defacement of the finest tracery of its moral feelings and apprehensions, and consequent loss of memory of them. The patient loses moral memory, so to speak, just as when, his mind impaired by deeper disorganisation, he loses intellectual memory.[2] Indeed some degree of impairment of intellectual memory may be detected sometimes after acute mania, as after the delirium of an acute fever, which passes away by degrees only as full strength of mind is regained. Worse still, now and then,

[1] They make the tone of the individual nature, the rhythm of its motion, so to speak, with which, even from the first, different impressions consciously and unconsciously harmonise or are dissonant.

[2] He forgets to feel finely just as he forgets to think fully. Owing to the way in which thought is held captive by words, we usually think of memory too narrowly, not considering what it means essentially: it belongs properly to other nervous functions as well as to thought—to moral feeling, to social feeling, to perceptions, to acts, and the like. There is no such thing as an abstract memory; there are so many memories. The failures of faculties which are described pathologically as mental blindness, mental deafness, mental insensibility, are instances of loss of memory. The psychological division of mind into artificial faculties and their designation by special names has been an incalculable hindrance to seeing and thinking things as they are.

especially after acute mania in children and adolescents, there is so much hurt done to the most fine and specialised mind-tissue that it never recovers its integrity and the memory of its function—a veritable moral imbecility or insanity is left; just as if the tender shoots of moral development, latest conquests of human culture, had been blasted and their fine nervous substrata laid waste by the violent commotion of the storm. In these cases, moreover, the mind has not always much to lose and forget, since moral insanity, whether in young persons or adults, almost invariably bespeaks the faulty structure of unsound mental heritage.

How long is an attack of mania, acute or subacute, likely to last? By what signs may we know that it is going to be long or short? Many times it is as hard to say why it stops when it does as why it ever stops at all. Nevertheless, we may sometimes feel pretty sure that it will be brief. Sudden storms are short, and when the mania breaks out abruptly without forewarnings and is violent, it may be soon over—perhaps in a few days, now and then in a few hours. When it thus comes and thus goes, it is usually where an unstable neuropathic temperament, inherited or acquired, has undergone a sudden shock or strain. And the attack is then more likely to be short when the cause of perturbation, being comparatively slight, might seem disproportionate to the effect. A young woman having suffered an abrupt shock of mind in consequence of a breach with her lover, whom she has chanced to surprise in the company of a rival, or from whom she has received a letter saying that he does not wish to see her again, presently drowns herself, or goes raving mad for a few hours or days. A nervous and over-nicely sensitive person, newly married, is so revolted, physically and morally, by the delicacy-hurting business of consummation that he or she falls into a post-connubial mania which may terminate soon. A man or woman has an angry altercation with a neighbour about some petty matter of disputed rights, and thereafter falls into acute mania. In such cases the apparent inadequacy of the cause, proving how easily the mental equilibrium was upset, may justly inspire a hope that it will be as easily restored. But an equal hope is not justified when the mind is crushed by a violent stress or shock. The victim of a brutal rape or attempt at rape who goes stark mad in consequence of the horrible fright and shock of the outrage would not be so likely to recover soon, if she ever recovered at all. Nor would the father or mother, whose mind had been overthrown by the sudden news of the sudden death of a beloved son or daughter, be so likely to have a short attack as if the derangement had been due to a foolish quarrel with a neighbour about the merits of a fight between their respective dogs or respective children.

Other conditions in which a mania of short duration, a *mania transitoria*, may be looked for are these :—A person who has once had a severe sunstroke or a concussion of the brain or an injury to the head, which occasioned serious symptoms for a time, is left, after recovery, with so great a susceptibility and instability of nerve-centres that he is made temporarily but positively mad, not drunk, by a little alcohol only or by a cause of moral disturbance which would produce the brief madness of anger in a fairly balanced mind. The molecular ties of his nerve-element have been so strained that they yield to the least extra strain. The violent fury which sometimes follows epileptic fits and sometimes occurs in their stead, blind, destructive and dangerous as it is while it lasts, usually comes to an end in a few hours or at most in a few days. When there is but a weak federation of the cortical nerve-centres, whether native or acquired, it is easily dissolved, and the dissolution is superficial; but when, being strong, it suffers dissolution, the mischief goes deeper and is of more serious import; not otherwise than as the passionate gesticulation, cries and fury of a native of the inconstant South, when he is in a rage, do not mean the madness which they look nor even such a depth of emotion as a similar manifestation would mean in a cold and self-contained native of the more constant North : in the one the excitement is from the top, in the other it goes to the bottom, of the nature.

CHAPTER IV

INSANITY WITH EXCITEMENT—MANIA

Chronic Mania.

RECOVERY not taking place, what other issues has acute mania? The next most common event is that it becomes chronic, the excitement subsiding but the derangement continuing. Then it presents diverse features according to the degree and character of the persisting derangement. Sometimes, though seldom, delusions in respect to one subject or to one class of subjects and relations remain, while the rest of the mind or the mind in relation to other subjects is clear and rational; for all the world as if the general disorder had now condensed and settled into a certain definite tract or area of morbid function. Such limited madness used to be described as *monomania;* and there can be no question of its existence, albeit that name is now generally discarded as misleading. It is not ever possible to make an exact line of delimitation between sound and unsound parts or areas of mind and strictly to circumscribe morbid function. Mind is not an aggregate but an organic whole; and a whole cannot be sound whose constituent part is diseased. We are never then in face of a loss only—of the simple negative effect of so much subtracted function that has gone wrong, and there an end—but have to do with the occult, subtle, yet positive workings of the special diseased function on the other functions of a so far weakened mind; effects which, being worked unconsciously, as in dreams, and known only by their accomplishment, cannot be foreseen either by the patient himself or by others.

With this so-called monomania, which is secondary to foregoing mania or melancholia, and more often to melancholia than to mania, there is always some weakness of mind, often much more than appears on the surface, and in different cases varying degrees of weakness down to actual dementia: the whole mind weakened throughout but the particular delusions retaining their pre-eminence.[1] Where should such a height of delusional folly grow and sustain itself save in a fit soil of mental weakness? The patient has not sufficient strength and unity of mind adequately to resent and reject the most glaring inconsistency between his real and ideal state. Shut up in an asylum, he refuses not perhaps to do the domestic work of it from day to day, revolting only during short periodical attacks of excitement which he has from time to time, though all the while he believes and declares himself to be a royal personage entitled to the homage of those whose orders he obeys; professing that his legs are dead or do not belong to him, he still uses them just as anybody else would do; having a commission from heaven to proclaim the destruction of the world by fire and flood within twenty-four hours, he prepares for successive morrows without regard to the superfluous trouble which he is giving himself. It is remarkable too how little he is surprised by his surroundings when he is in an asylum, and how little he appreciates the flagrant mental defects of his fellow-inmates, whom he takes little notice of, or perhaps, if they are particularly noisy and obnoxious, accuses of acting or being acted on to seem mad, or whose palpable insanity he denies. Harmless as he seems he cannot always be depended upon to do no harm, even when far gone in

---

[1] Differing therein from *primary monomania* (now sometimes called *paranoia*) in which some exaggerated passion summons to its sessions and holds in attendance a group of morbid ideas, while the rest of the mind outside the morbid area is fairly sound.

dementia. The persistence of such extravagant delusions as he has, so aloof from reason, so self-sufficing, implies the complete obliteration of the mental processes which constitute judgment; and with judgment gone and delusion liable to strange developments and uncertain throes of activity, it is impossible to foresee what chaotic train of unreason may go on in the impaired mind and what mad conclusion be the outcome.

Most often the continuing derangement after acute mania is a general incoherence with various delusions and a gradually increasing weakness of mind; a *chronic mania* or *craziness*, differing only from *dementia* in its less degree of mental weakness and sliding insensibly into it. Its varied and disorderly features betray so many modes and degrees of derangement of an exceedingly complex, intricate and delicate mechanism, the orderly functions of which are an unresolved nebula still beyond scientific ken. Many of the permanent inmates of asylums belong to this class: one distinguished by his interminable loquacity as he goes along absorbed in senseless conversations with himself or with imaginary persons; another, by his loud and angry declamations, his violent gesticulations, his defiant menaces against enemies who are the coinage of his sick brain; another, by his reserved and haughty dignity or proud strut expressive of delusions of greatness; another, by his grotesque antics, the singularity of his gestures, and his odd acts, which, dictated by absurd hallucinations or delusions, have no rational relation to external circumstances. If another walks with body half bent to the ground and head hanging down, bellowing like a cow from time to time and making headlong rushes to a ditch in order to drink its dirty water, it is because he is inspired by a dim delusion that he is a cow and must act accordingly; or if he tries to go on all fours and snaps or barks at those who pass by, it is that he imagines himself to be a dog. Not in such case a delusion that is whole, consistent, and constant in its operation, but partial, incoherent, and inconstant, since the patient who acts thus madly out-of-doors may sit down at table in-doors and take food decently like an ordinary mortal. Why not ? It would be as unreasonable as unjust to deprive a madman of the privilege of inconsistency when there is not an inconsistency or a contradiction of which human nature outside an asylum is incapable. Why refuse him the right to cherish a private monstrosity of belief when there is no belief so monstrous that it has not been entertained either as a dogma of philosophy or an article of religion sometime or somewhere ?

Chronic mania does not commonly run a regular course; exacerbations of excitement at irregular times and for uncertain periods, supervening for the most part we know not when nor why, give it an acute or subacute look while they last. What is remarkable is that recovery does now and then take place, against all expectation, after several years of disorder, and when its duration and degree had long since annihilated hope. Such unlooked-for recovery I have known take place after five and after seven years of almost continuous crazy turbulence. More surprising still are occasional sudden and short restorations to sanity where nothing seemed less likely. I have seen a day of full lucidity alternate regularly with a day of the utmost incoherence for some weeks in a turbulent hereditary maniac who had been under restraint for twelve years[1]; and I have known the same patient, after all that time, become regularly quite sane for two or three hours every morning and utterly and noisily crazy all the rest of the day. It is with eclipse not extinction of mind that we have to do in such case, disorder not disorganisation of its mechanism, dislocation not demolition of its molecular order; wherefore, when the molecular dislocation is reduced, so to speak, the function is instantly restored. Without doubt, the routine of an asylum, where no new impressions solicit new action of the thought-tracts, sometimes helps to keep up the monotonous round of disorder; the mental machinery reacting day after day to the same round of impressions

[1] The patient's father was confined in an asylum, hopelessly insane, and an only brother had died insane and paralytic.

gets set to the habit of its action, locked in disorder. Hence it is that removal from an asylum into new surroundings is sometimes followed by an unexpected recovery, the new circumstances having required and elicited new mental adjustments and so unlocked the habit of disorder.

Who are the chronic maniacs who make unexpected recoveries after long illnesses? Not the placid and passionless beings who move about in the same mechanical way day after day, going through the same routine of foolish speeches and grotesque antics. Nor the monomaniacs who, turning on one mental axis, so to speak, betray by their gait, carriage and address, the revolving of the same set of insane ideas round a fixed passion, such as pride, suspicion, religious exaltation, and the like. Nor again the dements whose vacant eyes and toneless apathy of look, gait, speech and demeanour disclose weakness or want of mind. They who recover are, I think, chiefly of two classes—either those who, not having lost passion, like dements, nor had it absorbed in a few fixed delusions, like so-called monomaniacs, are lively, aggressive, enterprising, perhaps boisterous and turbulent, evincing often by quick apprehension and keen feeling, which they are prone to express with incoherent anger and energy, mind behind the veil of disorder; or those who, looking as if they were sunk in senseless apathy and set to certain habits of unreasoning and quasi-demented behaviour, yet show by an occasional quick turn of expression, or a flitting glance of intelligent apprehension, or a significant word, or a composed gesture, or an act of social propriety, that they are not so lost to perception and reason as their vacant looks and demented doings might betoken. These latter are much actuated at bottom by perverse morbid temper, itself perhaps kept in automatic gear and play by the misconstrued and resented circumstances of their detention. Passionate incoherence is the note of the symptoms in the former, the individual being there but marred and masked by his frenzy; and when his frenzy is past he is himself again, or so nearly so as to present no more change than the suspension of his normal mental life and the lapse of time might account for. In both classes an insane heredity is usually present; symptoms which, were there no such predisposition, might forebode dementia being of less evil import because of the specially wry bent given to them by the innate warp of nature. Some of these patients might be thought to put their mad behaviour on and wilfully to keep up insanity, so histrionic do the symptoms look. But it is not entirely so, since there is a positively insane basis beneath consciousness which actuates and keeps up the seeming feigning. A rooted madness, subjugating the intellect to its service, finds conscious pleasure in the free play of its temper and nature.

When a person recovers not from acute nor glides into chronic mania, what other outlet has he ? He sometimes, though seldom, dies of it. Indeed, death may be reckoned an exceptional and accidental event, when it takes place, rather than a part of the natural history of ordinary mania. The conducive conditions of its occurrence, together or separately, are a frail constitution unable to withstand the exhaustion of the fierce turmoil; difficulty of getting sufficient food taken; the supervention of other bodily disorder, such as congestion of the lungs or actual pneumonia; and medical maltreatment by excessive use of narcotic drugs.

Acute Delirious Mania.

There is a small class of cases of acute mania in which the fury blazes so fiercely as commonly to expire only with expiring life. This is especially so when, after a sudden outbreak, the excitement mounts quickly in fierceness from the start to a pitch of very acute and incoherent frenzy; so much so that the form of illness, having more the character of delirium than of mania, was described not inaptly by old writers as *phrenitis*, and is commonly known now as *acute delirious mania*. Noteworthy then sometimes is the abrupt outbreak of the mania; which comes like a bolt from the blue, preceded only perhaps by sleeplessness, a morbidly keen sensibility to impressions, a strange gloom of heart as if chilled by the shadow of some overhanging illness or other calamity. By these symptoms the threatened brain forefeels and foretells the impending conflagration and ending of its functions.[1] Once the flame of fury has burst out it flares up quickly into delirious incoherence of thought and conduct.[2]

The features of *acute delirious mania* are as striking as they are instructive. They evince little sustained consciousness of surroundings, only flickering gleams of it for the most part, so confused is the frenzy, so frantic the behaviour, so wildly unreasoning the patient in his resistance to everything done for him, so insensible to words of comfort and acts of help. Being practically an embodied frenzy, it is no more use to talk reason to him than it would be to talk reason to a horse that was plunging and kicking madly in a panic of wild fright. With the thought-forms of his cerebral plexuses broken up and the wild riot of anarchy going on, there is a chaos of sense as well as of thought, and it is impossible that he should apprehend external things as they are. Tangled and confused hallucinations of sense, especially of sight and hearing, phantasms of fear and suspicion, shifting and fragmentary, are as many and confused as the formless and changing thought-currents of the frenzy into which the warped sensory impressions are wrested and translated when they are noticed and translated at all. Not that the unconsciousness is always so complete or constant as it looks; for there are transient gleams of recognition

[1] A lady of considerable poetical distinction whom I saw in this mania had, before she was attacked, summoned her sister from a distance, informing her that she was going to be very ill, made all her preparations and testamentary dispositions with composure and minute care, and then became delirious. She died, as she had predicted, though there did not at the onset seem good reason that she should die.

[2] It has been previously noticed (p. 206) that acute delirious melancholia differs from the corresponding mania only in the acuter distress shown and in the greater monotony of its manifestations. The latter, however, lacks the note of joy and exaltation of ordinary mania; there is a sort of undertone of fear or distress, and, at best, there is usually something bitter and aggressive in the excitement. The disorder, being serious enough to threaten the very life of the mental organisation, goes too deep to be compatible with joy. The similarity of symptoms—indeed the essential identity of disease—has necessarily entailed some repetition in the description of them.

of persons and circumstances even when things look their worst, and the wild and frantic behaviour fails not to exhibit fractions or remnants of method or purpose.

The movements are not entirely irregular and at random, they evince broken-up deeds or acts; nor are they actually convulsive in the ordinary meaning of the word, since they retain some purposive form or semblance, albeit evidently beyond voluntary control and convulsive in their involuntary intensity. The fearful struggles have the air of struggles of defence, of defiance, of opposition, of resistance, of escape, being violent pushings and clutchings, writhings and plungings and rushings, strikings and kickings; an attempt to minister to the patient in any way, whether to dress or undress him, to give him food, to put him to bed, or even to move him in bed, is enough to provoke the quasi-convulsive struggles of aimless resistance. What can the best services do to comfort one who sees in those who serve him demons endeavouring to torture or kill him, and fights against their attentions in a fearful fight for life?

Besides these more purposive struggles there are sometimes jumpings and jerkings in automatic, senseless repetitions, and quasi-convulsive contractions and shakings of the body and limbs; frightful grimaces, iterated snappings of the jaws, and gnashing or grinding of teeth; spasmodic closure or winking of the eyelids, which offer the utmost resistance to attempts to pull them open; horrible yellings and howlings in machine-like repetitions; half-sentences and fragments of sentences, or words and half-words, shot out and repeated with damnable iteration, the latter part of the word or its last syllable being sometimes prolonged into an inarticulate howl or cry; an incessant flow of incoherent chatter in rhyme-like cadences or in broken rhymes; continual inaudible mutterings or speech-like movements of the lips without any sound. We are confronted with so many disintegrate special wills or fractions of wills in automatic obstinacy of separate activity.

In the midst of all this turmoil the patient perchance makes a sensible answer to a question, puts out his tongue, or opens his eyes when peremptorily asked to do so, stopping for the moment his quasi-convulsive acts, or gives some other flitting indication of intelligence. Immediately afterwards, however, he drops back into delirium; the paroxysms of convulsive jerkings, grimacings and strugglings return; and he, spent with them when they have spent their force, lies panting, prostrate, bathed in perspiration. The evacuations are passed involuntarily. All this while he gets little or no sleep; either there is no sleep at all night after night, or he has only snatches of sleep or short slumberous dozes of which it is hard to say whether they are sleep or not. How distinguish between the delirium which is a bad dream and the scaring dream which is a delirium? Between the dream so vivid that it seems waking during sleep, and the hallucinations so vivid that they seem dreaming during waking? They run into one another without a break.

As the excitement continues so the exhaustion increases, and the difficulty of getting food taken, which from the first is a labour and anxiety, becomes very great even during the comparatively tranquil remissions. A little food is perhaps swallowed uncertainly and capriciously. What one observes and has to contend with for the most part is a regressive undoing of will and a confusion of acts marking sequent steps of the functional disintegration of the cerebral cortex; at first, a general wild and vague resistance to every offer of it, the patient being too much absorbed in his delirium to heed it or even so much as to know what it is and what he is doing in rejecting it—*distracted voluntary struggles;* then the most violent reactions of refusal and resistance, quasi-convulsive or reflex in character, so soon as it touches the lips—*mixed voluntary and reflex resistance;* lastly, inability to swallow it, especially if it be liquid, when it has been got into the mouth, where it is sometimes kept in the pharynx in a spasmodic sort of way for a short time before a little of it is perhaps swallowed with a violent gulp and the rest forcibly ejected—almost *entirely reflex reaction.* It looks then as if there was, as in hydrophobia, a purely convulsive reflex action of the muscles of the pharynx. When the patient gets up to stand or walk he may reel or stagger like a drunken man, his giddy and vacillating orderly movements being in marked contrast with the seeming strength of his disorderly doings: he cannot quietly and exactly co-ordinate his movements in mass to a definite end without signs of feebleness, because of the wild turmoil of his supreme motor centres in the cortex, although he exhibits excessive energy in the action of disrupted groups and separate fractions of them. So much higher in power and dignity, as it is slower and quieter in process of accomplishment, is co-ordination than disruption, association than dissociation, composition than corruption, development than dissolution, will than passion, reason than madness.

Here then is a fit occasion to note and apprehend the process of a gradual resolution of organised movement—in other words, the regressive undoing of the structure of doing. As in the anatomy of the bodily structure we have the primary *element*; then the *tissue* which is formed of elements; next, the *organ* built up of tissues; and, last, the *organism* or organic whole; so in the structural composition of action we have a like progressive scale of ascent—first, the *elemental reflex movement*; then the union of elementary movements in *associated movements*; next, the composite *purposive movement*, which is the organ, as it were; and, last, the full *voluntary action* of the whole being. When this order of gradual evolution or making suffers a swift and violent resolution or unmaking, then we behold, in acute and confused display, such phenomena of disintegrate will and act as *acute delirious* mania presents.

Whosoever, not having seen an example of acute *delirious mania*, would frame for himself a mental picture of its general complexion, let him imagine a convulsive intensification of all the symptoms of a bad case of acute hysteria. In both maladies there are the same strange and uncertain mixtures of consciousness, half-consciousnesses, and unconsciousness, the same airs of wilfulness and perversity in conduct that is not truely voluntary, the same disruptions of will, the same irregular decompositions of movement, the same abrupt variations of symptoms. Without doubt there exists a similar pathological condition of things in the cerebral cortex : with this important prognostic difference— that in hysteria the instability and disruption of nerve-centres is functional and transitory only, whereas in acute delirium the mischief goes deeper into serious disorganisation and paralytic exhaustion of them. Meanwhile the mental symptoms in acute delirious mania, before their structure is undermined, necessarily make the same kind of show ; so much so, indeed, that the quasi-hysterical complexion of acute delirium sometimes disguises its serious nature, and the deplorable mistake has been made, not once but many times, of pronouncing acute delirium due to meningitis or to abcess of the brain, or to other gross organic disease of it, to be no more than hysteria and of maltreating it by treating it as such.

Acute delirious mania runs a short and quick course, not often of more than ten days or a fortnight, seldom to recovery, most often to death. It is only in its milder forms that perfect recovery takes place ; for when death does not soon end the worse cases, they are likely, in consequence of the shattering turmoil which the mind-structure has undergone, to sink into chronic insanity of the demented sort. Not that there is uniform violence of symptoms throughout, even when the result is fatal ; there are remissions during which matters look hopeful. But the hopes are frustrated when, as too often happens, the tranquil periods are followed by relapses into frenzy and these at last by comatose exhaustion and collapse, in which the patient lies pale, with dry tongue, feeble and irregular pulse, lips and teeth covered with sordes, perhaps in muttering delirium.

The exhaustion-coma does not at first look so grave an affair as it is, because the patient, obeying a peremptory order, may open his eyes or put out his tongue, although at the same time he perhaps suffers a fly to crawl over his forehead or eyelids, without making the least attempt to brush it away. If food be given forcibly during the fury,

especially if it be given in large quantities, it may do little
or no good, because the vital energy necessary to digest and
assimilate it is wanting; nay, its presence in the stomach
and bowels in undigested state may do harm directly by
provoking discomfort and diarrhœa, and indirectly by
causing a reflex exacerbation of the nervous disorder. He
who, knowing the need of nourishment in order to prevent
death by exhaustion, is inclined to force all the food he can
down the patient's throat at any cost, might do well to recall
to mind and, were it possible, to feeling the sort of nourishment to sensation, mood and thought which undigested food
is in his own stomach. Thus he might put himself in the
way to realise how far it is likely to stimulate and inflame
the horrors of a delirious brain. Without doubt the patient
dies sometimes when enough food has been taken to prevent
death from actual want of it; still dies of inanition, from
sheer lack of nerve-force to infuse the desire to take and
the power to assimilate it. At the same time, if nourishment be refused from the first, it is necessary to give it
forcibly in sufficient quantity and in concentrated form
because of the danger of fatal exhaustion. A little while
before death when life is expiring in its ashes, all disorder
sometimes disappears, the mind becoming quite clear; food
is perhaps taken then without difficulty, but too late to
prevent death. If the case is not going to end fatally, the
patient generally begins to take food and to get sleep before
he is on the verge of death.

The temperature, like the other symptoms, is variable.
It probably rises at the beginning of the attack, sometimes
as high as 105° or 106°, continues unduly but irregularly
high throughout it, and is high when a fatal end is near.
Certainly the increase is not constant; remissions take
place and the rises and falls are apt to be abrupt and
irregular. The pulse is quick, small, feeble, and compressible;
the respiration rapid, shallow and sighing. If strong purgatives have been given to open obstinately confined bowels,
an uncontrollable diarrhœa may be a serious complication
and danger.

Such then is acute delirious mania: midway in nature and symptoms between ordinary mania and febrile delirium, wanting the system and elated tone of the former and the completer incoherence and acuter fears of the latter. In the three forms of delirium we have really to do not with distinct diseases separated by dividing lines, but with increasing depths of mental disorganisation which merge together through intermediate instances.[1] On the mental side, the steps of increasing disorganisation are—(*a*) systematised mania, (*b*) delirious mania, (*c*) delirium, (*d*) terminal coma; on the motor side they are (*a*) frenzied voluntary acts, (*b*) psychomotor convulsive acts, (*c*) convulsions, (*d*) terminal paralysis. Nor is it an unprecedented, albeit an unusual, event for one case to go through the several stages, beginning as ordinary mania, rising by increments of excitement to delirious mania, and ending in delirium, convulsions, and coma.

Although no one can tell why, or foretell when acute mania shall blaze into acute delirious mania there are certain conditions which may, I think, be set down as predisposing to that issue. These are—(*a*) a frail and highly sensitive neurotic temperament, acute in its susceptibilities, keen, mobile, almost volatile in its intensities of thought, feeling and energy, and of very delicate, if not unstable, equilibrium; (*b*) the allied nervous diathesis that sometimes goes along with phthisis, albeit perhaps without actual development of tubercle in any organ of the body; (*c*) the immediate precedence of such bodily diseases as acute rheumatism, pneumonia, pericarditis and heart disease, and occasionally of the puerperal state in a neuropathic subject; (*d*) the disastrous aggravation of ordinary acute mania by the excessive use of narcotics; (*e*) the violent sympathetic or reflex irrita-

[1] It is no wonder perhaps then that we find one author describing as acute delirious mania an extraordinarily fierce example of ordinary turbulent mania lacking the essential features of any true delirium; and another, with equal impropriety, describing ordinary acute epileptic mania as delirious mania. There is a variety of delirium tremens, however, frequently fatal, which does present symptoms of true delirious mania, so like in fact as to be by themselves indistinguishable.

tion, extraordinary in its intensity, which the presence of a tapeworm (*ascaris lumbricoides*) in the gullet has been known to produce.[1] Rare and singular rather than practically important as the last event is, it has its special interest from a pathological point of view; it is a signal illustration how much disorder a cause of irritation in any part of the gastro-intestinal tract can produce in the highest functions of a specially susceptible nervous system. There are neurotic persons whom a stomach-ache will make delirious. On the whole it may be said that, given the effects of one of the before-mentioned bodily diseases, especially acute rheumatism and pericarditis, upon a highly neuropathic temperament, we have then the concurrence of conditions most conducive to the production of delirious mania; and that, given a train of exhausting emotion, or one great moral commotion, powerful because of its sudden stroke, operating in these conditions, we have the most efficient exciting causes of the outbreak.

Essential factor of the causation in all cases is the native proclivity of the nervous structure; a lack of compact unity and strength of it, either in element or in organisation, whereby a cause of no uncommon power or character is able to effect a degree of disorganisation of mental function nearly approaching that which is produced in a more stable structure by a positive toxic agent, organic or chemical. Approaching but not actually reaching it, for notwithstanding their frenzy, there still is a measure of restraint in the disorganising processes of delirious mania which is not maintained in the delirium of fever or of poison. When a poison, like belladonna, causes the disruption of absolute delirium in one brain, and a more or less systematised mania in another, or when an acute fever or an acute pneumonia occasions violent delirium in one person and does not particularly affect another mentally, the different effects testify to a more

[1] In the *Annales Medico-Psychologiques* (1867), M. Laurent relates a case of acute delirium with refusal of food and death owing to the presence of tapeworm in a woman's œsophagus. His researches discovered other cases of violent delirious excitement, recorded by Esquirol and others, where a tapeworm had been present in the stomach or œsophagus.

or less weak and loose-knit mental organisation in the one than in the other.[1]

Alternating Recurrent Insanity (*Folie circulaire*).

There is still one issue more of acute or rather subacute mania which it remains to take notice of—where it ends by being transformed, its seeming ending being but the beginning of an opposite-complexioned disorder. When the acute symptoms are past, the thoughts restored to tranquil order, and recovery seems near or actual, the patient falls instead into an abject melancholy depression. Then he is just the opposite of what he was, paying for his long spell of joy and energy by an equally long spell of dejection and torpor: sad, silent, secluded, self-distrustful, pusillanimous, ashamed of his late exploits, and so bereft of energy to feel, think, and do that he cannot come to a decision on the least point, or so much as write a letter. A little while ago in the height of elated energy and ready to do anything, he is now in the deep gloom of inert despondency and can do nothing: quasi-extinction has followed quasi-ignition of function. However great his apathy, he is perfectly conscious of his own state and of what goes on around him. Onlookers, therefore, think he might rouse himself by use of will and urge him to do so, but he can no more raise up a will which he has not, by willing it, than he can, when in one state, help falling into the other, which he perhaps foresees clearly and acutely dreads. So he remains for weeks or months until at last the wretched incapacity to feel, think and act passes away and he comes to his true self. Quite sudden sometimes is the transition, especially when the attacks are short; the cloud lifts instantly and

---

[1] While great labour has been applied, by diligent collation of cases, to find out whether the delirium in these diseases has any relation to the height of bodily temperature, not an inquiry has ever been made, so far as I know, as to the exact hereditary antecedents and mental constitutions of the cases in which delirium occurred. Yet it depends upon the individual. Patients with temperatures of 105° often have none, while those with temperatures of 101° or 102° have it.

he, feeling perhaps as if something tight had given way in his brain, is at once as bright, alert and energetic as he was just now sad, slow and inert. During the apathy the pulse is often slow and soft, the respiration slow and sighing, secretions are lessened, the bowels constipated, but sleep is much better than in the excited state. Menstruation, too, may continue regular throughout.

The kind of mania which thus alternates with melancholy in recurrent attacks is generally *simple mania:* the mania without delusion which shows itself in insanity of feeling and conduct rather than of thought. Indeed the lucidity of intellect in it is a remarkable and disastrous feature; for it enables a person who, possessed with an inflamed energy and outrageous self-sufficiency, has lost all moral restraint, to devise and pursue injurious, if not ruinous, projects of dissipation, marriage, speculation, business, which he would not have dreamed of in his normal state; to do such follies too with amazing energy, with extraordinary cunning and skill, and with a cynical audacity, of all which he would have been incapable when in his right mind; yet at the same time it prevents him from being thought mad enough to be placed under restraint. He is in the unfortunate position of not being mad enough to be held irresponsible for what his madness does. He may scatter broadcast plausible letters of scandal or slander, may run riot in drink and lechery, may cripple or ruin himself and his family, and all the while be thought more bad than mad, or at any rate be thought to have brought on his madness by the intemperance and immorality which were really its first symptoms. Some of these cases in which the degeneracy runs into vice furnish the most striking examples of moral insanity—a veritable, vicious *folie raisonnante;* while others exhibit so much loose weakness of mind and such ridiculously exalted ideas and feelings, along with tremulous excitement, as to suggest, too hastily, a commencing general paralysis. Although the alternating mania and melancholy are usually without delusions, they are not invariably so; the mania may be an ordinary acute mania, and the melancholy be accompanied with delusions, or even with actual stupor.

In the three several states of excitement, of depression, and of natural health the individual is virtually three different persons, not really responsible for one another; so much so that it is sometimes a perplexity to friends to know which is the real person. A stranger or a casual acquaintance may think him wonderfully well and like him best when he is in his excited phase, repudiating the notion that he is not in his right mind, all the more strenuously if biassed in his favour by being sharers in his prodigality; his family who know what his mania is costing them in money and in peace of mind, would rather see him in the melancholic and manageable phase, sorry as the spectacle then is.

Mania followed by melancholia is not the invariable order of events; the melancholy may come first and the mania follow. Nor are the opposite phases always of the same duration, although they are often pretty nearly so; on the whole, the melancholy stage is apt to last longest. Their duration is very variable in different cases—for a day, or a few days, or a few weeks, or a few months. In one case, that of a middle-aged father of a family, whose official life had been decorous and successful, I witnessed an abject depression of six years followed by as long a period of excited activity and apparently thoroughly cynical immorality.[1] Very variable also are the lucid intervals between the recurrent attacks; sometimes they last for months, sometimes for years. Are they intervals of complete soundness of mind? It would seem so in most cases at first, and in some cases even to the last. I have known attacks recur periodically in a patient for thirty years, seldom at longer sometimes at shorter intervals than two years, without the mind being appreciably impaired during

[1] Pronounced by five experts to be suffering from general paralysis during the run of exalted excitement. Nevertheless the apparently characteristic symptoms—the unequal pupils, the tremulous speech, the extravagant projects, the high good humour—all disappeared; and during the later run of the excitement the patient was no more than thoroughly morally insane.

the lucid intervals. But from the first occasionally, and generally after several recurrences, traces of mental damage are betrayed by some degree of sluggishness of thought and apathy of feeling : a failure of the mind to be what it was, rather than any very positive disorder of it. The prognosis is always bad. The attacks may be expected to recur, the periods of derangement to grow longer, the mind eventually to become weaker in the sane intervals, and the disease to last for life. All sorts of remedies have been tried to stop the recurrences, but the results leave ample scope for new experiments. Like simple recurrent mania, the malady betokens bad hereditary antecedents.

It is proof how little we know of the essential structure and workings of mental disorder—of the molecular conditions at the bottom of it—that we cannot in the least tell why simple mania should be thus recurrent, or why in a class of cases it should pass into melancholy, any more than we can tell why it sometimes continues for an indefinite period and then ceases, without either growing into delusional mania or sinking into melancholy. There are ebbs and flows of normal mental function, and in persons of a particular nervous temperament the quickest transitions from one extreme to the other—from confidence to discouragement, from brisk decision to abject indecision, from pleasant sense of well-being to painful sense of ill-being.

Remaining Symptoms of Mania.

Having set forth at length the characteristic features of acute mania and its ways of ending, it remains only to complete the discussion of its adjuncts. Visible bodily disorder is no essential feature or factor of it, even when present, since it may run its course without any : that was implied in the old definition of insanity as an alienation of mind without fever. The pulse is often natural in force and frequency when it is not quickened by the patient's exertions ; whatever its condition, it is due more to his natural constitution, or the presence or absence of bodily disorder, or to the degree of turbulent activity, than to the mania. So with the temperature of the body; it is not perhaps raised sensibly when it is not raised by violent bodily exercise, except when the tendency is to death from exhaustion, or when another disease supervenes, of which a marked rise of temperature justly kindles a suspicion. Still one may be startled sometimes to observe abrupt and rapid rises of temperature, without apparent cause, in the pure and uncomplicated mania of highly neurotic subjects, especially young and delicate persons; the increases going as quickly and irregularly as they came, with nothing more than the nervous excitement to account for them. Sometimes the temperature of the head is higher than that of the body, apparently because of a fuller and faster circulation through the cerebral blood-vessels. The patient may feel much hotter than he is; whence the impulse to throw off the bedclothes, to strip off his clothes, to expose himself thinly clad to the coldest weather. Why should he thus feel hot when he is perhaps cold? For the same reason that he imagines unmoving objects to move round him when he is giddy: because the same kind of molecular state of nerve-element, its elemental energies being fired by the mania, has been produced by internal commotion as the external impression of heat would produce. A proof, if proof were needed, of the intimate molecular agitation betokened by the frenzy.

Other evidence to the same effect is presented by the disordered sensibilities of the senses. It is not at first that the patient is less keen to see, less quick to hear, or perhaps less sensible to touch, when ordinary impressions are made on the several senses, but he loses their more exquisite sensibilities and appreciations, the most specialised refinements, as distinguished from the grosser and more general perception-reflexes. Therefore it is that he extols music which it would pain him to hear, were he himself, pronounces wine choice which would disgust his healthy palate, sees artistic merits in bad pictures, and frequents loose company without repugnance. It might be said of him in respect of the loss of these fine-culture gains that, hearing, he does not appreciate; tasting, he does not savour; seeing, he does not perceive; being sociable, he is not social in the best sense. He is like the man who, demanding to be served with good wine and good company at the beginning of the feast, does not, when he has well drunk, resent bad wine and bad company. In the worst cases the deterioration of sensibility goes deeper, signal proof whereof are the savage mutilations and injuries which, with a martyr-like enthusiasm that usurps consciousness and blunts or destroys sensibility, he inflicts on himself——as when, for example, instigated by delusions, he thrusts his arm into the fire, chanting in delirious delight the while, or gouges out his eye, or cuts off his genitals, or bites off his tongue; and in the loathsome vitiations of taste and smell which hinder him not, at his worst estate, from eating solid and drinking liquid excretions with apparent relish. Certainly the derangement sometimes goes deep down into the ultimate elements of organic structure; then the secretions and excretions attest it by their peculiarly offensive smell; the nails and hair are dry, harsh and brittle, the latter perhaps turning rapidly gray; and the skin, when not flushed with exercise, is dry, harsh, withered, and imparts to the countenance a premature look of wrinkled age. The many diligent and elaborate chemical analyses of the urine which have been made by different inquirers in different countries, notwithstanding that the tabular expositions of them might fill a large volume, have failed to yield definite and constant results or to warrant any positive inference. Are not the morbid metabolic changes subtilties of disorder too fine to be translated into the terms of such ultimate coarse products of chemical decomposition as urea, uric acid, and phosphates? The menstrual functions are usually suppressed during the frenzy; they cannot abide so great a commotion. If they continue regular throughout it, as they sometimes do, their unconcern, betraying a constitution ready to accommodate itself to the turmoil of mind and body, warrants the suspicion of a distinct hereditary predisposition to insanity which has conferred a native ease of acclimatisation.

It is a common observation what little sleep acute maniacs get, and not a little surprising that they can go on as long and continue as strong as they do with the little sleep they get. Seldom do they sleep well, most often irregularly and indifferently, many times hardly at all night after night and week after week.[1] How is it then that they endure such a protracted wear-and-tear? There are some considerations which serve to lessen the apparent wonder.

1. Though they do not sleep they have brief periods of repose when they lie still in a half-dozing state, and it may be that these still intervals partly subserve the restorative functions of sleep. Any one who rests quietly in bed all night, though he get little or no real sleep, is less wan and weary, if not more fresh and fit, in the morning than he is when he has tossed about in his bed, scared by visions, through a restless night of horrid dreams. Sleep is a variable not a constant condition, differing in quality as well as in quantity; it presents every gradation between the shallowest layer and deep stupor; and it is wonderful how great a refreshment a few minutes' sound sleep sometimes yields. Moreover it is probable that one organ of the body may be more deeply asleep than another at the same time, or asleep when other organs are awake; one part of the brain perhaps fast asleep when another part, instigated by a wide-awake visceral organ, is at work. Are not the senses in acute mania much asleep, as it were, to natural impressions? The patient is practically like one who, when asleep, is dreaming deliriously; asleep in relation to the external world while his inner life is in full swing of disorderly activity. One thing is notable—that maniacs complain not of their loss of sleep and are not in the least distressed by it; they care not to solicit sleep, are not seldom worse the day after it, and laugh to scorn the reasoned need

---

[1] Morel, for example, speaks of "un violent accès de manie qui dura trois mois sans interruption et sans que la malade ait gouté un seul instant de sommeil." And yet the patient recovered.

of it. So unlike in that respect the melancholic whose last despairing words to the world he is quitting by his own act are—" I could get no sleep : I could bear it no longer."

Does the patient really need sleep always when he fails to get it in acute mania ? Will it be seasonable and salutary if violently forced on him ? No doubt he needs to get rid of his mania and to get natural sleep, but will he be helped to get rid of his mania by being put forcibly into an unnatural sleep ? These are questions which, though not asked, and it might seem absurd to ask them, may notwithstanding be proposed for sober reflection. An observation which the least skilled observer cannot want the occasion to make is that the patient is often worse after a night's sleep, whether it was natural or drug-compelled; and if there be one experience which is positive, and ought long since to have broken the habit of traditional belief and practice, it is that to drug him repeatedly into sleep, or that state of drug-enforced unconsciousness which passes for sleep, is to do him hurt not good. It is not absolutely impossible to render the most furious maniac unconscious by big enough doses of a strong enough narcotic, without killing him, just as it would be quite possible, without killing him, to render him unconscious by a stunning blow on the head measured to the proper nicety, or by making him inhale a nicely proportioned mixture of carbonic acid gas and air. But what is the usual result ? That he wakes after two or three hours' unconsciousness to renewed excitement and wilder fury, that the duration of the disease is prolonged, and that the risk of a demented issue or of death is enhanced. Perchance nature knows and does what is best for him when she suffers the fury of the storm to spend itself before she restores his natural sleep, wisely letting the restoration of it go along with the subsiding excitement. I do not count it a good omen when there is regular sleep from the beginning and throughout the frenzy; such a kindly taking to disorder may be suspected to betray a constitution which is not sufficiently shocked and put out by it.

2. A second consideration is that it is not the nervous structure itself which is directly consumed by the work; the source of the expended energy is the material supplied to it from the blood as fuel, and the nerve-structure is only the machinery of the work. It may well be, therefore, when the brain is on fire in acute mania, that there is a rapid and excessive oxidation of this fuel-stuff of mind and the discharge of its energy in irregular ways through the deranged mechanism, without much real damage to the structure itself so long as abundance of food is taken and assimilated.

3. A third and pregnant consideration is that the energy of raving madness is not truly a display of mind; not calm, contained, regular purposive work, but explosive, incontinent, random, purposeless; not function, but an inferior and degenerate activity the large, turbulent and dissipate displays of which are equivalent only to a modest show of true mental and bodily function. If sleep marks the regular reflux of the flux of function, how should that which is no function have regular sleep? To call furious madness hyperphysiological or an excess of function, when the very essence of function is form while it is formless, is as great nonsense as to call a man in convulsions a strong man, or to say that there is no essential difference between *compos sui* and *non compos sui*. In its frenzy there is a large volume of explosive energy proceeding from the decomposition of higher and more concentrated energy; destructive instead of constructive, disruptive instead of combining, anti-social instead of social—a kind of turbulent lightning-energy instead of silent light-energy. I might compare it to the current of high tension passing along an electric wire which, properly isolated and distributed, is a force serving the good function of lighting a thousand lamps and illuminating a city, but when not properly isolated and distributed is a destructive force which sets a house on fire or indifferently kills man or beast; *that* work then being *its* function.

Naturally then the loss which shows most conspicuous

in acute mania is the loss of self-control : how can a man whose self is decomposed have self-control? All the confederate energies of a compact mental organisation, which are in constant inhibitory use, silent or overt, by a sane person and form so large a part of his habitual mental expenditure, are abolished for the time. Therefore the patient is not really exerting and spending himself in the most expensive way, since it needs a higher kind of power, a finer and more abstract essence thereof, to hold self in than to let self go : he is a raging machine below the level of reason, his mental factors not reaching that height of composition, " full of sound and fury signifying nothing." To possess the soul in patience and to have the strength to be still,—that is the highest energy. There is a vast difference, in the degree of after-exhaustion felt, between the fury of one who, prone to passionate attacks, habitually displays them, and that of him who, habitually calm and self-controlled, is swept away by an exceptional torrent of passion ; the former is not much disturbed in mind and body by his outbursts after they are over, soon recovers his spirits, and feels little exhaustion, whereas the latter is profoundly and intimately shaken and spent by the storm, full of sorrow and self-reproach, much exhausted, and unable perhaps to get a wink of sleep the night after it. The difference is the difference between the cheap and common consumption of a lower energy and the rare and costly consumption of a higher development of energy. So perhaps it is with the acute maniac, who goes on with his habitual tumultuous activity of mind and body without evidence of exhaustion and without need of regular periods of natural sleep, getting casually in short and irregular sleep-snatches the necessary renewal of supplies and removal of waste to keep him going at his lower level.

4. A fourth consideration is that after an attack of acute mania there are often some signs, perhaps slight and transient, of exhaustion of mind and body ; a dull memory, a weakened power of attention, a sense of labour in thinking, which is slow, costs an effort, and cannot be sustained—a

sort of blunt indolence of thought and feeling; and along with these effects sometimes goes considerable bodily emaciation. The storm has bruised and numbed, so to speak, the exquisitely delicate mental machinery, which does not work again at once smoothly and with full efficiency, even when it has not been seriously damaged. Given a delicate and unstable nervous constitution to begin with, the injury done may be irremediable; an effect most likely to follow the acute mania of young children and adolescents where the fine and tender processes of a developing mental organisation are blasted. Then it is sometimes a hopeless wreckage which the storm leaves behind it.

Foretokens of its Mode of Ending.

How may we know whether an acute mania is going to end well or ill? What are the signs that recovery is drawing nigh? They are just the stray indications of a right mind struggling painfully to reassert itself; at first, fitful and uncertain glimmers, then more frequent and steady gleams of reason. The patient discontinues wild and senseless doings and has a more quiet and composed look and behaviour, from time to time showing more point in his remarks, doing natural acts in a natural way, preferring an intelligent request, or making a sensible inquiry concerning his position, his affairs, or his family. Instead of exaggerated elation of mood, pert and saucy or forward and blustering address, and the noisy parleys which he courted formerly, he is rather dejected, shy and embarrassed in manner and perhaps shrinks from observation and conversation; sometimes he is moody and irritable, feels cross and tired, grumbles at everything, looks weary and is unusually ready to retire to bed. His voice regains its natural intonation and his countenance comes to wear a more composed look, the lines of feature graven by morbid moods disappearing and its natural lines of expression being restored; intelligence shows itself in his eye, character in his gestures, self-restraint in his address and demeanour.

Other movements of bodily expression, regaining proper form and measure, restore the natural gait and carriage. He gives attention to his dress, which is no longer disorderly, and is more particular as to what food and what quantity of it he takes and in what manner he takes it; and he evinces the return of his natural feelings and affections by a reviving interest in his family, to whom he now perhaps writes a rational letter of inquiry, and in his own and the world's affairs. No surer sign of recovery can there be than the restoration of the father and the citizen, for it is the return of affections and interests. A gradual increase of bodily weight, which may have sunk much during the frenzy, is a good sign when it goes along with mental improvement; it is not a good sign when it occurs without any coincident mental improvement.

A modest dejection or sadness of mind after acute mania is not to be regretted; for it is a good omen of good recovery when the person feels that he has been very ill, shows some distrust of himself, thinks sadly of his damnified interests, and sincerely acknowledges the necessity of the measures taken to restrain him. But it is not a good omen, inasmuch as it may mark incomplete recovery or forebode relapse, when he continues to be elated, talks exultantly of his perfect health, ignores the prejudice which he and his interests have suffered by his illness, and is eager to resume work offhand as if nothing had happened—when he has not the logic of mind to realise what his illness means and to accept the logic of the altered situation. However, there are some persons who, being of a narrow, egotistic and suspicious nature, never entirely give up their distempered thoughts and feelings and who, resenting the humiliation to their keen self-love which the madness was, cannot sincerely acknowledge its true character; for them the removal of a restraint which they bitterly resent is sometimes the best treatment, notwithstanding that the release might seem otherwise premature. They do better when restored to the surroundings of their ordinary lives and to the free play of their peculiarities of nature than they do while chafing under a discipline of good sense and control to which their wry natures cannot adjust themselves. The illness was not so foreign to the character as to seem an interloping intrusion and to be felt as an alienation; their sense of unity of self in it and out of it goes deeper than any sense of alienation; they cannot therefore sincerely look back on it as a calamity which unselfed them, but nurse a secret rancour, perhaps institute an action-at-law, against those who treated them as insane.

An immediate augury of recovery in some cases is the return of an old bodily disorder which was suspended during the mania: it may be an old hæmorrhoidal flux, a leucorrhœal discharge, a chronic bronchial catarrh, a chronic skin affection; perhaps a chronic asthma which, disappearing during the frenzy, reappears when it is over; sometimes a neuralgia or so-called sick headache which, having been an almost life-long companion, goes and comes back in the same way; sometimes an habitual epilepsy which, suspended during the commotion of the mania, resumes its old course after it; or some variety of exaggerated hysteria which is swallowed up and lost for the time in the current of a fiercer disorder. "Where the greater malady is fixed the lesser is scarce felt;" wherefore, when the lesser begins to be felt again it is because the greater is getting unfixed; and it is perhaps so expected and welcomed. The restoration of the suppressed menses I look on as a good omen only when it goes along with or follows mental improvement; otherwise not. It is not the return of the function which is the cause of the approaching recovery, although it no doubt helps, occurring when it does, but it is the restoration of normal health which is the occasion of the particular recurrence of function as well as of the mental amelioration; for which reason it is not good treatment to try offhand to bring menstruation forcibly and prematurely to pass in acute mania. A like fallacy of inference may ascribe the outbreak of mania to the abrupt stoppage of menstruation which sometimes takes place immediately before or coincidently with it; when the two events may be only the concomitant effects of a common cause and the one no more the cause of the other than light is the cause of heat when the sun rises.

Sometimes the recovery from an acute mania is preceded immediately and seems to be determined directly by some pretty severe bodily disorder,—an acute fever, an inflammation of the lungs, an erysipelas of the head and face, a large sloughing carbuncle on the back of the neck or elsewhere, an inflammation and suppuration of the parotid gland, an abcess in some other part of the body. But the virtue of the seemingly salutary bodily illness lies in its opportune occurrence; for it may occur and go at the beginning or at the height of the frenzy without producing anything more than a temporary alleviation of the symptoms, even if it do so much as that.

What are the signs that recovery is not going to take place in acute mania? When the patient shuns intercourse with others, walking or sitting apart, stolidly absorbed in his own thoughts and feelings, and especially when he is also addicted to laughing and muttering to himself; when he exhibits abrupt unmotived changes of mood and behaviour, accosting the same persons amiably on one occasion and angrily on another without the least reason so far as they are concerned; when he continues, without the excuse of excitement, to mistake the personalities of others or his own personality, which he might excusably do when he was raving; when he makes sudden starts and exclamations that are not motived by and have no relation to what is going on around him, or continually repeats some odd gesture or motion which is not the natural expression of any normal thought or feeling; when he has a vaguely abstracted and vacant look of the eyes during a conversation with him, halting absently in the midst of it before he makes a reply, as if his mind were far away from the subject and had to be dragged back to it with a jerk, or perhaps turning his head aside as if listening to some one where no one is, or casting furtive glances of suspicion right and left. Such peculiarities of demeanour, having no rational relations to the conditions and course of things around, are bad prognostics when they remain after excitement has subsided; they betray actuating hallucinations or delusions in the background which distract the thoughts and distort the behaviour—are the tokens of absurd notions which he entertains, of unreal voices which he hears, of imaginary agencies by which he believes himself to be affected. They are good evidence sometimes even when a verbal acknowledgment of the secret motives cannot be obtained or when these are actually denied; for a crazy gesture, a grotesque attitude, a senseless act is the expression of an internal state and speaks in a dumb discoursive eloquence that is no less positive and significant than a foolish speech to one who has learnt by experience to comprehend its language. For the same reason it is a bad sign when the features do not resume their natural lines of expression, inasmuch as it shows that there has not been a return to the natural modes of thought and feeling: while incongruous features evince incoherent thought and feeling, an expressionless mask of face may reveal mental devastation.

Medical observation is still but coarse and crude; the subtilties of disease escape it. Besides the motions of face, lips and eyes that constitute the visible language of the features, there is a multitude of minute motions which are disordered in mania and in which the convalescent from it shows the return to his true self—in his finest gestures and exact gait; in his manner of coughing, speaking, blowing his nose and the like; in fact, in every the least movement of his that has individual character, as every thrill of it doubtless has were observation fine enough to perceive it. A man is distinguishable, perhaps as easily known, by his cough, or his sneeze, or the sound of his footstep, as he is by his face or voice; for such is the infinite possibility of variation and the almost infinite impossibility of exact coincidence in such a complex business that no two coughs, no two voices, are exactly alike any more than two leaves or two seeds.

How eloquent, if we rightly consider it, is the language of facial expression! More eloquent, more subtile, more sincere oftentimes the mute muscular expression than the spoken word! Consider how much silent intelligence and what a variety and delicacy of passion and sentiment two lovers can express by the language of eyes and features only. Without uttering a word, yet without the least misunderstanding, they can woo, repel, parley, languish, invite, pine, importune, quarrel and be reconciled, reproach and approve, make assignations and refuse them.[1] Did ever two lovers fail to understand each other and to compass their dearest delight, although both new to the complex business, because they had not been taught what to say and do to one another? Were two or three generations of men condemned to absolute silence they would converse almost as well by signs and gestures as they do now by elaborate articulate discourse. No doubt they would be obliged to dispense with much empty jargon of the parliamentary sort, but in return, being compelled to an economy of means and to charge every utterance with meaning, they could not help making things not words their concern and end, and thus could not fail to grow mightily in sincerity and solidity of thought and veracity of utterance.

Lastly, it is a bad sign when the patient shows no concern about himself, makes no inquiries about friends and affairs, expresses no wishes, entertains no projects, evinces no initiative, and at the same time perhaps grows stout; past care he is past cure, for he has reached the peace of a desert of mind when passions cease from troubling and curiosity and energy of intellect are extinct. Of the worst omen always are signs of paralysis of speech, face, or pupils, since they denote damage of nerve-structure, likely, when the mania is past, to end in gradually increasing mental impairment and accompanying bodily paralysis. It is important, however, not to be too swift to judge badly of mental obtuseness and slow and dragging speech when

[1] See Montaigne in one of his essays.

the patient has been drugged heavily with chloral and bromide of potassium; for the threatening symptoms may then disappear gradually after a stop has been put to the poisoning.

As the degree of degenerative fault in the native mental structure must needs affect the prognosis in a case of mania, it is proper to inquire what are the signs that betray morbid heredity. What are the neuropathic features in a particular case which warrant the suspicion or conviction that the mental derangement is not an original creation of the individual life, having no footing in the past, but the pathological outcome of a strain of degeneracy in the stock? The most suspicion-stirring circumstance generally is the eager haste of the patient's relatives, forestalling the thought even of inquiry, to repudiate vehemently the existence of insanity in the family and to wonder what can have caused it in this instance; so quick to protest and protesting so much, they fail not to instil or strengthen the suspicion which they would fain exclude. Putting this circumstance aside, the fact of most import from a scientific point of view is the coexistence of extreme madness side by side with singular lucidity of reason outside its limits of direct action. Even in an early and acute stage of mania, when it is yet too soon to forecast what the end will be, one may sometimes suspect a strong hereditary bias because of the outrageous madness of notions and conduct during lulls of excitement; grotesquely extravagant or absurd delusions and behaviour being in strange contrast with the general calmness of mind, when a corresponding abatement of them and improvement of conduct might justly be expected. How is it that, having so much reason, it should be impotent to judge and condemn and correct such mad thoughts and acts? It looks as if, not being outraged by them, it wanted the wish as well as the power to meddle with them. How is it that in a mind so insane in respect of them there should be so much reason as there is apart from them? The incongruity could not be if reason and unreason had not consorted in foregoing generations, having lain in the same egg and thus perforce come to a *modus vivendi* on terms of non-intervention. Custom of association has dulled the sense of incompatibility.

The extravagant delusions are not the consistent pathological developments of a system of morbid thought and feeling and have not therefore the character of explanatory outcomes—are not morbid *ergoisms*, so to speak; they look like independent creations, of inexplicable origin, spontaneous and unexpected, requiring no support from, nor susceptible to criticism or correction by, the adjacent sane functions which on their part seem nowise surprised or disturbed by them. Like the extravagant and fantastic creations of dreams, they witness to the natural powers and tendency of the human brain to create and dramatise, and in this case to do so according to inborn lines of structural incongruity. Its structure being informed by the incorporation of past function from age to age, no preparation to go wrong is needed where to go wrong is a quasi-natural instinct of the unstable mechanism. If the imaginations of a man spring from the deepest roots in his nature, the flowerage of its ideals will not fail to express character. And if we are ever to understand the mode of production of the creations of dreams and madness, so strangely bewildering in their variety, novelty, abundance, and dramatic intensity, we must not expect to find it in the field of consciousness; for a man becomes conscious of them only as products—as things *become*, not in the *becoming*—and would not conceive them consciously were he to spend his conscious life in trying to do it.

Other features of mania which point to its hereditary origin are these: abrupt outbreak and a similarly abrupt ending of the frenzy, in which case, though the immediate prognosis is good, the ultimate prognosis is bad, for the quick recovery is likely to be followed some time by relapses; great craziness of ideas from the first, and much irregularity and inconstancy of symptoms which never continue in one stay, being constant only in inconstancy—for example, contrasting delusions in immediate sequence, abrupt interruptions of the current of exaltation by fits of depression, transitory intervals of lucidity in the wild thought-rack; extreme affective or moral disorder, either with the special and specially urgent morbid impulses of so-called *impulsive insanity* or with the general immoral tendencies of so-called *moral insanity*, but without manifest impairment of the reason below its highest level of moral intuition; the surprising survivals of remarkable talents or aptitudes of a special kind which distinguished the person formerly, in the midst of a general wreck of faculties—such as a conspicuous memory for dates, names, and the minute details of events, a special musical sensibility, or some other artistic aptitude or accomplishment; lastly, the alternating phases of mania and melancholy which give its Janus-faced character to the alternating form of recurrent insanity. In all these cases of faulty mental fabric we may feel pretty sure of a morbid heredity; they are so many notes of a mental degeneracy in the stock.

Along with the betokening mental features go, in very marked cases, peculiarities of bodily conformation that are dumbly eloquent stigmata of morbid heredity to him who can read them. Unsymmetrical features, an unsymmetrical skull, unsymmetrical and badly formed or actually deformed ears, squintings and stuttering, and other impeding hindrances to and distortions of the forms of mental utterance, are the peculiarities which attract notice in such cases. Other significant signs are a want of harmony in the action of the features which, like a badly painted portrait, join incongruous expressions, or extraordinary and grotesque agitations of them, violent grimaces, spasmodic grinnings and jerkings during the mental efforts of conversing, especially under the stress of some emotion. It is impossible to describe the peculiarities of physiognomy, gesture and gait, so many, irregular and multiform are they, which nevertheless, when seen, everybody recognises as odd and calls " nervous." Incongruities of head, face and features will be of deeper import than might appear at first sight if outward asymmetry means unsymmetrical structure in the innermost, and they therefore are essentially the outward and visible signs of inward and invisible faults of the nervous organisation.

Certain it is that the loose nerve-centres are somehow not well organised to work together in perfect harmony of function when they thus function in odd incongruities of expression: perhaps in disjointed forms of expression, one part of the face being serious while the rest of it is wreathed in smiles; in smiling and giggling grimaces which are inconsistent with the mood and thought and with the gravity befitting the subject, or are fragmentarily commixed with fragments of serious expression; in sudden transitions from a laugh half accomplished to solemn gravity, the laugh being pulled up abruptly in its course and instantly transformed; in a singular, far-away, abstracted look of the eyes, as if the mind were away and at work elsewhere during ordinary conversation in which an ordinary part is being taken; in vague and aimless movements of the eyes which, everywhere at once, nowhere fixed, are now directed to the ceiling, now diverted to one or other side of the room, now rolled in restless mobility anywhere and everywhere about it; in a scared furtive look, like that of a startled wild animal, when he is accosted quietly and naturally, and in the mixture during conversation of the manner of a natural and present self with that of a suspicious, half-frightened and only partially present self; in these and like dislocations or incoherences of the component parts of the forms of expression, and incongruities between the mood and its natural expression. A man may, so to speak, squint, stutter, totter, stumble in thought as he may squint in vision, stutter in talk, totter or stumble in walk. Very notable in some cases is the extraordinary mobility of facial features which cannot any more than the volatile thoughts stay in the composure of form; quick, jerky, wavering dispersions of movement flit rapidly and at random over the face; and I remember one neurotic gentleman whose ears and the skin of his head were in continual rapid motions when he talked earnestly, as if in hurried, agitated superfluity of sympathy with the vocal expression. The condition of the mental organization in all such cases is presumably a condition of incompact unity and lacking harmony of its different parts or tracts whereby, wanting their due inter-inhibitions, they are prone to break loose from their unstable equilibrium and to go into disunited and irregular action on their own account. Thence follow so many and various examples of disintegrate wills.

The thoughts and moods may have no more stability and constancy than the mobile and incoherent outward expressions. Then a volatile and unstable mind, incapable, by reason of its loose and excitable structure, of a sincere touch and fast hold of facts, is devoid of essential sincerity or veracity of nature: unable to trust itself it is unable to trust others. When good counsel in time of need is given to those so mal-endowed they cannot logically accept it and consistently follow it; wherefore, falling deeper into trouble because of half-hearted, partial and inconstant acceptance of it and of fickle recourse to other counsels and actions to which they are in like manner not steadily faithful or are steadily unfaithful, they believe themselves to have been badly advised or wickedly deceived. The only opinion which they can take in is the opinion which jumps with the present mood. In the end they are the natural prey of knaves, for whose food-wants, as for those of all creatures elected for survival, nature has made beneficent provision in its vast and complex scheme.

CHAPTER V

INSANE DEFORMITIES OF MIND—PARAMORPHIC INSANITY

THE special features of mania and melancholia are, respectively, morbid caricatures of the two ordinary moods of depression and exaltation which affect all minds from time to time and are constitutional tendencies of some minds. In the vagaries of fanaticism and superstition these tendencies have had their morbidly extravagant, if not morbid, developments: on the one hand, as outcome of the sanguine and elated mood, the fanaticism of the inspired prophet or leader who, claiming supernatural authority, draws after him multitudes of disciples and perhaps changes the course of a nation's destiny; on the other hand, the gloomy superstition of the dejected and apprehensive mind which prostrates itself in abject fear before supernatural beings and labours to propitiate them by prayers and sacrifices. When these superstitious notions suited with the thought and feeling of the times they were not counted insane; they were in truth the natural products of primitive imagination lacking the basis of any knowledge of natural forces and laws and working to construct for itself somehow forms or species, necessarily provisional, of an unknown environment in order to deal with it at all. But were anybody nowadays to proclaim himself a prophet ordained directly by God to lead the world in the right way, or to declare himself possessed by Satan and given over to eternal damnation, he would probably be treated in the one case as a victim of mania and in the other case as a victim of melancholia; might anyhow be as great an object of gaping wonder, or of compassionate derision, as a person who appeared in the streets to-day in the costume of a bygone age and fashion. The wisdom which serves human development in one age becomes the madness which would serve its disorganization only in another.

Besides the two leading forms of general mental derangement with their opposite moods, there is a class of cases in which we are confronted, not with disease in the strict sense of the word, but with irregular and faulty mental development—with deformity or distortion of mind rather than with derangement proper. For mind may either be moulded by nature and circumstances into madness or distracted into it by disease. These systematised insanities are the mad maturities, so to speak, of varieties of insane temperament; and they vary in degree and kind from crankiness, where, the disorder being localised in the mental area, the functions of the rest of it are little, if at all, affected, to craziness where the whole mind is involved.[1]

Mania of Persecution.

One of the best examples of the growth of a mental deformity into madness is presented by the gradual develop-

---

[1] They used to be described under the name of *Monomania* or *Partial Mania*; but as these names were thought to limit the area of disorder too strictly, the tendency now is to abandon them in favour of a still worse-conceived name—*Paranoia*, which means properly nothing else than general insanity. Because *Monomania* expressed too little, though it marked well an essential feature of the disorder, those who are in love with a new term, without understanding it, and run gladly after a new thing because it is new, would supersede it by a name which marks not any special character of the disease, but really means just what it is not—general madness. To christen it mental derangement would appear plain nonsense : to call it so in Greek passes for scientific nomenclature. Thereupon, in accordance with precedent, the invention of the new name is supposed to be the discovery or discrimination of a new disease. Cumbrous but more correct is the descriptive designation of the kind of insanity as *Primary Systematised Mania*; for the name indicates how a system of insane thought and feeling grows gradually in the mind without previous acute disorder of it. If a Greek name be necessary, why not *Paramorphic Insanity*?

ment of a genuine mania of persecution out of an oversensitive and suspicious habit of thought and feeling; especially where the native infirmity, nursed in solitude and fostered by self-conscious exercise, has not been ballasted with the sound practical feeling and intelligent sense of proportion which come of converse and co-operation with men in the active work of the world. By an elective affinity working deeper than consciousness, ingraft in the base and building of the individual nature, the suspicious strain of feeling and thought summons congenial ideas and feelings to its secret sessions, gets silent reinforcements of support from them, and thus is nourished and strengthened; for it is the self-conservative instinct of a deformity or prejudice of mind, as of every living thing, to strive to maintain and increase its being. In the result we have a person who, of good common sense and sound judgment generally, perhaps very shrewd and capable, yet imagines himself the subject of special observation, slander, annoyance, insult, persecution in all sorts of incredible and impossible ways.

His enemies are not persons of his acquaintance only or at all, but persons whom he does not know, perfect strangers, whom he has never done the smallest wrong to, whose persistent meddling in his affairs is inexplicable, and the cause of whose hostility he cannot imagine. Why should so many people in many places be leagued in schemes and operations to watch and persecute him? That is the wonder of it, he will say, the amazing thing in the unheard-of network of villainy by which he is surrounded. But the huge improbability of the extraordinary circumstances, so far from shaking his belief, seems rather to strengthen it; like St. Theresa, the more impossible it is, the more he believes it. Thus believing, he discerns the evidences of hostility everywhere—in articles of newspapers covertly hinting or plainly pointing at him, in sermons at church preached at him, in the ordinary words or gestures of persons who pass him in the street, in a chair out of place, a drawer accidentally left open, or a curtain disarranged, in spoken words which he will admit, when challenged, sound quite innocent in their natural sense, but still suspect to have been infused in a mysterious way with another and ill meaning. Ordinary and natural circumstances acquire an extraordinary and mysterious significance; for his fixed, suspicion-charged notion of persecution has become an absorbing delusion which devours impressions and turns them to its nature and nurture.

Although nothing can be more positive than the certitude with which he iterates and reiterates his belief, it is a curious thing to see that he seldom acts consistently, as a sane person, believing as he did, might be expected to do. Complaining perhaps of insulting voices coming from the ceiling or underneath the floor, he makes no searching examination of those structures; and if asked why he does not, if he is so sure the voices come from those quarters, he will probably say that it would be of no use, since the rascals are too clever to be caught, or that they escape directly he begins to look for them, or that they contrive some way of sending sounds from a distance, or that the inquiry is superfluous folly when the thing is so certain and notorious to all the world. The truth is that, like the inspired prophet who works miracles, he has a latent feeling that things so entirely out of the domain of natural experience had better not be subjected to the tests of experience, an implicit certitude that exact inquiry would fail to disclose evidence to support his belief, an instinctive repugnance to bring his theory of belief to the tests of positive experiment; and so he distorts the impossibility of proof into proof of the impossible, the very incredibility of the thing into ground of its credibility.

He is not really one whole and compact mental being having one consistent belief, but a double being capable of two inconsistent beliefs, each of which is only a half belief; herein again like the religious fanatic professing to be inspired, who is one thing when strenuously acting among his disciples in his professional capacity, a more or less genuine believer then in his own pretensions, and quite another being, apparently hardly a believer in them, when he is talking quietly at his ease with his fellow-augurs or with people whom he knows to be unbelievers. His belief needs a favourable environment for its full force; an incredulous environment reduces it to a half-belief. When he has a violent quarrel with any one or has a real calamity befall him—loses his money or has his house burnt down—he does not impute that misfortune to his secret enemies, but suffers and treats it in a rational way very much as any sane man would do. His ideal life of deluded thought runs much apart from his real life in the common world.

Meanwhile he may go on with his work, performing it properly day by day, saying nothing of his troubles to those about him, exhibiting little or nothing in his conduct to attract notice or inspire suspicion. At most, he may be thought to be only reserved or absent in manner, and perhaps a little moody, odd, and uncertain in his behaviour. His reserve and aloofness spring from his wary distrust, for he fears to talk lest anything said by him may be used against him by his persecutors, and is on his guard not to give them that advantage. Those who see him thus at his daily work might scout the suggestion that he was mad and think it a cruel injustice to interfere with his freedom. But it may be quite otherwise with those who, seeing him in his intimacy when his thoughts are not diverted from himself by affairs, have abundant occasion to know how unreasonable and even dangerous his conduct can be; and it is unexpectedly otherwise sometimes with his fellows in work when he savagely, perhaps fatally, assaults one of them against whom he has conceived a violent animosity as the imagined principal in the persecutions of which he believes himself the victim.

Many and divers are the ways in which such an one imagines he is attacked. Every gateway of sense may be the channel of hostile operations. If through the sense of touch, he then feels strange shocks and thrills, perplexing pangs and pains, in his limbs and body: from the mysterious attacks he endeavours to insulate himself in a variety of ways, some more and some less successful, but always in the end finds that he has to begin again with new protective tactics. In another it is taste which is affected, when he suspects that deleterious substances are put into articles of food, which he refuses therefore to eat; rejecting food prepared for him at home, he goes out to buy it for himself, or takes meals irregularly in restaurants, leaving one place after another for a new one as each in turn is suspected; to such a pass may his suspicion go that he rejects one food after another until he is reduced to live on a single article of diet—perhaps milk, which he goes himself to see milked into a special vessel taken by him for the purpose; perhaps eggs, as food into which poison cannot be put, albeit such is the diabolic ingenuity of his enemies that eggs are not always safe. At another time or in another person it is the sense of smell which is offended: he perceives strange and suspicious odours which he has no doubt are caused by noxious vapours that his persecutors contrive to blow through the keyhole of the door, or through cracks in the ceiling, or through crannies of the walls; with the purpose of either making him ill, or of driving him mad, or of taking his life, or of throwing him into an unconscious stupor and thereby facilitating their evil designs against him. Awful is the diabolic power which they can thus exercise to cause horrible dreams, repulsive visions, loathsome thoughts, and disgusting sexual excitement. Oftentimes sight is the offended sense: he sees studied insults in the gestures of those who pass him in the streets; signals of treacherous meaning in the accidental change of position of a chair, a table, or a picture; secret masonic signs of conspiracy in the casual mode of blowing a nose, of lifting a hand, of twirling a moustache; a darkly hidden significance in the mysterious recurrence of a particular number or word in print, or of a particular word or phrase in conversation; persons dogging his footsteps wherever he goes, and the hurried escape of night-prowlers about his premises whom he catches glimpses of but attempts in vain to catch hold of.

Most frequent of all are hallucinations of hearing; so frequent that Laséque, who was the first to distinguish and describe accurately this mania of persecution,[1] considered them to be pathognomic features, and hallucinations of other senses to be rare. The class of cases in which they exist alone or predominate are certainly so distinct that they might form a separate group, but other senses are undoubtedly affected in cases showing the characteristic features of a genuine mania of persecution; indeed, in the specially hypochondriacal form of the malady other senses are more wrong than the sense of hearing, which is frequently not then affected at all. The frequent hallucinations of hearing are what might be expected, seeing that words are the signs of thought—the λόγος being both reason and word—and that it is through hearing that converse of mind with mind principally takes place; therefore if a person imagines that he is the object of ill-will, it is natural for him to suspect that he is ill spoken of, and in further course to hear the imagined words of evil-speaking and contempt. Then, as he grows more awry in mind, he goes on to hear snatches of insulting sneers, threats, comments, accusations as he passes along the streets; perhaps overhears discussions of himself and his affairs in the adjoining house, although it is impossible that articulate sounds can traverse the walls, and its inhabitants are entire strangers to him; complains that his thoughts are anticipated and voiced internally in his head, perhaps maliciously perverted there, before he himself conceives them, or that thoughts not his own are instilled into his mind, and voices into his ears from a distance, without words, by some mysterious means of communication. His mind, being sharpened by suspicion and distorted by the growth of it, is ever on sensitive watch, even in spite of itself, to discover secret and hostile meaning in the most innocent conversation which he hears and to detect allusions to him and his affairs in everything he reads.[2]

[1] *Archives de Médecine*, 1852.
[2] When a person, thus distracted, feels himself to be a double self, or rather perhaps feels in him a double which seems to be and yet not to be himself,

It is curious to see how the patient himself sometimes suspects that he is the victim of hallucinations and usually knows and complains that he is counted mad. But he cannot be brought to ascribe his hallucinations to their true cause—his own disordered nerves, any more than prejudice in a passion can; he protests that they are the diabolic work of his persecutors who, clever scoundrels that they are, are able to cause hallucinations artificially, and by that means hope to drive him mad or to cause him to be thought mad. Lost in conjectural maze as to the motives of such a system of artful cruelty, he tries to imagine an explanation: perhaps it is to destroy his individuality by making him think and feel not truly as he would do, but in a false character as they wish him to do, and forcing him to do what he would not do, while knowing not what he is doing; perhaps it is out of revenge because he is suspected of having discovered the secret sign of some secret society, or in pursuance of a plot to inveigle him into such a society; perhaps it is to make an expiation or an eunuch of him, by experiments at the cost of his individuality, for the benefit of science or for the sake of humanity. He would be happier if he knew the reason of the persecution, he protests, even if it continued. Very real are his sufferings, however indefinite and absurd the motives for which and the means by which he imagines that they are inflicted on him.

By his troubles and troubled imaginings the poor man is distracted from doing well his daily work, which otherwise he would be able and glad to do; for a while he goes on resolutely with it in spite of his distractions, though it is no little task to him; but in the end they so compel his attention that he cannot turn his mind to other things, but

each self thinks its own *thinks* or *things*—that is, thinks its own world; the true self, or what remains of it, perceives the world as it looks to sane persons, and the morbid self or double perceives it as a strange and hostile world. Therefore words and objects apprehended have strangely twofold meanings, the one familiar and natural, the other strange and unnatural. It is pitiful to listen to his unavailing attempts to explain how the word he knows has still somehow been made to have an ill meaning besides its natural meaning.

turns it exclusively to them. Without doubt, the more fully he is absorbed in work the less he suffers and the better it is for him, for the sane part of his mind is then exercised and strengthened by the sane use of its healthy tracks and the insane part of it weakened by disuse of its insane tracks; it is in work therefore that his best hope of salvation lies. How long he will be able to go on with useful work is a question of the growth of the unreasonable at the cost of the reasonable part of him, of the gradual displacement of a waning sound by a waxing unsound *ego*.

To ask him to muster reasons to demonstrate the absurdity of his mad delusion and to overthrow it, he being possessed by it, is virtually to ask it to resist and overthrow itself, and him to be other than he is; to set forth and rehearse reasons to prove its unreason is no better than to " charm ache with air and agony with words." Just as each sense is sensible of its proper stimulus only, not sensible of the proper stimulus of another sense, the eye seeing not sound and the ear hearing not fragrance, so a special tract of cerebral reflexes which is in a state of inordinate activity is susceptible only to the stimulus which feeds its activity, or construes the stimulus, whatever it be, into food of it— that is to say, when it has become a set morbid activity; for while the process of degeneration is going on, before matters have reached that pass, a strong restraining motive will sometimes hold it in check. For example, if the patient finds himself shut up in an asylum because of his unreasonable conduct, he may, in order to obtain his release, conceal, explain away, even deny his delusions; which are naturally less urgent when he is withdrawn from the special provocations and occasions of their exercise, and less confident when he is confronted with the startling surroundings into which they have brought him. Then he may disclose only in a moment of angry excitement, or of expansive confidence to a sympathetic listener, or in a letter to an outsider, what for the most part he does not say a word of —betrays only perhaps by a singular reserve, by a mysterious hint, by an equivocal gesture, by an odd act, by a refusal of a particular food, or by a peculiar manner of taking it. Sincere and consistent insanity is no more common a thing in a mad world than sincere and consistent sanity in a sane world.

That the brain is virtually a confederation of organs in intimate union of structure and function, and that no one of them can go wrong without the other suffering with it in some degree, would no doubt prove true if the inquiry into the general impairment were deep, subtile and wide enough—if, in fact, we could discern, trace and estimate those latent currents beneath the level of consciousness which underlie what appears in consciousness and are the source of what starts unconsciously into it. But it is proper to bear in mind, in this connection, how much of everybody's conscious thought, feeling and conduct is mere routine, local and automatic in relation to a uniform round of circumstances, and how well therefore a partial madman may go on performing habitual functions of life without the least apparent disorder. Only when the special faulty cord is struck is the false note manifest, or when the fault is so deeply rooted in the character and the habits of life as to invade or pervade the thought, feeling and conduct generally. Why should a cranky grocer not weigh currants correctly and debit the price of them correctly to his customer, when the work is done through brain-tracts that act in such capacity independently of the faulty tract, which on its part may be concerned mainly with speculative interests. I have known instances of persons who, sane in business, were still intolerably insane in their own homes. It is a different thing when the person believes that his persecutors persistently tap his thoughts, sap his health and vigour, or otherwise so afflict him in mind and body as to make him feel his misery every hour of his life; for then he is driven to leave off work, sometimes life, in despair.

As particular groups or sequences of thought, feeling, and will come into action in relation to particular groups or sequences of circumstances by which they were solicited in the first instance and to which they have been adjusted by exercise, they naturally recur, as particular movements recur, when their proper brain-tracts are fitly stimulated. So it comes to pass that a person is, or at any rate that the machinery of his personality functions as, one person in one, and quite another person in another, set of circumstances, sincere temporarily in both—an angel abroad and a demon at home, a rogue in his business and an honest man in his private relations, devout in his church or chapel and dissolute in his daily life, an impassioned preacher in the pulpit and the slave of a degrading passion out of it. The disgust which such seeming hypocrisies might excite may be allayed by the reflection that these persons have not unity and solidarity of mental structure ; they lack a whole self to hold in hand and make members one of another the separately acting partial selves or facets of self, the passionate activity of one of which extinguishes consciousness of the other and so makes an almost unconscious hypocrisy — at any rate, a hypocrisy which is not *felt* as such. Though they may *know*, they do not *believe*, themselves to be the hypocrites they are.

After the patient has given over his endeavours to ignore or despise the designs and doings of his persecutors, and has so far succumbed as to leave off work, he may still carry on a desultory and retreating warfare. He changes his lodgings repeatedly, perhaps wanders from place to place, always easier for a short time in new surroundings, and adopts all the expedients he can think of to countermine their plots. New surroundings are a relief, first, because, hoping to have eluded his persecutors, he does not expect and therefore immediately suspect their presence, and, secondly, because his attentions are diverted from himself and his suspicions by the new circumstances while they are new. So it is with other protective tactics which he adopts; they are successful for a short time because he expects them to be so, but after a while his troubles return in the same or in another form. In this way many go on for an indefinite time, perhaps all their lives, repeating the same complaints in the same stereotyped fashion, or getting better as the energies of passion wane and they, through age and custom, become more tame to endurance. From time to time, however, there are periods of excitement, in women at the menstrual periods especially, when they make appeals for protection to the magistrates or the police, are angry and abusive, protest that they can bear their sufferings no longer, and utter threats of violent retaliation. Some of them appeal and try to get access to queen or emperor as alone having power to make the persecution cease.

Other issues are these : (*a*) the derangement increases, the patients getting more and more distressed and distracted, until they boil over into an acute mania or sink into a deep melancholic stupor; (*b*) they become so impatient of their sufferings that they make a desperate and perchance fatal attack upon some one whom they suspect of injuring them ; (*c*) they are so miserable and so hopeless of relief that in despair they commit suicide, though suicide is not so frequent among them as their tale of sorrow might lead one to expect; (*d*) they undergo a gradual mental deterioration, the delusions which had a certain consistency and unity disintegrating and growing into incoherent and preposterous absurdities, until the mind is demented.

A mania of persecution is not always of gradual growth and chronic. When the disorder has a definite cause in alcohol, or sexual abuse, or extreme mental trouble, it may come on in periodical attacks, subacute or acute, which are characterised by great mental excitement, acute apprehensions, numerous hallucinations of sight and hearing, and much confusion of mind, all which pass away in due time.

The prognosis is always bad in mania of persecution when it has come on gradually. Still there may be recovery both from the acute mania and the melancholic stupor in which the disorder sometimes culminates. Indeed, an acute attack need not be deplored, for its storm may possibly sweep the mind clear of the poisonous vapours of suspicion with which it was infected ; and at any rate the patient is no worse after it. Now and then an acute fever or other acute disease has effected a secret healing revolution which medicine was powerless to achieve. When the patient is apparently recovered, it is not always certain that he has quite got rid of his delusions; they may not be a present trouble, but it is difficult for him sincerely to confess that they were entirely imaginary, and he may, while still at heart believing that there was something, feign to be convinced there was nothing, in them.

Such persons are prone to be dangerous at one period or another of their malady, notwithstanding that they may go on for years without doing harm to anybody, easing their complaints the while by appeals to magistrates and police for aid; for they are always liable, when despairing of help and out of sorts bodily, perhaps worn out by restless days and sleepless nights, to be so maddened as to lose self-control and to make a desperate assault on some innocent person who, incurring their suspicion, attracts the discharge of their explosive fury. One of my patients rushed up to a stranger whom he met in the street and struck him full in the face because he imagined that he had made an insulting gesture; and another entered the room of a surgeon who had operated on him successfully for fistula a year before, and, without saying a word, knocked him down because he believed that the latter had been in league with his enemies to expose him in some indecent manner during the operation. It is all the worse when they make fatal use of a revolver or other deadly weapon which they buy and carry for their protection. In such case the homicide is either (*a*) of a particular person who is suspected to be a principal in the conspiracy of persecution; or (*b*) it is homicide at large, being the killing of one who chances to present himself at the moment when the patient, swept out of himself in a fury of exasperation, resolves desperately to make some one pay for the iniquities of many; or (*c*) it is done with the deliberate resolve to enforce a public inquiry into his wrongs and thus to have justice done, the truth made evident, and their persecutors confounded; or anyhow to have done with the business one way or another, since it would be better to be hanged outright than to go on enduring such atrocious persecution.

In estimating the chances of danger in a particular case exact account ought to be taken of the individual character, which necessarily counts for much: the risk is never so great in women as in men, since they, being tame to sufferance, are not prone to attack others; nor is it great in men of gentle, timid and patient natures, since they, in the last resort, are more likely to do harm to themselves than to others; it is greatest in men of egotistic and aggressive natures who, unused to bend, passionately resent opposition and whose instinct is not to bear oppression tamely but angrily to resist it. Moreover, the danger is less when the patient, being more mad, has a crowd of imagined enemies, than it is when, being less generally deranged, he concentrates his suspicions on a single enemy against whom his anger is inflamed to a white heat of vengeance. This is one reason why those who suffer from alcoholic and hypochondriacal mania of persecution are especially dangerous; they are prone to fix on a particular person whom they believe to be the cause of their sufferings and to discharge their accumulated fury against him. They have also mind enough to feel bitterly their miserable state, to plan deliberate revenge, and to carry a desperate resolution into desperate effect; managing their delusions, if necessary, to the extent of dissembling or denying them for the occasion, and even of concealing them methodically for a purpose.

Another difference between the victims of alcoholic and of ordinary mania of persecution, which also helps to make the former more dangerous, was pointed out by Laséque: it is that the alcoholic patient is acutely fearful, keenly anxious and agitated, believing himself menaced by, and in a tremor of apprehension of, what *will* happen to him; his emotion is more acute, definite and consistent; whereas the latter is full of complaints of what *has been* done to him, never weary of telling over the tedious story of his persistent persecutions, ever lamenting what he has suffered rather than anticipating fearfully what is to come. He is not therefore really so unhappy; for as suffering lies much, often most, in apprehension, he who has an inflamed apprehension of it is sometimes more intensely wretched than he who can talk of his actual agonies, past or present. Moreover, the intellectual delusions are less and the hallucinations more marked in the alcoholic patient, who is prone to see strange animals and persons about him, perhaps corpses in the room, ceilings open and shut, flames of fire, and the like; the hallucinations, which are fleeting, changing and incoherent, being both of sight and hearing, whereas they are chiefly or entirely of hearing in ordinary mania of persecution. Still, when habitual alcoholic excesses act perniciously on a brain predisposed to mental disorder they sometimes give rise to a chronic mental derangement indistinguishable from ordinary mania of persecution; the only difference, if any, being that the emotional derangement is keener and more consistent with the delusions, which are themselves less absurd—indeed so little evident sometimes that the whole disorder may be mainly an abiding mood of insane suspicions and distrust dominating the conduct.

Such are the leading symptoms of mania of persecution proper. The chief varieties of it which might justify a separate mention are :—

(1) That in which the symptoms are chiefly *hallucinatory*, the disorder being concentrated mainly on the senses, and especially on the sense of hearing, and the infirmity or delusion of intellect being manifest principally in its impotence to weigh justly and to correct the false testimony which they give. So consistent indeed are the stories which these patients sometimes tell, so lucid are they in formulating their accusations, so rational do they appear apart from their particular unreason, that they are believed by those who do not know much about them; they may even infect with their delusions a person living with them, especially if it chance to be one who has a temperament tuned in unison and a rather weak understanding. Then "mad tales by mad ears believed be." Insane as they

really are, the personality is not transformed by the insanity, it is still preserved; the intellect is amiss in so far as it accepts certain false premisses of sense, but, approving and accepting them, it reasons pretty logically from them.

There is a sub-variety of these hallucinatory cases, in which the hallucinations have a specially hypochondriacal cast. Morel deemed hypochondriacal melancholy to be an invariable precursor of persecution-mania, describing it as part of the natural history of the disease. But that is too absolute a conclusion. Not all the cases of persecution-mania are either preceded or accompanied by special hypochondriacal symptoms, and some cases of hypochondriacal melancholy of persecution retain their special character throughout. These patients are for the most part occupied with watching their disordered sensations and with insane imaginings regarding the causes of them; they complain of anomalous itchings, burnings and prickings of the skin, and of strange feelings in their internal organs, which they ascribe to the sinister operations, magnetic or otherwise mysterious, of their enemies; not unfrequently the plaints are that the genital organs are being worked on, either to excite nasty feelings and seminal emissions or to weaken and destroy virile power. Very miserable is the man who imagines that he is being insidiously and iniquitously emasculated, and not at all unlikely to do harm to himself or others; very miserable also is the woman who imagines that she is tampered with and outraged sexually.

2. In this variety, already fully described, the symptoms are more distinctly and generally *delusional*, the disorder having got a deeper hold of the character and the intellect being manifestly deranged. A gradual and insidious transformation of the personality may be watched. The delusion of persecution, when it first enters the mind, is probably repelled as an intruder, the true *ego* being strong and lucid enough to reject it; but as it gains a footing and grows in strength, drawing to itself congenial ideas by an elective affinity and welding them by morbidly tempered feeling, a strong central delusional structure is organized round which

insane thought is systematised and revolves; and in proportion as this takes place is the true *ego* weakened and a new morbid *ego* formed. Then it is not the normal self but the metamorphosed self of madness which functions in thought, feeling and doing for the most part: the former is only occasional and partial, the latter pretty constant and general. For a time, while the process of transformation is going on, the individual is a sort of double being according as the one or the other of the contending selves rules, the true *ego* reasserting itself after its successive eclipses; but in the end it is so disintegrated, the morbid *ego* so completely integrated, the unreason such and so general, that the mental condition is an actual dementia.

3. This variety includes a class of very troublesome persons who are pests to themselves and to all who have to do with them or with whom they insist on having to do. They are really examples of moral insanity rather than of mania of persecution, seeing that their conduct exhibits much more moral than intellectual derangement. Without any distinct delusion or hallucination, they are more essentially unreasonable than if they had both; for they are utterly devoid of any just sense of proportion in their estimate of themselves and their relations to the world, their whole manner of thought and feeling being in that respect delusional. Inspired by a monstrous and exacting egoism, they deem themselves victims of persecution because they cannot have—what it is the implicit assumption of their selfish natures they ought to have—things all and always their own way; their failures, the inevitable results of their faults of character, they translate into wrongs done to them and proclaim themselves shamefully ill-used when it is they only who ill-use others. How faults and failures are bound together by natural necessity, the wholesome lesson which a wise sanity of nature soon learns, they never can learn: when they have wrecked their fortunes by their selfish follies, they have not the shadow of a doubt that others are to blame for their misfortunes. Self-indulgence is the note of their keenly self-loving natures, self-dis-

cipline the note absent from it; their only notion of self-denial is that others should deny themselves in order to serve them, their only notion of selfishness that it is very selfish in others not to do that. To help them once is a mistake and may be a calamity; for it is sure to entail new appeals for further benefits, not as favours rendered to them but as rights which they are entitled to, and to be made the justification of persistent persecution, angry abuse, and malignant calumny when the appeal is not answered, and answered in the ill-considered and impracticable way which they desire and enjoin. It is wonderful to see how quickly their fine sensibility is hurt and their dignity outraged by a refusal. Should they obtain the help they demand and fail again, as they are sure to do, they consider the new failure as a new wrong done to them for which they are entitled to recompense by renewed help. It is a good fortune to those who have to do with them if in the end they escape harassing lawsuits in addition to other such persecutions as abusive letters, insulting postcards, and the like. All the while the inspiration of their self-love is that they are virtuous persons contending against unexampled injustice.

As these persons only magnify monstrously the common qualities of exacting egotism and ingratitude, it may no doubt be plausibly argued that they are not mad. Certainly ingratitude and selfishness are common enough in the world; so common that a man of much experience in it naturally asks himself, when he hears one man speak ill of another, what favour the evil speaker has received from, or what injury he has done to, him whom he abuses. To belittle the benefit and to disparage the benefactor salves the humiliation to self-love which the solicitation or acceptation of help is. It is in the excess that madness lies—in the exaggerated development of natural passions of human nature, not in the appearance of new passions in it; and when self-love, in one or other of its various guises, has grown to such a height and so far astray as to make its possessor socially impracticable, he is justly accounted insane.

Thus much concerning the most characteristic varieties of mania of persecution. I now go on to take notice of an interesting pathological development which a mania of persecution frequently undergoes—namely, its transformation into an opposite state of exalted mania. From dejected notions of oppression the patient mounts to exalted notions of grandeur, from the melancholy of a humiliated to the conceit of an exalted self: a metamorphosis, if the comparison may be allowed, not unlike that of leaf into flower or of grub into butterfly. The manner of the change is something in this wise: he begins by noticing that persons look strangely at him, make peculiar gestures, throw out allusive hints, meddle with his doings in extraordinary ways, and is much perplexed and troubled with what he sees; brooding over it, he tries to think of some natural explanation, but in vain, since the whole affair is so mysterious and inexplicable; after a while, however, he suspects, and the dawning suspicion soon ripens into conviction, that he is a person of much greater consequence than he had supposed hitherto and that therein lies the secret reason of the singular attentions of which he is the object wherever he goes. Believing all the world to be concerning itself with him, he believes himself a person of sufficient importance to justify and account for the concern of all the world. Not entirely illogically, his premisses being granted; for to believe that so many persons in so many places connive to busy themselves about him and his affairs is such a colossal exhibition of unconscious egotism, such a grotesque exaggeration of his own importance, that his overgrown and distorted self goes on naturally to seek and find a conscious explanation of the mystery in his secret greatness.

This is the sort of pathological logic: such extraordinary persecution must be the work of some exalted person or persons having an immense interest in the business and able to command the requisite means and influence; how else could it be done? What then is the secret motive? He himself must be other than what he has hitherto been reputed to be—a great personage whose rights have been wrongly withheld from him. Or, astonished that he has been able so long to baffle the pertinacious plots of his enemies, he concludes that he has had secret protection and aid from some powerful quarter. Why such aid if he were no more than the person he is alleged to be? It has been given because he is not the real son of his reputed parents, but the son of some exalted, most likely royal, person, having been deprived of his birthright and placed in a mean station for secret reasons of state. Once it has got itself shaped and fixed, the delusion grows gradually, wresting support from the most trivial circumstances, until it mainly governs his thought and conduct; the chief interest and business of which it then becomes to discover the occasions of its confirmation and to put forward claims founded on it. He frequents royal processions or haunts the neighbourhood of royal palaces in order to receive secret tokens of recognition, sends statements of his claims to royal persons and prime ministers, perhaps tries to get access to the reigning sovereign or the heir to the throne, and becomes so troublesome at last as to require to be put under restraint.

It has been noticed—I have noticed three instances in my experience—that the transformation of a mania of persecution into a mania of greatness seems to take place with a more than accidental frequency of coincidence in persons of illegitimate birth. If the fact be so, the reason is not far to seek. An illegitimate person who is ignorant of his full parentage is naturally curious to know who his unknown parent was; nothing can be more interesting to him personally and nothing therefore is more likely to be oftener in his thoughts and speculations. It is beyond doubt that he will desire to have distinguished parentage—if he is an Englishman, nothing less than to be descended from somebody whose ancestors came over the Channel with William the Conqueror. Moreover, the illegitimacy being a humiliation which he cannot help having occasion to feel from time to time throughout life, he is specially sensitive on that score, apt to perceive and resent slights where none were intended, and quickly on the strain to assert his dignity. Unfortunately the sensitiveness and self-assertion are themselves a bar to wholesome social intercourse, partly because they render him averse to it and partly because they do not render him agreeable to others who, finding it difficult to get on pleasantly with him, are therefore disposed to shun him. Thus it comes to pass that he is first depressed and morbidly suspicious, ascribing his isolation to dislike or hostility, and afterwards goes through a sort of convulsive revolt into a mania of exaltation.

The steps of this pathological transformation are seldom so clear and logical as I have set them forth; in most cases they are more or less obscure and confused; sometimes they are altogether absent, so far as appears, the eruption of grandeur taking place on a sudden, without any apparent reason and without any previous conscious brooding over the process of it. Nevertheless it has had its sufficient reason; the processes of its gestation and maturation went on silently beneath consciousness, until, at the full time, the ripe product of infra-conscious workings emerged into conscious light. Always there is the *natura naturans* beneath the phenomena of the *natura naturata*. And of its essential workings how small a part is that which they reveal!

The transformation might be described technically as a passage from melancholia into mania, since there is often sufficient despondency in connection with the persecution-fancies to give the mental state the sad hue of melancholy. But that is a very superficial distinction, for many times the two characters persist and mix; the victim of persecution is sometimes more angry than sad, and self-conferred greatness which is kept out of its imagined rights by enemies is not always happy. The principal thing to note is that this sort of insanity, although chronic in character, is not secondary to any acute attack or other form of insanity, but is of primary origin: it begins so quietly in character that it is impossible to say when it begins, and grows gradually, once started, until it reaches such an irrational pitch as to be rightly accounted madness. We have not to do with disease in the sense in which delirium is disease, not with good mental machinery thrown out of gear by accidental disorder, but with ill-constructed machinery the propensity of which is to disorder—with a distorted rather than a disjointed mind, with deformity which, prone by the instinct of self-conservation to maintain and increase itself, becomes pathological.

Besides the misfortune of illegitimacy other causes which are a prejudice to the individual, rendering him conspicuous by some manifest bodily defect, and tending to isolate him in the social organization, act sometimes on an insanely predisposed temperament to inflame self-consciousness and ultimately to develop a mania of persecution. A bodily deformity, or a signal peculiarity of gait, feature, or speech, which is a social impediment and provokes notice, may be the starting-point in a weak mind, though a similar defect has spurred a strong mind to emulate and excel those who have no such prejudice to overcome. The almost masculine growth of a beard or a moustache in a woman has distressed her so much because of the ridicule and repulsion which she supposed it excited as to render her insanely suspicious and finally insane; and I remember one gentleman destitute of any hair on his body who, having been much teased and persecuted at school because of his defect and much afflicted through life by the consciousness of it, fell at last into a mania of persecution and tried to do murder. To be infirm in any way is to be at a disadvantage in a world in which every advantage is taken; and to be at a disadvantage in the struggle of life, whether from defect, deformity, age or other infirmity, tends naturally to breed envy and suspicion of enmity. Therefore it is that, as Bacon remarked, deformed persons, eunuchs and old men are inclined to be suspicious, jealous and envious; that weak-minded persons, who are usually very conceited, easily conceive notions of conspiracy and persecution; that delusions of persecution are symptoms of the insanity of imbeciles, children, and persons whose faculties are weakened by age, apoplexy, or softening of the brain.

A person of weak, timid and nervous nature sent to reside in a foreign city, to learn a business there among people whose language he understands not and whose manners and customs are alien to him, necessarily leads an isolated life at first, going little abroad perhaps from fear of what may befall him; solitary among strangers and brooding in his seclusion, he becomes suspicious and apprehensive of hostility, then conceives unfounded fears and fancies, and finally develops a true mania of persecution. I have met with some instances of that sort. In like manner, it happens sometimes to one who, being placed in authority over others, is not of strong enough character to maintain respect for his office, or is conscious of some painful incident in his past life which he fears may be known or suspected, to become morbidly sensitive to seeming slights, to imagine that those under him treat him with disrespect and defiance, veiled or open—as they probably may do if they dare—and thus to slide gradually into a positive persecution-mania. The likelihood of that issue is much increased if the solitary vice of solitary life has been contracted; which fails not then to intensify self-consciousness, to weaken self-confidence and self-command, and to aggravate the difficulties of healthy social intercourse. He must command himself who would command others.

Mixed Exaltation and Persecution.

Although mania of persecution is the most frequent it is not the only form which the insanity of mental distortion takes. From first to last the derangement has sometimes an exalted strain, the inflated delusion being erotic, religious, political or quasi-scientific. Common enough in the world is an intemperate conceit of self where there is not the least ground for any conceit; many times it reaches a degree of inflation which renders some one ridiculous who is not thought mad; sometimes it grows out of all proportion into the most irrational delusion. A person of not very strong mind, vain of his personal accomplishments, imagines that some lady of eminent station is in love with him, nurses the flattering notion in secret, discerns proofs of it in trifles light as air, and rejects all arguments and circumstances of disproof, be they never so cogent. There is no height of absurdity to which such a delusion may not grow: sometimes it is the most famous actress or singer of the day who is smitten with him; in another case it is a royal lady whose august favour he has attracted and whose hand he demands in marriage. Perhaps he follows the lady's movements from place to place without ever addressing her by word or letter, content with a distant admiration and the secret tokens of sympathy which he hopes to elicit or persuades himself he receives; or he pesters her with his pursuit, writing letter after letter couched in the same exalted strain and endeavouring to force his attentions on her in public. The tone of his letters is not that of a modest lover proffering a humble suit, but rather a tone of assured confidence, as of a favoured suitor to a lady who is kept from his arms by hostile machinations. If his letters are unanswered or answered only by a curt refusal to have anything to do with him, or if he accosts her in public and meets with an indignant repulse, he will not believe that she was acting with full freedom of will and meant what she did; he ascribes her feigned conduct to the lies and manœuvres of enemies who are plotting to keep them apart. Here we behold how the mania of exaltation is yet tinctured by a mania of persecution, as the latter is in some degree always by it; for in both cases he is, tacitly or expressly, a great personage, seeing that he is of so much consequence as to make it worth the world's while to engage in a conspiracy either to keep him out of his rights or to persecute him actively. If he is not unhappy, it is because he is happy enough to have too high a conceit of himself to be depressed by the hostility which he encounters.

Fool as such an one is, he is nowise a harmless fool always. The more fool there is in the delusion the more dangerous he may be, since conceit is prone to increase inversely as sense decreases; and with inflamed conceit uncurbed by sane reflection it is impossible to foresee the devious tracks of mad reasoning which witless thoughts will take and what their outcome in conduct will be,—in the end perhaps suicide or homicide. Not long ago a person of this sort in the United States who, after much persecution of a prominent actress with his attentions, had been at last sent to an asylum, from which he escaped, returned to it and shot dead the doctor whom he believed to have been in league with those who were plotting to frustrate his aspirations. Several other similar homicides have been recorded.

Women are prone, more prone indeed than men, to similar love-manias. Then it is usually a single woman or widow who sets her heart on some one, oftentimes a minister of religion, whom she believes to be in love with her and only prevented from proposing to her by some secret let or hindrance; she throws herself in his way on all possible occasions, never misses a religious service at which he officiates, pesters him with letters of love, and in the end perhaps makes a scandal by some public demonstration of it. Or it is some person of eminence whom she believes to be prevented by her enemies from declaring his love; to whom she writes loving letters and whose replies, if repulses, she maintains are not in his handwriting or not the expression of his real feelings, having been written under the constraint of others or in order to try her affection. Mad as the delusion is, there may be nothing mad in the general demeanour and conduct of such a victim of erotomania; who perhaps goes on performing the daily routine of her duties, notwithstanding that she is quietly sending letters abroad of a compromising and thoroughly irrational character. A master or mistress whose servant is behaving in that insane way may hear for the first time from outsiders of the strange things she is doing and of the reasons seriously to suspect her sanity.

Another flagrant case is that of the religious fanatic who believes himself to be the special medium of a divine revelation or a supernatural inspiration. Then the ordinary certitude of madness in face of directly opposing evidence is strengthened by the extraordinary conviction of a divine mission and miraculous doings. Moreover, because that which would be plain madness in all other domains of human belief, where it is reason's function to govern opinion, is nothing strange in matters of religious faith, where reason is foolishness and it is a Christian's express duty to become a fool in order to be wise, a person of this sort may draw after him a troop of credulous followers who revere his pretensions and make him the apostle of a new church. How far he believes in his own pretensions, how much of conscious deceit mixes with self-deceit in the mixed part of dupe and deceiver which he plays, it is hard to say; we meet with all degrees and kinds of blends between the predominant madness of a Joanna Southcote who believes herself with child by the Holy Ghost and the predominant imposture of the hypocrite who uses religion as procuress of his lust and spiritual intensifier of its sensual fruitions. Not that even he is the quite conscious hypocrite which he looks to outsiders; to be that a man must be capable of getting so far outside self-love and self-conceit as to obtain an objective glimpse of himself as he appears to others; whereas his being is so completely engulfed in a monstrous egoism that he can see no part of himself from the outside, not even his historical self. It is impossible to set rule or measure to the possible duperies of self-imposture; but it may be taken for granted that when any one goes to work to impose on others he will soon impose on himself, and that in proportion as he derationalises so will he demoralise himself. The genuine religious madman, whose own character and the character of whose delusions forbid any doubt of the sincerity of his derangement, is still capable of quite rational conversation and conduct in the relations of ordinary life; his daily doings going on in a routine of sane conformity with the ways of men and things around him, while the ideal life of greatness goes on its insane course almost aloof from it.

A third case is that of the person who imagines himself to be the discoverer of a secret conspiracy against the State, or to have penetrated the evil designs of some dangerous secret society which he would triumphantly unmask could he get himself listened to, as he fails not persistently to try to do. Although his supposed discovery is utterly irrational, it is remarkable how little his powers of just apprehension and reasoning are at fault in all matters that touch not the unreasonable part of him; if he gets himself shut up in an asylum, he is quite alive to the delusions and follies of other inmates and protests vehemently against the villainous conspiracy which has placed him in such company; it is only when he comes to expound his insane theories and to deal with the evidence which he cites in support of them that sense and reason desert him. Then the wildest improbabilities, the absurdest incredibilities, the most flagrant inconsistencies, affect not his conviction; if these are plainly and ruthlessly demonstrated to him the demonstration causes a pause of uncertain embarrassment only, followed by a vehement reiteration of his opinion or an explosion of angry abuse and imprecation.

If not a political discovery, it is perhaps an extraordinary discovery in mechanics, or in philosophy, or in prophecy, or of the right title to an estate or dignity, which he imagines himself to have made and which year after year he perseveres in pressing upon an unheeding world. If the letters in which he sets forth his claims and expositions be compared they are found to run in the same strain and almost in the same words, albeit there may be an interval of years between them. The same mad thought-tracts are limited to the same mad expressions. Exposition of the absurdity of his discovery only inflames his self-assertion; and to have listened to his arguments without being convinced by them, if it be not a personal offence, is proof of ignorant stupidity, or of dishonesty, or of jealousy, or of complicity with his enemies.

As time goes on, the delusions grow and spread, invading

more and more of his mind, which becomes proportionately weaker and more irrational, until he is virtually demented. In most large asylums are to be found instances of demented patients with incoherent ideas of grandeur who go on for the most part quietly and mechanically with the work they are employed in, talking sensibly when talking of it, but evincing their utter madness outside a few automatic tracks of thought. Here also, however, the law of uncertain periodic increase and decline which is witnessed in so many disorders of the nervous system fails not to show itself; for without any evident cause of disturbance they have their periodical excitements, when they are unfit to work, stirred by exacerbations of insane feeling and thought, and prone to unexpected and even dangerous acts.

Such insane persons are not likely ever to come to right minds: how can they when their right minds are at best more or less wrong minds? The disorder being no extrinsic and accidental disturbance, but an intrinsic and essential outgrowth of the nature, is too deeply rooted ever to be unrooted. Meanwhile there is nothing in the mental disorder to hurt the bodily health, which is commonly just as good as if nothing ailed the mind: lame in mind not in body, they perform their bodily functions as well as a distorted tree performs its functions of breathing, feeding, and putting forth leaves. The practical question which arises in connection with them is whether they are such discordant elements in the social organisation as to make it necessary or right to sequestrate them. Social nuisances they unquestionably sometimes are without being social dangers, and sometimes social nuisances which ultimately become social dangers. It is not quite safe to account them harmless, harmless though their mad pretensions may appear; for they are liable to become so impatient of the universal neglect of their claims and to be so exasperated by it and by their futile endeavours to obtain a hearing that they do something desperate in order thus effectually to force their grievances into public notice. Homicide or suicide may be the outcome although the delusions have no direct leading that way. When a mind is so much disordered as to be not merely out of tune but out of sense with the real order of things around and to find nothing but reinforcement of its disorder in every impression made on it, then it is impossible for a sane mind to foresee what distorted view of its relations to real things it may some day take, or what mad thought it may conceive and bring forth in action. To require a discernible link of cause and effect between the delusion and deed in order to excuse the doer from responsibility when he does something criminal, and to insist that the deed is not mad when no such connection can be traced—that is neither more nor less than to make sane thought the measure of insane thought and to postulate the necessity of a sanely logical order in the disorder of madness.

Insanity of Jealousy.

There are other passions besides excessive self-conceit which, attracting and inspiring their congenial ideas, stimulate them into an irrational growth. Notable is jealousy; a passion which, poisoning reason and blinding judgment, sometimes takes such ungrounded and unreasonable hold of the mind of a man or woman as to render it unsafe for them to live together in intimacy. For some trivial reason or without reason a husband, for example, conceives the notion that his wife is unfaithful to him, broods gloomily over his suspicions, finds arguments of confirmation in the most innocent circumstances, which he torments himself and her with persistently spying into and misconstruing, swallows greedily never so glaring improbabilities, and is blind to the plainest proofs of his unreason. He is psychically blind to them because reason in relation to them is suspended in him by an ecstasy of reasoning unreason. All the while he may not show any mental derangement away from home, so that no one outside his domestic circle has a suspicion of the insane way in which he is behaving in it. He is still able to go on successfully with work abroad requiring close and systematic mental application, notwithstanding that he is watching every movement of his wife at home, detecting evidence of her guilt in the most trivial and accidental circumstances of social and sexual intimacy, laying traps to convict her, discovering that the lock of the house door has been tampered with, surmising that the servants are in league to deceive him, and rendering her life intolerable by his suspicions, pryings, accusations, expostulations, adjurations, angry explosions and threats.

Knowing the frailties of his kind and the wiles and guiles of womankind, an insanely jealous husband might plead excuse for doubting the fidelity of a wife who lacked the effective protection of virtue which absence of temptation and opportunity is; but the marvel is that he cannot see the gross absurdity of the opportunities which he alleges, and that he torments himself for what, on his own showing, could hardly be more defiling than immaculate adultery with an invisible agent. A curious proof that the delusion is not the belief of his whole mind, but something which at bottom he but believes partly, is that he does not take steps to discard his wife, as a sane husband might be expected to do who was similarly convinced of her infamy, but pesters her with reproaches for her sin, lectures on its enormity, appeals to her conscience, and importunate entreaties to confess. His keenest grievance seems to be that she will not make a clean breast of it; if she would only confess he would forgive her and say no more, he protests. It is a foolish complaisance on her part if, seduced by his solicitations, she allows his importunity to extort a false confession of sin, with the aim of pacifying him, as I have known done; for the confession is only a fleeting sedative and is pretty sure to be adduced afterwards as confirmation of his quickly reviving suspicions. "She has deceived me once and will deceive me again"—is his natural and warrantable inference. It is futile error to make any terms or compromise with the delusion; the only course likely to do good is to face it firmly with a plain demonstration of its folly and with an unshrinking exposition of the perilous mental state which it betrays—to let a brisk gale of outside good sense blow through the close atmosphere of a narrow and stifling domesticity. The man may not be cured of his delusion, but his latent self-distrust will be strengthened, and he may haply be startled into self-control by the shock of rudely realising how others see it and how in the last resort they may resolve to treat it. That course failing, a separation should be enforced, the completer the better, and the ill-starred being will probably go on with his working life fairly well in the absence of the conditions which furnished the special stimuli to the unsound part of his mental structure.

The root of the insane jealousy in such case is, I believe, often sexual. Failing in desire or power or pleasure of coition, whether because of pre-nuptial abuse or post-nuptial excess or both, he finds fault with his partner, who may perhaps have shown some impatience of his sensual hankerings or his impotent pesterings, and straightway out of a mind nastily infested with sensual imaginings begins to suspect loss of affection and desire on her part because of attachment or indulgence elsewhere. Once launched on this track, he goes on in full sail of suspicion to multiply proofs of infidelity, torturing his ingenuity to devise cunning schemes of detection and ending perhaps by taking her dirty linen, which he purloins from its private receptacle, to a medical expert in order to have the stains on it examined microscopically. The pity of it is that these jealous-mad persons seem so sane to the world at large and tell their stories so plausibly that they are believed sometimes, when the affair is wholly a coinage of their brain-sick imagination; all the more easily since an imputation of unchastity in an unchaste world is not incredible. After all, it is not essentially jealousy but suspicion that they are mad of, which is the inborn note of their neuropathic natures; on that bad foundation the monstrous superstructure of their marital jealousy is built up into madness: a mad nature goes out in that development, the insane suspicion in its structure being the nursing mother of its madness. Therefore it is that their torturing thoughts perennially spring up and keep up without provocation, are impregnable to reason, proof against proof, crave the appeasements of indulgence, nay, appear positively to court and like their painful exercises. Paradoxical as it sounds, there are neuropathic natures which crave, even enjoy, the self-tortures they inflict; for every nature is prone and pleased to exercise its special idiosyncrasies, and one nature is by secret instinct as painfully fanciful as another is placidly prosaic.

As woman's end lies mainly in man, while man's end is mainly in himself, she is more dependent on the relations of marriage than he is and more prone to fall into insane jealousy. Although not limited to any period of wedded life, its development is most apt to take place at the change of life when, the age of pleasing being past, she perhaps covets and exacts proofs of a desire towards her which she has an instinctive apprehension of now failing to excite. It is always more likely to befall women who have not children and particularly women who are addicted to secret or open drinking. The craving of the barren womb expresses itself in feelings of disquietude and irritable discontent, in exacting demands, in uneasy suspicions; while the narrow domestic conditions of two persons who have lived much to and for themselves are ill adapted to effect a wholesome dispersion of feelings and interests. Moreover, the natural cooling of the sexual passion which goes along with advancing age, and usually follows the first ardours of nuptial lust, breeds a suspicion in some erotic and jealous natures of another than the true cause; the diminution of desire and zest being attributed, not to the natural exhaustion and blunting by use and wont, and to the satiety of easy fruition, but to illicit gratification elsewhere. Elderly men married to young wives are liable to fall under this suspicion. Fearful pests of frenzy are these jealous furies to their unhappy husbands, whose lives at home they render insupportable and whom they pursue abroad sometimes into their professions and businesses with such reckless passion as to blast their careers. At first the blazing outbursts of wild jealousy are limited to stormy scenes of reproach and violence, alternating perhaps with passionate sobbings and clinging ecstasies of affection, but afterwards they proceed to insulting abuse of those whom they suspect, either personal, or by letter, or by foul and abusive post-cards, and to public denunciation of their husbands. The destructive violence of their passions might seem incredible to any one who had not seen the effects: smashed mirrors and windows, wrecked furniture, shattered ornaments and crockery, jewelry trodden under foot or flung into the fire, and such exploits of violence to person as they are capable of. When the storm is past and the wreckage confronts them, they take neither shame nor blame to themselves; in this or that unimportant circumstance feminine reasoning finds the sufficient cause but for which nothing serious would have happened and the excuse of all that happened.

It is not necessary that there be the least evidence of a husband's unfaithfulness or any just ground of suspicion; for if he speak a few words of common courtesy to a woman, or make a casual remark about her as she passes, or chance to look particularly at her, it is enough to inflame the jealous fury and provoke a violent explosion. Not a female servant in the house can he speak civilly to but she is instantly suspected and perhaps dismissed. His letters are secretly inspected, the torn fragments of them gathered from the waste-paper basket and diligently pieced together, his blotting-book closely examined, in order to discover traces of a clandestine correspondence; and it matters not how innocent the words or expressions discovered, they are woven as warp or woof into the web of suspicion. Twice within my experience it has happened by a retributive justice—which happily chances just often enough to keep alive unreasoning belief in it—that a second husband who had been too loving to the lady during her first marriage, having been the confidant and consoler of the sorrows of a sad soul pining for finer and keener joys than the stale joys of domestic life, has been the victim of such jealous fury;

which failed not then to find in the remembrance of past illicit attentions to her argument of the certainty of present illicit attentions elsewhere. So bitter and hateful the sin done against her that was so sweet and flattering when it was done for her!

When matters have reached this pass there is no hope of mending them: it is best to end them once for all by a separation, since the conditions of married life perpetually provoke and inflame the mania. The difficulty with jealous-mad women is to induce them to consent to a separation; they cling tenaciously to a position which they protest is unendurable, as if they found an indispensable ease in the scenes of fury and violence which they provoke. When they consent to a separation they are still prone to pursue their husbands with abusive letters and post-cards, which they send to him and his relations and friends, causing sometimes no little mischief and misery in families by scandalous libels on innocent persons. If a legalised separation is impracticable, as it usually is with poor persons, then the situation is not always free from danger; for the confined elements of irritation may grow in heat until they explode in suicidal or homicidal frenzy. The desperate workman, if he be an honest man who will not desert his family, kills himself because he cannot bear his wife's suspected adulteries longer, or perhaps kills her and the children also; or the wife, maddened past endurance by her imagined wrongs, cuts her children's throats and then perhaps her own throat, partly out of angry vengeance and partly because she is resolved to remove them in their innocence from the contamination and misery of the situation. In neither case is the crime the product of simple jealousy, it is the outcome of insanity which has taken that development; and it may be pretty safely assumed that a close inquiry into the individual's hereditary antecedents would disclose evidence of an insane inheritance. Where so many degrees of disorder are possible the question of responsibility must needs be a difficult one; on the one hand, the jealousy might be so absurdly insane as to reveal a mental disorganisation which was almost dementia; on the other hand, it might be no more than the brief frenzy of the natural passion in excess. Let a man of insane mental temperament, known perhaps among his companions to be excitable and somewhat eccentric, fall in love with a woman, he is likely to be madly in love with her, his whole nature being rapt in an ardour of passion and recklessness of pursuit; if he kills her because she, after favouring his suit and accepting lavish proofs of his devotion, jilts him for some one who has more money to spend on her or more attractions to offer, he may well be mad for the time being, though not mad legally nor even medically.

Insanity of Avarice.

The extravagant growth of a special tract of the mental organisation into the deformity of a special madness is exemplified again by the monstrous development which avarice sometimes takes. Regardless of the ends to which money is a means, the sordid miser lives in the vilest and most wretched conditions imaginable, stinting himself of the bare necessaries of life and sometimes actually starving himself to death, while he is scraping and hoarding up every penny which he can get hold of and hiding his gold in secret places of his house. His greed is an all-absorbing passion to which not only every social feeling but every personal comfort is ruthlessly sacrificed. Were self-sacrifice by itself a virtue, no greater virtue could any man display, since no self-denial surpasses that which he practises. But the truth of course is that, like the religious ascetic, whom he equals in self-denial, he is really moved by self-love to gratify a deformed self: to endure the extremity of misery in the pursuit of his ideal is his supreme happiness. When he dies of starvation in the midst of his hoards of hidden gold he proves how small a worth human life essentially has, by proving how mean a passion may overcome the instinctive love of it.

What are we to say of so unhuman a specimen of the

human kind? He is not mad medically, for his mind is only deformed not diseased, its apt organisation having been moulded into a mere machine of money-getting. Nor is he mad legally, for it would be a principle of dangerous latitude to deprive a man of the control of himself and his affairs simply because he kills himself in the eager pursuit of wealth for its own sake, as he has the right to do. Nor is he quite mad socially, for he is not an intolerable pest or danger; and although, like a non-malignant tumour in the physiological organism, he grows entirely for his own behoof into a monstrous egoism which does nothing for the social organism but get its nourishment from it, he is not bound to value his kind as highly as his kind values itself; he may think human life at its best but a mean business, occupied with vanities and replete with shams, illusions, and hypocrisies, which at last nature will have to end and decompose, as it decomposes and gets rid of other organic nuisances. That being so, why should he not make his own self-development, to its fullest extent and agreeably to its inborn propensities, the one aim of his life? What has he, essentially egoistic and antisocial by nature, to do with altruistic efforts which, going entirely against his grain, would be futile labour and pain to him? Full inquiry into the particulars of his ancestral lines would no doubt show that he was the antisocial branch of an unsound stock.

The lesson of these morbid distortions or deformities of mind is a lesson of preventive hygiene; cure there is none for them. They represent bad mind-stuff, and the sooner it returns to nature's workshop to be worked up into new stuff, the better for the kind. When psychology has become sufficiently positive in its methods and practical in its aims to find out the exact ways by which they have come to be, it may be able to lay down rules to prevent their production in time to come. To do that successfully, however, it will have to substitute for the notions of *sin* and its penal consequences in a life to come after death the notion of fault of organic manufacture and its avenging consequences from person to person and from generation to generation in the life that now is.

The problem which mankind has to solve in its development is the right adjustment of the self-regarding and the social tendencies. A social organism is growing gradually at the cost of individualism, and in the process various transformations of egoism necessarily take place. Naturally, then, it does not fail to happen that certain exaggerated egoisms, incapable of social adjustment and transformation, are found to characterise so many more or less distorted and discordant minds in the social organisation, and that the beings so malformed mentally lay the foundations of antisocial structure in the mental constitutions of the children who spring from them. Being grounded in their natures, such structural tendencies are then instincts which cannot be eradicated entirely. When the training is good and the circumstances of life favourable to a wholesome development of mind, they may be held in check and show themselves, if they show themselves at all, only in the insane peculiarities of one whose general sanity is not questioned; but when circumstances have co-operated to nurse and nourish them, then they grow into the maturity of one or other of such special mental deformities as I have described—into the insane mental deformities which are pathological developments of the malformities of insane temperaments.

CHAPTER VI

CONDITIONS OF MENTAL WEAKNESS

THUS far I have considered the leading disorders of the mental organisation—those which mark quick, unbridled and dissolute reflex action of its cerebral tracts; those which mark dull, impeded and sluggish reflex action of them; and those which mark the distorted growth and function of certain special tracts of them. There still remains to be considered a class of disorders which ensue from, and denote the impairment or the obliteration of, a greater or less number of its cerebral reflexes.

At the outset it may be said that there is not an instance of mental derangement which is not essentially an example of more or less mental weakness. A machine so much out of order that it cannot do its proper work is certainly not strong in function, however strong it may be in random action that is the negation of true work. Patent as the weakness is in the case of the torpid melancholic who can neither think, feel nor act to any purpose, his mind being fixed cataleptically in one morbid track of gloomy function, and the rest of it temporarily paralysed, it is nowise so evident in the case of the raging maniac who, full of sound and fury, exhibits a tempestuous show of energy which hides the void beneath it. But what sort of energy is it? Frenzy of mind is not strength of mind. The function of mind being to think, the maniac is no more strong mentally than a man in convulsions is strong bodily, or than a political state is strong when, rent asunder by civil war, it is in violent internal commotions. In both cases there is motion enough, but it is motion without form and order; its tumultuous display of energy not the display of physiological function in the one, nor of national function in the other, both which are vastly weakened if not extinguished actually.

The states of mental weakness now to be considered are not, however, occasional and temporary states which pass away with the commotion which causes and accompanies them, but such mental disorganisations and impairments as are essential and permanent. Obviously there are two distinct classes of them :—(I.) A class in which the weakness is a constitutional defect, being congenital or at any rate proceeding from causes which operate soon after birth before there has been time for a real mental organisation. To this class belong so-called IDIOTS and IMBECILES, who are emphatically under a deprivation; examples of *Amentia*, seeing that they have to face the world without the capital of a fit mental structure. (II.) The class of cases of secondary mental weakness, in which the once competent organisation of cerebral substrata has been impaired or destroyed; examples of so-called *Dementia*, that is, of mental desolation after the ravage of a storm or other calamity —mind-lost as distinguished from originally mind-less instances.

I

IDIOCY AND IMBECILITY

The manifold varieties and degrees of congenital mental weakness do not come within the scope of present inquiry; they are such as in detail deserve special study and require a special description. I shall content myself therefore with a concise description of their general nature.

Most idiots betray their congenital defects by their bodily confirmation as well as by their want of mind. A broad examination of them might suggest the general conclusion that for some reason or other there is a constitutional defect of nutrition, limited perhaps chiefly to the brain and nervous system, but usually affecting the whole body. It is a question, indeed, whether idiots are ever physically sound, though here and there one may seem so. Their weight and stature are below the average of normal children of the same age : now and then an extreme instance of dwarfism, like that of an idiot in Earlswood Asylum, who, although twenty-two years old, was only twenty-eight inches high, exemplifies an extraordinarily deficient growth [1]; while the so-called sporadic Cretins, whose remarkable improvement in nutrition and intelligence when they have extract of the thyroid gland supplied in their food attests a definite and definitely cured defect of nutrition, are mostly dwarfs in greater or less degree. About 20 per cent of the admissions into the Royal Albert Asylum for idiots had a family history of phthisis, and some form of scrofulous or phthisical disease accounted for two-thirds of the deaths in it. Puberty is a perilous period for idiots, the demand made on their feeble vitality by its developmental changes leading to many deaths soon after it. In like manner premature senility is frequent among them; their low stock of vitality being unable to last the length of a normal life, they are old in youth and die of decay when still young in years.[2]

In some idiots and imbeciles, owing to defective nutritive processes, the normal growth of the bones is hindered and premature ossification of the sutures and closure of the fontanelles take place. The result, when the closure is general, is that the skull is a hard compact box which might be supposed to prevent the proper growth and development

---

[1] Or the case mentioned by Dancel of a girl, aged eighteen and a half years, whose bodily and mental condition was that of a child *æt.* three and a half ; or the case exhibited in 1857 to the French Academy of Medicine, by Baillarger, of a woman, *æt.* twenty-seven, who was three feet high and had only the intelligence and inclinations of a child *æt.* four.

[2] *Liverpool Med. Chir. Journal*, 1883, Dr. Shuttleworth : "Quite recently I had to certify *senile decay* as the cause of death in a patient aged only thirty-five, the autopsy showing no more definite lesion than worn-out mucous tissues and digestive organs."

of the brain inside it, and that when the closure is partial and local, the skull remaining narrowed or contracted there while other parts expand normally, various cranial deformities ensue. Though it might seem natural to ascribe the cerebral defect to the premature cranial synostosis, a later and more just theory is that both conditions are due to a common cause—namely, a constitutional defect of nutrition, whereby the formative elements of brain and bone lack proper vigour. A deep and narrow-shaped palate is not seldom met with in imbeciles of a scrofulous temperament; but it is not peculiar to imbeciles, though seldom, if ever, met with in persons of good constitution and strong mental capacity. On the whole, we may safely declare a want of unity, proportion, and prettiness to be the distinct note of the physiognomy of imbecility and idiocy.

In many cases *eclampsic* or *epileptic* convulsions and, in many more, paralyses with spasmodic rigidity or spasmodic movements coexist with the idiocy. Oftentimes the paralyses or contractions are of particular muscles, as in strabismus, club-foot, and like deformities. Occasionally there is paralysis and arrested growth of one side of the body owing to atrophy of the cerebral hemisphere of the opposite side; a condition of things which is then usually accompanied with epileptic attacks. Other frequent or occasional defects are—short and flabby fingers, or deformities of them and the hands; thickened and puffy skin, with abnormal harshness and dryness of it and perhaps an increased formation of epidermis imparting to it a branny look; dry, coarse and harsh hair; coarse and unshapely ears, which are not only malformed but badly planted low down and far back; ill-set, irregular, thick and carious teeth; tongue too large for the slobbering mouth and defective in its movements; unequal length or development of the arms and legs; sometimes, though not so often as is vulgarly supposed, deformed heads, which are abnormally small, or obliquely twisted, or much asymmetrical, or have the forehead framed like the keel of a boat. The popular notion that idiots commonly, if not necessarily, have small heads is not well founded. A certain proportion of them, perhaps about one-quarter, in whom a gross arrest of the development of the brain has taken place, are distinctly *microcephalic;* but Dr. Shuttleworth found, on comparing the head-measurements of one hundred normal children in an institution for orphans with those of three hundred idiots, that the differences of the averages for similar ages were but fractional. In respect of the frequency of abnormally small heads, as in respect of other deformities, it must be borne in mind that *non-congenital* idiots frequently have regular features and a good conformation of head and body; neither ugly nor deformed, their *acquired* idiocy may not mean any positive deficiency of formative force.

Such sensory defects as deafness, loss of taste or smell, and blindness, partial or complete, are frequent in idiocy. General sensibility too is often so blunt that primary reflex actions fail to be performed, and acquired reflex acts are but slowly and clumsily acquired, if acquired at all: the infant may not show any instinct to seek the mother's breast, nor be able to hold the nipple and suck when it is put into its mouth; now and then the reflex motions of swallowing are at fault; some of the lowest idiots do not even wink when the eyeball is touched; while the application of more than a year's patient labour in training an idiot's fingers to learn to button a button has been acclaimed as a triumph of, and proclaimed as an incentive to, perseverance. With reflex action, the fundamental factor of mental structure, so wanting, how could mental development take place even were there no defect of cerebral structure? How could the fine intellectual and moral reflexes ever be formed? Exact discriminations and fit apprehensions of things being impossible to the dull sensibility and the sluggish half-paralysed movements, it is impossible the creature should get mental grasp or apprehension of them. Alike in sensory, motor, trophic, and intellectual functions it is but half alive.

The mental defects of idiots vary in kind and degree, ranging from no mind in the worst instances through every grade of weakness of mind or imbecility to such feeblemindedness as passes muster in the world. Some are incapable of ideas and cannot be taught to speak or to learn, however persistent the pains taken to teach them ; some are capable of a few simple ideas and words, slow and dull, which they have learnt mechanically by frequent repetitions ; others can get as far as a few simple associations of ideas which, like the ideas, are dull, slow, and imperfect : others have capacity to respond to skilled and laborious training by a greater show of mechanical intelligence. It is the same with their feelings and desires ; in the lowest idiots, the satisfaction of their bodily wants is the one obscure desire they have and the motive of such vague cries and movements as they make ; those at a little higher level are distinctly pleased with toys and trifles ; others who reach a higher level of sensibility like tobacco and snuff, and manifest an animal-like liking for those who feed them and give them what they like. The wonderful stories told of idiots speechless from birth who suddenly, under the stroke of strong emotion or at the point of death, have given articulate utterance to blessed sentiments of affection or religion, thereby demonstrating the wholeness of a soul imprisoned vilely in a lame body, are pleasing tales which many people would rather believe proved without evidence, than believe disproved by incontestable evidence.

The movements of the lowest idiots, which seem to be automatic and meaningless or, if more or less voluntary at first, to become automatic, are continued mechanically for hours ; they are such as restless agitation of hands and arms, perpetual swaying to and fro of the body, grotesque grimacings of the features, snuffling or sucking movements, cries, shrieks, and howls. The idiotic movements proclaim the idiot mind ; like the ideas and feelings, they betray the wreck of mental machinery by broken memories of some rudiments of its functions.

There is a class of cases of hopeless mental deficiency, imbeciles rather than idiots, marked by abnormal excitability and extreme mobility of mind and body, but without epilepsy, paralysis, or bodily deformity. Their restless excitability is such that they cannot give a moment's steady attention to any object so as to learn its real meaning and qualities; they see it but cannot perceive it, turning away from it instantly to look at something else which they leave as quickly, or take hold of it and instantly loose hold of it and throw it down, without staying to apprehend it. Theirs is a monkey-like mobility of mind, and, like monkeys, they differ in degree of incapacity of attention and therefore of education. The result is that, although having a bright and alert look, they never can really learn, but remain troublesome imbeciles. Manageable at home while they are young and can have one person exclusively to look after them, they are apt to become unmanageable and practically insane at puberty. Some of them evince keenly active propensities to monkey-like mischief—to tearing, striking, hurting and destroying what they can; it is evident they take pleasure in the discharge of their destructive energies, for they howl, yell, kick, struggle and rage when they are prevented from indulging them. They generally own hereditary mental derangement. One sees in their bad mental machinery the extreme effects of a lack of power of patient attention and of an impatient discharge of irritable feeling; the hindrances which, in less degree, disable so many minds from ever seeing accurately and thinking clearly, and perhaps so disabled their forefathers in some measure.

A scientific classification of idiocy must obviously be a very difficult business, and certainly it has yet to be made. A division into congenital and non-congenital is simple and natural. The class of congenital idiots includes those in which there is gross cerebral defect or disease—*microcephalic, hydrocephalic, porencephalic*—and those in which, without any such gross defect or disease, the evidence points plainly to some general defect of nutrition, as in cretinoid and scrofulous idiots. In *microcephalic* or small-headed idiocy the brain is sometimes found to have suffered an arrest of development at some stage of fœtal life, after which it has continued to grow in whole or parts, so that, although presenting fœtal characters, it is larger than a fœtal brain at a similar stage of development. The result is perhaps a brain of fair size but imperfectly developed. It is never a reversion to the type of a monkey's brain, although its abnormal structure may approximate to what is normal in the monkey, any more than an idiot ever reverts to the monkey's mind, albeit exhibiting monkey-like traits; for it is not, as some have supposed, the reduction of a more complex to the state of a less complex mechanism, but it is a more complex mechanism malformed—strictly a pathological specimen. Too much has perhaps been made of the special animal-like features and instincts of certain idiots as instances of special reversions, out of a certainly superfluous curiosity to discover the brute within the man. The idiot brain which is arrested at different stages of its development along a path common to it and the lower animals for a long way, going on through stages at which they stay, will naturally suggest likenesses, without being a copy of them. Of the abnormally large heads met with in some idiots it must not be assumed off-hand that they are *hydrocephalic;* they may be the result of so-called *cerebral hypertrophy*, which is not really an overgrowth of nerve-element but of the neuroglia in which it is embedded: the large hydrocepalic head is globular, in the latter the head is more square-shaped. In the *porencephalic* brain there is a gap in brain-structure, though the skull may not show it, such as causes sometimes a paralytic idiocy.

Non-congenital idiocy is the result of causes that act injuriously on the brain after birth. Obviously a well-formed brain may thus be irretrievably damaged at the outset of its career. The principal causes are eclampsic and epileptic convulsions, the syphilitic poison in the blood, febrile diseases, bad food and starvation, the toxic effects of soothing narcotic syrups, the traumatic effects of falls, blows and the like, and the shock of fright or other violent emotion. A stroke of fright may produce exactly the same physical effect as a blow on the head, only by a subtler agency. In two idiots described by Hagen, whose brains were of good weight and well formed, without any hypertrophy of the connective tissue, the fault was presumably a very small heart unequal to sending a sufficiently brisk supply of blood to the brain: a fault of the same kind perhaps as that which hinders a giant in body from being a giant in mind, or that again which, owing to the ever weakening action of a weak heart in an aged person, sometimes makes a miserable mind and a melancholy end. Happy the old age which, soon overtaken by death, is not doomed to melancholise in a corner! The fate of acquired idiocy is all the more sad because for it there is no remedy, notwithstanding that its victims may be bright-looking, well shapen in body and features, without deformity of any sort; for the injury done to the very fine tissues of the brain and their occult molecular processes, although impenetrable by our most subtile means of research, is still so serious as to be irreparable. It seems to be a broad rule that the congenital idiot whose brain is arrested in development has more chance of improvement under training than the non-congenital idiot whose idiocy depends upon injury to a well-fashioned cerebral structure. Something may be done in the former to foster feeble processes of growth to sluggish habits of exercise, when nothing can be done in the latter to put right the damage of a delicate machinery.

The causes of congenital idiocy are still far from being accurately known. The fact of most certainty is that it generally denotes insanity or epilepsy in the stock. Morel regarded sterile idiocy as the natural term of human degeneracy when insanity went its way unchecked through generations. However that may be in an ideal process of degeneration, which seldom gets itself realised in practice, an excessive proportion of idiots has never been actually proved yet among the children of the multitude of insane parents who have been or are confined in lunatic asylums. Without pretending to scientific accuracy, I should be inclined to say that, barring positive weakness of mind in the parent, idiocy sprang as often from the sane as from the actually insane member of a bad stock; that some forms of insane temperament which never developed into parental madness were more likely to breed it than some forms of positive insanity were. That the insane predisposition is not the entire cause, but that something more is required to co-operate when it operates, is proved by the fact that while one child of a family of children is an idiot the rest of them may exhibit no mental defect. How could that be if there were not more special determining causes than the general predisposition?

It is a favourite opinion that intemperate parents are likely to breed idiotic offspring. But the often-quoted statement that out of 300 idiots in the State of Massachusetts 145 were the result of parental drunkenness is not the sober conclusion of science but the intemperate conclusion of an intemperate zeal for temperance. Were it an adequate and accurate estimate of causation, the wonder would be that so many habitual drunkards fail to beget idiots. Trusting to a general impression, without claiming to make a scientific statement, I should pronounce the most favourable conditions for the production of idiocy to be these— to be begotten by a drunken father off a half-witted mother.

A fact beyond dispute is that a complete idiot is sometimes born of parents who are apparently quite healthy and have other children that are perfectly normal. More surprising is it to see a whole family of idiotic children produced by parents who seem quite sound themselves, as in a case mentioned by Dr. Shuttleworth. We can do no more than conclude generally that as there are secret conditions of the germ-plasms utterly beyond our ken which render them unfit to combine at all, so there are secret conditions which unfit them to combine well and to generate a sound and vigorous product; and furthermore, that such conditions may be owing either to constitutional causes in the parents, or to special causes, mental or bodily, that act on them during the production of the germ-plasms and perhaps at the time of propagation.[1] Vain and void

---

[1] For an elaborate enumeration of such conjectural causes I might refer to Burton's *Anatomy of Melancholy*, who supports his statements in each case by

are all present speculations concerning what happens in the infinitely little, where, for aught we know, nay, so far as we can guess, there is infinite variety and nothing so infinitesimal as not to have its wondrous potency. Are two such relatively big things as two bacilli really ever exactly alike in form and properties? And how is it that the same bacillus which acts on one substance is not able to act on another substance having the same composition and qualities? or on isomeric bodies that have different properties?

Gross causes which act injuriously on the mother during her gestation, such as blows and like physical shocks, great fright and other serious mental agitations, irregularities and excesses on her parts, rightly rank as causes of congenital idiocy. So also occasionally does injury to the child's brain during parturition, whether the mischief then be done by the instruments used to aid delivery or, as some think more probable, by the prolonged pressure on the head during a difficult and protracted labour.

The intermarriage of near relatives, and especially of first cousins, is commonly assumed to be an occasional cause of congenital idiocy. It may well be so when there is a fault in the nervous structure of the stock which is intensified by the union of similarly frail and faulty germplasms. But when the stock is sound and strong there is no positive evidence that any harm ensues.

the authority of learned writers. "Old men's children are seldom of a good temperament and therefore most apt to melancholy"—"he that begets a child on a full stomach will either have a sick child or a crazed son"—"or if the parents be sick or have any great pain of the head or megrin, or if a drunken man get a child, it will never likely have a good brain"—"foolish, drunken or hair-brain women most part bring forth children like unto themselves, *morosos et languidos*; and so likewise he that lyes with a menstruous woman—*damnavit olim divina lex et morte mulctavit hujusmodi homines* (Lev. xviii. 20)—if she be over-dull, heavy, angry, peevish, discontented and melancholy, not only at the time of conception, but even all the while she carries her child in her womb, her son will be so likewise affected"—"if a man fast overmuch, study too hard, be over-sorrowful, dull, heavy, dejected in mind, perplexed in his thoughts, fearful, etc., his children will be much subject to madness and melancholy." Modern writers, so far as I know, make no allusion to the offence denounced in Leviticus: were the supposed bad effects entirely fanciful?

II

Dementia

Of Dementia two divisions may properly be made: (1) Primary or acute, when it follows some violent strain or shock, physical or mental, which paralyses mental function for a time or for life; (2) Secondary or chronic, when it follows other forms of mental derangement or other causes of a gradual mental disorganisation.

Primary or *acute dementia* is essentially a suspension, more or less complete, of the mental faculties. It has followed the shock to the brain caused by a serious attempt at strangulation. It is not unfrequently seen in some degree, sometimes in an extreme degree, after the violent molecular perturbation of the cerebral molecules accompanying an epileptic fit or a succession of such fits, especially in young persons of frail and delicate constitution; being then a stupor or confusion of mind with incoherent speech and behaviour and an inability to recognise anybody or anything, which lasts for a few hours or a few days. The acute insanity befalling in adolescents of fragile nervous constitution, especially those who have exhausted a weak nervous system by frequent self-abuse or other excess, is sometimes virtually an acute dementia. Again, it has been caused by violent moral shock and, as may well be believed, by the horrible combination of moral and physical shock which a brutal rape must needs be: witness the case of a girl, *æt.* seventeen, who, having been thrown down and violated by two ruffians in succession on her return home at night across some fields, fell into acute dementia from which she has never recovered. Under the name of sexual insanity Dr. Skae, a sagacious observer, described a form of acute dementia met with both in the male and female sex, but more often in the latter, which he ascribed to the effects of sexual intercourse upon an unstable nervous temperament.[1] In all cases the quick mental desolation bespeaks the effects of a great strain or shock acting on a weak nervous structure.

The most characteristic symptoms are—vacant and expressionless countenance; oftentimes dilated and sluggish pupils; confused and aimless excitement, alternating sometimes with periods of stupor; dulness of sensibility so that pain seems not felt or, if felt, only felt and responded to in a vague and confused way; seeing without perceiving, and hearing without understanding; no sense to take food, nor the sense to make definite resistance to it, but aimless and random opposition; speechlessness or incoherent murmuring, or senseless sentences or half sentences muttered or ejaculated; inattention to the calls of nature. There is practically a mental void, and there is no memory, therefore, after recovery, of anything having passed in the mind. With these symptoms go lowered reflex action, small and perhaps scarcely perceptible, but frequent, pulse, and bad nutrition; for the nervous collapse tells inertly on all the functions of the body.

Recovery takes place in a fair proportion of these cases when they obtain timely and proper treatment, and then usually within a month or a few weeks. If the disorder continue much longer, it is most likely to become a chronic and incurable dementia. A sound prognosis can only be founded on an exact appreciation of all the circumstances in the particular case—that is, on a knowledge of the qualities of the individual nervous constitution, of the character of the special damaging cause, and of the special mode and circumstances of operation of that cause on the individual nature at the time.

Chronic Dementia is most frequently, but not invariably, secondary to some other form of mental derangement. Its leading causes are :—

[1] In these cases it is not improbable that mental disorder, unobserved or unacknowledged, had been going on insidiously before marriage. Were it the rule in the marriage mart, as in the horse mart, to require a warranty of soundness, either many marriages would not take place which now take place, or many actions for false warranty would lie.

(*a*) Attacks of mental disorder which, instead of passing away in their due seasons and leaving a clear mind, lapse by quick or slow steps of degeneration into terminal dementia. Comparative peace reigns then, but it is the peace of a desert.

(*b*) Habitual alcoholic excesses, especially when such excesses have resulted in repeated attacks of *delirium tremens* or epilepsy. Here, however, it is necessary to presuppose a measure of special susceptibility to the hurtful effects of drink, since it is certain that a great many habitual drunkards do not go demented who could not fail to do so were drunkenness by itself a sufficient cause. Many persons can drink themselves into their graves who cannot drink themselves mad.

(*c*) Frequent fits of established epilepsy. The mental weakening then seems to be the physical effect of the violent commotion of the epileptic explosion in the cerebral cortex —of the tumultuous *detensions* of its morbid *tensions;* for it is remarkable how great a mental restoration takes place in apparently far gone epileptic dementia when, by some good hap, the fits cease. The shattered molecules go to work to reconstitute slowly their normal equilibrium and to regain their vital elasticity, as the inhabitants of a volcanic country set to work to rebuild their shattered houses after the earthquake.

(*d*) Positive damage to the mind-structure by physical injury of the brain, or by such gross cerebral disease as tumor or apoplectic clot. The damage in such cases is either direct, owing to destruction of structure or deadly pressure on it; or it is the indirect and later effect, inhibitive or irritative, of the local disease or injury.

(*e*) Failure of nutrition and deterioration of structure from the degenerative changes that condition the brain-decay of old age. The resulting mental decay is known as *Senile Dementia* or *Senile Imbecility*. Here an objection might be made to the designation of the dementia as secondary, since, although chronic, it is really primary. But old age is virtually the slow natural disease of which a man dies at last when he has no other disease; one need not scruple, therefore, to describe its dotage as secondary. Moreover, if that answer will not serve, there is the unanswerable argument that it is secondary to the feverish disease of life.

Most of the asylum inmates of every country are persons who have gone demented after one sort or other of mental derangement. Hospitals for mind-disease in a measure, lunatic asylums are in a larger measure the receptacles of mind-waste. I shall not vainly attempt the tedious and unprofitable labour of describing the varieties of mental wrecks met with there. Though they exhibit many individual differences in detail, they yield in the mass a monstrous expanse of dreary waste: like the leaves of the trees which in autumn fall withering to the ground in different stages of decay, no two of them exactly alike, but all so much alike in the general as to present one picture of decay. In a city which has been destroyed by earthquake or bombarded ruthlessly by shot and shell the houses are found in all stages of destruction: some battered and roofless with walls still standing to show what once they were, some with walls so shattered that their remains are only discernible here and there amid the ruins, others that are no better than heaps of dust and rubbish. So it is with mental wrecks: some dements, retaining many forms of thought-tracts, present the fair show of intelligence, talking quietly and reasonably on commonplace matters until, their weak attention exhausted or the most damaged tracts of their brain hit upon, they slide off into rambling and incoherent nonsense—they show a fair outside, but are roofless when we get inside them; some are habitually incoherent in their talk, but can on some occasions and for a short time so far hold their attention as to answer rationally simple questions put to them or give some account of their former lives; others are so entirely crazy that, although continually gabbling something, they never say anything sensible—their paths of mental association broken up or completely obstructed; others again, representing the last term of mental degeneration, are mere vegetative beings in whom all traces of mind are pretty nigh extinct, who must be cared for in every way, since they cannot take the smallest care of themselves, whose only utterance is a moan, a whine, or a cry, and whose few sluggish movements are monotonous and meaningless.

By attitude, gestures, features, carriage, gait, and conduct, as well as by speech, these persons betray their mental disorders and defects. One struts by in silent dignity with air of proud disdain and self-complacent conceit, who is possessed with the remains of exalted delusions of titled or royal greatness: such a caricature of the pride of greatness that he might be a study model for the small man who, having obtained a title of nobility or a high office of state, raises his chin, straightens his back, pouts his breast, and has high heels put on to his boots. The feeling which once gave force and consistency to the delusions is now so much weakened, or so nearly extinct, that he evinces little or no concern, if he takes any notice, when they are tacitly ignored or openly contradicted. Another continues to repeat with a most diligent industry the same singular gestures and antics, presenting a strange spectacle of odd and unaccountable conduct; he is acting under the delusion perhaps that he is busy doing some important work, be it the weaving of sunbeams into threads, or defending himself against some mysterious magnetic operations practised on him. A third who walks with low-bent head and stooping body, his pendant hands almost touching the ground, shouting or bellowing from time to time and making headlong rushes to a ditch to attempt to drink its dirty water, imagines himself to be a cow and behaves accordingly. Another is occupied continually in listening and replying to imaginary voices which ascend through the floor, descend from the ceiling, traverse the wall, float through the air, and cease not day or night; his words are incoherent nonsense, and from time to time he has outbursts of rage in which he shouts, gesticulates, declaims and denounces at large. One walks round and round, or backwards and forwards, with great diligence along a particular track of ground, of which he constitutes himself sole tenant, as if it concerned the fate of the universe that he should not leave it [1]; another stands or crouches in a particular corner, as though he would so stand or crouch unwearied to the world's end, were he left undisturbed; another diligently picks up pebbles, shells, pieces of string and other rubbish, whether because he invests them with an extraordinary value, not otherwise than the sane world does with its precious stones, or because like many sane persons he has lost sight of the end in the means and is dominated by the habit and mere pleasure of acquiring; another dresses himself in fantastic attire or bedizens his dress with straws, feathers, bright-coloured rags and the like, until he has more emblems of distinction, and is more proud of them, than the most distinguished politician or warrior is of the stars, crosses, and other decorations with which he adorns his clothes. But why go into further details? The vagaries of dementia would doubtless be as many and various, as fantastic and silly, as the follies of the sane, were it not that dements are damaged machines having only a few rusty springs left to move them, and that they are in a considerable minority in the world.

Many times it is hard, sometimes it is impossible, to find out the explanation of the ridiculous conduct. Perhaps it is that the behaviour is continued automatically after the originating mad motive of it has been erased from the mind; just like habits contracted by a sane person persist for which he can give no reason, and when he might be affronted if asked to give a reason for them. One dement is the very caricature of woe, for he is continually weeping and wailing and groaning and moaning and wringing his hands; another, the caricature of joy, who is perpetually laughing and grimacing and chattering in great

---

[1] Caricatures the first principles of the rights of property and the foundation of society—" I shall lie here: this piece of ground is mine "—by divine right, if he happens to believe, as kings once did, and emperors out of asylums still do, that he is there by supernatural ordinance.

seeming glee. In neither is there real depth, any more than the superficial show of, feeling in the mechanical business; for the monotonous manifestations of woe cease abruptly in the woeful patient, and of joy in the joyful patient, when his attention is attracted and diverted momentarily by some trifling circumstance, to begin again immediately after the respite. The preservation of an old habit of grave and courteous address and of quiet dignified bearing by a person who, being utterly demented, says little, may hide the waste of mind and quite impose upon a stranger who exchanges a few words of common conversation only with him. Such strength is there in silence and so true it is that the fool who opens not his mouth may be thought wise! But it is the evil fate of the fool that the one thing which for the most part he cannot do is to keep his mouth shut.

In some cases, no doubt, strange and disquieting sensations instigate the queer notions and grotesque antics. Such morbid sensations as in melancholia occasion bewildering distress and in mania of persecution are ascribed to the hostile operations of enemies become, in the tangled, confused and fragmentary thoughts of the uneasy dement, shocks of galvanic batteries that are rending his body, stifling gases that are suffocating him, poisonous vitriolic vapours and like horrible agencies of evil; of their reality he is as sure as he is loud in his complaints and denunciations of the tortures inflicted on him. Hallucinations, if we think of it, must needs be very real things in his disorganized mind, once they have arisen there; for, past associations being erased, they are, when active, his whole mind, and thus compel belief; with him too doubtless, as with the dreamer, ideal representations or notions become straightway vivid sensorial presentations or false perceptions, since they have few or no other paths of association to travel along. Derangements of muscular sensibility in their turn fail not to give occasion to very extravagant hallucinations with regard to the movements of objects around the body and its positions in space. How could his bed jump up and down in the night, he asks, his body be put in the extraordinary positions in which he finds it whenever he wakes, things around him move in the strange way in which they do move, ceilings ascend and descend, walls open and shut, except by the machinations of his persecutors?

A mental organisation being the most intricate and complex structure in the world, the most perfect thing which organic evolution has yet done on this inferior planet, it is no great wonder that we cannot for the most part trace method or system in the disorganisations of dementia. In order to do that successfully, it would be necessary to know the exact lines and order of its mental construction, not in the individual only but through foregone generations; then it might be possible to trace, in the ruins of each mind, the most firmly organised and fixed traits of its structure. In the slow and incomplete dementia following the mania of persecution, where the process of degeneration is marked by a gradual decline and fall from a sort of monomania or partial mania to weakness of mind, with persistence of the most absurd delusions of persecution, it is possible to trace the survival of such structural lines. The delusions then grow gradually in strength and area to such a prosperous perfection that they swallow up all resistance, and the patient, apart from the mere automatic offices of daily life, can think and talk of nothing else. Could we get inside the thought and feeling of one who has reached the lowest depth of this dementia, it might well be a hideous nightmare of horror. All in the mind is confused welter and ferment: sweet songs of birds are fierce, menacing cries; his body is shattered and his nerves incessantly exploded by frightful electric shocks; his saliva poisoned, his teeth corroded, and his food mixed with arsenic; his speech congealed, his stomach and entrails paralysed or destroyed, and his whole body rendered foul, corrupt and fœtid. Such are the monstrously extravagant delusions and feelings which dictate his odd gestures, violent gesticulations, uncouth attitudes, grotesque actions, his explosions of incoherent rage and his loud declamations; which last, uttered sometimes in the cabalistic words of an unknown language invented by him, are, like the speaking with tongues among religious fanatics, the incomprehensible expressions of ineffable states. The tangled and fragmentary speech betrays tangled and fragmentary thought-currents; its wreckage revealing the wrecks of their nervous patterns, even of delusional patterns which, once whole, have now been disorganised.

Short of such pronounced dementias are the so-called monomaniacs of asylums who, while giving utterance to their limited delusions with a quiet monotony of mechanical conviction and going on quietly with the automatic routine of their lives, hardly give cause to suspect the extent of their general mental disorganisation until something unusual happens to test and reveal it. Then it is surprising what mindlessness may be revealed at the back of what looks like very partial mental disorder. The old term monomania by which these cases used to be known was inappropriate literally, since it implied a too strict limit of mental disorder; moreover, it was applied to two different classes of cases—first, the primary forms of mental disorder ranging from insane suspicion or insane pride to the extreme delusion and the mental weakness in which the worst cases end, and, secondly, to the cases of chronic mania and dementia secondary to mania or melancholia, in which there is so much system preserved in the delusions as to lend a certain unity to the insane features of thought, feeling and conduct. It included, in fact, all sorts and conditions of mental disorder—from those in which the morbid feature was a striking flaw in an otherwise seemingly sound mind and was thrilled with a passionate intensity of feeling, to those in which the wreck of a disorganised mind was hidden under a prominent show of delusions, these being of quiet and monotonous character, uninspired by fit feeling, and expressed in a quiet and mechanical fashion.

Other cases of dementia in which we can trace a certain

order in the progress of disorder are those of *Senile Dementia* and some allied conditions of mental devastation. Here the notable symptom is the signal forgetfulness of recent events, while remote events, especially the remote events of early life, are remembered and related accurately. That means that the recent nervous adjustments of the cerebral cortex, the latest-formed patterns of its reflexes, are unstable, lapse quickly, and cannot be reproduced without the actual stimulus of the fit object; they can be formed then, but they cannot be reformed by a purely mental process and so be *re-collection* or memory. The patient sees a friend and, forgetting straightway that he has seen him, wonders why he never sees him; having told a story, tells it over again the next minute without any remembrance of the former telling; eats his dinner and in a little while asks if it be not dinner-time; expects his wife to enter the room, though she has been dead some weeks and he attended her funeral. His memory is not entirely gone, since he tells the same story in the same words, recognises familiar faces, and recounts in detail events of his early life: he remembers the impressions of objects and events which represent old and fixed patterns of nervous adjustments, but he is incapable, by reason of senile decay of structure, of bringing past experience into association with present relations, which to him indeed *are* only while they are actually present. He is in the main a worn-out machine of past performed functions which are now performed more or less lamely, he is no longer capable of function in relation to present experience. As matters get worse, he fails to recognize those about him, although they are old acquaintances or his near relations, mistakes the new faces of strangers whom he sees for the first time for those of old friends who are perhaps dead, and speaks to the son as if he were the father whom he knew in his youth, or to the daughter under the belief that she is her dead mother. It is not that he is blind of vision; he has not lost the sight of his eyes, but his mental sight or perceptive power; the old forms or habits of past perceptions being still retained, he translates present impressions into them. The latest and least fixed adjustments are effaced by the ravages of decay, while the older and more steadfast remain and perform their automatic functions.

It is probable that a similar order of decay obtains in those dements who, though much mindless, can play music, chess, draughts, or cards. The intellectual mechanism of the games having been firmly organised by practice, it preserves its form and performs its function automatically amidst the general wreck, just as when, the mechanism of the performance being left intact, a man writes his name rightly who cannot write a rational sentence. It would be impossible now, however, to teach them the accomplishment which they retain; they never improve in their play, being unequal to perceive and form new combinations; on the contrary, they are pretty sure to make mistakes and gradually to deteriorate as the residue of sound mechanism is involved in the progressive decay of structure.

The task of tracing an order of decay in dementia would be vastly facilitated if the operative causes acted generally and uniformly, denuding the mental strata, so to speak, equally in succession from above downwards. But this is not so: most often the destructive action is local and irregular; and the result is that some functions persist in comparative integrity while others of equal dignity are deeply damaged or extinguished. Nor is that all the difficulty in the way of an ideal scheme of mental dissolution from above downwards. The case is seldom, if ever, one of simple deprivation of function, of mere negative loss; for the disorder has its positive productive side, and that a process not of imperfect reproduction only but of new production also. There is evolution of a sort in the field of disorder. The features may witness plainly to the disorderly development of the functions that are left; not otherwise than as happens in dreams, where a partial and irregular mental activity only is possible; or in the motor domain sometimes, whenever the normal form of a complex of movements has been deformed by nullifying paralysis of some motions and positive distortion of the remainder. The powers of association and combination of ideas which belong to the sane and whole mind are not altogether obliterated because it is damaged and weakened—they continue in some sort so long as it is not bare of faculty; the surviving tracts or areas come into strange relations and create new products of an unforeseen character that are not perhaps imaginable by a sane mind; nay, as in dreams, they may sometimes actually work out a grotesque sort of systematisation of delirium. Thus it is that grotesque delusions, transient and fragmentary, spring up and instigate ridiculous conduct, or that dangerous impulses emerge suddenly out of the confused welter and discharge themselves in action when the morbid mood is one of morbid suspicion. It is probable that perverted sensations are dramatised in some mad mental ideation; and the danger is perhaps greatest when the sensations and delusions are of a hypochondriacally sexual or an obscene character. A demented patient who has worked quietly side by side with another patient for a long time makes a murderous attack on him of a sudden, instigated by an upspringing delusion or hallucination of which there was not the least forewarning and of which he cannot give an intelligible explanation afterwards.

Such hallucinations and delusions come and go, being present one week and gone the next; they presumably depend, as in dreams, on varying sensations and moods according to bodily states and external circumstances. Let it be borne in mind concerning them that, being formed by the surviving tracts in the mental waste, they have, like the simple ideas of young children before their ideational plexuses have been organised, few or no paths of association to travel along; they will, like them, therefore, be likely to be projected immediately into vivid sensory presentations or hallucinations. The senile imbecile who believes that he is being maltreated and robbed has not the least doubt that he hears the voices of thieves and the firing of guns, or that he sees persons prowling around the premises, and is urgent to be taken to his own home out of a house which is all the while his home. Painful exemplification of the gross allegorisation which perverted sensation can obtain in the impaired mind is furnished by the horrible and disgusting sexual hallucinations originating from morbid stimulation of the sexual organs in some demented patients who believe themselves to be nightly violated or outraged in the most abominable ways. No attempt to unravel the phenomena of dementia can succeed which does not realize that the inquiry must be not into the negative effects of dissolution only, but also into the positive effects of morbid evolution of mental function.

Thus much concerning the intellectual aspects of dementia. They must needs vary with the particular tracts of the mental mechanism that are impaired and with the varying degrees of such impairment. A manifest loss from the first is the loss of social and even of ordinary family feeling: the citizen disappears first; then the father or mother no longer exists; last is left only the individual incapable of social feeling of any sort. These patients make no inquiries about their relations, evince no curiosity about their doings, and, when visited by them, see them with indifference and part from them without concern. Some of them hardly recognize their nearest relations, others evidently not at all. Some do not even understand words. When the organised forms of cerebral tracts are so disorganised that the interpretations of impressions on sense are obliterated, the forms so undone that they cannot give form to the without, it must needs be that such impressions are simply an unknown language. For the same reason they show an entire indifference to what is going on around them in the household they belong to; it is all one to them who comes and who goes and what changes take place; some of them would see the house on fire and not stir a step to give the alarm; and they may be expected, unless they are wonderfully transformed meanwhile, to hear the last trumpet sound, without evincing a spark of feeling or interest in the awful summons.

Sensation is notably blunted in dementia, so much so in the worst cases that serious injuries cause no pain: a broken arm or leg or a severe burn is sustained with equanimity and elicits no sign of suffering. Tactile sensibility is more or less benumbed: its nicest and most accurate discriminations are altogether lost; and so slow to be excited and to be conducted is the sensory current of a grosser sensibility that a normal stimulus may provoke no reaction, and an extraordinary stimulus a tardy and sluggish reaction only. Smell and taste are sometimes extremely vitiated as well as blunted; disgusting odours exciting no repugnance or being entertained as pleasing, and hair, filth, live frogs, worms, and similar disgusting matters being sometimes swallowed with greedy relish. One patient perpetually licks the plaster off the wall as if it had a most delicious flavour, and another, urged by a singularly perverted appetite, so packs his stomach with stones, pieces of iron, and other rubbish, which he swallows surreptitiously whenever he has the chance, that in the end he dies of his strange greed. It may be noticed with regard to these perverted appetites that they are apt to come on periodically or to have periodical exacerbations, disappearing entirely or abating much in intervals of respite. Like other human pleasures, they cannot continue in one stay, since it is by remissions and intermissions that nature provides alike for the security of our pleasures and pains. An eternally uniform pleasure being by the nature of things pleasureless, and an eternally uniform pain painless, it might be argued logically, and hoped benevolently, that Heaven and Hell are equivalent.

The pity of it is that the remission of joy does not suffice always to revive its rapture, seeing that a regular and uniform intermittence of the same pleasure goes near to destroy all its relish. Satiety is sad, and the saddest longing is the longing for desire. Might it not be happier for men to rest in the desire and struggle to attain, foregoing the fulfilment? To let the pleasure go, when it had been overtaken, in order to relume the desire and renew the struggle of attainment? Perhaps so, were it not that, although accomplishment has its narrow limits and is a very finite affair, desire, while it lasts, is infinite, and thus man is beguiled in spite of himself, even against his better judgment, to go on struggling—to struggle for what, before he gets it he knows, but only when he has got it believes, is not worth the attainment.

It goes without saying that there is no recovery from chronic dementia. Still it is remarkable how bright a temporary kindling of intelligence can be produced sometimes in old-standing cases by the inflaming heat of an acute fever which has chanced to befall the patient. The fact proves that even in cases where from the symptoms we should least expect it we have not to do with actual destruction but with obstruction of the cerebral tracks; an obstruction which is temporarily overcome by their extraordinary molecular ignition in fever, but mostly, if not invariably, returns when the fever is over. The expectance of life in these people is on the whole less than in sane persons, notwithstanding that many of them, when properly cared for, live to a good old age, even to a patriarchal age if they come of a family of patriarchs, and then die just as sane persons might do. However, in some who are of weak constitution, mental and bodily deterioration goes on increasing until the patient either dies of a sort of general atrophy of brain and body, or is rendered an easy victim to such intercurrent disorder as pneumonia, tubercle, gangrene of the lung. Moreover, their dull sensibilities and stupid helplessness not only expose them to accidents, but render them unapt to feel and complain of the first motions of disease, always difficult to detect when it is beginning and perhaps curable; which thus gets itself firmly established and is discovered only when it is incurable, as for the most part disease easily is then. It may be as hard a matter to get definite information from them concerning the character and seat of their pains as it is from a sick animal. In some old-standing cases there is, besides the ordinary loss of intelligence in the features, a coarse mask-like look of the face owing to a slow infiltration of the skin of the forehead and round the eyes, with more or less thickening of the skin in the end; it is a myxœdematous degeneration of the same nature as the coarse thickening of the skin and subjacent connective tissue in the face of Cretins, and it denotes a deterioration of nutrition answering to the deterioration of nerve-energy. Perhaps it is an extreme instance of a larger principle—namely, that it is impossible to be out of sorts physically without being out of sorts mentally, and that there is not a mood of mind, good or ill, which has not its equivalence in a bodily state, functionally transient when it is transient, but liable to become permanent in structure when it is lasting.

PART III

THE CLINICAL VARIETIES OF INSANITIES

THEY (the symptoms) are so confused, I say, divers, intermixt with other diseases—as the species be confounded so are the symptoms; sometimes with head-ach, cachexia, dropsy, stone (as you may perceive by those several examples collected by Hildesheim), with head-ach, epilepsy, priapismus (Trincavellius), with gout, *caninus appetitus* (Montanus), with falling-sickness, head-ach, vertigo, lycanthropia, etc. (J. Cæsar Claudinus), with gout, agues, hemroids, stone, etc. Who can distinguish these melancholy symptomes, so intermixt with others, or apply them to their several kinds, confine them into method? 'Tis hard, I confess; yet I have disposed of them as I could, and will descend to particularise them according to their species: for hitherto I have expatiated in more general lists or terms, speaking promiscuously of such ordinary, which occur amongst writers—not that they are all to be found in one man; for that were to paint a monster or chimera, not a man; but some in one, some in another, and that successively or at several times.—Burton's *Anatomy of Melancholy*.

CHAPTER I

CLINICAL GROUPS OF MENTAL DISORDER

HAVING described the general symptoms of mental derangement and the leading forms which they assume in the course of its pathological development, I go on now to notice the special features presented by it when it occurs in connection with special physiological conditions of age, sex, and function, and with particular diseases. Whoever has to consider practically in a particular case what was its cause, what its course will be, how it will end, and what ought to be done to end it, will not care much to know whether it is maniacal or melancholic, but will inquire particularly whether it betrays a congenital mental flaw, or whether it is related to pubescence, to self-abuse, to childbirth, to the change of life, to the atheromatous degenerations of old age; whether it is associated with epilepsy, with commencing paralysis, with syphilis, gout or diabetes, or with any other disease. He will reflect, if he is wise, that there is no such disease as insanity, that there are really so many insane individuals to be treated in the concrete. Useless as drugs are directly to root up a morbid notion, to quell the riot of a frenzy, to disperse the cloud of melancholy, or to cleanse the mind of foul suspicions, they are not so useless when employed against the bodily derangements which are often associated with these mental troubles. Always will it be the first business in every case of mental disorder to put right coexistent bodily disorder—to attack the mental through the bodily humours. How many the ruptures, quarrels, suicides, and other calamities which the timely relief of a disordered liver might have prevented!

Insanities of Children.

How soon can a child go mad? Obviously not before it has got some mind to go wrong, and then only in proportion to the quantity and quality of mind which it has. Now, it has no mind, properly speaking, when it begins to be; for it is then little more than a pulpy organic substance, unshapen, endowed with a confused capacity to feel impressions and to make movements. Any discomfort or pain which it feels excites a movement to relieve it, and the movement, being a relief and in itself a pleasure, is prolonged and repeated; for infants agitate their limbs or body for the simple pleasure of the movement, as well as when they feel pain or want something the need of which is a pain,—laugh at large with their whole body, so to speak, before they can laugh specially with their faces. The movements they make, undefined and aimless at first, grow more definite and purposive by degrees. For when a movement is hindered or stopped by an external object, and a sensation of the obstruction thereupon excited, there is the dawn of an external world; and when movement is ever so little adapted to the quality of the external resistance, there is the beginning of the power to distinguish or discern. The exact sense of the particular movement being linked to the sensation of the object is thenceforth inevitably suggested by the object; it is the process of forming of its special sensori-motor reflex. The movement gradually acquires a definite, informed, purposive character—is instructed, built up in structure; not certainly in an overt definitely conscious way, but rather unconsciously as a *motor intuition* or *subaudition.* Suppress the actual sensation and movement, and in its stead make use of its sign in the supreme cerebral centres, that is to say, of the fit representative reflex which in due course is registered in the cerebral cortex, then the result is the pure idea or mental apprehension of the object.

The basis of the mental grasp or apprehension is always the sensori-motor grasp or apprehension : the notion is grounded fundamentally in the concrete experience, being its abstract image, so to speak.

A special educational process of this kind takes place in respect of the movements of the lips and tongue, which are the parts first exercised by the infant, sucking being the most deeply incorporate memory and earliest capacity of its mammalian nature ; and in respect of the movements of the hands, with which, unconsciously reminiscent of its remote quasi-simian ancestors, it makes so strong a monkey-like grasp soon after its birth that it can support the weight of its whole body by them, and which it frequently puts to its mouth afterwards, as it does everything else which it can. Thus the sensations and motions of the lips, which are the first inlets of knowledge, are followed by sensations and movements of the hands, lips and hands aiding mutually to instruct and develop. Soon the hand becomes more active, being used to grasp, to push, to pull, to put things to the mouth, and the like ; the young creature doing all it can to elicit from every objective experience all the sensations and adaptive movements which it can—that is, to distinguish and apprehend. Then, other senses coming into action and being similarly practised in relation to their exactly associated movements, numbers of definite perceptions of external objects are rapidly added to the mental structure, and their connections in it multiplied ; and thus steadily by multiplication and complication of cerebral reflexes is built up the fabric of the mental organisation. An aggregate of multitudinous reflexes with innumerable complex connections,—that is what the mental organisation of the cerebral cortex essentially is : its development a process of *instruction*, in the fundamental sense of a process of organising *in structure*.

The beginnings of the infant's mental mechanism being more of a sensori-motor or reflex than of a strictly intellectual nature, it follows that when it goes mad soon after its birth it must needs die in convulsions or present the symptoms of a deranged reflex or sensori-motor machine. Is there a surer sign of decay, when a bad nervous stock is dying out from progressive degeneration, than the early deaths of its dwindling children in convulsions? Badly constituted by reason of bad heredity, the nervous centres react in convulsive fashion to the first action of external stimuli, if not in external then perhaps in inward convulsions. That is very much what has happened in the rare cases in which, the mother having been insane when impregnated and throughout her pregnancy, the child has appeared to be mad from its birth; notably so in the remarkable case described by Greding in which four days after birth a child, brought to the workhouse as unmanageable, had paroxysms of such intractable violence and so much strength in its little legs and arms that four women could with difficulty restrain it at times. The paroxysms either ended in a fit of seeming laughter or else it tore everything which it could get hold of. "We durst not," adds the reporter, "allow him to be alone, otherwise he would get on the benches and tables and even attempt to climb up the walls. Afterwards, however, when he began to have teeth he died."

Reflection on the innate aptitudes of the nervous structure and on their tendency to separate quasi-convulsive action when the structure is defective, may abate the natural surprise which so extreme an instance of infantile madness might occasion. In the first place, every child has inborn aptitudes to certain co-ordinate acts corresponding to such instinctive acts in animals as those performed by the new-born calf or lamb which staggers on to its legs very soon after its birth, and by virtue of which, like the calf and the lamb, it requires little practice to learn them: they are silent memories which need only fit touch of experience to wake them. The infant grasps tenaciously with its hands and curls its toes into the dwindled remnant of a grasp as soon as it is born; and when it is a little older, it shows a natural propensity to push or strike with its arms, as a foal does to kick, a puppy to bite, a bull-calf to push with its ungrown horns. In like manner it exhibits an instinctive fear of falling from the nurse's arm and the instinctive motion of a fit muscular reaction against the danger before it has the least experience of what falling means, and performs the facial movements of smiling in response not to any mental conceit but purely to a pleasant organic stimulus from the viscera; not otherwise than as it makes the cross face of bad temper when it is suffering a visceral discomfort.[1] The second consideration is the extremely unstable nervous organisation and a consequent proclivity, on the occasion of an external stimulus, to a premature, direct, separate, and quasi-convulsive reaction of the nervous arrangements which are the basis of the natural aptitudes—that is, to convulsions more or less co-ordinate in character and will-like in aim. Such are the convulsive strength in the arms and legs which nurses hardly restrain, the uncontrollable fits of laughter without any evident reason, the furious graspings and tearings, the violent paroxysms of crying which cannot be checked by ordinary means. The little creature is an automatic machine stirred by sensory impressions to disorderly and destructive action.[2]

The mental derangement, such as it is, of these ill-born infants resembles that of the few animals which are known to go mad; for the infant is temporarily on the low level of mind which is permanent in the animal. The impressions made on the senses are for the most part translated directly into movements; few of them being reflected through higher ideational tracks, ideas are few, if any—there is no true reflection; morbid impressions instantly excite morbid actions. The elephant is known to be subject at

[1] Here I may call to mind the fact, little known or little regarded, that worms in the intestines, especially tape-worm, will give rise to laughings and sobbings, somnambulistic and cataleptic trances, and epileptiform convulsions in older persons of extreme neuropathic constitution.

[2] Of a mentally defective child, brought to me for advice, its mother said that from its earliest infancy it had been subject to unaccountable and uncontrollable paroxysms of violent crying which went on automatically, nothing availing to allay them, until it was carried out into the open air. She was always obliged to do that in order to stop them.

times to attacks of blind and dangerous frenzy in which it runs amuck, rushing about madly, trumpeting shrilly, and doing furious destruction; its whole mind, such as it is, is engrossed in the convulsive discharges, and its furious acts are the reactions of disordered motor centres to impressions on disordered sensory centres. Were the insane child as strong as the elephant it would be just as destructive; it is its impotence only which makes it harmless. The mad dog exhibits proof of a little higher development of mind and of a conformable higher quality of madness, since it is evidently much troubled with vivid hallucinations which distract it and provoke its fury.

With the rapid development of sense-functions in it, epitomising their slow devolopment through ages in the animal kingdom, the child soon passes beyond the simple reflex states of excito-motor function. Transient hallucinations are probably common; when it stretches out its hand and makes futile grasps, it is not always grasping at a real object out of its reach, it is sometimes mocked by a hallucination. The real world and the unreal world not being yet distinguished, its life is as much in the one almost as in the other; its natural talk, when it is amusing itself, is an incoherent prattle in which it does not distinguish its personality from things around it but speaks of itself in the third person as one of them. The least morbid irritation easily excites hallucinations; an infant, fourteen months old, having accidentally swallowed some seeds of the *Datura stramonium*, was continually stretching out its hands to seize imaginary objects in front of it; and an older child, poisoned by belladonna, was affected with the most vivid and various hallucinations of scenes in which it was eagerly and unceasingly occupied, sitting with hands busy in apparent play with companions, now singing, now quarrelling and striking, now intervening otherwise in the visionary drama. It is the same when the nervous centres are disordered by disease. Precocious children of highly nervous temperament, especially those predisposed to meningeal tubercle, create imaginary scenes and dramas which they see and deal with as actual events; instead of going to sleep perhaps when they go to bed, they lie awake prattling of visionary scenes as if real and they were taking an active part in them; so much so that their mothers are sometimes alarmed by their delirious chatter and think them light-headed. They are dreaming, so to speak, while wide awake, and with them, as with the dreamer, the notion is translated instantly into vivid sensory form; all the more easily, first, because there is no store of registered ideas to hold it in by their associate ties, and, secondly, because of its own vividness and intensity.

Although this sort of delirious dramatization is most apt to take place at night when outer objects are shut out by the darkness and quiet reigns around, yet in less degree it may take place in the daytime; then the child cannot be trusted always to distinguish between facts and fancies, may be accused of inventing the story which it tells and perhaps punished as a liar. The truth is that it does not distinguish between the very vivid images of real things which its intense imaginations are and the perhaps less vivid images which realities appear to it. How can it if the unreal is more real to it than the real? Such daydreaming is usually of a pleasant character, but the visions of the night are more likely to be terrifying. One child, scrofulous, with large irregularly shaped head, used to have terrific visions in the night, when not asleep, shrieking in a paroxysm of fright because it imagined there was something in the bed with it, and was particularly distressed by the moonlight because "it made so much noise."[1]

Of much the same character, though they befall in sleep, are the night terrors of nervous children who start up suddenly in the middle of their sleep, their eyes wide open but not seeing, screaming and sobbing piteously in the

---

[1] A nervous child, waking in the night, used to scream terribly until its mother came to it, giving the reason that the darkness "got up its nose and choked it." The physical accompaniments of the terror in darkness were probably much like those which would have accompanied the feeling of choking.

wildest fright and distress, clinging, clutching and writhing in a frenzy of agony, perhaps uttering heart-rending exclamations of anguish and incoherent sentences of appeal. They are not to be pacified, even when folded in their mother's arms, until the paroxysm is spent, when they sob themselves to quiet sleep again. In the morning they remember nothing of what happened. These trances of terror are likely to be provoked by any mental excitement of the child in the evening before going to bed, as well as by undigested food and like causes of abdominal irritation. Most children grow out of such night frights in due season, but now and then they develop into epilepsy. In other nervous children the night trance is a somnambulism in which the child gets up, walks about, perhaps leaves the room, and is taken back to its bed without ever waking.

Singular and unaccountable are the various special susceptibilities, the secret constitutional affinities and repulsions, sympathies and antipathies, manifested by the neuropathic temperament. It is impossible to foreknow what its likes and dislikes will be, or to know why they are what they are. One little creature used to shriek in an ecstasy of fright whenever another child or a dog approached it in the street, yet exulted with a frenzy of delight in a strong wind, no matter how violent; another would go straight up to any strange dog which it met and take instant hold of it, without the least apprehension, never coming to harm by its fearless behaviour. It is difficult for grown-up persons, unless perchance helped by a hateful memory of their own terrors in childhood, to realise the terrible agonies of fright and anguish which seize some nervous children when they are alone in the dark, or are left by themselves in a large room, or have to pass a room or closet of which they have conceived some formless dread, or are sent alone on a strange errand.

Although children of extreme nervous constitution are sometimes singularly precocious, perhaps showing special talents or aptitudes which seem quite out of keeping with their tender years, yet they are not likely to thrive well, and it is not without good reason that old women shake their heads gravely and doubt whether they are not too forward to live. A sad and repulsive feature of their degeneracy in some instances is a precocious propensity to self-abuse which, albeit a grotesque anachronism, is still so urgent and persistent that nothing avails to stop it. Being in them a motiveless act, without purpose although it has purposive form, it may be regarded as another example of the premature, independent, and quasi-spasmodic function of an innate aptitude. Outcomes of a process of degeneracy in the stock, the degenerate creatures represent, in various guises and degrees, a dissolution or decomposition of human development into its constituent factors and the disorderly exercise of the severed functions or fractions of functions.

Let it not be supposed that all children who have hallucinations often and vividly are necessarily without a future. A young child, when it has a hallucination, cannot help mistaking it for a reality any more than it can help its memory being incomplete and fallacious and its talk incoherent; for it has not in its mind the stored residua of experience enabling it to form and retain clear and distinct ideas, to correct sense by reflection, and to unify thought by just and complete associations of ideas. A special tendency to hallucinations no doubt marks an undue and unseasonable nervous excitability, but the nervous temperament which predisposes to them may be the basis of a particular bent of genius. Of William Blake, the strangely talented and eccentric artist, it is related that he first saw God when he was only four years old, God having put His head to the window and set him screaming, and that when he was eight or ten years old he had a vision of a tree filled with angels. And it was the habit of Hartley Coleridge, when a child, to marshal the phantasms which he saw into a regular drama. Not a habit to be commended either on general principles of sound education or for its particular issue in his case; for to encourage the mind empty of experience to weave fantastic fabrics of fancy is to hinder not to promote full and stable mental development, even when it is not to initiate positive disease. Because of its few and incomplete ideas and of their scanty associations the precocious imagination of childhood cannot at best be more than fancy; it must be occupied with images yoked together fantastically, often incongruously, by partial, casual, and whimsical coincidences, not with images welded into true unity by their essential and complete relations; and it ought therefore to be prudently checked as a danger rather than admiringly fostered as a talent. The wholesome practice in such case is patiently to solicit and steadily to train the child to converse with the realities of things; so to furnish and discipline its mind by experience and reason as to lay a sound basis of good material moulded into true forms of thought; and thereupon, if so be, to permit the rightly informed imagination to work in true and sober harmony with nature. Such the right principle, no doubt; but we may still suspect that some of these peculiar geniuses would be unequal to such a training, whatever the pains taken to bestow it, and that, were it carried rigorously through despite the repugnance of their natures, the result might be to kill the genius and not develop the reason in them. It being the way of nature to make use of all manner of instruments, bad and good, for its purposes, each used for the work which it is best suited to do and discarded when done with, for failures and successes alike there is the one peremptory and unanswerable reason—$\Delta\iota\grave{o}s$ δ' $\grave{\epsilon}\tau\epsilon\lambda\epsilon\iota\acute{\epsilon}\tau o$ $\beta o\upsilon\lambda\acute{\eta}$.

For the same reason that the imagination of children cannot rise above the inferior grade of fancy, their mania, when they have it, has more the character of *delirium* than of true *mania;* the fewness and incompleteness of ideas and the want of definitely organised associations between them preclude such a systematisation of disorder as characterises ordinary mania in the adult. Partial, fragmentary and incoherent ideas in the mental domain are the counterparts of partial, fragmentary and incoherent acts in the motor domain. In most cases therefore the mental disorder has a kind of absent, dreamy, quasi-somnambulistic look, the child talking and acting much as if it were in a dream. Three varieties of it corresponding to varieties of motor derangement might, I think, be described, according as their leading features suggest, respectively (*a*) chorea, (*b*) catalepsy, and (*c*) epilepsy.

(*a*) *Choreic variety.*—Notable are the extreme incoherence and automatic dreamy look of the mental disorder. The young patient is in perpetual but aimless movement, with vacant eyes that eye not, perhaps tossing the head or arms about in odd meaningless ways or performing a repetition of strange contortions and antics with his hands, making aimless and disjointed grabs, pushings and strugglings, gabbling incoherently or repeating mechanically one or two sentences or half-sentences, twisting the face into grimaces and grinning laughter, bursting into fits either of immoderate laughter or crying, whining, sobbing, or howling in a monotonous sequence. It may be possible to attract and hold the attention for an instant so as to get the child to tell its name or answer some other simple question, but immediately afterwards it lapses into its incoherent thought, speech and behaviour. All which does not prevent it from showing, after recovery, that it had noticed and apprehended more than it seemed to do or to be capable of doing at the time. Withal there is often manifest a mixture of pettish and obstinate humour, and the stupid mulish way in which it pushes, resists, and otherwise struggles is half wilful, half automatic. Complete or partial insensibility of the skin over different parts of the body is a remarkable and not uncommon feature; it is instructive evidence, like the similar local insensibilities in hysteria and in artificial hypnotism, how much out of gear the central confederation of nerve-centres is. Hallucinations, especially of sight, are probably frequent and vivid; seen most when the eyes are shut at night in order to go to sleep; seen then perhaps, although not seen when the eyes are open or shut in daylight. Such is the derangement when it is subacute:

when more acute, the excitement is greater, the conduct wilder, and there is more tendency to violence.

(*b*) *Ecstatic variety.*—The child falls into a sort of ecstasy or trance, in which it lies motionless for a few minutes or for hours, its limbs more or less rigid or fixed in strange postures, seemingly insensible or nearly so to what is said or done in its presence, at any rate so little sensible to pain that a pin may be thrust into its flesh without eliciting more than vague signs of discontent. Sometimes the ecstasy is an impassioned rapture of fright; then the child dances, stamps, screams in fits of frenzied agitation, all-engrossing and quasi-convulsive, or throws itself backwards with rigidly arched back and clenched hands, screaming wildly. A pretty and intelligent girl, *æt.* fourteen, about whom I was once consulted, used to start up suddenly from time to time in a paroxysm of wild terror, exclaiming, "Mother, I am dying," and then begin to pray aloud frantically in a rapid patter. She was the only child left to a mother who had had fourteen miscarriages, had lost three children at very early ages, and had herself suffered at one time from torpid melancholia; and this child, when born, was affected with choreic movements—ascribed to the mother's fright during pregnancy—which only left her when she was six months old.

In another variety the rapture is into the oddest acts of a quasi-voluntary sort—for example, a creeping frenzy, when the impulse is to creep along the floor on all-fours, as one little patient I once saw used to have sudden fits of doing; or a climbing frenzy, when it is to climb aimlessly up table, chairs, mantel-piece, perhaps up the chimney; or a frenzy to engage in some other quasi-spasmodic train of queer automatic action. Romberg relates a singular case of what he calls rotatory spasm in a girl ten years of age, and another case of a boy *æt.* six, who was from time to time seized with an irresistible desire to climb in spite of every impediment.[1]

---

[1] They may be compared with the peculiar symptoms of "lata," described at p. 147.

These and like strange seizures we may suspect to have a kinship with epilepsy, between which and them there is without doubt a direct connection by a bridge of intermediate instances. They naturally occasion great alarm to parents, but they are not so unconscious, nor so serious, quite as they look; and the more concern they cause the more likely they are to be repeated. Not that they are not genuine, but that when they have occurred once they are apt to recur on the smallest provocation. And the least opposition which the child experiences or the least indication of expectant alarm on the part of its parents is then a sufficient occasion. Nothing equals the acute apprehension which the morbid nervous system has of the situation and the subtle advantage it takes of it, playing aptly, as it were to its sympathetic audience. It is difficult therefore to treat such children properly so long as they remain at home under their parents' care; for although these may protest and think that they do not take too anxious notice of the child and that they are most careful to conceal any sign of apprehension or concern, the little creature is still more acute in perception than they are clever in concealment. Perchance it is the fond affection of an over-anxious and fidgety mother which is chiefly at the bottom of the business; in which case the practical difficulties are augmented by the impossibility of teaching her insulted affection that an exposition of the proper principles of treatment to be pursued is not a denial of the disease and a cruel imputation on her child's character and her understanding. The removal of it from home to the charge of some calm and sensible person who, having experience and tact in the management of children, will exert a quiet and steady discipline, and where it can associate with other children living a natural life of healthy work and play, will usually effect a cure; for children are very imitative, quickly assimilate the spirit of their surroundings, and learn and bear more from one another in a week than from grown-up persons in a month. I have known morbid raptures of the kind which disappeared soon in the family of a stranger soon reappear after the child was taken prematurely home.

(c) *Epileptic variety.*—A deeper degree of nervous disorder is reached by the positive epileptic insanity of children. Here it is most necessary to be alive to possible attacks of the so-called *petit mal* or minor epilepsy in one or other of its multiform characters; attacks so obscure and quick to pass away that they are easily overlooked or misconstrued, the associated mental disorder being accounted a spontaneous and unaccountable outbreak. If a boy or girl has from time to time seizures of a quasi-cataleptic kind in which he or she stands motionless for a minute or so, staring wildly or fixedly and perhaps murmuring incoherent words, the attacks being followed by mental excitement and disorder, we may be pretty sure that they are attacks of epilepsy, incomplete but likely to become complete eventually. If there be no history of any such seizure before the sudden outburst of a *mania transitoria*, then one of two things is probable: either that an unnoticed attack of minor epilepsy has gone before, or that the mania is essentially a mental epilepsy taking the place of the fit. For it is pretty certain that a short fit of mania may precede or follow or take the place of the convulsive seizure.

Abortive epileptic seizures and their kin are most various in degree and character; so many and divers indeed that no one has yet ventured to describe and classify them. One may suspect that transitory losses of sensibility of the skin, general or limited to local areas, occur in connection with, and are allied to, epilepsy in young persons sometimes, just as paroxysms of passing neuralgia are at other times in older persons; the local loss of function in the one case and the disorder of it in the other being the outward expressions of an inward local disorder in the cerebral cortex. Moreau relates the case of a boy who, after being expelled from several schools because of his unruly conduct, was at last sent to an asylum: there he was observed to be subject to periodical attacks of positive mania of conduct, in which he was rude, disobedient, and very violent, but in the intervals between them docile, affectionate and gentle; and the interesting circumstance was that he had complete insensibility of the skin when he was the bad self but normal sensibility of it when he was the good self. Along with the moral disorder of the bad periods in such cases will perhaps be found such symptoms of bodily derangement as foul tongue, disordered secretions, swollen belly, and constipation. The truth is that in practice we are confronted with all sorts of pathological deviations from the normal epileptic type, and with a variety of intermediate symptoms, sensory, motor, mental, and trophic, between those which are characteristically epileptic and such as are not really more than temporary physiological aberrations. More plainly too in the nervous disorders of children than in those of adults, we perceive that the divisions between them are not absolute; that epilepsy, catalepsy, and chorea merge into one another by gradations; that here as elsewhere nature respects its universal law of continuity.

The paroxysmal mania which occurs in connection with, or is in due season followed by, epilepsy is usually brief but furious. Young children, possessed with blind frenzy, will scream, bite, kick frantically, and tear or destroy at random; while older children may rush wildly about, speaking incoherently or shouting inarticulately, knock themselves against wall or furniture, and resist or even attack violently any one who goes to their assistance. One boy, *æt.* thirteen, whose mother and brother were mad, used to churn the saliva through his teeth into a froth, and when he was quiet poured forth a torrent of curses and obscene words. The outlook for children so afflicted is bad: when young, the process of mental organisation is arrested and they become imbecile or idiotic, although they may have been singularly bright and intelligent before they began to have fits; at an older age, the gradual effect of the recurring fits is to deaden and weaken the mind, albeit a remarkable revival of intelligence takes place even in bad cases when by some good hap the fits stop. The first aim therefore should be to search for and remove any condition of bodily disorder that may be acting injuriously on the nervous system to provoke the epilepsy; among which possible causes are worms in the intestines, habits of self-abuse, and the sequent effects of former injuries to the head.

Thus much concerning the excited or *maniacal* insanities of children. Owing to and in proportion to their state of imperfect mental organisation the features have a very incoherent and mindless character, and the effects, as I have said, are to arrest proper mental development and establish a permanent imbecility. When the excitement is not so great as to be the engrossing feature, but the mania is less acute and has more method in it, the lack of a moral development which has not yet had time to take place, in conjunction with the active disorder of feeling and conduct, necessarily gives the derangement the stamp of a moral insanity. The child seems bad because it shows much method in gratifying the excited instincts and impulses which actuate it and little or no trace of moral feeling. The occurrence of such a state of things at so early an age betrays a process of degeneracy in the branch of the stock from which it springs; a process now so far advanced that its continuance to extinction of the branch might be watched with scientific curiosity and accepted with philosophic equanimity.

As in adult, so in early life, insanity sometimes takes the *melancholic* form. Feeling going before thought in the order of mental development; its more primitive language of cries, grunts, exclamations, tones of sounds, gestures and features is used solely by the child to utter what it feels, before it can talk, and constitutes a large part of its utterance for a while after it has begun to talk. Thus it is that even babies which by ill fate are born with a nervous system lacking a proper tone of vitality, victims perhaps of hereditary syphilis, whine and cry perpetually, rest not night or day, cannot be soothed by ordinary means, and do not thrive; indeed, so burdensome and exhausting a care is the withered and wizened little creature that the patient endurance of a mother's love is overtaxed, and it is an unstifled sigh of relief which she breathes when she can think it has pleased God to take it. Essentially out of place as it was in the surroundings of this world, because it was entirely out of tune with them, every impression being a pain, why wish it to continue a sufferer in it? Older children of four or five years, sprung from a very neurotic stock, may have fits of moaning melancholy and apprehensive fears which, but for their neuropathic inheritance, might seem quite out of keeping with their tender age and to be inexplicable aberrations of nature.

At an older age still, the insanity sometimes exhibits the characteristic features of typical melancholia. A thin, delicate girl, eight years old, whose parents, a young mother and an old father, were both highly neurotic, and who herself was very precocious, among other things being a persistent masturbator, had positive and distinct melancholic delusions; she maintained that she could not swallow, that there was poison on her hands and lips, and showed much grimacing repugnance and struggling opposition to food; in like manner she asserted that there was poison in the water of her bath and resisted frantically being put into it. From time to time she had paroxysms, which were almost panics, of distress, when she talked of her great wickedness, declared that she was going to die, and begged her mother not to grieve for her. After some delay in overcoming the natural reluctance of the mother to believe that any one could understand and manage her child as well as she could, the parents were persuaded to send it from home into the family of a sensible clergyman; there it soon recovered under judicious management. I have met with similar cases of melancholic depression in boys from ten to fourteen years of age who, owning a distinct neuropathic inheritance and having themselves perhaps shown nervous peculiarities from an early age, have become moody and sad, imagining that they were suspected and shunned by their teachers and fellow-pupils, or that they were watched and followed by persons in the streets, or that they were very wicked and possessed by Satan. Prone to be hypochondriacal, they are disquieted with strange morbid sensations in the heart, head, abdomen, or genitals, which occupy and depress their minds. Restless and troubled in their sleep, they are unrefreshed when they get up in the morning. So genuine and deep is their misery that they may meditate and even attempt suicide.

In some of these cases there is manifestly an intellectual deficiency which, though not actual imbecility, is enough to prevent them from learning and doing like other boys. They are stupid and hard to teach, perhaps solitary and sullen, and, being so, are often teased and bullied by the boys with whom they cannot properly associate in play or keep pace in school-work. At the same time they have not seldom an over-sensitiveness which leads to excessive self-consciousness and to brooding introspections. Growing up, they are apt to become more dull, sad, morose, and moody, to have hypochondriacal fancies about their health, perhaps after much reading of the Bible to develop the melancholic delusion that the devil has got hold of them because of their sins. Unequal to the social ways and regular work of their fellows, they drift apart into idle brooding and sauntering, and, when they belong to the lowest classes, gravitate vagrantly into workhouse or gaol. From time to time one of this class commits arson, rape, or even homicide; not so much out of deliberate design as in blind discharge and relief of an intolerable feeling of internal unrest which must be unloaded somehow. Between them and the genuine epileptic criminal there are doubtless transitional instances. When they belong to a social class in which they can have special care, the common mistake is to try to educate them up to a level which they never can reach and to fit them for careers unsuited to their capacities. The aim of systems of education being to train boys to fit the approved standard exactly, to fashion them to feel, think, and be as much alike as possible, and the sin of social sins being a nonconformity to convention, a parent regards it as a calamity, even as a family shame, if his boy cannot go through the set course of social manufacture fixed for his class, and would rather have him dead or mad than see him earn his living by manual labour in a lower class. It is a mistake, not so often made now as once it was, to place such boys under the severe discipline of a stern master who expects to supplement nature's deficiency by his cruelty. Care should be taken, though it is often care taken in vain, that they do not, when they reach puberty, contract the vicious habit of self-abuse and thereby further weaken their weak minds.

Monstrous and unnatural as the event seems at so tender an age, suicide is an occasional result of melancholy in young children. The curious thing to see is that it is often done without any previous depression, on a sudden impulse springing out of the sad mood of the moment and the most trifling motive; not presumably with actual realisation of the momentous consequences, but rather perhaps as an outlet of temper or in unthinking imitation of a suicide which has been lately heard or read of. One boy, *æt.* 9, killed himself because he had lost a bird which he was fond of; another, *æt.* 12, hanged himself because he was shut up alone in a room as a punishment; a third, *æt.* 12, hanged himself because he was no higher than twelfth in his class; and others have killed themselves because of a rebuke, or of the threat of punishment, or of the refusal of a desired indulgence. It would be a wrong in fact and might be a wrong to others to assume that the deed implied previous exposure to a system of harsh and cruel treatment. The constitutional indifference to life and the ready impulse to end it betray a distinct neuropathic inheritance whereby, the love of life being lacking, a little jar strikes the life-weary note in the child's nature and easily precipitates its extinction. Let the inquiry be into the nature of the hereditary factor and its developments, in order to elucidate the steps of the particular process of degeneracy which has ended logically in the tragic event. This is the more necessary since the parents of such a child, being constitutionally unapt to believe that there can be any defect in their child, are inclined to impute any misfortune which may befall it to the mismanagement of those who have been entrusted with the care of it.

Perhaps there is no form of insanity occurring in the adult which may not occur occasionally, in modified form, in children, unless it be senile dementia. Certainly instances are now and then met with which, were they adult instances, would be called undoubted examples of *general paralysis* of the insane. Children who have been ordinarily intelligent up to within two or three years of puberty begin then to manifest symptoms of a progressive degeneration of brain which goes on increasing gradually until it ends in death within three or four years of its start; its symptoms being just such a progressive invasion and increase of dementia and of concomitant muscular paralysis as characterize the fatal paralytic dementia of adults. More than a dozen such instances have been put on record. Owing to some cause of weak cerebral vitality, inherent or acquired —perhaps an hereditary syphilitic taint — the brain is unable to respond to the stress of growth and the multiplying occasions of function; it wastes gradually when it should be growing gradually in organisation, dies of atrophy when it should be putting forth strength in the flowerage of pubescence.

Another group of insane children comprises cases of *moral imbecility* or *insanity*. Of the occasional occurrence of extreme moral deficiency in children who show no defect or no corresponding defect of ordinary intelligence there is no question. From an early age the boy or girl exhibits a complete moral insensibility along with the strongest vicious or criminal impulses, with an amazing skill in stealing and lying, and with an extraordinary cunning in devising the means and evading the penalties of its vicious gratifications. It is not that the thoroughly antisocial creatures do not know what is right and what is wrong in the abstract; on the contrary, they evince an acute intelligence in shunning the right and in choosing and doing the wrong; but they have no feeling of the right as right and of the wrong as wrong. Accordingly admonition, persuasion, appeal, example, entreaties, threats and punishments are all impotent to kindle real moral feeling and to make them do well. In order that morality may have a hold on conduct it is not enough to know it, it is necessary to feel it; instruction, to be translated into action, must be fired by feeling; it is not the sage who informs but the prophet who inflames a people that stirs it to great issues; and to teach a child knowledge without teaching it social feeling is perhaps as likely to make a social bane as a social boon of it.

When a boy of this bad quality is sent to a school he is usually sent back home after a time as incorrigible, and though school after school is tried the result is still the same. It is impossible to arouse any real sense of shame or sorrow in his nature, however urgent the appeal; the offence, though gross and palpable, never is confessed until the last available lie has been spent in denial of it; and when contrition is expressed and amendment promised neither sorrow nor promise has the smallest sincerity in it nor can in the least be relied on. Education is simply powerless to implant the lines of moral structure which are congenitally wanting. Seeing that a bad mental organisation is just as much a manufactured article as a bad machine, it is not a little pathetic to see parents amazed and aghast in face of such a product of them and their stocks; all the more so inasmuch as, though still sure that morality was not a natural product of human evolution but a supernatural gift to men from on high, they cannot now feel quite sure that immorality is a special diabolic inspiration and not a natural product of human depravity. The only education which is likely to be of real service to these ill-constructed creatures in the end is the education which they get when they are allowed to suffer the uttermost pains and penalties of their misdeeds: so long as they are again and again saved from the just penal consequences by the solicitous affection of fond parents or the more anxious dread of a public exposure of the family disgrace, they will go on sinning; but if they are allowed to touch the bottom of misery the sharp lesson may here and there teach one of them self-control enough to enable him to get a living in the low social conditions to which his nature gravitates and in which alone it is at home.

Besides the cases in which there is little or no defect of intellect to be noticed, the notable features being the vicious and criminal tendencies and the subtle activity of the intellect in their service, there are cases which manifest some positive intellectual deficiency, though not necessarily in proportion to the moral deficiency. Neither in imbecility nor in genius do moral and intellectual endowments necessarily go along together. An inability to apply the mind steadily and systematically to learn properly the ordinary subjects of tuition, perhaps to learn some of them at all, is not incompatible with a remarkable cleverness of a special kind or with an extraordinarily exact memory of details. One boy of this sort, who could never learn like other boys of his age, used to stand for an hour at a time before a map of the world and could tell every place on it where a ship would touch; he could also tell the times of stoppage of every train on the Midland Railway's main lines. Another boy, whose mental defect was not far short of imbecility, could tell correctly the birthday of every one of his relations and acquaintances and the birthday of every member of the royal family. A third, *æt.* sixteen, who broke the windows of several houses in the neighbourhood of his own home night after night, so cunningly too that detectives specially set to watch failed to discover the culprit, had an astonishing memory for what he had just read: it was said that he could repeat word for word a leading article in the *Times* immediately after reading it. Children of this description are seldom fit associates for other children, not even for their own brothers and sisters, since they are likely to demoralise them; all the more so when precocious sexual proclivities, which might seem incredible, constitute a special danger.

Nearly akin to the cases of general moral defect or perversion are the children who betray an unsound nervous inheritance by uncontrollable morbid impulses. The impulses are usually of a destructive or a precocious sexual character: witness the case recorded by Esquirol of a little girl, *æt.* five, who repeatedly attempted to kill her stepmother and her little brother, although the former had always treated her kindly; and another case, recorded by the same distinguished author, of a girl, *æt.* three years, who was constantly putting herself in the most lascivious attitudes of body and practising sexual motions to a pitch of spasmodic ecstasy against any suitable piece of furniture. Many more examples might be given in evidence. They are, so to speak, fragments of broken-up human being, embodying separate instincts or faculties of it in spasmodic action.

Whoever observes sincerely what a child's actual mind is, without being biassed by preconceived notions of its primal purity, innocence, and natural inclination to good, must see and own that its proclivities are not to good but to evil, and that the impulses which move it are the selfish impulses of passion. Give an infant in arms power in its limbs equal to its passions, and it would be more dangerous than any wild beast. Are not children natural boasters, apt dissimulators, quick to deceive and lie, prone to bully and be cruel? The thoughts, feelings and habits of boys or girls when they are together and not under suspicion of supervision are hardly such as a prudent person would care to discover in order to exhibit proof of the innate innocence, though he might watch them curiously as evidence of the innate animality, of human nature. Only by a patient, systematic and constant culture begun from the beginning of life, infused by the social atmosphere, enforced by social usages, instilled in the language slowly learnt, and applied deliberately in the long and tedious processes of education, are the lower tendencies repressed and the higher faculties developed and fixed.

Nor have the acquisitions of moral culture been yet so ingrained in human nature as to be fixed and stable instincts of the kind; for they are gained with difficulty and are lost with ease. If the child of civilized parents is carried off by savages and reared by them, it grows up a savage without the least memory of the lost conquests of culture; nay, if such a child be carried off by a she-wolf which suckles and rears it with her cubs, the creature, when discovered, goes on all-fours and has the tastes, feelings and habits of the young wolves. So precarious is the human, so powerful is still the animal, in mankind. History shows by many lurid examples, when the checks that curb and tame the brute within the man are removed and the passions set free, how the same horrible outbreaks of lust, rapine, cruelty and bloodshed invariably and uniformly follow; that the only difference between the savage and the civilized being then is that the latter uses his superior reason to devise and perpetrate more specialized refinements of savagery. A very simple reflection is instructive in this connection: that although man has now been in the habit of walking upright for unnumbered ages his body has not yet acquired perfect accommodation to the erect position, but suffers a variety of painful ills, such as varicose veins and hæmorrhoids, in consequence of his Godlike form. What wonder then that he betrays in so many ways the later and less stable acquisitions of his God-like faculties of mind? The child born with a mental organisation destitute of the fine nervous tracery which should subserve moral development is an example of a process of *dehumanisation*—that is, of the decomposition of the social nature of man, the rapid unmaking or stripping off of what has been slowly made or put on through the ages, the easy dissolution of a tedious process of evolution.

CHAPTER II

CLINICAL GROUPS OF MENTAL DISORDER

Pubescent or Adolescent Insanities.

I HAVE previously described the features of the revolutionary evolution of mind which goes along with the physiological changes of puberty. Being a travail of transition during which new sensations, new emotions, new ideas spring up, it is inevitably attended with some disturbance of the mental equilibrium, and sometimes, where that is unstable because of an hereditary strain of weakness, with a complete overthrow of it. The new-coming feelings and impulses have to find and make their adjustments within and without, and until they have done that they occasion much subjective unrest of a vague yearning kind—blind longings and cravings, undefined aspirations, tremulous pantings for the unknown, large and vague enthusiasms, accompanied by a dreamy sadness, a brooding want, a not altogether unpleasing melancholy. The thrill of the infinite in the individual has somehow to make its accommodations to the finite. So it comes to pass that out of the dim formless yearnings there spring up ideal forms in the domain of love or religion : either some terrestrial mortal whom the transcendent feeling invests with the glories of the ideal or gloriously invents outright, or a celestial object of devotion on which its expansive aspirations are fixed and spent. A mixed religious and erotic colour is indeed a striking feature of the insanity befalling at this period of life. Another notable feature, especially marked when the disorder occurs early in pubescence, and then imparting a characteristic complexion to it, is the mixture and contrast of the childish feelings and ideas of ending childhood with the pert self-sufficiency and self-assertive conceit of budding adolescence; a manner which, lacking the restraints wrought into character by riper experience, is apt to be rude, saucy, boorish. There is a time in the process of his development, while the metamorphosis is going on, when the youth is neither child nor adult: grub or butterfly, it is impossible to say which. The mind is stirred by obscure impulses, as the caterpillar's changing body is by its internal workings—by the putting off of the old and putting on of the new, forefeeling developments which it cannot foresee.

Females are on the whole more liable to the insanity of this period than males. In them the changes of pubescence are completed in a shorter time, and the reproductive functions exhibit their larger effects on mind by a larger development of the affective life in proportion to the intellect; while in the periodical function of menstruation there is furthermore not only a special cause of recurrent disturbances of the mental tone, disturbances bordering closely on derangement in some neurotic persons, but its irregularities and suppressions may become the direct occasions of positive disorder. Women again for the most part labour under the prejudice of having a narrow range of activity in life compared with the wider range open to men; they lack and miss the vicarious outlets of feeling and force in an equal variety of aims and pursuits; and they are debarred by social usages and physiological consequences from the illicit indulgences which in men are openly condemned, secretly practised, and tacitly condoned. Moreover, however much woman may exalt her rights and claim equality of pursuits and powers with men, she cannot, so long as she is susceptible to love and glad to bear its burdens, fail to find her main end in man and the family, not in herself. To comprehend how large a space in her nature the reproductive function fills and how mightily its fulfilment belittles other interests, it is only necessary to reflect on the extraordinary joy which she feels in bringing forth her first-born child and on the rapture of love which the half-animate creature stirs in her: though the performance is a common one which all sorts of women are doing successfully every hour of the day, she is as pleased and proud as if it had never been done before; and though her baby is neither better nor worse than scores of other babies, she is rapt in such loving admiration of it as to think it the most wonderful baby in the world, and nothing that she or any one else can do too much to do for it. Looking at the matter objectively in the dry light of reason, could anything be more ridiculous than all this affectionate fuss about what is essentially an excretory product and comes into the world by excretory ways? Moreover, there is nothing nice in the process of parturition nor in the base services which the child exacts of her, much on the contrary to provoke disgust, were it not for the strength and sanctity of the maternal instinct. What then must be the deep, subtile and far-reaching effects on her nature when that instinct is frustrate? The unrest of an organic dissatisfaction, a vague void of being, the dim craving of something wanting to full womanhood; a void which nothing else in the world will quite fill, albeit an abundance of wholesome work in pursuits which kindle desire and keep interest alive may yield a fair vicarious satisfaction. Very sadly, however, is she placed in the social body who lives unwooed and fades unregarded, having neither pursuit nor prospect to give a relish to the insipidity of life; who has instead the dreary prospect of dying to herself through a weary sequence of days without aim, without desire, without hope.

The insanity of this period takes either the excited form of mania or the depressed form of melancholia. Beginning in the former case with a short prodromal period of mental excitement marked by much self-conceit, loss of all diffidence or reserve of demeanour, pert impertinence of speech, rude extravagances of conduct, whims and caprices, wanton acts of folly or mischief, which are done the more and with greater glee the more distress or remonstrance they occasion, as if out of a wilful defiance of the proprieties and a delight in outraging them—it rises quickly to an acuter and wilder mania. Then there is much excitement of a noisy and tumultuous kind, with violent outbursts of laughter, loud singing, startling yells and cries, and ceaseless chattering; sudden starts, leaps, bounds and runs, and impulsive acts of apparently wanton mischief or destruction; paroxysms of aimless screaming, writhings, strugglings, pushings, strikings in resistance to control, all having a show of wilfulness yet without definite method or aim. There is no depth of meaning in the emotion and conduct; on the contrary, it is laughter without mirth, fury without passion, purpose-like violence without true purpose. Consciousness is not so extinct as the behaviour at the worst might seem to denote. The patient will recognize a person, realize the situation in a flash of perception, understand and partially answer a question, yield for the moment to a display of firmness, perhaps thrust out the tongue when asked, and then relapse instantly into the voluble and incoherent talk, turbulent behaviour and wild antics, all which are evidently a vast relief and delight to her. Sexual excitement shows itself frequently in the general complexion of the symptoms and specially in wanton words and gestures, indecent attitudes, loose exposures, even lascivious acts and attempts to strip naked; sometimes the excitement is interrupted by ecstatic or quasi-cataleptic states of speechless trance or stupor, in which with apparent insensibility to impressions there are rigid contractions of the muscles of the whole body or violent shudderings and contortions of them, all having the air of being wilfully set going and kept up; and sometimes the spasmodic motions of the ecstasy precisely forestall the movements of sexual congress. Self-abuse may be a repulsive feature of the mania, occasionally there is a veritable frenzy of it; with the increase of the mental degeneration the idealism of love is degraded into mere sensual lust, the imaginative joys of *erotomania* into the sensual fury of *nymphomania*. Mixed up with the erotic features there is sometimes a strain of religious babble, and the intact virgin chatters incoherently of religion, and of babies which she imagines herself to have had or to be going to have.

Such is the character of pubescent mania at its worst. But it differs much in degree of severity of symptoms and in their distribution in different cases. When the excitement is subacute only, the symptoms, though of the same character, are less violent and there is more show of moral perversity and wanton wilfulness; feature swhich, accentuating its histrionic complexion, are pretty sure to cause it to be described as hysterical insanity. But what profit or explanation is it to call it hysterical? Looking beneath words, the thing to apprehend is that different functional disintegrations of the confederate centres of the mental organisation in the cerebral cortex are at the bottom of the manifold and diverse disintegrations of consciousness and will which here, as in the various morbid states described under the vague term *hysteria*, impart the hybrid features of a psycho-motor convulsive activity—that is to say, the features of those convulsive volitions or volitional convulsions which, being intermediate between volitions and convulsions, consciousness and unconsciousness, had no chance of being understood formerly and still lack adequate scientific recognition.

In other cases, where the nervous constitution is frail and feeble, and the disintegration of the supreme centres greater, the movements of the patient are suggestive of a chorea gone mad, being of the most irregular description and repeated automatically in sequent aimless toil: hands and arms working continually in strange contortions and grotesque motions, the features of the face twisted into grimaces and distortions, the eyes prominent and glistening in fixed vacant stare, the pupils dilated; perhaps attempts, half voluntary, half convulsive, to creep, crawl, writhe, or otherwise disport and distort themselves on the floor.

However wild and turbulent the mania, it has its remissions, and it is not unusual for very lucid intermissions to occur two or three times before it ends in recovery or ends in dementia—its two possible issues. Recovery may be looked for hopefully under two conditions: first, that the best chances of it be given by removing the patient from the surroundings of place and persons, but especially persons, in which the disorder has broken out and placing him under conditions of wise treatment; secondly, that the foundations of nature are not of that weak and unstable degree which marks distinct degeneracy of the stock—in other words, that the patient bears not the badges of hereditary degeneracy. Here it is that good counsel is too often confronted and confounded by the insane strain in the parental temperament, which, asserting itself by a sympathy with the disorder and a sensitive repugnance to think it mental disorder at all, resents and rejects the notion of other than home treatment; while it is sometimes of that kind and degree of narrow egoism and moral obliquity which confers a worse heritage on children and exposes them to a more subtile contagion than actual madness in father or mother might do. Now and then recovery takes place after a few weeks or a few days only of disorder.

The prognosis is bad when the mania, becoming less acute, goes on from month to month through alternating phases of excitement and moody depression. It is as bad, if not worse, when the attacks are recurrent, with weeks or months of lucidity between them, as they are not unapt to become; for then the tendency is to more frequent and longer outbreaks of mania and to a gradual weakening of mind in the lucid intervals, the end being dementia. A sequel much more common than it need be, did not the determination to think and call the disorder hysterical and not to think and treat it as madness prevent the quick doing of that which, in order to be done well, ought to be done quickly. The tendency to recurrence is a marked feature in these cases; it is perhaps greater in women than in men, the probable reason being that the menstrual function, if it take place, or the absence of it, if it does not, suffices to overthrow the unstable equilibrium of a brain which has revealed its morbid susceptibility and weakness by breaking down under the physiological changes of adolescence.

Two things are notable in respect of this form of mania. One is how little the patient, after recovery, is concerned about her attacks; all the turbulent doings seemed the right things at the time, and she is not saddened by the past nor fearful for the future. The other is the close copy which the ideas, feelings and doings of one outbreak are of another, notwithstanding that these are hardly remembered in the lucid intervals; the two selves, sane and insane, pursue their respective courses apart, the one feeling no responsibility for, even if it so much as confusedly remember, the feelings, thoughts, and acts of the other.

The other leading form which adolescent insanity takes is melancholia. Growing dull and listless, moody and silent, apathetic and indolent, the youth or maiden loses interest in ordinary pursuits and pastimes, which are neglected, performed slovenly, or abandoned altogether, shuns society and lives much in solitude; is prone to be engrossed with hypochondriacal sensations and fancies, to relieve which various devices of diet, dress and physic, or external applications of plaisters, poultices and bandages, are perhaps used; is capricious and wilful in behaviour, perplexing and distressing parents by perverse whims, outbreaks of temper, rude speeches, and sullen defiance of their authority, and perhaps insisting pertly and obstinately on pursuing an independent course of life which is as unreasonable as it is unbefitting; all the while complaining bitterly of being misunderstood and ill-used when not allowed to have his or her exacting and impracticable way.

Such is the state of things at the outset. In further course morbid suspicions and fears ensue: fears and fancies of having done something wrong or of being suspected of wrong-doing, of not being loved by parents, of being disliked and spoken ill of by companions, of being watched and followed in the streets, of having been designedly put to an injurious or unsuitable occupation, of having been injured by a wrong diet or a wrong medical treatment; or with less distemper there may be deeper depression of feeling, because of tormenting ingenuities of religious scruples, which episcopal authority is perhaps invoked and fails to exorcise or ease, or because of dreadful thoughts, wicked wishes, sinful feelings which assault and harass the mind. Great as is the misery in which these patients profess to be, there is still no little self-conceit and self-indulgence in it, since notwithstanding their woe they are quick to feel and remember the least hurt to their self-love and bitterly resent any thwarting of their wishes or opposition to their selfish ways.

The disorder going still deeper, positive delusions are developed. One young woman, whose limited experience and capacity of wickedness belie the conceit she has of herself, declares that she is the wickedest person in the world, possessed by the devil and damned to all eternity in consequence; she spends hours on her knees in fancied prayer, refuses food or takes it most capriciously and irregularly, and perhaps makes abortive attempts at suicide. It would be a gross and grave error to treat her suicidal attempts as if they were mere empty pretences because they seem not very deep and genuine and have a histrionic look; they may be carried into full effect, either suddenly at the convulsive instigation of an overwhelming crisis of despair, or because a pretended or only half-intended attempt, once started, gets out of hand and accomplishes itself. Another young woman, translating desires into hopes and hopes into beliefs, maintains that some gentleman whom she has met in society but to whom she has hardly spoken or has not spoken at all is in love with her and would propose to her but for hindrances put in his way by others; accordingly she writes loving letters to him, takes and makes occasions to throw herself in his way, perhaps insists on leaving the house to go to him, persuading herself that there is a mysterious tie of secret spiritual sympathy, if not a spiritual marriage, between them.

In this as in the maniacal form there are convulsive tendencies on the motor side: perhaps fits of hysterical laughter or weeping, or even positive attacks of hystero-epilepsy; perhaps falls into quasi-cataleptic trances in which he or more often she lies mute, insensible to pain, with widely dilated pupils, and motionless, except for a quivering of the eyelids or for some spasmodic contraction of muscles. Out of the quietness of this cataleptic ecstasy, however, there are sometimes and from time to time the suddenest upstartings into explosions of violence.

On the whole the prospects of recovery in this form of mental disorder are not bright. Much depends on the native build of the mental fabric; if it be bad, and especially if a native degeneracy reveals itself in some weakness of mind going along with the depression, then the risk of a decline and fall into dementia is very great; but if the mental foundations be fairly good, then proper treatment may effect a cure. A gradual recovery takes place sometimes in those persons who are fortunate enough to meet with an aim in life which, kindling their interests and eliciting and engrossing their energies, draws them out of themselves: love and its sequel marriage, or a congenial pursuit which diverts self-devastating feelings into channels of outward activity and braces loose nervous centres into more compact stability by increasing and strengthening their relations with the outside world of not-self and therewith its hold on them. Perchance the accident of a severe bodily illness, a pneumonia or a fever, may in the same way do what art cannot accomplish. When, however, the mind becomes more and more absorbed in the things of a morbid self, its perverted sensations and imagined wrongs and suspicious apprehensions grow and get stronger hold, while its sane power weakens in proportion; the patient either develops fixed delusions, becoming a chronic lunatic, and goes on from year to year with his complaints, denunciations, and schemes to discover the causes of his sufferings and to frustrate their effects; or he gets gradually weaker in mind until he is practically mindless.

In the melancholy more perhaps than in the mania of adolescent insanity is it important to remove the patient from the home-care of those who, because of their former close relations with one who is now quite out of relations with them, necessarily provoke the disorder by their resented and misconstrued attentions and aggravate it by their exhibitions of concern and sympathy. It is hardly reasonable for a reasonable person to expect that a young mind should grow strong and right in the soil and atmosphere in which it has grown weak and wrong. Nevertheless the suggestion of a transfer of the patient from home into saner surroundings is pretty sure to be met with the protest of the sympathetic parents that it would make their dear child think itself mad and so drive it mad to be sent to the care of strangers, if it be not met with the indignant repudiation of an imputation of insanity as an insult. Whatever is done it must not be anything which suggests insanity : only a doctor who treats nerves, nowise one who has made a special study of mental disorders, must be consulted; at most a nurse who understands hysteria, certainly not one accustomed to attend on insane patients, can be employed; and above all must the utmost heed be taken not to treat the patient in any way as if he or she were out of his or her mind, or at any rate, while actually adopting most coercive measures, not to breathe the suspicion of mental alienation. Having thus anxiously and carefully protected the disease from any offence to its susceptibilities, they fondly hope that it will be considerate enough to get well. While it is natural for those who have bred the disposition to madness in the patients sensitively to resent the imputation of it and to be instinctively set on keeping them in the morbid track, the pity of it from a scientific point of view is that the insidious danger and ominous significance of the quasi-hysterical symptoms are out of all proportion to their seeming insignificance; for as the disorder continues to smoulder, the mind sinks down stealthily into increasing weakness, until at last recovery of its powers is impossible, whatever be done, and the wonder then is that a person who has never been out of his mind should have no mind left.

Having described the features of (*a*) the mania and (*b*) the melancholia occurring in connection with adolescence, it remains now, in order to make a complete picture, to notice a third variety of disorder—namely (c) the strange moral perversion and intellectual obliquity displayed in some cases of hysteria. To this category belong the young women who, believing or pretending that they cannot stand or walk, lie in bed or on a couch all day, week after week and month after month, objects of attentive sympathy on the part of their anxious relatives, when all the while their only paralysis is a paralysis of will which an opportune lover or other salutary moral impression might cure straight off; those, again, who, having the notion that they cannot speak, continue mute for months or speak with labouring efforts in a feeble whisper; those who hold their water for a long time, thinking or protesting that they cannot pass it, or who, passing it in secret, maintain that they never pass water at all; others again who exhibit strange substances which they assert they have ejected by vomit, or dejected by bowel; others who, by means of an acid or other corrosive fluid, simulate strange skin diseases which puzzle and sometimes impose on medical practitioners; near akin to them, those who, professing to live without food, attract the curiosity and excite the gaping wonder of the whole countryside, and sometimes, if their disorder obtains the fit food of a foolish sympathy and congenial surroundings, fall into ecstasies of religious transport in which, seeing visions or displaying the sacred stigmata on forehead, hands or breast they are deemed to be the special channels of a divine influx.

Although these people would never act as they do without a fit audience and require a sympathetic environment to keep up their parts successfully, they are not the entirely wilful impostors which a cool observer can hardly help thinking them; the dominating morbid notion in the loose-knit brain, setting the machinery to its lead, has inhibited or suspended the remaining thought-tracts except so far as they are wrested to its service; therefore while a full and true will is impossible to the patient, she is governed by the particular morbid development of the disintegrate will. To her the only world practically existent is the world within its range of activity. The result is that when she recovers and comes to her full self, she is not ashamed nor seemingly concerned at what she, being then not herself, was and did in her days of hysterical transport and mutilated self. Nay, such is the essential sympathy of nature here and there between a young person of this sort and her father or mother that to unmask the fraud which she is practising and to cure her off-hand may be deemed an unpardonable act of medical brutality.

The immoral vagaries of these hysterical persons sometimes show themselves in more mischievous guise. Indeed, whoever wanted to illustrate a systematic moral insanity could not find more striking pictures of moral degeneration than some of them present; nowhere more perfect examples of the subtlest deceit, the most ingenious lying, the most diabolic cunning, in the service of vicious impulses. Inventing stories that are pure fables, or large superstructures of falsehood founded on a tiny basis of fact, they make false charges of indecent assault or write anonymous letters of a defamatory or even grossly obscene kind; pilfer in tradesmen's shops; play secretly the most mischievous pranks in a household with such a cunning and pertinacious ingenuity that the inmates think the place haunted; peradventure set fire to the house for the impish joy of doing it; all the more active and pertinacious in their evil ways and doings the more commotion these excite. That their perverted moral state is somehow connected with the action of the reproductive organs on an unstable nervous system seems probable because it is mostly met with in unmarried women, is prone to exhibit erotic features, and is sometimes cured by marriage. All the more probable too because, besides the moral and intellectual disturbances, there are often local hyperæsthesias and anæsthesias on the sensory side, spasms and convulsions on the motor side, and various vasomotor and trophic derangements.

It is hard to believe that these people can always discriminate between reality and hallucination, between what has been actually and what they have only imagined vividly. Such incapacity to distinguish fact from fiction is the probable effect of the loosening of the confederate union of the cortical nervous centres and its accompanying degree of mental disorganisation; a condition of things which would tend to make the vividly imagined seem real and, as co-effect, the real seem unreal and visionary. It is very much then as it is with the habitual opium-eater who, living mainly under the influence of a drug which creates a visionary world and dulls the sense of the real world, making the things thereof pale, shadowy and distant, comes to relate as actual events what he has only dreamily imagined and is utterly untrustworthy in what he narrates. Another effect of the dissolution of the mental organisation is demoralisation—the destruction of true moral feeling and will, so that conscience is practically abolished. It is possible still to think of some degree of moral responsibility and will in connection with hysteria because some degree of unity of mind is preserved in it, but it is impossible to think of any true conscience and will in connection with the completer mental dislocations of hypnotism. A sound moral sense and a strong will are the supreme conquests of culture, the flowerage of a well-formed character; physically they signify the development of the highest cerebral reflexes in their full proportion and a just solidarity of the whole mental system.

Insanity and Self-abuse.

The mental disorder in the causation of which self-abuse has been a factor is not always to be distinguished from simple adolescent insanity; occurring about the same period of life, its early symptoms have the same general complexion and character. This they owe to the processes of adolescence, not to the particular vice. Then again it is hard to be sure that the particular cause has been entirely absent in all cases of adolescent insanity, or that, when present, it is not really more a symptom than a cause.

Furthermore, it is pretty evident that when self-abuse is the apparent cause of insanity, some hereditary nervous weakness is an essential coefficient; for it is in a small proportion only of those who have been addicted to the practice that the mind suffers permanent injury, and it is exactly in those persons who show the stigmata of morbid heredity that the most serious damage is done. In the result then the mental derangement attests the frequent excitement and exhaustion of a frail nervous constitution rather than a specific effect of the vice.

As a matter of observation, the worst effects are not so much to be feared in the openly vicious as in delicate nervous youths who, having been brought up quietly at home, perhaps in the company of sisters only, and not having mixed much with other boys in work or play, are thought to have been guarded from the least contagion of impurity. Shocked and hurt by the bare suspicion of such a vice in them, the parents think it impossible their boy could ever have learnt it and incredible that he should be guilty of the sin of it; not reflecting that the sexual instinct does not need to be taught in order to find out how to gratify itself, that the tendency to solitary indulgence may be more urgent where other indulgence is wanting, and that the guilt and risk of the evil habit are perhaps unknown to one who has been treated always as if he had no sexual organs or as if, having them, he ought always to think, speak and act as if they were a shame to him. It is not indeed by vigorous and manly boys who mix freely with their fellows in work and play that the habit is so likely to be contracted or, when contracted, so likely to be carried to a pernicious excess as by weak and nervous boys who, shrinking from rough companionship and sports, are naturally inclined in this as in other things to solitary broodings and secluded ways.

The hope of getting the habit abandoned lies less in moral strictures and urgent appeals to conscience than in the inculcation of a more manly tone of thought and feeling and in the stigmatisation of it as " bad form," dirty, base and degrading, which will not fail, if continued, to betray itself in the face and manners. Vanity and fashion being nearer and stronger motives than moral feeling to influence human conduct, since for one person who performs a self-sacrifice to do right there are five hundred persons who make greater self-sacrifices, sometimes the sacrifice of life itself, to gratify vanity and do wrong, we do not fail to elicit a more effective check by apposite appeals to the youth's vanity and to the fit social feelings of his age and class than by endeavours to stimulate higher moral feelings. In man's threefold nature, animal, social and moral, the animal, however it be covered and disguised, is fundamental and the strongest, hidden at the best not abolished; while the lower social feelings that spring from the direct relations of men living in a community are of older date, have a closer hold, and are of stronger sway to rule conduct, than the more abstract and refined moral feelings which decrease in force, as motives, as they increase in distance and refinement. It is not in the abstract principles of the Sermon on the Mount, but in traditional and customary social feelings, that we must seek for the working morality of individuals, sects, classes, peoples and nations. Rapt in exalted admiration of moral feeling as something divine in himself, man still fails not to be very human in his moral practice.

The symptoms of the mental disorder in these cases differ according as it befalls at or about the beginning of pubescence—that is, before the sexual function has entered into the mental life and transformed the whole manner of feeling and thinking; or as it occurs later in life when the thoughts and feelings witness to the evolution of sex in mind and the consequent revolution of character. In the former case we observe, along with boyish thoughts and feelings at the best and positive impairment of mental and bodily vigour at the worst, much pert conceit and marked moral deficiency; in the latter case, there are, in addition, special derangements of thought and feeling that attest the degradation of the sexual instinct in mind.

In the first case there is really nothing special in the symptoms to distinguish the disorder from pubescent insanity; it is in fact pubescent insanity stimulated and aggravated by the secret vice. A youth of seventeen or eighteen years of age who is at school or has been put to some business begins to neglect his work or to do it fitfully and badly; he is moody, indolent, apathetic; shows no interest in his pursuits or pleasures and puts no energy into them; is morose, sullen, insensible to remonstrance, and displays a conceit and self-sufficiency absurdly unbecoming his age and position. At home he is solitary and very selfish, perhaps slovenly, in his ways, altogether wanting in respect for his parents and in consideration for others, self-willed, egotistic, indolent, exacting. Taxed with his faults, he either denies them or denies that he is at all to blame, explaining or excusing them by putting the blame on the jealousy and hostility of others, or declaring the work to which he has been put to be beneath his dignity and degrading to a person of his genius and capacity. Put him to other work, and the result is still the same; one occupation after another may be tried but every experiment ends in failure. Much inclined to solitude and brooding, he spends a great deal of time in his bedroom or saunters about listlessly out of doors in a desultory fashion for the greater part of the day, his mind perhaps occupied with hypochondriacal feelings which he is addicted to treat by particular diets, exercises, appliances. Oftentimes the manner is downcast and sullen with averted eyes, the dress untidy and slovenly; sometimes it is pert and conceited and the dress priggish. The expression is apt to be dull, the complexion sallow, the pupils dilated, the hands cold and clammy, the breath bad, the tongue rather foul, and the circulation languid.

In some cases the morose gloom deepens into a genuine melancholy which may be accompanied by suicidal feelings and talk, perhaps by feeble suicidal attempts; in other cases it is followed by an outbreak of excitement, a sort of subacute mania, which then has the hysterical complexion of adolescent mania. In both the melancholy and mania there is usually a look of superficiality about the symptoms, a lack of genuine depth in them, which gives an air of conscious exhibition for dramatic effect.

When the insanity comes on later in adolescence, after the sexual development has transformed the feelings and ideas, the symptoms witness to the transformation. The patient is shy and constrained in society, especially in the society of women, although prone to fall in love, or to think himself in love, with one to whom he may have only spoken a few words or not spoken at all. Perhaps he nurses the feeling in secret without ever giving any practical expression to it, consulting one medical man after another about a variety of hypochondriacal sensations which much engross his attention and asking their advice whether he ought to marry or not. He caresses the alluring notion, without having the serious intention, of marriage, being probably at heart nervously apprehensive of physical incompetence, and beguiles himself with the belief that he only desires an authoritative medical opinion to do what he dares not do. Nowise satisfied when he has got his opinion, he goes through the same exposition of his symptoms and dubitations at his next visit, and when he is tired of or has tired out one adviser betakes himself to another to begin afresh his tedious story. If he gets himself engaged at last to some lady, urged to it by his or her relations or dragged into it by her persistent pull, it is then that his fears and doubts grow acute and overpowering; he puzzles and troubles his friends and his betrothed with doubts of his fitness to marry, his fears of incompatibility of character, his serious sense of the awful responsibility of bringing children into the world, and the like overstrained qualms and scruples. In the end he is not unlikely to break off the engagement on one pretext or another. Perhaps he makes the opportune discovery that the consummation of marriage is the degradation of love and that he cannot face such an abasement of his ideal.

Very remarkable is the strain of exalted sentiment and

lofty idealism professed by some of these persons. The
common ways of mankind are too gross and selfish for
their exquisite sensibilities and fine aspirations; they may
go so far as to make a solemn covenant with their future
wife to forego the sensual joys of marriage and to taste
only the more elevated joys of a union of pure souls; and
notwithstanding that they are sunk in a base sensualism,
perhaps emasculated by it, they will pour out high-pitched
moral and religious sentiments from a pedestal of lofty
conceit and take the world hotly to task for its low aims
and gross doings: all these superfine sentiments not incompatible with extreme egotism, exacting selfishness and
pitiful shiftiness of conduct; not incompatible perhaps
with a dirty dwelling of the mind on sexual subjects and
a nasty colouring of the ideas, feelings and behaviour by it.
Their dear delight is in the indecent exposures they make
of their moral persons. Certainly high spiritual development
from the basis of an emasculated manhood is anything but
a successful business with them, who by their examples
prove indubitably that the conscious enunciation and elaborate exposition of superior moral sentiments is no proof
of their moral presence in character.

It is a bad blunder to recommend marriage with a
view to cure such persons. Seldom does anything but
misery come of unions so contracted. The confirmed
sinner has little desire or power of natural intercourse, the
lust of a depraved habit having weakened or destroyed the
natural appetite; even when he is not entirely impotent,
he is still capable of going back to and on with his solitary vice after marriage. Coldness, indifference and petty
tyrannies on his part, discords, quarrels, explosions of rage
and violence, separation from bed and house—these are
probable sequels, while suicide or even homicide is not an
impossible consequence. The following instances exemplify
some untoward issues: a gentleman who, scared at the
terrible responsibility of begetting children which he was
about to undertake, had broken off his engagement a little
before the appointed marriage-day, was urged successfully

by advice and entreaties to go through with it later on ; the result was that he fell into an acute mania during the honeymoon, and nearly succeeded in throwing his wife out of the first-floor window of the house in which they were lodging. In another case, a gentleman, four months after marriage, attacked and attempted to strangle his wife in a railway carriage in which they were travelling alone, and afterwards threw himself out of it on to the track : being unapt or unable to perform his marital functions, he had fallen into melancholy with eventual delusions of suspicion and persecution. In a third case the result was different : a frail and highly neurotic gentleman, of a boyish look much younger than his years, possessed of extraordinary musical sensibility and singular skill in execution, who had been married fourteen months, confessing to a rarity of connubial congress which might suggest a cynical doubt of its success, was sent to gaol at the end of that time for indecently exposing himself to girls and young women in a field near his house through which a public footpath ran.

Up to the point of some compromising act on their part persons of this sort, although on the road to insanity, perhaps within its precincts, would hardly be accounted positively insane. What becomes of them in the sequel ? Some of them continue in much the same state for years without getting appreciably worse ; they may even get better as they grow older, and be fairly free from trouble when life reaches the natural season of reproductive decline, if they do not then develop a new swarm of morbid apprehensions. In other cases the disorder increases until it explodes in an attack of acute mania, which then perhaps exhibits a strong and unsavoury mixture of erotic and religious ravings and hallucinations, varied from time to time by rapt ecstasies, pleasant or painful, and different quasi-cataleptic forms and degrees of muscular rigidity or stupor. The acute attack over, the patient is frequently none the worse, sometimes he is the better, for it.

Lastly, others there are whose mental degeneration increases gradually into dementia. Notions of hostility and ill-feeling towards them bred of their morbid susceptibilities and exacting egotism undergo further morbid development into positive delusions; having forfeited self-respect, they suspect that other persons do not respect them, but slander and defame them, look and sneer at them, make gestures of contempt, perhaps utter insulting words; and they ascribe their disordered sensations and accompanying muscular starts, which are really the bad effects of their enervating vice, to streams of electricity made to play upon them, or to drugs secretly administered to them, or to the malicious use of mysterious magnetic or telepathic agencies. Queer gestures, odd tricks of movement, spasmodic jerks and ugly grimaces, which they contract a habit of making, burning sensations in the genitals of which they complain, rushes of strange feelings from the sexual or epigastric regions, sexual irritation and emissions, loss of manly vigour—all these are the effects of secret persecution. Their inability to control their wandering thoughts and to concentrate their attention, due actually, like their pains and starts, to their nervous exhaustion, they ascribe in like manner to telepathic, telephonic, or other occult agency by which their true thoughts are obstructed, tapped, turned on to wrong lines, answered by anticipation before they are conceived, and other thoughts not their own, disgusting, loathsome, perhaps blasphemous, are suggested to their minds. Hallucinations of vision may take revolting shapes, and hallucinations of smell are a conspicuous feature in some cases, especially in women. In the worst instances of extreme mental degeneracy there are delusions that persons steal into their rooms at night and play disgusting tricks or perpetrate foul offences on them.

Those who have sunk to this depth of mental degradation are not likely ever to rise out of it; they are more likely to get gradually weaker in mind, more shrill-conceited and extravagant in their delusions, and to sink at last into a moody and self-absorbed apathy. Then they sit or lounge indolently all day long when not obliged to move, or saunter about in a sluggish and slovenly fashion, muttering or laughing sillily to themselves and lost to all human interests. Pitiful mind-wrecks, some live out their full days in that state, or at any rate have not their lives appreciably shortened, dying at last from ordinary causes; others, of frailer and feebler native constitution, die sooner in a state of general and bodily marasmus, or fall easy victims, by reason of their nervous prostration, to some incidental disease. However early the death, it is never so early as to be premature.

In another class of cases, especially those in which the exhausting cause has sapped the easily excited and quickly consumed forces of a high-strung neurotic temperament, the chronic mental derangement presents certain tolerably distinctive features. These are they who, sensible in other respects and able to do their daily work in the world, are still haunted with urgent impulses to think, do, or say something ridiculous, obscene, or dangerous, and are in a perpetual fever of nervous apprehension and distress in consequence. Manifold and various are the besetting troubles. In one it is the continual intrusion of a blasphemous or obscene thought into the mind; another feels the impulse to speak aloud some indecent word in company, and that so urgently perhaps that he is obliged to keep his mouth tight shut and even to bite his tongue to prevent himself from doing what his frantic desire is not to do. Another cannot ever leave his room without a pursuing fear that he has left the fire unguarded, or not put the candle out, or has dropped a spark on the floor, or omitted to lock a drawer, and has no peace of mind until he has gone back to see, even if he has to get out of bed to do it, and is all the while quite sure that his fears are ridiculous. A fourth is tormented with anxious doubts, after doing something, whether he has done it rightly, and cannot refrain from going through the same harassing reflections over and over again, knowing well that he will be no happier when he has exorcised that doubt, since a new one is sure to spring up and haunt him until it in turn is supplanted by another; a fifth is in a fever of nervous agitation lest, when

walking out, he knocked something down which may have
hurt somebody, or, when driving out, that he may unawares
have run over somebody; a sixth is unfortunate enough
to get a particular number or a particular word into his
head and is impelled to be evermore looking for it and,
looking, to notice its recurrence with a strange frequency
that seems something more than natural. More wretched
still is he who cannot go into women's society, for fear
that they will be sexually excited by his presence or that
he will do some act of indecency, being overwhelmed, if
he ventures into their company, with a quaking apprehension, perhaps breaking out into a most distressing flushing
and profuse perspiration. All the while he is so far from
the least wish to do anything wrong that he loathes the
very thought of it. Then there is the person who is in
perpetual trepidation because he imagines that he has soiled
his fingers whenever he has touched something and must be
for ever washing and wiping them, or, having done some
trivial act, is constrained to do it over and over again,
making no end of his repetitions until a new " fad " supplants
it. Another must ask himself the cause or meaning of
something, and the cause again of that cause, and so backwards in endless metaphysical questionings which he cannot
for the life of him stop, although well aware how foolish and
futile they are. Lastly, not to prolong a tedious tale, there
is the unhappy being who, utterly horrified and disgusted at
his mental degradation, still cannot help picturing to himself how everybody whom he sees would look in some odd
or disgusting attitude and in vain tries to cleanse his mind
of its foul imaginations.

In these cases the essential distress is to have lost control of the mind and to feel under the sway, almost at the
mercy, of tyrannizing impulses which are ludicrous or loathsome. But the character of the impulse adds a keener
pang to its tyranny when, as happens sometimes, it is
suicidal or homicidal. If suicidal, its victim cannot bear
to go near a precipice, or a river, or a railway-engine in
motion, and if he reside anywhere in their vicinity falls into

periodical agonies of fright lest the opportunity should overtempt him some day to make away with himself. If homicidal, he cannot endure the sight of a knife, or a razor, or like instrument of possible harm, and has panics of distress because of his fear of the fear that he may one day succumb to the temptation to kill somebody. In bad cases the suicidal or homicidal impulse increases at times to an almost convulsive crisis, as if it must perforce discharge itself in deed, and then the sufferer is driven to pace the room in agitation or to rush furiously out of it, or to throw himself on his knees and to pray frantically to be delivered from the obsession. In vain he labours to make others comprehend a suffering which he feels and protests to be inconceivable, unspeakable; he can only say that there is no bodily pain, however great, that he would not a thousand times rather endure than suffer what he suffers.

It may be left to the metaphysical psychologist to excuse or accuse a will which is so helpless to help itself in such cases. Those who are content to observe facts as they are and simply to draw natural conclusions from them will usually discover in cases of the kind, if proper search be made, that the morbid impulse is seldom, if ever, a sudden outbreak in a healthy person; it is generally preceded by symptoms of nervous debility—vague and gloomy disquietude of mind, exaggerated susceptibility, feelings of restless irritability, and perhaps disordered sensations. Such symptoms of a neuropathic state are the customary precursors of a nervous crisis of some kind or other; and the upspringing tyrannic ideas or impulses are the analogues, on a higher nervous level, of the neuralgic pangs and muscular spasms of a lower nervous level. Indeed, there is good reason to believe that one may sometimes replace another—the idea-spasm, so to speak, taking the place of the pain-spasm or the motor-spasm, or either of these appearing in its stead.

Of the same nature with the just described cases are those singular nervous crises which befall persons who cannot cross an open place or square, being seized with an

overwhelming panic of impotence at the bare thought or attempt to cross: not a vulgar fear of being run over, nor yet a vertigo in the ordinary sense of the word, but a reeling of thought and feeling, an indescribable anguish, as if the foundation of self were sinking away; the knees perhaps trembling, the heart beating rapidly, and the perspiration pouring out over the body. For the life of him the person cannot cross alone, although he can do it very well when he is accompanied, even if it be by a child only, or can manage to do it perhaps if there be a cart or other object in the middle of the open place, or can go round it by the houses, which then yield him the required sense of support and confidence. The converse of this disabling panic is the panic of anguish arising from an overwhelming dread of being alone in a room, because of a then insupportable feeling that space is threatening or beginning to contract and the walls to close in; a feeling as of impending suffocation so overmastering that the sufferer cannot bear to remain in the room, but is compelled to rush wildly out of it. He has really much the same kind of feeling that would accompany, and makes much the same kind of convulsive effort that would follow, a commencing process of suffocation. Another singular effect I have noticed now and then in persons who had a marked neurotic inheritance but were not otherwise mentally affected: the inability to look over a large space, such as a wide expanse of plain or sea, without being attacked by an indescribable perturbation and distress, as if their very being were reeling out of being; and I call to mind the instance of one gentlemen, an intelligent and capable man of business, who never could occupy a room high up in a house or hotel, since even to enter it caused an instant panic of acute fright which impelled him to rush away frantically in spite of himself, conscious all the while how foolish and cowardly his conduct appeared.[1]
'There is no notion, however trivial, which, if it reach a con-

---

[1] The immediate cause of his consulting me was recent conduct of that kind on the occasion of a visit of inspection, as one of its directors, to the upper floor of a large hotel.

vulsive intensity of activity, may not thus possess the self and suspend the normal functions of mind.[1]

The general pathological conditions of these morbid mental states are an unstable nervous temperament rendered more unstable by exhausting causes. No doubt sexual exhaustion of one sort or another is a frequent exciting cause, especially in those cases where sexual features of the disorder seem to betray its direct agency; but the tyranny of the haunting ideas and impulses is owing essentially to the neuropathic constitution, and it is certain that other than sexual causes of exhaustion may act to excite their spasmodic activity. To conclude self-abuse to be the exciting cause in every case would be to conclude wrongly and to do wrong to the sufferer.

A more special pathological condition of the singular panics in respect of space is probably a disorganisation of the muscular sense, whereby the special mental forms or intuitions required to inform the proper purposive movements are rendered impossible. The mind being thus unable to form its fit grasps or apprehensions of the environment might naturally reel in impotent alarm, transferring its subjective disorder to the external world, as the giddy person does when he seems to see things turn round him. If there be an accompanying or following perturbation of the sympathetic system, such as is notable often in panics of anguish and dissolution of self-confidence, then perhaps all the necessary conditions of the symptoms exist.

Besides the chronic mental derangements which go along with self-abuse it is sometimes the exciting cause of an attack of acute insanity in a predisposed subject. Then

---

[1] When crossing the sea to the United States, I made the acquaintance of a gentleman, a medical man of good sense and capacity, who never dared to go to bed at night during the voyage for fear the boat might go down. He used to wander about, sitting and sleeping here and there, all the while as conscious as anybody else of the absurdity of his apprehensions but unable to master them. He had crossed the Atlantic six times and, always under the same conditions of unreasoning fright, had never been able to occupy his berth at night.

the acute disorder is either a positively acute dementia, or it is such a mixed state of excitement and depression that it might be styled indifferently mania or melancholy. Whatever its predominant mood, it usually has a distinctly demented complexion. There is no real method in it: obstinate mutism, incoherent mutterings and mumblings, a word, sentence or half-sentence repeated automatically aloud or in a whisper, perhaps aimless yells and howls from time to time; pushings, writhings, dragging movements of stupid resistance which look wilful, being kept up with a mulish obstinacy in a mechanical way; sometimes quasi-cataleptic states in which the patient, not actually unconscious, stands or lies in one fixed position, mute and more or less rigid, the precarious quiet liable to be interrupted by abrupt starts into excitement and violence; dazed attempts perhaps to unbutton his trousers and expose his person or openly to masturbate; refusal of food, not with definite purpose but with an aimless, confused obstinacy, as if from a perverse spirit of stupid opposition; lessening or loss of sensibility, so that he does not seem to feel pain, or, if he feels it, to feel it only in an indefinite and confused way prompting the vaguest movements of defence or escape; lowered reflex action and inattention to the calls of nature. The pupils are often dilated and sluggish, the heart's action weak, the pulse feeble and frequent, sometimes hardly perceptible, and the general nutrition bad.

That is the most characteristic form of the acute insanity, but it is not always so characteristic. On the one hand, it passes by intermediate instances into acute noisy mania of the ordinary type, and on the other hand into the stupor of dementia; while in some cases alternating periods of mania and stupor are marked and very untoward features. Bad as the outlook is at all times, it is not always hopeless in these acute cases; occasional recoveries take place, albeit perhaps only after the closest escape from dementia. The proclivity to dementia, always great, is greatest where the patient bears in his person the stigmata of hereditary degeneration.

CHAP. II CLINICAL GROUPS OF MENTAL DISORDER 413

It is probable that the vicious habit is not so frequent in women as in men nor so hurtful to those who practise it. Pelvic and ovarian pains, neuralgias and other sensory troubles, palpitations, syncopes and hysterical crises are more common effects than mental disorder. Still the habit may be suspected sometimes, and confessed occasionally, in those cases in which the patient imagines that her hands are soiled whenever she touches anything, and occupies most of her time in repeated washings of them; or is in perpetual torment of fear that her clothes are impregnated with dirt or infected with insects, of which there is not the least trace, and must for ever be inspecting and brushing them; or thinks that she has done harm by touching something whenever she has entered a shop, and is impelled to go back to see; or has over-minute scruples of conscience lest she said something not with the precise degree of proper accuracy and which, since it may be misconstrued or misunderstood, she is in conscience bound to correct or explain; or gets a particular intruding word or ridiculous thought into her mind, which she cannot expel, and fancies that it has some secret, equivocal, and perhaps indecent meaning; or is tormented with over-scrupulous doubts as to the true meaning of some passage of Scripture which has fixed itself in her mind and which she imagines must, if rightly interpreted, condemn or inculcate a particular mode of diet, dress, behaviour, or religious observance; or is in a desperate fear of damnation because of horrible thoughts, indelicate or impious, which invade and haunt her mind; or after a long and slow process of deterioration of will, brooding fancies, moody depression, and decline of moral sense, develops the delusion that she has been made pregnant in some impossible way—as, for example, by sitting opposite a gentleman in a railway carriage, as one young lady maintained, notwithstanding that the journey was made in broad daylight and that her brother, a young man six feet high, sat by her side all the way.

Perhaps the morbid idea is that she is followed and watched by persons who say offensive things of her and call her foul names, make comments on her person and remarks about her affairs, and that they have contrived some extraordinary apparatus for seeing or listening whereby they can watch or overhear everything which passes in the privacy of her bed-chamber. If she gets engaged to be married, it is not improbable that she may refuse to be married when the time comes, or, if she get married, refuse sexual intercourse, perhaps putting on armour or adopting elaborate devices to defend herself against an assault shocking to her overnice delicacy. In the end she falls into melancholy or mania. It is inconceivable the misery which a woman of this sort is capable of causing in a household by her exacting caprices, passionate temper, morbid suspicions, unreasoning perversities, false representations, and selfish and intolerable habits, while the slow and tedious process of mental degeneracy is going on. She is sometimes the veritable incarnation of a repulsive moral insanity; and it is an inestimable relief to everybody who has anything to do with her when she becomes so incontestably mad that she can be put under restraint in an asylum. It is a rare piece of iniquity, though not the rarity it should be, to palm such a woman on a man in marriage.

CHAPTER III

CLINICAL GROUPS OF MENTAL DISORDER

Insanity and Child-bearing.

WHEN a woman falls insane soon after she has gone through the labour of child-birth the mental disorder is properly called *puerperal insanity*. But some predisposed women become insane during pregnancy, owing seemingly to the perturbation of the bodily economy which they then suffer: a perturbation which may obviously be of a twofold nature—either (*a*) partly or wholly the reflex or sympathetic effect of the uterine change on an unstable brain; or (*b*) due, partly or wholly, to changes in the quality and circulation of the blood and in the processes of nutrition. On the other hand, I have met with occasional instances of women who, melancholic, irritable and restless when not pregnant, became placid and cheerful directly they were so. Of the insanity of pregnancy it may justly be suspected in many cases that it is really the continuation of mental disorder which existed before marriage and for which marriage was recommended as a cure and acted as a temporary relief; while the happy effect of pregnancy on the mental sanity will, I think, mostly be in women who, having suffered from mental excitement in consequence of a sort of irritable and feverish lust which has been satiated by pregnancy, then became stable and composed in mind and body.

It is alleged that a large proportion of the insanities of pregnancy occur in first, and then most often in illegitimate, pregnancies. That women married late in life are more liable thus to suffer is probable, seeing that their bodily system, having lost much of its elasticity, is less fit to make the new accommodations required by the uterine changes. Melancholia is the form which the disorder most often takes: profound depression of mind, undefined fear and despair, sometimes positive stupor, perhaps refusal of food and suicidal feeling being the leading symptoms, but not really distinguishable from those of melancholia otherwise caused.

In these cases the special physiological condition gives a special interest to the prognosis. How is the disorder likely to end? When it is accidental — that is to say, is not essentially the sequel of disorder previous to pregnancy—as many as half the patients recover before delivery; where it is such a sequel, however, there is a decline into dementia, which pregnancy quickens or only temporarily checks; a few patients continuing melancholic up to parturition, fall into acute insanity after it, commonly acute mania, and perhaps then recover eventually. Here and there an exceptional instance of instant recovery after parturition serves to strengthen the popular expectation of that happy issue. To bring on abortion in order to cure the insanity is an experiment which, although it has been tried sometimes, has neither the warrant of reason to excuse nor of success to justify it.

Puerperal insanity proper comes on within a month or so, usually about the fourth or fifth day, after parturition. It may be a mania or a melancholia: a mania usually when it breaks out a few days or a week after the event, a melancholia when it does not occur until three or four weeks after. The suppression of the milk is a frequently assigned cause, whereas the suppression goes along with the diminution or suspension of other discharges, such as the lochia and the urine, all being common effects of the general perturbation of mind and body. Nevertheless the vitiation of the blood by the absorption of septic matter from the uterus and the suspension of proper discharges might obviously be a cause of hurt to the nervous system.

Preceding and presaging the mania are such symptoms as irritability, sleeplessness, excited look and talk, restless agitation and suspicion, accompanied or followed by sullen fits of gloom, indifference to the child, perhaps angry aversion to it and to the husband. Sometimes the natural joy and elation after the event, rising fast to an immoderate pitch, runs on directly into excited and incoherent talk and ends in an outburst of mania. The mania is acute, turbulent and incoherent: the patient, who is noisy, restless and sleepless, shows little method in the mad things which she says and does; rolls, writhes, or wriggles aimlessly on the bed, twisting the bed-clothes into coils round her body and limbs or tossing and kicking them off, or jumps on or out of the bed, unconcerned at the nakedness which she may chance to uncover; snatches wildly at anything which she can catch hold of—hand, dress, or ornament of any one standing near, and holds on to it with a tenacious grasp which it is not easy to unloose; one minute keeps her eyes and mouth tightly shut, taking no notice of requests and resisting attempts to open them, and another minute glares fiercely with a scowl of angry and defiant suspicion, which of a sudden perhaps changes to a pleasant smile or laugh and the offer of an embrace; apprehends abruptly some part of what is said to her or said in her hearing and whirls it into the chaotic turmoil of her frenzy, not always without a jocose comment or apposite sarcasm; evinces a lascivious flavour of thought, feeling, and behaviour, and is prone to be dirty in her habits. Hallucinations of vision, many and changing, are marked features and are betrayed by the way in which she stares at imaginary objects or talks to imaginary persons and by the gross mistakes which she makes concerning the identities of persons around her, calling them by wrong names, smiling at the same person one moment whom she frowns at the next moment, asserting perhaps that her nurses are men and addressing her medical attendant, whom she may believe to be her husband disguised, in terms of unbefitting endearment. There is often a look of demented stupidity in her acts, habits, and hallucinations, which would bode ill in ordinary mania but is not of such grave import here; indeed, sometimes the excitement ceases soon and the prevailing condition is one of vacant stupor in which she seems to see but not apprehend, to hear but not understand, in fact dazedly to missee and mishear everything around her.

The bodily symptoms are not always in accord with the violence of the mental turmoil, for in many cases the pulse is quick, small and irritable, the face pale, drawn and pinched, and the general condition feeble. It would not be safe to exclude the hazard of suicide, for although the deed is not likely to be done deliberately it may be either the convulsive outcome of a vivid hallucination of sight or hearing or a purposeless incident of the unreasoning fury. Of the same character is the killing of the baby when it is rashly left in the patient's possession.

In keeping with the acute and incoherent character of puerperal mania while it lasts is the little remembrance which the patient shows of its events when it is past, a fragmentary circumstance or expression here and there perhaps alone being remembered; as also is the fact that women come out of it generally with less after-depression, less concern about their doings in it and the calamity of it, and with more self-confidence than out of an attack of ordinary idiopathic mania. One lady had no recollection, after her recovery, that she had had a baby; another could not be persuaded to own the child she had borne and never showed it a mother's affection, although she tolerated its presence and passively suffered it to be brought up with her other children; a third, the chief interest of whose life before marriage had been dogs and horses, showed no anxiety about her first-born baby when she recovered from a very acute attack, although she quite remembered its birth, but made her first eager inquiry about a particular dog of which she was fond. In some cases there is manifest, after all excitement has gone, much lingering confusion, apathy, and apparent weakness of mind—a sluggish, dreamy, demented looking state, from which, however, there is a gradual recovery of mental powers.

It is a mania in which good hopes of a good result, sometimes within a few weeks, generally within from three to six months, are justified; if it last longer, the outlook, though darkened, is still not hopeless. First labours are attended with most risk. In not a few cases women who have been deranged after the first labour go through subsequent labours without hurt. In some the attacks of mental derangement only follow two or three out of several parturitions, as if capriciously, but then probably because of some moral trouble, or of bodily shocks or excesses, or of neglect of bodily health during the susceptible period of pregnancy. Here and there women have and recover from as many manias as they have children, but they are not unlikely to become incurably insane at last, more especially when succeeding attacks increase in duration and severity. Death is a rare, but an occasional, result of puerperal mania; the pulse becomes rapid and feeble, the tongue dry, little or no food is taken, the secretions are scanty, and the patient, falling into a stuporose state, dies in a coma of cerebral collapse. When she has been drugged deeply with narcotics in order to quench the excitement, death, if the immediate issue, or dementia, if the later issue, owes more to the drugs than to the disease. If there is a rise of bodily temperature which continues irregularly a suspicion of septic absorption may justly inspire some anxiety.

Of the melancholy form of insanity after child-birth it may be said truly that its features are not so characteristic as to enable the most skilful observer who did not know what had gone before to distinguish it from other melancholias. Beginning commonly with a dislike or suspicion of husband, nurse, and others around her, it is often accompanied with suicidal impulse and sometimes with the impulse to kill the child. The delusion, prone to be of an extreme character, as for example that her children have been murdered, is sometimes in singular contrast with the general lucidity of mind, sometimes accompanied by a positive mental stupor. As in puerperal mania, so here, the existence of a definite physical cause of disturbance justly strengthens the expectation of ultimate recovery.

The melancholy into which some women fall while they are suckling has been called the insanity of lactation. It is an ordinary, nowise distinctive, melancholia, caused by the debilitating effects of suckling in conjunction with such depressing moral influences as a husband's unkindness, worries about servants, or other domestic chagrins and anxieties; essentially an insanity of exhaustion and preceded usually by such neurosthenic symptoms as headache, ringing in the ears, dimness of vision, neuralgias, and a very weary feeling of weakness; and it is best cured, after the child has been weaned, by a system of good nourishment and by rest of brain through change of scene and surroundings. As man evinces and vindicates the prerogative of his superior animal nature by the cultivation and gratification of an unintermitting procreative lust, it is not superfluous to add that abstinence from sexual intercourse will be helpful, and may be needful, to remedy a condition which imprudent self-indulgence or amiable compliance with a husband's exacting appetite has perhaps co-operated to produce.

Insanities of the Decline of Life.

The cessation of the menstrual function in women marks a definite stage of life's decline. To do for the last time in life, as the result of waning life, that which has been a regular function of the best part of it is a momentous change which may well be a startling intimation of mortality and an occasion of sadness. Moreover, the crisis often entails various feelings of bodily distress which only pass away by degrees, and not seldom a mental depression and unrest which here and there deepens into actual mental disorder. The disorder, usually a melancholia, is known as *climacteric.* That the disturbance of the balance or the composition of the blood-supply may be a factor in its causation is made credible by such instance as this: a lady, whose menstruation ceased at fifty years of age, fell straightway into an apathetic melancholy with refusal of food so persistent as to make it necessary to send her to an asylum; after some months she had bad bleeding piles and thereupon recovered her reason, remaining well for ten years; then, having undergone an operation for the radical cure of the piles, because of the distress and debility which they occasioned, she had an immediate recurrence of her melancholia, characterised by vague fears that she could not pay for anything, that she was shunned by her friends, that she was to be carried off and something dreadful done to her; all which fears, although she was sensible of their folly, caused her the most poignant distress. Another lady, whose menstruation ceased at forty-eight years of age, became melancholic after suffering from a feeling of fulness in the head and various nervous troubles; although formerly active in household affairs and in concern for others, she was now active only in tormenting herself and them with the continually repeated tale of her sufferings, which were that she could not believe in the reality of things, that people looked changed, that the houses appeared smaller and the streets narrower, that the trees were not natural, that everything was strangely altered and unreal. In this state she lingered for eight months, when, the menses having reappeared and resumed a regular course, she became and remained well.

Without doubt moral causes often co-operate with the physical changes in such cases, and sometimes they predominate. The physiological change in women marks abruptly a decline which is later and gradual in men, and in both is accompanied by mental changes. For the first time it is now realised that the conventional description of life as a vapour, a dream, a fleeting shadow, a passing show, a vanity of vanities, which has been reiterated mechanically hitherto with a sort of melancholy complacency, is not a mere form of empty words but a grim earnest. He who had been content to know begins henceforth to believe that he must die. Life has to be lived without the relish and energy which made it seem worth living; duties to be done without the former zest in doing them; troubles to be faced without the eager faith that the result is worth the pains, nay with the silent certitude perhaps that it is not; so much of the thrill of feeling extinct in thought that the sense of reality and interest of things seems gone, and belief but the shadow of what it was; lowering doubts and dim questionings whether there is anything essentially of more constancy and worth in the being and events of human life than in the changes and vicissitudes of the physical world; the future a prospect not now, as once it was, a long vista illuminated by hope, but a short and dark vista, death-bounded, within the easy compass of imagination; the past a disenchanted retrospect of extinct desires and achieved vanities. Disillusionment is pretty complete, the reason of it being that the mortal has ceased to be a part of evolutional nature and is no longer thrilled and beguiled with its energy and aspiration: faith and hope therefore almost gone, unless perchance they find footing in the imagination of a world to come. Obviously there is in such circumstances the sufficient reason of a mental collapse when a character has not been so moulded by previous discipline into good habits of thought and feeling as to be able to encounter the processes and pains of declining life with a calm front of resignation and to bear the burden of them with quiet stoicism. Should the former life have been a life of habitual self-indulgence, frivolous pleasures and vain display, and the desire to attract admiration still linger when the power fails, while other actors on the stage obtain the coveted and once monopolised applause, the burden is all the heavier and the will to bear it all the weaker.

The melancholia of climacteric insanity is often marked by vaguely vast and formless fears and delusions, such as the foregoing instances exemplify: boding fears of a great but undefined calamity, something dreadful which the patient is sure is going to happen, although she cannot tell what it is; confused feelings that the world is turned upside down and everything in it strangely changed; or such more definite delusions as that she is reduced to the direst poverty and must starve, or will be stripped of her clothing and turned destitute into the street, that she has neglected her duties throughout life and lived a wicked life of deceit, that her memory and other mental faculties are completely gone, that the sins she has committed are so many and so great that it is impossible she ever can be forgiven. An old maid is perchance in agitated distress because she ought to have accepted an offer of marriage which was made thirty years ago, or which, never made, she is sure would have been made had she only given the proper encouragement, and is in despair now because the word not said never can be said, the mischief done never can be undone. Now and then instances are met with in which along with extreme irritability, agitated distress, and the bitterest self-reproach strong erotic impulses are urgently felt: one lady, the respected mother of a respectable family, protested piteously, in the midst of passionate exclamations of anguish and denunciations of herself as the vilest of the vile, that she was sure she should rush out into the street some day and offer her embraces to the first man she met. It is indeed remarkable in climacteric insanity how lucidly conscious of her state the patient often is; so much so that, while firmly holding to her delusions and declaring that she ought to be sent to an asylum in order to prevent her from doing harm to herself or others, she expresses in the same breath the utmost horror of such a fate, exclaiming that it would kill her or drive her entirely out of her mind, and protests that she never can recover, whatever be done. " It is all in vain; you don't believe what I say; but I know it is true—oh dear! oh dear!"—such is the burden of her pitiful lamentations.

    Suicidal feelings are sometimes strong, and a persistent refusal of food may necessitate forcible feeding, because of immediate danger to life from exhaustion, or excuse it because of an increasing debility which exposes her to the intercurrence of a fatal congestion of the lungs or a low pneumonia. It is a common but mistaken notion that these patients do not recover; a fair proportion of them, perhaps as many as half, get well eventually, although their illness is prone to drag tediously until their constitution has had time to accommodate itself to the new conditions of its being. Here, as always, the right question is not whether the disease is one likely to end in recovery but whether the particular sufferer from it, being what she is, is likely to recover.

Such is the most characteristic sort of climacteric insanity. Another form which it takes sometimes, I think, is an insane jealousy which, rooted in an instinctive apprehension of the loss of power to provoke and please male desire, shows itself in unfounded or exaggerated suspicions of a husband, in gross accusations of his unchastity, in intolerably exacting claims for attention, in explosions of jealous fury. Matters are then apt to be made worse by indulgence in alcoholic stimulants, which were perhaps taken in the first instance to relieve feelings of bodily sinking and mental depression well-nigh too great to be borne.

It is natural to ask whether men ever have a similar climacteric insanity. In them the physiological changes of sexual decline are gradual; they are spread over a longer period, and there is certainly no such definite crisis, mental or bodily. But as growing age brings with it a gradual decline, and abuse a premature extinction, of the function, there is good reason to father on it a form of melancholy which is met with in some men who unwillingly own and vainly regret their expiring powers; most often in those who, having made the gratification of lust the sole or main end of their lives and in pursuance thereof given themselves up without restraint to its fruitions, are confronted with the insipidity of a life out of which the relish has gone, and find themselves stranded, without aim, without interest, without any pleasure to live for and any pleasure in living; and who, unlike some women similarly bereft, cannot obtain for themselves compensating joys and interest in the spiritual raptures and devotional exercises of religion.

Worn-out desire and sated lust are certainly not ill adapted to make human life a hell.[1]

The melancholy into which such persons sink is apt to be of a very hypochondriacal and quasi-hysterical character. The wretched sufferer recounts and bewails the wearisome particulars of his sad mental and bodily state; complains of anomalous sensations and pains in all parts of his body, which he maintains cause him the greatest agony, being a perfect hell of torture, and doctors do not understand in the least; protests that his stomach is wasted away and that food is torture to him, though he eats and digests sufficiently well; asserts that he never sleeps, a complete privation which others do not observe, that he cannot do anything to occupy or amuse himself, and that he suffers frightful pains when he forces himself to make the least exertion, notwithstanding that he can make the exertion and apparently support easily if not enjoy it actually— perhaps he goes so far as to sit down in the street when he walks out or to stand or crouch there in some grotesque posture and protest that he cannot move, not so much from a real incapacity to walk as from a sudden giving out of his will, or from a perverse will to demonstrate in dramatic fashion how bad he is; laments that he has no interest in anything, cannot read, cannot remember, cannot think, cannot use his mind in any way, albeit his faculties prove themselves as acute as ever they were when he is tempted to exert them, as he does more often and more than he pretends; declares his condition to be hopeless, the agony which he endures every moment of his life to be insupportable, and repeats over and over the wearisome story of his sufferings, never failing, however far off from them the subject of conversation is, to bring it soon back to himself and them.

The routine of his wailing refrain is liable to be interrupted by paroxysms of excited anguish in which he shrieks aloud or shouts out curses and obscenities, batters his face

---

[1] "All this the world well knows, but none knows well
To shun the heaven that leads men to this hell."

with his hands, bangs his head against the wall, throws himself headlong on the ground, or makes attempts at suicide which, though they seem pretended or only half-intended, are sometimes carried into instant convulsive effect and sometimes do such immediate injury as entails a fatal effect later. His suffering is genuine, notwithstanding that his insane sayings and doings have the histrionic air of wilfulness or wilful exaggeration. Sad and ignoble as the spectacle is, it has its interest for the philosopher and the moralist. The latter may see in it proof of the maxim, old as the hills, that the way of true life lies not in self-indulgence but in self-renunciation, and that in order to attain its best development self must be used and spent for the not-self. The former may see in it proof how large a part of the illusion of life is inspired by the generative force of nature; how much keener are the altruistic joys of the propagative instinct, though they spend and weaken, than the egoistic pleasures of the self-conservative instinct, though they sustain and strengthen; and how stale, flat and unprofitable life becomes when the fading illusions of time are not replaced in the imagination by the unfading illusions of eternity.

These persons seldom recover: they are more likely either to commit suicide, or to drift into an acuter melancholia, or to continue in chronic misery until they waste and die from ordinary bodily disease. In some cases diabetes, or a glycosuria ending in diabetes, has appeared to me to go along with the mental disorder. Then the continued presence of sugar in the urine, testifying to an abiding disorder in the processes of cerebral metabolism, may yield a presumption that the mental disorder is of a like essential and hopeless character: the weak and wailing mental function the reflex of the weak and waning cerebral nutrition.

Senile Insanities.

Under this head I include the mental disorders which are caused by the decay of brain in old age; premising only that old age is relative and that some persons, old in middle age, exhibit its proper degenerative changes some time before others of the same age, as told by years, show any trace of them. The best known form of disorder is that extreme mental decay or dotage called *Senile Dementia* or *Senile Imbecility* which, coming on by degrees, is the effect and exponent of a gradual degeneration and wasting of the nervous elements of the brain: the second childhood of waning faculty through which the mind sometimes goes regressively when it is ceasing to be, as it went progressively through a first childhood of waxing growth when it was going on to be. But before this extremity is reached there are initial disorders of cerebral nutrition, subtile, secret, and known only by their effects, which forebode the decay and ending of its functions and give rise, in some constitutions, to positive mental derangement. This prodromal disorder, which is either maniacal or melancholic, might be said to mark the response of the cerebral nerve-element, in the one case by active resentment, in the other case by sad dejection, to the menace of an impending extinction of its function.

Senile Mania I should describe as characterized by a subacute excitement and a diffuse, elated activity of thoughts, feelings and acts; a state of exulting optimism and acute self-sufficiency which now and then looks so much like the mania of general paralysis as perchance to be mistaken for it. Sanguine, elated, and restlessly doing, the busy old man eagerly broaches schemes or launches into speculations of a rash, dubious and perhaps altogether foolish character; transacts business in a reckless, loosely sanguine and fussy way, without the least self-distrust, though in not quite so absurd and methodless fashion as the general paralytic; although hitherto a sober and decent member of society, now indulges freely in alcohol, frequents low company, visits haunts of vice, or goes about in public with loose women, for his enkindled organic energies assert themselves in a dream, perhaps in a revival, of sexual desire. Thence also it comes to pass that he is liable to get into serious trouble for sexual offences, natural or unnatural, or to be got hold of by some vile and designing man or woman who, flattering his vanity and ministering to his foibles, exploits his weakness and robs him of his property. Impatient of advice or of the least opposition to his wishes, he resents jealously any interference, however unobtrusive and considerate, on the part of his family, of whose motives he is keenly suspicious and whose remonstrances, if they venture to make any, irritate him into fury against them. They, meanwhile, are in the utmost perplexity and distress, knowing not what to do and fearing to do anything; if they attempt to thwart or check him he may abandon and disinherit them; if they take legal measures to have him declared a person of unsound mind they may fail, since he has mind and means enough to employ the agency of an unscrupulous defence; and, failing, they may incur vast expense, his bitter revenge, and the public suspicion and odium of having tried, for their own base ends, to make a sane man out to be a lunatic.

When the excitement subsides, as it does abruptly sometimes, he is likely to exhibit weakness of mind which passes eventually into the dotage of senile dementia. However, he may recover without appearing to be any the worse for his attack; but it is then probable that in no long time he will have a recurrence of mental disorder, if he has not a stroke of paralysis or some other attack of gross cerebral disease.

In another variety of senile mania there is little or no exaltation of feelings and ideas with its active outcome in answering projects and speculations, but predominant ideas of suspicion and hostility give the disorder the character of a mania of persecution. The exacting egotism of the old man, unconscious of his failing faculties and tenacious to the last to be what he was at his best, resents jealously the least suggestion of anything amiss in his ways and doings, repels indignantly any attempts, secret or open, to help him in the work which he has hitherto done, and glides easily into suspicions of hostile intentions and designs against him. Ingrained in his nature is the experience that the world is not a world of doves and lambs; and as he feels implicitly, though he confess not explicitly even to himself, his failing powers, he shields himself behind the natural defences of weakness—suspicion and cunning. In the end perhaps, as his suspicions grow, he imagines and denounces vile schemes to slander, rob, ruin, or poison him. The decay of brain still proceeding and the mind weakening with it, he forgets where he puts things and, not finding them at hand, believes that they have been stolen; gathers all sorts of things about him in dirty disorder or thrusts them incongruously into drawers, corners, and the like; perhaps carries coals in his pockets or stores food in his boots; wanders about his room with lighted candle at night to look for what he has lost, without knowing what it is that he is looking for; will not allow a servant to enter his room to clean it or even to make his bed, and neglects or refuses to change his linen and wash himself.

A second leading form which the insanity of commencing senility takes is *melancholia*. The ground-tone then is one of affective apprehension, and the disorder, being marked by great agitation, is a true *melancholia agitata*, increasing sometimes to a positive delirious melancholia. In a fever of agitated alarm about his health, the patient thinks and exclaims that he is dying, or, similarly agitated about his affairs, which he declares to be ruined, paces up and down the room or wanders from room to room in a restless anguish of apprehension; bemoans his dreadful fate, because he will be turned naked into the street and must starve, or because some other dreadful calamity is impending over him and all belonging to him; receives soothing words and reassurances as if they were alarming menaces and keeps up a continual moaning or an iteration of the same ejaculations of distress, such as, " Don't say that "—" Oh don't say it "—" It is too dreadful "—" I have no money to pay," and the like; distractedly pushes, writhes and struggles or aimlessly strikes and kicks those who attend upon him; sometimes rejects food with frenzied energy, believing it to be drugged or poisoned, or to be filth, carrion, or human flesh, or protesting that he cannot swallow. From time to time the distress amounts to paroxysms of acute anguish in which he shrieks or yells, tears out his hair, smashes what is within his reach, runs his head against the wall, or bursts out into some other destructive explosion. His frantic movements are the unloading of his frantic unrest; his frantic unrest, with its keen fears and suspicions, the reaction of labouring nerve-element resenting its threatened extinction. Sometimes the words and acts betray fierce sexual excitement, and now and then a frenzy of self-abuse afflicts old women. Noteworthy in this active melancholia are the acute perception and memory shown, notwithstanding the delirium, and the clearness of understanding when the mind can be moved for a moment off its morbid tracks; the patients are much more conscious of what is going on around them and in relation to them than they appear to be, and there is more of perverted and distracted volition in their doings than a superficial observer might suspect. Not infrequent are short intermissions or intervals of tranquillity during which there is a singular lucidity of mind and after which the raptures of distress recur.

What are the issues? In no case favourable. Either the distressed excitement increases to a true delirious melancholia, as occasionally happens, and the patient, who gets no sleep and rejects all nourishment, dies from general exhaustion or from the special coma of brain-exhaustion; or the excitement abates and the disease continues in a chronic form, the delusions then being of an extravagant character—as, for example, that persons and things are not real, that some organ of the body or the whole body is dead, that he is not himself but somebody or something else, and the like, and being accompanied with mental weakness.

Senile Dementia, the typical mental disorder of old age, is that imbecility of mind which is the term of the natural decline of the faculties when they suffer great decay before death. It is the occasional fate of the person who, having every bodily organ except the brain sound, has no lurking disease in friendly waiting to carry him off before, dying by the brain, he sinks into dotage and mere oblivion. There is reason to think that it is less common now, when old people by exercise keep their minds, like their bodies, alert and active up to and through old age, than it was in the days of our forefathers when, mental life being less varied and more sluggish, dull minds and bent bodies seemed the natural adjuncts of old age.

The symptom to attract first and most notice is a marked impairment of memory of recent events; the events of yesterday or of a few hours ago, although perceived correctly and with apparent interest at the time, being clean forgotten, while long-past events are remembered and talked of as if they were affairs of yesterday. The remote being thus brought near and the near razed out, there results a striking want of congruity between the actual circumstances of daily life and the manner of thinking and talking about them; an incongruity which may give the show of greater imbecility than the facts, when strictly examined, disclose. For if simple questions with regard to present circumstances be plainly put to the patient, he may still apprehend them rightly and answer them correctly at the moment, although, when asked about them a few hours afterwards, he has no recollection of what took place and babbles of things which happened fifty years ago as if they were things of yesterday. So it comes to pass that he asks the same question over and over again several times within a few minutes, forgetting immediately on each occasion that it has been asked before and answered. Apprehension and memory, however, vary at different times according to bodily states; he may know a person and remember an incident on one day or on one occasion, notwithstanding that on another day or occasion he does not recognise the person or remember the incident. This also may be noticed sometimes—that he will easily utter in conversation the particular name of a person or place which, if asked directly to tell it, he is utterly unable to recollect. In the further course of his mental decay his powers of perception are gradually impaired, almost erased at last;

he does not recognise familiar faces and places, but accosts as an old friend a person whom he sees for the first time, and this notwithstanding that the friend he mistakes him for has been dead many years; not unfrequently confounds generations, talking to a son as if he were his dead father or to a wife as if she were his dead mother; does not know the familiar objects around him in his own house but, believing that he is in a strange house, urgently demands to return home. Perchance he speaks of his wife as if he were accustomed to see her daily or wonders why he has not seen her to-day, though she has been dead some time and he saw her last in her coffin. Meanwhile, if his manner be grave and composed, his speech reserved, and he preserve a formal habit of polite behaviour, he so dignifies imbecility that a stranger who is with him for a short time and asks him a few ordinary questions about ordinary things, not probing the real state of his mind, may not suspect what a wreck it is beneath its fair show.

As decay's effacing process deepens and spreads, more tracks of mental function are obliterated. The patient cannot now either apprehend or remember; his perceptions and memories are a confused and incoherent jumble; and his conduct has little or no relation to his external conditions. He will insist that it is bed-time at noonday and get up in the middle of the night believing that it is morning; maintain that he is occupied regularly with work which he has not touched for years and will never touch more, or rail against those whom he supposes to be hindering him from going to work; listen to and seem perhaps to understand a simple question, put quietly and distinctly to him so as to give time for the sound of each word to excite his dull sense and to arouse his sluggish apprehension, and straightway begin a reply which, his feeble attention collapsing after the first word or two, scatters at random into unmeaning nonsense; or he fails to understand at all what is said to him and, in seeming reply, says something utterly irrelevant and incoherent.

Along with the increasing waste of mind there are in

some cases morbid suspicions and delusions that he is being
robbed, perhaps hallucinations that he sees strangers in the
room or hears thieves about the house; and the paroxysms
of noisy excitement into which he falls in consequence are a
great trouble to those who have the anxious care of him.
Such paroxysms are worst and most frequent in the night,
when the absence of outer impressions on the senses leaves
the dilapidated brain to the free constructive play of its
disorder; the more so as these patients are apt to get what
sleep they get in the daytime and to be restless at night.
Social feelings are involved with intelligence in a common
ruin of oblivion; he is no longer citizen, friend, or father;
all the definite feeling which he shows is anger at the supposed plots against him and the injuries which he imagines
to be done to him; and from time to time he has outbursts
of sobbing distress and tears of dotage which, coming on
and going off anyhow and anywhen, have as little foundation in real feeling as the babbling glee displayed at other
times or in other cases. The habits are prone to be unclean.
At last, after long lingering superfluous on the stage, he
dies when the descending degeneration of his brain reaches
the deeper-lying nervous centres that subserve the vital functions of respiration and circulation. He dies as an organic,
after having ceased to be a relational, being. But it may be
a slow process and go on for years, unless some other disease, such as bronchitis, heart-disease, kidney-disease, apoplectiform or epileptiform attack, helps to bring life to an end.

These symptoms of progressive mental decay present the
long detail and tedious chronicle of that which, in initial
stages and various degrees, marks the mental decline natural
to old age. For the keenness of the senses being then
blunted, they are less susceptible of both weak and fine
impressions, and, conduction being slackened, stronger impressions take a longer time to awaken a duller apprehension;
suppleness and energy of mind are lessened, ideas more
sluggish, prone too, new adjustments being difficult, to run
mainly on old tracks, and some of their associations so
obstructed that memory begins to fail; language, like other
movements, more slow and measured, and judgment stiff,

hesitating, and formal. The old man's appreciative interest in current events is weakened, whether he knows it or not; he cannot well and truly assimilate new experiences, cannot, being in a state of stagnation or incipient dissolution of mind, take full part in a process of evolution, and he shrinks naturally from new enterprises; even if still sagacious in counsel, he is not good in execution where decision and vigour are required. If perchance, being endowed with an extraordinary physical vitality, he goes about to interest himself ardently in present movements and to plunge enthusiastically into them, so that men behold the spectacle of senile energy with admiring wonder, he is really weaker in wisdom than his admirers acknowledge, who do him no good service when they encourage him to go on doing ill what he can no longer do well.

Being what he is, he cannot organically assimilate new movements, they being what they are: either he makes partial and imperfect assimilations of them whereby he deludes himself that he is a man of his times, albeit he is governed mainly by his past order of thought and feeling; or throws himself recklessly into them, taking violent leave of his past, and prosecutes them impetuously with a fierce egotism and weak judgment similar in kind to, if less in degree than, that which characterizes senile mania. The failing mind which goes along with failing brain and feeble vitality may be obstructive and negatively mischievous, but the failing mind which goes along with failing brain and vigorous bodily vitality is prone to be rash and positively mischievous. For an insidious moral deterioration creeps on stealthily along with the other degenerations of senility, showing itself in loss of the finest moral sensibilities, in irritable vanity, in exacting jealousy, in egotistic self-will, in self-regarding habits, in blunted feeling for others. Even when there is no very positive moral deterioration, second childhood, like first childhood, tends to absorption in self; the aged man or woman to whom friends dread to announce the sudden death of the nearest and dearest, lest the shock should be fatal, receives the news with tranquil stoicism and goes quietly to bed and to sleep.

CHAPTER IV

GENERAL PARALYSIS

UNDER this name it is usual to class a number of cases of mental derangement which, having some characteristic features, run a pretty definite and comparatively short course, and are specially remarkable for the concurrence, and in the main concurrent increase, of motor and mental disorder. The mental disorder is most often of a signally elated type, marked by exultant feeling and wildly extravagant notions of health, wealth, strength, wit, birth, grandeur; the motor disorder a paralysis which, beginning insidiously in speech, increases and spreads gradually until it involves the whole muscular system; and the course of the disorder downhill to death within two or three years of its start. Its victim, who, all unconscious of the wreck he is and of his doom, believes himself to be wonderfully well and strong in mind, body, and estate, loses steadily the power of performing ideas and movements and gets worse and worse until he dies. Essentially the disease is a progressive paralytic dementia, masked though the mental weakness is at the outset and in its early stages by the tumult of elated excitement: its fundamental and constant elements the mental and motor feebleness and their concurrent decline into dementia and paralysis, and the extravagant delusions which come and go on the way the usual but not invariable accessories of the decline.

Typical General Paralysis.

What are the distinctive features of a typical example of general paralysis? After some precursory symptoms, brief or prolonged (to be described later), which may or may not have been manifest enough to attract special notice, the person exhibits an abrupt transformation of character and habits which occasions no little surprise to his friends: he becomes extraordinarily elated and buoyant, prolific in projects, sanguine in prospects, and restlessly busy in his doings; discourses freely of his affairs with expansive geniality to all comers, and shrinks not from communicating to casual acquaintances matters of private domestic concern which, were he his true self, he would not breathe to any one; indulges a wanton freedom of speech, makes coarse jokes, and is pleased to brag of his affairs and enterprises. Alike in speech, manner, and behaviour he betrays the loss of refined feeling and of quiet self-restraint; not out of wilful offence to social proprieties but serenely unconscious of his lapses. Indeed, his look, talk, and ways are so like those of one who is half drunk, that he is pretty sure to be suspected of having taken too much to drink, whereas he may have taken no alcoholic liquor at all or taken a little only by way of good fellowship.

It is when inquiry is made into the nature of the schemes which he has in project that a startling disclosure of mental dilapidation is made. They are wild, extravagant, reckless, perhaps preposterously absurd; just the mad imaginative outcomes of the insane elation of feeling with which he and they are infused. He is going to make an immense fortune with the greatest ease by some capital speculation which, although it is very simple, no one was ever clever enough to think of before; or to do wonders by an extraordinary mechanical invention which he has thought of; or to become famous and wealthy by a superlative voice for singing which he has discovered that he possesses; speculations, talents, and inventions being alike the silly follies of a frenzied fancy. Flushed with exulting self-confidence, he can undertake anything and is sure that everything he undertakes will be a superb success; is in such a dream of foolish joy that he treats the things of the real world with the freedom of a dreamer. Never in his life was he in such splendid health, he protests, never so fit for work nor so clever in it, never so happy in himself. Sometimes he is in a perpetual unrest of diffuse activity, as though he were prodigiously busy and had not a moment to spare: walking up and down the room, hurrying to and fro from one thing to another, having many things in hand but accomplishing nothing, all the while talking rapidly, almost breathlessly, of his projects; covering note-paper, scraps of newspapers, or any available piece of paper with notes of his multitudinous business or with nonsensical scribblings; sending off telegrams, letters, post-cards to all sorts of persons and places; driving about in a cab from place to place and keeping it waiting for reckless periods, in random pursuit of business which is devoid of real method or purpose.

Seldom does he stay long in projects only of riches and greatness. As his disorder deepens and the bonds of his mental union are more loosened, his extravagant imaginations, lacking the restraining ties or inhibitions of their associations, grow into monstrous proportions and into more vivid realities to him; not otherwise perhaps than as a particular group of movements becomes exaggerated and deformed when it is deprived of the adjunct or opposing muscular contractions which normally accompany, support, restrain, and steady it. Then he declares himself to be possessed of immense wealth, his vaguely vast feelings rather than notions of which require terms of indefinite thousands and millions to express themselves and, after all, are not adequately expressed; in like manner, he has notions of personal greatness so spacious that he heaps titles on himself, proclaiming himself count, duke, prince, king, even king of kings; notions of personal strength and activity such that he can lift with his little finger as great a weight as the strongest man could lift with both hands, or perform any feat of agility, even were it to travel on a tight-rope to Australia; so great notions of his powers and resources that he makes nothing of a plan for bridging the Atlantic Ocean, or driving a tunnel through the centre of the earth, or buying up half London in order to clear the ground and cover it with palaces of marble; notions of personal graces and virility such that he is going to marry a princess and to have a harem of all the finest women in the world. If it is a woman who is afflicted she may boast of having a million husbands, while a man may exult in the belief that a benevolent nature is increasing the number of his testicles. Everything in the undermined imagination is weakly colossal, and the superlatives used to express it are, like the rapturous utterances of religious ecstasy, endeavours to express vague feelings of grandeur, not to convey definite ideas: the language, like the language of love, is a perpetual hyperbole.[1]

In accordance with his expansive feelings and notions he makes extravagant purchases in reckless and foolish fashion, buying what he has not the least need of and deeming everything which he buys superlative of its kind: jewelry of all sorts; carriages for which he has no accommodation; horses which, though they are sorry jades palmed on him by an unscrupulous horse-dealer, he maintains to be the finest horses in the town and he will easily sell at an enormous profit; pictures which he boasts are by Titian and Rembrandt, or some other great master, though they are the worst rubbish of the worst picture-shops. Little craft is required to cheat one whose inflated feelings run eagerly into pleased collusion with the fraud; for by lending magnificence to common objects and transforming them into paragons of excellence, they make mean things the means of their pleasing self-discharge. As he considers not what he does when he makes his reckless purchases, so he soon forgets what he has

---

[1] The result is that he has not that full and distinct belief which he has when feeling and thought run in harness together; he believes only partially, as it were, deceiving himself for the moment by his vague imaginations. Though he would unhesitatingly give a cheque for millions, he might hesitate to give sixpence out of his own pocket.

done. If the articles which he has purchased are delivered at his house, it is probable that he has forgotten all about them; still it is all right when he is told they have arrived, and if they do not arrive he commonly forgets to wonder why they have not been delivered.

Big as the delusions are in such cases the note of them is mental weakness; indeed, their very extravagance proclaims their origin in mental dilapidation.[1] There is nothing logical in them; they are not the consistent products of a systematic train of disordered associations, nor spring consistently from the data of former life and habits; they are the direct and random miscreations of a disorganised cerebral cortex—of disrupted and inflamed imagination. The fundamental weakness beneath the inflated show reveals itself furthermore by other evidence: by the gross loss of memory which, although a marked feature often from the first, is in such singular contrast with the mental and bodily activity displayed that, being unsuspected, its revelation is a surprise; by the facility with which for the most part the patient can be diverted from his present schemes of folly by transparent devices which he is weak enough not to see through; by the grossly absurd, inconsistent, changing, and even contradictory delusions, whereby it happens that although he is a duke one day he is a prince another day, that although he is married to a princess he acknowledges his real wife when she visits him, that although he possesses millions he begs for a pipe of tobacco, that although he is going to do wonders he never wonders that he does not set to work to do them; by the complacent unconsciousness of any flaw in his absurd schemes or in himself, despite their impossible nature; and by the weak way in which he gives utterance to his extravagant delusions—at first with an exuberant and childish glee, later on with an air of fatuous satisfaction, and, later still, with a flabby smile or a burst of imbecile laughter. So flagrant is his folly that the asylum-patient

[1] If it were legitimate to revive an old term, used by Bacon, I might describe the state of mind as inflamed *ventosity;* the term expressing well the big-swollen emptiness.

is far gone in dementia who does not perceive and deride the madness of the general paralytic.

It is another result of his mental weakness and forgetfulness that he is sometimes prone to take what does not belong to him ; not from a wilful design to steal, but from the mere unrecking impulse to possess what attracts his notice and his no-memory of the difference between *mine* and *thine;* taking what he has no need of or makes no use of when he has got it, and usually without making any attempt to conceal his theft. If challenged with the theft, he may deny it with the cool imperturbable sincerity of absolute oblivion. From the same mental confusion and oblivion it proceeds that he sometimes offends against public morals by making an indecent exposure of himself; not again wilfully, but by performing legitimate acts without regard to legitimate times and places. So it comes to pass that he is apt to get into trouble and to be sent to prison for these two classes of offence.[1]

Along with the first mental symptoms in some cases, after them in most cases, and before the least show of them in a few cases, special motor troubles appear. These are noticed first in the process of articulation, the very fine, exact, and special movements of which have to execute the most delicate and complex work with the nicest precision, and especially in the pronunciation of words beginning with and abounding in consonants, where a demand is made on a variety and complexity of precisely adapted movements. First symptom of all to attract attention, though it may pass unnoticed for a time, is a brief halt before the pronunciation of a word beginning in consonants, after which check it is uttered rightly, perhaps a little accentuated : there is no real fault of articulation, once it has got itself started, only a moment's pause or embarrassment in thinking and starting the fit utterance. It is the motor intuition or

---

[1] Of thirty - eight prisoners transferred from prison into one county asylum in five years nine were general paralytics (*Report of Rainhill Asylum for* 1888). Much similar testimony has come from other county asylums.

subaudition of the word in the cerebral cortex, so to speak, which flags and lags, the impediment not being so much in the execution of it as in silently thinking and bringing it and its steps to execution. Sometimes, with ever so little pause, there is a labouring twitch or tremulous motion of the muscles about the mouth before and during the utterance. Matters getting worse, the scarce sensible halts or jerks become more marked, although they are never a proper stutter or stammer, and so affect each syllabic movement that the speech, instead of flowing in even modulations, is broken into a succession of jerks, irregular in time and degree, and becomes staggering and tremulous. Or the stumble at the syllable, laming the exact pronunciation of it, blurs its distinct form, dislimning its contour, so to speak, and so either makes the speech shuffling and indistinct or now and then, by omission of syllables, occasions a clipping of words. Sometimes the syllabic defect leads to a distinctly heavier leaning on each vowel-sound, whereby speech becomes a slow and mouthing drawl. In the end it sinks by degrees of increasing defect into a mumbling indistinctness. The early tremor might signify the break-up, into interrupted discharges, of the rhythmical succession of waves in sequent flow which, being many though seeming one, constitute the continuity of the normal nervous discharge and its sequent muscular contraction. Later on it is evident enough even when the patient's talk is pouring out in a voluble torrent, as it oftentimes is. Then also there is often a tremulousness of the adjunct muscles of the lips and face, which quiver or twitch or grimace spasmodically when he speaks or smiles. When these motor symptoms go along with the special mental symptoms they are of fatal omen; they are the first visible signs of an oncoming motor paralysis which betrays itself distinctly in the minutely fine and complex movements of speech before it is revealed in the grosser movements of locomotion; and they render the diagnosis of general paralysis and the doom of the patient, which might still be uncertain without them, pretty nigh certain. Although there are many more finished examples, there is

not in the world a more glaring example, of nature's irony
than the immense joy and exultation exhibited, even unto
the last sometimes, by the general paralytic who, fatuous and
death-struck from the first, rejoices, like a giant, to run his
course.

Other motor failures follow in due time. The tongue
is not paralysed, but in the later stages it either cannot be
put out or is put out with labour and difficulty, perhaps
thrust out and pulled in by a succession of spasmodic jerks,
trembling when protruded; if not tremulous as a whole,
there is a frequent fibrillar quivering of its muscles. However, it is not invariably tremulous either in whole or in
part; whether it be so or not depends somewhat on the
way it is put out, at any rate in the early stages; for the
same tongue which, when protruded quickly with contracted
muscles, is perfectly steady, may be jerky and show considerable tremor when it is put out slowly in a relaxed state. I
have seen as much fibrillar quivering of the tongue in a
healthy neurotic subject after a night's debauch or a sleepless
night of pain as in any case of general paralysis. A common
but not constant symptom is a marked inequality in the
size of the pupils; though not characteristic, it is a bad
omen when it goes with other symptoms; but it is sometimes absent from first to last in general paralysis, and it
may be present in other cerebral disease. Moreover, it has
no constant relation to other symptoms, mental or motor,
or to any stage in the process of the disease, so far as is
known; for it occurs either early or late in it, before mental
symptoms or before bodily symptoms, varies in degree at
different times, and comes and goes irregularly. Now and
then it is curious to see inequality of the pupils for many
months before any mental or motor symptom of a general
paralysis which ultimately supervenes. In most cases the
pupils are sluggish to light, in some quite inactive, and in a
few there is an almost pin-point contraction of them which
disappears perhaps later and is followed by inequality.

The next motor failure noticed is in the walk, which is
observed to be not quite what it was, though it may be hard

at first to say what the change exactly is. Very much doubtless what it is at the beginning of the speech-fault—that is to say, a slight halt and seeming embarrassment in the starting of the movement, followed perhaps by a brief stay on it, whereby the gait, losing its ease and freedom, may at first have a look of stiffness or even quasi-aggressiveness; and, later on, a succession of partial halts and failures in the steps of its performance, whereby it is rendered springless, shuffling, heavy and feeble. The patient takes unconscious care to bear on both legs in standing and plants his feet in walking with an exaggerated but somewhat slack energy, thus supplementing his failing fine adaptations by grosser movements of support, and he cannot stand well at ease. Asked to step on to a chair and stand on it, which he will mostly be pleased to do energetically in order to show his prowess, he betrays a loss of quickness, quietness and precision of co-ordination which otherwise might not be apparent; or if, after being ordered to march straight forwards he is asked to face round suddenly at the word of command, he may sway or totter a little before he gets a firm hold of the ground and starts afresh. He has not lost actual muscular strength; *that* he has in full force when he exerts it rudely; but he lacks the nice control and management of it necessary to grace and skill of performance: the skilful skater fails to execute the difficult figures with his old grace and skill. Meanwhile he is not aware of his defect though it be considerable, but perhaps brags exultantly of his superb muscular power and skill in walking, running, leaping and the like. The disease deepening, the motor trouble worsens, going through all degrees of tottering, shambling, stumbling incompetence until it reaches the depth of locomotive impotence. The shambling and stumbling steps are of the same nature as the slurred and clipped words; just as the distinct form or outline of the special syllabic movement is blurred, so that one syllable is run into another before it can get itself exactly executed, or is left out altogether because it does not get itself executed in time, so the several component movements, simultaneous and successive, of the purposed act of walking are blurred and partially missed.

The invasion of paralysis in the hands and arms may be detected, if it has not already been noticed in some loss of grace and ease of gesture, by the inability of the patient to perform the most nice and special movements of a manual art in which he was an adept—for example, by the inability of the clever seamstress to sew neatly, of the accomplished violinist to bring out the finer tones of his instrument, of the distinguished painter to paint the delicate touches of expression and colouring, of the skilful marksman to kill his birds. In each case the artist loses the finest manual language of his art, so to speak, just as he loses the finest movements of speech. That the hand has forgotten its cunning is a literal statement of the truth, if we translate the hand into the representative form or pattern of its functions in the cerebral cortex; for its incompetence is essentially of the same kind as the losses of memory which seem so much more mental. Every clumsiness or coarseness of thought, feeling, or conduct shown by an individual who once possessed refinement in that particular is neither more nor less than an instance of loss of memory; for it is the effacement, temporary or permanent, of the fine traceries of cerebral reflexes which subserved the lost niceties of function.

It is strange to see how placidly unconscious of his state the patient remains, notwithstanding that every one about him is deeply concerned at it, and how content he still is with his slovenly failures as they grow steadily worse. One eminent painter who, going from bad to worse, took to executing his pictures at last by emptying the ink-bottle over his canvas, boasted of the fine flowing outlines and broad effects which he was thus able to produce, and anticipated exultantly the immense fortune which he would soon realise by the multitude of magnificent pictures he was going to paint at a prodigious rate of speed and sell at prodigious prices. The monstrous lack of judgment, like the monstrous delusions, is the effect and evidence of the dissolution of the forms of the cerebral thought-tracks and of their associations;

the razed forms of past experience being only a "formless ruin of oblivion," comparisons and inhibitions are impossible, and the outer world is now framed anew, and accepted offhand, in such shapes of inflamed notions as chance to be formed in the wreckage.

As might be expected, the handwriting eventually betrays loss of nice control over its finely specialized movements; but many times not so soon as other symptoms would lead one to expect. The defects are these: the lines of the letters, especially large letters, stiff and shaky, sometimes zigzag; the transitions from letter to letter and the forms of letters angular and irregular, their easy flow lost; omissions of letters or words, halting execution failing to keep pace with thought, sometimes repetitions of letters and words when the letter or word chances to loiter in the mind by reason of the stay on its particular execution; spasmodic stoppages in the middle of words or lines, and repetitions of words and partial sentences. As every letter represents a special purposive movement, and every word, much more every sentence, a succession of such movements, it follows that every such purpose or train of such purposes may falter or fail; the faults or failures in the component movements of writing being of the same nature as those which cause the disorder of speech and of walking. Let the patient try to write when he has got near his worst, he will perhaps bring the whole hand and arm into a ludicrous supplementary help of his failing special movements; just as, when asked to take hold of some small article quietly with forefinger and thumb, he will bring to the work the jerky co-operation of his other fingers and his hand; and just as, in process of further nervous destruction, he supplements the special work of the hand with movements of the arm, and the special work of the arm with movements of the body, until his whole frame is grotesquely and uselessly agitated.[1] In the same

[1] He is brought to a stage in the degenerative process of unmaking complex and special movements like that which a child goes through in the developmental process of making them.

way, when, being near his end, he makes vain endeavours to speak, the muscles of his mouth, face, head and neck are sometimes involved in useless grimaces and antics. That the handwriting is not lamed soon, but the patient writes well when he cannot perform other less special and complex acts, and for the life of him could not write a sensible letter, is no doubt because writing, being so early acquired, so much practised, and so automatic an art, survives the decay of less fixed and stable acquisitions. It is just for the same reason, in other forms of insanity, that one who can hardly ever speak sensibly may write a sensible letter when it is confined to commonplace inquiries and the stock phrases of conventional expression; for when he sits down with pen in hand, the undamaged part of the damaged machine is prompted to begin and do its automatic work.

As the disease reaches its last stage before death, the paralysis of body is general. The patient, unable to stand on his legs, is confined to his bed or couch, his sphincters lose their power, he cannot feed himself, and he has difficulty in swallowing the food given to him. Food must be put into his mouth in a minced or liquid state; otherwise he runs a risk of choking himself by a lump of insufficiently masticated solid which, sticking in the partly paralysed pharynx, blocks the opening of the larynx, or slips into it past the dull guard of its sluggish reflexes. He can no longer rely on the fundamental reflexes—those which were gained and framed for his kind ages before the prophetic spirit of organic evolution ever dreamt of him to come. If he has sense enough to understand what is said to him when he is asked to put out his tongue, he either protrudes it only partially with a jerk, or he fails entirely to do it despite his laboured attempts; or he perhaps raises his hand feebly as if to help him to do it, his hand having just enough confused and fragmentary remembrance of its helping use to move to help where it cannot help in the least. His tongue has lost its memory entirely, its cerebral centre being completely disorganized, but the hand is not in quite so bad a case. And here one may make the reflection, though it be a digression, how each instrument of the body which does purposive work has not merely a general memory but as many special memories as it can perform special acts. The face is often a vacuous blank over which a flabby smile flickers from time to time and loses itself in the waste, but it may present a pretty study of incongruities : a corrugated forehead perhaps gives to its upper part a stern look of reflection while the lower part is flabby and devoid of any expression ; or the upper part is a complete blank while mouth and nose are sternly compressed or are working in energetic movements; or a feeble smile begun in response to a word of cheer turns into a spasmodic grimace of weeping; or some other incongruity witnesses to the disintegration of physiognomical expression. Rigid contractions of particular muscles, especially of the arms and legs, sometimes come and go, and a continued monotonous grinding and grating of the teeth, horribly discordant to hear, or a persistent champing of the saliva, or a perpetual smacking of the lips, or the automatic repetition of a fearful howl or yell, is not uncommon in the latest stages. The muscles of the mouth are fixed in a sardonic grin, the knees perhaps drawn up to the chin in rigid contraction, and the torpid remnant of humanity, who can do nothing else, is sometimes strangely persistent in the mechanical industry of diligently rolling up the bed-clothes with his hands as fast as they are unrolled.

Mental is involved with motor power in a common ruin, mind at last as palsied as movement. Even exalted notions vanish, or fragments only of them are attested by mumbled words about dukes, millions, and the like. The patient does not recognise persons, seems not to see them, although his eyes are not blind ; he is simply incapable of perception, mentally blind, like a pigeon which has had its cerebral hemispheres removed ; his disorganized hemispheres have been practically removed by the denudation of disease. The remnants of delusion, when there are any, like the residues of decomposed acts or the residual acts of decomposed conduct, are so many fragments of function-patterns surviving feebly in the waste of mental disorganisation.

Such is the general aspect of the paralytic decay of mind and body. As regards particular symptoms, it is evident that with the motor decline goes hand in hand more or less decline of sensibility, general and special. The false good news which the muscular sense gives is proof of its inability to do its duty; sharing in the general elation, it declares a fictitious feeling of extraordinary bodily strength and skill at first, and later on fails entirely to make the patient sensible of his motor incapacity. It may be suspected that the impairment of its special sensibility, both in its lower concrete form of sense and in its higher abstract representation in the cortex as a factor in the motor intuition, plays a considerable part in determining the special motor and mental features of general paralysis. Assuredly it is not muscular power which the patient lacks in the first stages of the disease, or even in later stages when he is maniacal; he has plenty of power when he gets it grossly exerted; but it is the fine power of exactly actuating and executing the precise purposive movement which fails him. He has a difficulty in performing the special adjustment of a nice motor apprehension because, by reason of the impairment of its proper cortical reflex, he has a difficulty in informing it with its fit representative mental apprehension. The consequence is that although he fails in exact accomplishment he does not know that he fails; which would not be the case if the failure in act and in intuition did not go together—that is, if the intuition were perfect and the defect only in accomplishment. Having lost his sensory touch and measure of the forms and things of the external world, the forms of real experience no longer exist for him; at the same time he is filled with an inflamed feeling of wellbeing and power: what conditions could be imagined more fit to produce the disruption of the unbridled and inflamed self into monstrous and incoherent delusion-selves?

The nicest discriminations of tactile sensibility I believe to be impaired or lost at an early date. It is all one for the most part whether the impression made on touch be fine or coarse. Not that there is the much-blunted sensibility which is notable in chronic alcoholism, where the peripheral ends of the nerves are almost paralysed, but that the sense is somewhat blunted; and at a later stage there is a signal insensibility to pain, so that a broken rib or other injury elicits no complaint and seems to cause no suffering. Local anæsthesias, which come and go and change their places in irregular fashion, are not uncommon at one period or another of the disease; they are the probable occasions of such delusions as that a part of the body is dead, or has been cut or torn away, or has been transformed in some strangely impossible way. In the last and worst case dulness declines into complete deadness of sensibility; then the patient who is accidentally burnt gives no other notice of what is going on than the penetrating odour of his charred flesh diffuses abroad.

How soon and how much the special senses are affected are questions very difficult to answer, seeing that applied tests cannot be trusted to elicit exact replies; but it is evident that the finest discriminations of every one of them are soon lost, since they welcome gladly coarse impressions which would have jarred painfully erewhile. Doubtless there is a progressive defacement or effacement of special reflexes, and the degeneration, limited at first to the most special and refined functions, extends by degrees to the more general and less complex functions. Certain it is that smell and taste are often clean gone towards the end of the disease and sometimes much impaired early in its course. Hallucinations of sense, especially of sight and hearing, occur in many cases at one time or another; they are prone to change and come and go, and, like the delusions, are of an extravagant and absurd character: flights of angels, showers of gold, and the like perhaps when the disease is of the elated type; hallucinations of the body or a part of it being dead, or being changed into something else, or of having its passages sealed up, very like the extravagant hallucinations of alcoholic dementia, when it has the dejected form.

2 G

Overt reflex excitability, usually unimpaired at the outset, is lessened in the cerebral nerves as the disease advances; sometimes it is heightened in the spinal cord when the brain is diseased and the cord is not. Of the so-called knee-jerk or patellar reflex nothing constant can be predicated, since it may be either increased or lessened or natural; and there is no discernible connection between its state and the state of the pupils, since it may be greater or less indifferently whether they are affected or not. An inflamed sexual desire, with an excited display and immoderate indulgence of it, is not infrequent at the beginning of the disease, but for the most part without power equal to desire, and both desire and power fail later. Perchance such failure has been one of the hidden griefs of a preceding depression. Moreover, from the first the person loses all the refinements of feeling and expression which transform and ennoble its brutal nature: it is no longer love, it is only inflamed lust.

Such are the symptoms of what might be called typical general paralysis. It runs a fatal course usually in two or three years from the start. Now and then there is the rarity of a quick short course of only two or three months or even less; in that case the symptoms are generally acutely melancholic, perhaps with a stupidity which is almost stupor, while the signs of bodily paralysis are so slight as to make it hard to recognize the real nature of the disease. It is probable that there were unregarded symptoms of nervous weakness for some weeks before the actual outbreak and that the whole course was not quite so short as it appeared to be. An irregular deterioration with remissions of symptoms is the rule; the remissions sometimes so complete as to be intermissions which are mistaken for recoveries. When the intermissions last for a few months we may admit them to be properly so called, but when they last for years, as it has been said they have sometimes done, we might perhaps question the existence of a disease which hides itself so well for so long a time. It is in its early stages especially that symptoms are apt to disappear; then every trace of paralysis may vanish while the mental symptoms remain, or every mental symptom vanish while the symptoms of paralysis remain, or both motor and mental disappear together so completely that the patient's friends, seeing nothing wrong in him, tax the diagnosis with error. It is not well to be too swift to judge in any case, it is better to wait and watch. Watching closely, it may be noted that the person is not quite what he was before his illness: that his refinement of thought and feeling is a little tarnished; that he has lost something of his wonted delicacy and reserve in conversation and conduct; that he has a heavier look and a tamer manner of talk and walk; that he is not equal to the same intellectual efforts as formerly, but is sooner fatigued mentally and bodily; and that, although he goes on well while he lives quietly and nurses his strength in retirement, he shows symptoms of illness again directly he goes back to real work. That is not only because real work puts a strain on his brain which it cannot bear, but because return to it, involving the returning use of the special tracts of thought, feeling and action which failed him, reveals an incompetency likely to pass unnoticed when he is taking rest and making no demand on them. Commonly after a few months at most, though now and then the interval may be longer, there is a return of the bad symptoms, perhaps suddenly, and the disease, as if it had gathered force of fury during its lull, runs a rapid course through acute mania or convulsions to a fatal ending.

Whether lasting recovery ever takes place in general paralysis is an uncertain and disputed point. On the one hand, it is possible to mistake the complete intermissions for recoveries, as has certainly been done; on the other hand, it is always possible, when a lasting recovery has taken place, to say that the diagnosis was wrong and that the disease then was not real general paralysis, only a mania simulating it, a pseudo-general paralysis. It does not appear why a person should not recover occasionally in the early stages when, although there is abundant exaltation of feeling and ideas, there is no sign of loss of memory or of other mental weakness betokening positive disease of structure, more especially when the life thenceforth led is quiet, regular, and free from stress or excitement. The signal disappearance of motor and mental symptoms for a while at later stages of the disease, when there is no reason to question its paralytic nature, tells certainly in favour of that view; and for my part I believe that paralytic dementia is not the inevitable, though it is the usual, and might be called the logical, termination of the peculiarly exalted mania which so often goes before it. I have known a patient present all the characteristic features, motor and mental, of general paralysis, so that no one entertained the least doubt of the nature of the disease, in whom nevertheless every characteristic motor and mental symptom disappeared, he living for seven years afterwards in a state of ordinary dementia and dying at last from kidney-disease.

Outbursts of acute mania may occur from time to time in the course of general paralysis; they are apt to be furious frenzies. The patient has got the secret of going a long way—namely, an infinite belief in himself and an infinite disbelief in any power outside himself; wherefore, being madly exultant in his might and unchecked by any impeding doubt, or by reflection of which he is incapable, he displays reckless violence of conduct and is not cowed, as one suffering from simple mania generally is, by the large show or use of restraining force. Thus it is that, struggling with a blind fury, he is dangerous to those who have to contend with him and a danger to himself because of the injuries which he is liable to inflict or sustain in the desperate conflict to restrain him; all the more so when, as sometimes happens, confused notions of danger to his life, whirling wildly in the anarchy of his mind, actuate his furious conduct. Sometimes, where the frenzy has a more melancholic or stupid colour, there is an aimless struggling for hours together in a stubborn stupid fashion with a sort of mechanical constancy, the patient pushing, or pulling, or writhing, or grabbing in monotonous repetitions until he is bathed in perspiration. Whatever the special features of the mania, its general looseness, incoherence, methodless activity, hazy consciousness of surroundings and insensibility to external control, bespeak a deeper dissolution of the thought-tracts and more general disorganisation of mind than obtains in ordinary mania.

Furious as these manias are, they are not the direct danger to life which they may seem to be at the time ; for although death occasionally takes place in one of them, they usually subside and perhaps recur more than once before the end. When, however, the mania is of acute delirious intensity from the very outset of the disease, as it now and then is, there is some danger of a short and fierce flare ending in typhoid exhaustion and perhaps death. Seeing that when it so begins and so ends it may not be known for what it is— that is, the acute mania of general paralysis ; seeing too that when it does not end in death but subsides, it is followed by the usual exalted symptoms of the disease, which then goes on to run its ordinary course ;—one might fairly ask, Is not acute delirious mania or melancholia essentially an acute general paralysis ? It may be pretty safely set down, I think, that anyhow we have to do with a rapid quasi-inflammatory disorganisation of the cerebral cortex ending, on the one hand, in death or recovery, and, on the other hand, in chronic and deepening degenerative changes.

The attacks of excitement which occur late in the disease, when deeper cortical disorganisation is betrayed by an almost demented condition, are of a dazed, silly and incoherent character : much silly laughter, childish bragging, busy and senseless activity by day and night, incoherent gabble, fragmentary delusions of grandeur, facile changes from mood to mood, spells of convulsive laughter without joy and of convulsive sobbing without woe, which come on abruptly without appreciable cause and may go on mechanically for hours ; and, in addition, perhaps proclivities to tear and strip off clothes and to the dirtiest habits imaginable.

Another striking feature of general paralysis is the

occurrence of epileptiform or apoplectiform attacks from time to time, sometimes early in its course but most often in its later stages, when undigested food, or a loaded colon, or a full bladder is particularly liable to start them. They are generally accompanied by complete unconsciousness, frequently by strong convulsions which are often more marked on one side than on the other, sometimes almost limited to one side, and are preceded by flushed face, heated head, and a general rise of bodily temperature. It must not, however, be taken for granted that a fit of the kind is coming because of a rise of temperature only, since such an intercurrent rise may be caused by a full bladder or a loaded colon and pass away without any following fit. Unlike an ordinary apoplectic attack, they pass off in a few hours usually, albeit not so soon as an ordinary epileptic attack; but they leave behind them some paralysis or convulsion of one side or one limb, which in its turn passes off in a few days. Although the general weakness, mental and bodily, is usually greater after them, yet it is remarkable sometimes how much better temporarily both mind and body are, for all the world as if the cerebral cortex had been eased of a load of disorder by the explosion; the patient who could not speak intelligibly nor stand on his legs before the fit will then speak and walk fairly well after it. Charged with energy which, by reason of its nature or their disorganised state, they cannot discharge and distribute in regulated function, the cortical tracts discharge themselves in some violent explosion—in a furious mania, or in violent epileptiform convulsions, or perhaps in an hæmorrhagic outburst on the surface of the brain. Occasionally one of these attacks ends in death—either, in the apoplectiform state, from slow gradual cessation of the circulation and respiration, without recovery of consciousness; or, in the epileptiform state, from exhaustion after a rapid succession of fits, between which there may or may not have been a recovery of consciousness, partial or complete. It is wonderful how many epileptiform fits, one after another in quick sequence, with or without intervals of some consciousness, a patient will sometimes have—more than a hundred in twenty-four hours —and, though expected every moment to die, still recover so far as to get about on his feet again. If the fits are not fatal, the patient gets weaker and weaker from week to week, until at last, being no more than a bed-ridden mass of organic life, he tediously expires as the residue of his vitality slowly ebbs. Bed-sores, bronchitis, congestion of the lungs, or pneumonia then perhaps help to bring the dragging scene to a wearily awaited end. Cold has a bad effect on these patients; they deteriorate markedly in cold and rally wonderfully in warm weather. In women the disease usually runs a slower course than in men, and Morel made the observation that the slowest course of all was in persons sprung from an insane stock; in them, too, as in other hereditary insanities, remissions are most marked.

It is curious to see how little the general bodily nutrition suffers as a rule. At the outset of the disease there is apt to be a loss of weight, but the patient grows stout and flabby as he becomes demented. Sores and wounds heal singularly well in the earlier stages; even later, large bed-sores begin to heal directly he so far rallies as to be able to sit or stand up: one instance I call to mind in which, both heels having sloughed away owing to their own pressure on the bed, healing began and a skin-graft was even successful, although the man was a helpless log who died two or three weeks afterwards. This being so, it is curious to find that the ribs, and other bones in less degree, are sometimes soft and friable after death; their structure has undergone degeneration and they are soft, dusky-red, easily cut through, and contain much blood. That is one reason why general paralytics who are violent are liable to get broken ribs in asylums. Another reason is their dulness of sensibility and sluggishness of motor reaction, whereby it happens that the intercostal muscles are not put into timely action to fix the chest and meet the impending blow or fall which, so expected and guarded against, might be comparatively harmless.

Such is general paralysis when it answers the ideal

notion of it : a characteristic and fatal disease. But here as elsewhere in nature the manner in which things are is oftentimes different from the manner in which they ought theoretically to be. The cases which do not run the typical course are almost as many as those which do, and the deviations from the type differ also among themselves. Before going on to consider these diversities it will be convenient to speak of the precursory symptoms which herald and usher in the disease and of the different modes of its invasion.

Precursory Symptoms and Modes of Invasion.

However seemingly sudden the outbreak of general paralysis, forewarnings have seldom been wanting, if adequate inquiry be made, though they may not have attracted their due notice at the time. These are its principal modes of invasion :—

(*a*) Most frequent, I think, is a period of mental uneasiness and depression, a vague disquietude and undue susceptibility of mind, when the person's sleep is bad, noises affect him intensely, and he is very irritable and prone to explosive outbursts on slight occasions : a state of irritable weakness witnessing to nervous exhaustion which, though short and transient in some, may be traced back for weeks or months in other cases. Further causes of distress are a sluggish and failing memory, difficulty in thinking, inability to do accustomed work without pain and labour, sad and vague anxiety, perhaps a boding sense of impending calamity or a gloomy fear of going mad. The weakened nerve-element, menaced with dissolution, forefeels its danger and declares it by strange and vague apprehension. With these symptoms in some, without them in other cases, there may or may not be headaches, transitory local hyperæsthesias, neuralgic pains in face, head, or elsewhere; the pain so severe now and then that the sufferer yells in agony. Suddenly, as if by magic, all troubles vanish in an outburst of the characteristic wild exaltation.

(b) A direct outbreak of the insanely exalted thought and feeling occurs without, so far as appears, any forewarning signs: a bolt from the blue, so to speak, if such bolts ever come.

(c) There is a prolongation and a deepening of the precursory depression into positive melancholia which may continue and be the disease mentally or be followed after a while by elation.

(d) There is an insidious invasion of moral and mental weakness, so gradual that it is hard to say when it begins and when it is actual disease. The symptoms are—blunted moral and social feeling, indifference to family, intellectual apathy, unwonted acts of indelicacy, coarse language, loss of memory, stupidity and confusion of mind.; and these deepen into complete dementia, the quiet course of which is apt to be interrupted from time to time by outbreaks of elated excitement.

(e) There is an abrupt outbreak of the maddest mania, such as I have already described, either following symptoms of nervous depression, or without any presages so marked as to have attracted special notice.

(f) Apoplectiform or epileptiform attacks, puzzling the observer, occur without evident reason and are followed after a time by elated excitement, which throws light on their nature. Such attacks are of all degrees and sorts: the epileptiform seizures varying from convulsions like those of true epilepsy to spasms of one side of face, or of one arm, or even of particular muscles, and followed by greater or less degree of motor paralysis; the apoplectiform, from light to deep coma. Sometimes they are no more than a so-called giddiness or momentary faintness, with a temporary loss of speech, recurring irregularly; sometimes there is only a temporary loss of power in the lower limbs, either without the patient falling down and entirely losing consciousness, or enough to make him tumble, when his illness is pretty sure to be ascribed to his fall.

One conclusion the early as well as later symptoms of the disease, whatever form they take, plainly point to—

namely, exhaustion of the nerve-energy of the highest tracts of the brain: a weakness of its supreme organisation over a large area, shown—first, in a blunting of moral sense and fine social feelings, uneasy depression, intellectual apathy, as well as in the various incipient sensory and motor troubles; afterwards in explosive outburst of silly mania and convulsions; and, last, in a pretty nigh complete paralysis of mind and body. Whatever the cause of the disease, we have the right to expect it to be a cause of spent force—something by which somehow the most refined and sublimed vitality of the cerebral centres has been drained away.

Proceeding now to the diversities which general paralysis presents, we find the traits of the two leading varieties prefigured by the melancholic and the demented modes of onset. There is a form of the disease which has a marked melancholic complexion throughout, and there is another form of it which has a demented complexion throughout.

Melancholic General Paralysis.

In the melancholic variety the palsied mind is possessed with preposterously absurd delusions of the gloomiest hue: the patient protests that his eyesight is completely lost, at the same time that he looks quietly in the face of him whom he addresses; that he is deaf, although in the same breath he replies to doubts by reiterated assertion of his calamity; that his throat is entirely closed and he cannot swallow a morsel of food, which all the while he makes no scruple to swallow or swallows in spite of scruple; that he has no stomach or intestines and that nothing ever passes through him, notwithstanding the most positive assurance and evidence to the contrary; that his body has dwindled to a grain of sand or is otherwise strangely transformed; that he is dying or is actually dead in whole or in parts. So often and so much do the delusions relate to some transformation of the personality that the disease may have the look of a monstrous caricature of hypochondria. But they are not, as some have thought, invariably of that nature: one person protests that he has been ruined in some absurdly impossible way, having lost treasures of wealth which he never possessed; another, whom I saw from time to time, used to expatiate in placid droning complaint on the outrageous persecutions to which he was subjected, among the rest that insects as big as horses were persistently put into his food; one imagined that another patient had got hold of him in his bed and was tormenting him by causing the convulsions with which one side of his body was convulsed; another maintains that the persons about him are committing multitudinous adulteries with his wife and loudly denounces her conduct, descanting triumphantly on the action for divorce which he has brought and the hundreds of co-respondents whom he has cited; another may bemoan the extraordinary ravages which some wonderful disease is making in him, a disease such as no man ever saw or heard the like of before or will ever see or hear the like of again. These woeful plaints are apt to be made in a placid, monotonous, sometimes almost complacent way, not as if they proceeded from a corresponding underlying woe, but rather as expressions of suffering without sorrow and indignation without anger; they may even be poured out half-exultantly, as if the bigness of the affair was a sort of triumphant solace. Concurrent with such mental symptoms, which may prevail throughout the disease or for the most part of its course, are the characteristic symptoms of motor paralysis; and the decline, as in the elated variety, is to death.

The misery in melancholic general paralysis is not always so quiet and unmeaning. Where the disease is more acute, there is keener and more consistent distress, and the patient, believing something vaguely dreadful is going to be done to him, is in an agitated state of dazed fear and trepidation, or falls into a positive melancholic stupor. Although it is not usual to think of suicidal tendency in connection with general paralysis, still the possibility of it ought not then to be overlooked: I have known such a patient kill himself by severing his femoral artery with a common table-knife in the most determined manner.

Demented General Paralysis.

In the demented variety there is a quietly encroaching weakness of mind which deepens into complete stupidity, embarrassment of speech and other muscular weakness going along with it. The patient, serenely unconscious that anything is wrong with him, is dull, inert, stupid, makes mistakes and muddles in his business or apathetically neglects it, while believing that he is doing it properly, forgets on one day or at one hour what was said or done the day or hour before, leaves letters out of words or words out of sentences in writing. His infirmities may excite the anxious notice of his colleagues in business before they cause alarm at home, where his apathy of manner, his indifference to his family and domestic affairs—formerly his anxious concern—an excessive drowsiness, and an undue irritability are perhaps ascribed to worries in business and natural exhaustion. After a while, however, he startles people by grosser defects: talks freely, even to those below him, of private domestic matters, and disregards ordinary social proprieties and even common decencies of behaviour in the most quiet matter-of-course way—for example, coolly lights a cigar in the drawing-room of a lady on whom he is making a call, goes into another person's bed-room and quietly undresses there, not in the least put out when his mistake is pointed out to him, makes water in the middle of a busy street or on the carpet of a room. The present impulse meets with no restraining reflections, because of the utter dissolution of the bonds of his cerebral reflexes. With these symptoms goes sometimes a propensity to theft, not out of malice aforethought, but from a simple impulse to take and an oblivious inability to perceive any reason for refraining from taking that which is not his. The mood is usually placid, easy, good-natured, though it is not constant, being liable to be interrupted by periods of gloom and irritable temper, when he resents angrily direct contradiction or opposition; sometimes it is marked by silly and absurd suspicions of persecutions; now and then it is an inert apathy which almost reaches the depth of stupor. The course of events is from bad to worse, but not always by regular descent; indeed the patient so far gone that he seems near his end will sometimes rally in a wonderful manner, remaining comparatively well for a time, after which he has an attack of acute mania or a succession of epileptiform fits and dies. This demented form is more common in women; they do not for the most part evince such lively exaltation and energy as men, and they have quieter and less assertive delusions of grandeur conformable with their gentler natures and the quieter currents and conditions of their lives.

Mixed Forms of General Paralysis.

In the three forms of general paralysis described we should have three pretty distinct varieties if only they would stay within their respective bounds and keep up their respective characters there. But that is what they seldom do; they are apt to intermingle, and there is not a mixture of symptoms which is not to be met with at one time or another in one case or another. Common enough is an interval of depression, perhaps with occasional paroxysms of convulsive sobbing, lasting for an hour or a few hours or a day or two in the course of the elated variety; in some cases there are pretty regular changes from meaningless joy to meaningless woe, periods of depression alternating with periods of elation after the manner of so-called circular insanity; here and there a patient who is in a whining melancholy, refusing to take food and so feeble and emaciated as to seem near his end, passes quickly, as by magic transformation, into lively exaltation with delusions of grandeur, whereupon he displays a ravenous appetite and quickly recovers strength and activity.

More strange to see occasionally are exalted delusions in company with dejected delusions, an uneasy and dejected exaltation along with a placid and half-exultant discontent, the utterance of great notions being intermixed with the whining dolorous tale of such woes as that he cannot see, has no blood, no inside, and the like. There is not enough strength of fit feeling to infuse and sustain consistent notions of either sort: the weathercock of fatuous delusion, so to speak, answers not to the uncertain current of weak and wavering feeling, sometimes sticks contrary to it. As with melancholy, so it is with fatuity when it is the predominant feature. On the one hand, in a case which is running the elated course symptoms of elation will disappear and the disease sink suddenly into dementia; on the other hand, in a case beginning with symptoms of dementia and keeping that form for the main part of its course, elation may supervene and continue to the end. One thing is pretty certain always: that whether the patient be elated or depressed he is essentially more or less demented; and that it only needs the removal of the eclipsing glare in the one case, and of the eclipsing gloom in the other, to reveal the fundamental weakness of mind.

Similarly inconstant are the relations of the mental and motor symptoms. The most paradoxical thing of all is that one person may die of general paralysis of the insane without ever being insane and another die of it without ever being paralysed; in other words, there is a progressive general paralysis ending in death without any particular mental symptoms, and there is an exalted mania with weakness of mind which ends in death without bodily paralysis. Calmeil has recorded one instance of characteristically exalted delirium which continued for three years, and Bayle one which continued for six years, before there was any sign of motor trouble; and Westphal described under the name of masked general paralysis occasional cases in which the patients die with characteristic mental symptoms without any motor defects. On the other hand, Baillarger, Skae, and others have insisted that bodily symptoms may exist and go on to a fatal termination with little or no appreciable disorder of mind—at most with only some weakness of it before the end. In such cases it is probable that a closer examination might detect a much earlier loss of the finest sensibilities of mind, social and æsthetic, and some obtuseness of moral feeling. These anomalous instances after all do but maintain, throughout their exceptional course, a condition of things which is occasional and temporary in some ordinary cases — that is, the persistence of motor symptoms during a suspension of the mania, or the disappearance of them when an attack of mania supervenes.

In face of its different forms, manifold variations, and incalculable inconstancies are we entitled to say that there is such a disease as general paralysis ? What we can say is that there is a progressive degeneration of the cerebral cortex beginning in its highest and most finely organised networks and spreading by degrees to its coarser forms ; that such degeneration, although it has a wider area and goes deeper than ordinary mania for the most part, is not universal and uniform throughout the cortex, but may have different main sites and be of different degrees, thus giving rise, according to its place, area and depth, to different symptoms and varying mixtures of them ; that it is at first a functional dissolution only of the organised forms of thought-tracts, whence the coming and going of symptoms ; and that it is serious structural disorganisation at last when the disease, whatever form it has had, reaches the dead uniformity of dementia and paralysis. It is a probable surmise that from the first the disorder has a deeper strain of damage in it than ordinary insanity, seeing that it does not tend to recovery but evermore tends to dementia and death ; and a reasonable conclusion therefore that the individual has some native weakness of nerve-structure predisposing to early bankruptcy of it under the stress of exhausting causes. Were that not so, why should it not follow ordinary mania or melancholia, especially the manias which present very elated feelings and exalted delusions ? So far is general paralysis from being predisposed to by a previous attack of simple insanity, that we might venture to predicate of one who has had such an attack that, however many more attacks he may have, he will not have general paralysis.

Exaltation in other Insanities.

Inflated feelings and delusions are nowise the exclusive appanage of general paralysis. There are varieties of mania which present so exalted a strain of thought and feeling as to make it hard or impossible to say whether the disease is going to be general paralysis or not. That is sometimes notably so in the excited phase of so-called circular insanity, where the large projects, the eager and perhaps tremulous talk, and the exultant busy activity may deceive experts into the belief of an oncoming general paralysis. Perchance the sequent phase of torpid apathy is then a saving change, by cutting short the excitement before it topples over into degenerative weakness; by collapsing into the exhaustion of an opportune torpidity the over-excited brain may thus stay its waste and recover its powers. Again, in the alcoholic mania of a person having a strong hereditary predisposition to insanity the delusions are sometimes of a very elated and grotesquely extravagant kind. One patient, so suffering, who had been occupied in watering diamonds that were to grow in his garden when I saw him, affirmed that his body had been cut through with a sword and had healed again, that he had been dead and was alive again, and in exalted strain recounted the events of his past history, which he jumbled up with preposterous delusions in admirable confusion. After two or three weeks, he entirely recovered his reason, as he had done once before from a similar attack. Again, singularly elevated delusions and conduct mark acute idiopathic mania in some cases where there is a strong hereditary bias to madness; delusions which in respect of their rapid rise and grandeur seem to be the concentrated silent memories of generations of irrational thought and feeling. Lastly, the senile mania which ushers in senile dementia is prone to exhibit signal exaltation of ideas, projects and behaviour; and its likeness to general paralysis is all the greater when it is accompanied by the tremulous speech and manner of a threatening apoplexy or commencing gross disease of brain.

How can we distinguish the strained exaltation of these cases from that of real general paralysis? For the most part we miss in them the quavering note of mental weakness perceptible in it. The patient is not so facile and mobile, not so oblivious, does not exhibit the same weak and expansive good-humour, is more consistent in feeling, less loosely incoherent in manner and behaviour; the *ego* being in a better state of preservation, his gestures retain more of their normal firmness, precision, and perhaps grace; there is more of personal reserve and dignity in his movements, and he evinces more method and less silliness in his exalted mania: altogether there is more residue of restraint, less loose abandonment, in his madness. The symptoms betoken a shallower dissolution of the cortical nerve-patterns which are his thought-forms. He is possibly somewhat sarcastic, self-assertive, imperious; and whenever that is the case, one may entertain a doubt whether his disease is general paralysis, or suspect, if it be, that he will so far recover as to have a suspension of it. The conclusion of the whole matter is that in general paralyis we have the mania and melancholia of ordinary insanities superposed on the basis of a deeper degeneration of structure and deriving their character of silly extravagance from that fundamental weakness.

Causes.

What are the causes of general paralysis? It has already been inferred that they must be of an exhausting nature; and it may be assumed that there is a constitutional frailty of the structure of the cerebral cortex whereby, when disordered, it is liable to run into such rapid degeneracy. Were there not something exceptional, why should simple manias not go on to dementia and paralysis?

The favourite temperament is, I think, that of the man who puts passionate feeling and unreserved energy into the work which he is sanguine to undertake and ardent to accomplish; who is prone to keep his feeling as well as intellect on the stretch, being eager in pursuit and in possession too;[1] who is liable therefore to impatient worries when affairs do not run smoothly and to bursts of passing passion when he encounters a check; and who, social, genial, expansive, and pleased to please, eats, drinks, and enjoys himself in a similar whole and ardent way; who, in fact, using up his reserves, pursues his life-voyage with all sails full set. It might be said perhaps of such a nature that the organic life pours itself too freely into the life of relation, so that when exhaustion comes the capital of vital energy is spent; its misfortune being to have a sympathetic nervous system in such free communion with the brain that there is no saving power to shut off feeling from thought. However that be, in one way or another he keeps up a tension and activity of the cerebral structure and circulation, without periodic relaxations, which passes at last into a quasi-inflammatory hyperæmia of its cortex—that is, into the turgid state of vasomotor dilatation which is characterized by turgid emotion, turgid notions, and turgid actions. It may happen that the immediate occasion of the outbreak is a moral shock of some kind which, coming on the top of the habitual overstrain of powers, precipitates the catastrophe and perhaps gets the whole credit of it. In a structure so strained and weakened any cause, moral or physical, might easily start the degenerative process.

Two facts in regard to causation stand out unquestioned: that the disease occurs during the season of fullest mental and bodily activity, seldom before thirty or much after fifty years of age; and that women are much less liable to it than men, the women most liable being of the lowest and loosest classes in large towns. Were it right to ascribe it to any single cause, I should fix on sexual excess, and still hold the opinion despite the dissent of those inquirers who find no evidence of such excess. It is natural for one not to find who looks not, or knows not how to look. Many

---

[1] "Mad in pursuit and in possession too;
Had, having, and in quest to have, extreme."

medical men, not suspecting a pretty frequent cause of nervous troubles that are apt to be attributed to other than their main cause, might think it an outrage to hint the most delicate inquiry concerning rites which, like a vast number of non-medical persons, they may innocently suppose cannot be abused so long as there is an appetite for them and they are licensed by marriage. But licensed is not anywise less hurtful physiologically than unlicensed exhaustion, nor does the blessing of the Church avail to multiply manly vigour.

It will suffice to advert briefly to certain considerations of which due account is seldom taken. Sexual excess, like other excess, is relative, the quantity of indulgence which would not hurt one person or at one age being pernicious to another person or at another age. And not the quantity only but the quality counts; for there is much difference between the dull, stale, satiating pastime of the sleepy bed, mechanically performed and mechanically enjoyed, and the eager, ardent desire, the acute orgasm, the spasmodic intensity and the exhaustive abandonment of other circumstances and of special temperaments. Illicit relations provoke more passionate indulgence, since custom stales and stolen pleasures are sweet; and I have known general paralytics, married as well as unmarried, whose secret illicit amours, quite unsuspected until disclosed by the calamity, were thus pathologically avenged. In this connection I might perhaps cite in evidence the vascular streaks and spots due to dilatations and minute ruptures, which are directly caused in some men, after middle age especially, by the passionate strain of laboured performance, and which are particularly noticeable in some general paralytics. If not the effects of sexual overstrain, they are evidence of a delicacy and easy dilatability of the small arteries, which may have a special interest in relation to the quasi-inflammatory hyperæmia of the convolutions prevailing at the beginning of the disease.

The tendency of the general paralytic temperament is to spend itself in all ways. Now as the organism is a complex mechanism which, charged by rest and nutrition, discharges its energy in its several sensory, emotional, intellectual, motor and trophic tracks of function, it is plain that when it spends its forces excessively in one way it has not them available for expenditure in other ways, and that when it spends them excessively in all ways it necessarily suffers a weakening which, functional only at first, passes into organic deterioration if a stop be not put to the debilitating drain. Is there any single act occupying so short a time which is so expensive a strain and drain as the sexual act? Representing at its best a unique combination of intense and special sensory, emotional, motor and secretory energies, it is a transporting discharge of them which is of the essence of the whole being; for as the seminal germ represents in its substance every part of the parent organism, so its discharge during the transport of the sexual orgasm may represent every energy of individual character, mental and bodily. How manifestly hurtful then must too frequent repetitions of it be! It is not the immediate and temporary exhaustion only of which account must be taken, but also the more distant and lasting effect of continued excess—the irritable weakness of nerve-element, shown by extreme susceptibility, quick irascibility, hysterical emotion, loss of intellectual grasp, self-confidence, and silent strength of self-control, which causes the ordinary impressions of life to be extraordinary provocations and its ordinary business an extraordinary strain and burden.

If these things be so, there is good reason why men are attacked by the disease at their best age and why women are much less liable to it. Women are not subject to the same strains and pains of thought and feeling which men undergo, nor do they suffer so much as men from the excesses of love or lust, even when they are as much addicted to them. The argument that sexual excess cannot be a cause because prostitutes do not become paralytics, not as single victims but in troops, argues but a poor judgment in him who uses it.[1] Prostitutes would be in a

[1] M. Trélat of Paris has recorded the opinion that of the young women suffering from general paralysis a large proportion were prostitutes, and it seems to be pretty certain that the public asylums in England which contain

bad case did they not become the mere mechanical agents of a joyless commerce which, but for local wear and tear, they might go on practising to the edge of doom without serious prejudice to their health, could they live so long. If, like members of other trades and professions, they begin by putting heart into their work, they soon, like them, learn the wiser economy of suspending feeling and performing their functions automatically; indeed, use-worn sensibility will do that for them without conscious co-operation on their part. For that reason it is, I think, that lewd women who are not professional prostitutes are more prone to break down in general paralysis; women who, soliciting and pursuing sensuality as a pleasure, not as a trade, make lust their business, not their business lust. It is certainly a rare thing to meet with an instance of the disease in a lady, and in that rare event it might be worth inquiry whether the victim had lived a gentlewoman's life.

Some authors set down alcoholic intemperance, others syphilis, as the principal cause. Were either of these ills sufficient of itself, there would undoubtedly be many more general paralytics in the world than there are. Frequent and indisputable is the occurrence of the disease in sober men; not a physician of experience but could tell of such cases; so that when it follows drinking it must do so either independently, or with dependence on it only as an auxiliary.[1] *Delirium tremens,* alcoholic mania and dementia are the normal insanities of habitual drunkenness; and neither alcoholic mania, which is usually an acute mania of persecution, has the characteristics of the mania, nor alcoholic dementia, which is non-paralytic, the characteristics of the

---

most such sufferers are those which are so placed as to receive the lowest and most dissipated classes of large towns. Other contributory excesses are no doubt probable in such cases.

[1] Total abstainers, virtuous in preaching against a vice they have no mind to, are sometimes extremely intemperate in sexual indulgence. Human nature being what it is, and what it is likely for a long time to be, seeing that it requires some 10,000 years to make one 10,000th part of its progress, it is a rule of pretty wide application that impassioned souls and noble spirits have their private passions and intemperances.

dementia, of general paralysis. Still the exceeding exaltation of the acute mania excited by alcoholic excess in a person who has a strong hereditary predisposition to insanity, so like general paralysis sometimes as to be mistaken for it, might be cited to support the opinion that its more chronic action will help to produce the degenerative changes of that disease. In that case it is probable that a little liquor has been taken habitually many times a day in the form of a social glass or "pick-me-up," rather than much at a time; either by way of spur to overtasked energies, or in pursuance of a habit of work and pleasure at an artificial strain of excitement.

The obvious resemblance between the character and course of the symptoms of general paralysis and those of ordinary drunkenness has not failed to attract notice. Compress the former within the brief compass of a few hours, or stretch the latter out to a length of two or three years, and the likeness would be all the more evident. What do we behold? At the beginning of intoxication, elated excitement, expansive geniality, elevated notions, sanguine schemes, bragging talk, and a vast conceit of self; then, as the wave of excitement is getting spent and the association of nerve-plexuses loosened, rambling notions, incoherent talk, embarrassed speech, and staggering gait; lastly, as the highest plexuses are paralysed, blunted sensibility, deepening stupidity, and inability to walk or talk. The alcohol manifestly produces in the cerebral cortex a swift sequence of temporary changes similar in character to those wrought slowly and permanently in general paralysis; it may well therefore sometimes play a part in the causation of it.

That syphilis has any special power to cause general paralysis is a conjecture based on the undoubted fact that many general paralytics have sometime had syphilis. It could hardly be otherwise seeing how many persons contract syphilis. What it would be proper to have explained is how it comes to pass that syphilis causes general paralysis in one out of a multitude and not in the large remainder. Now and then we certainly meet with cases of syphilitic dementia so like its dementia as to be indistinguishable from it; the true diagnosis then being at best a guess based on a previous history of syphilitic infection and the happy results of antisyphilitic treatment. In such case it may be supposed that the syphilitic infiltration, being diffused through the cortex, has caused a widespread degeneration of it very like that which prevails in demented general paralysis; not otherwise than as happens in the diffused damage of the dementias of lead-poisoning and pellagra, both which might sometimes be mistaken for that of general paralysis. When the same morbid changes in the cerebral cortex have been brought about, albeit by different causes, it would be ridiculous to expect the symptoms to be different.

The notes of syphilitic dementia, so far as they are distinguishable, are these: a previous history of severe headaches, especially severe in the night, of acute sleeplessness, of intense nervous susceptibility; delusions of a weak-minded, muddle-headed and incoherent sort, seldom of grandeur and ambition; an absence of the special motor symptoms in lips, tongue, face, and of the placid mental exaltation which gives its characteristic complexion to general paralysis; definite local paralyses, especially strabismus and ptosis, which are rare in general paralysis—in fact, any motor failure that is more a localized paralysis than a general ataxic feebleness; the onset often sudden, with irregular quasi-apoplectic or quasi-epileptic seizures without loss of consciousness; the course of the disease more, sometimes singularly, irregular and uncertain; the prognosis not absolutely bad. The one hope of recovery for the patient in a doubtful case is that the disease may be syphilitic; there is just a chance then that it may yield to specific treatment. But it is a small chance; for when the morbid condition of brain producing such symptoms has been brought about, the effect is likely to continue and increase of itself after the original cause has ceased. Revolutions go on, gaining speed as they go, when those who rashly make them would have them slacken and stop.

Here and there the exalted symptoms of general paralysis supervene on locomotor ataxy. The sequence is not common nor, when it occurs, necessarily one of cause and effect. In locomotor ataxy the mind is for the most part clear to the last; if symptoms of mental disorder show themselves, they are either those of a progressive dementia, or those of extreme irritability, depression, morbid suspicions, querulous complaint, and even delusions of persecution. I remember one case in which the characteristic exaltation and delusions of general paralysis followed the usual symptoms of locomotor ataxy; and the remarkable thing is that, although that occurred twenty years ago, the patient is still alive, but demented, subject to paroxysms of exalted excitement from time to time, and with the lower half of his body completely paralysed. Certainly the symptoms of locomotor ataxy and disseminated sclerosis may look like general paralysis, especially in the early stages: why not, if their degenerative changes threaten or attack the cerebral cortex?

Baillarger has recorded some cases in which he believed that erysipelas of the face was the direct cause of general paralysis: an interesting causation, if real, in relation to the hyperæmic state of the convolutions in the first stage of the disease. It was the conclusion of his admirable study—and no better conclusion has since been formulated—that cerebral congestions played the most efficient part in its causation; which must be sought therefore in such causes of frequent cerebral congestion as alcoholic and venereal excesses, the mental strains of a plethoric constitution, the suppression of bleeding piles, injuries of the head, and the like. I have certainly known the disease follow directly the removal of old bleeding piles in a man of middle age who had lived an active life of business and sensuality.

So much concerning the causation of general paralysis. The different opinions entertained as to its causes, and the absence of any assignable cause in some cases, are proof that the chief determinant lies not outside but inside the individual—in the build of his nervous constitution. Moreover, seeing that the usually assigned causes continually act on multitudes of persons without ever making them general paralytic, they must perforce meet with secret co-efficients in the natures of those in whom they do produce so rapid and fatal a degeneration of nerve-structure. There is no evidence that an inherited predisposition to insanity plays any special part in the production of the disease; on the whole, general paralytics seem not often to have insane ancestors, and are perhaps less likely than other insane persons to have insane progeny. The particular ancestral temperament predisposing to it seems rather to be that which is prone to end in apoplexy.

The pathological process at the bottom of incipient general paralysis I take to be an enkindling of organic energies translating itself into exuberantly buoyant feeling and its congenial ideas, and, as co-effect or consequence, a suspension or destruction of the finest functional forms of the cortical network. Thrilled with an inflamed sense of self, the individual naturally and necessarily sees the world in the colour of his feeling and in the forms of his notions — proudly and triumphantly from a standpoint of exultant strength and freedom; just as one who is cast in timid mould cannot choose but see it in formidable shape and aspect, and everybody see it according to the mould in which he is cast. As the *ego* rises in feeling of power and confidence the *non-ego* sinks in might and awe; as the *ego* sinks in feeling the *non-ego* rises in power and authority. Here we might properly call to mind and reflect on the physiological analogues—like in kind though less in degree—of the pathological state. Consider, for example, the natural egotism and almost ludicrous conceit of young children before experience has distributed overflowing organic energy into various channels of activity and its steady discipline has organised controlling forms or habits of thought and will: so full of self are they, and so naturally prone to be boastful, braggarts, arrogant, cruel, deceitful, and ready liars, that it is curious to think what they would be if they were left entirely untaught and undisciplined. Consider, again, the inflated feeling, the pert conceit, and the absorbing sense of self which accompany pubescence, when a new and large supply is added to organic feeling from the new and special store of reproductive energy; an exuberance not to be tamed until the travail of transition is over, and sobering experience, weaving its hard web of disenchanting reason into the structure of the mental organisation, has re-formed the world in sober hues and proportions. Consider, once more, the flaming feelings, the tumid notions, the enchanting imaginations, the hyperbolic language of love; for there is nothing in the world more like the pathological exaltation of general paralysis than its sexually thrilled physiological state. Lastly, might be cited the wonderful things done in happy dreams, when, the external world being shut out and the life of relation suspended, a pleasant organic feeling runs riot in the creations which it inspires and illusively overestimates. Are not such physiological states suited to teach the same lesson which the exuberant feelings and notions of general paralysis teach in larger and coarser type?

In the main it is a lesson of the intimate participation of the organic life in the life of relation; a lesson, therefore, of the important part played in the pathology of general paralysis by the sympathetic nervous system with its vasomotor distributions throughout the entire visceral system. In no case is the sympathetic so separate from the cerebro-spinal system as it was formerly believed to be; essentially it appears to be the splanchnic distribution of the cerebro-spinal system; and at any rate the sympathy between the two systems differs in different temperaments, being much less marked in some than in others. Reflect how emotion instantly blanches the face, deranges the secretions, paralyses the muscles in one person and not in another; how the whole organic life is so agitated by passion in the one that his heart beats rapidly, he cannot eat a morsel of food, he is sleepless all night, while the other feels so little ill effects from a like passion that his pulse hardly varies in stroke, his appetite is not hurt, he does not lose a wink of sleep; how one person might drop down dead from fear, his heart paralysed by the shock as suddenly as by a stroke of lightning, when the effect on another might be to make him gird up his energies to confront the menace; how completely one is disabled from sexual congress by the least untoward impression on sense or feeling, to which another would be entirely insensible; how he who suffers from the nervous headache called *migraine* feels inwardly a sort of tremulous visceral tenderness and sinking, and an accompanying weakening or dissolution of self-confidence and will, which are quite unknown to those who never have such headaches. Brace up the sympathetic system of the organically sensitive person by good health or good news or good wine, and he is another being, brisk, confident and energetic. It is impossible to calculate the advantage in the rough work of a rude world which the comparatively insensitive person, whose pulse beats quietly while he is in a passion, has over him who, being sensitive and having quick and easy conduction between the agitations of his organic life and his life of relation, suffers many things and cannot suffer a moral jar or a physical trouble without its vibrating painfully through his entire system. The former is not incapacitated by anxieties at the time nor exhausted afterwards, it is not so easy for him to spend himself in excesses, and he might be supposed to be less likely to break down in general paralysis.

Thus much concerning general paralysis, a disease which exhibits the extremest oppositions of optimism and pessimism. Certainly, if all people on earth were general paralytics, the great majority of them would entertain extravagantly optimistic views of life, but there would still be a small remnant who entertained extravagantly pessimistic views of it: on the one side there would be so many who, fooled by an optimistic frenzy, presented a picture of optimism gone mad, and on the other side so many who, crushed down by a melancholy frenzy, presented a mad caricature of pessimism. Naturally too the former would disdain with jubilant scorn the views of the latter as morbid and cowardly. In both cases, however, alike beneath the glory of the one and the gloom of the other, there would be discernible the same fundamental basis of mental weakness. Less extreme differences of natural temperament, optimistic and pessimistic, no less due to molecular causes, are they of any more validity in the eternal order of things? The vanity of mortal things was a conclusion reached alike by Solomon, the wisest of men, who had traversed all the heights of human joy, and by Job, the most afflicted of men, who had sounded all the depths of human sorrow.

CHAPTER V

EPILEPTIC INSANITY

UNDER this name I include the mental derangements which, occurring in connection with epilepsy, appear to have to it relations either of causation or of kinship. Most distinctive and best known is so-called epileptic mania, which differs chiefly from ordinary mania by the extremity of its blind fury and reckless violence. During the paroxysms of frenzy the patient, little conscious or misconscious of his surroundings, struggles and fights against the dangers by which he believes, oftentimes vividly missees, himself surrounded and threatened; he is prone to make the abruptest and ugliest rushes from time to time, and, when stopped in his headlong fury, yells, shouts, roars, kicks, strikes and fights frantically. When the storm is spent he remembers not at all, or only hazily, what he was and did in it. The mania may be short, lasting only for an hour or a few hours, but is liable to recur, or it may continue for days with only partial abatements. As the attack comes on, so it goes off, pretty suddenly, leaving the mind sunk in hebetude or partial stupor, slow of comprehension, dull and sullen in feeling, and sluggish and confused in memory; a state out of which he comes gradually to himself, either to plunge soon into new fury or to remain sane for months or longer before he has another bout. The recurrent outbreaks are usually determined by the recurrent fits which they follow; and these befall, we cannot say why or when, at widely different intervals in different cases—at long intervals, every month, every fortnight, or oftener. The longer the sane interval after an attack of mania the longer, as a rule, is the next insane attack.

Considering the great and general commotion of mind in epileptic mania, its tumultuous disorder which might seem to preclude any show of method, it is a surprise to observe the amount of coherence which may be evinced in speech, to receive perchance pretty direct answers to questions in the midst of it, and to perceive that the patient partly apprehends the circumstances, though he misconstrues their purport. Stormy and destructive as his action is, he does not rage quite aimlessly, but makes more or less determinate, though senseless, attacks on persons and things; for example, he will maliciously watch his opportunity and, seizing the basin, fling it violently in the face of the attendant who is endeavouring to feed him out of it. Another feature which it is curious to see in some cases is that in the midst of his fury he is seized with a localized convulsion of will and suddenly betakes himself to some odd action which he repeats automatically with spasmodic frenzy for a short time—throws himself on his knees, for example, and furiously gnaws the floor or the furniture, or has a spell of violent jumping up and down repeatedly, like a dancing doll —and then perhaps reverts to his furious conduct with renewed violence.

The general acts of violence are without doubt the reflex quasi-convulsive outcomes of vivid and confused hallucinations and delusions: delusions of menace and terror springing out of the surly, irritable, suspicion-charged mood; vivid hallucinations of spectres, wild beasts, assassins, blood-red flames or luminous halos before the eyes, sulphurous, stifling smells in the nostrils, loud roaring sounds or imperative voices in the ears: a hideous nightmare of horror, to which he is all the more prone perhaps because epileptics are prone to horrible dreams and nightmares. In the tangled welter and confusion of the cerebral currents not only are unreal objects present to sense but any real object which presents itself is invested with a strange and unreal character; lifeless objects seem to threaten his life, and the compassionate face of a friend becomes the menacing face of a foe. The most innocent impression on sense, a word, a smile, a look, being madly misconstrued, suffices, like a lightning-conductor, to determine the incidence of a discharge of desperate violence: surcharged with a sullen fury of suspicion, he kills a child of whom he is very fond because it then chances to meet him and ask a simple question, or kills his wife, or father, or mother because of some casual remark or a kindly act of natural attention. Like a mad dog, he missees and, misseeing, attacks a friend as a foe; for it is not to the real persons and things around him but to the unreal surroundings created by his mental anarchy that his frantic behaviour answers. Another feature of the epileptic homicide is the superfluity of destructive violence often used; the victim being not only killed but perhaps desperately battered or mutilated, or one person after another who happens to present himself at the time being attacked with fatal fury.

Such is the most common and characteristic form of epileptic mania: that which the name at once calls up in mind and which renders its victim the most dangerous of lunatics. But epileptic mania is not invariably so violent; sometimes it is of a subacute character, more busy than wild, with voluble and incoherent talk, agitated and restless movements, and perhaps with singular exaltation of feelings and ideas. Then the patient is prone to entertain very elevated notions of himself; and if he is addicted to much reading of the Bible, as epileptics sometimes are, he may develop the delusion that he is an inspired personage and has a divine gift of interpreting Scripture or a divine mission to reform or redeem the world. As he alone in the world is then possessed of the light of inspiration, while all the rest of mankind are enveloped in fogs of error, he will not shrink from fulfilling his mission by means that may be startling to ordinary intelligence and traditional modes of action.

What relation has epileptic mania to the ordinary epileptic fit ? (*a*) Most often it follows a fit or a succession of fits; and this it does sometimes when the fit, having been one of minor epilepsy, has passed unnoticed. The usual order of events is for the convulsions to be followed by a period of stupor, the so-called epileptic coma, of varying length from a quarter of an hour to several hours, after which the mania bursts out. (*b*) The mania precedes the convulsive explosion now and then, ending in or ended by it. This also has been observed occasionally: that fits of mental disorder, having the distinctive characters of epileptic frenzy, occur at intervals for months or even years and are then superseded by regular epileptic fits—the convulsive mental by the convulsive motor explosion. (*c*) Now and then instances are met with in which an attack of mania appears to take the place of an attack of convulsions, the mania being a sort of vicarious epilepsy. A patient subject to epileptic fits at irregular intervals has not his customary fit but in its stead a sudden and impulsive fit of frenzy in which, starting up abruptly, he jumps violently up and down or rushes furiously forward and strikes blindly about him. In that case some argue that an unnoticed attack of the *petit mal* in one or other of its various forms has preceded the outbreak of frenzy and is all the explanation needed. Whether it has or has not is of no great moment, seeing that the *petit mal* is not something definite, but a name covering a variety of transient seizures, differing in degree and character, which themselves stand in need of definition and explanation. It is not to be doubted that medical science would advance rapidly if it were as useful as it is hurtful to its progress to ascribe something requiring explanation to a learned name given to something else, not itself defined, and thereafter to treat the name as an explanation.

Is there any abrupt, abnormal, obscure and transitory nervous disorder that might not be put down to incomplete epilepsy? A passing vertigo, a momentary eclipse of consciousness, a transient pallor or spasm, a strangely odd sensation anywhere coming and going quickly, a startling smell with no outward cause of it, or an imperative voice heard where no voice is, a passing shadow or cloud before the eyes, much more a vivid visual hallucination, an aphasic halt in conversation or the utterance of a few irrelevant words, a sudden dreamlike presentation of some ideal scene or of a new actual scene as if it were a reminiscence, an abrupt access of inexplicable distraction of self and urgent suicidal impulse,—all these and I know not how many more symptoms might be deemed of an epileptic nature and called minor epilepsies. From them at any rate it is possible to pass through every grade of allied seizure in ascending scale of disorder to regular epilepsy. One may wonder perhaps that no one has yet described as epileptic the strange incoherences of thought, the fragmentary memories, the abrupt hallucination of a spoken word, and the phantasmagoria of vision which often occur in the most unaccountable way immediately before sleep; all the more since in alcoholic and epileptic mania the phantasms become vivid hallucinations. The varieties of the so-called *aura* going before the complete attack are essentially so many minor epilepsies which do not stop there but go on to the consummation in convulsions. As in the complex and specialized structure of the cerebral cortex the tendency to nervous explosion, which is the note of the epileptic temperament, may be carried into either general or limited effect, so the local discharges of groups of cells at different spots must, according to seat and area, needs occasion all sorts of irregular sensory, motor, ideational, and trophic explosions, which might be called incomplete epilepsies.

In this relation it is necessary to take notice of the strange and anomalous states of consciousness which are observed in epileptics. During an attack of the *petit mal*, when consciousness seems to be suspended for a few moments, a person will sometimes go on with the mechanical work which he was doing at the instant of his seizure; a tailor continuing to stitch, a musician to play his instrument, a pedestrian to walk. Why not, seeing how much automatic work the body does habitually when consciousness is engrossed in some act of reflection? But it is important to apprehend that such a state of suspended consciousness and mental automatism in connection with epilepsy is not always momentary; it may be prolonged through a considerable period of time and a methodical sequence of acts. Then the sufferer, who seems to lookers-on to be conscious, although perhaps so dazed and dreamy that he is suspected of being drunk, may wander home or elsewhere in a mazed mechanical way, perhaps take up and carry off on the way something which does not belong to him, or go through some other train of coherent action which looks deliberate; he is very much like a somnambulist, for he is all the while unconscious of his normal relations, and oblivious, when he comes to his true self, of what he did in his trance—may find himself somewhere without the least remembrance how he got there.

Now this kind of acted dream is either of such an everyday character and evinces so much coherent sequence of events that those who merely take a cursory look at the person fail to observe his abnormal state; or it is odd and ridiculous, perhaps even dangerous. Is he altogether or always unconscious of what he does? Or is it not that consciousness is enthralled rather than abolished, so that while it is bound to the train of strange doings it is thereby suspended in relation to the functions of normal life? Certainly he is sometimes so far conscious of himself and his surroundings that, while doing foolish things, he knows what he is doing, but feels impelled, in spite of himself, to do them. Moreover, he is not always entirely oblivious of what has happened, when he comes to himself, for he can sometimes so far recall the circumstances bit by bit as to obtain a hazy and confused remembrance of them. It all depends, I imagine, on the degree of the thraldom of consciousness whether he remembers at all or how much he remembers: the more complete that is, the less he remembers of his strange self when he comes to his true self. But an interesting thing is that each recurring attack is an excellent memory of every former attack; for he has the same feelings, thinks the same thoughts, does the same sorts of deeds, without the least consciousness how well he is remembering; not otherwise than as in some cases, before the epileptic fit, the same idea, the same reminiscence, the same hallucination invariably recurs and ushers it in, or as one epileptic fit is usually a pretty exact memory of a previous one. The same order of thoughts, feelings and acts on each occasion necessarily betokens the same definite process of cerebral disorder, beginning, proceeding, and ending in the same way: the epileptic mental just as uniform a process as the epileptic bodily fit.

Is it possible for an epileptic, while in the above-described state of abnormal consciousness and mental automatism, ever to exhibit so much plan and method of performance as to make his deed, when it is homicide, look like deliberate murder? Certainly the features of epileptic homicide have sometimes so cold, calculated, and ferocious a look that, on the face of them, they might denote deliberate plan and execution. But there is as much evidence of design in the doings of the somnambulist whom nobody accuses of going deliberately to work; and it is the just conclusion, not of analogy only but of observation, that a person may plan and perform, while in the inconscient epileptic state, what he does not remember when he comes to himself and what his sound self would never dream of doing. It will obviously be difficult to say positively of a particular case that it was pure mental automatism, because exact observation is pretty sure to be wanting; and all the more difficult because there is no actual dividing line between the extraordinary and some ordinary mental states. Consider, for example, the abrupt and dangerous transformation of personality, the thoroughly distempered mood of acrid and sullen feeling, which frequently precedes or follows an epileptic fit, prelude or after-clap of its cerebral commotion, and more often follows an incomplete than a complete attack. Superficially the mood has all the look of morose temper, surly suspicion, crabbed irritability and violent passion; but it may really denote a strange anguish and intolerable unrest urging or driving the patient to unburden himself of its load at any cost, or it may mean a distracting impotence, indescribably distressing, to collect his ideas, to feel his being, to realise himself, or it may cover an awful broil of horror and suspicion. It is out of such sullen ferment of acrid emotion that violent and destructive outbreaks against persons or things either precipitate themselves abruptly or take the slower sequence of premeditated and planned effect. Then a simple remark or a friendly joke which would have been received amiably in health may be vindictively brooded over as an insult or provoke a startling outburst of fury. The asylum attendant who knows his business takes good care to leave such a patient alone or to appease him with a soothing word of flattery, which has sometimes a wonderful effect. Although the epileptic may know what he does when he does homicide, it is still not himself but a transformed self who knows and does it; a being incapable of the sane feelings and thoughts of his natural self, capable only of the insane feelings and thoughts of his morbid self.

It looks as if the mental atmosphere of sullen gloom and suspicion, or, speaking more correctly, the nervous commotion at the bottom of such mood, must discharge itself by an explosion of some kind, as the electric charge of the atmosphere must discharge itself by a thunderstorm: either (*a*) by the epileptic fits; or (*b*) by an epileptic mania; or (*c*) by a convulsive and irresistible impulse to violence, perhaps homicidal. It is pretty certain in that case that the homicidal deed, like the epileptic fit or mania, is often preceded or accompanied by a vivid hallucination of sight or hearing which determines its incidence, for its victim is not seldom one whom the patient, when himself, has liked and looked on as his good friend. In the fits, in the mania, in the hallucination, and in the homicide we discern the same epileptic note — the note of convulsive rapture of disordered energy.

Besides this epileptic state of sullen, acrid and suspicious feeling there are other abrupt changes of feeling that go before the fits in different cases: in one case we see great dulness of feeling, sluggishness of thought, loss of memory and much mental torpor; in another an abnormal gaiety, a singular self-sufficiency and self-conceit, and an unusual loquacity which run on almost to maniacal excitement; a third assumes a cringing and fawning manner, perhaps thrusting his face close to the face of the person whom he speaks to as if he had something confidential to communicate, and uses a style of obsequious address unlike what is natural to him. The changes all go to show how complete and involuntary is the unconscious transformation of the personality, and how unjust as well as unscientific it is to regard acts done in them or within the shadow of them as the expression of the true self. Insecurely stands the *ego* which stands within the precincts of epilepsy.

The behaviour, after the event, of an epileptic who has done homicide in the abnormal mental state is of medico-legal importance, since it may be cited to prove that he did or did not know what he was doing at the time and to settle that he ought or ought not to be hanged for his epileptic exploit. How far does he remember what he felt, thought, and did? In some cases there is every reason to believe that he is so rapt from himself in the transport of his fury that when he comes to himself he remembers nothing; he is simply amazed and confounded when he realises what not he but his madness has done. The alienation of self was so complete that the normal self has no real memory of what happened, no sense of responsibility for it, cannot own it: the convulsive rapture being no more a part of his mind's function as mind than a convulsion of the body is part of its functions, there is complete oblivion of it by the whole and sound mind. In other cases there is no such blank of oblivion: stupefied and dazed immediately after the paroxysm is past, he recollects bit by bit, partially and indistinctly, what he has done, just as a person recalls by degrees the events of an almost forgotten dream; the process of labouring recollection being suggestively helped by the circumstances of the catastrophe when he comes to perceive and realise them. So dazed is he at first, however, and so dreamlike does the whole business seem, that he may sit or lie down, even go to sleep, by the side of his victim, or stolidly confess to the first comer what he has done, or wander away in a stupid, aimless way, urged by a vague instinct to escape. When he is interrogated closely as to the motive which actuated the homicide he can give no sensible explanation: because of his partial and confused recollection he perhaps tells such a lame and inconsistent story that he is suspected of feigning to forget and of playing the imbecile; or he can say no more than that a cloud came over him, or that something rose in his head, like a mist, whereupon he lost his senses and knew not what he did; or if, being a person of dull intelligence and low cunning, addicted to lying for lying's sake, he has a dreamlike confused memory of what he thought and felt at the time, he may either deny the plainly undeniable deed altogether, or may conceal the insane motive springing from hallucination or delusion which actuated him, fearing to confess it and the crime, and invent what he thinks a less guilty and more clever story, hoping thereby to exculpate himself. He unluckily recollects enough of the motive to make him solicitous to dissociate himself from it; thus out of a stupid insincerity and foolish cunning manufactures false evidence which may be used afterwards to prove that he knew what he was doing and knew that he was doing what was wrong. It is not unlikely then, when he is put on his trial for murder, that the stupid turnings and windings of a dazed intellect, the characteristic ferocity of the epileptic crime, and the unconcern shown after it may be pounced upon and denounced as shocking evidence of cold-blooded brutality and plain proof of legal responsibility.

Having said enough of acute epileptic mania and of the anomalous states of epileptic consciousness out of which anomalous acts emerge, it remains now only to deal briefly with chronic epileptic insanity. Although the acute attacks, when they first occur, usually disappear in a short time, recurring only with the recurring fits, yet their tendency is to produce, sooner or later, a chronic mental disorder which lasts through the intervals between them. Then the patient is sometimes intolerably irritable, suspicious, quarrelsome, full of querulous complaints of insults, wrongs and ill-usage; complaints which are concocted and formulated with such a circumstantiality and show of truth as almost to deceive and dupe those who know his mendacious character and their injustice. Always with these persons it is others who are to blame and they who are the innocent sufferers; to hear them talk, one might think them the most affectionate of husbands, the most devoted of parents, whose self-sacrifices were requited with cruel ingratitudes and wrongs; the offences springing from their inward state of ill-humour and hypochondriacal distress they impute to the ill-will of their attendants, on whom they make treacherous and violent assaults; they cannot realise that they give any provocation even when they are the aggressors, and put down to persecution every thwarting of their inclinations, every opposition to their unreasonable doings, every uneasiness which they suffer. Ignoring their malady and its consequences, they peremptorily demand their release from all restraint. It is curious to see how much display of religious sentiment and exaggerated devotion they mix with their deceit, lying, treachery, and monstrous egotism, and how unoffended their piety is by the habitual self-abuse which they sometimes practise. They are made thorough moral degenerates by the ravages of their disease; at the same time they exemplify a temper and disposition of mind which, in less extreme degree, is met with pretty often in the world, and of whose fierce egotism and lacking altruism a bad mental organisation is the explanation, perhaps the excuse.[1]

The abiding insanity of epilepsy is not always of this acrid and irritable sort, it is sometimes marked by good-humour and exaltation. An excessive vanity with corresponding exalted delusions is then a frequent and striking

---

[1] A milder phase of it has been described previously as one variety of the insane temperament, and an insaner phase as a variety of mania of persecution.

feature, and it is curious to note how often the delusions are of a religious character. During certain phases of his malady the patient is much addicted to reading his Bible and prone to develop a delusion that he is some great personage, perhaps a god or Christ, or that he has received the Holy Ghost, or that he is a direct channel of divine inspiration in some other special way. He may see vivid visions or dream vivid dreams during the epileptic stupor or trance; the memories of which, if they vanish after the fits are past, or the hallucinations of them, if they still continue to vibrate in his mind throughout the quiet intervals, are well calculated to strengthen and uphold his notion of a divine mission. Therefore it is that even the good-humoured epileptic is liable to be an uncertain and dangerous creature; instigated by an overpowering hallucination, he may explode in destructive violence without notice. A patient of this class, mentioned by Dagonet, saw angels whose voices commanded him to commit homicide and he, obeying their commands, nearly killed a companion who was lying near him; and some years ago a labourer in the Chatham dockyard who had once been confined in an asylum on account of epilepsy and mental derangement, suddenly and without the least provocation split open with an adze the skull of a labourer who was working near him; his reason being that a little while before he had received the Holy Ghost, which had come to him as a bright light, his own eyes having been taken out and balls of fire put in their places. Why a man should do murder because the Holy Ghost has entered into him does not clearly appear, but there can be no question that patients thus impregnated are liable to give unexpected proof of their high-mightiness in a startling way.

The ultimate effect of the continuance of mental disorder is a gradual weakening of mind with great loss of memory —a state of epileptic dementia, which differs from the dementia of ordinary insanity only in being more accompanied by hallucinations, more prone to be interrupted by outbreaks of excitement and violence, and more dangerous because of the evil conjunction of hallucinations and excitement. As the mind is sooner impaired by the incomplete attacks of the so-called *petit mal* than by the full explosions of epileptic convulsions, it is all the more strange to call the former by a name which might imply that it was the lesser evil.

Casting a retrospective glance over the features of epileptic insanity, we perceive that its most distinctive notes are the convulsive rapture of the frenzy, with the subsequent oblivion, partial or complete, of the events of it; the extremities of its explosive violence, whereby so much more than the necessary destructive energy is used; the vivid hallucinations of sense, which are calculated to instigate deeds of violence or to lead to beliefs of supernatural experience; the acrid perturbation of feeling in some, and the singular exaltation of feeling in other cases; the periodical outbreaks and exacerbations. In these features we see morbid exaggerations of the natural qualities of the epileptic temperament, at any rate of the principal variety of it. Transports of exaltation rising up to states of ecstasy, frantic enthusiasm and intrepid energy, vivid imaginations translating themselves into hallucinations, inflamed conceit with alternations of melancholy self-distrust, —what are these but the factors and characteristics of the inspired prophet who, being epileptic, used once to be thought to have a divine disease and to see visions and hear voices from heaven?

That epilepsy has kinship with insanity and often brings mental disorder in its train is certain, but it is also certain that many epileptics go on having their fits all their lives without ever having their minds notably impaired. There is much uncertainty about the occurrence of mental disorder both in minor and major epilepsy, and we cannot tell the reason. Three facts stand out pretty clearly: that mental disorder seldom goes along with epilepsy at its outset, but usually comes on either after it has lasted some time or has recurred frequently in a short time; that it is most likely to follow where the seizures are incomplete or abortive; that their ultimate tendency, when long continued, is to produce weakness of mind. It might be conjectured that it is because of a double predisposition to epilepsy and insanity that epilepsy acts with special effect to produce insanity, just as any other cerebral commotion might do, and then in further surmise that it is because of the double predisposition that the epilepsy, distracted thereby from its regulur course, misses its full stroke and is abortive, being more mental than physical. Is there any good reason why diseases so near akin should not intermix and produce hybrids?

However caused, epileptic insanity has a bad prognosis. It is likely to recur with the recurring fits until the mind is permanently impaired. As it is natural to think that there would be no more mental disorder could the epilepsy be cured, it is natural to endeavour to suppress the fits by the large and frequent use of bromide of potassium. The practice is useful perhaps in the beginning, at any rate not hurtful, but at a later stage, when the epilepsy is well set, it is doubtful whether the repression of the fits by such measures does not result in a worse and longer attack of mania. The patient had better on the whole have his epilepsy with its brief mental derangement than have, as he is not unlikely to have in the end, a long and furious mania, instead of fits, and to fall sooner into dementia. Assuredly more evil than good is done by attempts to stifle or cut short the acute mania by the use of large doses of chloral, opium, or other narcotic drugs; the stuporose unconsciousness, miscalled sleep, of two or three hours will probably be followed by worse excitement and a prolongation of the attack. There is not the same objection to the administration of a narcotic dose in the stupor after the fits; a treatment recommended by some as useful to prevent the outbreak of mania which might else occur, the non-occurrence of mania in such case being counted proof of the drug's success.

Notwithstanding that epileptic dementia is cureless, it is remarkable sometimes how much mental improvement, albeit incomplete at best, takes place when by good hap the fits cease. Let a patient, for example, accidentally hurt himself seriously in a fit, breaking his leg badly so that the broken bone is thrust through the skin, or burning his face, head, or body by falling into the fire, he will probably have no fits during the healing of the injury, though he had them daily before it; meanwhile his mind may clear up wonderfully. But when the healing is nearly or quite done the fits begin again and soon matters are as bad as they ever were. That is commonly what happens also when the skull is trepanned with the aim of curing epilepsy; the fits cease for a time, but after a while they come back. Only where there is depressed or damaged bone, or other distinct evidence of local irritation, is such operation likely to do permanent good. Now and then instances occur in which, an old-standing epilepsy ceasing of itself—no one can tell why—instead of mental improvement also taking place, a chronic mania follows and seems to take its place. Moreover, epilepsy is observed to supervene in some cases of old chronic mania. From all which it may be concluded, I think, that the pathological conditions of epilepsy and insanity are such as hardly to warrant the expectation that, when they have co-existed for a long time, the cessation of the one will be of much benefit to the other.

CHAPTER VI

ALCOHOLIC INSANITIES

IF a person suffers from mental derangement after alcoholic excesses the vulgar opinion is that he is not ever insane, but at most has an attack of *delirium tremens* which will soon pass away, and which, having brought it on himself by his misdoings, he is justly responsible for. But that is an error. The abuse of alcohol is sometimes the cause of a positive insanity, maniacal or melancholic, which has nothing of the special features of *delirium tremens*. Moreover, *delirium tremens*, when at its height, is essentially an acute insanity, although it lacks the systematization of ordinary mania, just as febrile delirium or acute delirious mania does. Like them, being a delirium rather than a mania, it witnesses to an acute, deeper and more widespread molecular perturbation of the cerebral mind-tracts.

1. The attack of *delirium tremens* is usually preceded by a very unquiet depression: lowness of spirits, apprehensive anxieties, gloomy forebodings and suspicions, extreme nervous agitation, nausea and loss of appetite, unrest and sleeplessness; the little sleep obtained being disturbed by a succession of frightful dreams out of which the patient wakes in terror, panting and bathed in perspiration, and because of which, though he longs for sleep, he dreads to fall asleep again. His troubles are worst in the night season, when he is at the mercy of himself, for the impressions and incidents of the day help to distract him

from himself. Upon this depression follows mental excitement with delirium, the delirium characterized by acute fear and trepidation and accompanied by terrifying hallucinations and extreme restlessness. Although the terror and apprehension which are the chief note of it might seem to be caused by the hallucinations, the truth is that it is the threatened nervous element which translates the menace to its life into conscious alarm and engenders its hallucinations; and it is not to be imagined that the patient endurance of a saint or the stoical resolution of a philosopher would avail to teach composure of mind in such circumstances of physical agitation.

The special character of the hallucinations and their comparative constancy in different cases merit consideration. They evidently point to a special and pretty constant action of the alcoholic poison on the nervous system, perhaps some such action on its peripheral nerve-endings as, in greater degree, manifests itself in chronic alcoholic paralysis. Most common are the visions of rats and mice, snakes, beetles and other creatures running and crawling on the floor, walls and bed, of bats flying about the room, and the like, but sometimes they are the more alarming spectres of dead persons, of thieves, of assassins. The patient is therefore very agitated and restless, his hands in continual tremulous movements as if aimlessly trying to get hold of something or to push away the invading vermin, and he may start up wildly and jump out of the window either in pursuit of or in escape from the phantoms which threaten him. The hallucinations are not fixed, but transient and changing.

The pulse is quickened, small and compressible at the wrist, but full and throbbing in the carotids, the heart's action violent, the perspiration profuse, and the breathing panting and irregular. After three or four days of delirious horror he falls perhaps into a long and deep sleep and then quickly recovers. When the issue is not into life, as it usually is, but into death, then he either (*a*) sinks by degrees into a low muttering delirium accompanied by all the symptoms of typhoid exhaustion and ending in coma, or (*b*) he expires suddenly, perhaps quite unexpectedly, from collapse, or (*c*) the delirium becomes very fierce, with symptoms of meningitis, great rise of temperature and perhaps an invasion of pneumonia.

Recovery, when it takes place, is usually pretty rapid and in the end complete, although some weakness of mind may linger for a while even after a first attack and remain permanently after several attacks. In a few cases the mind does not clear up, but continues more or less weak and confused, clouded with morbid suspicions, vexed with hallucinations of hearing, gloomy and inclined to suicidal feelings. Then we may justly suspect a predisposition to insanity and fear a lapse into a chronic course of it.

2. Characterized by the chronic display of symptoms like those which are exhibited by *delirium tremens* in an acute form—an expansion of them, as it were, in space and time—*alcoholic mania* is a sort of chronic *delirium tremens*. It may be acute, subacute, or chronic. After the premonitory sleeplessness, scaring dreams, unquiet distress, nausea and loss of appetite, the growing mental disquietude, instead of culminating in an acute outbreak, develops into intense morbid suspicions and into delusions and hallucinations of persecution. The patient imagines that his friends are hostile to him and plotting against him, that persons are set to watch him who even contrive to keep up a system of espionage through the walls of his room, that detectives are everywhere about, that thieves get into his premises and rob him, that poison is put into his food, that his wife is unfaithful to him; and with delusions of this sort go hallucinations of the different senses, but especially of sight and hearing—hallucinations which vary from mere sparks of fire or flashes of light in the eyes and confusing sounds in the ears to a misseeing of scornful gestures and hostile movements and to the mishearing of threatening, accusing, and insulting voices. These hallucinations of the senses are a distinctive feature of the mental disorder; perhaps they are the allegorical interpretation, by the disordered brain, of the perverted sensations caused by

the alcoholic injury to the nerves. Neither they nor the delusions are constant and systematized, but come and go and change; and they are liable to fierce exacerbations which discharge themselves sometimes in violent deeds. Indeed, the mental state is a dangerous one because the feeling of injury is keen and the condition somewhat acute, and a violent-tempered man, driven to desperation and resolved to make the scoundrels pay for persecutions which he can no longer endure, is prone to execute a wild justice of revenge.

If a patient of this sort be placed under proper restraint, so that he cannot get drink, and be carefully nursed and fed, he gradually recovers. The hallucinations disappear first in the daytime, the mind being fairly clear then, although it is as deranged as ever during the night; then they become less troublesome at night, being most vivid in the stage between sleep and waking; at last they are indistinguishable from scaring dreams or nightmares, of which indeed they appear sometimes to be the waking continuations. For the distinction between the bad dream of a troubled sleep which is scarcely sleep and of the waking delirium which looks like a bad dream is lost in the passage of the one into the other. Some patients I have seen who, when the illness was coming on and when it was passing off, have had a partial hold of their hallucinations, being able to start them or to let them start at will.

Victims of alcoholic mania seldom continue well, when they recover, for they soon return to their drink and soon fall ill again. Although they may make good resolutions and solemn promises to reform, no trust can be placed in what they say, perhaps believe, they will do; they have so paralysed their highest cerebral reflexes that moral feeling and will are effaced in them. The proclivity of the gradually weakening mind is into *alcoholic dementia*.

3. Another form of mania, a *mania of exaltation*, lighted up sometimes by alcohol, has a quite different complexion, being characterized by much less acute excitement but by great mental conceit, by diffusely busy activity, and by

delusions of grandeur so like those of general paralysis that it is sometimes mistaken for it. As a rule, however, a close examination of its symptoms reveals more trace of mental power—less silliness, less facility of moods, less looseness and incoherence in the delusive notions, more proneness to suspicion, more aggressive behaviour, more consistency of feeling, than in the mania of general paralysis. It is in accordance with the preservation of more mental continence and unity that recovery generally takes place from this exalted mania in a few weeks. The alcohol, I think, acts on a distinct insane predisposition in such cases; the disorder being in fact essentially an hereditary insanity kindled into flame by it, rather than an essentially alcoholic insanity.

4. In consequence of a certain predisposition in the brain to disorder, a distinct instability of it, the excess of a single alcoholic debauch sometimes occasions an *acute transitory mania* which ends perhaps after a few hours in a heavy sleep or continues for a few days. It differs from ordinary mania only in its acuteness and destructive violence and in the confused memory or entire oblivion, after the attack, of what went on during it; two features in which it much resembles epileptic mania. In truth it is not unlike a sort of mental epilepsy; and just as a person on coming out of epileptic coma passes sometimes into furious mania, so it sometimes follows the waking from a heavy drunken sleep. Then violence or even murder may be done on the least provocation, perhaps under the influence of a vivid hallucination; the whole affair a sort of alcoholic mental convulsion. Such convulsive impulses and destructive violence are worst when alcohol and epilepsy go together to cause the mania; then the two seem to unite their evil forces to produce a most fierce attack.

When alcohol causes a transitory insanity instead of an ordinary intoxication we may always expect to find either a strong hereditary predisposition to insanity in a weak and excitable nervous constitution, or an acquired infirmity of brain in consequence of injuries to the head, or of sunstrokes, or of previous attacks of mania, or of recurrent epilepsy.

A mind of unstable equilibrium, easily overset, is then thrown into delirium by a little alcohol just as it is by the heat of a fever or by comparatively small shocks or strains. The person is not drunk, he is mad for the time being, and capable of violent or foolish conduct of which he would have been incapable when he was sane and sober: gives himself up to the police as the perpetrator of some recent murder of which he has read, but with which he had nothing whatever to do; gets into trouble because of some indecent offence which he has perpetrated; makes an unprovoked assault on some one against whom he has conceived an unfounded suspicion; sets fire to hay-stacks and farm-buildings from mere impulse of destruction. The delirious ideas which may spring up are various; for the alcohol may be said to intoxicate silliness in the silly, melancholy in the melancholy-minded, suspicion in the suspicious, violence in the violent, vanity in the vain, and thus to stimulate the different dispositions to take their own forms of mad thought-imagery in the delirious brain. To censure or sentence a person of this sort for the mad things which he does when in his state of alienation as if he were only drunk, is more expedient socially perhaps than just scientifically; for he is so little himself at the time that he is but hazily conscious of what he does, and only realises truly what he has done when he comes to himself.

5. *Alcoholic dementia*, like senile dementia, is the result of an organic degeneration of brain produced by the continued action, but not to be cured by the present disuse, of alcohol. The mental symptoms are due to the degeneration of structure, not to the alcohol; they are permanent, therefore, like those of senile dementia and of the dementias of gross cerebral diseases which they resemble also in character. The erasure of memory is particularly notable: the patients forget recent events as soon as they are over, so that they know not what happens from day to day or even from hour to hour, and speak of remote as if they were just past events— talk perhaps in a quiet way of their doings abroad yesterday when they have not left the house for months. Sensibility

is much blunted and conduction retarded; they not only do not feel what they felt before but feel more slowly what they do feel. Preceding the loss of sensation or going along with it there are various perversions of sensation: prickings and itchings of the skin, and creepings of it as if ants or other insects were crawling on or under it; or the more painful feelings of burning, biting, cutting, as if the flesh was being torn out violently or burnt with a red-hot iron. The pains are worse at night. They usually begin first in the legs, afterwards in the arms, but sometimes simultaneously in arms and legs. Although the blunting of sensibility to pain and touch may pass ultimately into almost complete loss of it, the anæsthesia is seldom quite complete, and is sometimes strangely local, as though the alcohol selected special areas of devastation.

With the sensory deterioration goes loss of motor power in the arms and legs: the tremulous hand cannot easily take hold of an object or grasp it steadily, the tremor being increased visibly by the eagerness of the attempt, perhaps drops it helplessly when it has got hold of it; and the patient has eventually to lie in bed because he cannot use his legs, which bend under him as if the bones or joints were softened when he attempts to stand on them, though he can move them freely as he lies in bed. Meanwhile he suffers from terrible draggings and cramps in the muscles, especially in the calves of the legs, as if they were being traversed by thousands of electric shocks; the cramps are the forerunners of general epileptic convulsions which befall when he continues to saturate himself with alcohol. The order of events in the progress of deterioration in fact is tremor, spasm, cramp, convulsion, paralysis. The epileptic convulsions may recur from time to time, sometimes several following one another in quick succession; then the urine will probably contain a quantity of albumen.

Hallucinations, especially visual, of an extraordinary and extravagant character are common, and are worst at night—*e.g.* of insects crawling over the skin or burrowing in the flesh, of vermin gnawing it, of cats driving their claws into it, of knives and broken glass thrust into the limbs, of corpses lying about on the floor, of frightful animals in the room, of living persons cut to pieces, and the like monstrosities of demented imagination; all which the patients narrate in a quiet matter-of-fact way, as if they were ordinary incidents, and without the least apparent consciousness of the absurdity of their stories.

This condition of dementia may be brought about gradually by a continued course of drinking, especially in women, without being preceded by active symptoms of acute insanity. I have sometimes asked myself whether it has not followed, and been precipitated by, the abrupt and entire cutting off of alcohol from a regular sot; but dubiously only, seeing that the occurrence of alarming symptoms may well have been the occasion of the enforced abstinence.

In a few cases the delusions of alcoholic dementia are of a very exalted kind, just as they are in one form of alcoholic mania, being as grand as, but more fixed and continued than, those of general paralysis. One patient loaded himself heavily with a variety of collars and decorations of pewter which he maintained to be the order of the Golden Fleece, and declared that he was to be crowned and live at Buckingham Palace; another was to undergo a mental discipline of three years in order to regain for himself and mankind the vast power which women had obtained and concentrated in convents, after which he was destined to have supreme power over all the world. Neither of them suffered from the least motor paralysis. Both were quiet and courteous in manner and by no means inclined, like the general paralytic, to babble of their delusions incontinently to all comers; indeed, they showed rather a tincture of suspicion and reserve when asked directly about them. The existence of a distinct morbid heredity might warrant the opinion that the special features of the mental disorder testified of it rather than of the alcohol.

One cannot expect a person who is in a state of chronic alcoholic dementia to recover his full mental faculties. He may improve a little in memory and mental power while he is under restraint; but as his moral sense and will are pretty nigh obliterated, and his mind continues weak, he can neither refrain from drink nor take proper care of himself, if left to himself. He is liable to be the easy prey of designing persons who set themselves to gratify his craving and perhaps to rob him or defraud his heirs of his property. The paralytic weakness often disappears entirely, when the mental weakness does not, under a regime of compulsory abstinence, and the person may live a pretty long and peaceful life of dementia. Now and then one whose mind seems gone beyond hope of restoration recovers it in a quick and unexpected way; then, however, the disorder will probably be found to have been a sudden invasion and to have the character of an acute alcoholic dementia.

6. There is yet another form of alcoholic insanity which has distinctive features—namely, the so-called *dipsomania*. In its exact and proper meaning the name does not apply to the common sot who drinks day after day and is seldom sober for days together; he is just the habitual drunkard who has no more insanity about him than the insanity of a vicious craving and an habitual self-indulgence. Dipsomania proper appears rather to be akin to recurrent mania, being a *recurrent alcoholic mania;* for its outbreaks are paroxysmal and periodic, occurring in persons who in the intervals are sober and decent members of society, untormented by any craving for alcohol. After long periods of sobriety, during which they evince no trace of moral or intellectual disorder, they suffer a sort of indescribable anguish and feverish unrest, with a strong craving for alcohol, to relieve which they begin drinking and go on drinking day after day, taking little food and getting little sleep, until no food at all can be swallowed, vomiting perhaps sets in, and the craving for drink is satiated and exhausted. Then they are in the lowest and most abject misery for a short time, tremulous, fearful, ashamed to show themselves, and utterly prostrate in mind and body, after which they rally and return to the steady performance of their duties until the next outbreak. It is strange to see how men and women of good social position and

high intellectual accomplishments will thus abandon themselves to debauches of drink—defiant of social proprieties, reckless of consequences, to the grievous injury of themselves and their families, either secretly in their own houses or in wanderings from place to place, like vagabonds, and in consortings with low company—notwithstanding that when the paroxysm is spent they are bitterly sorry, sadly penitent, and make the best resolutions for the future. Such resolutions vanish instantly when the next attack comes on; for the moral nature is then entirely changed, sense of truth and right depraved, and the will to resist the bad inclination extinct: the self of *now* which breaks, is not the self of *then* which made, the vows.

The disorder is manifestly very like a recurrent mania —in its periodic nature, in the profound change of moral character which it entails, in the exact copy which one outbreak is of another as regards onset, features and course, and in the complete recovery of the mental powers during the sane intervals. In the end, if the attacks recur frequently, a permanent mental deterioration, especially moral, takes place. Sometimes the outbreaks, becoming less fierce and frequent with the advance of age, cease at last, and the old man then perhaps shows little trace of hurt from the debauches of his manhood. In women they seem to be liable to occur, or to be worse, at the menstrual periods.

Its neuropathic nature is further attested by these facts: first, that it is commonly found to own a morbid nervous inheritance, such as ancestral insanity, epilepsy, or drunkenness; and, secondly, that it is sometimes acquired as the sequel of an injury to the head, or of a sunstroke, or of a regular attack of acute insanity.

Lastly, in relation to it, I may call attention to an observation which I have had occasion to make of similar outbreaks of vagabondage without any special tendency to drink. A gentleman, *æt.* thirty, who was happily married and had one child, had always been an excellent husband and was so much esteemed in the office in which he was employed that his periodical irregularities were overlooked and condoned. When anything went wrong, however, whether at home or in business, he brooded over it anxiously, though it was a small thing which he knew very well was not worth troubling about, until he had an overwhelming feeling that he could not face it, that the responsibility was too great, that he must go anywhere, anywhere away from it. Thereupon he wandered off without giving any one the least notice, ashamed of himself, distressed beyond measure at what he was doing, not knowing nor caring where he went, caring only to go on and on, sleeping in the lowest lodging-houses or lying under hedges at night, living scantily on the cheapest food, but not drinking any alcoholic liquor. This vagrant life he continued for two or three weeks or a month, giving no sign of himself to his family the while, until he was at the end of his resources, when, returning to the neighbourhood of his home, he used to write to his wife in deep penitence and abasement. She would then fetch him home secretly by night, being ashamed for him to be seen by the neighbours in his dirty, unwashed and dilapidated state. The story, as told to me by himself, seemed to be perfectly truthful. In the case of another person who had been addicted to similar outbreaks of a vagabond mania matters had been made more serious, on the occasion of my being consulted, by his having cashed a small cheque, which he ought to have paid away, and spent the money. Such prolonged aberrations of conscience and will, viewed scientifically, might suggest a likeness to the shorter epileptic disorders of consciousness in which the patients, knowing all the while what strange things they are doing, still cannot help doing them. No doubt also they might prompt a suspicion whether all the essential facts, which confessions commonly do not confess, had been stated.

INSANITY AND PHTHISIS.

The frequency of phthisis among the insane in asylums is an old story. But the inference that insanity directly predisposed to phthisis has been invalidated by proof that since the diet, warmth, clothing, and general sanitary surroundings of insane patients in asylums have been improved the proportion of phthisis in them has vastly diminished. Still it was the positive opinion of Schroeder van der Kolk that the one disease directly predisposed to the other; and Dr. Clouston maintains, as the result of his statistical inquiries, that the mortality from phthisis in asylums is still three times that of the mortality from it in the general population. Assuredly a great many idiots—as many as two-thirds of them, it is said—die of phthisis. As the nutritive processes are sluggish and feeble in some forms and phases of insanity, where a low vitality of the tissues of the body is a concomitant or sequel of a low vitality of the brain, the bacillus of phthisis will find there little resistance to its attack and a favourable soil to flourish on. In the majority of cases in which the two diseases coexist the mental disorder appears first. Instances of one or other, perhaps of both, of them are pretty sure to be seen in a decadent family which is in process of extinction; and I think there is no inter-breeding of diseases more fatal to a stock than that of phthisis and insanity. How can it be otherwise when a nervous system unequal to the animal life or life of relation meets in the same person with an organic system unequal to its life?

When the two diseases begin about the same time in the same person the features of the mental malady are often, though not invariably, peculiar in some respects; so much so, however, that Dr. Clouston has given much time and pains to define and describe a distinct clinical variety which he styles *phthisical insanity*.[1] Starting together in the individual, the one disease cannot be looked on as the cause

[1] *Clinical Lectures on Mental Diseases.*

of the other; but the concomitant quickening of the two morbid heredities, and the special features of the mental symptoms, might betray a nervous temperament which was weak and essentially consumptive or phthisical in character. For assuredly there is a special nervous temperament in many cases of phthisis—that is to say, quick and susceptible, prone to be irritable and exacting, keen, eager and sanguine, but more fickle than stable, brilliant in fancy but wanting in depth, breadth, and stay of thought; there is something fitful and intense in its moods, its projects, its imagination, its energy, as if the hectic were in its thoughts, feelings and actions. Very remarkable is the singular hopefulness which so often prevails throughout the disease; day by day the patient, who is slowly and surely pining away of his disease, speaks hopefully of himself as stronger and, sanguine of recovery, even to the last makes projects for morrows which he will never see. Nevertheless his sanguine confidence is liable to be interrupted by intervals of despondency, sometimes by successive days of irritable depression, and now and then a mental and physical prostration lasts throughout.

When a person of this temperament becomes insane one might certainly expect the complexion of his disorder to witness to the special features and variable course of its moods or phases. And that appears to be much what happens. The derangement is not fierce and violent, it has the general character of a mild mania or melancholia, or of a sort of monomania of suspicion. When acute, the acute stage, whether maniacal or melancholic, is short and does not run into the ordinary sequent chronic form nor into positive dementia; it lapses quietly into an irritable, excitable, moody and suspicious state of weakness of mind without fixed delusion. Indeed, very often the disorder begins and grows in that way by a gradual alteration of disposition and conduct. The acute mania is sometimes marked by considerable mental exaltation with great conceit of self, sometimes by delusions of grandeur of the general paralytic sort and a keenly passionate excitement or even a quasi-spasmodic intensity of action when the delusions encounter opposition. The mania reflects the keen irritability and sanguine intensity of the phthisical temperament, and its short duration reflects the instability of it. Conformably to the moods of dejection or the occasional continued despondency in phthisis, the insanity in other cases is a melancholia, which is also prone to be intense and variable. Then there may be a refusal of food, partial or complete, owing perhaps to the suspicion of poison in it, or to a conviction that the inside is corrupt or blocked and cannot digest it, or to the delusion of a foul disorder in the mouth or throat.

But the most special insanity in connection with phthisis, that which is thought to be a clinical variety, is a chronic mania of suspicion coming on in an insidious way without any previous acute attack and without any marked excitement or depression; characterized by irritability, waywardness, caprice, and a progressive weakening of intellect, and, at a later stage, by brief attacks of subacute excitement in which the patient is obstinate, wilful, impulsive, and resists whatever he is asked to do or is done for him, with a mulish perversity or with a passionate intensity that leaves him pale, panting, and exhausted afterwards. There is more show of dementia in his conduct than there is actual dementia, for when not under the active sway of his disorder he may talk and act in an intelligent way contrasting strangely with his general aspect and conduct; from time to time may exhibit fitful gleams of animation and energy that come and go, like the feverish rises of bodily temperature which are the probable occasions of such transient revivals of mind.

Does the insanity affect the progress of the phthisis? Some observers have thought that the insanity checked the phthisis, for the patients do not cough, nor expectorate, nor complain of pain, as a rule; but the truth is that it only masks it, and that, as Dr. Clouston has pointed out, exact examination of the lungs, of the bodily weight, and of the evening temperature day by day discloses no real improvement. During the passing attacks of maniacal exaltation when the patient is brisk, animated, energetic, and feels wonderfully well, the vivified tissues will naturally offer greater resistance to the morbid process and may thus occasion a temporary arrest of it. But it is a question whether it does not then soon regain lost ground by a quicker pace after the inspiring energy has disappeared.

Such then is the character of so-called phthisical insanity. Why phthisical? Certainly there are formidable difficulties in the way of accepting such a name or such a variety. First, it is certain that phthisis by itself is not a known cause of insanity, only a small proportion of the many persons who contract phthisis ever becoming insane, and that when the diseases occur together some other factor than the phthisis must be the main determinant of the insanity— both of its invasion and its character. Secondly, it is not less certain that exactly the same sort of mental disorder, indistinguishable positively by its symptoms, is met with in some cases where there is neither suspicion of phthisis nor of special predisposition to it—for example, in the insanity going along with self-abuse in certain frail neurotic temperaments and in the insanity befalling some persons of thin intense artistic or poetic temperament. It is the temperament not the phthisis which gives its complexion to the insanity. Thirdly, in a great many cases in which insanity and phthisis coexist the insanity has nothing special about it, not so much as one of the characteristic features, so far as they are characteristic, of the so-called phthisical insanity. How then rightly style phthisical a clinical variety of insanity which may exist and run its course whether phthisis coexists or not, and not exist when phthisis and insanity coexist? The scientific aim will be to define and describe the special nervous temperament which, when worked upon by a cause, phthisical or not, of deteriorated nutrition, presents the special clinical features. If a person has two morbid heredities in him, an insane and a phthisical one, and if he gets into such bad health or circumstances as to light them into flame, he will present the special features of both; but if he has only one of these morbid heredities, then that which he has, whether phthisis or insanity, will exhibit its independent and special features. The name cannot, I think, be accepted as convenient to designate a clinical group and succession of symptoms, since it has just the faults which a name so used should not have : it does not denote what it professes to denote and it denotes other things than it professes to denote. There is no phthisical insanity anyhow; there is an individual who, being insane and consumptive, has sometimes a particular form of mental disorder going along with his consumption, when the two disorders chance to begin and go along together.

INSANITY AND GROSS BRAIN-DISEASE.

The symptoms of the impairments and disorders of mind that go along with gross cerebral diseases are not within the scope of this treatise; they belong to the diseases which they forbode or accompany. Still as they are sometimes so like the symptoms of uncomplicated mental disorder as to be mistaken for them and disastrously misconstrued, it will not be amiss to make brief mention of them.

It is well known that a person may have gross disease in his brain or lose a part of its substance without showing any mental defect or disorder. The presence of a tumour, abscess, cysticercus, or other gross product in it is compatible with the full exercise of its mental functions, provided that the morbid product does not directly encroach on, or hurtfully press on, or indirectly disable by irritations and inhibitions, nervous or vasomotor, the essential nervous substrata of mind. As these are the several modes by which it acts on mind to disorder it, it is obvious that the mental disorder will differ according to the seat and extent and mode of operation of the morbid deposit in the brain and must needs present various and irregular symptoms. In no case do we get the typical symptoms and regular course of an ordinary form of insanity. If the symptoms of mental disorder are acute, they have more of the incoherence of delirium than of the method of insanity; they lack the systematization of morbid action, the definite organizations of disorder which characterize its forms. Moreover, they are liable to appear and disappear in a sudden and complete way when they are reflex effects of the morbid product; for we may assume that when they thus come and go abruptly they are not due to structural mental disorganizations. However, no one can venture to diagnose such gross disease of the brain as tumour by the mental symptoms only; it is necessary to seek the guidance of more special symptoms— to wit, intense paroxysmal headaches, attacks of giddiness, affections of one or more of the special senses, paralysis of sensation or motion in eyelids, muscles of eye or face or elsewhere, the presence of optic neuritis, perhaps a suddenly supervening loss of consciousness and epileptiform or apoplectiform seizures and coma.

The ultimate injurious effects of gross cerebral disease on mind are increasing intellectual feebleness and stupor. The weakness of mind is for the most part an aimless and restless stupidity with loss of memory, the patient, who perhaps confusedly feels but is incapable of intelligently apprehending the measures taken to guard him, making vague efforts to escape or resist them. The stupidity is likely to deepen into stupor, is sometimes accompanied by a progressive motor paralysis, and ends at last in fatal convulsions or coma. In the desolation of mind there are no wrecks of systematic delusions, such as are met with in the dementia following mania or melancholia, and even sometimes in the dementia of general paralysis which its symptoms most resemble.

The mental symptoms which precede serious organic disease of the brain have a particular and very practical interest; for they have been misinterpreted, being regarded as merely hysterical or hypochondriacal, before their true significance was made plain by the sequel. Most notable are the sense of loss of mental power and interest, the painful incapacity to think, the difficulty to do customary work, the forgetfulness of words and phrases or the use of wrong words and letters, and the great emotional susceptibility which distress and depress one whose brain-ruin they forebode. I have met with instances—once in three members of one family—in which symptoms of what seemed a hysterical or hypochondriacal sort of melancholia, and was thought so at first, increased quickly to a muttering somnolent delirium, passed thence into stupor, and ended soon in coma and death from acute degeneration of the brain. In such cases a considerable rise of bodily temperature, a semi-conscious stupor, with perhaps repeated yawnings, from which the patient can be roused to open his eyes or to put out his tongue, an overwhelming sense of weariness and prostration which might be mistaken for indolence, are ill-omened symptoms; still more so when hallucinations of smell go with them.

The subjective symptoms of mental distress shown before a tumour of the brain declares itself by positive symptoms are sometimes of so strongly hysterical a character as not to be recognized for what they are, that is, the general nerve-weakness of brain caused by the yet undeclared local mischief, and to be mistaken for what they are not, that is, the similar constitutional nerve-weakness of hysteria or hypochondria. All the more is this likely to happen because of the complete intermissions of them, since a patient who protests at one time that he is blind or deaf, or that he cannot walk, when it is plain at another time that he can see, hear, or walk, might naturally be suspected of exaggeration or feigning. These are the kind of symptoms: an unspeakable feeling of weariness which incapacitates him from exertion but, since he may be urged to make some temporary exertions, looks like apathetic indolence; swaying and staggering walk of giddiness when he stands up to walk, the features of his failure showing so much staggering of will as to suggest a suspicion that he is not trying his best; extreme prostration without fever and great loss of appetite and disinclination to food without gastric disorder; moaning self-pity, and wailing complaints of sufferings which, being knowable only by himself, may not obtain the consideration they merit; an intense sensibility to sounds, which, jarring his brain and frame terribly, are shrunk from with acute apprehension; periodical paroxysms of headache, the agonizing pains of which cannot fail to distress an onlooker by their outward and visible manifestations. It is beyond doubt that in many instances the gravity of symptoms of this kind has not been realised and that sufferers sick unto death have been treated as if they were only fanciful or shamming.

The fact is that the organic disease produces in the rest of the brain not directly affected by it a general condition of nerve-element like that which prevails throughout the brain in such functional distempers as hypochondria and hysteria and gives rise therefore to similar neurasthenic symptoms: a molecular disturbance which means a destruction of molecular elasticity and sluggish molecular action, and may, if the morbid product be removed, disappear entirely. It is an obstruction to thought which temporary excitement may overcome even when it is destined to go on to destruction of nerve-element and death.[1]

Having regard then to the condition of things in the brain, it is not surprising that the opposite mistake is sometimes made of treating a patient who is only hysterical or hypochondriacal as if he or she were afflicted with organic disease of the brain. I call to mind the particular instance of a young lady of nervous inheritance and hysterical temperament who was pronounced by an eminent physician to be suffering from tumour of the brain and to be doomed to an early death. At each recurring visit ophthalmoscopic examination of the eyes revealed an optic neuritis which confirmed the sad prognosis. After a time, however, as matters went on without much change, her

[1] As, for example, in an aged clergyman who, after detailing his painful symptoms of incapacity, wrote—"Though these symptoms occur when I am speaking to my very small congregation of agricultural labourers, I find myself able to address a hall of educated people for an hour and a half without unusual effort and without any hitch whatever. . . . I seem to get better under high-pressure."

parents placed the patient in the family of a lady of good common sense who, having brought up girls of her own, was not so gravely impressed by the symptoms as the eminent physician. She professed to discover the main cause of a tangle of hysterical symptoms in extreme tight-lacing, habitual constipation, and other like sins of omission and commission; and, having enforced such vigorous hygienic measures as seemed requisite, was rewarded by the speedy recovery of her patient.

The symptoms of cerebral tumour witness to the tumour only, not to the nature of it. Therefore it is that the syphilitic morbid product, when localized as a gumma, produces just the same symptoms as any other tumour in its position and growing at the same rate would do. The diagnosis of syphilis, if it can be made, will rest mainly upon a previous history of syphilitic infection and upon observation of its traces on the body; upon the occurrence of severe nervous disorder at an age—from twenty-five to forty-five years—when such disorder from other cause is rare; upon the absence of any other discoverable cause; upon the irregular character, association, and sequence of the symptoms, and their great variability; and upon the happy results, if they are happy, of specific treatment. Sometimes there is a general tenderness of the scalp on pressure, especially where the pain in the head is partial and local; in which case, as Dr. A. Robertson of Glasgow pointed out, percussion of the skull by the finger may assist the diagnosis by eliciting distinct pain in a spot where it was not previously localized.

Of course the syphilitic product is not always localized as a gumma; it may be a diffuse gummous meningitis, or it may infiltrate and thicken the coats of the small cerebral arteries and so lead to thrombosis, which will then act just as thrombosis otherwise caused would do. Though mind may be gradually destroyed by such morbid changes, in no case can we say properly that there is a special syphilitic insanity. What we can say is that there is more or less impairment of the mental functions of the brain according to the seat, extent, character and morbid action of the syphilitic deposit in it; and what we may justly expect is that the mental disorder, if not quickly removed by specific treatment, will pass into destruction of mind—into a dementia which, when accompanied by paralysis, is sometimes hardly distinguishable from the dementia of general paralysis.

PART IV

THE MORBID ANATOMY AND TREATMENT OF INSANITY

Qu'est-ce qu'un homme dans l'infini ?
Mais pour lui présenter un autre prodige aussi étonnant, qu'il recherche dans ce qu'il connaît les choses les plus délicates. Qu'un ciron lui offre dans la petitesse de son corps des parties incomparablement plus petites, des jambes avec des jointures, des veines dans ces jambes, du sang dans ces veines, des humeurs dans ce sang, des gouttes dans ces humeurs, des vapeurs dans ces gouttes ; que divisant encore ces dernières choses, il épuise ses forces en ses conceptions et que le dernier objet où il peut arriver soit maintenant celui de notre discours ; il pensera peut-être que c'est là l'extrême petitesse de la nature. Je veux lui faire voir là-dedans un abîme nouveau. Je lui veux peindre non seulement l'univers visible, mais l'immensité qu'on peut concevoir de la nature, dans l'enceinte de ce raccourci d'atome. Qu'il y voie une infinité d'univers dont chacun a son firmament, ses planètes, sa terre, en la même proportion que le monde visible ; dans cette terre, des animaux, et enfin des cirons dans lesquels il retrouvera ce que les premiers ont donné ; et trouvant encore dans les autres la même chose, sans fin et sans repos, qu'il se perde dans ces merveilles aussi étonnantes dans leur petitesse que les autres par leur étendue ; car qui n'admirera que notre corps qui tantôt n'était pas perceptible dans l'univers, imperceptible lui-même dans le sein du tout, soit à présent un colosse, un monde, ou plutôt un tout, à l'égard du néant où l'on ne peut arriver ?—Pascal, *Pensées*.

First, therefore, in this, as in all things which are practical, we ought to cast up our account, what is in our power and what not ; for the one may be dealt with by way of *alteration*, but the other by way of *application*. The husbandman cannot command neither the nature of the earth nor the seasons of the weather ; no more can the physician the constitution of his patient nor the variety of accidents : so in the culture and cure of the mind of man two things are without our command ; points of nature and points of fortune : for to the basis of the one, and the conditions of the other, our work is limited and tied. In those things, therefore, it is left unto us to proceed by application.—Bacon, *Of the Advancement of Learning, Divine and Human.*

CHAPTER I

THE MORBID ANATOMY OF INSANITY

THE morbid anatomy of insanity would take little room were speculation rigidly excluded and it limited to what is actually seen and known.[1] Nor does that which is seen, it must be confessed, throw much light on the symptoms; though very minute, owing to improved powers and methods of observation, it only carries us a little farther in that direction than the cruder observations of our forefathers. Ardent proposals to found a scientific classification of insanities on morbid anatomy may for the present be coldly ranked with not less fondly fanciful proposals to define and describe in a nerve-tract the thrill of love, the quiver of anger, the physical conditions of a warped thought or a morbid suspicion. In the end it may be easier to discover in the nerves why a man feels hot or cold than to discover why he rages in mania and despairs in melancholia.

The intimate chemical and molecular changes which are presumably the conditions of mental disorder go on in a domain of nature the subtilties of which yet far exceed the subtilties of observation. If a molecule of nerve-element is more complex in constitution and intestine motions than the solar system, it is obvious that we have yet much to do in subtilizing our means of research before we can reveal the ways of its workings. What is seen at best after

---

[1] The description of it will need the less space here because of what has been said at length in the chapter treating of the pathological causation of insanity.

death is the dead matter of dead structure, not the living motions in a living structure; something quite different, therefore, from the swift flux of vital changes which obtains during life. The essential in dead things is the *matter*, in living things it is the *form*. Nor is the matter which we see after death necessarily just that which it was during life—it may be but the wreckage of it; for so momentous a change as death might well make changes in substance so exquisitely delicate as nerve-element that would invalidate any conclusion from what is seen to what is not seen. All the more so when the dead substance has been affected by the reagents used to stain and make it visible, and undergone the manipulations required to preserve it. What is to hinder the making visible that which was invisible from being an important condensation or modification of its substance? the colour-stain from being, as it were, a nature-stain?

Chemical agents are vastly more subtile than microscopical observation to detect differences of constitution in nerve-cells. A moderate dose of alcohol which affects the nerve-cell of the cerebral cortex appears to have no appreciable effects on the nerve-cells of the spinal cord, while a dose of strychnia evinces just the opposite elective affinity. No observation of either cell which we can make discloses the least reason why strychnia thus poisons the one and not the other, or so much as a difference between the poisoned and the unpoisoned cell. Why is it that a dose of alcohol which would certainly make a sane person drunk has no visible effect on a brain in a state of inflamed activity? Though pathology cannot tell us why, it may justly point to the non-effect as proof that the nerve-structure is then in an abnormal molecular state.

There is abundant evidence that molecular and chemical changes somewhere are somehow the conditions of function of nerve-element. It is exhausted by severe exercise so that it cannot work again until rest and nutrition have restored its energy; its activity involves oxidation-changes which render its reaction acid and give rise to constant products of retrograde metamorphosis very like those which are the result of muscular activity; the molecular changes in its interior when it is active are, as Matteucci and Du Bois Reymond demonstrated, accompanied by modifications of the electric currents which circulate in it;—these are facts of observation which rightly warrant the inference of a composition and decomposition of structure, a tension and de-tension of energy, in nutrition and function.

The nice measurements which can now be made of the rate of conduction by nerves have modified the old notions which used to be entertained of its metaphysical speed. Though Haller first proposed to measure the rate, and even made a calculation of it for man which was pretty near the truth, the eminent physiologist Müller thought it impossible, because the time seemed to him too brief to be measurable. In reality, the speed is not only measurable but comparatively moderate—far below the rapidity of light and electricity, less even than the rate at which sound travels, about the same as that of an eagle's flight, only a little quicker than the speed of a racehorse or of a locomotive.[1] As might be expected, the time-rate of propagation is lowered by cold; it is some ten times less in a cold than in a normal nerve; and in a cold-blooded animal like the frog it is normally only about half what it is in man. Differing a little naturally in different persons, it varies much according to varying conditions of health, ranging from inordinate rapidity to an almost complete stand-still.

Not only is the time-rate of propagation along a nerve measurable, but the time-rate of a volition can also be measured experimentally. This too differs constitutionally in different persons, everybody having his personal equation, and differs in the same person according to the state of his attention and to his varying bodily conditions. Thought is no less at the mercy of nerves than movement is, and the speed of the one no more unconditioned than that

[1] To say nothing of the miserable show which its slow pace makes when compared with a speed of 380 miles a second, which is the calculated pace of Arcturus in its leisurely travel out of the infinite somewhere into the infinite somewhere.

of the other. In all thinking we have a physical basis and process to reckon with, and the notion of thought flashing over sea and land with inconceivable rapidity is just an absurdity of poetical fancy. When it does travel in an instant from London to Pekin, it only travels from one thought-track in the brain to another not far from it, and then only at a moderate pace. If all the past events of his life seem to flash on the consciousness of a drowning man —as, since Admiral Beaufort's well-known graphic description of his experience, it has been the fashion for them to do—it is that the letters of their registers in the brain are suddenly illumined and read, much as the details of a wide landscape are vividly and instantaneously impressed on the eye when presented to it suddenly out of the surrounding darkness by a flash of lightning on a dark night.

That the volitional response made to a given sensation by a concerted muscular signal is notably quickened by expectant attention, may be reckoned proof that such attention signifies a certain degree of molecular tension of nerve-element, which renders it quick to feel and react.[1] The psycho-physical researches of Fechner and Weber long since demonstrated the existence of stimuli below the level of consciousness which rise above its threshold when a little addition is made to the latent stimulation. We may conceive then how much activity, pleasing or jarring, may be going on in the brain without our being aware of it, and how small an impression here or there may instantly raise it into pleasing or painful consciousness. A melancholic is, so to speak, in a general state of expectant melancholic attention, ready on the least stimulation to feel and think sorrowfully; a commencing maniac, like a sanguine optimist, in a state of expectant joyous attention, ready on the least stimulation to feel and think jubilantly.

As every mental act takes and requires a definite time, it may be inferred that its proper nervous action, if the duration thereof be longer or shorter than a required

---

[1] Aptly expressed in a line of Shakspeare's:—
To set his sense on the attentive bent.

maximum or minimum, will not excite consciousness and be consciously mental. The current may be too quick or too slow for consciousness, just as auditory vibrations audible by one ear may be too quick or too slow to be heard by another ear. Perhaps it is too rapid when an act which was gradually and consciously acquired is performed at last instantly and unconsciously. However that be, it is pretty evident, on the one hand, that the torpid melancholic who remains for successive months in a state of mental stupor in which he feels not the lapse of time and is perhaps unconscious of self as something separate from the not-self, is for the most part an example of nervous action too slow for true consciousness; and, on the other hand, that the acutely delirious maniac may be deemed an example of nervous action too rapid for true consciousness. A latent stimulation and an over-stimulation are alike incompatible with the mental function of the nervous mental substrata.

Whatever be the intimate molecular conditions beneath thought and feeling, they may be profoundly deranged and still yield no visible evidence of the morbid change. By their mental effects alone do sluggish or mobile molecules testify of themselves; and they can pass almost instantly from the one state into the other, as they do when melancholic stupor is followed suddenly by active mania, without anybody being able to tell why or what the change is. The disappearance of a reflex or sympathetic mental disorder, just as a reflex neuralgia or convulsion sometimes disappears, when an eccentric cause of morbid irritation is removed, proves how mobile and transitory are the morbid physical conditions. However one might wish it to be otherwise, and however sure that it will one day be otherwise, it is still the fact that mental disorder may exist during life without the least morbid change being visible in the brain after death.

Leaving these conjectures as to what takes place in a domain into which observation cannot yet enter, I go on to describe the morbid changes which have been discovered in the domain of grosser processes. Three factors in the structure of the brain have to be taken account of—(*a*) The blood-vessels; (*b*) the nerve-cells and fibres; (*c*) the neuroglia or connective tissue and the lymph-channels. What are the vascular changes? What the changes in the nerve-elements? What the changes in the connective tissue and in the lymph-channels? Within the compass of these questions lies the known morbid anatomy of insanity.

Common enough in old-standing insanities are changes in the membranes of the brain and especially in the *pia mater*, which, as the name implies, has so pious a motherly relation with the cortex. The *dura mater* is sometimes thickened, the *pia mater* oftentimes much so, in senile insanity, in chronic alcoholic insanity, and in general paralysis; and the *pia mater* may be so firmly adherent to the surface of the brain, especially in general paralysis, that it cannot be stripped off without tearing parts of the cortex away with it. But some thickening of the membranes, though not to the same extent, is often found in the bodies of persons who have not been insane. Schrœder van der Kolk gave two reasons why such inflammatory changes might take place without implicating the cortex. The first was that inflammation does not spread readily from one kind of structure to an adjacent structure of a different kind—not by easy continuity of motion from like to unlike as it does from like to like element: witness, for example, the escape of the intercostal muscles in acute costal pleurisy; the little implication of the muscular wall of the intestine in peritonitis; the soundness of the heart-substance in acute pericarditis with effusion into the pericardium. The second reason was the manner of distribution of blood-vessels in the *pia mater*. He was of opinion that while most of the arteries in it passed down from it into the cortex and there formed a most abundant network, the blood being brought back by a corresponding series of veins, there were in addition direct channels between the arteries and veins in the *pia mater* itself; an anatomical provision, as he thought, by which storms of temporary disturbance in its circulation might pass over, without hurting, the cortex.

In acute insanity, especially acute delirious mania, the appearances of acute hyperæmia of the *pia mater* are marked: they are great vascular injection with minute extravasations of blood, visible sometimes by the naked eye or a low power of microscope, both on the surface of the convolutions and between them where it descends into the sulci. It may be said generally that the morbid appearances in the membranes are those of acute hyperæmia in acute insanity, of chronic hyperæmia in chronic insanity. But there are no yet distinguishable differences between the morbid conditions that are seen in mania and those that are seen in melancholia; certainly not such as would enable the cleverest pathologist to tell which form of insanity had existed during life.

That the extremely fine networks of nerve-cells and their connections in the cerebral cortex are richly supplied with extremely fine networks of blood-vessels is a fact of observation; and that an active supply of the material of nutrition and function to the nerve-element by the blood and an active removal of waste products take place regularly is as certain as if the stream of vital changes had been actually watched. It had long been known, and has now been exactly demonstrated, that the flow of blood through the brain is increased during active function, and falls to the lower level of its mere organic requirements when active function is suspended. If the hyperæmia persists, instead of passing away, because of some morbid irritation in the parts, then it becomes morbid; the condition of things is a kind of sub-inflammation—for between transitory hyperæmia and acute inflammation there are all gradations—such as we believe to accompany the inflamed mental activity of commencing mania. Is the increased flow of blood then primary, or is the molecular change of nerve-element primary and the blood-flow secondary?

The change in the elements of the tissue is presumably the first step in mania, as it is the first step in inflammation. Such order of events is pretty evident in mania caused by mechanical or chemical injury to the nerve-cells; for it can hardly be supposed then that the instantly damaged function is due to increased vascularity, any more than the directly damaged structure. By the experiments of Claude Bernard it was shown that the modifications of the circulation which alcohol produces were—(a) hyperæmia, corresponding to the period of excitement; (b) anæmia, corresponding to the period of insensibility. But the vascular changes were not the cause of the drunkenness; that was due to the presence of alcohol in the blood and to its direct action upon the nervous elements.[1] So when an explosion of joy, anger, or other passion marks a nervous explosion, the passion is presumably the direct expression of the molecular commotion, and the vaso-motor dilatation its immediate, perhaps reflex, sequel. Prolong the strain of the passion thus blood-sustained, so as to cause an actual mental disorder, the result is gradually such detriment to the nerve-element, with accompanying vascular disturbance, as is done instantaneously to it by chemical or mechanical agency. The order of events appears to be the same in the two processes —only that it is acute in the one, chronic in the other.

A fact of physiological observation which ought to be borne in mind in this connection is that the effects of the activity of vaso-dilator fibres are essentially local in character. When any set of them comes into action the limited vascular area which they govern is dilated, little or no change being produced in the vascular system in general. Evidently then a local area of the cerebral cortex may be involved in morbid nervous action and concomitant vascular disorder, the rest of it being unaffected: it might be very active while the function of the rest of the cortex was suspended, the very excess of its exclusive activity acting to inhibit the rest. One may behold in it perhaps the mechanism by which a fixed passion or fixed idea

[1] Magnan has also seen and laid stress on the hyperæmic vessels of the membranes and cortex of the brain in alcoholized dogs.

exists and grows into madness. When any one solicits or procures sleep which will not readily come, compelling it at last, as it were, by fixing his mind and keeping it fixed on one subject, not ever allowing attention to wander, he appropriates and holds the available energy to a local activity, effects such a tension of it as to make it exclusive attention. Localizing the function of a limited cortical area he allows, indeed helps, the subsidence of the activity of the rest of the cortex and of its vascular circulation: he cures his general sleeplessness, so to speak, by keeping a local area monotonously awake, which necessarily then becomes itself very much a dream.

It is pretty evident that the very similar symptoms of commencing mania and of drunkenness own very similar conditions of disorder of nerve-element and of vascular circulation. Animated circulation and increased animation of mind, such as a glass of wine or a piece of good news might occasion, pass into the hyperæmia and mental ignition of mania and of drunkenness; whereupon elated ideas, feelings, and conduct express an activity in excess, an activity which is not true function in excess because it lacks the supreme continence or restraint of true function. Mental incontinences, however slight, express the nervous and vascular incontinences.

To have established a connection between mania and disorder of vascular circulation is only to have made a beginning, not a step towards a knowledge of the intimate changes that follow in the metabolic processes. It is natural to think that the bright glow of maniacal activity signifies a sort of flaming oxidation or combustion; the more natural to think so if we accept the conclusions which Claude Bernard drew from his experiments—namely, that the oxidation-processes or other chemical changes go on more rapidly in a part when its sympathetic nerve has been cut, not only because of a direct vaso-motor effect, but because of a direct effect upon the chemical processes in its tissues. He observed, when the cut nerve was galvanized, that there was not only contraction of the vessels, but a direct lowering of chemical changes; and maintained therefore that its influence on nutritive processes was inhibitory, both through the capillaries and directly through the tissues. If that be so, a maniacal ignition of thought might well betoken an excessive combustion, the flame of thought be a sort of inflammation.

Here we come to a point at which it is difficult to think that what is true of mania can be exactly true of melancholia. Certainly acute melancholia might own much the same physical conditions of combustion, since there is little real difference between the symptoms; so little sometimes that it is dubious whether to call them maniacal or melancholic. But what of chronic melancholia, where all the signs betoken sluggish or smouldering activity? Moreover, we may fitly call to mind how often a brief period of melancholic depression precedes an attack of acute mania, just as if a chill or contraction of the tissues were followed by a glow and dilatation of them. Have we then a transient inhibition of the proper metabolic changes? If so, is there a chronic condition of the kind—a deficient oxidation, so to speak—in melancholia that is not acute? These are questions to which it is easy to make answers that are surmises, but not yet possible to make scientific answers.[1] Long ago Andral pointed out, and others have insisted since, that an anæmic condition of the brain is as favourable as a hyperæmic condition of it to the production of delirium. It is virtually all one to the nerve-element whether it is living in the midst of a congestion of unfit food which it cannot make use of, or of an anæmia by which it is starved of fit food, so long as it lacks what it needs: in both cases it will show its sufferings in the same way by a delirious energy—that is, by energy off the tracks.

[1] Meynert professed to have found distinctly hyperæmic appearances after death in 47 per cent of maniacs, but only in 9 per cent of melancholics, and thereupon concluded that mania marked a state of cerebral excitement, melancholia a state of cerebral exhaustion. But why cerebral exhaustion in the 9 per cent in whom there was hyperæmic evidence? And if in them, why not in the 47 per cent of maniacs? And what of the 53 per cent of maniacs in whom there was no hyperæmia?

Now if a lack of blood may be the starting-point of delirium, why not of mania also? Why not an anæmic as well as a hyperæmic mania? And what then becomes of the hyperæmic condition which many authors postulate as the invariable accompaniment, and some as the primary cause, of mania.

Passing now to the next steps of degenerative change, what happens when an active hyperæmia, a sort of sub-inflammatory state of the cerebral cortex, persists? Very much what happens under similar conditions in any other delicate tissue of the body. Sluggish blood-stream, cramming of small vessels with swaying columns of red corpuscles, infiltration of their walls with leucocytes and bulgings of them here and there, proliferation of epithelial cells, and escape of corpuscles, leucocytes, and albuminous plasma into the surrounding tissue. These vascular exudates have been observed in acute insanity which has been fatal; and it is presumed that they occur to some extent in acute insanity which is recovered from, but are then got rid of through the lymph-channels. When they cannot be thus carried off, as they are at first when the channels are in good state and not overloaded, they break down in degeneration, and the waste or refuse of them and of blood-pigment is seen to cumber or clog the lymph-spaces in cases of old-standing insanity. Then follow thickening of the walls of the vessels, which become tortuous, varicose, sometimes atheromatous, an increase of connective tissue, and degeneration or atrophy of the nerve-cells; deteriorations of structure that are apparently due partly to pressure and partly to interference with nutrition.[1] In further process of degeneration ensue atrophy of the cortex, local or usually general, owing to the obstruction of the vessels, the destruction of the nerve-elements, and the contraction of the connective tissue, and finally the replacement of the wasted brain-substance by serous fluid.

[1] Various experiments made to produce and keep up artificial hyperæmia of the cortex have shown the main results to be hypertrophy of the connective tissue of the vessels and of the neuroglia.

There is not much to be said about changes in the nerve-cells in recent mania or melancholia. When the disorder of them is such as can be recovered from, it is not likely that the microscope will tell us what it is; only when old disease has ended in dementia is there visible evidence of atrophy, degeneration, and fragmentary disintegrations of them. Cloudy swellings of them, granular appearance of their protoplasm, and obscuration and displacement of their nuclei have been noticed in acute cases which were rapidly fatal.

The lymphatic system of the brain plays an important part in the pathology of insanity, for by it the waste matters of nutrition and function are believed to be removed. Clearly if such matters are not duly cleansed away, they cannot fail to obstruct and poison the delicate nerve-cells, since these, like mortals, create for themselves a poisonous environment which would soon be fatal to them were they not regularly disencumbered of it. All the more pernicious must the waste products be when, besides an excess of them in quantity owing to an excessive activity, there is perhaps also a more virulent quality of them owing to the disorderly character of the activity. If the hyaline sheath of the blood-vessel be connected with a capsule surrounding each nerve-cell by a spur-like process, as the latest theory has it, there is obviously an ideally complete apparatus by which its refuse is discharged into the perivascular sheath and carried thence away. Equally obvious is it that if the capsule and its process get blocked, the nerve-cell must be in a very ill plight—somewhat in the case of a man buried under a fall of earth who dies half crushed and half poisoned.

To the agents that work to clean away the refuse of metabolic processes in the cortex it has been proposed to add an active ally. As the larger, branched cells of its connective tissue—the so-called spider-cells or Deiter's cells—increase in number and are much more evident in certain morbid conditions, Dr. Bevan Lewis has propounded the theory that they are connective elements in the lymphatic system which perform the work of "scavengers" by devouring the refuse.¹ They increase rapidly in conditions where there is increased waste of cerebral neurine, especially in senile insanity, he believes, and are then very active in the removal of the products of disintegrate nerve-cells and fibres and of vascular effusions. In the end, when they are overwrought and beaten by stress of their work, as they are in chronic insanity, their processes undergo hypertrophy, take the place of the normal neuroglia, and form a net-like structure which, contracting, damages nerve-cells and fibres and narrows or obliterates the channels of minute blood-vessels. Except in very acute cases of insanity, especially of acute mania and general paralysis, where they are numerous and distinct, they are not many in the early stages.

As might be expected, it is in chronic insanities where disease has gone deepest and farthest and where permanent weakness of mind is manifest that the degenerative changes in the cerebral cortex are most marked—in senile dementia, in alcoholic dementia, and especially in general paralysis. Thickening of the membranes of the brain, especially of the *pia mater;* thickenings and degenerations, atheromatous and fatty, of the walls of the tortuous blood-vessels; increase of the connective tissue; atrophy and destruction of the nerve-cells; colloid and amyloid degenerations;—these and the ultimate general wasting of the cortex are certainly as emphatic evidence of structural degeneration as the mental incoherence and weakness are of functional degeneration. From shrunken, degenerate, and perhaps broken-up nerve-cells nothing better than a dementia of function can be looked for. General paralysis might be said to present the morbid changes of ordinary insanity in distinct and

---

¹ *A Text-book of Mental Diseases.*—They are figured in some excellent plates representing the microscopical morbid anatomy of the brain by Dr. Palmer of the Lincoln County Asylum in the *Journal of Mental Science* for 1887 and 1888. He believes them to be protoplasmic exudations from the arterioles, larger than ordinary leucocytes, which no doubt form part of the phenomena of inflammation. Exactly similar bodies can be seen in repair-tissue at the margin of an injury, and in the inner coat of the wall of any arteriole after thrombosis.

accentuated characters, so that they are more easily read, as it presents their symptoms in more dramatic form—all the inflammatory signs and products at first, followed in due succession by the degenerative and destructive effects. But its morbid changes are at bottom much the same as those of senile insanity and of chronic alcoholic insanity; indeed they may well be so, seeing how difficult it is sometimes to distinguish these insanities by the symptoms from general paralysis.

A morbid event which is most common in general paralysis, though it occurs sometimes in other forms of chronic insanity, is a so-called *Pachymeningitis* or *Hæmatoma of the dura mater*. It is an effusion of blood into the arachnoid cavity on the surface of the brain. Virchow thought that the hæmorrhage was from the rupture of a delicate, new-formed vessel of an inflammatory exudation. But a later and better-grounded opinion is that an effusion of blood from the ruptured vessels of the *pia mater* over the gyri is the primary event and that the clot then undergoes more or less organisation. Dr. Wigglesworth, who has made a special study of such clots, attributes the vascular rupture to the wasting of the hemispheres and the congestion of the degenerate vessels in the meninges.[1]

Examinations of the brains of idiots have disclosed degenerative changes similar to those of demented insanity: local obliteration of capillaries in the *pia mater* and convolutions, the capillaries having the appearance of dirty yellow bands of connective tissue; more or less marked atheromatous degeneration of arteries, veins, and capillaries; and coarsely granular nerve-cells, with disappearance of their nuclei, and their processes more or less abortive or degenerate. The so-called hypertrophy of the brain met with sometimes in large-headed imbeciles, especially epileptic imbeciles, is due really to an increase of the neuroglia, not of the nerve-elements themselves, which in fact, like the capillaries, undergo atrophy.

Formerly a great deal was made of *Hæmatoma auris* or

[1] *Journal of Mental Science*, January 1888.

Othœmatoma as a consequence of serious, and a sign of hopeless, insanity; it was called "the insane ear" and deemed to have the worst prognostic import. It is simply a bloody swelling of the ear produced by a gradual effusion of blood under the perichondrium, or within the layers, of the cartilage of the ear. The blood may remain for some time in the cystic state, but absorption of it takes place eventually, and the ear then becomes dry and shapelessly shrivelled. Some ascribe it to violence done to the ear, while others argue strenuously that its gradual manner of coming on, its appearance, and its duration distinguish it positively from a contusion. The fact that the shrivelled ear is seen in the statues of ancient wrestlers and is not unknown to football players of the present day points pretty plainly to a traumatic origin. Certainly it is not the sign of hopeless insanity which it has been pronounced.

The laborious inquiries made into the coexistence of thoracic and visceral disease with insanity have not revealed any special connection; although all diseases of all organs are met with from time to time in different cases, no disease can be said to occur in constant relation to a particular insanity. Cancer of the stomach or liver has been observed where there was a delusion that some animal was present in the belly gnawing it; and in a well-known case recorded by Esquirol, where a woman had the most preposterous delusions concerning the enemies who were fighting one another in her inside, a chronic peritonitis had glued the intestines together. Disease of the uterus, a prolapsus of it, an ovarian cyst has also sometimes seemed to impart a sexual colouring to the insane delusions. But similar disease of every organ, thoracic and abdominal, has been met with in the insane without any traceable connection between the complexion of the insanity and the particular disease. Still, without such special relation, disease of any organ of the body may be expected, by reason of the consensus of parts in an organic whole, to conspire with other predisposing or exciting causes to produce and aggravate mental disorder.

CHAPTER II

THE TREATMENT OF INSANITIES

I. *Preventive*

To prevent insanity, when possible, were a better thing than to cure it, which is often impossible. The discussion of its causation, while showing how prevention would have to be done, has shown also how difficult it must be ever to get it done and how unlikely it is that it ever will be done. An ideal aim requires for its achievement an ideal human being capable of ideal virtues.

The two principal ways of its prevention obviously are: (1) To hinder its propagation from generation to generation, and (2) to employ that training and culture of self which is best fitted to repress and suppress its germ in one who is predisposed to it. Not to breed it were best, but, having bred it, it were good not to rear it. The misfortune is that both ways of well-doing run directly on the bed rock of human selfishness and usually end there.

1. The good of the kind being an end which men count it right to strive for, it would seem wrong, abstractly speaking, for insanely predisposed persons to marry and procreate. Nevertheless it is certain that reasons are never wanting to justify or excuse the wrong in the particular instance. Those who absolutely reject interest as excuse for such a marriage, counting it but base selfishness, still hesitate to pronounce so absolutely against love as a motive, and may even discover a sublime unselfishness in it. They

can think that when a man and woman have conceived a violent love for one another, they belong to one another by a higher than human law, a divine law of nature transcending human conventions and insight, and thereupon believe that the affair is not their concern but may be safely left to the universal plan, which will provide for its own fulfilment in its own way. Perceiving plainly that human continuance and development through the ages have not been dictated by reason, they find a divine sanction of passionate love in the evolutional impulse of nature which has so often made man go onward blindly against reason. The pity of the principle is in its logical application to passionate lovers whatever the obstacle, whether husband, or wife, or madness, which separates them.[1]

There is always an excuse for risky marriages in the complete want of exact knowledge of the laws of heredity and in the impossibility of laying down precise rules in face of the complexities and practical difficulties of the subject. Balancing the gain against the harm, would it be right or wrong to breed children with the certainty that one might be specially talented, perhaps something of a genius, and another insane? Would the world be the better or the worse off if it lacked the explosive enthusiasms and narrow fanaticisms which help so much to break the tyrannous thrall of custom and to free thought and feeling? There is more promise of progress in explosive variations which strike out new paths than in sober uniformities which cannot leave the trodden paths of ancestors; and if man is ever to reach the ideal heights of evolution

[1] The mighty, often terrible, effects which have been caused on earth by the passion of love—that is to say, by a secret sympathetic thrill, a consensual vibration of nerve-molecules, between two beings, may be taken in two ways : either as evidence of its quasi-divine nature and sanction, or as evidence of human vanity and of the vanity òf human things. Pascal says :—" Qui voudra connoître à plein la vanité de l'homme, n'a qu'à considérer les causes et les effets de l'amour. La cause en est un *je ne sais quoi* (Corneille), et les effets en sont effroyables. Ce *je ne sais quoi*, si peu de chose qu'on ne peut le reconnoître, remue toute la terre, les princes, les armées, le monde entier. Le nez de Cléopâtre, s'il eût été plus court, toute la face de la terre aurait changé."

which good people expect in time to come and fanatics are frantic to foresee near at hand, he cannot afford to dispense with the inspirations of neurotic beings. Human life, its record soberly regarded, has always been so much a madness that to eliminate the madness might be to end the life. Those who, living now, will not admit this to be true of the present, being, like most madmen, unaware of their madness, cannot help seeing it to be true of the past.

Whoever has a cool and sober regard to the prospective peace and repose of his own life will certainly shun marriage with an insanely predisposed person. Setting aside the risk of insanity in her or her children, such a union at the best is not likely to be restful; it will probably expose him to uncertain recurrences of unseasonable desires, fidgety impulses, flighty fancies, and jarring disquietudes of thought, feeling and conduct which he cannot cure and only afflicts himself in vain if he tries to cure, and which, but for the ease or even liking of endurance conferred by custom on the patient husband, might render his condition insupportable. Interesting to see is the special sympathy of nature by which two persons of unsound neurotic temperament are sometimes attracted to one another as lovers, being both inspired by its intense sentiments and idealistic aspirations of the unpractical kind, and how ill they bear the disillusion and discord which the dull and prosaic duties of domestic life fail not to entail. Despising the low ways and sordid ideals of the crowd, they discover, when they become part of the crowd, that to leave the common road is to go astray to disaster, and that there is nothing for it but to condescend to its aims and to go its ways. If domestic life and love in Eden was so sad a satiety that Eve was driven by curiosity for a new experience to forfeit its monotonous happiness, it is not surprising that two intense temperaments prone to overstrained imaginations cannot always bear its dull yoke patiently. They are doubly unfitted—first, because they cannot bear and forbear in the mean and unheroic trials of daily life, whence ensue frequent discords and ruptures; and, secondly, because of an impatience of dull routine and a craving for the excitement of more ideal experiences, whence dissatisfactions, recriminations, unrest. Without doubt a naughty curiosity for new experiences has counted for more than passion as a motive in some adulterous ventures; and it may be that a liberal gratification of the craving has sometimes preserved from insanity one who otherwise might have fallen into it. After all, if we reflect on it, the indulgence of the special want of a warped nature may sometimes be the necessary condition of any adjustment at all of it to the environment.

A young man in love with a young woman predisposed to insanity is in a rather evil case, for he is not only blinded by passion so as to see what he desires in her and to see nothing else, but he may expect to have all her relatives in a tacit conspiracy to keep him blind. They are capable of persuading themselves that she is only hysterical and that marriage will be sure to cure her of her ailments, or they hold in a commercial country the commercial maxim that it is the seller's business to sell and the buyer's business to take care of himself. Even if she has had an attack of acute mania it is not certain that he will be told of it or told frankly what it was; at most he may hear of an attack of strong hysteria. To say so much will be a sufficient discharge of conscience to them, loth to believe what they would fain not believe, and a sufficient assurance to him, eager to believe what he wishes to believe. So, in conformity with the established custom of mankind to regard not what the thing is itself but what it is called, they are glad he should marry, and he is glad to marry, madness when it has been christened hysteria. The cold scientific truth which a prudent suitor in love should apprehend and ponder is that any mental disorder occurring during the years of pubescence in a person who inherits a predisposition to insanity is not a light but a grave thing, and that if passion blind him to its gravity or generosity move him to esteem it lightly, he may have to reckon ultimately with an insane wife, or with insane offspring, or perhaps with both. The practical rule of worldly caution which he will do well to bear in mind is that behind what he sees and hears there is always something, sometimes a great deal, which he does not see nor hear.

Is then a person who is prejudiced by insane inheritance to be condemned to celibacy and to the privation of life's best joys? Are we to apply strictly to the human kind the rules which a breeder of any select species of animal would accept without question and enforce as a matter of course? So hard a decision is naturally hard to come to; and it is no wonder if the two persons concerned declare that they are quite willing to assume the responsibility and face the risk of one another—nay, sincerely persuade themselves that the calamity of insanity, if it come to either, will be a trial of loving self-sacrifice and be met by a heroic devotion of which the other feels quite capable. But that is the ardent utterance of passion which is fleeting, not the cool wisdom which proceeds from reason and is lasting. They know not nor can know what it is they propose to do, until the calamity befalls and they are face to face with the sad, dreary and ugly reality. For there is nothing lovely in madness, and it must be a deep well of love which is not sooner or later emptied by its irksome exactions. Moreover, the question arises whether they have the right to breed children under conditions that entail a possible heritage of woe on a single human being to come. If, thinking not, they still decide they will marry but will forbear consummation or frustrate procreation, they adopt conditions of life which are most likely to precipitate the overthrow of the ill-balanced nature. Is the right thing then not to marry? If so, is it wrong also for a married person who has been insane and has recovered to have any more children? The woman who has once had puerperal insanity, is she to be debarred ever afterwards from childbearing? Peremptory prohibition once begun, it is hard to say where it ought to begin and end.

All the more questionable is peremptory prohibition, since madmen are neither so hurtful to themselves and others nor so miserable as they are vulgarly supposed to be.

Many persons not insane do as little good in the world as they do, and a vast deal of harm which they are precluded from doing. Why should noxious sanity be freely granted a right to be bred which is grudged to innocuous insanity? One may suspect sometimes that all the insane persons of a nation, if they had been let loose in it, could never have done it the damage in one generation which a single person has done to whom it has raised monuments of admiration in marble or in bronze. But it will be said perhaps that madmen are such miserable wretches that it is a pain to them to live. That is a hasty opinion which sane persons form because they cannot help attributing to them the feelings which they, being sane, would have were they in their position; which is as ridiculous as it would be to think that a sore-sick or dying man must be dreadfully distressed because he cannot run, ride, toil and moil, when all the feeling he has is that it is strange, hardly credible, that people are caring to run, ride, toil and moil. Some insane persons, it is true, are unhappy because of their melancholy fears and delusions; others, however, have a joy in their madness which madness only knows; while the majority of them, having no particular feeling either of misery or of happiness, would go on indifferently living their mechanical lives for ever were that immortal satisfaction granted them. Where is more devoted love ever seen than that sometimes lavished by a fond mother on her idiot child, in whose inarticulate howls and meaningless grimaces she detects, in spite of disproof, proofs of intelligence and affection which are an unspeakable joy to her heart? And is not such joy worth as much as the joy with which the multitude acclaims a politician's eloquent babble, or a victory at football or on the battle-field, or a display of superiority in any other of the occupations and diversions with which man distracts himself from thinking seriously how poor a creature, engrossed in pursuing poor ends, he is.

If the greatest blessing is to be well born, and it would be a blessing for the human race if only those who are sound of body and mind should marry, as Ferselius said long ago, then one may do well to take serious account of the considerations which have been set forth in the chapter treating of the causation of insanity. But every one must make his observations and reflections before he falls in love, for he cannot observe and reflect when he is in love; on the contrary, he will then see in the manifest imbecilities of his mistress only innocent prettinesses, in her unreasoning impulses only pretty caprices, in the sacrifices which she inflicts on others only rights withheld from her or wrongs done to her. Let him study her character in her history. What has been her life at home as a daughter? Little things are not of little significance when they are rightly read as revelations of character. In Othello's eyes it was a loving virtue in Desdemona to deceive her father for his sake; but if Othello had not been as thick-witted as he was brave, he might have suspected that a maiden of so refined a breed and nurture, who, in spite of nature, country, credit, everything, grossly and heartlessly deceived her father to throw herself into his coarse, sensual embraces, would be pretty sure insidiously to deceive herself and finally him if the sufficient temptation ever presented itself.[1]

If he is minded to carry his critical inquiries further, let him take particular notice of the physical signs, if there are any, which betray degeneracy of stock—of any malformations of the head, face, mouth, teeth, and ears. Outward defects and deformities are the visible signs of inward and invisible faults which will have their influence in breeding.

---

[1] No juster warning could have been given than that contained in her father's last words to Othello—

> Look to her, Moor, if thou hast eyes to see:
> She has deceived her father and may thee.

And how pitiful the inept insight shown in Othello's reply!

> My life upon her faith!—Honest Iago . . .

By bringing so close together the confidence in her faith and Iago's honesty Shakespeare may have intended to indicate something more than the Moor's simplicity. Might not the murder be after all a sort of anticipatory vengeance for a crime which was maturing in the womb of time and would one day have been delivered?

And let him not forget that there is almost as much risk from marrying some mental obliquities as from marrying insanity.

2. The second principal consideration is for the person who has a predisposition to insanity. How shall he so discipline his mind and manage his life as not to become insane himself and not to propagate insanity in his progeny? There is no lack of wisdom to help him, since he has ready at hand for use all the wise sayings of philosophy, the maxims of morality, and the principles of religion to inspire his heart, to instruct his intellect, to govern his conduct, to strengthen his will. Had it sufficed to know wisdom, mankind would long ago have been mighty wise. Not in the knowledge but in the practice of wisdom is there scope for improvement. But they have ever been reckless enough in the mass to obey the inspiration of feeling and to hope, rather than to regard the lessons of reason and perchance to despair. As for the individual, the misfortune is that he who has least need of wise dogmas can readily assimilate them, while he who has most need of them can make no use of them; they are excellent where they are least, useless where they are most, wanted.

A perfectly balanced mind could not well become insane from moral causes; its equilibrium would be too stable to be overthrown by any commotion which it could suffer. Being thoroughly logical and mathematical in structure, it would see things, itself included, in their causes and consequences and see them truly, see them in their true proportions and see them whole; the ratio in it would prevent it from growing irrational. It is an easy counsel then to give every one to acquire the just balance of a quiet mind and a calmly strong will, but in many cases it is as futile as to recommend a short man by taking thought to add a cubit to his stature. What boots it to preach to one who is lame of mind a system of philosophy which only the best-made minds can live, and live only when they are at their best? Advice, to be practical, must have regard to what is and what is not within a man's powers, which his nature and fortune are not; a mind that is naturally lame and deformed being no more able than a lame and deformed body to attain the ideal of development —the ideal, that is, of strength, activity, and beauty. To learn to have a strong will is to learn to develop that compact confederation and unity of well-fashioned mental centres of which a strong and large will is the conscious expression, and which it is the defect of the insanely predisposed person to want. Fit practice on a fit basis—that is how every perfection of will is attained; no more to be had otherwise than is perfection in dancing or in swimming.

As the loose-knit and irregularly formed parts of an unsound mental organisation do not work well together in just ratio and compact unity of consent, so they are easily deranged, easily losing such unity as they have, and break up into self-conscious turmoil. There are nervous temperaments so sensitive that they are put out of sorts by a cloudy sky, an east wind, an electric change in the atmosphere, and so mobile that they pass by a quick transition from gloom to joy in a ray of sunshine, a south wind, another state of the atmosphere. Their whole bodily system is affected in its inmost, whether they will or not; they cannot help feeling their moods even if they restrain the outward expression of them; it is impossible therefore that they should think coolly and act composedly as if they had them not. To ask a person who is suppressing the display of an irritable sensitiveness to think quietly is like asking a thing to be hot and cold at the same instant. The level of inhibition, and with it the level of consciousness, being lowered throughout the whole nervous system, they live on a lower than the sanest plane of cerebral plexuses and are terribly self-conscious in every function of mind: over-sensitive in sensation, over-quick in emotion, over-excitable in thought, unsteady and explosive in will, incontinent and spasmodic in action; they have a self too irritably conscious of itself to receive quietly and assimilate the stimuli of ordinary impressions, which its excessive irritability at once makes extraordinary. They lack self-suppression, order of thought, perseverance : it is easier for them to pass from one extreme to another than to stay in a quiet equilibrium of orderly thought and action : steady application is repugnant to them and soon exhausts and wearies them. When such neuropathics have some special talent or genius they are the degenerates or decadents who distinguish themselves in some display of morbid art, literature, or social activity ; when they become actually insane they are full of their morbid sensations and self-consciousness and can think and talk of nothing else. A lowered level of inhibition in a complex organic union means a tendency to discursive action of its constituent parts : to transform turbulence into stillness is a transformation of lower into higher energy. Co-ordinate and integrate action is composition, disordinate and disintegrate action is decomposition of reason and will.

How is the fault to be mended ? As it has been made —by function. But by good social function which works for consolidation, not by such bad function as in the past has tended to disintegration. Now good function which is to be steady, lasting, and naturally prone to exercise, is not the accidental acquisition of an hour or a day : it is a slow affair of gradual incorporation in structure through patience and constancy in well-doing. It will always be impossible entirely to undo in one generation what has been formed through generations ; but if a character is to be so much as modified materially the process must begin early in life and be continued steadily through childhood and youth. A wholesome system of feeling and discipline must steadily ingrain in structure a set habit of feeling and doing well, if an acquired nature is to be developed to counteract or supplement the defects of an inborn nature. Everybody's moral character is practically formed before adolescence. The child steadily assimilates the social medium in which it lives, accepting it without question as the natural order of things which could not be, or it cannot think to be, otherwise ; and if it has been formed badly then, no after-training will undo the mischief which omission or commission has done. A childhood of indulgence is necessarily a manhood devoid of endurance and self-restraint. It is the way of Nature to exact rigid observation of its laws and never to remit the inexorable penalty for a breach of them, whether the fault be wilful or unwitting. If education and training be not based on the same stern principle, the individual will suffer the inevitable consequences in follies that are faults, in misfortunes that are misdoings, in sufferings that are sins—perhaps in suicides that are Nature's ultimate means of getting rid of a structure unfit to continue in it. When a person is weary of life, it is that life in Nature is weary of him.

Given a nature predisposed to go wrong mentally, an ideal counsel of ideal perfection might be to take its training out of the hands of those who bred that inclination in it—from the parents who, by a pathological sympathy of nature, see its faults with indulgence, if they can see them at all, nay perhaps behold them with loving admiration, and shrink from the pain to themselves of inflicting the pain of a fit discipline on it. In order to rule it as it should be ruled, they would have to rule their own minds as they should be ruled and to change the whole tone of the domestic atmosphere. Children are very quick to assimilate unconsciously what they feel and see around them; mimic habits of thought and feeling as they do habits of gesture and speech; are actors who take advantage of and play excellently well to the situation without knowing how well they do it; easily contract perhaps a pretty fair chorea from a choreic, pretty finished convulsions from a convulsed, child.[1] They cannot thrive sanely within the insane precincts of parental morbidity, for it is the tone and feeling of the social atmosphere around it which the child breathes continually that unconsciously determines the tone of its nature. In the end it is not the instruction of intellect but the instruction of feeling, not the cramming in of

[1] A tendency to mimicry is a natural instinct of the human nervous system, whether it be a reminiscence of simian or pre-simian ancestors or not. One sees a remarkable display of it in some imbeciles who, lacking reason and utterly destitute of common sense, can still imitate wonderfully, remember well, and perhaps discourse volubly.

knowledge but the formation of a good tone of nature, which is the best gift of early education. On the whole it were better to misguide a child in knowledge, which it can remedy later, than to mistone it in feeling, for which there is no remedy. A jarring note implanted in its nature might spoil the music of its life, a melody of feeling implanted in it make music of its life.

Not many natures predisposed to insanity but might be saved from it were they placed from their earliest days in exactly those circumstances and subjected to exactly that training most fitted to counteract the innate infirmity. To apply fit counteraction fitly to the wrong bias, however, it would be necessary to have a full and exact knowledge of the construction of the individual mind as well as of the proper remedy : to know the particular character, the special fault of it, the kind of disorder to which the fault was prone to lead, and the exact conditions of life which would be the fit remedy; for different pursuits might wisely be used as so many remedies for different defects of character. The example of the Jesuits, who alone among educators seem to have aimed to adapt specially a system of training to the special qualities of individual character, proves at any rate how much can be done to mould a human being to feel, think, and believe in a particular way and to find the happiness of his life in the automatic exercise. In the mental organism we have really a plastic machinery which, if taken in hand sufficiently early, may be manufactured to almost any desired pattern of feeling and belief. By severing the child from general experience, placing it in conditions that force it to work to a certain fashion of function, and giving it the exclusive training of a constant special experience through youth into adult age, it might be so moulded that the man would think and believe in the prescribed track, feel the truth of his belief with an intuitive certitude transcending contradictory experience, and pride himself exultantly on a faith robust enough to believe not only what was above but what was contrary to reason. In the history of mankind nothing has been so firmly believed as that which was absolutely incredible. Obviously then, if a sane mind may be trained to believe any madness, it ought to be all the more practicable to train a mind predisposed to madness to a pattern of sane thought and feeling. An advantage which the Jesuits possess is that they have a definite standard of man whom they desire and work definitely to form, whereas the world in general would be puzzled to say what is the standard of man which it ought to aim to fashion. A being professing to be what he is not and aspiring to be what he would be sorry to be can hardly be the final aim of its developmental *nisus*. Moreover, the psychology which should have supplied it with principles and methods has been so much in the clouds, so entirely divorced from realities, that it has given no help.

The work of education is to mould a mental organisation with inherent differences of tendencies which can, within certain limits, be fashioned by fit exercise in doing. By doing and not otherwise. To develop a good moral and intellectual character by a process of introspection and reflection, whereby wrong impulses are to be curbed, right impulses to be roused and exercised, and a strong will, able to rule despotically, to be formed deliberately—that is at best only a devout imagination of the closet. Such a method of procedure by itself is likely to do more harm than good by intensifying self-consciousness, even if it do not actually stimulate wrong impulses by the attention given to them in order to realise and reprehend them. Let anybody from his earliest years live in conditions in which he must, as a daily matter of course, without thinking of it, practise self-denial and self-control, subdue self-regarding impulses, feel, think, and act for others, he will, unless the original structure of his nature is hopelessly bad, be shaped into a good social unit and rule himself wisely. Let him, in the absence of such conditions, occupy himself in reflections on his wrong impulses, in penitential broodings and catechetical self-communings, and in making good resolutions how to feel and do well in the future, he may succeed now and then, but his success will be occasional and uncertain, not in the central stream of his nature, of ungracious evidence, and of small manufacturing value. The fact that he needs consciously to make many good resolutions proves that they are mostly made in vain; that the good principles of a working philosophy have not been grounded in his mental constitution. For it is in the constant system working silently, not in irregular jolts of regret and jerks of resolution, that the construction of a sound and virtuous nature lies. Were a man capable of looking at himself from outside and of satirising himself as a fool among fools when he makes a fool of himself, the practice would be a wonderful preservative against insanity. Thereupon follows naturally the excellent counsel for one in need of it to cultivate a habit of seeing himself in others and therefore as others see him—a habit of detachment and objective study of self. But that is just what he who has a predisposition to insanity cannot for the most part do; for an intensity of self-consciousness is the usual infirmity of his nature and an insuperable hindrance.

No doubt it would be most helpful to him to fix a good aim in life within his compass to attain, to which he should work resolutely, constantly, and definitely; for that would steadily shape his nature as a whole by moulding its divers parts to work together definitely in common consent of rule and order to the appointed end. Consider what a passion like love or ambition—love in youth and ambition in manhood—may do to brace the energies of a feeble neurotic; how it can subdue overgreat sensitiveness, subjugate self to a discipline of self-denial, and enforce strenuous and systematic work. Without need of vows and resolutions, the motive inspires the method and the work; consciousness of the end swallows up self-consciousness in the doing. It is a good fortune then for the neurotic who, incapable of larger and more sober aims, gets himself absorbed in some fanatical project and devotes all his energies to its pursuit. An opposite exemplification of the same truth is the misfortune of the neurotic who, having retired from work in which he has been strenuously and successfully engaged, becomes the most miserable of men, occupied all day with vexing himself about trifles and with watching his pulse and his sensations. The truth is that it is a dangerous thing for a man to be continually thinking about himself, because he then runs a risk of feeling and finding himself to be such a wretched creature that suicide seems the only sensible issue. From that gloomy thought and issue he is saved by the distraction of an ambition in which he forgets himself, no matter whether it be ambition for distinction in work or in play—to be the first politician or the first billiard player in the world, the first in the game of golf or in the game of war.

The wisest thing, perhaps, which a person predisposed to insanity could do to hinder its development would be to make a complete change of his surroundings and to begin a new life in a new country. To change the constitutions of individuals and to prevent the diseases to which they are hereditarily prone, Hippocrates taught that they ought to be placed in entirely different circumstances from those in which their parents lived and they were born. Certainly other circumstances than those in which an insane strain of mind has been bred are the most fit to counteract it; for, by the disuse of old tracts of mental structure and the use of new tracts in order to make new adjustments, they tend to produce salutary differentiations. Oftentimes the transplantation might advantageously be into the simpler and ruder conditions of a young country and cruder civilization, where there would be more to do with the realities and simplicities of men and things and less to do with the artificial conventions and hypocrisies of a complex society. For these constitute a system of irritating rules and checks to which the nature cannot perhaps accommodate itself, and which its very intensity of self-feeling may render insupportable. But custom is tyrannical: not to conform to its established rule is counted eccentricity or want of reason, perhaps a gross social offence, though little reason may be needed to prove the custom to be utterly unreasonable. It is not only that the refusal to conform is something which most minds cannot even imagine and in any case a sore trial of mental fortitude, but success in life depends on conformity to the approved opinions and manners of the society in which a person lives: he who cannot bend to them must be very strong if he does not break under them. To get away into the new circumstances of a young country is, as it were, to strengthen vitality by contact with mother earth; for the change may not only impart the rude animal vigour which it needs to a constitution of frail nervous structure, but fortify it by full freedom of exercise in simple and general functions. Moreover, a rude and turbulent nature may find there fit outlet for its tumultuous energies.

A complete transplantation might be specially beneficial sometimes, I think, in the case of a proneness to adolescent insanity. The conditions of life in the complex society of a large city not only conduce to develop a keen activity of the nervous system generally, which becomes irritable and excessive activity when that system is inherently weak, but tend specially to enkindle sexual sensibility and precocity. For the sensuality of a great city is not merely the large accumulation of it in one place: it is the production also, from the fermenting mass, of a sort of hothouse sexual atmosphere which stimulates the development of sexual passion and favours its degeneration into lubricities and depravities. Nothing can be better therefore than to remove an insanely predisposed youth, prone by his very predisposition often to an irritable sexual precocity, into the cooler, fresher and more wholesome atmosphere of a simpler and ruder life in direct converse with nature; from the corruptions and artifices of human nature when congregated in complex society—the social toxins which hitherto have always been bred in it to poison it—to the salutary simplicities and sincerities of physical nature.

II. *Curative.*

The purely medical treatment of insanity which is not maltreatment might be comprised within a narrow compass.

Drugs can no more directly quell an insane delusion than they can eradicate an envy or abate an ambition. Their best use lies in their beneficial action on any bodily disorder which is co-operating to cause or keep up the mental disorder. Always must the prime aim of medical treatment be to put right the bodily health when it is wrong.

The first thing to do, then, in a particular case is to find out what is the bodily disorder, if there be any. Is the patient gouty? If so, treat the gout. Is he syphilitic? If so, treat the syphilis. Is he diabetic? If so, treat the diabetes. Is he badly nourished? Use the proper means to improve his nutrition. Just attention to these considerations may obviously warrant the treatment of the same form of mental disorder by nearly opposite methods and of different forms of mental disorder by the same method—the treatment, for example, of melancholia in an overfed, gouty man quite differently from its treatment in a half-starved, feeble woman exhausted by suckling and domestic worries. Neglect of them may lead to gross maltreatment by stuffing a gouty melancholic with food the changes of which in the metabolic travail act as direct poisons to the nervous system, or by purging away the vitality of a feeble melancholic on the theory that a sluggish liver is the cause of the mental illness. Worse still, it has led, and may lead again, to the cruelty of feeding forcibly with the stomach-pump an unfortunate melancholic whose refusal of food was due to an overlooked cancer of the stomach.

In the medical treatment of insanities it is of the first importance to encounter and, if possible, check the beginnings of disorder. They may be prevented then sometimes, though little or nothing can be done to abate them when they have once got headway. In that premonitory stage of moody dejection, unrest and apprehension which goes before positive melancholia, oftentimes also before an outbreak of acute mania, when sleep fails, a grain of opium or a quarter of a grain of morphia at bed-time for two or three nights will sometimes stop a habit of sleeplessness, allay the vague distress, and put an end to the trouble. Instead of a single dose of opium at bed-time, the administration of a small dose of morphia (gr. $\frac{1}{8}$ or $\frac{1}{6}$) three times a day has sometimes the best effects; for such dose dulls the keen sense of misery, pushes troubles, as it were, to a distance, and acts as a stimulant rather than a narcotic on the nervous system. If the treatment has not an immediate good effect, it is no use continuing it night after night or day after day. With it too should always be combined measures to improve the general health and to obtain change of scene and rest of brain.

As opium does not suit every constitution, it is possible that sulphonal, chloral, chloramide, or paraldehyde may suit better. Of these drugs sulphonal is the mildest, paraldehyde perhaps the most certain, though the nastiest, and chloral the most stupefying in immediate operation; while it may be said of their remote effects that, though none are harmless, those of chloral are the most hurtful. The aim should be to mitigate to the utmost their use, when they cannot be disused—to use so as not to abuse them.

When the attack is not stopped, but the disorder drifts into positive melancholia, no good is done by the continued use of narcotics in order to procure sleep. Most melancholics sleep more than they say or think they do; when they sleep not one night, they perhaps get a fairly moderate sleep the next night. They are more likely to sleep sooner and to get a better sleep after plenty of quiet exercise in the open air, or even only after sitting out-of-doors for most of the day and watching the sea, or the horizon, or the clouds, or the trees. A bicycle or a game of golf is oftentimes a better sleep-producer than any drug in the pharmacopœia. Very useful sometimes is a warm bath at night, in which the patient lies for five or ten minutes; for it is not only pleasant to the skin but, by its soothing effects on the cutaneous nerves, it exerts a reflex soothing effect on the central nervous system, and may have tranquillizing when it has not sleeping effects. The best results are perhaps obtained by rubbing the body or some part of it gently with the hand, for it is astonishing how soothing, out of all proportion to its seeming simplicity, is the regular stroke of a gentle hand, even when limited to the forehead, arm, or the back of the hand only. A calm and sympathetic nurse may do much to solicit natural sleep in that way, or by reading softly to the distressed patient. But the tone must harmonize if it is to soothe; if not, it will irritate. An unfit nurse, by her jarring presence and ways, will drive sleep away; and it is too ridiculous, while subjecting a sick brain to such untoward influence, to try to soothe it by narcotic drugs.

The sleeplessness of the melancholic is, I think, of two sorts: either he cannot get to sleep when he goes to bed, though he felt sleepy before going to bed, and tosses about all night, getting only short and shallow dozes at the best and thinking in the morning that he has not had a wink of sleep; or he goes to sleep when he goes to bed, but wakes up abruptly after two or three hours and gets no more sleep for the rest of the night. In the former case he should take his sleeping draught at bed-time, if he takes one; in the latter case he may properly defer taking it until he wakes up in the night. But in both cases he might sometimes find a small cup of warm soup or beef-tea or milk or the like to be as efficacious as, and more refreshing than, a sleeping draught. Instead of tossing restlessly from side to side in bed, when he wakes up suddenly in the middle of the night, let him get up, walk about the room for a short time, brush his hair, go through some bodily gymnastics; it will be easier then to go to sleep when he goes back to bed.[1] Only to sit up in bed with the head leaning back against a pillow will sometimes help, especially when quick and irritable palpitations of the heart aggravate the unrest. A more heroic measure, to which few are equal, but which I have more than once known to be adopted successfully, is to plunge into a cold bath or to undergo the douche of a

---

[1] Aubrey says of Harvey:—"His thoughts would many times keep him from sleeping, in which case his way was to rise from his bed and walk about his chamber in his shirt till he was pretty cool, and then return to his bed and sleep comfortably."

shower-bath. The best posture to take in bed is no doubt that which is felt to be most comfortable, but it is certain that one who cannot get to sleep with limbs stretched out will sometimes do so if, bending his knees almost up to his chin, he curls himself up after the manner of a cat or dog. He must not, however, then soon change his position, but steadily maintain it for a reasonable time, resolute, if he is to remain awake, that he will remain awake in it.

There is no doubt that by strong and steady exercise of will a person may gain a certain power of hypnotising himself into natural sleep. If he fix his attention on one thing, the more monotonous the better, rigorously barring the intrusion of wandering thoughts which disquiet him, he finds that just when he succeeds he goes to sleep. That is the real virtue of the various plans recommended to induce sleep—counting slowly up to a hundred, repeating slowly lines of poetry, the continuance of slow, measured respiration with the undistracted imaging of some regular and monotonous movement, and the like. Unlike the use of sleeping draughts, it is a practice which gains, instead of losing, virtue by repetition. But it is not of much use giving such counsel to the melancholic, who would not be melancholic if his will were not weakened, and whose torturing reflections are too acute to be banished by it. It is his weakness that he cannot resolve and persevere in little or great things; though he laments the misery of his sleepless nights and protests that it is intolerable, he has not the resolution to get out of bed in the night and try what a little exercise will do for him. Faith and hope are lacking; he looks for the prophet to do or bid him do some great thing; and the latter, if he recommend such simple measures, must enjoin them as the absolutely indispensable pre-essentials of the big thing which a dose of some harmless drug will then be sure to do.

The best of all hypnotics in some suitable cases is a grain or so of blue-pill at bed-time. The sleep so produced is singularly sound. A domestic remedy which seems to produce a like sleep, probably by a like action on the liver, is the common onion. There is no doubt of its hypnotic qualities when taken in food in the evening; and I knew one gentleman who affirmed that he combated sleeplessness successfully by supping off a stewed Spanish onion. Bad sleep and bad dreams are often caused, in whole or in part, by disorder in stomach, liver, or intestines; and when a deranged abdominal sympathetic nervous system seems to produce a deranged sympathetic disturbance of the heart and of the vascular circulation of the brain, the removal of the disorder by suitable measures is called for, not the further stupefaction of an oppressed brain by narcotic drugs. To dine between eight and nine o'clock at night and to go to bed two hours after a heavy dinner of mixed foods may occasion bad sleep in one who would sleep well after a simple meal at mid-day and a light meal in the evening. Most persons in England take two or three times as much food daily as is necessary and therefore good for them; and those who eat their fill of so-called butcher's meat twice a day perhaps merit more commiseration than those whose sad fate a silly sentimentalism compassionates because they only eat butcher's meat once a week. It is quite possible to be perfectly well nourished and to enjoy the best health without tasting meat once a week, and would be quite possible for many families, rich and poor, to live well for a fortnight on the food which they eat and waste in a week.

Attention having been given to the improvement of the general health and to the removal of any special disorder, a nerve-tonic may be given. I have found useful small doses of arsenic in its acid or alkaline solution, according to circumstances, and doses of two or three drops once or twice a day quite as beneficial as larger doses oftener. With it two or three drops of liquor strychniæ may be combined. Of especial service in some cases is the combination of minute doses of morphia with the arsenic. When there is evidence of anæmia, iron is the remedy indicated, and if the nervous constitution is frail and feeble, cod-liver oil and maltine do great good, especially in young persons.

Constipation is a common trouble in melancholic insanity.

Although pills of colocynth and mercury, black draughts, and other strong purgatives will act freely one day, they leave the over-stimulated liver and bowels less inclined than ever to act naturally afterwards. Milder laxatives, such as liquorice powder, confection of senna, extract of cascara, are to be preferred for frequent use; but a great deal may be done to obtain regular action of the bowels by stewed prunes, stewed pears, tomatoes, or the like, especially if they are taken the last thing at night or the first thing early in the morning. A remedy which is of some use, if it be continued, is a tumblerful of hot water drunk immediately on getting up in the morning before beginning to wash and dress; if the hot water alone has no effect, the addition of some saline water helps satisfactorily. When a regular purgative pill is necessary, a grain or two of extract of aloes, with a quarter of a grain of extract of belladonna every evening, sometimes acts well on the sluggish lower bowel and induces a regular action which may then go on of itself. One patient of mine who had tried many drugs in vain got the best results from taking a light repast of Revalenta Arabica before going to bed; to it he attributed the cure of his constipation and his eventual recovery from melancholia. In some cases the use of an enema two or three times a week is necessary, either because the patient refuses to take any medicine or because the repetition of purgatives day after day is not advisable; then an enema of warm water is best for regular use, though a drachm of glycerine acts excellently as an occasional enema.

Above all things in melancholic insanity, it is proper to enforce a regulated life of exercise, of diet, and, if possible, of doing. The want of hope in the patient is accompanied by a want of faith in remedies that have not an immediate result; he soon, therefore, abandons them as useless, even if he adopts them, unless he has somebody constantly at his elbow to sustain his resolution and to hold him to a continuance in well-doing. His lacking will must be supplemented by a will from without. To wail and despair is the natural utterance and morbid self-indulgence of his misery, and to leave off efforts which it is a pain to make is a part of that self-indulgence. Had he the resolution, despite what he feels and thinks, to ignore himself, convinced that weeping and wailing cannot help and that he must live the nightmare out, and for a few weeks to do steadily as sane persons do, he might discover, at the end of that time, that he was feeling and thinking as they do and was cured of his melancholy.

Forcible feeding by the stomach-pump or by the nasal tube is necessary for some melancholics who positively refuse all food because of a strong delusion that they cannot or must not eat, when there is nothing in the state of their bodily health to prevent them from eating. But it ought to be ascertained clearly beforehand that there is no bodily disorder which accounts for the refusal and might be removed by suitable medical treatment. A vigorous purgative will sometimes bring appetite back by producing a free action of the bowels, when forcible feeding would do no good and might be a positive torture. Owing to the blocking of the bowel by hardened fæces, especially in women, it may be necessary to remove the obstruction by mechanical means; and I have once known recovery directly follow the relief. To cram a melancholic with food which the liver cannot properly manipulate is quite as foolish as the old practice of purging away violently the black bile which was assumed to be the cause of the morbid melancholy; for the inactive and overcharged liver must then let crude matters pass unaltered into the blood which will oppress the nervous system and increase its depression.[1]

---

[1] That is a sort of experiment with regard to which one may dissent from the author of the Report of the Morningside Asylum for 1882, when he says—"I don't suppose any one will object to such 'experiments on living beings' on any ground but the cost." The same author in another place relates two painfully instructive cases: a woman, æt. 58, deeply melancholic and in hopeless despair as to her religious state at first, and afterwards as to the condition of her inside, protesting that she had no gullet, could not live, and refusing all food, got steadily worse, notwithstanding that she was fed thrice a day by a tube through the nose "and very frequently vomited the meal." Her bowels were obstinately constipated, and she died four months

In melancholia, when it is not acute, travel with a suitable companion may be desirable, or residence in one place at the seaside or in the country if the patient dislike travel or is unfit for it. A hydropathic establishment, where rest of brain, regulated diet, and daily exercise can be had, is sometimes of great benefit; and a series of baths there may serve usefully to occupy and inspire the imagination, if they do nothing more. In deciding what change of place to recommend, special regard should be given to the stage and character of the disease and to the individual character. It is not of much use to send a melancholic to travel who cannot tolerate travel when he is well; nor is it of much use to send one who is in the depth of his melancholy to travel from place to place and to go through the dreary routine of hotel life, when he has not the relish to enjoy and lacks the energy almost to endure it. When the worst is over and convalescence is setting in, or when disorder of feeling and thought lingers after the worst symptoms have

after admission. After death the intestines were much distended, particularly the large intestine. In it "huge masses of hard fæcal matter were found which must have been there a considerable time." On the surface of the intestines were found extravasations of blood and traces of inflammation. "One huge mass of fæcal matter seemed to block up the external orifice of the intestinal canal."

The second case was that of a woman, æt. 58, who was wretchedly melancholic, imagining herself to have been very wicked and to be lost for ever. She was worn, anxious, slept badly, had no appetite, and sometimes altogether refused the food forced on her, so that she was once fed with the stomach-pump. Very disinclined to take exercise, she prayed every morning to be allowed to remain in the house, "as she was too weak to walk," and protested against the cruel treatment when she was compelled to go. "This idea at times almost amounted to a delusion that she was persecuted by the attendants." Gradually she became weaker and weaker, until she died. In the brain, after death, was found a cancerous mass growing from the upper part of the petrous part of the temporal bone, and partly embedded in the brain; in the stomach, at its pyloric end, the orifice of which was contracted, were several small secondary masses of cancer.

In the Report of Bethlehem Hospital for 1882, its author says: "I make it a rule that if patients are not taking as much food as I think they should, and if they are losing flesh, to have them fed artificially for a time; by this means one can judge if the wasting be due to physical disease or simple starvation." A rule which the patient with a cancer of the stomach might not feel the same approval of!

disappeared, a voyage may do great good. But care should be taken not to send abroad any one who is sickening for an acute attack of melancholia or of any other insanity.

If the repeated use of narcotics is hurtful in melancholia, it is still more hurtful in mania. Nothing is more pernicious, though nothing more common, than the practice of giving repeated doses of them day after day and several times a day with the aim of subduing the excitement of acute mania. How many the minds and lives that have been destroyed in that way! So many that one may soberly believe that if a narcotic had never once been given in acute mania the recoveries would have been more, and the deaths and dementias fewer, in number than they have been. It seems to be an implicit notion in many minds that the fury is a sort of raging entity which has attacked and taken possession of the unfortunate patient and must be subdued or exorcised by the drug; if there is a revival of the fury after each short period of drug-enforced stupor, as there almost invariably is, it is only proof that larger doses are necessary in order to stifle and still it; and the natural result, seeing that there is no such thing as mania but an individual who is maniacal, is that the heroic measures used to kill it act to kill him or his mind. If a raging entity in him be not assumed, it is at any rate assumed that the mind is on fire, like a house on fire, and that it is necessary to put the fire out. A pretty conceit no doubt, were there good evidence that an inundation of narcotics is fitted to put the fire out, and no evidence that, though they may damp it temporarily, they do not help it to blaze more fiercely afterwards and to keep it going until the mind is put out. Mechanical restraint, except under surgical necessities, was formerly abandoned, not only because use was sure to become abuse, but because it was deemed better for the patient to let him have the relief and self-respect of pretty free exercise than to keep him tied up like a mad dog, and it is not now defended as in itself beneficial by those who have gone back to its use; but it may be doubted whether its coarse bonds did as much harm as has been done by the finer means of chemical restraint which have been used to paralyse the brain and to render the patient quiet.

As the organism is not really attacked by a something which is disease, but is a mechanism that falls into various disorders in consequence of various hurts to it, so it always strives to right itself when the cause of hurt is removed and its processes of restoration are not obstructed by unwise medical meddling. Certainly he is the best physician who, having made the general conditions, internal and external, as favourable as possible, meddles the least with processes which he understands not by drugs the operations of which he understands not. To my mind he who endeavours to stifle acute mania by ever-increasing doses of narcotics is much like one who, thinking to cut short an acute fever, would search out and employ a number of drugs for the purpose of suppressing every external sign of it; or like one who would, if he could, go to work to suppress, because it is violent and destructive, the furious gale which is Nature's way of restoring the equilibrium of the earth's atmosphere.

Having taken care that the patient gets plenty of good nourishment and made proper provision for his security, the best thing is usually to let him work off his excitement by exercise in the open air, if possible : by purposive exercise, if he can be solicited to it, but if not, by the disorderly exercise in which he delights. The meddlesome attendant who, always apprehending that he is going to do something wrong, interferes continually with him, only irritates and keeps up the excitement; the patient is susceptible and suspicious, and, like a startled animal, prone to retaliate by an instant attack; to a tactless environment his disorder reacts automatically in continued disorder. But let him have about him calm attendants who, being cool and tactful, meddle with him as little as possible, and then only with firm composure, the result is that they gain quietly a certain measure of control when they must interfere. Having gained that much, they may go on by patient degrees to solicit and obtain more orderly exercise and thus steadily to develop his self-control, which is the necessary beginning of recovery. Orderly exercise and occupation are not only beneficia lby discharging turbulent nerve-currents—the limitation of action to a definite purpose or end being the arrest of dissipate currents of disorderly activity—but by framing and keeping the mind to obedience, order and method. Any method in thought and action is so much gain ; it is so far to recompose what has been decomposed.[1] This much or this little may certainly be said on behalf of mechanical restraint, that it might do less harm than a bad attendant; but the evil of its use is its inevitable abuse, since those who are most fit by character and experience to use it wisely are those who do not require to use it, while those who are least fit to use it are most quick to use and sure to abuse it.

There is no doubt that a sedative given at the right moment appears sometimes to have an excellent effect in mania. A good sleep follows, the excitement subsides, and recovery perhaps begins : what stronger proof of its remedial operation could be desired ? But when this happy effect takes place it is not at the outset or during the height of the fury, it is usually when it has lasted some time and the worst is over. The salutary virtue of the drug oft lies in its opportune use, and it might be suspected that the good result would have ensued without it. The drug which has failed a hundred times to do the wonder may do it once, and the drug which has done it once not do it again. Still the experimental use of a sedative occasionally is not to be condemned absolutely, especially of opium or morphia in frail and feeble constitutions and in old persons : if it does no good it can soon be abandoned. It is the doctrine of stifling the excitement by the repeated use of such narcotics

[1] Dr. Kandinsky, the Moscow physician whose personal experience of madness in himself I have previously cited, points out how much the active work of the supreme cerebral mental tracts helped to inhibit hallucinations ; these gambolled and luxuriated in him when the former were exhausted by delirious activity, as he believes hallucinations are naturally prone to do when the supreme functions are feeble by nature and training.

as choral, chloramide, and opium day after day and night after night, albeit the enforced temporary quiet is followed by no mental improvement but by ever-renewed excitement, which is to be deprecated as false in theory and pernicious in practice. With the view not of stopping by strong doses an excitement which will run its course, but of abating it by moderate doses without doing harm, bromide of potassium alone, or in combination with tincture of henbane, tincture of digitalis, tincture of Cannabis Indica, tincture of belladonna, or dilute hydrocyanic acid, may be employed. The active principle of henbane, its alkaloid hyoscine, has of late come into great vogue, and the hypodermic injection of it has been extolled for its excellent effects. But what effects? The reports of its successes, when examined, are mostly naïve reports of its success, not in curing but "in quieting the patient." Not a word is said of, apparently not a thought given to, the question whether it helped to bring about recovery or to hasten dementia. There can be no question that it will quiet for a time the strong and active maniac who is conscious of and delights in his turbulent doings, as a knock-down blow on the head which stunned him would do, and perhaps do him no great harm when it is not too often repeated, though it may do him no permanent good; its benefit then being possibly due to the moral shock of the utterly helpless feeling which it produces in him rather than to any medicinal virtue in it. But if there be bodily weakness and a tendency to delirium in the mania, and especially if there be difficulty in getting proper food taken in proper quantity, it may do a great deal of harm—first, by the dryness of throat, difficulty of swallowing, and loss of appetite which it occasions, and, secondly, by the consequent aggravation of bodily weakness and of the delirious tendency.

Even bromide of potassium in large doses often repeated —all the more so when given in combination with chloral, as it often is—ought to be avoided. For what happens when a person has drachm-doses of bromide of potassium given to him three times a day for week after week? A positive enfeeblement of mental powers, which are dull, sluggish, requiring hours to do work which was normally done in half an hour; slow, uncertain speech, one word perhaps being substituted for another having a similar ending and the right word for the idea being found with difficulty; failing memory; stooping gait; heavy eyes and features a state of things artificially produced which, were it to occur naturally, would be thought to portend apoplexy or softening of the brain, but which disappears gradually when the use of the drug is stopped. It is hard to discover in these effects anything to warrant confident expectation of a curative operation in mania; easy to suspect in them the push of a temporary artificial dementia given to the natural tendency to dementia.

Of sleeplessness in mania and of the use of narcotics to combat it I have already spoken at length and shall say no more.[1] It has yet to be proved that the sleep which they produce is beneficial sleep. When a person is rendered unconscious for a time by the inhalation of a suitable gas like chloroform, the unconsciousness is not called sleep, nor is it pretended that it serves the purposes of sleep: why then assume off-hand that when he is rendered unconscious by swallowing a drug like chloral, the perhaps similarly produced effects of which pass away after a while, the case is altogether different? Why expect a disorder of violently acting molecules, which has been caught and fixed, cramplike, by a strong chemical restraint, to take on a quick and orderly action when it is released? It prefers naturally to resume its suspended motion more fiercely; that which the drug has done perhaps is to refresh the mania—to restore its elasticity, so to speak, to supply it with the tension for a subsequent de-tension.

Constipation in mania, if troublesome and not medicable

[1] Page 283.—In speaking so strongly against the abuse, not the prudent trial, of narcotic drugs in acute insanity, I only repeat what I have been preaching all my life. Although the mischief still goes on, especially in private practice, in two or three large public asylums, each containing more than a thousand inmates it has been found practical almost entirely to abandon the use of them.

by suitable diet and simple laxatives, is best dealt with by the use of a simple enema three or four times a week. It is not necessary that the bowels should act every day, and the use of strong purgatives to compel them to do so is meddlesome and mischievous. For exceptional use on urgent occasion a drop of croton oil in a cup of coffee, or two or three grains of calomel in the food, may be given, but the administration of drugs in food is to be avoided as a rule, for any taste or suspicion of them might engender an aversion to food and a delusion that it was poisoned.

The foregoing remarks concerning the treatment of mania and melancholia apply generally to the treatment of the mania and melancholia of general paralysis. The tendency in it, however, being to active cerebral disorganisation, two cautions are necessary : to be more heedful not to do harm by giving drugs in strong doses in order to produce immediate and positive effects; and to treat it as grave disease by insisting more on rest and quiet exercise than on vigorous activity. Whether acute maniacal delirium be, as I have suggested, a sort of acute general paralysis or not, its proper treatment unquestionably is seclusion, nutrition, and as much rest as possible.

The treatment of the class of insanities which I have described as paramorphic, or mental deformities, is obviously only medical incidentally. If any good is to be done, it must be by fit moral management of the native bias of character applied methodically from the cradle onwards into adult life. The principle to be kept in view is to place the individual in surroundings which will steadily and unconsciously ingraft in him the silent conviction that he is not distinct from the rest of his kind and extinguish the desire to be particular and to distinguish himself from them.

The one thing to be desired, if recovery be desired, in all forms of mental derangement is early treatment. Statistics have proved indubitably that the proportion of recoveries rises in proportion to the prompt adoption of fit treatment. Seldom, however, is such treatment put in force, and that exactly because it involves the application of force and all its painful concomitants and consequences, social and legal. The special misfortune of the malady is that the sick man generally does not know that he is sick, nay oftentimes believes himself to be wonderfully well; for it is the organ which should feel and judge that is deranged and now entirely misfeels and misjudges. Not perceiving that his mind is wrong, how can he be expected to submit to any restraint of doings in which he delights, in order to have it set right? His relations and friends cannot take fit action to control him against his will, even if they recognize the beginnings of illness in him: if they are not deterred by their own dread of throwing on him or on the family the stigma of madness, they are confronted with insuperable social and legal obstacles. Suppose them resolute enough to interfere effectually, they still incur most serious risks; for if he recover soon, it will be thought by others, and not improbably by himself, that he has been very unjustly used by them and they may be mulcted in heavy damages in an action at law. The very promptness of the timely action, which ensured recovery and perhaps prevented suicide, will be deemed the weightiest evidence against them, because they did not wait for the furious madness or suicide to prove the necessity of interference. Thus cases are rendered incurable which early treatment might have cured; thus many suicides, and some homicides, occur which might be prevented; and thus no harsh check is put on the propagation of madness by madmen from generation to generation: rather than endanger the principle of individual liberty it is deemed better for madmen to become hopelessly mad, commit suicide, and propagate madness.

In all dealings with the insane a frank sincerity ought to be aimed at. It is wrong to pretend to agree with his delusions, though it may be of no use to argue against them. A clear and distinct expression of disbelief in them as groundless, made with quiet firmness, has sometimes a beneficial effect in the end, though it seemed useless at the time. Many times the maniac is not nearly so confident as he looks, having at bottom a latent distrust of himself, and is impressed, if not oppressed, by calm sanity of discourse; the wise word wisely spoken stirs in him a subconscious distrust and reflection which subdue insane belief to a sort of half-belief for the time and may perchance suppress a half-belief altogether. A kind word of real sympathy, a cheering expression of hope, a genial pressure of the hand, a good-humoured satire—a little thing of that sort will sometimes do much to hearten the melancholic and to initiate hope, reflection, and recovery. All-important is the manner of saying and doing what is said and done; for a good manner is as good a passport to the confidence of insane as it is to that of sane persons. The suspicious and irritable susceptibility of mania is offended instantly by the least misliked and therefore misconstrued expression, which he is quick to catch —by a too curious look, an angry frown, the least expression of scorn, an aggressive or constrained address, any hurt to his self-love, which, resented at the time, is remembered bitterly after recovery. Bitter too are his feelings then sometimes if he was removed forcibly from home to an asylum without explanation, or was sent there by deceit; for he remembers how the apprehensions and delusions of his insanity were aggravated by his unexplained arrest, and by finding himself in a position utterly unintelligible to him, and how his disordered mind was harassed by all sorts of horrible imaginings to account for the situation and to escape from it.

In the management of insane persons exact account should be taken of the individual character, and the circumstances of attendance and treatment be adapted accordingly. It would be absurd to treat medically the insanity of a feeble pubescence exactly as one would treat the melancholia of a gouty climacteric; and queer people are sometimes best managed by queer people, a fellow-feeling being the foundation of confidence and influence. It is of no use to try to enforce systematically a mode of life which goes contrary to the strong bent of a particular nature; since such a warp, wanting a particular way, must have its way for the most part, or else it will wreck the whole structure.

Always the rule of rules should be to treat an individual who is sick, not an abstract disease.

It has been proposed lately to call in the aid of surgery to cure insanity. After a serious injury to the skull, causing depression or fracture of the bone, a subsequent moody, irritable, and passionate change of character sometimes takes place, ending perhaps in positive mania or epileptic fits; and there are a few striking instances on record in which the removal of the depressed or damaged bone by the trephine has been followed by mental restoration. But the new proposal is to remove a portion of the skull with the express purpose of relieving a pressure on the brain which is assumed to exist and to act perniciously in some acute insanities. Although the proposal has even been put in practice in a few cases of general paralysis, it can hardly be said yet that the success of the operation has been such as to warrant its general adoption or to confirm the theory of speculative pathology on which it is based.

However successful the treatment of insanity, it is at best successful in bringing about recovery in only fifty per cent of the persons attacked. As the result of his exact and careful inquiries, Dr. Thurnam concluded that on the whole it might be said that of ten persons who fall insane five recover and five die sooner or later without recovery. Of the five who recover not more than two remain well for the rest of their lives; the others have subsequent attacks, it may be after long intervals of sanity, during which at least two of them die.[1] Hardly so favourable even were the results of Sir A. Mitchell's inquiries into the histories of 1297 persons who were admitted into the asylums of Scotland in one year—1858. Twelve years afterwards, in 1870, the intermediate histories of 1096 of them were ascertained. Of these no less than 454, nearly half, had died insane, and 367 still lived insane: a total, that is, of 821 or 74·91 per cent insane. Only 78 had died, and 197 still lived, not insane. In general terms, then, three-fourths were insane, while only one-fourth was sane.

[1] *Statistics of Insanity.*

A physician who had spent his life in ministering to diseased minds might be excused if, asking himself at the end of it whether he had spent his life well, he accused the fortune of an evil hour which threw him on that track of work. He could not well help feeling something of bitterness in the certitude that one-half the disease he had dealt with never could get well, and something of misgiving in the reflection whether he had done real service to his kind by restoring the other half to do reproductive work. Nor would the scientific interest of his studies compensate entirely for the practical uncertainties, since their revelation of the structure of human nature might inspire a doubt whether, notwithstanding impassioned aims, pæans of progress, endless pageants of self-illusions, its capacity of degeneration did not equal, and might some day exceed, its capacity of development. Fain, though in vain, would he question the Genius of the human race, mute and inscrutable, musing of the seeds of time and dreaming prophetically of things to come.

> Es horcht der Verbannte
> In nächtlichen Höhlen
> Der Alte, die Lieder,
> Denkt Kinder und Enkel
> Und schüttelt das Haupt.

INDEX

ACQUIRED characters, inheritance of, 39
Action, madly purposive, 142, 269
  the structure of, 271
Acute fever, insanity after, 116
Adolescence, mental changes of, 387
  insanity of, 145
Ages, diseases of different, 45
  mental characters of, 46
Agoraphobia, 228, 409
Albumoses, poisonous, 114
Alcohol, action of, 108
Alcoholic insanities, 492
Altruism, 26
Amentia, 335
Andral, 524
Aphasia, 143
Apoplectiform attacks, 454
Appetite, perverted, 358
Apprehension, mental and bodily, 9
Aptitudes, innate, 13, 366
Arsenic, in melancholia, 550
Art, decadent, 70
Articulation, in general paralysis, 440
Ascaris lumbricoides, in the gullet, 275
Ataxy, locomotor, 472
Atonement, law of social, 65
Atropine, poisonous effects of, 109, 368
Attendant, character of, 548, 555
Attention, nature and effects of, 139
Aubrey, 548
Automatism, mental, 481
Avarice, morbid, 75
  mania of, 331

BACON, 60, 318, 514
Baillarger, 222, 472, 482
Bayle, on general paralysis, 462
Bees, cleverness and stupidity of, 7
Belief, artificial formation of, 15
Belladonna, poisonous effects of, 368
Bernard, Claude, 138, 522, 523

Blake, William, hallucinations of, 371
Blood, cerebral circulation of, 105, 158
  vitiated, 108
Boulepsy, 148
Brain, action of vitiated blood on, 108
  circulation of blood in, 105, 158
  measurement of time by, 122
  reflex mechanism of, 5
  the double, 221
  ignition of, 238
  in idiocy, 340
  tumour of, 511
  syphilis of, 511
  anæmia of, 524
Breeding, law of variation in, 37
Bromide of potassium, in epilepsy, 490
Browne, Sir Thomas, 221
  in mania, 557
Burton, Robert, 162, 343, 362

CALIGULA, 31
Calmeil, on general paralysis, 462
Cerebral cortex, complex structure of 12
  hyperæmia of, 521
Cerebral hemispheres, dissentient action of, 209, 221
Cerebral hypertrophy, 341
Chateaubriand, 61
Chatham, Earl of, 113
Child-bearing, insanity and, 415
Children, insanities of, 364
  night terrors of, 368
  moral character of, 385
  moral insanity of, 382
  egotism of, 473
  suicides of, 381
Chloral, 547
Civilization, insanity and, 27
Claustrophobia, 228, 410
Cleopatra, 531
Clouston, Dr., on phthisical insanity 503, 505

Cohnheim, 106
Cold, nervous effects of, 133
Coma of cerebral exhaustion, 272
Conscience, 84
Consciousness, and mental function, 8, 9
   lowered level of, 538
Consentience, 84
Constipation, in melancholia, 208, 550
   in mania, 558
Crankiness, 298
Craziness, 298
Cretins, 336, 360
Criminal, born not made, 10
Criminal nature, the, 78-83
Cross-fertilization, benefits of, 55
Culture, the conquests of, 239, 259
Custom, tyranny of, 544

DARWIN, Charles, 55
   George, 55
Datura stramonium, poisonous effects of, 368
Death, in acute delirious melancholia, 207
   in ordinary mania, 267
   in acute delirious mania, 275
   in puerperal mania, 419
   in general paralysis, 447
Deformities, bodily, mental effects of, 318
   mental, 297
   in idiots, 337
Delirium, 274
Delirium tremens, hallucinations of, 219
   symptoms of, 492
Delusions, forms of, 149, 189
   stimuli of, 151
   melancholic, 188
   delimitation of, 196, 306
   of persecution, 299
   concealment of, 305
   of general paralysis, 437
   of alcoholic dementia, 499
Demagogue, the, 22
Dementia, 333, 345
   acute, 345, 412
   chronic, 346
   senile, 354, 430
   of general paralysis, 460
   syphilitic, 471
   alcoholic, 497
   morbid anatomy of, 527
Desdemona, 536
Devolition, 244, 250
Dipsomania, 500
Disease-tendencies, hereditary, 46

Disillusionment, 422
Dislocation, mental, 17
Dreams, creations of, 122, 293
   organic causes of, 123, 151
   horrors of, 130
   of flying, 156
   and delirium, 270
Drowning, sensations in, 518
Dura mater, thickening of, 520
   hæmatoma of, 528
Dysnoia, 127
Dysthumia, 127, 240

EAR, deformed, 337, 536
   hæmatoma of, 528
Eccentricity, 59, 60
Ecstasy, nature of, 18
   cataleptic, 395
Education, power of, 43, 539, 541
Ego, the basic unity of, 128
   disturbances of, 128
Egoism, the transformations of, 333
Egotism, morbid, 65
   natural, 473
Elephant, frenzy of, 368
Emotion, organic basis of, 127
   expressions of, 127
   the wear and tear of, 30
   organic effects of, 474
Environment, the social, 31, 57
Epilepsy, minor, 376, 480
   mania of, 478
   mental automatism of, 481
   homicide in, 483
Epileptics, the offspring of, 53
Epileptiform attacks, 454
Equilibrium, mental, 537
Ergoisms, pathological, 150, 293
Ergotism, symptoms of, 110
Erotomania, 321, 390
Esquirol, 275, 385, 529
Eunoia, 127
Eunuchs, envy of, 318
Euthumia, 127
Exaltation, mania of, 319
   in general paralysis, 436
   in other insanities, 464
   in epileptic insanities, 479, 487
Excesses, sexual, 466
   alcoholic, 471

FAMILY feeling, effects of, 35
Fanatic, the religious, 321
   the political, 323
Fanaticism, physical basis of, 18
   of belief and conduct, 66
   mental basis of, 297
Fears, morbid, 168, 169, 407, 413

Features, the language of, 291
Fechner, 518
Feeling, the tones of, 125
  sympathy of, 126
  forms of, 127
  distempers of, 129
  exaltation of, 131
Fever, effects of, in dementia, 359
Flying, dreams of, 156
  hallucinations of, 156
Folie circulaire, 240, 276
Food, refusal of, 552
Fortune, good or ill, 58
  altars to, 82
Freewill, the doctrine of, 36
Frenzy, a climbing, 374

GALEN, 152
General paralysis, in young persons, 382
  in adults, 435
  invasions of, 456
  melancholic, 458
  demented, 460
  mixed forms of, 461
  causes of, 465
  morbid anatomy of, 527
  treatment of, 559
Genius, inheritance of, 40
  breeding of, 54
  and madness, 60
Germ-plasms, secret modifications of, 39
  incompatibility of, 53, 343
  combinations of, 54
  ill-constructed, 53
Gesture, language of, 290
Glycosuria, mental state in, 113
  in melancholia, 426
Goethe, 33, 43, 61, 563
Gout, insanity of, 112
  mania of, 115
Greatness, mania of, 315
  delusions of, 437
Grief, organic effects of, 139
  organic causes of, 163

HAFIZ, 214
Haller, 517
Hallucinations, motor, 156, 352
  of special senses, 216
  genesis of, 218
  prognostic of, 214
  in acute mania, 246
  of persecution, 301
  in epilepsy, 488
  in alcoholic dementia, 498
Handwriting, impairments of, 143

Handwriting, in general paralysis, 445
Hartley, on the images of dreams, 156
Harvey, 548
Head, size of, in idiots, 338
Heat, nervous effects of, 133
Hereditary predisposition, 47
  suicide, 213
Hippocrates, 106, 544
  the sons of, 40
Homicide, impulse to, 182
  in melancholia, 215
  in mania of persecution, 309, 321 324
  in mania of jealousy, 330
  in insanity of self-abuse, 409
  in puerperal mania, 418
  epileptic, 483
Hope, effects of, 171
Howden, Dr., 204
Hydromania, 112
Hyoscine, in mania, 557
Hypnotism, nature of, 17
Hypochondriacal melancholy, simple 229
  delusional, 230
  demented, 232
  in gross brain-disease, 509
Hysteria, the phenomena of, 135
  moral perversion of, 397
  in gross brain-disease, 509
  miscalled, 533

IDEALISMS, narrow, 70
Idiocy, 335
  causes of, 341, 342
  morbid anatomy of, 528
Idiosyncrasy, peculiarities of, 97
Idiot, the, 3
Ignorance, two infinities of, 11
Illegitimacy, mental effects of, 316
Imagination, non-inheritance of, 41
  and reason, 62
  of childhood, 372
Imbecile, the, 3
Imbecility, 335
  senile, 354
  moral, 382
Impulses, morbid, 170, 184, 407, 413
  resistance to, 185
Individual character, scientific study of, 19, 47, 76, 90
  influence on delusions, 159
  treatment of, 186, 561
Individuality, the conception of, 22
Influenza, insanity after, 116
Insane temperaments, varieties of, 63-78
Insanities, symptomatology of, 160
Insanity, definition of, 1

Insanity, social study of, 18, 21
　alleged increase of, 27
　pathological study of, 93
　causes of, 44
　predisposition to, 47
　moral causes of, 83, 117
　organic causes of, 105
　paramorphic, 297
　adolescent, 387, 535
　puerperal, 415
　of pregnancy, 415
　of lactation, 420
　of decline of life, 420
　senile, 426
　alcoholic, 493
　phthisical, 115, 503
　of gross brain-disease, 507
　morbid anatomy of, 515
　and visceral disease, 529
　preventive treatment of, 530
　curative treatment of, 545
　surgical treatment of, 562
Instinct, nature of, 7
　reason and, 7
　instances of, 366
Interbreeding, incestuous, 56
　evils of, 55
Interest, as excuse of marriage, 531
Intermissions, in mania, 251
　in melancholia, 225
　in general paralysis, 450

JEALOUSY, mania of, 325, 424
　homicide from, 330
Jesuits, as educators, 541
Joy, organic cause of, 133
　in mania, 325
Judgment, reflex nature of, 9
Jumpers, 147

KANDINSKY, Dr., 247, 556
Kant, 26
Knee-jerk, the, in general paralysis, 450

LACTATION, insanity of, 420
Lamb, Charles, 59, 255
Lasègue, on mania of persecution, 303, 310
"Lata," phenomena of, 146
Law, the moral, 26
Lead-poisoning, the symptoms of, 109, 110
Lewis, Dr. Bevan, 526
Life, the basis of love of, 177
　the decline of, 421, 424
Liver, effects of disordered, 112, 120
Loquacity, in mania, 248

Love, the attraction of, 121
Love, the infatuation of, 191, 533, 536
　the exaltation of, 474
　as excuse of marriage, 531
Love-manias, 321
Lucid intervals, 250, 265
Lust, display of, 244
Lymph-channels, blocking of, 525

MALFORMITIES, mental, 16, 63
Mania, the counterpart of convulsions, 20
　the symptoms of, 234
　simple, 240
　recurrent, 240, 252, 390
　acute, 240
　varieties of, 249
　the issue of, 256
　transitoria, 260, 376, 496
　chronic, 262
　acute delirious, 267, 453
　of persecution, 298
　primary systematized, 298
　of greatness, 315
　of avarice, 331
　choreic, 373, 391
　ecstatic, 374
　epileptic, 377, 477
　adolescent, 389
　puerperal, 417
　senile, 427
　of general paralysis, 452
　alcoholic, 494
　vagabond, 501
　morbid anatomy of, 521
　treatment of, 554
Marriages, consanguineous, 55, 344
　propitious, 57
　of morbid heredities, 531
Matteuci, 517
Mean, the happy, 88
Mechanical restraint, 554
Medium, individual and, 2, 74
　the social, 23
Melancholy, organic causes of, 133
　self-indulgence of, 194
　symptoms of, 163
　simple, 165
　panics of, 173
　delusional, 188
　with stupor, 198
　acute, 205
　acute delirious, 206, 453
　issues of, 226
　varieties of, 228
　hypochondriacal, 229
　in children, 378
　adolescent, 393

INDEX

Melancholy, puerperal, 419
  climacteric, 420
  senile, 429
  morbid anatomy of, 524
  treatment of, 546
Memory, after mania, 254
  losses of, 259
  in recurrent mania, 255
  in imbecility, 384
  after puerperal mania, 418
  in senile dementia, 431
  in general paralysis, 439, 444
  after epileptic homicide, 485
Menstruation, suppression of, 288
Mental mouldings, 15, 75
Mental organization, innate aptitudes of, 13
  nervous substratum of, 5, 18
  variability of, 14
  derangements of, 18
  building up of, 365
  mental weakness, states of, 334
Metabolism, disordered, 107
Milton, 130
Mimicry, nervous instinct of, 540
Mind, deformities of, 4, 297
  distortions of, 365
  malformities of, 16, 63
Mitchell, Sir Arthur, on proportion of recoveries, 562
Modern life, the hurry of, 28
  the self-indulgence of, 32
Monomania, 263, 298, 353
Montaigne, 291
Moral insanity, in children, 382
  in young women, 397
  in circular insanity, 278
  in mania of persecution, 313
  in epilepsy, 487
Moral nature, instability of the, 50, 81, 92, 386
Moral sense, the, 25
  absence of, 77
Morbid heredity, intensification of, 53
  mitigation of, 53
  neutralization of, 53
  modification of, 53
  in mania, 292
  stigmata of, 294
Moreau, case of moral insanity, 376
Morel, case of inert stupor, 201
  contrary hallucinations, 220
  sleeplessness in mania, 282
  sterile idiocy, 342
Morphia, the effects of, 134
  in mania, 554
  in melancholia, 546
Motor hallucinations, 156, 352

Motor intuition, 364, 440
  tension, fine degrees of, 154
  impairment, 157
Müller, 517
Muscular feeling, sluggish, 155
  irritable, 156
Muscular sense, loss of, 153
  in general paralysis, 448
Muscular tonicity, 175
Mussulman, the education of, 15
Myths, heroic, 102
Myxœdematous insanity, 114

NAPOLEON, 58
Narcotics in melancholia, 547
  in mania, 554
Natura naturans, the, 317
Natural selection, the law of, 25, 36
Nature, the social, 21
  the family, 33
  the individual, 37
  the criminal, 78
Nero, 31
Nerval, Gérard de, 235, 242, 245, 247
Nerve-tracts, forms or patterns of, 13
Nervous conduction, speed of, 517
  hierarchy, 6
Nervousness, morbid, 70
Neuroses, transformations of, 51
New ideas, hostility to, 102
New Zealand, the native of, 30
Nutrition, in mania, 237
  in general paralysis, 455
Nymphomania, 390

OLD AGE, sluggish perception of, 157
  decay of mind of, 433
Opium, in melancholia, 546
  in mania, 554, 556
Optimism, physical basis of, 99
  in general paralysis, 475
Organic intelligence, 152
  mechanism, the reactions of, 93-105
  qualities of tone of, 125
Organisms, limited relations of, 11
Orgasm, the sexual, 174
Othæmatoma, 529
Othello, 536
Overstrain, 28, 44
  the conditions of, 101
Overwork, as cause of insanity, 86
Oxaluria, mental state in, 113

PACHYMENINGITIS, 528
Pains, anomalous, 172
Palmer, Dr., on morbid cerebral anatomy, 527
Panic, melancholic, 173

Paraldehyde, 547
Paramorphic insanity, 297
Paranoia, 263, 298
Pascal, 514, 531
Pellagrous insanity, 111
Perception, reflex nature of, 9
   loss of, 431
Periodicity, of nervous functions, 252
Periodic mania, 252
Persecution, mania of, 298
   alcoholic, 310
   hypochondriacal, 310, 312
   hallucinatory, 311
   delusional, 312
   reasoning, 313
   senile, 428
Pessimism, physical basis of, 99
   in general paralysis, 475
Pia mater, thickening of, 520
   hyperæmia of, 521
Phosphuria, mental state in, 113
Phthisical mania, 115
Phthisis, in idiots, 336
Pregnancy, insanity of, 415
Prostitutes, general paralysis in, 468
Proteids, changes of, 114
Psychalgia, 240
Pulse in melancholia, 208
Purgatives in melancholia, 551

REASON, nature of, 8
   instinct and, 7
   imagination and, 62
Recovery, in mania, 254
   in melancholy, 226
   in hereditary mania, 258
   foresigns of, 286
   in general paralysis, 451
Recurrent mania, 252
Reflex action, 5
Relapses, 258, 287, 293
Relatives, a good use of, 49
   morbid sympathy of, 64
Religion, as cause of insanity, 85
Remissions, in mania, 250
   in melancholia, 225
Responsibility, legal criterion of, 216, 325
Reymond, Du Bois, 517
Rheumatism, acute mania in, 115
Romberg, on rotatory spasm, 374
Rousseau, Jean Jacques, 61

ST. CHRISTINA, hallucinations of, 156
St. Dunstan, hallucinations of, 156
St. Theresa, 218, 299
Savage, the, 29, 34
Self, the changing, 96, 104

Self-abuse, propensity to, 371
   insanity of, 399
Self-confidence, loss of, 165, 173
   excess of, 234
Self-consciousness, the pains of, 72
   the nervous conditions of, 144, 170, 538
Self-conservation, alarmed instinct of, 164
Self-hypnotism, 17
Self-indulgence in melancholia, 552
Self-inspection, 72
Self-love, insane, 66
Self-sacrifice, the self-indulgence of, 331
Self-torture, morbid mental, 169
Self-utterance, need and joy of, 237
Seneca, 214
Sensation, morbid, in melancholia, 172
   in dementia, 351, 358
   in insanity of self-abuse, 406
   in other insanities, 201
Sense, discriminations of, 154
   hallucinations of, 216
Sensibility, differences of, 96, 99
   levels of, 101, 538
   in melancholia, 208
   in idiocy, 338
   in general paralysis, 448
Sex, insanity and, 86
Sexual excess in general paralysis, 466
Sexual passion, decline of, 424
   loss of, 132
   display of, 243
Shakspeare, 42, 58, 61, 518
Shuttleworth, Dr., on idiocy, 336
Shyness, morbid, 71
Sin, meaning of, 76
Skae, Dr., 50, 345, 462
Skull, premature ossification of, 336
Sleep, in melancholia, 209, 547
   in mania, 282
   drug-enforced, 283, 558
   self-inducement of, 549
Sleeplessness, 548
Social reflexes, 24
Speech, incoherence of, 248
   in general paralysis, 440
Stammering, movements of, 144
Stock, morbid strain in, 35, 47
   regeneration of, 57
   variation of, 59
Stomach-pump, use of, 552
Strychnia, selective action of, 516
Stupor, in melancholy, 198
   degrees of, 200
   transience of, 201
   horrors of, 203

Stylites, Simeon, 2
Suicide, thought of, 166
 fear of, 168
 impulse to, 175
 concealment of, 176
 motives of, 177
 feigned attempts at, 181
 from delusions, 211
 in melancholic panic, 212
 inherited tendency to, 213
 in mania of persecution, 308, 324
 in children, 381
Sulphonal, 547
Superstition, mental basis of, 297
Suspicion, morbid, 35, 63, 64
Sweating, partial, 209
Sympathetic system, disorder of, 211
 in general paralysis, 474
Sympathy, morbid family, 35, 64, 540
 organic, 117
 reflex nature of, 137
Syphilis, in general paralysis, 471
 cerebral, 511

TALENTS, inheritance of, 41
Tapeworm, in the gullet, 275
Temperament, insane, 62
 over-sensitive, 69
 the epileptic, 489
Temperaments, the bodily, 97
Temperature, in delirious mania, 273
 in mania, 279
Tertullian, 218
Theft, in general paralysis, 442
 in epileptic automatism, 482
Thought, active, 158
 laboured, 158

Thought, in mania, 236
Thurnam, Dr., on statistics of insanity, 562
Thyroid gland, atrophy of, 114
 juice of, 115
Time, measurement of, 122
 loss of sense of, 171
Transplantation, 58, 186, 226, 544
Travel, in insanity, 553
Treatment, early, 559
Tumour cerebral, 511
Twins, insanity of, 49

VAGABONDAGE, mania of, 501
Van der Kolk, Schrœder, 520
Vanity, morbid, 73
 in epilepsy, 487
Variation, tendency to, 59, 61
Vaso-dilatation, 522
Vaso-motor nerves, action of, 38
Virchow, 528
Virgil, 214
Volition, rate of, 518

WALK, in general paralysis, 432
War, the good uses of, 26, 35
Waste-products, cerebral, 107
Weber, 518
Westphal, 462
Wigglesworth, Dr., 528
Will, demoralization of, 136
 disintegrations of, 142, 245, 249, 269
 good basis of, 538
Witchcraft, belief in, 2
 delusions of, 189

THE END